Guy de la Bédoyère has written a large number of books on the Roman world over the last thirty years, most recently *Gladius: Living, Fighting and Dying in the Roman Army*. He was part of Channel 4's archaeology series *Time Team* for fifteen years. He has degrees from Durham, London and University College, and is a Fellow of the Society of Antiquaries. He has lectured in Britain and abroad, mainly Australia, and is an accredited lecturer of the Arts Society.

A Radio 4 Book of the Week

'De la Bédoyère, a prolific historian [. . .] manages an impressive amalgamation of scholarly research with popular history . . . The subject has enormous appeal because of the popularity of Tutankhamun' *The Times*

'A scrupulous yet accessible history of ancient Egypt under the 18th dynasty . . . Complemented by striking illustrations and valuable appendices, this impressive survey will be welcomed by ancient history buffs' *Publishers Weekly*

'Superb . . . de la Bédoyère lays out the elusive history of Egypt's 18th dynasty' *Library Journal*

'Packed with big names, from Tutankhamun to Nefertiti, and de la Bédoyère sets their stories alongside those of the populations they so often exploited . . . Along the way, he offers an evocative account of an era of epic riches and ruthlessness' *History Revealed*

'De la Bédoyère tells the story with not just an archaeologist's eye for accuracy but also a broadcaster's nose for a colourful story . . . His book is peppered with lively details' *Radio Times*

# PHARAOHS OF THE SUN

### How Egypt's Despots and Dreamers drove the Rise and Fall of Tutankhamun's Dynasty

## GUY DE LA BÉDOYÈRE

abacus
books

ABACUS

First published in Great Britain in 2022 by Little, Brown
This paperback edition published in Great Britain in 2023 by Abacus

3 5 7 9 10 8 6 4 2

A CIP catalogue record for this book
is available from the British Library.

Paperback ISBN 978-0-349-14474-0

Typeset in Spectrum by M Rules
Printed and bound in Great Britain by
Clays Ltd, Elcograf S.p.A.

Papers used by Abacus are from well-managed forests
and other responsible sources.

Abacus
An imprint of
Little, Brown Book Group
Carmelite House
50 Victoria Embankment
London EC4Y 0DZ

An Hachette UK Company
www.hachette.co.uk

www.littlebrown.co.uk

This book is dedicated to my grandchildren
Nell, Willow, Rufus, James, and Oliver

*I will speak to you, all people:*
*I have been rewarded with gold seven times before*
  *the entire land,*
*And also with male and female slaves*
*I have been endowed with many fields*
*The name of a brave man is in what he has done.*

*I conveyed the Dual King, Thutmose I,*
*As he sailed south to Khent-hen-nefer*
*To crush rebellion throughout the lands*
*And to drive off intrusion from the desert regions*
*I showed valour in his presence at the cataract.*

From the tomb biography of
Ahmes-Ibana, soldier and
naval commander

# CONTENTS

# MAPS AND PLANS

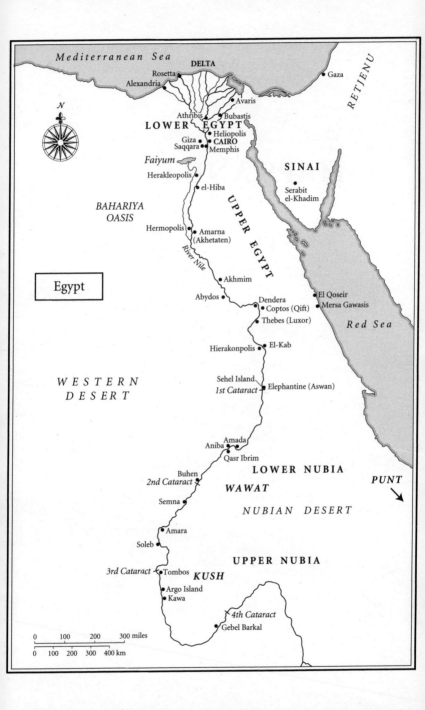

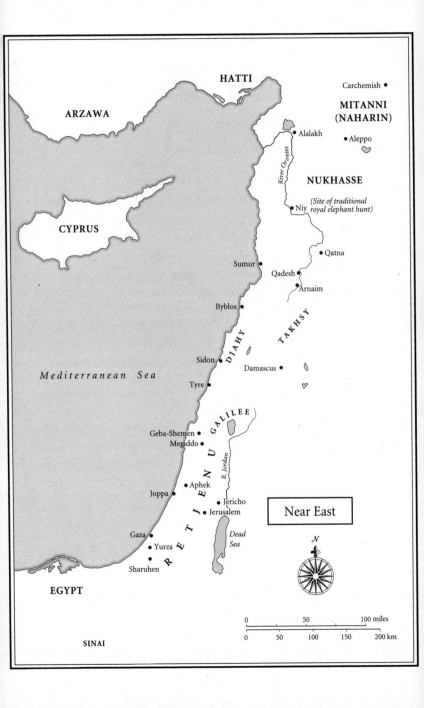

HATTI

ARZAWA

Carchemish •

MITANNI
(NAHARIN)

• Alalakh

• Aleppo

CYPRUS

*River Orontes*

NUKHASSE

*(Site of traditional
royal elephant hunt)*

• Niy

• Qatna

Sumur •

Qadesh •
• Arnaim

Byblos •

D I A H Y

T A K H S Y

Sidon •

*Mediterranean Sea*

Damascus •

Tyre •

G A L I L E E

Geba-Shemen •
Megiddo •

*R. Jordan*

Aphek •

Near East

Joppa •

• Jericho
• Jerusalem

Gaza •
• Yurza

*Dead
Sea*

𝒩

Sharuhen •

R E T J E N U

EGYPT

|   |   |   |
|---|---|---|
| 0 | 50 | 100 miles |

|   |   |   |   |   |
|---|---|---|---|---|
| 0 | 50 | 100 | 150 | 200 km |

SINAI

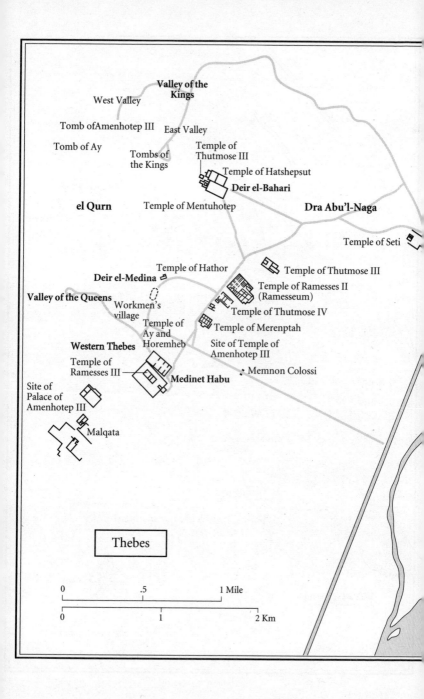

Valley of the Kings

West Valley

Tomb of Amenhotep III    East Valley

Tomb of Ay

Tombs of
the Kings

Temple of
Thutmose III

Temple of Hatshepsut

Deir el-Bahari

el Qurn        Temple of Mentuhotep                    Dra Abu'l-Naga

Temple of Seti

Temple of Hathor

Deir el-Medina                                    Temple of Thutmose III

Valley of the Queens                             Temple of Ramesses II
                                                 (Ramesseum)
            Workmen's
            village                              Temple of Thutmose IV

            Temple of        Temple of Merenptah
            Ay and
Western Thebes   Horemheb                Site of Temple of
                                         Amenhotep III
Temple of
Ramesses III                             Memnon Colossi
                    Medinet Habu

Site of
Palace of
Amenhotep III

        Malqata

Thebes

0            .5              1 Mile

0            1               2 Km

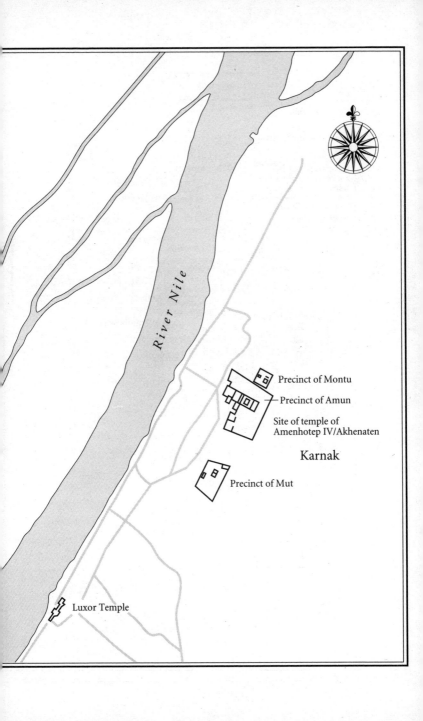

River Nile

Precinct of Montu

Precinct of Amun

Site of temple of
Amenhotep IV/Akhenaten

Karnak

Precinct of Mut

Luxor Temple

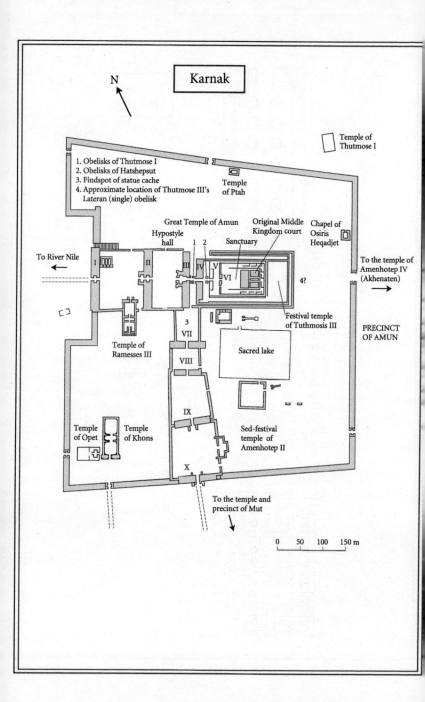

N

Karnak

□ Temple of
Thutmose I

1. Obelisks of Thutmose I
2. Obelisks of Hatshepsut
3. Findspot of statue cache
4. Approximate location of Thutmose III's
   Lateran (single) obelisk

Temple
of Ptah

Great Temple of Amun        Original Middle        Chapel of
                            Kingdom court          Osiris
Hypostyle                   Sanctuary              Heqadjet
hall          1  2

To River Nile ←                              To the temple of
                                             Amenhotep IV
                                             (Akhenaten) →

4?

Festival temple
of Tuthmosis III

PRECINCT
OF AMUN

Temple of
Ramesses III

Sacred lake

Temple        Temple
of Opet       of Khons

Sed-festival
temple of
Amenhotep II

To the temple and
precinct of Mut

0    50    100    150 m

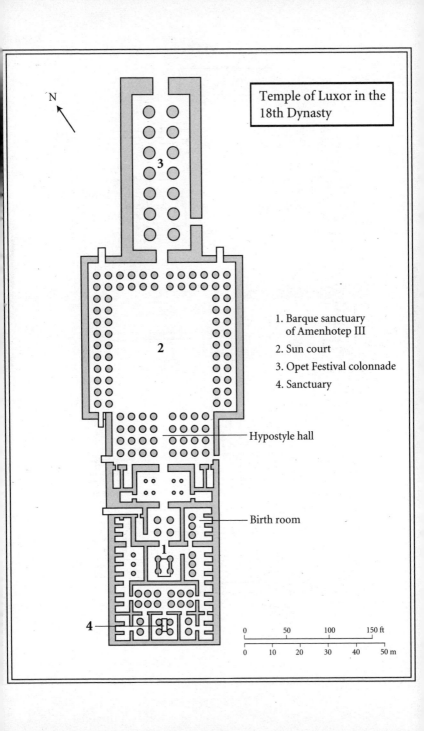

N

Temple of Luxor in the
18th Dynasty

3

2

1. Barque sanctuary
   of Amenhotep III

2. Sun court

3. Opet Festival colonnade

4. Sanctuary

Hypostyle hall

Birth room

1

4

| 0 | 50 | 100 | 150 ft |
| 0 | 10 | 20 | 30 | 40 | 50 m |

Royal Tombs

Thutmose III
KV34

Thutmose IV
KV43

Amenhotep II
KV35

Royal
Mummy
Cache

Amenhotep III
WV22

Tiye

W = Well shaft
BC = Burial chamber
S = Sarcophagus
KV = Valley of the Kings
WV = Western Valley
TA = Amarna Tombs

Treasury

BC

S

Annexe          Antechamber

Tutankhamun
KV62

'Meketaten suite'

β  γ

α

BC

S

Akhenaten
TA26

Entrance →

Horemheb KV57
Burial Chamber only

0   5   10 m

# FOREWORD

In 1972, like thousands of others at the time, I queued for several hours to see the Tutankhamun Exhibition at the British Museum in London. The experience of seeing the displays was overwhelming and unforgettable, even life changing. Tutankhamun was one of the last, and most obscure, kings of Egypt's 18th Dynasty (c. 1550–1295 BC). In November 1922, when Tutankhamun's tomb was discovered, he became a household name and has remained so ever since. Many of his predecessors were far more illustrious or notorious than him, including Hatshepsut and Akhenaten. Some, like Thutmose III, were the most powerful kings of their era.

Another half-century has passed since 1972 and I still have some of the books and souvenirs acquired at the time, the first part of a still-growing personal Egyptology library. Countless weekends were spent in the Egyptian galleries at the British Museum. At Durham University I studied Egyptology as part of my first degree.

Modern tourism in Egypt was well established by the 1970s but nothing like the colossal industry it became before fears of instability in the Middle East crushed it almost out of existence. In 1983 I made my first trip to the Nile Valley. It was still possible to wander easily among the monuments on the West and East Banks at Luxor (Thebes) without seeing many other people. I was filled with wonder, most by the arduous walk in the baking late summer heat from the

Temple of Hatshepsut and up over the hills across to the Valley of the Kings. Several other visits to Egypt followed. It was also my good fortune to visit major exhibitions of material from Tutankhamun's tomb and the Amarna era in Los Angeles and Denver. For nine years I worked as a teacher and took trips to Berlin where one of the annual pleasures was introducing students to Akhenaten through the magnificent Amarna collection at the Egyptian Museum there. Some of those students said in later years that seeing the bust of Nefertiti had been the most memorable experience of their historical studies.

There can be no other ancient civilization that is so instantly recognizable to modern eyes as that of the Egyptians. Stories about Egypt and antiquities trickled into Europe for centuries, especially once Octavian (afterwards Augustus) seized Egypt in 30 BC for the Roman Empire. The popes in Rome recovered buried statues and obelisks brought there by the Roman emperors.

Awareness of Egypt's exotic past and landscape spread gradually among the cognoscenti of Europe in the seventeenth and eighteenth centuries, but it was Napoleon's Expedition to Egypt that had a truly dramatic impact. By publishing magnificent illustrations of the monuments, many since damaged or destroyed, the French explorers caused a worldwide sensation. In 1799 they found the Rosetta Stone which would change everything by revealing a path to deciphering hieroglyphs. Travelling to the Nile Valley soon became a more common pastime, at first only for the privileged rich and daring, reviving a tradition that had existed as far back as the fifth century BC when the Greek historian Herodotus visited an ancient Egypt already well into decline.

As Egypt opened up in the 1800s, explorers and excavators sailed up the Nile. They were fascinated by the monuments, strange gods and stranger customs, the gold and the cryptic language, just as visiting Roman senators had been in their time. Once the hieroglyphs had begun to give up their secrets, Egypt's history began to emerge back into the light along with the discovery and clearance of ever more monuments. European museums were the first to start packing their galleries with astonishing finds and works of art. Many major museums in the world have outstanding collections of 18th Dynasty relics, but the most important of all is in Cairo. No one who visits any one of these or is lucky enough to explore Egypt can fail to be staggered by the vastness of the sculpture, the beauty of the hieroglyphs and the sheer mystery of this remarkable and unique civilization.

The enthusiastic amassing of museum collections in the nineteenth century and later could be just as easily seen as the despoliation of ancient Egypt. Many archaeologically valuable sites and locations were destroyed in the search for exciting pieces. Some places were excavated with care, but the standard of recording varied wildly. A great deal of ransacking, especially of tombs, went on in the hunt for valuable artefacts to sell to the antiquities market. It cut both ways. The results included sensational discoveries, like the first cache of royal mummies found in 1881, and drawings or paintings made of reliefs and carvings that no longer exist, at least in legible form.

Since the ancient Egyptians spent a great deal of time despoiling one another and anyone else within their reach it is hard to be too judgemental. At least nowadays the buildings and artefacts housed in museums are safer than they have ever been. The greatest threat a pharaoh's burial and monuments faced was from his successors rather than nineteenth-century collectors, and the same applied to almost any private burial or possessions.

In the meantime, the work inspired ever more assiduous searches, the sand and rock being swept aside in the relentless hunt for the literal crock of gold. The discovery of Tutankhamun's tomb is unlikely ever to be matched, let alone exceeded. In recent decades work has been more concerned with long-term projects, such as restoring Hatshepsut's memorial-mortuary temple, mapping and recording Akhenaten's city at Tell el-Amarna, together with workers' villages and cemeteries, and the reconstruction of his reliefs from the blocks used as filling in later pylons at Karnak. The new National Museum of Egyptian Civilization in Cairo is the latest great initiative. In April

2021 it was the destination of the Pharaohs' Golden Parade when the royal mummies, including some of the most important 18th Dynasty rulers, were moved there and watched by the world.

Ever since the unravelling of the Egyptian language, the 18th Dynasty has gradually been restored as a historical era like no other. For all that, Egypt remains strangely impenetrable. The modern name of the country comes from the classical *Aegyptos*, itself a Greek rendition of Egyptian words that sounded something like Hewet-ka-Ptah.[1] This meant 'Mansion of the Spirit of Ptah', the city of Memphis, rather than the country itself with which the name came to be synonymous. Among the names the Egyptians applied to their country were Kemet, 'The Black Land', a reference to the Nile silt, and Tameri, 'The Beloved Cultivated Land'.[2] The Hittites called Egypt Mizri, a word of uncertain origin but which might be derived from an Egyptian word that meant something like a 'walled-in place of treasure'.[3] It survives today as Misr, the modern Arabic name for Egypt.

The ancient Egyptians have a unique capacity to confront us with our own mortality. It is impossible to look at the photographs taken in Tutankhamun's tomb when it was discovered and not be transfixed by the thought that the boxes, chairs, chariots, vases, statues and all the rest had already been precariously balanced in position for a thousand years when Alexander the Great invaded Egypt in 332 BC. The everyday paraphernalia of a young and fabulously wealthy king is the evidence for a whole life lived thirty-three centuries ago from birth through childhood and into young adulthood and death piled chaotically into a very small tomb. The glitter has always overwhelmed those lucky enough to see his celebrated solid gold mask and coffins, but the ephemera has more power to humble us: the reed that Tutankhamun cut one day to serve as a stick, or the golden throne battered by his impatient infant feet.

The images of Howard Carter and his assistants carrying each piece out back into the Egyptian sun leaves one with the thought of being in the tomb when it was closed and seeing the last people leaving, among them surely Tutankhamun's queen Ankhesenamun, before they disappeared into history. Soon afterwards there were disturbances when the tomb was robbed twice and then total darkness and silence for an eternity until Carter broke through the blocking, pointed his light in, and gasped. He described what he saw with words that had not come into use until thousands of years had passed after the tomb was sealed. At that moment Carter met the 18th Dynasty head-on and even briefly breathed its air as he gazed in bewilderment at the scene of glistening clutter that met his eyes, with no idea yet of the wonders waiting beyond the blocked wall to the burial chamber. In between that moment and Tutankhamun's burial lay a trackless, 160-odd generations-worth of billions of human beings, almost all of whom have been vaporized without trace.

The abundant evidence for lives led thousands of years ago, ranging from everyday items that look as if they were last used yesterday to the desiccated bodies of their owners, is spellbinding. The Egyptians' tireless efforts to commemorate and preserve their love of life and their landscape in their tombs is a powerful reminder of the short time we have available to share these pleasures ourselves. Add on the passage of vast tracts of time and the enticing mystery that envelops ancient Egypt, and it is easy to see why the modern world is addicted to the subject in all its manifestations.

Throughout its history, but especially so in the 18th Dynasty, the whole teetering Egyptian edifice was built on the systematic exploitation of its people, its neighbours and the resources the state could lay its hands on in an endless cycle of greedy imperialist wars and tribute demands. Wealth and labour were poured into the hands of the king and his family, his acolytes, and the state cults. They were used on colossal building projects and tombs that formed an integral part of the ever more extravagant myth of the king's semi-divine status and entitlement, backed up by a self-serving aristocracy that managed the administration of the state and religion. This was all applied to keep the population under control, suffused with the opiate of cult and ritual that dominated Egyptian society.

Egyptian society was controlled by a collective cultural conspiracy, locked in a timeless and reassuring recycling of custom, character-ized by oppression and exploitation. There is no point in judging a Bronze Age state by modern standards. The inequality was normal for the period and taken for granted as such across the region. Monarchical power was absolute. Opposition and protest were virtu-ally non-existent because that way of life was accepted as the price of security and stability. The difference is that in Egypt enough evidence exists for us to be able to see this happening in a chronological and historical framework at an early stage in the development of the modern nation. Egypt represents the supreme form of the Bronze Age absolutist state, and thus a vital stage in the process of political development and consciousness.

Some of the 18th Dynasty's rulers have attracted endless attention, in particular Hatshepsut, and Akhenaten and his queen Nefertiti. This can marginalize the wider historical context in which they ruled, as well as their predecessors and successors, the nobility and the general population. They deserve more than simply being pre-ambles or epilogues to the biographical works of a very few favourite rulers. These men and women of the 18th Dynasty deserve in every way to be seen alongside those of other important historical peri-ods. In their lives we can see all the dynamics that drive history from ambition, greed, temptation and radical ideas to creativity, self-destruction and a craving for immortality. This was set against a backdrop of one of the most sensational landscapes in the world.

The miracle of Egypt is that we have learned so much about a civili-zation from thousands of years ago. Yet at the same time the subject remains tantalizing and obscure, especially to the uninitiated. In this book I have tried wherever possible to focus on what we do know and to be frank about the nature of the evidence, laboriously pursuing and scouring the prime Egyptian sources wherever it was possible to do so. This is a subject where something purporting to be historical fact often turns out to be based on one translation of an ambig-uous and obscure term or very partial interpretation. References to the detailed evidence that lies behind the main text have been placed in the extended endnotes which contain full details for those readers who wish to follow them up. Egyptian terms, usually in transliterated form, are also to be found mainly in the endnotes and appendices.

The structure of this book is broadly chronological by reign. This is a conventional approach for which I make no apology. The Egyptians defined and measured their history in terms of their kings, and it is the best means of understanding the surviving evidence and identifying change and continuity. The dates given in this book are approximations. There is no consensus about the absolute dates for most of ancient Egyptian history and nor will there ever be. The reasons for this are explained fully in Chapter 1. Likewise, there is no agreement about or consistency in the spellings of proper names and place names. I have tried to use forms that appear most often in the existing literature.

The nature of the evidence, as so often with the ancient world, means that speculating to some extent is unavoidable but relying on it is a particular issue with Egypt. I hope I have kept mine to a minimum. Too much speculation interweaved among, and even overwhelming, the evidence has an unfortunate habit of being unintentionally read, and treated, as fact even by those responsible for it.

I have utilized examples from other historical settings to help amplify and emphasize certain points, particularly dynastic aspects of England in the 1400s when another extended royal family exerted itself to maintain a hold on power, dissolving into civil war. Although the contexts may appear to be very different from Egypt, and indeed were in important respects, there is value in trying to draw Egypt more closely into more general historical themes, rather than invariably focusing on Egypt's peculiarities. Power, ambition, and self-interest and their consequences are always defining features of the human experience.

Guy de la Bédoyère, Welby, Lincolnshire 2022

# 1

# EGYPT IN THE 18TH DYNASTY

*. . . The gates of monarchs*
*Are arch'd so high that giants may jet through*
*And keep their impious turbans on without*
*Good morrow to the sun.*[1]

William Shakespeare

The events and history described in this book took place for the most part in ancient Egypt and beyond its borders to the north in the Near East or Western Asia and to the south in Nubia (Sudan). The timescale runs from the middle of the sixteenth century BC to the early thirteenth century BC, straddling the middle of ancient Egypt's dynastic historical era of almost three thousand years. Literacy made Egypt one of the first nations with the ability to record its history permanently. The Egyptians were fully aware of this. A wisdom text from not long after the period covered by this book said, 'Man decays, his corpse is dust. All his family have perished. But a book makes him remembered through the mouth of its reciter.'[2]

The deeds and conceits of the kings and queens, and the elite, who presided over this remarkable nation were recounted and celebrated across Egypt's monuments and on papyri. As history this astonishing

1

archive leaves much to be desired and needs to be understood in the context of a completely different perception of the past. That record is nonetheless without parallel for the period and provides us with our first opportunity to witness in detail an early civilization at the height of its power.

Egypt's famously unique geography has always made it a two-dimensional country. The vast bulk of human settlement in pharaonic times was stretched out along the Nile Valley and across the Delta. The oases of the Western Desert accounted for most of what habitable land remained. For the most part the Egyptians were engaged in sophisticated farming on the fertile land of crown, temple, and private estates saturated annually by the Nile's inundation. Quarrying and mining took place in scattered locations in the Eastern Desert across which trade routes led to the Red Sea. In the broader context of human activity in the area even the grand antiquity of ancient Egypt accounts for only a tiny proportion. Tool-using peoples were present in the region as much as 400,000 years ago, and it is certain that human beings had been there for at least as long again before that after the first made their way north out of east Africa.

Within Egypt two of the most important places were the administrative capital Memphis in northern Egypt (close to modern Cairo), and to the south the religious capital at Thebes, on part of which the modern city of Luxor stands. Memphis and Thebes were the cities' much later Greek names. In ancient Egyptian times they were referred to in various ways, explained later. During the 18th Dynasty, the first of the so-called New Kingdom, the kings spent much of their time at Memphis. The city's profile has suffered in modern times because thanks to the shifting of the Nile almost nothing visible survives there today, apart from the pyramids, tombs and other religious structures of the nearby necropolis at Saqqara. Thebes is a different matter. On the east bank of the Nile the vast ruins of the temple complexes of Karnak and Luxor are among the most impressive ancient buildings of all time and in any place. Across the Nile on the west bank are the remains of the mortuary temples and royal and private graves. Much of what is visible today is of 19th Dynasty and later dates, but a significant proportion belongs to the 18th Dynasty.

The 18th Dynasty and the rest of the New Kingdom owed a great deal to the four centuries of the Middle Kingdom (c. 2055–1650 BC), despite an intervening era of instability known today as the Second Intermediate Period (see under The Evidence below). During the Middle Kingdom, Egyptian society and culture developed ideas about kingship, bureaucracy and government, monumental architecture, an awareness of the outside world in the form of trade and technical innovations, and a more sophisticated identity and sense of self. The *Teaching of Ptahhotep*, for example, is a 12th Dynasty philosophical work concerned with how old age brings weakness and decay but also how wisdom only comes with age.[3] It was one of many old writings known and studied in the New Kingdom.

Under the 18th Dynasty kings Egypt's territorial ambitions were directed mainly to the north into Syria and Nubia to the south. Both places became major sources of wealth and resources, including manpower seized in war or levied as tribute. Egypt was one of several significant Bronze Age states in the region. Others included the Hittites from Hatti in what is now Turkey, Mitanni in Syria, Minoan Crete, and Mycenaean Greece. These nations were all ruled by versions of despotic monarchies. There was no sense of personal autonomy or self-determination, and no means of expressing or coordinating dissent. Political representation for the population lay centuries in the future, and then only in other emergent nations.

By the middle of the second millennium BC all these places exhibited growing signs of sophistication and had advanced skills in literacy and technology. The copper alloy known usually now as bronze was the basis of weaponry and tools. Iron was scarcely known in Egypt and elsewhere other than from meteorites. This explains why an Egyptian word which seems to have been used to refer to iron, *bỉw*, was phonetically virtually identical to the word for heaven. Iron did not become more widely available in Egypt until

c. 500 BC and did not become an everyday metal until the Ptolemaic and Roman periods.

The Egyptians had mastered their use of the Nile as a highway and could sail further afield in the Red Sea. The cul-de-sac of the eastern Mediterranean provided an extensive three-sided coastline which guided an endless procession of merchant vessels whose crews risked being wrecked on the rocky coasts that separated the ports. Their voyages through what the Egyptians knew as the 'Great Green', personified as a fertility deity, meant a continuous process of disseminating news, ideas, innovations and skills throughout the region.[4]

For the most part the fate of each nation relied on the personal qualities and prestige of individual rulers. We are most familiar with Egypt. No official records of contemporary rulers of Mycenaean Greece or Minoan Crete survive, or their deeds. Only the folk memories of the Trojan War in Homer's poetry and other myths tell us anything 'historical' about that era, though the results of archaeology are compatible with the Homeric image of chieftain-based city states either in alliance or at war with each other. The picture is a little fuller for the Western Asiatic states, with written evidence for some regimes, such as the Hittites, and their activities.

The evolving states had bureaucrats who compiled and managed archives, which in Egypt included laws recorded on the '40 skins' (leather rolls).[5] Egypt had been one of those first nations to lead the field over a thousand years before but was no longer exceptional. Collectively these states were laying the foundations for the ways modern governments operate, communicate, manage resources and control their populations. Apart from Egypt, the sequence of rulers, events and history are often lost, leaving us with merely the relics of their citadels and graves, serving at best as only glimpses into their society. The remains of imported goods found in Egypt, the adoption of innovations like chariots, Egyptian exports and surviving diplomatic correspondence prove that Egypt was a dominant and advanced player in the Bronze Age world.

## WHY THE 18TH DYNASTY?

The 18th Dynasty lasted about 255 years from approximately 1550 BC to 1295 BC. This was roughly midway between the age of the pyramids and the end of Egypt as an independent country in 30 BC when it was absorbed into the Roman Empire. The 18th Dynasty was the latest manifestation of native royal power in Egypt which already stretched back well over fifteen centuries and is known to us as the first phase of the New Kingdom.

The history of the 18th Dynasty serves as an allegory of unrestrained ambition and greed for all times. A combination of factors brought into being a line of kings who presided over what became temporarily the wealthiest and most powerful nation in the region. Regardless of their individual abilities or lack of, they gradually discovered the extent to which they could indulge themselves by exploiting a population contained within a despotic system designed to ensure continuity and control. This propelled Egypt towards domination of the Near East, a position it had reached by the mid-fifteenth century BC. With that went so many other characteristics of an imperialist state: violence, the systematic extraction of resources and manufactured goods from conquered or vassal states, slavery, and a self-glorifying ideology based on the idea of a divinely backed monarchy. However, it also brought stability.

During this time Egyptian culture reached full maturity, benefiting from the evolution of skills and crafts to an exceptionally high standard. Egyptian society was capable of fielding major armies, working gold and silver into fabulous works of art, fashioning vast stone obelisks and monumental statues, and building gigantic temples. Literacy was well established in a minority of the population made up mainly of the elite classes which included the priesthood and professional scribes, and specialized artisans. Literacy was integral to the development of a sophisticated bureaucracy that governed the country and managed all these projects.

Much of this effort was expended on conspicuous waste, apart

5

from creating an illusion of permanence. State vanity building projects were designed to glorify and perpetuate the regime as part of that mirage. The justification that drove this was immersed in a powerful and intoxicating religious ideology of the king as a living god. His living career and his journey to an ecstatic afterlife required an unmatched level of devotion and commitment. The king ruled as the sun god falcon Horus. At his death he became Osiris, Horus' father who had been killed by his brother Seth and was brought back to life by his wife Isis, mother of Horus, and was succeeded by his son, the new Horus. The cycle was perpetual.

This way of life held Egypt together, bonding Egyptian society together in a shared ideology of existence in this life and the next. The system created livelihoods for the wider population through the trickle-down distribution of food and other goods necessary for subsistence, gifts of livestock and land and sometimes more valuable items by the king and the elite. For most of the time the celebrated fertility of the Nile Valley, thanks to the annual flood, guaranteed an unusually reliable source of food. Similarly, the power of the Egyptian state in the 18th Dynasty protected the people from the threat of foreign invasions, which became a serious issue in later times.

The system was founded on a narcotic sense of timeless stability, oppressive conservatism and total dependence on the state. The great monuments and the all-encompassing framework of religion existed primarily to serve the self-interest of the king and the elite by reinforcing control and acquiescence, even if the consequence was also to create security and dispel fear of chaos.

The idea of investing Egypt's wealth in technological and social development for the greater good did not exist. When innovations emerged, usually from abroad, they were used only to benefit the interests of those in power, for example in the form of advanced military technology or luxury items. Wealth served to enrich the king and his family, and through gifts and endowments also the state cults and the elite. This was normal for a Bronze Age nation, but the scale on which it took place in Egypt's 18th Dynasty was unprecedented.

Nothing was spent on public entertainment or associated facilities, apart from showcase religious processions, the promenading of the king in his chariot and the triumphal display of captives and their executed leaders. Music and hunting existed as leisure pursuits but were mainly the preserve of the elite who left a rich record of their lives compared to the vast bulk of the rest of the population. They are largely undetectable now apart from the monuments on which they laboured and occasional discoveries of their modest graves.

Trade today is a means by which the surplus production of a nation's economy is exchanged through international markets. In antiquity the movement of goods was as likely to be determined by a nation's ability to extort goods by force. Egyptian products of the 18th Dynasty could and did turn up elsewhere, for example in Cyprus, Rhodes, Crete, and Greece. In general, the movement of goods was more in Egypt's favour, at her behest, and with coercion. The appearance of Cretan-style bull-leaping frescoes in an early 18th Dynasty palace in the Delta, and a temple to the cult of the Syrian goddess Astarte at Memphis, shows that the influences were not all one way.

Egypt under the 18th Dynasty operated an international state protection racket. Minor city states sometimes actively welcomed the insulation Egypt offered them against their stronger neighbours. The army played the most important role in turning Egypt into an imperialist predatory state. The legitimization of the 18th Dynasty was founded on the achievements of its first king, Ahmose I, who used the army to expel the Asiatic Hyksos kings from the Delta region and thereby reunified the nation. His successors followed his lead, seeking opportunities to invade Egypt's neighbours to the north and south. Thereafter, apart from the occasional insurrection after the death of a pharaoh, the mere threat of an Egyptian invasion was normally enough to keep Egypt's neighbours meekly handing over tribute. Eventually the rise of new nations, such as the Hittites, introduced fresh tensions towards the end of the 18th Dynasty. One of New Kingdom Egypt's weaknesses was the failure to create a colonial administration to govern its possessions, but this reflected the country's relatively primitive development as an imperialist state.

The king posed as the bastion between the people and the forces of chaos which the Egyptians dreaded. Everything was invested in his ability to maintain order under the auspices of the gods, enshrined in the goddess Maat (who personified the primeval state of Truth and Harmony), a concept deliberately fostered to maintain control and suppress dissent. The same principle lies behind every state and is fundamental to the contract between the ruling government and the people. Enriching the state cults that presided over keeping the wider population in order allowed the king to develop the myth of his status as a protective superman. As the nation's wealth and power grew during the 18th Dynasty the inherent weakness of Egyptian absolutism became clear. The kings ruled unchecked. They could indulge themselves on an unprecedented scale. Consanguineous marriages were sometimes used as a mechanism of holding on to power within the dynasty. This was particularly conspicuous earlier in the dynasty, but circumstantial evidence suggests the royal circle later in the 18th Dynasty included individuals appointed to high office who were also blood relatives of the kings. This helped ring-fence the crown with loyalists, as well as diminish the chance of factions emerging.[6]

There was no professional judiciary or independent legal system. Legal cases were heard in a type of regional court known as the *kenbet*. These courts were not made up of professional magistrates (who did not exist in Egypt), but, rather, the governor of the area concerned together with senior priests and other officials who of course owed their positions to the king. Their seniority was treated as a qualification to hear cases. There was no government assembly of any sort.

Egypt's glory days of the 18th Dynasty were built on a hierarchy with gold-bedecked kings at the top and the broken bodies of labourers, including children and prisoners of war, at the bottom. These kings presided over a population most of whom died before their thirties from disease or other hazards. They were often youthful themselves. The 18th Dynasty rulers mostly succeeded to the throne as children or very young adults. It is quite a comment on the system that by and large it withstood such a hazard. The implications and dangers of being ruled by juveniles, especially those brought up in a culture built on posturing and violence, were considerable and are better attested in the Roman Empire and the Middle Ages. There was little opportunity to assess an Egyptian king's ability to rule. Each had grown up within the confines of a royal household that jealously guarded its prerogatives and imbued him (or her) with a sense of unconditional entitlement. At best, Egypt could hope the young king would be guided by advisers, including his mother, and experienced ministers. At worst, the country was vulnerable to being subjected to the passions and obsessions of adolescent whims, flattered by lackeys in search of position and profit. Few kings lived to their fifties.

The dramatic evidence from workers' cemeteries at Akhenaten's city of Amarna paints a picture of a largely young workforce afflicted by disease, skeletal fractures, other injuries and premature death. These impoverished and illiterate people were a world apart from the extravagance of the upper classes, whom they lived alongside. This was the first great historical era of conspicuous and staggering inequality, with the gap between the rich and the rest widening rapidly.

Such woes were omitted from the idealized depictions of everyday life in Egypt found in private tombs, our main source for everyday life. There is, however, the exceptional evidence of the tomb of the sculptor Ipuy at Deir el-Medina (TT217) with its paintings of workers in action around 1300 BC, including among other detail an image of one man apparently having a dislocated shoulder set by a colleague.[7] The Edwin Smith papyrus from the Old Kingdom, with its itemized guidance for the examination, diagnosis and treatment of injuries, shows that the Egyptian medical profession was quite familiar from early on with the physical consequences of dangerous hard work.[8] This went hand in hand with knowledge of disease and treatments.[9] However, downtrodden labourers at Amarna seem to have benefited little, if at all, from such skills.

Injuries added to conditions typical of any pre-modern society such as blindness, dental problems, arthritis, tuberculosis and other diseases. References to these are also unusual. An exception was the priest Ruma who served in the temple to the Syrian goddess Astarte at Memphis, itself an unusual example of Egypt adopting an interest in a foreign cult. Ruma was shown with an atrophied right leg and a so-called 'equine' deformity of the foot, a characteristic of poliomyelitis.[10]

Bronze Age warfare meant extreme face-to-face violence and brutality meted out to the losers. At Horemheb's Saqqara tomb, constructed while he was a general under Tutankhamun, an Egyptian soldier is shown casually smashing his fist into a Nubian prisoner's jaw while others in manacles are dragged before the king.[11] Such scenes and others formed part of a cycle of triumphant iconography that commemorated the humiliation and degradation of Egypt's helpless and broken foes who had been subdued by the king. None of this made Egypt necessarily any different from other Bronze Age states at the time or since, but Egypt's dominance during the New Kingdom meant it was in a stronger position to inflict brutality than suffer from it.

Complex rituals, especially for death and burial, were engaged in and at vast expense, especially by the elite. They were conducted against a backdrop of institutionalized and casual theft operated on a grand scale. The larceny which characterized Egypt's relations with its neighbours was endemic within the country. An industry of tomb robbing was at work, made viable by a largely undetectable web of complicity involved in dispersing the goods stolen from tombs, especially portable metal items that could be melted down and untraceable oils or unguents. The thieves were prepared to risk being interrogated with beatings, and the prospect of having their limbs amputated or being executed, confident there was an excellent chance they would escape punishment thanks to their friends in high places.[12]

Meanwhile, kings usurped or demolished the mortuary temples

and monuments of their predecessors or even sometimes helped themselves to the contents of their tombs. Each king depicted the past as a prelude to his own blaze across the firmament. The posthumous prospects of his predecessors were not a priority. The reasons for this are complex. Usurpations to a modern eye look aggressive and acquisitive. Sometimes that was true, especially where there was a desire to suppress the memory of a previous ruler such as Hatshepsut. However, in Egypt notions of individuality were more fluid, especially in a royal context. The king's public image was also a conflation of his own identity and achievements with those of his predecessors, thereby creating a more imposing and cumulative manifestation of power renewed with each reign. Usurpation of a predecessor's monuments to help achieve that was part of the tradition of blurring change and continuity.

The king went to war to glorify and enrich himself in the name of Amun, the king of Egypt's gods with unmatched powers as a creator and solar deity and whose name meant 'secret' or 'hidden'. The ultimate exponent was the 19th Dynasty king Ramesses II for whom the whole of Egypt's history was merely a canvas on which to portray himself, but the pioneers were the warrior rulers of the 18th Dynasty such as Thutmose III. There was a remorseless inevitability about what happened towards the 18th Dynasty's end. By the first half of the fourteenth century BC Egypt was under the rule of the otiose Amenhotep III and his queen Tiye who lived in unmatched luxury, spending astronomical sums on extravagant monuments to themselves. They were followed by their religious revolutionary and narcissistic son Akhenaten whose reign turned Egypt upside down.

Monarchs, especially such luminously powerful and wealthy ones as these, have always attracted opportunists like leeches. A continuous parade of parasitic chancers sought position and fortune for themselves and their families. Their principal outlet was the competitive building of their own prodigy houses, tombs and mortuary chapels. These were designed to impress the king and rival courtiers with flair, novelty and extravagance deployed in traditional contexts.[13]

Through their private monuments these officials displayed their status and achievements, each claiming to be the sole focus of the king's admiration and appreciative beneficence. These were the literal and natural expression of a culture completely absorbed by the need to invest in an afterlife. The prodigy tombs and chapels were also the principal Egyptian permanent manifestation of temporal status, just as great houses or similar forms of competitive conspicuous consumption are found in the history of other cultures. The wealthiest imitated the 18th Dynasty kings by having separate memorial chapels and burial chambers. Just as important was the visibility of the work in progress that made such projects considerable matters of note. After the great man's death, the chapel served to perpetuate his reputation or, ironically, acted as a handy target if he had fallen into disgrace in some way.

Some of these overmighty courtiers gambled everything to rise to extraordinary heights and then just as quickly disappeared having been overtaken by events, their greed and misjudgement, and the scheming of their rivals. The nature of their fall is usually obscured by time, but their elaborate tombs and chapels were often abandoned and unused, their walls desecrated, and their mummies and reputations thrown to the winds.

## THE EVIDENCE

Egypt provides just enough historical evidence to form a true chronological outline. Recreating that has been a triumph of research. However, the nature of the evidence is often tenuous and cryptic with the result that modern histories of ancient Egypt frequently veer towards the suppositious and sometimes overwhelmingly so (see Chapter 13 especially). The position is, however, considerably better than it is for contemporary societies and regimes.

By classical times the historical information available in Egypt to Greek writers like Herodotus and Diodorus Siculus was confused and patchy. Herodotus said he was dependent on what the Egyptians and their priests told him, much of which was manifestly spurious (to us at least, if not always to him).[14] The 'history' the priests had at their disposal consisted largely of myth and anecdote, but they may also have been enjoying themselves at Herodotus' expense. Had regnal coinage existed in Egypt in the 18th Dynasty our knowledge of rulers and lengths of reigns would be transformed. But coinage was not invented until the seventh century BC in Lydia and in Egypt did not come into regular use until the Ptolemaic pharaohs.

Manetho, an Egyptian priest of the third century BC, wrote down in Greek a chronology of Egyptian rulers based on a series of dynasties, but provided little supplementary information. This has formed the structure of Egyptian history ever since but just like Herodotus, Manetho had garbled information to hand that he did not fully understand. Moreover, his original text only survives in extracts by later ancient authors.[15] Some of the kings he listed are recognizable, but many are not. Even more confusingly, his account does not always correspond with surviving king lists the Egyptians had compiled long before. The 'Palermo' Stone is the name given to fragments of a royal annals of kings and major events from the 1st to the 5th Dynasties, though its original findspot is unknown. The damaged and incomplete Turin Canon papyrus appears to be a private checklist of kings compiled in the late 19th or 20th Dynasties from official records and includes many obscure or ephemeral rulers. King lists found at Abydos running up to the 19th Dynasty frequently do not correspond with Manetho, as well as omitting 'undesirables' like Hatshepsut and Akhenaten who may have spectral presences in Manetho.[16] Manetho supplied lengths for reigns but did not take account of overlapping dynasties and possible co-regencies, having no real idea about exactly when these kings had ruled.

Manetho's system is the basis of grouping of dynasties into the 'Old Kingdom', 'Middle Kingdom', 'New Kingdom' and the 'Late Period', each separated by episodes of disorder and political confusion known today in a rather utilitarian way as the 'First, Second, and Third Intermediate Periods' (see Appendix 2 for a breakdown of these periods and approximate dates, and Appendix 4 for Manetho's 18th Dynasty). To these have now been added the 'Predynastic' era at the beginning, and at the end Manetho's own time as the 'Ptolemaic' period when Egypt was ruled by the descendants of Alexander the Great's general Ptolemy (Ptolemy I Soter of Egypt, 305–282 BC). The Ptolemies were followed by the Roman imperial era which brought ancient Egypt to an end and eventually saw the wholesale displacement of Egyptian religion by Christianity.

Individual Egyptian rulers were keen to record their own accomplishments. Kamose, whose exploits helped bring an end to the Hyksos era and laid the way open for the 18th Dynasty, erected stelae at Karnak which described his war against the Hyksos and his victory. Other inscriptions on, for example, temple walls were used to celebrate a king's achievements.

A royal stela was a stone plaque, usually with a curved top which framed a panel containing a relief showing the king and suitable gods together with their names and honorific slogans, and the year of the reign. This preceded a more discursive and often lengthy text which explained in variable detail whatever was being commemorated. Stelae were posted at suitable locations, erected in temples, or carved into living rock.[17] Their size depended on whose name they were in, and their purpose. They and other inscriptions were unlikely to have much direct impact on the wider population who might have had little or no access to them and could not read them anyway. Stelae were often buried, reused for their stone, or smashed in the course of time.

Stelae served as a symbolic means of consolidating official history. A typical royal example might recount a military expedition in an extravagantly complimentary way, for example likening the king to 'a young panther', occasionally with useful but more often opaque detail. Others were erected by prominent individuals, for example the Egyptian viceroys of Kush (Nubia), but these similarly were

14

designed to publicize their personal achievements in the service of the king and their loyalty to the state. They lack any objectivity and almost invariably obscure the role or contribution of anyone else. References to Egyptian losses or mistakes are virtually non-existent on any stela. Nonetheless, such records contain references to specific events about which we would otherwise know nothing.

Dismissing these records as propaganda is too simplistic and is based on seeing Egypt from a modern perspective, though there are similarities to the publicity produced by some modern totalitarian regimes. The Egyptians invariably reimagined the specific events of their own times within what they regarded as perpetual and essential truths. One of those was that the divinely backed king was always victorious, that Egypt was superior to anywhere else and had been preordained to be so. Consequently the 'facts', or what passed for them, were adapted into semi-mythologized accounts that also served as ritualized and reassuring confirmations of those 'truths'.

Much of what we know (or think we know) about the events of individual reigns comes from a small number of sources, often found by chance. Ahmes, son of Ibana (hereafter Ahmes-Ibana), was, or so he claimed, a brilliantly successful soldier under Ahmose I, Amenhotep I, and Thutmose I. His military exploits were detailed in a career inscription on the walls of his tomb at El Kab.[18] He had an acute sense of being at the centre of events, and a similar notion of his own importance in the eyes of his king. Without Ahmes-Ibana's tomb texts we would know virtually nothing about the military history of those three kings and in particular the fall of the Hyksos capital Avaris (Hutwaret) to Ahmose I.[19] That momentous event set Egypt on the path to reunification and established the 18th Dynasty.

Ineni the architect served under several of the earlier 18th Dynasty kings. He proudly described on the walls of his tomb at Western Thebes (TT81) the great building projects he claimed to have been responsible for. Such men were primarily concerned to record their own masterful achievements as well as their loyalty to the king but

their accounts are still priceless. Their accounts are typically obsequious and packed with references to their outstanding fulfilment
of duty, and the gifts showered on them by the grateful king. It is
precisely the comparative *absence* of such individual narrative career
biographies for the reigns of, for example, Amenhotep III, Akhenaten
and Tutankhamun that means we know less about the sequence of
events later in the 18th Dynasty. There are plenty of other examples
of senior officials or soldiers, but none of them left anything like Ineni
or Ahmes' accounts, or at least that have been found.

Men such as Ahmes-Ibana and Ineni were all success stories, or
so they would have us believe, and are in that respect alone obviously self-selecting. As sources, their biographies are simultaneously
invaluable and unsatisfactory. The dangers include taking these
half tales masquerading as truth at face value, mistaking rhetorical
claims for literal accounts, or selectively accepting or rejecting the
content to suit preconceptions. They were also compiled potentially
many years after the events they described, perhaps even sometimes
by descendants, making it possible and even likely that there were
errors in detail and sequencing. Similar problems apply to the artistic depictions of kings in action or at war, or portrayals of everyday
life. The cinematic format of paintings and reliefs relied on idealized
images, not realism. A scene of a gigantic king firing arrows from his
chariot at his diminutive and traditional enemies as he ran over them
was an allegory of his and Egypt's position in the universe, even if
in some cases it purported to record an actual event. Consequently,
the image was easily usurped by one or more of his successors, just
as any verbal account might be. Whittling away the puff to reveal the
truth, if there was any, is often impossible.

Such pitfalls imperil the study of all historical periods, but Egypt
has been unusually badly affected, as the late Egyptologist William
Murnane observed:

One of the more vexing problems Egyptologists face is the
interpretation of what we are pleased to call historical records.

Since most of these texts are public statements, 'published' on tomb- and temple walls for a variety of commemorative or propagandistic reasons, they are generally assumed to be tendentious – but paradoxically, Egyptologists go on taking them at their face value as raw materials for history.[20]

The same considerations apply to Egypt's neighbours whose accounts are equally susceptible to be accepted at face value today.[21] Many current controversies in Egyptology have been going round in circles for over a century.[22] The reason is simple: the evidence does not exist to resolve them. Another scholar has said, 'the materials for ancient history often do not permit us the luxury of deciding what we must believe, but only what it seems reasonable to believe'.[23]

History as a discipline begins when disagreements start about what took place at a given time. This usually commences when the events are still happening, leaving even contemporaries confused by what was going on around them, especially in an era of disorder. This is true of all periods, but in Egyptology there is a particular love of foundering on minutiae in an endless quest to unravel a definitive narrative when no such thing existed even at the time. The belief is that the tantalizing truth is anxiously waiting to be released from anonymous mummies and illegible or cryptic inscriptions by bombarding them with hypotheses. The latter part of Akhenaten's reign and its immediate aftermath is the best example. The arguments over reconciling the apparent identity of certain royal mummies with various and often conflicting scientific evidence for their ages at death and other physiological data for sequencing and relationships have also proved to be equally inconclusive and interminable.[24] This would never normally be possible for any other ancient line of rulers (for example, not a single Roman emperor's body is known) and the effect in Egypt's case has been only to muddy the waters more than it clears them.

If historical nihilism ever existed in Egypt, it had no voice.[25] Nor did any Egyptian independent historian emerge in later generations to compose a revisionist account of past events like Hatshepsut's rule or Akhenaten's revolution, even if the authoritative records to do so had ever existed which they probably did not. We are left instead mainly with occasional official or private references to contemporary events. Records such as Kamose's stelae are easily dismissed as unreliable in some way, but this overlooks how bias serves as a defining characteristic of the era. Their bombastic conceits tell us a great deal about how Egyptian kings and their supporters saw themselves and wished to be seen. This is even the case if it is obvious that the contents of these texts are flagrantly one-sided and exaggerated. The Egyptian king, like every other ruler of his era, had no choice. Presenting himself as all-powerful and successful was essential to his prestige and continued tenure.

Military scribes are attested recording events, but their accounts do not generally survive. The text as written on a temple wall, stela, or scarab is very unlikely to be identical to the original version. The reliance on stock phraseology and the aesthetic arrangement of hieroglyphs is apparent from extant inscriptions. The potential for changes, mistakes, or invention, and at the very least the blurring of specific detail beneath clichés and repetition, is obvious. Some include stock passages that were based on earlier texts. Second-rate carving on the inscriptions, compromised by circumstances and poor rock, especially in tombs, as well as disintegrating plaster and partial loss of painted texts, creates endless difficulties of interpretation.[26] Many texts are incomplete thanks to damage incurred over the enormous length of time involved.

There are also surviving contemporary diplomatic letters in cuneiform, a method of writing commonly used by some of Egypt's Western Asiatic neighbours. However, it is not even possible always to identify the correspondents, including the Egyptian king being written to. The best-known are the Amarna Letters which provide a fascinating archive recording correspondence of the courts of Amenhotep III and Akhenaten with various foreign powers in Western Asia. The Amarna Letters represent only a tiny part of

18

what must have existed, limiting their wider relevance. The contents are also notoriously undated, cryptic and written in languages few can read today, resulting in dependence on translations and all their vagaries.

## DATES

The given chronological dates for ancient Egypt today vary wildly, depending on the book or article being read. As one review has put it, 'the variables in the evidence far outweigh the facts'.[27] Nonetheless it has been possible to draw up a relative chronology of the kings and some of the major events, even if these vary depending on the assessment of the length of reigns.

The only contemporary dating information normally available comes from inscriptions on temple walls or stelae, and notes (known as dockets) on stone, papyri, or pottery sherds. These referred only to a king's regnal year, counted from accession, and sometimes might have involved parallel sequences if there was a co-regency (see Appendix 7 for regnal years). They do not supply absolute dates that can be tied to our calendar. Complications arise if the text is partially illegible, incomplete, or contradicts another. There was no continuous system of numbering years. When a new king came to the throne the count started again with his 1st regnal year. The highest known regnal year serves only as a *terminus post quem* ('time after which') for the death of a king, not the maximum length of the reign. Although this is an elementary archaeological concept, in Egyptology the highest known regnal year is often treated as evidence for the end of a reign or soon after. The discovery of a single new inscription on something as mundane as a potsherd or a quarry face can have a dramatic impact on the known length of a reign.

The only reliable way of pinpointing an historical event would be the ancient record of a solar eclipse in Egypt, tied by some piece of written evidence to a specific regnal year of a pharaoh. The absolute dates of past solar eclipses and their paths of totality are easily calculated. There were several major eclipse events during the period covered by this book, including partial and annular eclipses. A total solar eclipse passed across Thebes on 1 June 1478 BC. Another crossed a wide swathe of central Egypt, including the site of Akhenaten's new city at Akhet-aten (Tell el-Amarna), on 14 May 1338 BC.[28] These indisputable events must have been occasions of enormous significance but there is no known Egyptian reference to either. Many attempts have been made by Egyptologists also to use Egyptian lunar dates, and to tie to Egyptian chronology what seem to be references to eclipses in other sources, such as Hittite texts for the eclipse of 24 June 1312 BC and the Bible, for example Joshua 10.13 and the eclipse in Canaan of 30 October 1207 BC.[29]

The subject of eclipses as a basis for establishing absolute historical dates is really beyond the scope of this book but there are some important considerations. No ancient Egyptian record of a solar eclipse exists, even though Diodorus Siculus reported that the Egyptians were able to predict solar and lunar eclipses based on past observations.[30] The only known pre-Islamic record of a solar eclipse visible in Egypt is of the event on 10 March AD 601.[31] Non-Egyptian ancient sources like the Hittites tend to refer to such astronomical events with euphemistic or allegorical terminology (if at all), making it difficult to know even if an eclipse is involved, quite apart from when, exactly where, or whether it was partial, annual, or total. This usually means more than one eclipse is a possibility, making a firm link to modern computed eclipse events in antiquity very difficult.

Ancient records of eclipses are unreliable for another obvious but usually overlooked reason. In the past the idea of associating an eclipse with a major event was an attractive prospect even if the two had not actually coincided, and so was exaggerating the eclipse. The eclipse of 30 April AD 59 was described as total in Rome by the Roman historian Cassius Dio to emphasize the importance of the omen after the murder of Nero's mother Agrippina, but in fact was only partial in the city. The Anglo-Saxon Chronicle mentions a solar eclipse on 2 August 1135, describing it as a portent of the death of Henry I of England on 1 December 1135. The eclipse occurred on 2 August 1133 and appears to have been placed in 1135 in the Chronicle either by mistake or for the sake of a better story.[32] These discrepancies are only apparent because the absolute chronology in both cases is known. It is obvious that even if an ancient source did refer to an eclipse, any coincidence with an important event might be false or manipulated, making conclusions about the actual date of the event wrong.

There are very few other ways of estimating absolute dates in Egyptian history. The Egyptians were fully aware that the solar year lasts 365¼ days.[33] However, they operated a civil calendar that ran only for 365 days, made up of twelve 30-day months and five inter-calary days added at the end to make up the difference. The months were grouped into three seasons of four months: flood, growth and low water.[34]

The civil calendar system began in or around 2781 BC. It was marked by the Egyptian New Year's Day on what we call 19 July. This was the day when the star Sirius was first observed in the dawn sky rising at the same time as the sun (the 'heliacal rising of Sirius'), a phenomenon that appeared just a few days before the annual inundation of the Nile every year. Thanks to the civil calendar's annual shortfall of a quarter of a day 'grave consequences' ensued.[35] After four years of being in alignment, the civil calendar moved a day ahead of the solar year for the next four years. After forty years the civil calendar was ten days ahead for four years. After 400 years it was 100 days ahead. Of course, Sirius was still rising at the same point in the solar year as it ever had, and still does, but by then it appeared to an Egyptian that the heliacal rising (and the imminent Nile flood) was occurring 100 days after the civil calendar's New Year's Day.

It took 1,460 solar years (4 × 365) after 2781 BC for the civil calendar to fall back into alignment with the solar calendar which it did for four years between c. 1321 and 1318 BC before drifting once more.[36] The alignment returned in AD 139–42 during the reign of the emperor Antoninus Pius (AD 138–61), by which time Egypt had been a Roman province for 168 years. This was treated as so important that it was marked by a special issue of coins at Alexandria for the beginning and end of the four years concerned.[37] A century later a Roman writer called Censorinus recorded the occasion, specifying the exact year.[38] The phenomenon was known as the Sothic Cycle and as the celestial *apocatastasis* ('the return of the stars to their original position'), though in fact it was the civil calendar which had temporarily returned to its original position. The AD 139 event is the key absolute date which allows us to count back to 1321 BC and 2781 BC.

The relevance of this engaging example of Egyptian madness is that some records survive of the civil calendar date on which the heliacal rising of Sirius was observed. By calibrating these records with the point in the Sothic Cycle it is possible to estimate an absolute date. One such observation was apparently made during the reign of Amenhotep I in the early 18th Dynasty on the 9th day of the 3rd month of the season of low water in his 9th regnal year appearing as an incidental calendar reference written on the verso of the Ebers medical papyrus.[39] The date of the heliacal rising was thus 309 days into the civil calendar, which means that by then 1,236 (4 × 309) years had elapsed since 2781 BC, making the year c. 1541 BC. However, we do not know which of the four possible years the same observation could have been made, so we can only say that the potential range was 1544–1538 BC. That would place Amenhotep I's accession to 1553–1547 BC, but of course other estimates of the absolute dates exist.[40]

Thanks to Sirius's own movements in the heavens, and the place in Egypt where the observation was made (not always specified), the heliacal observations can at best get us only to within about two to three decades of the true date. This is better than nothing and it does mean that our dates for Amenhotep I are probably not much more than thirty years in either direction from the truth. From that we can estimate the dates for his successors but there is great uncertainty about how long many of the reigns were, or the incidence of possible co-regencies, increasing the margin of error. Much scholarly positioning on the subject has appeared over the years but pursuing the topic in search of further precision is futile.[41] For this reason the dates given for Amenhotep I in this book match one of the currently used chronologies but strictly on the understanding it is only an approximation.

Much of Egypt's history cannot be linked to dates of any other civilization of the period because no other contemporary societies' records can be tied to absolute dates either.[42] The only time we have any sense of parallel but undated chronologies is when, for example, diplomatic correspondence makes a reference in one letter to a named ruler of Egypt, and a king of Babylon or Mitanni, but such instances are rare. What matters most, then, is Egypt's relative chronology: the sequence and lengths of reigns, and when events took place during them.[43] Nonetheless, the Roman natural historian Pliny the Elder, writing in the AD 70s, referred to Ramesses II 'who ruled at the time of the capture of Troy'.[44] He had no idea about the dates involved but the Trojan War, or at least the context in which the myth was set, is today usually associated on an archaeological basis with roughly around the time Ramesses is believed to have ruled in the thirteenth century BC. It is not until 664 BC, when Egypt's history can be tied to firm classical sources which are fixed to absolute dates, that precision is possible.

Other archaeological methods of absolute dating, for example radiocarbon dating, are generally less precise than the methods outlined above. For example, radiocarbon dating only provides a statistical probability of an organic item belonging within a range of dates which need calibrating against tree-ring data. However, there has been some success recently in dating organic items found in Egyptian tombs such as seeds which have tended broadly to confirm the approximate chronologies already used.[45]

# NAMES

Modern Egyptology throws up endless variant spellings and names forms, the most obvious of which are Thutmose/Tuthmosis ('Thoth is born') and Amenhotep/Amenophis ('Amun is satisfied'). These examples are partly attributable to the survival of the names into Greek versions (here the second version given). They differ from transliteration of the hieroglyphs, themselves subject to variations even for the same ruler, and are used for convenience today. They bear little resemblance to their original forms. For example, Thutmose is sometimes pronounced from hieroglyphs by Egyptologists as *Djehutymes* but was possibly vocalized by the Egyptians as *Tahati'missaw* though even that is uncertain. The same problem afflicts the records of lesser individuals. Djehuty was a senior official under Hatshepsut. He is to be found today in books called either Djehuty or Thutiye. To the uninitiated it is easy to assume two quite different people are involved.

We blithely use the royal birth names of pharaohs, qualified by our addition of numerals in the manner of medieval monarchs, such as Thutmose III, because it suits us to do so. The Egyptians never differentiated their rulers by number. Although the birth name was prominently displayed it was usually depicted alongside the king's regnal (throne) name in a pair of cartouches. The other three names held by a king were not contained in cartouches and did not usually appear on monuments. In Amenhotep III's case we read his throne name as Nebmaatre ('The Lord of Truth is Re'). The throne name (sometimes called the prenomen) was also the name by which the king was generally known outside Egypt. When references turn up, for example on the cuneiform diplomatic correspondence found at Amarna, they can give us an alternative idea of the pronunciation, at least as the words sounded to foreigners. Nebmaatre was written by Asiatics as Nibmuwareya (or variants of).[46]

Variant spellings complicate even the use of indexes when researching a topic in various articles and books. To some extent this is unavoidable, and sometimes the only means of distinguishing two contemporary individuals of either sex who shared the same name. The lack of consistency is often infuriating. The best example is Ahmose or Ahmes ('Moon Born'), a very common name for both men and women. Its pronunciation was probably more like *y-'hames*.[47] Many members of the 18th Dynasty were called Ahmose, sometimes helpfully provided with a second part of the name like the queen Ahmose-Nefertari, while commoners might distinguish themselves by referring to their fathers, Ahmes-Ibana being a good example. In one recent work summarizing the members of the royal families the only resort was to allocate some letters such as 'Ahmes B', the queen and mother of Hatshepsut.[48]

These inconsistencies in modern works, avoidable or otherwise, are matched by almost every other aspect of Egyptian history and culture. During the research for this book, it frequently turned out that what appeared to be two different pieces of evidence were the same one, the confusion created by variant spellings and translations, variant place names, and alternative chronologies. This is made more complicated by using different referencing systems, and there being no established series of core source material in bilingual texts as there is in Greek and Roman for the classical world.[49]

## THE EGYPTIAN LANGUAGE

The sensational unravelling of the tortuous Egyptian language is an extraordinary story. It is our portal into ancient Egypt in all its manifestations and the single greatest source of revelations about its history and society. The result has been the ability to read the career inscription of the old soldier Ahmes-Ibana, the conceits of Hatshepsut, a grumpy letter from Amenhotep II, and of course above all some of the revelations about the extraordinary reign of Akhenaten. Nonetheless, the obscure meanings and colloquialisms of Egyptian, together with completely different forms of expression, mean that while the language has brought us immeasurably closer to the Egyptians, it has simultaneously shown us how far apart we are from them.

Hieroglyphs were pictograms used to represent whole words, individual sounds and syllables. Some words that we rely on, such as forms that indicate tense in verbs, did not exist and neither did punctuation. Hieroglyphs could be written in any direction. There was a handwritten form known now as hieratic, used for papyri or dockets on pottery sherds or on a tomb wall, and a much later and even more abbreviated form called demotic. Literacy was greatly admired in Egyptian culture, but proficiency varied among the literate, depending on an individual's training and personal or professional needs. This impacted on what was written down and how, contributing to problems understanding texts.

Pioneering modern introductions to Egyptian are available today but these are primarily pathways to familiarizing oneself with basic elements of the language.[50] They are successful and imaginative approaches, but function very much in terms of conventional 'accepted' translations of stock formulae and phrases.

To make Egyptian more coherent (and convenient to typeset), a modern convention is to transliterate the hieroglyphs into letters that are easier for us to reproduce. Since some of the sounds, insofar as we understand them, are not normal for English or other European languages this has meant introducing additional symbols and letters. These are listed in Appendix 1. In this book the transliterated font has been used to show these words, but most are consigned to the appendices and notes.

There has not been a human being on Earth who would recognize ancient Egyptian as it was heard, or could speak it as it was uttered, for over 1,600 years. In the late fourth century AD the Roman historian Ammianus Marcellinus published a translation in Greek of the texts on one of the obelisks in Rome made in the time of Augustus 350 years earlier by a Greek called Hermapion. Ammianus also made some basic comments on hieroglyphs and how they differed from the alphabetic letters the Greeks and Romans were familiar with.[51] Before long even that knowledge had faded.

Despite the ingenious decipherment pioneered by Jean-François Champollion (1790–1832), and the work done since, knowledge of the ancient Egyptian language remains incomplete. For all their beauty and elaborate design, hieroglyphs were not a comprehensive written form of Egyptian, at least not in a way we can now fully understand. Alan Gardiner described 'the absence of vocalization' in hieroglyphics as having irritating consequences. This was a marvellous understatement, yet he was only referring in that instance to the impossibility of transcribing proper names.[52]

Some words are still not fully understood, and many can be translated in several different ways. The grammar remains afflicted by ambiguities. The multiple possible meanings of hieroglyphs and absence of other important features such as tense and mood in the written language mean we will always be distanced from it. This is especially likely when faced with an unusual text that does not contain the usual stock phraseology. The study of the language is a specialized pursuit and many Egyptologists have only a passing familiarity with it.

Had it not been for the survival of some ancient Egyptian words into Coptic, used in early Christian Egypt, we would be even worse off. The first scholars of Egyptian unravelled what words the hieroglyphs represented by comparing the Egyptian symbols with the Greek translation of the same text on the Rosetta Stone, which dates to 196 BC. Words that had recognizably survived into Coptic provided clues to meaning and pronunciation. Coptic uses letters based on the Greek language with the addition of signs from demotic and derived many of its words from late Egyptian. The creation of Egyptian vocabularies and grammars in modern times is a startling achievement, but it would be a mistake to assume this means scholars are always capable of identifying exact meanings. Moreover, the Rosetta Stone used a late form of Egyptian, differing in many ways from the so-called Middle Egyptian in use in the 18th Dynasty. By the time of Egyptian's last manifestation in Coptic, Middle Egyptian was as remote as early Anglo-Saxon English is to us.

James Breasted described 'how helpless our incomplete knowledge of the Egyptian dictionary leaves us as soon as we pass from the conventional language of the few classes of monument familiar to us, to some untrodden path'.[53] Although he wrote that in 1906, his essential point holds true to this day. Alan Gardiner added in 1938, 'the uncertainties of Egyptian translation are indeed deplorable'.[54] Both observations are still valid today as salutary warnings to Egyptologists trying to reconstruct precise family relationships or sequences of events from texts that include obscure phrases or vocabulary.

Hieroglyphs are much closer to certain early modern forms of shorthand in the way sounds and words are represented, haphazard and varied types of abbreviation, omission of vowels and a reliance on context to resolve ambiguities in use of signs which include symbols and simplified pictograms. Shorthand exists today in several different types, but it is rarely used now and thus less familiar than it once was. The English diarist Samuel Pepys (1633–1703) used a system called Thomas Shelton's Tachygraphy which the present author is fluent in. The similarities to hieroglyphic expression are striking, and especially with transliterating what is, by definition, an incomplete representation of the spoken language.

When using shorthand, the omissions and ambiguities do not trouble the composer, but for anyone else trying to read the text back, problems often arise. Written Egyptian, like shorthand, is prone to selective and inconsistent abbreviation, potentially confusing to anyone other than the person who composed the text. This is especially true where the medium, such as a scarab, is small and where the text is also poorly executed. Add on the distance of thousands of years and trying to read a remote and obsolete ancient language and the danger of assuming a reading is correct becomes obvious.

Another issue is the need to introduce elements to make good the normal omissions, or unintelligible signs, and thereby create a comprehensible translation. This sometimes results in assuming these additions to be as valid as the direct translation of the signs that do exist. Time after time it turned out while writing this book that a translation, however well intentioned, had been based to some extent on restored texts where whole words or even phrases have been supplied by the translator or transcriber to make good gaps. Obviously, this is often unavoidable, but it does mean the translations are not what they sometimes appear to be. Just to compound the problems, many Egyptian texts are damaged and incomplete, some only existing now in old drawings or photographs. Much surviving written Egyptian was formal and formulaic. It rarely veered into the vernacular or served as an authentic written form of everyday spoken Egyptian. Only in the Amarna period during Akhenaten's reign did this become more common, even in official texts, reflecting the more intensely personal characteristics and realism of art under his regime.

Egyptian words could be written in various ways, using different hieroglyphs to represent the same sounds. The phonetic results were thus identical or similar, but the appearance of the written forms in hieroglyphs could be noticeably different. The same sequence of hieroglyphs may represent both the phonetic sounds of a single word, or individual words in a phrase, depending on the context.

Just as with forms of modern shorthand, Egyptian words were normally represented by signs that represented only their consonants. The same symbol or symbols might also be used to represent other words which happened to have the same consonants but different meanings. The use of determinative signs alongside phonetic signs sometimes clarifies the meaning in Egyptian, but not always. The 'determinative' was a sign that confirmed the meaning of a series of phonetic signs, for example a pictogram of a horse after the letters of the word for a horse (*ssmt*). A determinative could be used on its own either to indicate that same word, or to serve in another way as a quite different phonetic value. It could also be omitted, or another determinative substituted.[55] The governing principle seems to have been either the space available or individual taste on the part of a person whom we might regard as the equivalent of a typographical compositor. Word order was complicated by something now called 'honorific transposition'. For example, the name of a god normally took precedence even if it formed the later part of a king's name. Tutankhamun, for example, was written Amun-Tut-Ankh.[56]

Understanding of the language is now sufficiently advanced that for the most part translations provide us with plausible versions of the original meaning. But the ambiguities and obscurities remain. Consequently, translations of the same original text often vary considerably. Elementary scrutiny of many translations reveals them to be pastiches of a text probably correct in terms of the general meaning, but which could easily have been translated several different ways. There are countless examples of translations of rare or even unique specific terms in Egyptian that are suppositious, sometimes with optimistic significance then being attached to the translation which often ends up being treated as definitive. This is less of a problem with standard texts like dedication stelae or religious texts where the content was matched by many similar examples.

Despite these problems, for the most part texts can now be translated with a good degree of relative accuracy. 'Relative' here means compared to other far better understood ancient languages like Greek and Latin where most of the enduring problems with Egyptian do not exist. Apart from standard brief notices like dockets and dates, successfully translating Egyptian is most likely with longer texts where the context is clear and helps to unravel difficult phrases and terms. More challenging are colloquialisms (which might easily be overlooked now and taken literally), obscure or anachronistic references, epithets or titles found in isolation, and especially when any of these have few or no parallels. Many of the 'rules' of Egyptian grammar are modern conventions, devised to make sense of a language that will never now be fully understood.

# KINGS AND QUEENS

The words for kings and queens are particularly good examples of the distance between the way we express these concepts and the ways the Egyptians did. For example, in transliteration *ḥmt-nsw* was 'king's wife' or 'royal wife' and variations such as *ḥmt-nsw-wrt*, 'great royal wife'. We often substitute words like 'queen' but a more literal translation from Egyptian would require a descriptive phrase in English. The word for a king that appears here (*nsw* or *nesu*) means 'he of the (sedge) plant', a symbol of divine royal power. Appropriately it was represented by a hieroglyph in the form of that plant.[57] Thus, what we would call a 'queen' was in Egyptian represented by words that meant 'woman/wife of he of the sedge plant'. The term did not have to mean a conjugal relationship, a crucially important distinction from today and often leading to unwarranted and over-literal interpretations. By the late 18th Dynasty, the eldest daughter could serve her father as great royal wife, fulfilling the role in a formal and symbolic way.[58]

There were other ways of indicating a queen was meant, for example the addition of a determinative hieroglyphic sign showing a woman wearing a diadem and holding a flower, or another for the uraeus symbol of monarchy. Incorporated in a royal cartouche that contained the signs for her name, this made it clear the individual was a queen but a queen-consort in our terms. In this respect the Egyptian queen served less as a separate royal identity and more a widening of the concept of kingship as a 'male-female composite'.[59] This makes it much easier to understand why the position of queen could be filled by the king's mother, his daughter, or his wife. It shows similarly how a queen, such as Hatshepsut, could reverse the process and try to create the same composite when declaring herself king (see Chapter 7).[60]

The word for king, *nsw*, is of very obscure origin and symbolism. It is now understood to be a reference to the spiritual institution of kingship, and was usually paired with another word, *bity* (shown as a bee), which meant the living king ruling in the temporal or mortal sphere. However, the sedge plant was formerly believed to be symbolic of Upper Egypt (the Nile Valley), and the bee of Lower Egypt (the Delta), confusing the symbolic concepts of kingship with the geographical zones of the country. This arose from the Greek text on the Rosetta Stone which used words that can mean higher and lower land or spiritual and mortal concepts, leading to the ambiguous former English translation 'King of Upper and Lower Egypt'. Nowadays *nsw-bity* is usually translated as 'Dual King', meaning king in the divine and temporal senses. This is explained in more detail in Appendix 7. Of course, the geographical distinction between the Nile Valley and the Delta remains, not least because the Egyptians recognized them to be quite different by using the red crown of Lower Egypt and the white crown of Upper Egypt, combined in a double crown to symbolize the unified nation.[61]

There were many other words or terms related to what we would call a king, but which translate more literally as 'majesty', 'the perfect god' or 'Lord of the Two Lands'. These have been placed in Appendix 7 with their transliterated equivalents. Some of these terms could be and were feminized when appropriate with the simple addition of the letter 't'. For example, 'Lord' which in Egyptian is *neb* became *nebet*, meaning 'Lady' or, perhaps better in an Egyptian context, 'she-Lord', though it is also to be found translated as 'Mistress'.[62]

Today the word 'pharaoh' is often used for an Egyptian king. In the Old Kingdom the word for pharaoh, made up of the signs for a house and a column (*pr-ꜥ*), meant literally 'Great House'. It was used as we use the word 'palace', for example to refer to where an official worked. By the late 18th Dynasty, the term was a synonym for the ruler, used in a letter from a steward in Memphis to Amenhotep IV (Akhenaten), in this instance 'Lord Pharaoh, may he live, be prosperous, and be healthy' (the latter exhortations often abbreviated to l.p.h. by Egyptologists).[63]

All these terms were conventionally male because the positions were usually held by men, and that is why we translate them as 'king'. Our word 'king' is, however, matched by our word 'queen',

*Egypt in the 18th Dynasty*

applied when a woman is either the consort of a king *or* rules in her own right. With no such word for a female ruler in Egypt the closest was a feminized version of the word usually translated as 'sovereign' (see Appendix 7). This still meant that on those occasions when a woman did assume supreme power, she had no choice but to adopt the terminology of a male ruler, even if it was sometimes feminized.

The word for mother (*mwt*) was the sign for a vulture feminized with the letter 't'. Combined with the word for king it became 'mother of the king'. Of course, the vulture headdress was worn by Egyptian queens and women who ruled as kings and was the symbol also of Mut, the mother goddess and consort of Amun, whose name was the same as that for a mother.

A term such as 'son' or 'father' served equally well in Egyptian to describe more distant or even only symbolic connections. In the absence of any specific words for grandson, 'son' might also mean 'grandson' or even descendant, or an honorific statement of proximity and intimacy.[64] The same applies to 'daughter', 'brother', 'sister', 'father' and other similar terms for which the Egyptians also had no alternatives like 'grandfather', 'uncle', 'cousin', or other extended family relationships. Formulae were sometimes used. By multiplying the determinative 'f' in the word for father two generations or more could be indicated, but even this could be symbolic rather than exact. This makes unravelling connections within royal families difficult since it is often impossible to know what the relationship was, because the Egyptians did not always make such precise distinctions.

## OFFICIALDOM

Egypt's administration on one hand can be seen as a well-organized structure of departments or ministries that took care of everything from construction to mining, administering royal estates, managing the royal household, and taking care of regional and local government. On the other, the glitterati of the 18th Dynasty court circle and the bureaucracy enjoyed an array of elaborate, often ambiguous and overlapping, titles and responsibilities that defy precise understanding today. Many held several posts. The system was riven with nepotism and jobs were often handed down in families, rather than competed for, as was normal for the ancient world. This problem is made worse by the inconsistency in the way Egyptologists refer to these positions. There was, however, the so-called *Onomasticon* of Amenope. This work of instruction, of which several examples are known, was compiled at some point in the 20th to 22nd Dynasties and was based on older traditions. It is divided into categories of various aspects of Egyptian life, including sections on occupations, towns, buildings and classes of food. The text provided a detailed breakdown of what the jobs involved were called, and thus served as a sort of handbook.[65] These sections provide important evidence for how Egyptian society operated and was structured, and the terminology employed.

The most senior position was that of vizier. The English word 'vizier' derives from an Arabic word *wazīr* via Turkish which meant viceroy, but was probably ultimately derived from *wazara*, 'to bear a burden', or in other words something akin to the bearing of the obligations and duties on behalf of the monarch. Its closest equivalent now is 'chief minister' or 'prime minister' though by the middle of the 18th Dynasty there were two 'viziers', one in the north and one in the south, which helped cope with Egypt's geography. The vizier represented royal authority in his area and presided over a hierarchy of other officials and scribes who dealt with taxes, administering the goods and products which needed processing and storing.[66]

The memorial chapel of the vizier Rekhmire (*temp.* Thutmose III) (TT100) contains a description of the duties and rituals involved. He described himself as second only to the king. This reflected the way Rekhmire's home would have exhibited the same information about his status.[67] Like all such men, Rekhmire was also keen to include references to how 'greatly loved' and 'greatly respected' he was, as well as being the beneficiary of royal favour.[68] The vizier basked in an array of supplementary honours and titles listed in Rekhmire's career autobiography.[69] The chapel's main purpose was to record and advertise his status in life. It was an extravagant facility that can only have been paid for out of the profits of high office, whether legitimate or otherwise.

Rekhmire featured a speech by the king in his chapel that made much of how difficult the job was. Thutmose III exhorted the vizier to be restrained, conscientious, to follow the letter of the law, and even not to be over-zealous in a way that would impoverish people.[70] Rekhmire's tomb texts explained how such a vizier sat in a chair with a cushion upon a dais with the '40 skins' law code laid out before him, named after the skins on which it had been written. Other officials were arranged around him in two rows according to precedence. These men reported the current state of their individual spheres, such as frontier fortresses and income and expenditure. The assembly included scribes to record the proceedings. In his turn the vizier would proceed to report to the king via the chief treasurer. Petitioners were brought in to make their cases.

Rekhmire's uncle had held the vizierate before him. These men, some of whom undoubtedly had blood connections to the royal family, owed their advance to the king and were often able to rely on their positions becoming effectively hereditary, ensuring their families' prominence in future generations. Despite his importance and claimed popularity, the state of the memorial chapel and the desecration of his images show that Rekhmire fell from grace at some point. The fate of his three sons who were thereby denied the chance to succeed their father is unknown.[71] Rekhmire is only one of several 18th Dynasty officials believed to have been summarily deposed after falling from favour.

In Egyptian the word for a vizier was pronounced something like 'Tat(y)'.[72] The hieroglyph was an image of a nestling duckling, its literal meaning, but it had the same phonetic value as the first part of the word used for a vizier, along with the additional '*t*'. In Egyptian it was possible to drop the additional *t* and provide only the duckling sign, and still mean 'vizier' with the understanding being reliant on the context. The explanation comes from the fact that the phonetic value of the duckling sign resembled the word for a curtain, used as the determinative sign in some references to a vizier instead. The vizier was thus 'he of the curtain', perhaps an allusion to what he sat behind while waiting to receive other officials.

The English word 'viceroy' is now normally applied to the 'King's Son of Kush' and variants.[73] This powerful position was conferred on the man placed in charge of Nubia on behalf of the Egyptian king. By calling the incumbent a son of the king, the status was emphasized but this was not a reference to any blood relationship. This kind of terminology can be confusing to the modern mind, leading to some literal (and naïve) inferences, especially on the basis of a shared and very common name.[74] Similar problems arise with other honorific titles like 'God's Father' where the god involved was the king. The term could be used for what we would call the king's father-in-law.

Another recurrent example is 'mayor', normally elaborated in English to 'mayor of Thebes'. The Egyptian word denoted 'foremost' or someone who took precedence over others, perhaps 'the one in charge'. Other possible meanings include 'prince' and 'governor'. Together with a determinative the word was qualified. For example, a figure of a seated man might be used to indicate he was a man whose role placed him above others. The obvious problem with the possible translations is that they all have quite different and more precise meanings in English, whereas the Egyptian was an all-purpose term.[75]

The official usually described today as a 'chamberlain' supervised royal domains. He also acted on the personal authority of the king. There were several words or phrases for this position. One meant something like 'the first man under the king'. Another meant 'he who is front of [others?]'. The fact that multiple English words are used sometimes adds to the confusion. The titles 'chancellor', 'treasurer', and the most literal 'royal seal-bearer (or wearer)', all appear in modern books. The term was made up of the words for the kingship in the mortal sphere and a cylinder seal on a necklace. The combined meaning seems to be 'the bearer/wearer of the royal precious seal', hence the various English options which all amount to the same thing: this official was a royal treasurer whose office was symbolized by possession of the royal seal.

The use of words 'Steward', 'Overseer', 'Chief', 'Superintendent' and even 'General' in English translations of Egyptian look like several distinct supervisory posts. They are good examples of how various terms have been used to translate what is largely the same phrase in Egyptian, often including archaisms drawn incongruously from the vocabulary of nineteenth- and early twentieth-century English estate management, reflecting the time at which Egyptian dictionaries were being compiled. The Egyptian term (*imy-r*) for all these positions was a colloquial phrase that meant something like 'he who is in the mouth [of those under him]'. The Egyptian phonetic version of the term was more usually represented only by the determinative for an ox tongue which had the same phonetic value as the individual alphabetic signs.[76] 'Overseer' would, for example, never now be used to describe a modern supervisory job but has a resilient presence in contemporary translations of Egyptian. It is also translated as 'master', as in the title Master of Horse.[77] The consequence is that this one term ends up now being translated into various words implying several different jobs existed when the Egyptians were referring to only one type of supervisory role.[78]

Another word, using the sceptre determinative sign, meant 'he who was in control/charge'. It served a similar purpose but is also translated in various ways, for example 'leader'.[79] Just to complicate the matter further, the sign for the sky could be used for 'chief' or 'commander', indicating someone literally above others. It could be used interchangeably with *imy-r*, even by the same person to refer to the same position.[80]

These titles were often clarified with a descriptive specification of office.[81] There was, for example, the Overseer of the Army, normally translated as General, or even Great Overseer of the Army, perhaps what we might call Commander of the Armed Forces.[82] The Overseer of the King's House resembled the modern British office of Master of the Household of the Sovereign. Another good example is the Overseer of Works on the two great obelisks Amenhotep, who worked for Hatshepsut (also sometimes translated as her Chief Steward).[83] At the same time he held other positions which were similarly explained with their own specifications of office.

There are no agreed conventions for translating these posts in Egyptology. This can be confusing when consulting two different books, obscuring how two individuals had held the same position. This is of additional significance if the two are thought to have been related because of the habit of treating such posts as hereditary.[84]

Quite what any of these officials really did in these jobs in Egypt, apart from profiting out of them, is another issue altogether (see Chapter 11 for Amenhotep III's father-in-law Yuya and his astonishing array of honours). Some of these positions were largely honorific conceits that granted status, influence and wealth, while all the work was carried out by underlings about whom we know little. Men like Rekhmire, or Setau who was Overseer of the Workhouse of Amun at Karnak some time between Amenhotep II and his grandson Amenhotep III, dressed in a manner that befitted their stations. Setau, for example, was portrayed wearing a full-length kilt under a tunic, and a complex double-tiered wig that amounted to a headdress of rank.[85] Rekhmire's memorial chapel described an elaborate ceremonial audience with him as the vizier, but this mainly consisted of him being reported to rather than Rekhmire doing anything substantive. The occasion was clearly the apex of a system that involved an array of lower tiers of officials operating at a local level, mainly exacting (or extorting) taxes and tribute, distributing funds and settling disputes over land, all conducted with untold quantities of record-keeping. Many of these individuals enforced their prerogative in ways that were based on precedent, frequently involving abuse of privilege. Surviving correspondence suggests the men involved took every opportunity to flaunt their status by berating their underlings with pompous admonishments and warnings.[86]

The overlapping spheres made for jealousy, rivalry, and factionalism – thereby diverting energy into feuding which might otherwise have been used to challenge the ruler, particularly later in a reign. Such jockeying for position and the ear of the monarch or leader is routinely attested in places as divergent in time and place as the Tudor court in England and Germany's Third Reich. It can be an effective way to rule. This also suggests posts were invented as rewards rather than out of any substantive need for another bureaucrat.

Egypt's officialdom was also obviously open to corruption. Holding such a position could be very profitable for the incumbent and his family. Some jobs were undoubtedly obtained with bribes. There is little direct evidence for this, though complicity on the part of senior officials in tomb robbing is one area that is recorded (see the Epilogue). Examples from other periods show that the most profitable offices were sought by any means. The Roman emperor Claudius's wife Messalina notoriously presided over the blatant selling of positions and privileges under her husband's nose.[87] In the English Tudor court royal patronage included the distribution of profitable monopolies and these were routinely squabbled over by jealous members of the aristocracy.

These are only some of the issues affecting our understanding of ancient Egypt. There is no doubt that we are at a greater distance from understanding the Egyptian world than we are from, say, the Greeks and Romans, in almost every way. This is an essential ingredient in our appreciation of Egypt's fundamental uniqueness, a phenomenon that was no less evident to other contemporary ancient societies.[88] Yet, one of the most gratifying experiences of exploring the ancient Egyptians' culture and history is the endless opportunity to discover their humanity. They were prey to the same temptations, ambitions and flaws, even if they sometimes found different ways to deal with and express them.

# 2

# TWILIGHT OF THE HYKSOS
## c. 1555–1550 BC

*For a century, northern Egypt had been ruled by a line of Asiatic kings known as the Hyksos, whose capital was at Avaris in the Delta. Although the Hyksos adopted Egyptian traditions their presence was resented and had left the country divided in an era now known as the Second Intermediate Period. A new dynasty of Theban kings headed down the Nile Valley and began the fightback, culminating in the short and bloody reign of Kamose. His premature death left Egypt on a precipice.*

In the mid-sixteenth century BC or thereabouts a visitor to the Thebes (now Luxor) area of Egypt would have been presented with a very different scene from the one that prevailed by the end of the New Kingdom. Thebes was known to the Egyptians as Waset ('sceptre district'), which referred to the administrative zone in which the city lay. On the east bank of the Nile the huge complex in Thebes now known as the Temple of Luxor, dedicated to the renewal of kingship, lay in the future. The temple, known as the 'southern place', came into being under the Thutmosid kings, including Hatshepsut.[1]

Amenhotep III replaced their work with a larger structure, extended during the 19th Dynasty.

To the north about 1.75 miles (3 km) away was the temple of Amun at Karnak. Although Karnak had been established during the Middle Kingdom 400 years earlier, the place was still minuscule compared to the sprawl of pylons, courts, obelisks and shrines it would become over the next few centuries. Karnak was known by various names including 'most select of places', and 'Throne of the Two Lands' (the opposite sides of the Nile).[2] It evolved during the 18th Dynasty into a highly visible and public form of monumental architecture that displaced existing settlement.

Karnak is a peculiar and haphazard complex. Once the main east-west central shrine area was established, few kings appear to have had much idea of how to contribute to Karnak other than adding monumental pylon gateways, embellished with colossi of themselves and obelisks which they either commissioned or usurped from one of their predecessors. Ostensibly for the glorification of Amun, the purpose was really to glorify the kings, each concerned to outdo his (or her) predecessor. The technical limitations of Egyptian architecture played their part.[3] The result was that over time, the western and southern approaches became extended with one more pylon, pair of obelisks, hypostyle hall and courtyard after another, complicated and sometimes obscured by usurpations, demolitions, rearrangements and unfinished work. There was little attempt at symmetry or order. Additions continued through late dynastic times and into the Ptolemaic and Roman periods, adding to the bewildering jumble. In its final form Karnak covered around 304 acres (123 ha), or around three times the size of the Vatican City. The whole precinct was cluttered with statues and stelae and was linked to the nearby subsidiary precinct of Mut.

Karnak and the Temple of Luxor served as the end points of the great processional Opet Festival when boat shrines and cult statues were transported between the two. Many other temples were built across the country during the New Kingdom, or existing ones were repaired and enhanced. Enough of Karnak and Luxor survives to show how imposing the buildings were, intentionally drawing on conventions of fortified architecture. Amenhotep III's memorial-mortuary temple in Western Thebes across the Nile was specifically described on a stela recording his building works as an 'eternal, ever-lasting fortress'. In practice it turned out to be anything but.[4]

These temples were the essential permanent ingredients in 18th Dynasty royal theatre and state ideology. Although today's son et lumière presentations at Karnak can hardly compare with the great processions and rituals conducted there in antiquity, the narration and music echoing round the ruins at night leave a lasting impression on any modern visitor. To an ordinary Egyptian 3,300 years ago the sight of a garishly painted Karnak or Luxor glittering with gold and electrum, choked with countless statues of gods, kings and private individuals, the air filled with the smell of incense and echoing to the raucous sounds of ancient musical instruments, must have been overwhelming especially on the day of a religious procession or the presentation of the spoils of war.

All this was paid for from Egypt's colossal New Kingdom wealth, gained from war, tribute and taxation. It was carried out by untold numbers of workers and slaves, managed by a complex hierarchy of officials.[5] The extent of slavery is hard to assess since slaves are largely absent from the record. Many were prisoners of war. However, the evidence from cemeteries at Amarna under Akhenaten is that it would be difficult to distinguish the lives of Egyptian labourers, most of whom were children or young adults, set to work on pharaonic building projects from those of slaves. In any case the distinction between 'free' and 'enslaved' in the way we understand it did not really exist in those days.

The temples were vast administrative and industrial machines and storage centres, and therefore formed an integral part of the state. A painting from the tomb chapel of the chief sculptors Nebamun and Ipuky (TT181) shows artisans hard at work somewhere in the Karnak complex manufacturing items such as *djed*-pillar symbols of stability, collars and boxes, one decorated with the names of Amenhotep III.[6] These products were destined for use in rituals and tombs. Temples were the recipients of revenue from conquered states, gifts and endowments from the king, and income from vast estates which included mines. The priests fed and paid their own administrators who managed the labourers and tenants working the land, farming animals, and supplied in the form of a tithe some of their produce to the temples as offerings.

Cults, and that of Amun at Karnak was by far and away the most important, were therefore vast vested interests. Above all else, the priests who controlled them were concerned to maintain the status quo.[7] So, too, were many of the men and their families who worked the land. They enjoyed some protection as a result. The temple reserves of surplus grain and other foods could help to overcome a bad year, for example when the annual inundation of the Nile was lower than usual. They were thus essential to legitimating the state's power. The enriching of the temples was a means of filtering, storing, administering and disseminating state wealth. Their role was echoed on a local and regional basis by lesser temples which were supported by their immediate communities and served similar functions, as well as also being a way through which prominent families of those communities could assert their status.

In Western Thebes the cutting out of tombs in the hills and foot-hills was well established, but the Valley of the Kings was yet to come into existence. Memorial-mortuary temples on the plain between the Theban hills and the Nile were only just starting to appear. At Deir el-Bahari, nestled into a recess at the bottom of the east-facing cliff, was the terraced platform mortuary temple of the Middle Kingdom pharaoh Mentuhotep II (2055–2004 BC), though that was already in ruins.

By the end of the New Kingdom 500 years later, Western Thebes had also changed out of recognition. The wreckage of Mentuhotep's temple was dwarfed by a similar, but larger and more impressive, structure that had utilized the far better site a few metres to the north. This was the memorial-mortuary Temple of Hatshepsut. It was already battered and a shadow of its former self, the result of damage inflicted after her death. A series of other royal memorial-mortuary temples of various sizes and layouts had proliferated, some robbed to yield stone for new ones during the process of frantic construction, belonging to almost every reign of the 18th to early 20th Dynasties. They were supplemented by an 18th Dynasty temple of Amun-Re-Kamutef at Medinet Habu.[8] Each year a statue of Amun-Re was brought across the Nile to act as the centrepiece in a procession that visited these temples, finishing up at the one belonging to the current king.

Behind the hills that formed the backdrop lay the Valley of the Kings and the Western Valley of the Kings. Here tombs had been prepared for many of the principal royal figures and most senior officials from early in the 18th Dynasty right down to Ramesses XI, the last king of the 20th Dynasty.[9] The Valley of the Queens was developed too but despite its modern name was mainly used for officials to begin with, only becoming the routine burial place of princes and queens in the 19th Dynasty. In the foothills near the mortuary temples other officials and ordinary people continued to be buried in numberless tombs. Another workforce, based at the village of Deir el-Medina near the Valley of the Queens, carried out the continuous excavation of the tombs and their decorations. These were routinely desecrated by generations of tomb robbers, some of whom were drawn from among the workers and others who willingly participated and helped disperse the loot.

Almost all this work had taken place across a short period of Egypt's history. The Old Kingdom's pyramids belonged to a remote past between about 2670 and 2500 BC. They were for the most part located much further north in what had become the vast necropolis of Memphis at Saqqara. The latter had been established by an Old Kingdom pharaoh called Pepy I (2321–c. 2287 BC). He named the pyramid cemetery *mn-nfr-ppy*, 'Pepi is established and perfect'. In time part of that name was transferred to Memphis which was known (among other names) as *mn-nfr*, 'Established and perfect'.

Thebes and its surrounding area might have dominated the architectural work of the New Kingdom, but the period also included the construction of tombs by officials at, for example, Saqqara, the shrine of Osiris at Abydos and an early temple at Dendera, long replaced by the magnificent and extant Graeco-Roman version. There were many others, not least the temples and the new city built at his new city at Tell el-Amarna by Akhenaten as well as the temple to the Aten he commissioned at Karnak. These were all cleared away or fell into ruin after his death. From the Delta in the north to Nubia in the south numerous temples were built or altered by a long list of kings.

## THE HYKSOS

The development of Thebes and other New Kingdom monuments such as Abydos lay in the future. By 1550 BC for around a century northern Egypt had, to the shame of the Egyptians (or so the story went), been ruled by foreign kings during an era known to Egyptologists in a memorably banal way as the 'Second Intermediate Period'. This began in the early eighteenth century BC but reached its most significant point when the Hyksos kings of the 15th Dynasty took control of the Delta region and neighbouring areas. A central dogma of the 18th Dynasty kings was that the first of their line, Ahmose I, had been personally responsible for leading the fightback and expelling the Hyksos. His 18th Dynasty successors all basked in his glorious achievement by descent in that grand pharaonic tradition of transferable accomplishment.

Manetho provides us with at least what seems to be a late Egyptian version of what had happened. 'Invaders of an obscure race', whom he called the Hyksos from 'the regions of the East', were said to have invaded Egypt with a chariot-based blitzkrieg. Chariots were the Bronze Age's high-speed dive-bombers and tanks that tore into enemy infantry. It was one of those points in history where possession of a single innovative piece of technology by one side in a war was the decisive factor, or so at least it appears. The Hyksos allegedly attacked so rapidly that they seized northern Egypt without even having to fight. They toppled the native rulers and embarked on a ruthless campaign of destroying cities and temples, while murdering and enslaving the inhabitants.[10]

By depicting the Hyksos as unified and villainous, their subsequent expulsion only appeared to be a more triumphant achievement. The story was a classic liberation myth which had its foundations in a form of the truth and legitimized the New Kingdom regime. The Hyksos sphere of control was limited to the Delta and northern Egypt, but they had only taken advantage of Egypt's self-inflicted weakness.

The native 13th Dynasty controlled most of Egypt from its capital at Itj-tawy somewhere in the Faiyum Oasis area. Itj-tawy was originally founded in the 12th Dynasty, probably to provide a stronghold against an incursion from Asia, anticipating perhaps the Hyksos invasion. But the 13th Dynasty ended badly with part of the Delta breaking away to be ruled by the spectral 14th Dynasty, with an even more obscure and unnumbered dynasty ruling at Abydos. This fragmentation weakened Egypt and laid the way open for the Hyksos.

The word 'Hyksos' was a much later Greek version of the Egyptian term *heqa-khast*.[11] It meant 'rulers of hill countries', a way of showing that the Hyksos came from somewhere recognizably quite unlike Egypt. The name 'Hyksos' was a convenient catch-all label used by the Egyptians who wanted an easily defined enemy, defined as aggressive interlopers. They became known in later tradition as 'shepherd kings'. The Hyksos did not form a coherent movement, but they originated in Western Asia (which means what we call Iraq, Turkey, Syria, and Palestine today for the main part). In a world where controlled borders did not really exist, the migration of peoples was inevitable.

By the eighteenth century BC Western Asiatics of Palestinian origin were living in Egypt at Tell el-Dabʿa in the eastern Delta, identified now as the Hyksos capital of Avaris. Avaris was founded in the Middle Kingdom by Amenemhet III (c. 1855–1808 BC), but its funerary monuments demonstrate a blurring of Palestinian and Egyptian traditions. The details of what happened hinge on fragments of evidence as small as individual scarabs bearing the names of spectral rulers, a thoroughly unreliable basis for constructing any sort of viable chronology and even less for measuring the extent to which they yielded power.[12]

This phase culminated in the Hyksos eventually taking control of the Delta and northern Egypt as far south as Cusae, a little beyond Hermopolis (now el Ashmunein), their most southerly stronghold. The Hyksos kings, classified by Manetho as the 15th Dynasty, kept up trade and contact with the kingdom of Kush in Nubia by using a desert route that hopped from oasis to oasis through the Western Desert and bypassed the Theban zone. The Hyksos also claimed to rule the rest of Egypt.

Avaris became a major target for the Theban fightback. Until it fell, the Hyksos worshipped Egyptian cults, maintained an Egyptian-style bureaucracy, styled themselves with regnal names embellished with Egyptian epithets such as 'beloved of Re' and used hieroglyphs. An obscure 13th Dynasty king called Imyremeshaw had erected a pair of colossal statues of himself at Memphis dedicated to Ptah. These were usurped by the Hyksos king Apepi of the 15th Dynasty, who removed them to Avaris.[13] He had them inscribed with his name and a dedication to the god 'Seth, lord of Avaris'. Seth's cult was already established at Avaris, but the Hyksos were especially interested in him.[14] A pyramidion (a pyramid capstone) from the 13th Dynasty was found in Kataana in the Delta where it would have been impossible to build a pyramid.[15] The stone must have come from a now-lost pyramid in the Saqqara-Dashur area and was probably a Hyksos trophy.

The Hyksos even commissioned new editions of older Egyptian texts. One of the most famous is the Rhind Papyrus carrying a 12th Dynasty text.[16] It includes the resolution of various mathematical problems including a computation of $\pi$ as 256/81 (3.1605, a tiny error). This version was made during the reign of Apepi in the mid-sixteenth century BC. There are, however, no Hyksos historical accounts of their time in Egypt. Our perception of the Hyksos era is thus primarily based on archaeological evidence and the way the later Egyptians described them.

One possibility is that the Hyksos lacked any cohesive identity of their own and were genuinely enthralled by Egypt's ancient culture. Another is that they were confronted by a people whose traditions were so well established that it would have been futile to try and rule their part of Egypt any other way. Nonetheless, Egypt's adoption of Hyksos fighting equipment at the beginning of the 18th Dynasty and the inclusion of Minoan-style bull-leaping frescoes in the Delta region at Avaris after its capture by Ahmose I show that the Egyptians did not ignore outside influences.[17]

Egyptianized foreigners and invaders proved to be an enduring phenomenon. They all tended to adopt Egyptian ways, such as the Nubians who became loyal Egyptian administrators in the New Kingdom. Over a millennium later the Ptolemaic pharaohs intro-duced Greek as the new administrative language and established a regular coinage system. They otherwise posed as Egyptian rulers (as the Roman emperors did), built Egyptian temples, worshipped Egyptian gods and allowed hieroglyphs to be used on all their monu-ments. Some Greek and Roman immigrants to Egypt had themselves buried in an imitation of the grand tradition of Egyptian burial and its rites, combining classical-style portraits and death masks with a perfunctory and degenerate form of mummification.

However hard they tried to go native, the Hyksos would never be accepted, this despite the technical improvements they brought to warfare and transport in Egypt, serving as a conduit for innovations that had emerged across the region. These included armaments such as the composite bow and the chariot. These lightweight vehi-cles were rapidly becoming an indispensable feature of Bronze Age elite warfare across the region. The Hyksos cannot have been the only source of influence. The eastern Mediterranean was already a thriving commercial thoroughfare. The transference of ideas was inevitable sooner or later.

Merely possessing these improvements was not enough. Had posturing in war chariots been the pre-eminent basis of military superiority and used to that end, the Hyksos might have taken control of all of Egypt. But they did not. Thus, they left the way open to the Theban Egyptians to utilize and improve the new methods of warfare.

A nationalist pulse was beating in the south. A hatred of the Hyksos and a thirst for revenge were already building. At least that was how Egyptian tradition would later record what happened. Naturally, the eventual Theban victory made sure that the Hyksos version of events never saw the light of day.

The Theban 16th Dynasty is little known. This probably reflects a very fragmented picture in which settlements were ruled on a primarily local basis by local chieftains, for example at Abydos and Thebes. Bombastic liberation rhetoric was a favourite pastime of the Theban rulers, but the groundwork had already been laid. The short-lived Neferhotep III ruled from Thebes during the 16th Dynasty (c. 1650–1550 BC). His modest sphere of control extended only 50 miles (80 km) upriver to El Kab, but he did not hold back from making extravagant claims. The stela that records him saying he ruled from 'victorious Thebes' and had saved the city from starvation also mentions for the first time in Egyptian history the *khepresh* (blue) crown, so commonly seen worn by 18th Dynasty kings in a variety of contexts.[18] Neferhotep's other names included the title 'the might of Re who nourishes the Two Lands', which suggests the famine was a real event though whether his remedial efforts were as successful as he claimed is another matter altogether.

Neferhotep III's stela marks a stage in the evolution of identity and religious ideology integral to the imminent 18th Dynasty. By the 17th Dynasty these were becoming more clearly and consistently defined with the king at the head of a militarized hierarchy in control of Egypt between Abydos and Elephantine. His role was as the manifestation of divine will on Earth with Egypt as the beneficiary, and at the apex of a patronage structure in which office and the fruits of conquest were distributed. The severance of ties with the north of Egypt was an advantage. The burgeoning Theban regime had to reconstruct its own authentic Egyptian tradition based on what was still available to them, which at the time did not include the scribal archives to the north at Memphis.

In around 1120 BC tomb robbers, after being tortured, agreed to testify to their desecration of a royal tomb of the 17th Dynasty in Western Thebes. One of the gang members admitted that he and his accomplices routinely robbed tombs in the area but normally targeted noble tombs.[19] The thieves came across the king's pyramid tomb and dug down, using their copper tools.[20] Based on other nearby examples the modest pyramid was probably about 43 ft (13 m) high and 36ft (11 m) square at the base. Equipped with candles, the gang explored the intact tomb and found the bodies of the king and queen. Despite whittering on about the nobility of the occupants, the squealer admitted that he and his associates had found gold and jewels on the mummies which they stole before setting the coffins on fire.[21]

The macabre testimony also tells us that by the sixteenth century BC the Theban kings of the 17th Dynasty were wealthy enough to write off precious metals and other valuables which were withdrawn from circulation when buried. Evidently, the kings were able to acquire and hoard wealth, derived, it seems, from pushing Theban power further south into Nubia. The thieves discovered that Sobekemsaf had been buried with a sword, probably the king's personal weapon, based on other attested instances of arms buried with pharaohs. The 17th Dynasty king Intef VII was buried with two bows and six arrows. The image of the warrior king was well under development. Nonetheless, it is easy in the mind's eye to turn the description into a vision of extravagance and opulence. The surviving coffin of Intef VII was made of sycamore with gold leaf and painted blue.[22] In comparison with what was to come in the 18th Dynasty the coffin was not only crudely carved but also made of poor materials.

Elephantine, an island in the Nile close to Aswan, had been autonomous but by the 16th Dynasty the mayor of Aswan had been absorbed into the Theban power structure. That suggests the kings at Thebes were gaining access to the products of the gold and copper mines of the land of Kush (Nubia). Kush was still closely tied to Hyksos-controlled Lower Egypt via the oasis route, but these links were threatened by rising Theban power. The populations of the Egyptian forts of the Second Cataract turned initially to the kingdom of Kush for protection. In return they fought for Kush. The Thebans needed to push back to Kush to secure the forts and thus weaken the Hyksos first before turning on them directly.

The penultimate king of the 17th Dynasty was Seqenenre Tau II who ruled in the few years around 1560 BC. His reign was brief, and he died in battle. The only clue we have to the context is an account written on papyrus during the 19th Dynasty.[23] In the story Seqenenre was ruler of Thebes, embroiled in a row with the Hyksos king Apepi. Apepi's metaphorical grievance was that he was unable to sleep because of the hippopotamus noise problem at Thebes and wrote to Seqenenre to tell him so. The Egyptian hippopotamus god was the female fertility deity Taweret but here the significance is more likely to have been the notoriously aggressive habits of the male of the species. If so, Apepi was insulting Seqenenre by likening the Theban ruler and his men to the very animals a pharaoh might traditionally hunt and kill to demonstrate his power and skill, perhaps because Apepi had heard about anti-Hyksos sabre-rattling at Thebes. In later times the story was taken literally, obscuring the wit of the sneer. Either way, Seqenenre called his councillors to discuss the crisis. There the tale ends. We have no idea what came next, except that Seqenenre lost his life during an unnamed battle against the Hyksos.

Seqenenre's mummy survives, famously mutilated by vicious injuries which include large cuts to the head.[24] He had been struck at least twice in the face by an axe that smashed one of his cheekbones and left a gaping wound. Once face-down on the ground a dagger was driven into the back of his neck. There are few other examples from antiquity that so vividly display the visceral brutality of an ancient war fought at close quarters, especially where the victim is a known individual.

Seqenenre's battered corpse was returned to Thebes for burial. Much later it was transferred to a cache of royal mummies found in 1881. The ghastly, tortured grimace on his face and the huge hole in the front of his skull are reminders that this type of war was largely conducted by violent and aggressive young men trained from childhood to kill and who exulted in that culture. They took the risks because the fighting was exhilarating, and the rewards were glory and riches.

# KAMOSE (WADJKHEPERRE, 'AMULET OF THE MANIFESTATIONS OF RE'?) c. 1555–1550 BC

Seqenenre Tau II's son Ahmose was too young to succeed, at least safely. Instead, Seqenenre Tau II was succeeded by Kamose, probably a close relative and perhaps his brother. That sidestepped the succession problem, at least temporarily. Kamose was another Bronze Age fighting leader given to extravagant and shameless claims of his own importance and military credentials. It would have raised eyebrows if he had behaved differently. In the event Kamose was not to last much longer than his predecessor but he set in train a series of events that would ultimately end the Second Intermediate Period and rule by the Hyksos.

The most important source of evidence for the reign of Kamose, which lasted for three to five years at most, survives on the two stelae he erected at Karnak.[25] Their bluster blurred the truth. Kamose complained to his nobles that he was trapped between an Asiatic in Avaris and a Nubian in Kush and in the north was unable to advance beyond Memphis. To this general grievance he added the specific one that the Egyptians in the Hyksos zone had to pay imposts. There is no mention of Seqenenre's death in battle, but this must have been a factor. The nobles were reluctant to fight, pointing out complacently that their part of Egypt was in a good state, and arguing they should only fight if attacked. Kamose was frustrated by their reluctance and expressed his desire to wreak revenge by splitting open the Asiatic's belly. The sense of being sandwiched between enemies to the north and south was not just a casual rhetorical position. The Hyksos and Kush continued to bypass the Thebans by using their own lines of communication via the oases of the Western Desert.

Kamose's grievances contributed to one of Egypt's most enduring tropes during the 18th Dynasty. In Tutankhamun's tomb, which dated to more than two centuries later, was a walking stick with an elaborately carved handle depicting the intertwined bodies of a Nubian and an Asiatic, their hands tied with thread. There was also a pair of marquetry veneer sandals, each decorated with a Nubian and Asiatic captive so that the young king could trample them underfoot as he walked along.[26] Egypt's traditional enemies had by then been reduced to fashionable decorative motifs, compliant diplomatic contacts and sources of tribute, as well as philo-Egyptian administrators and attendants. Successfully keeping these foes at bay was the principal ideological claim of the 18th Dynasty kings even during times of peace. Kush was always 'wretched' or 'vile', the latter being a translation of the word *ḥḥtsy* that had connotations also of being feeble and mean-minded. Along with Western Asia, Kush remained the target of sustained Egyptian campaigns and the victim of derogatory references for generations after Kamose's time, despite the absorption of Asiatics and Nubians into Egyptian society.

Kamose began the war against the Hyksos in his 3rd regnal year. It was only one episode in a conflict that would last a generation, characterized not by sustained fighting but by intermittent campaigns and battles. The battles were probably no more than frantic skirmishes that are unlikely to have involved more than a few hundred men. Egypt's landscape did not help the movement of huge armies, especially far beyond its borders, and stretched communications and supply lines to a withering extent.

Kamose styled himself 'mighty ruler', 'strong', 'brave', the 'protector of Egypt', and bragged that he enjoyed the backing of Amun. The language and phrasing were modelled on earlier examples dating back to the Middle Kingdom, though they also anticipated the more specific tone of the 18th Dynasty.[27] Kamose led at least two expeditions into Nubia, recapturing the fortress at Buhen which may have been lost during the first Nubian foray. Kamose next took his soldiers north and defeated the Hyksos garrison at Nefrusy, north of Cusae. It was a clever tactic. Cusae was instantly cut off from Hyksos territory. Kamose continued his advance, probably planning to continue the campaign the same way. However, his actions had already caused great concern to the Hyksos king Apepi. Apepi dashed off a diplomatic letter to Kush asking for help. 'Come north!' said Apepi, 'do not hold back. There is nobody who will stand up to you in Egypt. See, I will not give him a way out until you arrive! Then we shall divide the towns of Egypt, and Nubia shall be in joy.'[28] The letter was dispatched down the Western Desert oasis route. Unfortunately for the Hyksos, the messenger was intercepted. Apepi's plan was rumbled.

Reacting quickly, Kamose sent a detachment to the Western Desert with orders to destroy the Bahariya Oasis settlement and thereby break the link to Kush. This was successful. Kamose could continue his campaign into the Hyksos-controlled Delta with his rear secured. He reached Avaris. Having come by water he had the necessary vessels to blockade the city. Oddly, given the comical rhetoric of the two speeches he claimed to have made, he held back from goading Apepi into a fight. Instead Kamose contented himself with mocking his enemy. In the first speech he bragged, 'Watch your back, evil one – my army is after you,' he promised, adding the dire warning that 'the women of Avaris will not conceive, nor will their hearts open in their bodies, while the road of my army is heard'.

In the second speech Kamose boasted to the 'wretched Asiatic' that he was taking whatever he wanted, wreaking gratuitous

destruction like hacking down trees. The passage included an especially vivid and authentic sounding section where he describes seeing
Apepi's 'women on his housetop, looking through their windows to
the riverbank. Their bodies would not open when they saw me, as
they peeped through the nose-holes on their walls like the young
of [the meaning of the word here is unknown and does not appear
in any other text – perhaps the jerboa] in their burrows, saying "it is
an attack".' Kamose dismissed Apepi's citadel as a form of burrow-
dwelling rodent colony. The literary implication of course was that
Kamose and his men were therefore predators in the manner of lions
or dogs in pursuit of prey.

One of the most striking references is in Kamose's list of loot at the
end, using a term that meant 'this belonging to spans [of animals]',
probably an attempt in Egyptian to refer to Hyksos chariots and their
horse teams that had been 'carried off'.[29] It would be a while before
a specific Egyptian word was introduced for a chariot. The make-do
phrase proved enduring and is found in later examples in the New
Kingdom (see Chapter 11). Chariots were soon to evolve into one
of the most important display symbols of high status in Egyptian
society, as a mark of individual prestige and for officials going about
state business.[30]

Once he was bored with posturing, Kamose left with his booty
and sailed upriver to Thebes where he was greeted with delight by an
excited populace, or so he said. However, the truth was that Kamose
had failed to capture Avaris, seize control of the Delta and expel the
Hyksos. We do not know if he had ever entertained such ambitions,
even though his actions suggest he had the ability to have prosecuted
a more wide-ranging war. On the other hand, his intelligence may
have led him to take the view that it was better to test the water,
spy out the land, see how Apepi reacted and assess the prospect of a
more decisive campaign. Kamose had shown his hand and lost the
element of surprise but in the Nile Valley it is unlikely that there was
any surprise to be lost.

Kamose's Hyksos war might have been followed by another

campaign. It did not because of unexpected circumstances. Before long both he and Apepi were dead, probably for natural reasons since there is no suggestion violence was involved. Kamose had lived in the fast lane and vanished just as quickly, deprived even of enjoying a heroic death in battle. All the momentum he had achieved evaporated. The Hyksos could sink back into the comfort of controlling the Delta. Had it not been for the Karnak stelae and the Carnarvon Tablet, which makes good some of the stelae's missing sections, Kamose might have disappeared from history.

Kamose left no obvious successor. It is not even certain if he married. The only candidate appears to have been another woman unhelpfully called Ahhotep (sometimes now known as Ahhotep II); unless Kamose married Seqenenre Tau's widowed sister-wife of the same name.[31] Kamose's mummy was found in 1857 at Dra Abu'l-Naga. After the end of the 20th Dynasty when his tomb was inspected and supposedly found to be in good order the body had been removed, buried in what seemed to be rubbish, presumably in an attempt by tomb robbers to hide the evidence of their handiwork.[32]

By bowing out when he did, Kamose lost the chance to go down in Egypt's annals as the nation's liberator. His posthumous cult was maintained for several centuries and the main reason we know about him, his Karnak stelae, remained on show until the late 18th Dynasty. One was later used by Ramesses II as the base for a statue — helpfully preserving it. Kamose had blazed a frenzied path across the firmament. In the world of the Bronze Age chieftain his death created a vacuum into which it would have been easy for one of Egypt's enemies to fill or for a court faction to seize power. It was a dangerous moment, but luck was on Egypt's side.

# 3

# THE DAWN OF THE NEW KINGDOM c. 1550–1525 BC

## AHMOSE I (NEBPEHTYRE, 'THE LORD OF STRENGTH IS RE')

*Ahhotep's regency maintained Kamose's momentum and protected her son till he came of age. Ahmose was celebrated by the 18th Dynasty as its progenitor and the key figure in the liberation myth that defined the era. Ahmose expelled the Hyksos, reunified Egypt and established the image of the 18th Dynasty warrior king who had pushed back the nation's enemies to north and south.*

Seqenenre Tau II's son Ahmose was too young to rule when Kamose died. The Hyksos missed their chance. Power shifted to a woman, and not for the last time under such circumstances, in this case Ahmose's widowed mother, the queen Ahhotep.[1] Ahmose later credited his mother with assuming charge of military affairs during this time and of saving Egypt at a moment of crisis. According to an undated stela at Karnak, Ahhotep 'took care of Egypt, recruited its infantry, secured it, gathered its deserters, calmed Upper Egypt and drove out its rebels'.[2] The stela was more concerned, though, with praising Ahmose, providing a detailed list of the gold and silver vessels, necklaces of 'real lapis lazuli', gold amulets, an ebony harp and a barque made of cedar from Lebanon for the cult of Amun at Karnak in Ahmose's name. This greatly resembles the list of similar material recorded on another stela, which is dated to his 18th regnal year.

Queen Ahhotep's tomb was found in 1858 at Dra Abu'l-Naga. Its disastrous, unsupervised excavation resulted in the wholesale stripping of the mummy, which was then, incredibly, thrown away. Fortunately, the antiquities were recovered. They go a long way to substantiating Ahmose's claims about his mother's achievements. Ahhotep was buried with a gold dagger with an inlaid handle, and a ceremonial axe made of copper, gold, electrum, and with a wooden handle covered in gold plating. It was extravagantly decorated in the Minoan (Cretan) style, a mark of the foreign influences Egypt was increasingly open to.[3] One side of the blade bore Ahmose's name, and the decoration depicted him wearing the new khepresh crown while symbolically smiting one of his enemies. Other items included the military decoration for valour of three gold flies.[4] Ahhotep certainly lived on well into the reign of her grandson Amenhotep I, at least as far as his 10th regnal year.[5]

# THE CAMPAIGN AGAINST THE HYKSOS

Ahmose was a diminutive man with the dynasty's characteristic overbite. He was about 5ft 5in (1.64 m) tall, a little under the average for an Egyptian, but he was by no means the shortest member of the 18th Dynasty royal family.[6] He took the throne name Nebpehtyre ('The Lord of Strength is Re'). His reign was long and eventful enough to change everything by finishing off the work begun by Kamose. In a rare instance of Hyksos evidence, some notes on the back of the Rhind mathematical Papyrus recorded news as it arrived from the front during the 11th regnal year of a Hyksos king. A 'southern prince', presumably Ahmose, had targeted Hyksos strongholds.[7]

This war was so significant that it featured in reliefs prepared later for Ahmose's temple at Abydos. It also appeared in the biographical inscriptions and illustrations placed on the walls of the tomb at El Kab of Ahmes-Ibana, one of Ahmose's soldiers who rose to become a naval commander under the early pharaohs of the 18th Dynasty.[8]

The war against the Hyksos, which included the crucial fall of Avaris, was Ahmose's principal achievement because it ended with Egypt's reunification. This harked right back to Egypt's earliest historical times just before 3000 BC when Narmer, the country's earliest named king, was believed to have brought Upper and Lower Egypt together under his sole rule. Ahmose's feat was therefore of enormous significance. Just as Narmer had wrested order out of chaos, Ahmose had restored that order. Ahmose celebrated the conflict during his lifetime, and so did those who had participated. The war rapidly took on such mythical proportions that some subsequent rulers such as Hatshepsut made preposterous claims to have been personally responsible.[9] The pharaohs of the 18th Dynasty defined themselves and expected to be defined as the liberators of Egypt. It was the foundation of their legitimacy and justified their wealth and power.

Ahmose commissioned reliefs that depicted the war for his cenotaph temple at Abydos.[10] Equipped with naval transport, chariots and new weapons such as the composite bow and the *khopesh* curved scimitar, the Egyptians under Ahmose had the good fortune to be led better, or at any rate more inspiringly. The Hyksos are inevitably shown as the fallen victims and bound captives. These include the earliest known images of horses and chariots from Egypt. Avaris was mentioned, as was Apepi. While these panels may well once have been set out in narrative format, the ruined nature of the temple and the fragmentation of the reliefs mean that the chronological detail has been lost.

The Abydos evidence is thus eclipsed by the narrative from the tomb of Ahmes-Ibana, a highly successful military officer. His career spanned the reigns of the first three 18th Dynasty kings, and he lived well into affluent old age. His father had been an officer under Seqenenre, and Ahmes-Ibana was to take his place as a soldier on a ship called *Fighting Bull*, proceeding to serve on several other vessels, too.[11] Kamose goes unmentioned. Ahmes-Ibana rose to the dizzying heights of 'commander of the troop of rowers' and benefited also from seven gifts of gold, and land grants, for his services. These tomb reliefs are the only detailed surviving record of Ahmose's achievements in expelling the Hyksos.[12]

Ahmose headed north, leading from the front in his chariot. Ahmes-Ibana sailed downriver before following his king with the infantry on foot, a reminder that chariots were expensive prestige items. The siege at Avaris involved fighting on land and water, Ahmes-Ibana being promoted because of his achievements. The hands of dead enemy soldiers were severed and handed over for counting. Ahmes-Ibana participated and received gold as his reward, following this up with two more victims, the second of whom was carried back 'as if he had been captured on the way from the city', earning him yet more gold. The defenders had clearly put up a spirited defence, but they would have known what to expect when the city fell. Egyptian soldiers burst in to sack Avaris. Ahmes-Ibana rounded up one man and three women as prisoners for the king who gave them back to Ahmes as slaves along with more gold. If the war was a profitable one for successful soldiers, it was a great deal more lucrative for the king. For a man like Ahmes-Ibana, slaves did not have to work for him alone. Their labour was a tradeable commodity sold on a day rate, and thus a useful source of ongoing income.[13]

Once Avaris had fallen, Ahmose's army pushed the Hyksos back into Palestine. The Egyptians holed themselves up in a fortress at Sharuhen, which led to another siege that lasted for three years.[14] Whether that was continuously or was renewed over successive campaigning seasons is not clear. The logistical difficulties involved in sustaining a siege for three years at such a distance from home, and while Ahmose was still asserting his rule, would have been exceptionally challenging.

# THE ARMY OF AHMOSE I

Ahmes-Ibana tells us little about the Egyptian army's hierarchy and structure, organization, supply lines, and even less about strategy and tactics or weaponry. He never mentions Egyptian losses or mistakes. The purpose was only to celebrate his personal achievements and honour his service under Ahmose and his successors. It is unlikely Ahmes' personal contribution was unique. Other soldiers of his rank must have been similarly rewarded, though naturally he said nothing about them.

Ahmes-Ibana described an army led personally by the king. Strategy and tactics were made up on the spot based on the prevailing circumstances. Ahmes does not mention a headquarters, a chief of staff, officers, or indeed any form of structure at all, though they must have existed in some form. The army could move by water and land, with Ahmes' testimony suggesting either was used as required. Although Ahmose had a chariot, we can assume that an elite component of the force went to war in chariots, too, even at this early date. Ships were mainly for transportation, not fighting. Both modes of transport required support networks.

Until the 18th Dynasty the Egyptian army was relatively unsophisticated. In the Old Kingdom, the king relied on the levying of Egyptian nationals on an as-need basis. By the dawn of the New Kingdom soldiers were armed with a variety of weapons that included bows, clubs, daggers, spears and slings, but wore little apart from leather jerkins to protect themselves apart from shields. Thereafter the kings started to hire mercenaries, such as Nubians, who served in return for land grants and gold. Soldiers were organized into centuries of 100 men, with each century further divided into two groups of 50, subdivided into five bands of ten men. The five bands were themselves arranged in a hierarchy. The leader of the most senior unit took command of the whole 50, with the commander of the first 50 being in overall command of the 100-strong century. In practice these numbers were probably nominal, with sickness and desertion affecting unit strength at any given time.

By the 18th Dynasty the army had evolved into a standing force that was the principal means by which the Egyptian state could assert itself in war and domestic security. The army also supervised forced labour on state building projects. Recruits were raised in Egypt, and from Nubia and Syria. It became commonplace for the 18th Dynasty king to appear in a chariot during a parade accompanied by a military escort. Weaponry had improved. Scimitars, probably introduced by the Hyksos or via one of the extensive trading links across the eastern Mediterranean during the Second Intermediate Period, were available to the highest ranks. For the same reason swords were also available.[15] The most important metal used for weaponry was bronze.

Supplying an army across Egypt and into enemy territory necessarily entailed a military bureaucratic division as well as extended transport networks of pack animals, probably donkeys, where water transport was impossible. The further the campaign from Egypt the more difficult this became, doubtless with serious implications for the size of an army that could be realistically supported. Thutmose III's extensive campaigns in Palestine and Syria depended on naval support.

The most radical changes occurred at around the time Kamose and Ahmose were fighting the Hyksos. By adapting the heavy four-man Hyksos chariot into a lightweight version that carried only the charioteer and a warrior, the Egyptians transformed their armies. The Hyksos chariot had suddenly by comparison become ponderous and vulnerable. Since a few royal chariots from the late 18th Dynasty have survived intact it is easy to see why the new version was successful: protection was sacrificed for speed. A wide wheelbase made for stability while executing high-speed manoeuvres on the battlefield, but there was a price. Even a small number of chariots, with two horses apiece, meant a significant change in logistical problems. Horses had to be fed and watered, cared for and replaced. That meant grooms and a supply chain built around the animals alone. Ahmose's mortuary temple at Abydos includes representations of horses, the earliest known in Egypt.

The chariots were flimsy, requiring maintenance of the wooden, leather and metal components. They were capable of being dismantled for storage and transport since a fighting chariot was not robust enough for long-distance transport. Chariots needed frequent repairs, and therefore also dedicated engineers, carpenters and smiths continually on hand during a campaign. The written evidence from the Mycenaean and Minoan civilizations shows that their citadels had sophisticated in-house workshop systems for making, repairing and managing stocks of spare parts. Pylos in the western Peloponnese is known to have had almost 300 smiths, as well as officials tasked with securing supplies of metal. The inventories at Knossos in Crete included a record of 117 available pairs of usable wheels and those which were in a serviceable state.[16] Similar arrangements must have existed in Egypt if Ahmose was to make any reliable use of his chariots, especially in the much more pressured conditions of a war.

The evidence of the chariots from Tutankhamun's tomb, where six chariots were found, is that considerable differences in design detail existed, depending on the purpose of the individual vehicle (most of his were unused and primarily ceremonial). Fighting or hunting chariots, for example, were undecorated and lighter than the more elaborate versions intended for victory parades. One of Tutankhamun's hunting chariots had wooden wheels with tyres reinforced with a hide binding and bark, and bronze ties that secured the tyres to the six spokes of each wheel.[17]

Ahmose's stunning victory over the Hyksos was probably down far more to luck than judgement. He had taken a huge gamble by extending himself so far north. Success must have brought other problems. Ahmes-Ibana had found himself the recipient of gold and slaves, as had other men of his rank and achievements. However prestigious these awards were, they were also serious liabilities for a soldier so far from home. Gold had to be guarded, slaves had to be fed and land had to be taken care of. On the other hand, the acquisition of land and the labour to work it improved the long-term prospects of a man such as Ahmes and his family.

Ahmes-Ibana was not alone in profiting from the war. A 'commander of ships' called Neshi was also given a land grant by Ahmose, only known about today because of the dispute that erupted among his descendants centuries later who were arguing about their share of the original parcel of land.[18] Egypt's growing wealth was being built ever more on the back of a culture of complicity in slavery, whether these men, women and children were handed over to work for individual families or disappeared into the quarries or backbreaking labour. Only very rarely did the story turn out well for any one of them.[19] Some found their way into the Egyptian army, especially Nubians who played a significant part fighting for Egypt in the wars of Ahmose's successors (see Chapter 5).

## THE END OF AHMOSE'S WARS

Ahmose was no fool. He consolidated his hold over former Hyksos territory in Egypt by beginning the construction of a palace at Avaris, and re-establishing Memphis as an administrative centre. Near Thebes work began to enlarge and develop the Amun complex at Karnak. Today Ahmose's work at Karnak amounts to only a few visible traces. They include an inscribed lintel, now dwarfed by later construction, modifications and commemorative stelae, but his efforts marked the start of the 18th Dynasty's long tradition of investing in the cult of Amun which continued unabated until it was briefly suspended during the reign of Akhenaten. He added Heqatawy ('Ruler of the Two Lands') to his throne name, integrating his achievement with his identity as king.[20]

Ahmose had taken a major risk by leaving Egypt vulnerable to attack from Kush. He must have been fully aware that the alliance between the Hyksos and Kush was bound to mean a response. No sooner had Sharuhen fallen than he had to turn his army about and dash south into Nubia as far as the Nile's Second Cataract to attack Kush. Given that his men were now laden down with booty he cannot have taken them all with him. He needed to move fast.

Ahmes-Ibana reported that a huge slaughter took place, which included his success in killing three men and capturing two others, for which he was presented with yet more gold and two women. Two rebellions followed. The first was led by one 'Aata' who mysteriously entered Egypt from the north by water up the Nile. It is possible he was a Nubian mercenary who had fought for the Hyksos. Aata was captured along with his ship, Ahmes taking two prisoners and receiving as his reward five captives and a '5 arourae' plot of land (about 3.3 acres, 1.3 ha). The second rebellion was home-grown. An Egyptian called Tetian, perhaps a soldier and barrack-room troublemaker, had recruited malcontents to lead a rebellion. He was killed and his force wiped out, Ahmes collecting another three captives and another 5 arourae of land.

With Tetian obliterated, Ahmose had brought all of Egypt under his control. The Tetian Revolt is an interesting episode because it suggests that Ahmose did not enjoy universal support, that the distribution of the spoils had angered some of his army, or that Tetian had spotted a chance to challenge Ahmose and try and seize supreme power for himself in post-Hyksos Egypt. The Tetian Revolt may have been a relatively trivial threat, but it is also possible that it could have derailed Ahmose had it been successful.

The protracted siege at Sharuhen suggests that five years was a bare minimum for Ahmose fighting against the Hyksos alone, quite apart from the war in Nubia which followed immediately, and then the two rebellions. Eight to ten years in total is a reasonable estimate. Ahmose reigned for around twenty-five years but much of that time included his childhood while his mother Ahhotep was in charge. It is likely, then, that most of his adult reign was taken up by fighting.

Several stelae were set up at Karnak to commemorate Ahmose's achievements. Three are mainly concerned with his beneficence to the Temple of Amun, but this had begun while his mother Ahhotep was ruling as regent. One recounted how Ahmose had bought a 'Second Priesthood of Amun' for his sister-queen, Ahmose-Nefertari, which therefore acted as a mechanism by which he could pay over some of his wealth to the cult. Another from his 18th regnal year laboriously specified expensive and extravagant items Ahmose supplied for use in the observation of the cult. These include cups and vessels made of precious metals, decorative embellishments for statues and a barque to carry the cult statue in processions. These may have been new replacements for items melted down during the Second Intermediate Period, material lost in a natural disaster (see below), or additions to his earlier gifts. The content resembled that on the undated stela of the reign mentioned earlier that detailed the achievements of his mother Ahhotep. It may therefore have been a purely symbolic list, perhaps repeating earlier donations rather in the manner of a modern government recycling news about funding from last year or the year before.

There was a natural disaster during the reign. Such calamities provide an opportunity for the ruler to show his mettle and justify his existence. One of the most remarkable records surviving from Ahmose's reign is the so-called Tempest Stela, also found at Karnak. The text records disastrous weather:

*[Then] the gods [caused] that the sky come in a tempest of [rain], with [dark]ness in the condition of the West, and the sky being in storm without [cessation, louder than] the cries of the masses, more powerful [than . . . while the rain howled] on the mountains louder than the sound of the underground source of the Nile that is in Elephantine.*

*Then every house, every quarter that [the storm and rain] reached [. . . their corpses(?)] floating on the water like skiffs of papyrus outside the palace audience chamber for a period of [. . .] days [. . .] while no torch could be lit in the Two Lands.*

*Then His Majesty said: 'How much greater this is than the wrath of the great god, [than] the plans of the gods!' His Majesty then descended to his boat, with his council following him, while the crowds [on] the East and West had hidden faces, having no clothing on them after the manifestation of the wrath of the god. His Majesty then reached the interior of Thebes, with gold confronting gold of this cult image, so that he received what he desired.*[21]

The stela describes Ahmose organizing aid for victims and ordering immediate repair and restorations, noting the flooding and destruction of tombs and funerary monuments, pyramids and temples. The stela is unique, and therefore probably a record of a real event. However, it was in Ahmose's interests to have the occasion depicted as having been as serious as possible. It was a rare instance of an Egyptian king going the extra distance for the greater good; though under the circumstances he had no choice. He was already able to pose as the liberator and the man who had reunified Egypt. Now he was also the saviour of the nation – he had stepped up to the mark when Egypt needed him most. The wealth his wars had brought the country could be used to rebuild it when the disaster abated. The catastrophe had provided Ahmose with the perfect opportunity to fulfil the expectations of his people as the literal bastion against the forces of chaos.

While this could have been an exceptional once-in-a-century catastrophic weather event of a type attested in the region, it is also possible that the storm was caused by the epic volcanic eruption which took place at the island of Thera, north of Crete, and caused the destruction of the Minoan civilization. It has never been possible to pin down the exact date of the eruption due to a discrepancy of a century between archaeological (c. 1500 BC) and radiocarbon dates (c. 1600 BC) and other suggestions.[22] However, recent work to calibrate the radiocarbon dates has moved the estimated date for the eruption to a band across the middle of the sixteenth century BC.[23] This would provide an explanation for the devastating weather, but the evidence of Cretan influence surviving in the early 18th Dynasty building work in post-Hyksos Avaris suggests otherwise.

To the Egyptians it mattered not a jot what caused the destructive wind, rain and floods, whether an eruption in the Aegean Sea or disruption to normal weather patterns.[24] What mattered was that the storm had occurred at all, and that – assuming Ahmose can be believed – they had a ruler on hand who had the ability and means to try and ameliorate the worse effects on the ordinary population. Effective leadership and rapid action will have reinforced Ahmose's authority and that of his family.

## AHMOSE'S FAMILY MATTERS

Ahmose married two of his sisters, the senior one being Ahmose-Nefertari, one of the most prominent royal women of the 18th Dynasty.[25] Together they formed the first major male-female royal composite of the period. Sibling or consanguineous marriage would recur during the dynasty, though not invariably. Ahmose-Nefertari was celebrated with several special titles that distinguished her variously as the King's Great Wife, his Sister, the King's Daughter, and most importantly and often as the 'God's Wife' of Amun.[26] She also became the head of a semi-autonomous economic household unit within the royal hierarchy which had its own accounts and staff, known as the 'God's Wife of the House of the Adoratrice'.

Ahmose-Nefertari was made the holder of the Second Priesthood of Amun, funded by an endowment recorded in the so-called Donation Stela found at Karnak. Ahmose provided the necessary investment, including land and servants, which befitted the office and allowed his wife to generate her own revenue. The subtext, of course, was that this was the easiest way the crown could assert control over the Amun cult while simultaneously integrating its ideology with the dynasty's entitlement to rule. Various rhetorical declamations of her impoverishment were made, and she expressed her gratitude to Ahmose: 'he clothes me while I have nothing, he causes that I am rich'.[27] The possession of the priesthood and her right to transmit it to future generations was protected by Amun in whose presence the transaction took place at Karnak. In this capacity

Ahmose-Nefertari became a major figure in the observation of the cult, officiating at ceremonies and becoming one of the very few people allowed access to the innermost sanctums.

The positions Ahmose-Nefertari held granted her considerable power, prestige, wealth and the ability to bestow her riches on worthy causes and to do so in her own right. She did this in the form of dedications at several locations in temples at Thebes and Abydos. One other, more unusual, location was a temple in Sinai dedicated to 'The Lady', now recognized as a form of one of the Egyptian goddess Hathor's titles.[28] The temple, which had an underground chapel, was first built in the Middle Kingdom but became the subject of renewed focus in the 18th Dynasty and was substantially extended under later 18th Dynasty kings. Ahmose-Nefertari was routinely depicted with black (or blue) skin, a symbol of resurrection that associated her with one of Egypt's identities as Kemet, 'the Black Land', a reference to the fertility of the soil that had been fertilized by the rich waters of the annual inundation.

Ahmose-Nefertari survived her husband by many years, living well into old age. Despite being his sibling, she bore Ahmose at least two sons (including his successor Amenhotep I) and three daughters. Her prominence as Ahmose's sister-queen and during the reign of her son was so great that she was posthumously deified and worshipped for centuries. She appears, for example, being greeted by Ramesses II around 250 years later, shown on a relief at Karnak. Her commanding presence there, wearing the Hathoric crown, is in stark contrast to the grisly remains of her mummy, found in the Deir el-Bahari cache of royal mummies (TT320, and possibly originally her own tomb, but see p. 378). By the time she died, Ahmose-Nefertari was almost entirely bald. To compensate, the mummy was fitted with stylized (and obvious) hair extensions. She shared her brother's prominent congenital overbite and allowing for shrinkage had stood around 5 ft 4 in tall (1.61 m), of similar height to him.

Ahmose-Nefertari's overbite was shared by her nurse Rai who was found with her and a third unidentified woman.[29] This makes it likely these two were related to the royal household, suggesting that senior staff were drawn as far as possible from the clan. If so, this practice probably continued and may lie behind the complex family relationships in the latter part of the 18th Dynasty for which most of the bodies are unknown or are unidentified (see Chapters 12–14).

In or around 1525 BC, and certainly not much later, Ahmose I died. Since he apparently succeeded as a child, the likelihood is that he was no older than his early to mid-thirties, which would fit with his minimal dental wear.[30] This early death, probably from natural causes, corresponds with the evidence that the dowager queen, his mother Ahhotep, lived at least until his successor's 10th regnal year.[31]

Ahmose had invested heavily in a substantial cenotaph temple and funerary complex at Abydos. The central feature was a pyramid, the last built in Egypt by a ruler, which was a modest 165 ft (50 m) or so high, though only the bottom two rows of casing stones have survived. Like so many major royal building monuments in Egypt, the pyramid was robbed out by later kings. The practice of building pyramid tombs was adopted instead by commoners and became a frequent sight of the Theban necropolis area on the West Bank. The pyramid stood beside Ahmose's mortuary temple, the only one of the 18th Dynasty not to be built at Thebes, with its showcase reliefs of his war against the Hyksos, displayed (he hoped) for posterity.

Ironically, Ahmose's successors, who were so keen to associate themselves with the 18th Dynasty's triumphant beginning, did little to preserve this monument to the events that had given them the power they so enthusiastically flaunted. The complex included a structure built in the style of a traditional mastaba tomb which was dedicated to his low-born grandmother. A stela records Ahmose stating that he specifically discussed this with Ahmose-Nefertari, before ordering work to start.[32] Given his grandmother's origins the memorial was a striking compliment, clearly intended to help amplify Ahmose's family and improve its lineage. The mastaba was not designed to be used – there was no proper burial chamber – nor is there any evidence that Ahmose was buried at Abydos. His body turned up in the cache of royal burials at Thebes (TT320), as did that of an unknown woman tentatively identified as his grandmother Tetisheri. It is more likely that Ahmose was buried from the outset at Thebes at Dra Abu'l-Naga. Until it was robbed out, his complex at Abydos served only as an impressive cenotaph and monument to his achievements. This was a radical departure from earlier burial practice. From now on the burial and the mortuary temple became physically separated. Royal tombs were deliberately concealed with no surface monument to mark their locations. Ahmose's Theban tomb has never been found.

Ahmose's greatest achievement was to write the script and create the 18th Dynasty's template of power, which his successors tried in various ways to follow. He demonstrated how as king he had single-handedly rid Egypt of chaos and protected his people. Like all such claims, it was as much fiction as fact but that did not matter. Ahmose had restored the idea of Egyptian kingship and reunified the nation. He laid the foundations for the absolutism and the determined control of Egypt's resources and population that would define the history of the next two centuries.

# 4

# MOTHER AND SON
## c. 1525–1504 BC

### AHMOSE-NEFERTARI AND AMENHOTEP I
### (DJESERKARE, 'HOLY IS THE SOUL OF RE')

*Amenhotep I consolidated the 18th Dynasty's hold on power. He developed the system of disseminating wealth won through war and tribute as a way of building his power base and began a programme of building works to amplify the image of the king and state. His mother, Ahmose-Nefertari, was an integral component of his regime and the two were to evolve into a pair of significant deities, worshipped by later generations. However, he did not leave an heir.*

When he became king, Amenhotep I may already have been ruling alongside his father briefly as his co-regent. This would have ensured the succession, but such arrangements are notoriously hard to confirm. In any case, Ahmose-Nefertari ruled on her son's behalf until he came of age. She retained her prestigious titles through his reign of 'Great Royal Wife' and 'God's Wife'. By maintaining these positions for the dowager queen, the family helped reinforce the king's legitimacy and keep power within the family. This was also derived from the myth that the king's mother had been impregnated by Amun in the guise of his father.

Amenhotep ruled for at least twenty-one years but not much more, denying him the chance to celebrate a *heb-sed* jubilee festival after thirty years, though he had undoubtedly been planning such an occasion. The term literally meant a 'feast festival'. The occasion was designed to commemorate a specific passage of time in a reign, and to rejuvenate the king in a series of religious ceremonies and processions. With a thirtieth anniversary behind him, a surviving king might go on to have further jubilees at much shorter intervals thereafter. There were several instances in the 18th Dynasty of rulers arranging jubilees when it suited them to do so. Jubilees were important pretexts for royal building programmes in the 18th Dynasty.

The nation's reunification made possible the identity and expectations of a king as a predatory warrior. Amenhotep I fought at least one Nubian campaign, attested in the tomb biography of Ahmes-Ibana. Ahmes was, according to the old soldier at least, in command of the transport arrangements to take Amenhotep and his army south into Kush. The purpose was to 'extend the border district of Egypt' or, in other words, to push the country's frontier further south at the expense of Kush.[1]

The expedition went well but given Ahmes-Ibana's track record as a dedicated follower of his kings it is unlikely that he would have described it any other way. The Kushites had no idea Amenhotep I was approaching and were caught by surprise, the Egyptians surrounding them so efficiently that not a single enemy soldier, or so it was claimed, was able to get away. Ahmes-Ibana reported the direct confrontation between Amenhotep and the Kushite king: 'His Majesty smote that enemy bowman dead in the middle of his army'. The death is described as happening almost as soon as Amenhotep arrived on the scene and corralled his foe. It is highly unlikely that Amenhotep was able to charge right into the enemy and kill the leader in person. More likely is that soon after the fighting started a lucky arrow or spear found its mark. It was not necessarily fired by the king though of course no one, and especially Ahmes-Ibana, would ever have had the bad taste to say so. The main word used for the felled Kushite leader was 'bow', followed by the determinative sign for a fallen enemy.[2] The most literal translation therefore is 'fallen enemy bowman' and nothing more.

Their nameless leader's abrupt demise was certainly a shock to the Kushites. It cannot have been less of a surprise to Amenhotep. The Kushites solved the problem of what to do next by obligingly fleeing the scene immediately. That they were able to do so suggests the Egyptians were no longer in formation around them. Either way, the Kushite flight allowed the redoubtable Ahmes-Ibana to participate in or even lead the chase to kill as many of the enemy as possible.

The battle over, the Egyptian army as usual set about plundering the ordinary people, taking some of their cattle. Ahmes-Ibana gleefully helped himself to more booty, adding to the gifts from Amenhotep, but this time he was promoted to the position of Warrior of the Ruler. This amounted to Ahmes being placed in supreme command of the army. After this display of derring-do, the victorious Amenhotep headed for home in Ahmes' fleet, where suitable celebrations and triumphant swaggering could follow when he arrived.

A stela found in the ruins of a Christian church south of Aswan shows Amenhotep I and Ahmose-Nefertari making an offering to Horus of Miam (a manifestation of the god in Lower Nubia) and is dated to his 8th regnal year. The stela's presence is impossible to explain unless it was placed in a now long-vanished temple and was perhaps linked to the campaign.[3] It is a mark of how reliant we are on Ahmes-Ibana as a source for this war, which appears only to have lasted a single season, that there are no other sources that might corroborate his account. For the same reason we know almost nothing else about foreign policy during Amenhotep's reign. Given how enthusiastic Ahmes-Ibana was about recounting every one of his marvellous military achievements, invariably depicting himself as the epicentre of the action and as if he was the only senior soldier on hand, we can be fairly sure there were no other major wars or at least ones in which Egypt triumphed during Amenhotep's reign.

Another of Amenhotep's senior officials was Ineni, the king's chief architect and engineer who said with the usual hyperbole in his tomb autobiography that he was 'in control of all craftsmen', and that 'all offices [were] under the supervision of my command'.[4] The 18th Dynasty saw an increasing proliferation of these posts, all with grandiose titles and nebulous overlapping remits bestowed by the beneficent king as part of his patronage. Just because Ineni depicted himself as the architectural supremo, and we happen to have his account, does not exclude the possibility of other high office holders who believed they were of similar importance and engaged in similar tasks.

By Amenhotep I's reign the royal family was becoming self-contained as a matter of policy. The cache of royal mummies found in 1881 included several princesses who were either married to kings or not married at all. They are most easily explained if such women were prohibited from marrying anyone apart from the king. This helped avoid bringing ambitious men into the family as husbands who might mount a challenge to the crown.

The personal possessions of princesses born to the great royal wife, the senior consort, were likely to be marked with statements of parentage. These said that the princess was the daughter 'of the king's body', without being more specific, though her mother, the great royal wife, was named and her rank made clear.[5] This seems to have been a formula that specified these princesses as those of the principal royal female bloodline. Not surprisingly, this led easily to consanguineous unions to preserve power. Such arrangements did not offend sensibilities at the time. A disputed succession risked dividing the country once more and reversing the territorial and economic gains of recent years. There was thus a faultless logic about the principle of the closed royal family though it contained the potential for dangerous hereditary congenital conditions. In practice, the risks of such unions were to some extent circumvented, probably unintentionally, by the kings' freedom also to marry non-royal Egyptian women and foreign princesses. Sons born to these unions could and did become king in the absence of an heir born to the senior wife and queen. They had a better chance of being healthy, Thutmose III and Amenhotep II being cases in point.

One of the frustrating facts about 18th Dynasty history is that princes were far less likely to be recorded on their fathers' monuments, unlike the wives, sisters and daughters of the king, probably to guard against dynastic wars of succession.[6] Instead, if we hear about these boys at all it is usually only from the personal monuments of their nurses and tutors, and other scattered pieces of evidence that occasionally attest them in senior administrative, priestly, or military positions under their fathers if they had lived long enough.[7] This makes it difficult to know why any one individual prince ended up succeeding his father. The theology of kingship also helps explain their obscurity. The living king was the Horus who had succeeded his deceased predecessor, the Osiris. There was no place in that framework for a prince especially if there was more than one. Only when his father died and became Osiris could the prince emerge like the risen sun to assume the guise of Horus himself. Throughout the 18th Dynasty the existence of the heir apparent was veiled by this tradition (but from the 19th Dynasty on this changed and the intended heir was openly publicized). It also helps explain why hard proof of co-regencies is so elusive.

The balance was precarious. Such states rely on a sustained income from war and tribute to fund the building programme, other projects and administrative and military infrastructure to provide the opportunities to be a beneficiary of patronage. They also depend on the person of the king being able to live up to the expectations of his senior followers. Failure of the male line risked instability.

Ineni claimed to have presided over building work which Amenhotep I commissioned at Karnak as a priority, and which continued after the king's death into his son's reign. The worship of Amun at Karnak was now unequivocally positioned centre stage as the 18th Dynasty's state cult. Amenhotep had the time and opportunity to commission such prestige projects. Much of his reign was peaceful. Ineni's description relies on vague references to metals and other goods and the establishment of festivals. This is reflected at Karnak today where there is little attributable to Amenhotep I, thanks also to some of his unsentimental successors removing his contributions. Ineni oversaw the construction of Amenhotep's small (4.5 × 6.8 m) chapel made of alabaster from the Hatnub quarries.[8] It was a powerfully symbolic installation designed to house the barque shrine of Amun during its processions, and to link the cult with his own and his mother's, while also creating a clear link between Amenhotep's reign and the Middle Kingdom work at Karnak. Unfortunately, his efforts counted for little in the years to come. This 'Alabaster Chapel', which was decorated with reliefs portraying Amenhotep's heb-sed jubilee, was demolished over a century later by Amenhotep III. Its stone was reused in his new Third Pylon along with spoil from several other buildings, fortunately ensuring its survival and reconstruction in modern times.

Ineni was probably also in charge of works commissioned by Amenhotep at Abydos, and the mortuary temple the king shared with his mother Ahmose-Nefertari at Dra Abu'l-Naga. This temple was an important gesture even though little is known about it today. It made Amenhotep I the first New Kingdom ruler to build a mortuary temple in the Western Thebes area and, even more radically, one that was separate from his tomb. Nearby was another chapel for the sacred barque of Amun for when it was brought across to take part in the Beautiful Festival of the Valley.

Amenhotep I's tomb has not yet been identified though his mummy was found in the great cache of royal mummies in 1881 (TT320), which included his mother's remains. The body has never been unwrapped due to the beauty of the work. Like his father, he stood around 5 ft 5 in (1.65 m) tall. One candidate for his tomb is KV39 in the Valley of the Kings.[9] This has produced material from as late as Amenhotep II's reign. Its curious plan, consisting of an entrance corridor leading to two separate corridors each with a burial chamber, was an arrangement perhaps suitable for Amenhotep I and his mother, even if one of the corridors was a later addition used for a *reburial* of Amenhotep I.[10]

Another proposal is that KV39 was originally dug for a sister-queen of Seqenenre Tau, because dockets on three royal mummies found in the same royal cache refer to them having been removed to 'the "high place" of Queen Inhapi in which Amenhotep I lay'.[11] This disparate evidence is typical of the sort of problem Egyptologists face and means no conclusions can be drawn about the time Amenhotep might have devoted to his original tomb.

The essential priority remained producing an heir. Amenhotep was probably married to a woman called Meryetamun. A statue labelled as hers was later placed next to one of Amenhotep I by Karnak's Eighth Pylon. Her titles, also only attributed to her later, including 'King's Sister', 'King's Daughter' and 'Great Royal Wife', make it likely she was his sister.[12] If the intention was to secure a successor who was descended only from Ahmose I and Ahmose-Nefertari, the plan failed, at least as far as we know. Since the marriage was one more in a sequence of consanguineous unions in the 18th Dynasty royal house it is not hard to understand why they might have failed to have children. Amenhotep died around the age of thirty, Ineni only telling us that the king had lived 'good years in peace'. The throne passed to a military man of unknown origins called Thutmose, but who is also likely to have been a relative (see next chapter).

Amenhotep I's most unusual posthumous achievement was to be worshipped as a god along with his mother, particularly from the 19th Dynasty on when cult statues and stelae of them were made. The cult was popular with private individuals but was also observed by later kings.[13] The deification of a deceased king was not new. At death he became identified with Osiris, as did every king. The difference with Amenhotep and Ahmose-Nefertari is that their cult was popular and long-lasting, serving as the prime divine symbols of the ruling house.[14]

Amenhotep and Ahmose-Nefertari evolved into the protective deities of the tomb workers' village across the hills at Deir el-Medina (see Chapter 10). They were depicted in reliefs with Amun centuries after their respective deaths as part of a very widespread and long-lasting cult.[15] Eventually, the 7th month of the year was named for Amenhotep as 'Pa-n-Amenhotep'.[16] This Egyptian term survived into Coptic as Paremhat (Παρεμϩατ), 'the Festival of Amenhotep', and in Arabic today as Baramhāt, an extraordinary example of transmission to modern times from the 18th Dynasty.

Ahmose-Nefertari's exalted position of the God's Wife of Amun gave her exceptional privileges to participate in some of the most important rituals at Karnak. These included a symbolic sexual role as the physical stimulator of the god. So great was her prestige that people made offerings to her in the hope that she would help them with whatever their problems were. The deification of Amenhotep I and his mother formed part of the evolving ideology of the 18th Dynasty's ruling house. The claim to be the chosen kings of Amun formed a fundamental validation of their right to rule and thereby excluded everyone else.

### The Mummy of Amenhotep I

In late 2021 news emerged of the results obtained from a CT scan of Amenhotep I's magnificent mummy which had been found in the TT320 cache of royal mummies in 1881. So remarkable was the quality of the rewrapping performed in the 21st Dynasty that it has been left untouched, and thus the body has never been seen. The scanner revealed that like his mother Ahmose-Nefertari, Amenhotep I had the family overbite and a profile that shows a very strong family resemblance. The University of Cairo team also concluded that Amenhotep died in his mid-thirties, corresponding with existing evidence for the length of his reign.

# 5

# FIRST OF THE THUTMOSIDS
## c. 1504–1492 BC

### THUTMOSE I (AAKHEPERKARE, 'GREAT IS THE MANIFESTATION OF THE SOUL OF RE')

*Thutmose I's reign, of uncertain length, was a major turning point. His principal qualification was merit. This energetic and ambitious king took Egypt to war in a series of successful campaigns that consolidated the 18th Dynasty's hold on the country and control of its population and resources. His daughter Hatshepsut would turn out to be one of Egypt's most remarkable rulers.*

Ahmose-Nefertari outlived her son Amenhotep I, surviving into her seventies. As a mark of her importance, she was interred in an astonishing coffin that, thanks to its headdress, was 12 ft 5 in (3.78 m) tall. In the 18th Dynasty theatrical considerations were equally important in the afterlife. It was just as well that she lived so long, providing useful continuity since Amenhotep had left no heir. Perhaps she arranged the solution. Thutmose ('Thoth is born'), a dynamic man of elusive origins, was a middle-aged soldier and a well-established figure in the court circle. He was also probably a member of the royal family though in what way we do not know.[1] His descendants for example exhibited the overbite already detected in Ahmose-Nefertari.

Thutmose featured his otherwise-unknown mother Seniseneb on his monuments but only ever called her 'King's Mother', for example on his coronation decree when she was still living.[2] Had she enjoyed a more exalted title, such as King's Daughter, it would surely have been mentioned, especially on such an auspicious occasion. However, Ahmose-Nefertari was alive well into the new reign and remained the principal female member of the royal dynasty.

Thutmose's father is unknown. In his victory stela erected at Tombos, Thutmose refers to having become king by 'taking possession of his inheritance (or heritage)', which might suggest he had been earmarked as a successor before Amenhotep I's death in the absence of a son, and that he had some dynastic entitlement.[3] The word for inheritance was expressed as '*iwˁt*', a curious term that used the sign for a joint of beef as the phonetic determinative.[4] It was associated with several similar words, all of which denoted the ideas of succession and heirs. Although Thutmose's claim was in the form of a rhetorical phrase this does not mean there was no literal truth involved.

Thutmose's principal wife was inconveniently (as far as we are concerned) also called Ahmes whose origins are therefore even harder to establish than they might already have been.[5] Her importance to history is that she was the mother of Hatshepsut, who explicitly commemorated her parents and a sister.[6] Queen Ahmes was only subsequently referred to as 'King's Sister' and 'Great Royal Wife', and never as 'King's Daughter', which makes it improbable she was both Amenhotep I's sister and a daughter of Ahmose I. It is more likely she was Thutmose I's sister or half-sister, but that gets us no nearer knowing who their father was. Thutmose I was also married to Mutnofret, a lesser wife who was mother of his son and successor Thutmose II. Unlike Ahmes, she appears to have been a member of the royal family, possibly a sister of Amenhotep I's, and would have strengthened Thutmose I's legitimacy (see next chapter).[7]

Thutmose I's apparently undisputed accession only makes sense if he had a cast-iron claim by being the offspring of a senior member of the royal family. Amenhotep I's uncle Sipairi, brother of Ahmose I and Ahmose-Nefertari, was a minor royal who enjoyed unusual posthumous prominence. That might be explained if he was Thutmose's father but there is nothing to prove a connection.[8] Given the importance of keeping power within the royal family it is likely that Thutmose and Ahmes were related to Amenhotep I in some way, but Thutmose I's paternity is likely to remain unresolved.

Thutmose made offerings and gifts to the shrine of Osiris at Abydos which bypassed recognition of his 18th Dynasty predecessors in favour of directly addressing the god as his father. 'I am a king excellent because of what he [Osiris] has done,' he proclaimed. The only reference to his forebears was his claim that he had 'increased the work of others, the kings who have been before me'.[9] Given the potent reputations of Amenhotep I, his mother Ahmose-Nefertari and Ahmose I, it would surely have made sense to link himself to them more explicitly if he had been able to do so by descent. However, he completed Amenhotep's Alabaster Chapel at Karnak as a gesture of loyalty – he did not, for example, replace his predecessor's names with his own. Once Thutmose was crowned, how he became king ceased to matter, even if it ever had.

## THUTMOSE I'S WARS

Estimates of Thutmose's reign vary from around seven to fourteen years, an excellent example of the uncertainty surrounding the chronology of the period. He made the most of his short time by embarking on a series of apparently decisive military expeditions, beginning with one into Nubia in his 2nd regnal year. At the First Cataract a canal dug out in the 12th Dynasty was found to be choked with rubble, preventing navigation. Thutmose ordered it cleared.[10] Remarkably, the old soldier Ahmes-Ibana was still serving

82

in high office and provides us with his version of events with himself, as usual, in the vanguard and no one else in sight. As Warrior of the Ruler and by then surely beginning to approach middle age, he took charge of transporting Thutmose and his army south to Nubia beyond the Second Cataract.[11] Thutmose's own inscription at Tombos (see below) said the campaign took place in his second year. The pretext, real or fabricated, was the outbreak of rebellion in Nubia and attacks from the desert. Perhaps the change of regime was treated as an opportunity to challenge Egypt. If so, it was a mistake.

The campaign was particularly challenging because the vessels had to be pulled upriver past the cataract. Ahmes-Ibana presumably meant that the crews had to disembark and pull the vessels by rope past the hazardous stretch, or even carry them.[12] He was immediately promoted. Bursting with pride, he told posterity that he was made Commander of Rowers, a term often mistranslated as admiral.[13] That has rather misleading connotations of being at the head of a separate wing of the armed forces involving ocean-going vessels. In the 18th Dynasty ships or boats were an integral part of the army mainly used for transporting troops up and down the Nile or later along the coast of Syria.

The ensuing battle began with Thutmose 'as angry as a panther', Ahmes-Ibana deploying a Homeric-style simile for the king who allegedly fired the first arrow and struck the enemy. He claimed the fighting rapidly degenerated into a rout, resulting in carnage.[14] Thutmose was able to round up the enemy as captives and head north. The story is typically both triumphant and perfunctory. It also resembles aspects of Amenhotep I's campaign, suggesting that it was at least partly compiled from stock passages. The most memorable section is the grisly description of how the corpse of the Nubian leader was hung head downwards over the prow of Thutmose's own vessel and taken to Karnak. This was a ritual form of humiliation which appears in accounts of similar events at other times.

No mention is made of Egyptian losses, a topic Ahmes-Ibana studiedly avoided to paint both himself and his king in the best possible light. He was emulating the kings whom he served. Only the enemy could suffer such humiliation. The account therefore cannot be wholly true. The same consideration could be applied to other aspects of the whole campaign and indeed almost any other account of a war by an Egyptian.

Other references to this war have survived including one commissioned by Thutmose I which was carved into the living rock near the Third Cataract at Tombos.[15] It was short on detail, though it does specify the 2nd regnal year, but long on bombast and imaginatively colourful gore. Thutmose bragged that so many of the enemy archers had been killed that the valleys were 'flooded with their innards' and it was beyond the local birds to carry off all the body parts. Apart from telling us that Thutmose wanted to claim he had presided over a murderous rout the text is useless as an account of what had really happened in the battle.[16] But then it was never intended to do any such thing. Like most self-respecting Egyptian kings Thutmose was only interested in depicting himself as a superman. He returned from the campaign in what was by then the 3rd regnal year.[17] Following the war, a fortress was established at Tombos.

A buoyed-up Thutmose next campaigned to the north in Canaan and Syria, territory called Retjenu by the Egyptians, reaching as far as Naharin, the Egyptian word for Mitanni. Both names seem to have been phonetic, transcribed sound by sound into Egyptian consonantal hieroglyphs but with the addition of key determinatives: Naharin with a throw stick determinative, associated with foreign warfare, and the other the hill-country sign used to indicate foreign territory, Retjenu in this instance with just the latter.[18] Mitanni then controlled a large region in northern Syria, stretching into what is now south-eastern Turkey.

Catching the enemy unawares (of course) and apparently in the process of manoeuvre, Thutmose inflicted a 'massacre', followed by the cryptic phrase '[there was] no census (or total) of captives living' followed by the words for 'brought [by] His Majesty from his victory'.[19] This could mean either that Thutmose had captured so many live prisoners that they could not be counted, or that the massacre was so comprehensive any living prisoners could not be counted because they were all dead. In English this would read better as 'no one was taken alive'. The text was obviously rhetorical in the sense that it deliberately avoided giving a number in favour of making an extravagant claim. The use of a firm negative here is, though, more suggestive of a wholesale massacre than unlimited captives being taken. Egyptian also had the term for a number so large that it could not be specified, not used here.[20] The text can be read either way.

The tireless Ahmes-Ibana naturally placed himself in the thick of the action, capturing an enemy charioteer along with his vehicle and horse (the vehicle is indicated by the new word *wrryt* and a determinative pictogram making the meaning certain). He handed them over to Thutmose in return for gold. He does not mention, but it was recorded later by the king's daughter Hatshepsut, that Thutmose had indulged himself by hunting elephants. The relief concerned is badly damaged and the reading relies to a large extent on comparing the few surviving components with a similar elephant hunt referred to later by Thutmose III.[21] Ahmes-Ibana moved straight on from the end of the battle to explaining that he had grown old, still in receipt of honours and finishing up with a named list of his slaves. The implication is that his death preceded Thutmose I's or came soon afterwards. One of the female slaves had the interesting name Hedetkush. The first part seems to be a feminized version of an Egyptian word for punish, so it perhaps meant 'the punished woman of Kush'.[22] If correct, she must have stood for thousands of others like her, endlessly reminded of their inferior origins by their Egyptian masters.

Another soldier, Ahmose Pen-Nekhbet, also fought in these wars. Apart from boasting about his responsibility for capturing various prisoners, killing some and seizing a chariot during Thutmose I's campaigns in Kush and Naharin, he tells us nothing else of any use.[23] For men like him and Ahmes-Ibana the world was merely background noise to their own individual blazes across the firmament, the exclusive focus of the admiring monarch's gaze.

Thutmose I marked the southern boundary of Egypt with a stela placed on a huge natural rocky outcrop called Hagr el-Murwa near Kurgus, which lay between the Fourth and Fifth Cataracts. It was designed to advertise Egypt's power to the Nubians, and the new king's prowess. The text said Thutmose had been accompanied by his queen Ahmes, as well as a prince called Amenmose (who would predecease his father), and a princess who was either Hatshepsut or her sister.[24]

The wars led to Nubians being recruited for the Egyptian army. They may have welcomed the opportunity if the alternative was slavery. Nubian goods, and graves containing young adult male skeletons with Nubian features, have been discovered at an early Thutmosid palatial precinct and military stronghold town on the former site of the Hyksos capital at Avaris. Thutmose enlarged the palace at Avaris, which in a striking development was painted around this time with bull-leaping frescoes of Cretan Minoan style, an unusual example of cross-cultural tradition in Egypt. He also developed the palace at Memphis, which thereafter served as the 18th Dynasty's principal administrative headquarters. The two locations, and the stationing of the Nubians, showed how Egypt's attention was turning towards Canaan and Syria and beyond.[25]

## THUTMOSE I, THE BUILDER

With so much new territory secured by his 3rd regnal year, an exultant Thutmose claimed that he had 'made the boundaries of Egypt as far as that which the sun encircles'.[26] He was well placed to start major building work, largely motivated by a desire to repay Amun as well as developing the image of the all-powerful 18th Dynasty king. Thutmose embellished Karnak, where the works were supervised by the architect Ineni who claimed to have been an autodidact. 'I received no instruction from an elder,' he boasted, apparently having been born with his skills.

Thutmose was not the first king of the 18th Dynasty to invest the spoils of war in glorifying Amun, but he did a great deal to institutionalize and enlarge the trajectory of booty and tribute in that direction. Little or nothing was done specifically for the greater good of Egyptian society. The official story, such as it was, remained completely focused on the king, his achievements and official cults.

The Egyptian imperialist state had no concerns about the human cost of its ambitions. Nor was anything ever said about the levels of coercion that must have been applied, or punishment for non-compliance. Ineni explained that the staff he needed were provided by the king along with the necessary supplies which were sent from the palace.[27] Records of Egyptian building work bear more resemblance to the propaganda output of latter-day totalitarian states such as the German Democratic Republic. All we normally hear about or see are the magnificence of the achievements, along with images of energetic workers enthusiastically applying themselves to the tasks in hand. These cannot be the whole truth or anything like it, even if the effect of the management measures – whatever they were – was the successful execution of some quite remarkable civil engineering projects. The US phase of constructing the Panama Canal (1904–14) ran to over 5,600 deaths, despite the provision of medical treatment, catering and accommodation.

According to Ineni, Thutmose I's work at Karnak included a lake, hypostyle halls made of 'papyrus columns', pylons, flagpoles made of Lebanese cedar tipped with electrum, and two granite obelisks undoubtedly quarried at Aswan. These were the first obelisks of the New Kingdom, but the idea was not new. The oldest known, still standing in its original location, is at Heliopolis (Al-Masalla), erected in the 12th Dynasty.[28] There was a new gate at Karnak fitted with Asiatic copper and dedicated to 'Amun, powerful in magnificence'.[29] The cedar and the copper help illustrate why Egypt had a practical interest in controlling territory beyond her borders. With almost no natural timber of its own, Lebanese cedar played an increasingly important part in Egyptian building. The works at Karnak also included completing embellishments to the Middle Kingdom core of the temple which had been started by Amenhotep I.

A huge freighter was built to bring the obelisks downriver from Aswan to Karnak, where the lake was also being dug out on the west side of the temple complex.[30] One obelisk still stands on its original plinth, a rare relic of Thutmose's reign in its original place. The northerly one (which has now fallen) was left uninscribed and was later taken over by Thutmose III.[31] Ineni was at pains to point out his role as a supervisor with overall authority, 'all things were entrusted' to him. There is little sense of what he did apart from tell other people to do what the king had instructed him to carry out, taking the credit and flaunting his exalted status.

## THE TOMB OF THUTMOSE I

Thutmose's other great project was his tomb in the Valley of the Kings. There is little doubt about where it was. Ineni claimed to be in charge of choosing a suitable location for the tomb and also the idea of using 'fields' of 'clay' or 'mud' to cover the tombs. This presumably meant spreading layers of wet soil over the ground to conceal the entrance.[32] These, he said, were precautions never adopted before. Thutmose had apparently commissioned what ended up as one of the most ambitious, even reckless, royal tombs. Ineni used a word (*ḥrt*) that just means tomb though it has been variously translated as 'rock tomb' and 'cliff tomb' with the general intention of supporting its identification as the extraordinary KV20. Neither adjective appears in the hieroglyphs – another example of translations supplying unsubstantiated precision, even though in other ways KV20 fits the bill. The hieroglyphs for the word in this case include a determinative with the generic meaning of hill-country.[33] This sign was sometimes used to distinguish foreign territory from Egypt. It is therefore much more likely to refer to the general landscape in and around the Valley of the Kings; in other words it was merely a 'hill-country tomb', as opposed to one on the east-facing lower slopes of the Theban hills on the west bank of the Nile which Thutmose's predecessors had preferred.

Ineni said the work was done secretly, 'not seen, not heard'. That was more wishful thinking than anything else since he obviously did not dig it out by himself. The Valley is still littered with tomb builders' spoil. Creating this royal tomb and the ones that followed required a workforce which evolved into a specialized one. They and their families lived nearby in the village of Deir el-Medina to the south. All of them would have had some access to knowledge of the tombs' locations and it only needed a few to be tempted either to rob the burials themselves or to sell the information (see Chapter 10). It would also have been impossible to carry out the project without a sharp-eyed local noticing.

KV20 was cut into the Valley of the Kings early in its use as a royal necropolis almost two-thirds of the way up a 350 ft (91 m) cliff at the far end of a branch in the south-east sector. It is primitive in design and lacks the technical or architectural sophistication introduced over the next two centuries. Later kings continued to commission the construction of tombs either in the Valley of the Kings or in the adjacent Western Valley of the Kings for several centuries.[34] Other family members were sometimes buried there, as well as some selected nobles.

The work on the tomb had two phases. The first amounted to only a quarter of its eventual 700 ft (213 m) length which is at least compatible with Thutmose I's short reign. An inscribed calcite jar sherd found there by Howard Carter names Queen Ahmes making a dedication to the body of the deceased Thutmose I.[35] If a mortuary temple was ever constructed for him, it has not been found and Ineni does not mention one. Thutmose was subsequently commemorated in a chapel constructed by his daughter Hatshepsut in her vast memorial-mortuary temple on the other side of the cliffs. His posthumous cult was certainly still in operation two centuries later.[36]

The exact burial arrangements for Thutmose remain unclear because Hatshepsut was to extend KV20 dramatically so that she could be accommodated with him, a topic we shall return to later. Wherever Thutmose I was buried within the tomb became an irrelevance. Under his grandson Thutmose III he was removed to KV38 to be interred in a place free from anything to do with Hatshepsut.

The work necessary to create a tomb in such a location was gruelling in the extreme. First a spot had to be chosen and the outline of the entrance marked out. This needed to be wide and long enough to accommodate the slope of the entrance corridor and its steps. The men's copper tools (which had constantly to be handed to smiths to re-sharpen) produced vast quantities of limestone flakes that had to be removed and dumped nearby. The Valley of the Kings is today filled with this debris which has been endlessly moved around ever since. As the entrance corridor progressed down into the rock so the temperature inside steadily rose. The Egyptians had several terms for tombs, for example 'house of eternity', but appropriately another was the 'house of corridors'.[37]

Even today advancing only a few metres into an Egyptian tomb is to immerse oneself in a suffocating oven of unbearable humidity. The walls prevent the movement of air with the effect that each person's sweat saturates the immediate atmosphere. Without modern fans and air coolers, walking down into a tomb is claustrophobic and oppressive. Physical exertion is unthinkable. When the tombs were being dug, the corridors were filled with dust and noise, and far more people than would ever be allowed in today. Ventilation was only possible with hand-operated fans. As the tomb deepened, each of these hazards increased dramatically, exacerbated when rockfalls occurred or by faults that necessitated abandoning shafts or changing direction. The work must have been responsible for high rates of severe respiratory conditions, accidents, and deaths. The workers in the Valley of the Kings were considerably hardier than most people today and accustomed to the blistering heat of the Nile Valley, but the labour must still have been ghastly. The only means of alleviating the hazards would have been to reduce or suspend the work during the summer, and to operate the digging with rotating teams, each with its own gang master. The men who dug out Thutmose I's tomb were among the first to experience these conditions in the Valley, but they were nothing to those that must have followed when KV20 was extended in what seems literally to have been an attempt to dig a pathway to the underworld.

Thutmose I's cause of death is unknown and so is his body. The mummy once believed to be his, found in the 1881 royal cache, is almost certainly of a family member but has been rejected as someone too young and who had died from an arrow wound.[38]

There is no question that Thutmose's time as king developed some of the most enduring traditions of the 18th Dynasty. Egypt was moving beyond being a state whose fortunes rose and fell entirely on the prestige and achievements of an individual ruler. Men like Ahmes-Ibana and Ineni were essential to how Egypt functioned with its increasingly sophisticated use of manpower and resources. The succession was organized on internal family arrangements to exclude other challengers or those with claims. Thutmose I left two significant children, the half-siblings Hatshepsut and Thutmose II. Just as their father had apparently been married to his sister, they were married to one another. This prevented them fighting with one another over primacy, but was also part of keeping power within the family. This plan, however, did not protect against either predeceasing the other, or Thutmose II having children by another woman. Both eventualities, as it turned out, were to determine what followed.

# 6

# BROTHER AND SISTER
## c. 1492–1479 BC

### THUTMOSE II (AKHEPERENRE,
### 'GREAT IS THE MANIFESTATION OF RE')
### AND HATSHEPSUT

*After the death of Thutmose I, the 18th Dynasty entered its most remarkable phase to date, but he had laid the groundwork. As so often in history, events turned on unexpected circumstances. In this instance the early death of Thutmose II was to have dramatic consequences. That left his half-sister and wife, Hatshepsut, to serve as regent for his son Thutmose III by a lesser wife. Hatshepsut fulfilled that role briefly, before making one of the most dramatic decisions in Egyptian history.*

Thutmose II succeeded his father in 1492 BC, but only because two brothers had already died.[1] His reign was short, though just how short is unknown. Thutmose II's mother was Mutnofret, one of Thutmose I's other wives, but her titles recorded on later monuments included King's Sister and King's Daughter. Mutnofret was therefore probably a sister of Amenhotep I and a daughter of Ahmose I.[2] Thutmose II's half-sister and queen Hatshepsut had a strong claim since her mother was Thutmose I's principal queen and probable sister Ahmes. The solution was to marry Thutmose II to Hatshepsut. They were probably at least teenagers at accession, but there may have been a significant age gap. Either way, the marriage reinforced Thutmose II's entitlement to rule and helped secure the family's hold on power. It also had an unintended consequence. Thutmose II lived long enough to father a daughter by his half-sister, but his early death left Egypt with a queen who had a claim of her own.

The name Hatshepsut was not uncommon, with no special significance, but there was a tone of accidental prescience to its full form, Hatshepsut-knenemet-Amun.[3] The first part 'Hat' means 'front' or 'foremost' to indicate a person who took precedence over others. The second, -shepsw-, meant a person of nobility. The addition of the sign for *t* at the end feminized the whole name and thus it meant 'foremost among noblewomen'. The last part means 'joined with Amun', which she adopted, a notion Hatshepsut constantly returned to. As queen she enjoyed an unassailable suite of titles: King's Daughter, King's Sister, God's Wife, and Great Royal Wife.[4]

Hatshepsut was shown married to Thutmose II at Karnak, together with their daughter Neferure. Her prime position as her brother's queen was dependent on him remaining alive. The fact that she produced only a single daughter during the marriage was a disadvantage. Had she borne Thutmose II a son her status would have been assured during his reign and afterwards, assuming she outlived him. Hatshepsut was vulnerable to being marginalized were the throne to be passed to a son of Thutmose II's by a lesser wife – which was exactly what happened.

Thutmose II reigned at the most for about thirteen years, dying in c. 1479 BC. Other estimates make his reign far shorter at only three to four years or even less, but without knowing his age at accession it is impossible to be more precise. There is no evidence that Thutmose II made a major contribution to the building programme begun by his predecessors. A gateway at Karnak commemorated his joint rule with Hatshepsut on reliefs but may have been commissioned later by her. It only owes its survival to the reuse of the blocks in the Third Pylon by Amenhotep III. At Elephantine the Middle Kingdom temple of the ram god Khnum was added to with a court by Hatshepsut during her brother's lifetime.[5] There are other scattered but largely inconclusive examples.[6]

The few scarabs produced under Thutmose II, or, more correctly, the few found, can be used to argue for a short reign. The scarab represented the dung beetle believed to propel the sun through the night so that it could rise again in the morning, just as a real dung beetle was observed rolling a ball of dung. It was thus a symbol of renewal. Scarabs were used as amulets, issued as commemoratives of important occasions. They usually bear an inscription on the underside, often a cartouche of the king or queen, and sometimes a more detailed text recording an event. Nothing is known about the factors that determined their production at any given time, or who by, and there is no guarantee they were all made only at the times to which they refer.

The news of Thutmose I's death inspired some Kushite chancers to try their luck. In his 1st regnal year, the only one attested for Thutmose II, news had arrived from a messenger that 'vile Kush' was preparing a rebellion with the express intention of breaking into his father's fortresses and stealing cattle. An unnamed north-ern Kushite ruler organized a conspiracy with other chieftains and family members which Thutmose II, or those acting in his name, moved swiftly to crush by sending an army south to Tapedet. This name meant 'Land of the Bow' and served both as a synonym for Nubia and Egypt's administrative district on the border.[7] From here the army marched on into Kush. The text of an inscription at Aswan inevitably describes the campaign as brilliantly successful but implies that Thutmose II missed the action, 'his Majesty when in the palace, his fame is mighty; the fear of him is in the land'.[8] He was probably too young or too ill to take part.

There was no battle because the expedition had been too fast for the Kushites to organize themselves. In Egyptian royal military lore, the enemy was always branded as cowardly and incompetent. The conspirators and their men were allegedly massacred with the sole exception of one son of the Kushite king and his followers. The prince and his men were taken (apparently) to Thebes to be dragged before Thutmose to general exultation. Kush was reduced once more to being subject to Egypt. The Kushite prince's fate is unknown, but one possibility is that he was to be indoctrinated into serving as a pro-Egyptian client king in Kush, paying for his life with loyalty thereafter.

One of the participants in the Egyptian army in Kush was the senior soldier Ahmose Pen-Nekhbet, who was before too long to become the nurse of Thutmose and Hatshepsut's daughter Neferure.[9] In his biographical inscription he also records fighting for Thutmose II in Naharin (Syria) and in Shasu, supposedly in Sinai or Palestine.[10] Since Ahmose Pen-Nekhbet also refers to Naharin there is every possibility that Thutmose II did what several kings of the 18th Dynasty did and used his army to assert himself to the south and north.

According to the architect Ineni, Thutmose II died soon after, but gives us no cause. Thutmose II is unlikely to have been much older than his late twenties when he expired but his baldness and skin suggests either that he had lived rather longer than that or experienced premature ageing from whatever killed him. There were no signs of violence on his body, just indeterminate signs of disease. His mummy measured a little over 5 ft 6 in (1.68 m). Thutmose must have prepared a tomb for himself, but it has yet to be found. His was one of the bodies transferred to the royal mummy cache found in 1881 (TT320). There is no evidence of a memorial-mortuary temple unless the one known as Hatshepsut's was begun by him and intended for them both.

Thutmose II's premature death by c. 1479 BC was not a disaster for Egypt though it may have created a fleeting succession crisis because his son (see below) was still an infant. In the short time Thutmose II had been on the throne enough had been done in his name to ensure there was no obvious reason for a pretender to try and seize the throne. It was in any case not the first time a pharaoh had died before his time.

A member of the harem called Iset had conveniently already provided Thutmose II with a son, also called Thutmose. There is no evidence Iset was related to the royal family. If not, her new blood may have helped her son who was to be much longer lived than either his father or grandfather. The young Thutmose, still no more than a toddler, succeeded as Thutmose III-Menkheperkare. He only used this version of his throne name during the co-regency with Hatshepsut, modifying it later. Iset was awarded the title Great Royal Wife during her son's rule, a curious phenomenon we shall return to later and explained by reasons that will become obvious.[11]

Thutmose III was about two years old when he became king. This suggests two possibilities. One is that he was the only viable candidate, despite his age, and there was thus no choice other than to rely on his half-aunt ruling as regent until he reached adulthood. The other is that he had been deliberately chosen by Hatshepsut from the harem nursery as her patsy, possibly at the expense of other half-brothers. He would then fill the role of king while she ruled as regent until she changed course and made herself king in her own right. Thutmose II might easily have fathered more sons by other women of his harem. Omitting or even deleting them from the records was a simple and obvious way of creating a narrative to show that the successor was predestined to rule.

We can be sure that Hatshepsut was involved with Thutmose III's accession since the boy played an integral part in her programme to legitimate her rule. She often had herself and Thutmose III depicted as equivalent monarchs, with him sometimes shown as king independently of her.[12] Regardless of Hatshepsut's motives, her regency was a pragmatic solution. Whether her plans were fully formed at this stage or not is impossible to know, but her path to becoming king was undoubtedly more easily achieved by increments than organizing a dynastic coup. It also gave her time to use her patronage to build up a support network first.

Until Hatshepsut's death Thutmose III was a virtual irrelevance other than in official records. There is no need to assume that Thutmose III had to be named as successor by his ailing father to pre-empt any designs on Hatshepsut's part, for example by arguing that Thutmose II knew Hatshepsut was so rapaciously ambitious she had to be kept in check after his death. It is possible she was that sort of person, but she can hardly have known how circumstances would end up advantaging her. There is no evidence to suggest she was in any sense implicated in her husband's death or that she had designs on the throne before the opportunity unexpectedly presented itself.

In later life Thutmose III was keen to record his predestination. The story was recounted in the coronation inscription at Karnak, created between his 15th and 22nd regnal years. According to this the young Thutmose had been resident at Karnak, in training to be a 'prophet/priest' in which he would necessarily have become literate, a privileged skill. One day, or so Thutmose said, a procession of priests was carrying a statue of Amun in the boat shrine through Karnak's Hall of Cedar Columns. The occasion was a ceremony in which his father Thutmose II was making a sacrifice to the god when Amun appeared searching for the young Thutmose III. The boy prostrated himself before the god who placed him in front of his father as the successor, at which point 'the doors of heaven' were opened to him.[13]

It does not matter that the story is obviously not true. Since Thutmose III was only a small child when his father died it is not even a plausible account of an experience later reimagined. What matters is that Thutmose III felt the need to present it as a sign to justify and authenticate his position as king. It would certainly have helped displace any belief that Hatshepsut was the instigator of his accession. Whether he genuinely believed the incident to have happened is another issue entirely. In the context of the era that is entirely possible.

Thutmose III's story belongs to a long series of similar prophetic claims from other places and times, including at other points during the 18th Dynasty. Obviously unverifiable, these stories usually involve claiming supernatural intervention in human affairs in which omens indicated a ruler's predestination. They were always recounted retrospectively, the accession being the 'proof' of the veracity of the stories. The Roman historian Suetonius described various omens that were interpreted as signs of the future greatness and semi-divinity of Augustus. This included one that his mother had been impregnated not by her husband but Apollo in the guise of a serpent, echoing claims that various Egyptian kings made about Amun impregnating their mothers.[14] In the meantime, predestined or not, the person in charge was Hatshepsut. As regent, she executed the outward face of royalty with all the prerogatives, her ambition growing with every year.[15]

# 7

# KING OF EGYPT, DAUGHTER OF AMUN c. 1479–1458 BC

## HATSHEPSUT (MAATKARE, 'TRUTH IS THE SOUL OF RE')

*Hatshepsut spent several years serving as regent for her half-nephew Thutmose III before making herself king alongside him. Hatshepsut's remarkable reign as king of Egypt challenged tradition while at the same time being depicted with all the usual male conventions and devising her own destiny myth. However, she found herself trapped in a paradox she could not escape.*

Although women had already taken on prominent roles in the 18th Dynasty, these had been in the capacity of a king's mother or wife. After Thutmose II's death, Hatshepsut was neither. The simplest solution would have been to serve as the widowed regent for her infant nephew Thutmose III until he came of age and then withdraw. She could not marry someone else, or remove Thutmose III, without risking civil war. She needed Thutmose III to justify her role as regent. The crunch would come when he reached adulthood and automatically superseded her, assuming both lived that long.

By 1473 BC, after six years of serving as regent, Hatshepsut metamorphosed herself into being a joint king alongside Thutmose III, claiming to be the predestined heir of her father Thutmose I. The boy, of course, was still far too young to raise any objections. In this new version of the myth, Amun had chosen her by impregnating her mother Ahmes in the guise of her father. Thutmose II was conveniently omitted. There was nothing especially unusual about Hatshepsut's version of events. Her destiny story was a trope which other kings of the 18th Dynasty followed.[1] The only difference was that a woman was in the process of making herself king. She resolved this with the simple mechanism of writing herself into the traditional route to kingship. Since she was 'chosen' she was therefore by definition the rightful king.

It was a lateral solution possible in Egypt, where symbolism always outflanked reality. The regnal years of the joint reign were dated from Thutmose III's accession with Hatshepsut as co-regent. This system continued even when Hatshepsut declared herself king in the 7th regnal year, conveniently backdating her accession as king to Thutmose II's death. She ruled in this capacity until the 21st regnal year when she died. Hatshepsut's transition to kingship was not straightforward. Once Thutmose III came of age, he was unlikely to tolerate a joint monarchy, especially with a woman. There were also technical issues about kingly titles which were traditionally male, and which had to be adapted into feminized versions.

In practice Hatshepsut established a conspiracy of collusion in her scheme and carried it off with considerable panache. Nonetheless, she was, unless she commissioned an assassin, unable to stop Thutmose III growing up. This made it likely that sooner or later she was liable to be challenged. In the meantime, she was exceptionally focused on her own lineage, particularly as the daughter of Thutmose I, and on her legacy. These themes dominate the evidence for her reign.

Ineni the architect's high-profile career continued unabated, having spotted where his best interests lay. As a result, he was contentedly descriptive of how 'Hatshepsut, the King's Sister and the God's Wife, governed the land' while Thutmose 'ruled'.[2] The distinction in the Egyptian in this case is quite clear. The word *mḫrw* meant govern in the sense of actively running a country, whereas *ḥḳȝ*, for 'rule', used here for Thutmose (whose role is brushed over quickly), was more of a generic description of a nominal role. Ineni, who described Hatshepsut's abilities in power with far more detail and at length than Thutmose's, made no bones about the unsolicited praise and material rewards he received in return for his 'excellence at court'. Hatshepsut gave him property, gold and silver. Ineni repaid the gifts by comparing the 'she-lord who utters commands' to the ropes at either end of a ship holding the nation together, one tied to Lower Egypt and one to Upper Egypt.[3] Hatshepsut was clearly in charge. She was the one with the patronage to bestow, not Thutmose. Those who were smart enough to realize that had much to gain, for the time being at least. Hatshepsut was also smart enough to appreciate the value of the honours and titles she could distribute to loyalists.

Ineni died during his generous mistress's reign. He rounded off his account with a reference to how compliant he had been and how similar benefits would accrue to those who did 'good deeds' like him. Ineni's life was an allegorical tale of the loyal servant at Egypt's height. He was not alone in being a high official Hatshepsut inherited from her brother and father.[4]

## THE IDEOLOGY OF HATSHEPSUT'S KINGSHIP

It is impossible now to know if making herself king had been Hatshepsut's plan all along, or whether she became aware of what might be possible as her position and the reality of her power gained acceptance. Hatshepsut was not playing a game. She explored the idea that the concept of a king could be separated from its physical manifestation in a man and treated as a distinct idea. In this ingenious reimagining of the concept, kingship became a mantle which could be adopted by a man or woman and conflated in either. This way Hatshepsut created her own version of the male-female composite of Egyptian kingship in which both parts were vested in her.

Hatshepsut embarked on a publicity campaign to show she was Amun's chosen, preordained to rule and superior in all the necessary attributes to do so. It is possible she subscribed to a more general idea of female entitlement to rule, taking as her immediate inspiration her own forebears such as Ahmose-Nefertari. Thereby she constructed a theological and dynastic framework that both justified and legitimized the role she was carving out for herself. One of her titles was 'hereditary princess, daughter of Geb [the Egyptian god of the Earth], heiress of Osiris', clearly indicating the importance of divine descent as part of her claim.[5]

Hatshepsut was surely aware of Sobekneferu, the last ruler of the 12th Dynasty. Hatshepsut's sarcophagi carried inscriptions identical to those on Sobekneferu's sister's coffin. These must have been transmitted by an indirect route, but they suggest Hatshepsut was interested in replicating older traditions.[6] Sobekneferu was the probable wife and half-sister of Amenemhet IV, succeeding him as ruler of Egypt. She ruled between c. 1806 and 1802 BC. Her position resembled Hatshepsut's, the main difference being there was no male heir for whom Sobekneferu could serve as regent. She took the ruler's title 'beloved of Re' and was named on a cylinder seal found in the Faiyum as Sobekneferu, the Dual King.[7] Sobekneferu was also depicted in statues wearing simultaneously a woman's dress and the clothing of a male ruler, the *nemes* headdress and the kilt. She also experimented with modified headdresses and wigs designed to conflate male and female royal conventions.[8]

Sobekneferu found ways a female Egyptian ruler could adopt the attributes of a ruler even if those were conventionally male.

Sobekneferu venerated her father and added to his building works, thereby emphasizing her lineage and entitlement, just as Hatshepsut did. Sobekneferu was regarded by Egyptian posterity as a legitimate king. She was included in a 19th Dynasty king list found at Saqqara called Sobek-ka-ra, and the contemporary Turin Canon.[9] Hatshepsut replicated Sobekneferu's titles, and the interchangeable use of male and female ones, and had them proclaimed at her coronation.[10] Like Sobekneferu, Hatshepsut saw no need to change her name. Her new role as king was an extension of her existing identity and not a new one. She took the titles of a Dual King, along with her throne name Maatkare.[11]

A statue of Hatshepsut now in New York shows her as king of Egypt in the emerging style of the era, characterized by a serene expression which was to be even more obvious in some of her successors. The features are feminized and softer, with a small mouth and chin, reflecting the curious ambiguity Hatshepsut had created. On the back she had conventional queenly titles, 'the perfect goddess' and 'she-Lord of the Two Lands', the feminized versions of the male equivalents.[12] The radical element was associating them with Hatshepsut in the guise of a king. Loyalists followed Hatshepsut's cue, commemorating Hatshepsut on their own statues as 'the perfect goddess, she-Lord of the Two Lands', while Thutmose III was called 'Lord of the Two Lands'.[13]

Hatshepsut extended the ideological basis of her gender-composite kingship to her predecessors, principally her father Thutmose I in his chapel at her Deir el-Bahari memorial-mortuary temple (see below), as well as Thutmose II and Thutmose III in his minority. This was an effective way of deradicalizing her innovations and in theory made it possible for males and females to occupy the same royal composite position. Thutmose I was therefore also portrayed with a variety of male and feminized titles, in one instance 'the Perfect Goddess' and 'Lord of the Two Lands' in the same passage.[14] This blurring of gender was matched in Hatshepsut's own statues where she was depicted as a man but with feminized titles, or even with inscriptions that combined male and female forms.[15] The obvious counter-argument would be that the mixture of male and female identities was the result of simple confusion about how to represent a female as a king. But the feminizing of, for example, some of Thutmose I's titles and the dissemination of the practice among her loyalists makes it more likely the practice was deliberate and fitted Hatshepsut's agenda.

The conflation of the male and female had the additional advantage of elevating the king even closer to the gods, especially those with androgynous identities. The creator god Atum had female counterparts.[16] The creator goddess Neith had no known male partner but was associated with a range of female and male attributes.[17] She was, for example, a warrior deity and a mother goddess, and could be shown with weapons or a sceptre of power. It is obvious that such ideas would have been useful to Hatshepsut. Some of these feminized titles escaped deletion during later usurpations and give away her work. However, Hatshepsut was invariably shown as a male ruler, an essential emphasis if she was to present herself to the public as a joint king with Thutmose III. The feminized titles were only accessible to the literate, which meant the priesthood and the elite. What she was trying to achieve probably seemed opaque and uncomfortable to some of them at least.

The Egyptian word (*nsw*) we interpret as 'king' meant the status of being a ruler. While this was normally treated as male, and is usually translated now as king, there was no theoretical contradiction with the idea that Hatshepsut was also 'daughter of Amun', and 'his beloved one' and 'daughter of Re, of his body'.[18] The words usually translated into English as 'queen' or 'great royal wife' meant literally 'wife/woman of the ruler/king', and were therefore useless to a woman ruling in her own right. Neither Sobekneferu nor Hatshepsut had any choice but to style themselves as king even if by convention that came with male attributes.

One way to understand what Hatshepsut was doing is to consider a monarch such as Elizabeth I of England who ruled as queen in her own right. She was able to do so because the concept of the queen regnant had become accepted. In Egyptian terms it would have been necessary for Elizabeth to call herself king so that she could rule in that capacity. This was not therefore necessarily a question of Hatshepsut lacking a suitable female role model and needing to identify herself with her father to rule. Hatshepsut had no conceptual alternative to adopting the only available Egyptian titles for a ruler but had found an ingenious ideological basis for doing so. Hatshepsut would not be the last such female king either. Nefertiti served as a co-regent with Akhenaten and briefly continued as a king in her own right after his death. There were other female kings in later Egyptian history, particularly during the Ptolemaic era.[19]

Hatshepsut could thus be shown as a king, and even with the false beard worn by male rulers. In the reliefs and texts displayed at Deir el-Bahari, the memorial-mortuary temple which became her principal architectural work, her mythical conception by Amun in the guise of Thutmose I who lay with her mother Queen Ahmes was displayed. Amun informs the overwhelmed Ahmes of the prospective daughter from their union who he says will be king over all Egypt.[20] To reinforce the point Hatshepsut's reliefs at Deir el-Bahari which depict this cycle showed her visibly pregnant mother being escorted by the ram god Khnum, a symbol of creation through the procreative force of the ram, assisted by the female frog deity Heket whose role was to oversee the development of the foetus and birth. The scene has no parallel. Hatshepsut clearly felt the need to go beyond the metaphorical and symbolic to depict the myth of her predestination as a literal sequence of events. Once born, she was presented to Amun by Hathor. A delighted Amun announces, 'come to me in peace, daughter of my loins, Maatkare, you are the king that takes possession of the diadem, on the throne of Horus of the living, eternally'.[21] This passage was Hatshepsut's way of demonstrating her credentials and unequivocal entitlement to be king of Egypt by descent and destiny.

**The pregnant Queen Ahmes with Khnum and Heket**

This sort of validation was essential to Hatshepsut. Divine right was an essential ingredient in 18th Dynasty royal ideology. Thus, she appeared on scarabs and in various other contexts as 'united with' and 'beloved of' Amun. On the inscriptions at Deir el-Bahari recording the Punt expedition she was 'the sacred image of Amun, she whom he wanted to be on his throne' and the 'rightful image of Amun-Re'. Hatshepsut therefore posed as fulfilling the god's earnest desire by being king. Crucially, though, she made no attempt to remove Thutmose III. Hatshepsut clearly knew that there was only so far that she could go with her radical transformation, even if his role for the moment was purely as a figurehead.

## HATSHEPSUT'S WARS

In Hatshepsut's coronation inscription the gods promised this 'daughter of Amun-Re' that among other activities she would attack the various enemies of Egypt, specifying various targets such as Syria. For this, Egypt would be rewarded with 'myriads of men'. It was a conventional rhetorical statement and not a meaningful manifesto of campaigning plans. Elsewhere in the Punt reliefs in her memorial-mortuary temple she claimed that such was her prestige she 'had no enemies among the Southerners' and 'no enemies among the Northerners'.[22] Both served in different ways to flaunt Egypt's supremacy and how these other nations were subservient to her, would willingly hand over tribute and had been placed in this role by Amun.

Hatshepsut may have had personal experience of being on campaign. A princess had travelled with Thutmose I and Queen Ahmes on the campaign into Nubia in his 3rd regnal year, mentioned (but not named) on the stela near Kurgus.[23] Leading a campaign was an obvious way for a male ruler to win prestige at the head of a victorious army (as the outcome would inevitably have been described). For Hatshepsut such a feat would have put the final stamp on her claims of entitlement to rule. There was, however, a danger of losing control at home if she left to fight a war beyond Egypt's borders. Delegating military leadership to an experienced general meant risking losing the prestige of any victories to him, and with it the loyalty of the army.

The trouble with almost any reference to a pharaonic war is unravelling the truth from the spin. In the event Hatshepsut's hand was forced by circumstances. Any hint of political instability or weakness risked risings on Egypt's borders. Either would undermine the 18th Dynasty royal ideology of the ruler as the central figure in Egypt's military power. Several campaigns apparently took place during her rule. Some of the evidence is on fragmentary reliefs at her Deir el-Bahari temple that refer to Nubian and Asiatic foes 'under the feet of this good goddess', adding for good measure that 'the fear of her possesses all countries . . . she sends her horses among all her enemies'. A reference to a specific campaign of hers was added to this general description of Hatshepsut's wars, but also acknowledging that she was doing as her father had done. The name of the enemy is lost but the routine slaughter and the severing of hands survives. There is also a mention of 'horses on mountains', which might mean the foe concerned was Asiatic. This is uncertain. It may be the undated Nubian campaign mentioned below.[24]

Thutmose I's ruthlessness in Kush did not prevent further rebellions. Perhaps the bowmen of 'vile Kush' regarded the rule of Hatshepsut as regent alongside the underage Thutmose III as a sign of useful weakness. By the 12th regnal year of their combined rule, Hatshepsut had sent out an army into Nubia against one of these risings. There was at least one other campaign into Nubia about this time, either before or after the 12th regnal year effort, which Hatshepsut apparently participated in personally. One of Hatshepsut's senior officials, a Chief Treasurer (or Overseer of the Royal Seal, or Chancellor, depending on the translation), called Ty left a graffito on the island of Sehel near Aswan. He said he 'followed' Hatshepsut as part of her entourage and had personally witnessed 'him' (expressly using the masculine pronoun $f$) defeating the Nubian, 'destroying the land' and receiving the chiefs as prisoners.[25] Referring to Hatshepsut as 'him' neatly circumvented the incongruity of a female warrior king.

What we cannot unravel is whether these campaigns amounted to major events or were more akin to policing expeditions contrived to allow Hatshepsut to make suitable claims of her prowess. There are no extant depictions of Hatshepsut in a chariot as a warrior king. Whether Thutmose III was involved in any capacity is unknown.[26]

There is one curious postscript to Hatshepsut's foreign policy. In the British Museum is a diminutive obelisk 6 ft (1.83 m) high, now broken into three pieces. It is badly worn and battered but enough of the hieroglyphs can be read to show that it was in Hatshepsut's name. It was found at the citadel of Qasr Ibrim in Nubia in the ruins of a Christian church where it had been reused as a step. This obelisk, which must have been one of a pair, was probably installed in a temple that marked the presence of either Hatshepsut or her army in this remote location and which dated back at least to the reign of Amenhotep I on the evidence of a stela in his name.[27]

## SENENMUT

Hatshepsut was so successful in her endeavour to be king that she was able to rule for fifteen years before her death. As far as we know she was not challenged, either by Thutmose or a faction operating on his behalf. The most important in her support network of officials was Senenmut, today one of the most famous non-royal Egyptians.

Senenmut ('brother of Mut') was the son of Ramose and Hatnefer, provincial commoners whose tomb at Sheikh Abd el-Qurna near his own tomb chapel (TT71) was found intact (see below). Ramose was only called *z3b* (zab) in the family tomb, a generic word for a 'worthy' or 'dignitary' which could be applied to someone who also held a particular high office.[28] Ramose held none. The word is therefore best treated as a way of describing him as an esteemed member of his community without specifying anything more. Hatnefer ('Foremost in beauty') was equally vaguely called 'lady of the house'. In the English seventeenth century, the nebulous term 'persons of quality' circulated. It would have described Ramose and Hatnefer perfectly. Senenmut must have been regarded as a family phenomenon who emerged from obscurity to become the principal royal favourite.

When Hatshepsut made herself king, Senenmut's elite professional career was already underway as Steward of the God's Wife and Steward of the King's Daughter in the service of Hatshepsut and Neferure during the reign of Thutmose II. In the latter capacity Senenmut replaced the senior military officer Ahmose Pen-Nekhbet, and proudly commemorated his responsibilities for Neferure with statues at Karnak. The text on one described his position as Neferure's 'nurse' retrospectively but referred to Hatshepsut's new role as king. It reads: 'I brought up the eldest daughter of the King [i.e. Hatshepsut], the God's Wife, Neferure (may she live!) and I was given to her as father of the goddess, through the greatness of my serviceableness to the King.' The fact that Neferure was described as the God's Wife, as Hatshepsut had been, suggests she was intended to follow her mother in the honour.[29]

Senenmut probably started his palace duties under Thutmose I, carrying on into Thutmose II's reign. Once Hatshepsut became regent after her half-brother's death Senenmut's role expanded, and Neferure was passed to the care of another steward. Senenmut never married, raising questions about Hatshepsut's demands on, and choice of, her principal retainers that made her the sole focus of their attention (see below, this chapter). Once Hatshepsut made herself king, Senenmut was placed in charge of secular activities as Chief Steward of Amun, his most senior post. Hatshepsut presented Senenmut with a statue of himself kneeling before a Hathor-headed sistrum in her name and Thutmose III's for the temple precinct of Mut at Karnak. The text was composed as Senenmut addressing a viewer in the first person, sharing his exalted status with the world, and including 'I, the great of greats in the whole land . . . I, the King's true trusted one, favoured by the Lord daily, Overseer of the Cattle of Amun, Senenmut, justified'. His name was accompanied more than once elsewhere in the list by the honorific epithet 'justified' (also translated as 'triumphant' or 'true of voice'), more normally applied to the esteemed dead. Several words of related meaning were used in this sentence for emphasis, overegging the pudding in a very pointed way. His other claims included his ability to make correct decisions, that he was unbiased, and that the Lord of the Two Lands was content with him.[30] The statue was even reproduced in miniature versions for the Mut precinct and perhaps elsewhere.

The statue's texts are exceptional, even for Senenmut whose ego and reputation always marked him out. The need to acclaim his role as the authentic 'true trusted' smacks of court rivalry because it implicitly dismissed other dignitaries as inconsequential. The statue and its texts, its royal donation, and its prestigious location were thus an official declaration of Senenmut's pre-eminence, but his fame was bound to have been bitterly resented by others passed over for such favours. Exactly who the target readership was is far from clear. Only the priests in the Mut precinct would have been able to read the text, assuming they had any inclination to do so. Perhaps Senenmut was the one who derived the greatest pleasure from reading it, or merely knowing it was there while his enemies festered in the background. He had also gained wisdom through his unique access to the prophets, 'there is nothing in what has happened since the very first moment that I have not learned with the intention of perpetuating the origin (of things)'. Senenmut used here an old form of expression, not the only time he looked for inspiration in archaic writings. It was surely another way in which he sought to outclass everyone else around him.[31]

Thanks to his startling abilities, Senenmut had overall responsibility for Hatshepsut's building works at Thebes. One of the most unusual aspects of Senenmut's career is the exceptional number of sculptures of him, matched or exceeded only by members of royalty.[32] These include several unprecedented types which depicted him in various capacities such as Neferure's nurse. The so-called 'block' statues with Neferure are remarkable for the way the child is depicted as enveloped within the clothing, and almost the body, of Senenmut. The composition primarily symbolized his proximity to Hatshepsut and her daughter. The statues were still being produced after Senenmut had given up the role of nurse. Hatshepsut was personally involved in the commissioning of some of the statues which were already being made while she was still acting as Thutmose III's regent.

Senenmut's statues played an important role in making good his lack of prominent forebears by creating new traditions of his own and gratifying his own narcissism. In the absence of children, they would also serve as his legacy. This was a point he explicitly made by having some inscribed with his claim that he had designed the compositions himself 'from the devising of my own heart'.[33] An oddity is that Senenmut was always depicted wearing the most basic clothing, usually just a knee-length kilt, instead of the more elaborate costume of a high official, though he did wear a wig.

Senenmut experimented with symbols that made up his mistress's name or which referred to her attributes. One of his most distinctive rebus designs showed Senenmut kneeling while holding a so-called cryptogram made up of a cobra uraeus (Maat) placed between the pair of upraised hands representing the soul ('Ka') surmounted by a solar disk in a pair of horns (Re), the Hathoric crown. This made it a symbolic depiction of her throne name Maatkare ('Truth is the Soul of Re').[34] The *ka* was the expression of the king's integral spiritual association with his deceased and divine forebears. The cobra uraeus evoked both royalty and a goddess, in this case Maat but probably conflated with a variety of other goddesses, all gathered within Hatshepsut's identity. This cryptogram was also used as a motif in friezes at the Deir el-Bahari temple and was unique to Hatshepsut's reign, though most of the ka symbols were later defaced and the arms removed. Another of Senenmut's designs incorporated the sceptre hieroglyph, symbol of power, with the 'ankh' sign for eternal life.[35] Both cryptograms can still be seen at her temple today. There was also one showing Senenmut kneeling and grasping a large sistrum, symbolizing Hathor who appears on column capitals at the Deir el-Bahari temple.[36] At the temple, a project which he oversaw, Senenmut installed reliefs which depicted him in devotional postures along with inscriptions naming Hatshepsut, presumably with her explicit endorsement.

Senenmut created an innovative visual style for Hatshepsut and her regime. He was taking established themes and motifs but recasting them in ways that set Hatshepsut apart, while at the same time asserting her fully integrated identity as an Egyptian king. His work fulfilled Hatshepsut's ideological interests, and his own needs to do it in ways he believed would be both beautiful and interesting. If Senenmut was the genuinely creative polymath he appears to have been, the prospect of being able to work like this was probably irresistible, especially if he idolized Hatshepsut. He certainly idolized himself.

Senenmut's role was fundamental to Hatshepsut's successful consolidation and maintenance of power. His portfolio of titles included being Overseer of Amun's granaries, cattle, gardens, fields and weavers, as well as being Hatshepsut's principal architect and Overseer of Works. These gave him unmatched influence and pre-rogative. His days were not necessarily filled by rushing from one location to another to deal with everyday micromanagement. His multiple prestigious offices positioned him in an exceptionally close and conspicuous orbit around Hatshepsut. How close Senenmut was to her personally is a matter for debate and some ribald comment, then as now.

## SUSTAINING THE REGIME

Hatshepsut depicted herself as not only the favourite child of Thutmose I, but also as the daughter of Amun. She faced a variety of potential existential threats in Egypt from among the nobility and the wider population as she aged. In the role of a female king with Thutmose III waiting in the wings, her time in the sun was likely to wane as he grew to adulthood. She must have realized that those with ambition would drift away from her and focus instead on him for patronage.

Hatshepsut made her grand statements at Thebes, clearly more concerned about preserving her power in Egypt than beyond. In any case Hatshepsut would have struggled with some of the conventional diplomatic tactics to manage neighbours and allies to Egypt's advantage. She could never source a foreign prince as her husband to secure her bloodline, assuming she was able still to have children. Any such prince would instantly have become a major threat to Egyptian autonomy and demolish the ideology she had created of herself as the male-female composite king.

Moreover, while it was quite acceptable for an Egyptian king to have a principal wife and several other lesser wives, and father children by any or all of them, the nature of Hatshepsut's kingship obviously precluded that option. This was one of several areas in which Hatshepsut had cornered herself. Sobekneferu had faced a similar problem. In her case there was not even the option of a nephew successor. The 12th Dynasty ended when Sobekneferu died. Nefertiti was to find an ingenious technical solution much later in the 18th Dynasty when she ruled as a king alongside her husband Akhenaten and then on her own after his death. Their daughter Meryetaten ('Beloved of Aten') served as their mutual great royal wife, a role she remained in during Nefertiti's brief sole rule before the accession of Tutankhamun (see Chapters 13 and 14).

No such arrangement seems to have occurred to Hatshepsut. Nor would it have avoided Thutmose III succeeding her anyway. In the meantime, Hatshepsut's daughter was in a similar position to her mother. The obvious marriage for Neferure as a princess would have been to Thutmose III. Any children would have secured Hatshepsut's bloodline. There is only the most tenuous evidence for such a union (see next chapter). She probably died during her mother's reign or very shortly afterwards.

Hatshepsut therefore had few, if any, options. All she could do was consolidate her power at home during her lifetime and hope that her life's achievements would echo through eternity. This mirrored Senenmut's career. With no wife or children, his career was never going to result in securing his family's prominence down into later generations. Hatshepsut faced the same sort of oblivion, but this did not stop her throwing her time and resources into her legacy-building programme. Hatshepsut was able to draw on resources from territory under Egypt's control and other luxury goods that were brought in on trade routes. The principal beneficiary, apart from Hatshepsut and her court, was the cult of Amun with which Hatshepsut regarded her interests as inextricably intertwined.

# THE DEIR EL-BAHARI TEMPLE

Hatshepsut and Senenmut's greatest triumph was the memorial-mortuary temple at Deir el-Bahari. Known as Djeser-Djeseru ('holy of holies') the temple was described by Hatshepsut as the 'garden' she had constructed for 'my father Amun'. It was embellished with trees and plants acquired in Punt. Within the porticoes painted reliefs displayed Hatshepsut's accomplishments, including both the voyage to Punt and the erection of her obelisks at Karnak.

The reliefs within the temple included those that portrayed the myth cycle of Hatshepsut's conception and predestination as king. The work was in large part delegated to the care of Djehuty (in some modern works called Thutiye), Overseer of the Treasury, literally the 'double houses of silver and gold', among other titles which he listed in his tomb, each proudly prefixed with 'noble'.[37] The work was supported by various other loyalists who knew the sense of being seen to participate. Puyemre, Second Prophet of Amun, was one of several who provided special votive stones bearing Hatshepsut's name which may have symbolized more substantive involvement in the project.[38]

The new temple was not the only or even the first such structure there. Mentuhotep II of the 11th Dynasty had built his temple at Deir el-Bahari five centuries before, in a less advantageous position just to the south. Its design pioneered the notion of a terraced structure accessed by a ramp and built into a recess in the Theban cliffs. Hatshepsut's new temple was larger and consisted of two pylons (which are long gone) preceded by a causeway of sphinxes with Hatshepsut's features, and then three courts, the upper two accessed by ramps on the main axis. It may have been originally conceived as the memorial-mortuary temple for herself and Thutmose II and begun before his death, even if it was primarily her project.

Almost all the features used, including decoration, had some precedent so the temple could not be described as truly original.

The real achievement was the scale, setting and overall success in realizing a masterpiece ensemble. The façade of each level of the temple was defined by covered porticoes of rectangular columns with each level reflecting the strata in cliffs immediately behind. No later mortuary temple ever used the Theban backdrop this way. The uppermost façade's columns were fitted with attached Osiride figures of Hatshepsut, a type already known in the area from the lost temple of Amenhotep I. The overall design was based on the use of squares and rectangles, and the triangles of the ramps. The recessing of each level is not obvious on the approach thanks to the deliberate use of foreshortening. It is only as one walks up each ramp that the size of the courts becomes apparent, though this is best appreciated by looking down from the cliffs above.

At the rear of the upper court was a complex of three chapels which served important functions in royal ideology surrounding a central rectangular courtyard. On the south side was the chapel dedicated to Hatshepsut's future mortuary cult and on the north a chapel and solar dedicated to Re-Horakhty and Amun. At the rear of the courtyard was a narrower and smaller chapel that protruded back into the cliffs. Here Amun was worshipped in the company of cult statues of the Ennead deities of Heliopolis and Thebes housed respectively in nine niches on each side of the entrance to the chapel. On the terrace below were shrines to Hathor and Anubis.

Although its primary function was as a memorial-mortuary temple, the building played a much more important religious role during Hatshepsut's reign. It took at least fifteen years to construct, making the work alone a prominent ongoing event throughout her time as king. As well as accommodating religious activities, the temple served as a monumental example of Egyptian royal theatrical architecture by showcasing Hatshepsut's status and achievements, in particular the voyage to the land of Punt of which she made so much.

The Amun chapel was the focal point of the entire temple structure which ensured that it was aligned towards Karnak. Thanks to the huge amount of extensive modern rebuilding and restoration by Polish archaeologists, the temple can now be seen from Karnak today just as it was in Hatshepsut's time. In antiquity they were connected by the Beautiful Festival of the Valley processional route that crossed the Nile. Hatshepsut's temple still stands among the greatest architectural achievements of all time.

## THE EXPEDITION TO PUNT

The expedition to Punt in the 9th regnal year was publicized as one of the defining events of Hatshepsut's rule.[39] Through an oracle, or in consultation, Amun had allegedly instructed her to send the expedition by land and water to Punt, a land of which Hathor was mistress. Punt was now 'given' to Hatshepsut by Amun which he had created for his own pleasure, from which she could bring back exotic goods. The people of Punt had no say in the matter. The expedition was made up of a flotilla of five ships, each of which was about 70 ft (21 m) long, and carried 210 men including troops. It was organized under the supervision of an official called Nehsi who held several senior positions at Hatshepsut's court including one described variously as either Chancellor or Wearer of the Royal Seal (see Glossary). For more about Nehsi see Loyal Foreigners below.

The Punt ships probably left Egypt from a harbour just south of Mersa Gawasis or at El Qoseir. Both lie on the Red Sea to the east of Thebes. Mersa Gawasis was certainly used for expeditions to Punt during the Middle Kingdom and earlier, several hundred years before Hatshepsut.[40] The location of Punt remains unknown but was probably further down the Red Sea or on the north coast of the Horn of Africa in modern Somalia.

A long eulogy of Hatshepsut was included, 'quoting' Amun, which added the useful messianic endorsement that Amun had foreseen her coming and planned all this long ago. He had softened up the inhabitants of Punt so that they would welcome Hatshepsut's expedition. They would hand over the myrrh trees for installing in the temple garden and other exotic items including ebony, ivory, animals and even labourers together with their families. All these are described and illustrated as being joyfully loaded onto the Egyptian ships to return to Karnak along with princes from Punt who followed behind. The presence of Egyptian soldiers must have been the real incentive for the people of Punt to comply. The reliefs also include Parihou and Ati, the king and queen of Punt, who were shown greeting the anonymous Egyptian 'king's messenger' with his escort of eight soldiers and an officer. The queen of Punt was famously depicted graphically as morbidly obese, evidently a source of fascination to the Egyptian artist responsible.

For all the boasting about the enterprise, Hatshepsut did not participate in her venture to help herself to the fruits of paradise. It was not a risk she could take. Given the precise detail in the reliefs, especially the depiction of the queen of Punt, there is good reason to suspect the expedition took place much as described. Among the officials receiving the incoming spoils was Djehuty, the Overseer of the Treasury. Described as scribe and steward in the Punt expedition reliefs, he is seen busily supervising the measuring and counting.[41]

The extent of the haul brought back was exaggerated. The number of men sent out on the ships, the relatively small size of the ships and the need to avoid overloading them, as well as the people from Punt supposedly brought back to Egypt, meant freight had to be limited, especially the live animals. There was another practical consideration that went unmentioned. Records of an expedition to Punt under Ramesses III (1184–1153 BC) explain the arrangements necessary on the return leg. The goods had to be offloaded and carried across the desert for about 95 miles (150 km) by road by men and pack animals from the Red Sea to the Nile port town of Coptos (modern Qift) where they could be reloaded onto boats for the triumphant journey by river, either to Thebes or Memphis.[42]

Hatshepsut claimed the expedition had been a tribute-gathering exercise. It was also possible sailing to Punt had been part of expanding Egypt's long-distance trade routes, albeit coercively. This was already happening through the normal commercial traffic in the Red Sea and the Mediterranean. Bronze Age shipwrecks show that maritime traffic was routinely transporting commodities around the region, and probably often as private enterprises, but the work was dangerous and expensive. In Egypt, the crown was ultimately the principal beneficiary. The Punt expedition's purpose was to provide a consignment of luxury goods for Hatshepsut and her court circle, not improve the lives of Egyptians more generally.

## LOYAL FOREIGNERS

Nehsi (literally 'the Nubian') was one of many prominent foreigners who made their careers serving Egypt during the 18th Dynasty.[43] Employing foreigners increased Egypt's control through cultural assimilation, even if it meant them having to live with Egypt's insulting disdain. Nehsi's loyalty to Hatshepsut was later repaid by his likeness on the Punt reliefs being hacked out along with hers. Ruiu was a Nubian who served as deputy to the viceroy of Kush in the province of Wawat, Egypt's name for the territory of northern Nubia between the First and Second Cataracts, during the co-regency and before that under Thutmose I and II. Ruiu's sons followed their father into the same job, one enjoying such titles as Vigilant Agent of the King's Daughter to begin with. This was adapted as Hatshepsut's position changed, becoming Vigilant Agent of the she-Lord of the Two Lands. These men commemorated themselves with tombs and personal monuments in fully adopted contemporary Egyptian style.[44] People like them have served imperial states ever since. The Roman Empire relied on utilizing provincial elites this way, and so did the British Empire. The advantages to some individuals clearly outweighed other considerations in their minds.

# HATSHEPSUT'S KARNAK

Hatshepsut's works continued at Karnak with Senenmut's assistance. Her Karnak obelisks included at least two pairs and possibly a third.[45] Senenmut organized the quarrying at Aswan of two obelisks in Hatshepsut's name though the inscription recording this has no regnal year.[46] These were probably the two obelisks erected by her at what was then the entrance to Karnak. They no longer exist, apart from the tip of one and a pair of bases, and nothing is known about their inscriptions.[47] They may have been the pair which is shown being transported in reliefs on the walls of Hatshepsut's so-called Red Chapel (Chapelle Rouge) at Karnak. This was a small shrine built at Karnak in her 17th regnal year to accommodate the sacred barques of Amun and Mut, and other gods. It was probably originally positioned between these lost obelisks. The reliefs show how two obelisks were placed on a huge wooden barge which was towed north by twenty-seven boats powered by 850 rowers, helped of course by the current. The scenes show troops at the ready to offload the obelisks before a reception committee of priests and other worthies, with acclamations in Hatshepsut's and Thutmose III's names, including '[Amun] increased the years of his daughter who makes his monuments!'. Thutmose's name appears only at the end for the sake of form, uncredited with any specific achievement.[48]

Cutting the last pair of obelisks out of the Aswan quarry took seven months from Hatshepsut's 15th regnal year into her 16th regnal year, a job tackled by Amenhotep, Overseer of Works on the two great obelisks, and in whose career the task had clearly been a high point.[49] They formed part of the celebrations for her sed festival which Hatshepsut scheduled for that year. The obelisks were shipped on raft freighters north to Karnak. They were erected in the hypostyle hall between the Fourth and Fifth Pylons, which had been built by her father Thutmose I, on either side of the processional way through the middle of the temple. Several of Thutmose's columns had to be removed to make way for them. The obelisks' inscriptions state that

Hatshepsut 'made (them) as a monument to her father, Amun' under his command, and that their caps were plated with electrum.

Hatshepsut wanted those in the future who might gaze upon the obelisks and wonder why they had been made to know they were for Amun 'in order that my name might last'.[50] Posterity was a particular concern of Hatshepsut's and she returned to this theme repeatedly. The words she used, although often translated as 'future', had subtler connotations of eternity and the notion of the swathe of time between past and yet to come. She also used a strange idiomatic Egyptian phrase, little understood today, that evoked the way her imagination ran riot just musing on what people of later ages would say about her achievement.[51] This was driven by her professed conviction that she was the medium through which Amun acted by following his orders, and that through her works she replaced and improved upon those of her predecessors. Accordingly, she expected to be recognized and admired for this by future generations.[52]

The obelisks were 97.5 ft (30 m) high. Djehuty said that he had been responsible for the electrum plating in his capacity as Overseer of the Treasury which amounted to about 12 bushels (around 440 kg).[53] They were supposed to emulate but exceed the obelisks Thutmose I had raised between the Third and Fourth Pylons. They would have been clearly visible to the east from Deir el-Bahari, especially in the early evening as the electrum tips reflected the sun as it began to drop down behind the Theban hills in the west. Hatshepsut also proclaimed that the obelisks were in honour of Thutmose I and without precedent, 'the ignorant like the wise know it'. One of this pair is still in its original location in Karnak and is the tallest standing in Egypt today. Its southerly companion lies shattered nearby where it fell centuries ago.

The 15th regnal year sed festival jubilee was recorded on reliefs at Karnak and Deir el-Bahari. The Overseer of Works Amenhotep claimed to have been the main impresario.[54] In theory Hatshepsut ought to have waited another fifteen years, but it was already about thirty years since Thutmose II had succeeded to the throne with her by his side. It was another opportunity to promote her rule and justify her prestige building projects. To offset any sense that she might have gone too far, Thutmose III was incorporated into the celebrations. She also embellished Amun's barque shrine in the heart of Karnak by adding rooms which showcased her mythologized journey into divine approval. The Eighth Pylon was added to Karnak's south side, elaborating the southern entrance to the temple.

Hatshepsut complemented the work at Karnak with additional contributions to the Mut precinct, which included the monumental statue of Senenmut mentioned earlier. She also added to the Temple of Luxor. The purpose was theatrical. Hatshepsut was the central figure in the cycle of rituals and theology that associated all three religious centres, including, for example, the annual eleven-day Opet (in Egyptian *Ipt* from a name for Karnak) Festival which she initiated. This involved Amun's cult statue, and those of Mut and their son Khons, being transported on barques from Karnak for a sojourn at Luxor before being returned. Hatshepsut installed way-station shrines on the route between the temples. The festival was how the reigning king's mortal identity and spiritual identity, the ka, were conflated at Luxor. It is obvious why this was so important to Hatshepsut.

The first court at the Temple of Luxor, built by the 19th Dynasty king Ramesses II, has a triple barque shrine for the statues of Amun, Mut and Khons that looks as if he was responsible for that too. However, at least two instances of the word 'beloved' are visibly in the feminine form. Ramesses had evidently ordered one of Hatshepsut's shrines to be dismantled and reused in his court. The sculptors were told to usurp the components with his name but overlooked this grammatical gender technicality, making it possible to identify the components as belonging to one of Hatshepsut's original barque shrines.[55]

More temple building and restoration took place further afield. Hatshepsut constructed a new temple at Elephantine, later dismantled and its components reused in a Ptolemaic temple. It was dedicated to a goddess called Satis who oversaw Egypt's southern borders and the Nile's annual flood, on which Egypt's very existence depended. Much of Hatshepsut's other building work involved adding to existing structures.

At Beni Hasan (about halfway between Abydos and Memphis) Hatshepsut had two shrines to the lion-goddess Pakhet constructed by Djehuty in the cliffs. The larger of the two was later given the Greek name *Speos Artemidos*, 'grotto of Artemis'.[56] Her dedication inscription said that she had restored various temples which had lain in ruins since Hyksos times, and thanks to a reference to the Punt expedition must date to after the 9th regnal year. She announced, 'I have restored that which was in ruins, I have raised up that which was unfinished after the Asiatics were in the midst of Avaris of the North-Land, and the barbarians were in the midst of them, overthrowing that which was made in the midst of their ignorance.'[57] It is more than likely that she included in this general claim work that had been executed by her predecessors, subscribing to the normal practice for an Egyptian king of stealing a predecessor's achievements. Hatshepsut's mission was also to depict herself as a major agent in the restoration of Egypt.

## THE BENEFITS AND PRICE OF LOYALTY

Although Hatshepsut's reliefs and texts are usually described as propaganda, few people were able to see them, and even fewer were able to read them. This contradicts the purpose of propaganda, but they must have formed the ideological basis of how Hatshepsut presented herself in more public contexts. Doing this depended on the support of loyalists. It must have been these to whom Hatshepsut was primarily addressing her message in its most sophisticated forms. Senior officials were well rewarded, at least for most of the reign, for supporting Hatshepsut. They were able not only to invest in elaborate private tombs for themselves and their parents but also

apparently to do so competitively, including decoration that honoured Hatshepsut's regime.

So intertwined was Senenmut with Hatshepsut's regime and her
identity as king that some contemporaries believed the two were in
a sexual relationship. A scurrilous graffito found in an unfinished
tomb close to her temple at Deir el-Bahari shows a ruler of ambiguous gender in a submissive position, having intercourse with a
non-royal male.[58] It is impossible to prove they represent Hatshepsut
and Senenmut, but the idea is certainly plausible. Neither was
married to anyone else, and Hatshepsut could not have considered
marrying again without compromising her status. On the other
hand, gossip aside, it is equally possible therefore that there was no
sexual relationship and that Senenmut acted as more of a protective
buffer zone around Hatshepsut.

Senenmut and Djehuty were not alone among Hatshepsut's senior
officials in making no mention of a wife or children in their tombs.
There are further echoes here of Elizabeth I of England and the jealousy she was susceptible to if her favourites, principally the earls of
Leicester and Essex, gave a hint of preferring any female company
to her own. While family members may have been tactfully kept in
the background, their absence raises the interesting possibility that
Hatshepsut had a very particular idea of what loyalty meant. It would
certainly be consistent with her focus on herself and her concerns.
It is conceivable that she prohibited any such marriages and children
to ensure that her officials had no distractions from attending to her.
That way she could exert a total and proprietorial focus on her affairs
and interests. This could not have happened the other way round
since there would never have been a male ruler relying on female
high officials. It is also possible that, in Senenmut, Hatshepsut found a
talented, flamboyant, and innovative man whose personal inclinations
precluded him from either having a sexual relationship with her or any
other woman, but who venerated her and was fully prepared in every
other way to devote himself and his creative skills to her interests.

Senenmut became so wealthy that he was able to commission a

major tomb complex in Western Thebes, the largest built by a commoner at the time. Today it is catalogued as two, consisting of a tomb chapel (TT71) and a burial chamber (TT353), designed as a private version of a royal burial. Senenmut had a quartzite sarcophagus of a type more appropriate for royalty, perhaps a gift from his mistress though it was never finished. Senenmut's burial arrangements marked him out as exceptionally privileged. The one oddity is that in his tomb scenes, roles that would have been normally filled by a wife and son were carried out by his parents and one of his brothers.

Senenmut also invested in a nearby tomb for his parents Ramose and Hatnefer; apparently also transferring into it six predeceased family members to join them. Since the tomb's equipage was primarily suitable for a woman it looks likely that only his mother Hatnefer had lived long enough to enjoy her son's success.[59] Hatnefer's death was used by Senenmut as the occasion on which to rebury his father and the others with her. The tomb and its contents demonstrate how success at court could impact on the status of a family, even if most of the members were already dead and where there were no descendants who could benefit from inherited status and position.

Senenmut is last recorded on an ostracon found close to his unfinished tomb which is dated to the 16th regnal year of Thutmose III and Hatshepsut (the 9th year since Hatshepsut had made herself king).[60] The length of Senenmut's known career suggests that he may have been in his fifties when he died. A natural death is a plausible explanation. There was, however, more to the story.

# THE LATTER DAYS OF HATSHEPSUT

It is often stated as a fact by some Egyptologists that Hatshepsut died on the 10th day of the 2nd month of growth in the 22nd regnal year of the joint reign.[61] The date comes from a stela found at Armant.[62] This is a close correlation to the twenty-one years and nine months of Manetho's 'Amessis' which is then taken to verify the stela in a classic circular argument.[63] The stela says no such thing. The date given is the one marking the beginning of Thutmose III's sole reign from that day forward but even that is implicit, and not explicit. There is no mention of Hatshepsut or her death, which had only *presumably* occurred on or before that date. That she had died is a legitimate inference but no more than. Either way the date was 160 days into the Egyptian civil calendar, which by 1458 BC was on or around the end of January or early February by our reckoning, even allowing for a significant margin of error of at least two weeks either side.[64]

If that was when Hatshepsut expired, she cannot have been much older than forty and may have been several years younger. Hatshepsut had prepared for her afterlife in a more comprehensive way than any of her dynastic forebears. Hapuseneb, a high official who as usual held several posts, specifically claimed to have worked on Hatshepsut's tomb (her name in his text being later replaced with Thutmose II's) on the basis 'of the excellence of my plans', he said. Unfortunately, since she appears to have had at least two tombs we do not know which one he was referring to.[65]

Hatshepsut's first tomb, probably created while Thutmose II was still alive, was in a remote valley to the west of the Valley of the Kings. Exceptionally difficult to access, the entrance was 231 ft (70 m) up an almost vertical cliff.[66] When found, it still contained Hatshepsut's unused quartzite sarcophagus, the first one ever created for an 18th Dynasty ruler. Once she became king in her own right Hatshepsut transferred her attention to the more appropriate Valley of the Kings. Here she ordered an extension to the tomb probably used for Thutmose I (KV20). If that is correct, the change of plan would have been in context with Hatshepsut's loyalty to the memory of her father.

Being Hatshepsut, her modifications had to make the tomb a great deal more impressive. Hatshepsut's new burial chamber was 700 ft (213 m) from the entrance at the end of a winding and precariously steep corridor. The remarkable depth of the excavation and its direction suggests that it was originally planned to run right down under the cliffs to meet another burial chamber below her mortuary temple. The scheme was unsurprisingly abandoned and instead the corridor had to turn back on itself. A burial chamber was prepared. She contributed two quartzite sarcophagi, both originally for her, one of which was converted for Thutmose I's use by adapting its inscriptions.[67] Whatever the abilities of the tomb builders, and the oppressive and lethal conditions in which they were compelled to work, this tomb went too far.

Hatshepsut's body has not been identified with certainty, though a second mummy found in the tomb (KV60) of her childhood nurse Sitre-In with its left arm crossed over the chest in the posture of a royal woman has been claimed as a possibility. Naturally, the identification has been roundly dismissed by some Egyptologists and equally obviously there is no means of verifying the views either way.[68] Although there is little doubt that Hatshepsut was buried in KV20, she did not remain in the tomb. Parts of a wooden coffin of hers were found in the tomb of Ramesses XI (KV4), used centuries later as a processing facility for recycling royal burials for valuables (see Epilogue). The 1881 cache of royal bodies (TT320) also contained several objects which included a wooden box bearing Hatshepsut's names. Inside the box were mummified viscera and a tooth. The tooth has been claimed to be the one missing from the KV60 female body's skull.[69] Even if this confirms the body to be Hatshepsut's, and most Egyptologists not surprisingly refute the theory, it makes no difference since the fact is that she had died and whether we have the body or not does not change that.

# THE AFTERMATH OF HATSHEPSUT

In 1962 Hatshepsut was described as Thutmose III's 'now-detested stepmother' who had frustrated his efforts for almost two decades to get rid of her, though there is no basis for such a view.[70] In recent years she has been more widely admired for her vigorous programme of works and imaginative adaptation of Egyptian royal ideology. While it is true that late in his reign Thutmose began a campaign to remove or conceal her monuments for the most part that did not come for at least two decades after Hatshepsut's death. One might have expected a more impulsive and explosive campaign of destruction had he really been nursing so much pent-up rage.

Hatshepsut's legacy was considerable. She was a competent ruler and had employed able officials. Her rule had seen the fruits of her predecessors' conquests invested in major building projects, mainly designed to amplify, assert and perpetuate her own status and reputation. The story of the Punt expedition, though doubtless amplified, had illustrated how easily Egypt could impose itself on lesser states. Conversely, if Thutmose III's first campaign after her death was as necessary as he claimed it was, there is a possibility that Egyptian control of its allies to the north was breaking down. However, such ructions were quite normal after the death of a king, and Thutmose had clearly not been prevented from growing into a successor who could tackle such problems.

There has never been any evidence for Hatshepsut's death being at Thutmose's behest or that of any other faction with an interest in his becoming sole ruler and toppling Hatshepsut. Had there been an active group of court malcontents we might have expected the reign to come to an end sooner and by force. On the other hand, it is easy to imagine that once Thutmose was into adulthood and perhaps supported by a band of hotheads of his own age, he might have sought the chance to neutralize Hatshepsut by first getting rid of her chief acolytes. If her daughter Neferure was dead, then there was even less reason to maintain any loyalty to Hatshepsut.

Perhaps as Thutmose III became older, tension grew between him and Hatshepsut. This could have led to Senenmut's assassination to rid the court of such an overmighty subject and explain why Senenmut's tomb and chapel were never used. There are many historical parallels that would make this plausible, such as the organized murders of the Roman emperor Septimius Severus' praetorian prefect Plautianus, and the Tsarina's favourite Rasputin. Both involved court factions nursing resentment of a single individual's power and influence, and the impact on their opportunities for advancement. The extent of this kind of jealousy within the neurotic and intense context of a court should not be underestimated.

Despite the bumptious ostentation of Senenmut's tomb chapel, it had been dug out of poor-quality limestone which subsequently started to collapse. Like the tomb proper it was also later desecrated. The chapel included unparalleled recessed panels carved with the overmighty subject's name and titles, including Steward and Keeper of the Diadem, the latter including a convenient phonetic allusion to Hatshepsut's name. Senenmut's name was crudely chiselled out.[71] Also desecrated was the tomb (TT11) of Djehuty where the damage even extended to hacking out most of the representations of his parents. Like Senenmut, there is no evidence to prove he was ever buried in his tomb either.

The wider damage to these tombs and Senenmut's monuments was haphazard and inconsistent, making it possible that there were several unrelated bouts of vandalism stretching on for years well after Hatshepsut's death and which were driven by different motives. There is also little evidence, though some exists, that the damage was simultaneously aimed at both Senenmut and Hatshepsut. It is possible that the target was Hatshepsut, and that Senenmut's statues and other inscriptions were only ever susceptible to collateral damage. Inebny, viceroy of Kush, had been in post at the latest by the 18th regnal year (and possibly as early as the 10th). He was replaced after Hatshepsut's death, though without any similarly sinister evidence for attacks on his memory.[72]

One statue of Senenmut, originally created during the joint reign of Thutmose III and Hatshepsut, was subsequently installed in Thutmose III's temple at Deir el-Bahari which was not built until the 42nd regnal year. That was two decades after Hatshepsut's death and more than twenty-five years since Senenmut was last attested as being alive and in service. Although the statue is damaged now from later rockfalls and an earthquake, Senenmut's name had not been defaced. The only deliberate damage was to a reference to Hatshepsut's throne name. The statue also carries Thutmose's throne name as well as the name of the new temple. The piece is a mystery since it appears to be evidence of some sort of rehabilitation of Senenmut which would only make sense if Hatshepsut had turned against him for which, like all the other possible explanations for his disappearance, we have no evidence. The statue only adds to the mystery surrounding Senenmut's career and its aftermath.[73]

Being on Hatshepsut's staff was not an automatic means of committing career suicide. Some of her officials remained in service into Thutmose III's sole reign, suggesting that there were special considerations when it came to Senenmut and a few others. For example, the treasurer Ty, who had been on campaign with Hatshepsut, was still in post thirteen years later in Thutmose's 25th regnal year.[74] The Second Prophet of Amun and in charge of the Treasury of Amun, Puyemre, who had been so keen to be involved with the Deir el-Bahari temple, had even built his tomb (TT39) overlooking the approach to the building. References to Hatshepsut in his tomb were tactfully replaced with those of Thutmose III, which suggests Puyemre ordered the changes as he greased his way into the new regime. Puyemre not only remained in post, but his sons also served as lesser priests during his reign.[75]

Hatshepsut's reign of about twenty-two years was a respectable length of time to rule, and with around fifteen of them as king in her own right. The likelihood is that Hatshepsut died in her own time of natural causes, even if Thutmose III had begun the process of pushing her to one side. An important achievement of her rule, whether planned or not, had also been to avert the possibility of a challenge to the crown. It was thus preserved within the family until Thutmose III came of age. She had lived long enough to allow Thutmose III to take up his birthright at an age when he was equal to the role. Her death could not have been better timed.[76]

Hatshepsut would not be thanked by Thutmose III or his

successors for shielding him for so long. As well as the desecration of her monuments she was subsequently obliterated from the official king lists. Her experimentation with female kingship was too radical and too disruptive for contemporary sensibilities, though she was not the last female king of the 18th Dynasty. The first three kings who succeeded Hatshepsut took steps to prevent their wives ever repeating her experiment.

Hatshepsut remains an enduring and inspiring historical figure who transcends the time in which she lived. It is easy today to see her as an icon, a clever and resourceful woman who asserted herself in a creative and forceful way by challenging convention. No other Egyptian ruler can compare with her. However, she also belonged firmly to the 18th Dynasty royal tradition of ruthlessly using Egypt's resources and energy in pursuit of her own interests and those of the ruling family. This is easily forgotten when celebrating Hatshepsut's achievements and the beguiling beauty of her Deir el-Bahari temple.

# 8

# WARRIOR KING
## c. 1479–1425 BC

### THUTMOSE III (MENKHEPERRE, 'ETERNAL IS THE MANIFESTATION OF RE')

*Thutmose III was the most militarily successful king in Egyptian history. His campaigns ensured Egypt was now the most powerful and richest state in the region. The image of the superhero ruler, backed by Amun, was enshrined in depictions of Thutmose smiting his enemies, and his lavish building projects. A self-serving elite scrambled for honour and favour. Inequality was at an unprecedented level.*

After Hatshepsut's death Thutmose III burst onto the stage with such vigour and determination that it is difficult to believe how opaque his existence had been hitherto. He was around twenty-four years old and in theory he had already ruled Egypt for twenty-two years since c. 1479 BC. In practice he had been largely eclipsed by Hatshepsut, despite the way she continued to maintain his presence in monuments as her joint monarch. He marked his sole rule by changing his throne name Menkheperkare to the more familiar form of Menkheperre.

According to his own testimony (see Chapter 6), Thutmose began his education by being trained for a priesthood in the cult of Amun. From this we can assume that he was also literate. Although we know little else about his childhood, largely because he was kept in the background so successfully, his adult career suggests that he must have spent most of his youth in military training. He may also have participated in or at least witnessed some of the campaigns that took place during his co-regency with Hatshepsut.[1] He emerged soon after his accession as an accomplished warrior and charioteer as well as an effective leader, strategist and tactician. He was also violent, impulsive and inclined to take risks.

Thutmose III's mummy was in a wretched state when it was found in 1881 but was measured at 5 ft 3.6 in (1.62 m). Even allowing for shrinkage, he can have been no more than 5 ft 5 in (1.65 m) in height. Like some of his dynastic forebears he exhibited the royal family's congenital overbite of the upper teeth. His mummy is that of a man in his late fifties (he died in about 1425 BC) and gives little hint therefore of the dynamic individual Thutmose was in life.

Thutmose was determined to maximize Egypt's control up through Syria and beyond. The number of wealthy and warlike states in the region had increased. The leaders of these states spent their time on commercial and territorial disputes, seeking the prestige and power that came from widening their spheres of influence over lesser nations or cities, and competing over international trade. Thutmose III's long-term plan was to take Egyptian power out of the Nile Valley and into Asiatic territory, and thus secure a reliable stream of income to enrich Egypt and ensure its primacy.

Like his grandfather Thutmose I, by casting himself as the personal catalyst for making his country wealthy Thutmose III was amplifying the role and importance of the king beyond managing domestic stability and security. All the resources of Egypt would be subverted to that end, regardless of the individual prices paid, whether in battle or in construction projects.

Thutmose posed as a predestined superman, a warrior who

was metaphorically bigger, more powerful and accomplished than anyone else. This was the validation of his entitlement to rule, the human manifestation of Amun's vision and intent. He was also a showman and a narcissist. Thutmose did more than any other Egyptian king to date to cultivate the image of the vast and towering figure on temple reliefs leaning down to smite his pathetic enemies. This went hand in hand with his self-professed reputation as a supreme athlete and sportsman. The chariot and the horse's arrival in Egypt in the 18th Dynasty had already done a great deal to create the idea of an elite class of mobile warriors. Thutmose developed this into the trademark image of the Egyptian king.

## THUTMOSE III'S WARS

Thutmose felt no need to stay in Egypt in the short-term to make sure of his hold on the throne after Hatshepsut's death, which might support the idea that he had been responsible for removing Hatshepsut's principal officials before she died. It is equally possible that Egypt was stable and that his orderly assumption of sole rule reflected well on Hatshepsut's management.

Thutmose III's military exploits were recorded in his so-called *Annals*, a series of inscriptions installed on the walls of the enclosure round the main shrine at Karnak. They cover his seventeen campaigns and were set down on his orders in his 42nd regnal year. They were composed as a chronicle, but the contents are highly selective and tendentious. In this regard they bear some comparison with the purpose of the better-known *Res Gestae* of the Roman emperor Augustus in which he set out his achievements for posterity. Thutmose's Annals vary considerably in detail. Most of the accounts of the annual campaigns are readable in some way, but there are gaps due to damage and some years are completely lost. Nonetheless, they form the longest and most detailed historical record from Egypt.

The source of the Annals was a journal kept by a royal scribe, military officer, and eyewitness called Tjeneny (also sometimes given as Thanuny) who claimed that he wrote down a factual account of events. Much later, the general Horemheb's tomb reliefs at Saqqara, which depict military engagements during Tutankhamun's reign, specifically showed army scribes recording the occasion when foreign enemies capitulated on the battlefield.[2] Thutmose III must have had the same arrangements, the archives providing the material from which the official version of events on the walls at Karnak could be composed.

The Karnak Annals amounted to score sheets, composed to record each campaign, the booty gathered and the tribute. The annual records vary, depending on whether any or how much fighting took place. The fourth campaigning season, for example, was not even apparently recorded. The record of the first campaign, which took place in Thutmose's 22nd–23rd regnal years, has the fullest account. The war was triggered on the pretext of border rebellions to the north and 'ordered' by Amun, the default justification put up by every self-respecting Egyptian ruler for almost anything he or she did. No information is supplied about the size of the army, its make-up, the logistics, or supply chains other than incidentally as the story progressed.

Thutmose headed initially into Gaza via the fortress at Tjaru (known in classical times as Sile) on the road that led north out of Egypt into Canaan. He left Tjaru in about mid-April as his 22nd regnal year ended.[3] Thutmose stopped at Gaza to prepare himself and his army 'to overthrow that wretched enemy' and 'to extend the borders of Egypt'. These nebulous aspirations thus blurred claims of a need to punish recalcitrant neighbours with opportunism. The campaign was to last just under six months, or 175 days, into the second week of October when he returned to Thebes.[4]

Within eleven to twelve days, Thutmose had advanced to Yehem (Khirbet Yemma in the Sharon). He held what passed for a council of war with the officers. He told them that their unnamed enemy of Qadesh had taken the city of Megiddo (in what is now northern

Israel), as well as organizing an alliance with various princes who had formerly been Egyptian allies together with others who included the Mitanni of the Naharin region. Thutmose claimed to have had a report that the Qadesh leader had announced he would wait at Megiddo to fight the Egyptians. It was in Thutmose's interests to depict his foe as being confrontational and over-confident. Having presented his men with this prospect, Thutmose 'got together with his strong soldiers' to discuss the plan.[5]

At this stage we get a hint of the size of the Egyptian army, in the sense that it was large enough to mean it could be dangerously extended. The 'strong soldiers', who must mean here the officers, expressed their concern about advancing up the road through the pass via Aruna (Wadi Ara) that became narrower, stretching the army out with men and horses marching in single file. This would expose them to an ambush resulting in the first part of the force being attacked while the rest were unable to dash up to support them. Clearly the Egyptians had advance knowledge of the territory, either gained during the campaigns of Thutmose's predecessors or because of their own scouts. Two alternative routes were suggested by the officers, either of which they thought preferable with one even being able to take the Egyptians right round to the north of Megiddo.

Thutmose outmanoeuvred the officers by pulling rank and insisted he was heading up the Aruna road. He explained how this avoided looking as if he was scared. Quite why he had bothered to consult his men is not clear unless he wanted an opportunity to assert himself, take a reckless risk, gambling that if he carried it off his prestige would be greatly enhanced. His announcement that he would personally lead the army along the road encouraged them to acquiesce.

Within three more days Thutmose had successfully brought the vanguard of the army out of the pass at Aruna. His gamble had paid off. There had been no attacks on his men. The real prize was discovering that the enemy had never expected the Egyptians to arrive up the road through the narrow pass. The enemy army was divided to the north and south, presumably having planned to surprise the Egyptians if they had come up either of the alternative routes. Thutmose was so confident that he ordered an immediate halt while the rearguard caught up and the Egyptians could re-form in the open. He then led the men on to Megiddo where he made camp and abandoned the advantage of surprise, though it is unlikely by then that anything could have been kept secret.

The following day and the seventeenth since they left Gaza, a buoyed-up Thutmose rolled the dice once more and went into battle. A less impetuous general would have waited for the enemy to capitulate and saved himself the trouble of fighting, and the lives of his men. Thutmose could not resist the temptation. Thutmose, naturally protected by Amun and with 'the strength of Seth in his limbs', positioned himself between the northern and southern wings of his army in his chariot, its description of being made of 'fine gold' (electrum) recalling some of those found in Thutmose IV and Tutankhamun's tombs.[6]

The description moves on abruptly at this point. There is no information about the enemy army which had formed up on the plain outside Megiddo. We are only told that Thutmose overwhelmed them by leading from the front. As usual, no Egyptian casualties or problems were mentioned, let alone referred to in detail. In pharaonic myth, the enemy was always hopeless, made up of witless cowards and led by arrogant incompetents who folded the moment the Egyptian king appeared on the scene at the head of his army of heroes. The paradox, of course, is that if every battle was a walkover the achievements of the king seemed trivial but that did not trouble unsophisticated Egyptian triumphalism. The Qadeshi and allied forces dutifully collapsed on the spot, panic breaking out as chariots were abandoned and their occupants fled along with the rest back to Megiddo. Confronted by sealed gates they had no choice but to be hauled up over the walls by hanging onto clothing thrown down by the people inside for them to grab onto.

The battle took a dangerous turn. Control broke down. The

Egyptian troops were distracted by helping themselves to everything left behind by the retreating enemy, recounted in the Annals without any criticism. This is no surprise. Ahmes-Ibana in earlier times was fixated by booty, presenting it to the king and waiting for some to be handed back as his reward. The Egyptians had lost the chance to break into Megiddo, but this was of no concern at all. Like locusts they scoured the dead, hacking off the corpses' hands to make a body count, while looking for 'live prisoners, horses, gold and silver chariots', and other valuables which included the enemy leader's tent decorated with silver. These were duly presented to Thutmose who triumphantly reminded his men that they had incarcerated the entire enemy confederation behind Megiddo's walls, adding the ludicrous brag that capturing Megiddo was the equivalent of capturing a 'thousand cities'.[7]

The result was that the Egyptians were now confronted with a great deal of additional work preparing for a siege. Trees in orchards around Megiddo had to be laboriously felled to provide the timber for a palisade around the city, along with a ditch that had to be excavated. Thutmose ordered the construction of a fort to the east of Megiddo named after his throne name Menkheperre with the epithet 'Trapper of Asiatics', a term suggesting the enemy had been caught like animals.[8] The Siege of Megiddo had begun. He also ordered an official record to be compiled of what each unit of the army had achieved that day. This was recorded on a leather roll which was transferred to Karnak but obviously does not now exist. The date was the 23rd regnal year, 21st day of the 1st month of the 3rd season, and it was a new moon.[9] Based on the out-of-synch civil calendar this occurred on about the day we would call 11 May in the year concerned, with a margin of error of several days on either side.

The siege continued into the summer until the various leaders trapped inside Megiddo gave up. They meekly emerged to swear fealty to Thutmose, handing over valuables, food and other supplies. They were forced to give up their positions as kings or chiefs, Thutmose appointing replacements as his stooges for all the nations represented. The Karnak relief itemized the booty with covetous precision. It included 924 chariots from the enemy army and allied princes. The Egyptians also took 'one fine bronze coat of mail belonging to that enemy'. Among other livestock there were 20,500 sheep taken, as well as several thousand slaves and a 'silver statue with a golden head'. The inventory listed everything from knives to 'one large jar of Syrian workmanship', as well as 207,700 sacks of wheat. Intoxicated by his success, Thutmose continued the campaign north that year capturing several more towns and adding more booty and prisoners. When he returned home, he associated his success with the cult of Amun, establishing a five-day 'Feast of Victory'. Huge quantities of gifts were handed over to the god. These included the tribute revenue from three Syrian cities, along with slaves, livestock, and other valuables.

The account of the Megiddo campaign is broadly credible, even if the content was highly selective. The enemy remains largely anonymous. There are no references to any heroic rearguard actions or indeed any resistance at all. No individual Egyptians are mentioned other than Thutmose himself, apart from the conference of the officers whose only contribution was to ignore their own advice and follow the king with whom they were so enamoured. The account of the Megiddo campaign was to promote Thutmose III as a military genius, despite depicting the enemy as imbeciles, who with divine backing had pulled off the greatest military gamble in Egyptian history to date.

For a young king setting out to make his mark, Thutmose's audacity and luck had resulted in a dramatic kick-start to his adult career. The outcome convinced Thutmose that he could go where he pleased and strike where he pleased, with the willing support of men who had seen how rich they could become under his leadership. Over the next eighteen years Thutmose would set off repeatedly with his army to seek out cities and settlements as targets of opportunity, eventually claiming to have captured over 350. None would have quite the same impact as Megiddo. For example, the second campaigning season (24th regnal year, 1456 BC) was really a victory parade. Thutmose toured Syria and Palestine collecting tribute from local leaders anxious to avoid fighting the conqueror of Megiddo. Gifts even arrived from Assyria, much too far away to be vulnerable but clearly concerned to solicit friendship rather than pick a fight. Likewise, the third campaign amounted to no more than a collection of flora and fauna from Syria.

The sixth campaigning season took place in the 30th regnal year (1450 BC). Unlike its predecessors it involved a waterborne landing at Simyra (Sumur) in Syria. That saved a tedious overland expedition but may not have included the entire expeditionary force. The target was Qadesh, which Thutmose attacked and captured, the Egyptians maliciously 'hacking down its trees' and 'cutting its grain'. The following year Thutmose used ships again so that he could advance up the Syrian coast, exacting tribute from various cities and requisitioning supplies. The strategy seems to have been a pernicious preparation for the eighth campaign in the 33rd regnal year (1447 BC). The war once again took Thutmose up the coast before heading inland to cross the Euphrates, defeating the king of Mitanni ('Naharin' in Syria) in one of at least three battles fought that year, including one at Carchemish.

The Mitanni soldiers 'fled like a herd of mountain goats', a predictable Egyptian description of the feebleness of an enemy.[10] Over the years ever more tribute was delivered, along with the goods seized in the annual campaigns that involved fighting. Mitanni was the principal place listed in the 42nd regnal year, the last of Thutmose's campaign seasons. Various states lined up to hand over tribute, including the Hittites, making their first appearance in history.[11] The places listed supplying tribute include Kush and Wawat (the latter is sometimes now called Lower Nubia, but Nearer Nubia would be a better description from an Egyptian perspective) on Egypt's southern borders, as well as Punt. Thutmose was also to secure foreign wives this way. One, a princess from Retjenu (Canaan-Syria), had been recorded in the Annals at Karnak for the second campaign (24th regnal year), though her name is unknown.[12] Others are known from their burials in Egypt (see below).

Amenmose was one of the senior officers who did well out of serving his bellicose king. He became a Commander of Troops as well as Overseer of Northern Territories and was able to build himself a tomb (TT42) in the Theban necropolis that befitted his station. The decoration includes a painting of tribute being handed over at Negau (in modern Lebanon) during one of Thutmose's campaigns. Like so many of these accounts or depictions the tribute consisted of the usual litany of captives, commodities and military equipment including chariots. Amenmose's career was to last so long that he was still in service under Amenhotep II.

Another senior army officer who fought alongside Thutmose was Amenemheb. A man of some panache and enamoured of his heroism in the field, he saw to it that his own version of the campaigns was placed in his tomb (TT85), beginning with the sixth campaigning season. Despite its chaotic order and lack of precision, Amenemheb's account bears some modest comparison with the far more organized royal Annals. From this we can infer that the official texts were founded in some truth.

Amenemheb was given to adding some rather more colourful detail than the Annals. During the siege of Qadesh, the enemy prince sent out a mare towards the Egyptian army. Amenemheb claims to have raced out after the horse, caught up with it and disembowelled the unfortunate animal before cutting off its tail to present to Thutmose.[13] On another occasion Thutmose decided to amuse himself at Niya in Syria by hunting 120 elephants for the sake of the tusks. In another example of his recklessness, Thutmose badly misjudged the animals and found himself confronted by the largest. Amenemheb claimed to have intervened and cut off the animal's 'hand' (the trunk) to save the king, receiving the oddly disparate gifts of gold and 'three changes of clothing' as a reward. When the stela was set up at Armant honouring the king's achievements (see below), this incident had been spun into Thutmose's successful killing of all

120 elephants himself, an interesting exposé of how foolish it would be to take pharaonic tales of bravado at face value. The round figure ought to excite suspicion, quite apart from considering the difficulty and danger involved in killing that number of enraged large animals with hand-thrown projectiles and arrows. For good measure, Amenemheb's tomb included a painting of himself fighting a large hyena with a stick, doubtless a reference to one of his other leisure pursuits on campaign.

Djehuty served as a general under Thutmose III. His tomb was found intact at Saqqara in 1824. The early date of discovery was unfortunate because few records were kept. However, the dispersal of its contents to museums does mean it is still possible to gain an idea of the sort of wealth a king could bestow on his most senior servants and by which these men set so much store as conspicuous proof of their status. These included a golden bowl decorated with lotus leaves and bulti fish with a presentation inscription by Thutmose III. The bulti fish was a symbol of rebirth and the sun, as were the lotus leaves. They were often used together in the New Kingdom in decoration.[14] Djehuty also received a golden bracelet inscribed 'the good god Menkheperre, given life'.[15] It was an affirmation of Thutmose's recognition of Djehuty's loyalty. By wearing it Djehuty also made it clear that he belonged to the king.

Djehuty was also the subject of a literary, and possibly apocryphal, version of the capture of Joppa under Thutmose III, recorded on a papyrus.[16] The tale was a form of Trojan Horse and Ali Baba and the Forty Thieves-style deception organized by Djehuty who was encamped outside Joppa with his army. He invited the prince of Joppa to his camp only to whip out his mace and unchivalrously knock the prince unconscious. He next hid 200 of his soldiers in grain sacks and had them tied onto pack animals. They were sent off to Joppa with a message to the inhabitants that he and his army had surrendered and were handing over tribute. The people of Joppa took the animals in, which allowed the Egyptian soldiers to burst out and seize the city. The story precedes the written version of the Trojan Horse by several centuries and even more so that of Ali Baba but they probably all grew out of earlier blurred traditions, based on events well before when they were set down. It is impossible to say whether Djehuty was responsible for such a ruse though there is little doubt that at some point around this time Joppa fell to Egypt. The story may even have been transposed to Djehuty as a plausible historical protagonist, especially if he enjoyed special fame in his own time and after as a clever and wily general.

Compared to the picaresque tale of Djehuty, the Annals are generally baldly factual about the places captured and the booty. Thutmose and his advisers were clearly capable of planning strategically. Water transport played an important role in transporting his forces and supplies and shipping back the booty. Harbours were used, and steps taken to make sure they were properly equipped to support the annual campaigns. Occasionally the Annals provide inspired gems. In the seventh campaign (31st regnal year) Thutmose was described as capturing a coastal city called Ullaza (location unknown) 'in a small moment, and all its goods were as easily captured', which included 490 live prisoners, 26 horses and 13 chariots.[17] In other words, the city fell in the blink of an eye, or so it was claimed. Perhaps the inhabitants had already decided it was smarter to capitulate to the warrior pharaoh than bother with resisting. An alternative possibility was that being controlled by Egypt was a more attractive option than being ruled by the current incumbent.[18]

The concentration on Asiatic targets meant that Thutmose III paid far less attention to Nubia than some of his predecessors, probably because it was now regarded as relatively under control. The Armant Stela (about 12 miles or 19 km south of Thebes) summarized the king's greatest achievements. The stela, the bottom half of which is lost, was set up no earlier than the 29th regnal year and included a specific reference to a campaign into the 'southern land of Ta-Seti', an administrative district on the border with Nubia, to seek out a rebel leader.[19]

Egypt's imperialist wars were driven by the prospect of profit. The growth of the country's wealth was accelerating. Other nations were being drawn into the net and resistance diminished. Thutmose III had refined the warrior image of the 18th Dynasty and although the costs of endless warfare were mounting, his spirited career helped to sustain both his domestic prestige and Egypt's dominance abroad. This was helped by a developing trope that gold was as common as dirt in Egypt, or so Tushratta, king of Mitanni, told the dowager queen Tiye a century later.[20] It was better, safer and more profitable for Egypt's enemies to maintain good relations.

## CLIENT KINGS, LOYAL FOREIGNERS AND SLAVES

We have already met Nehsi, 'the Nubian', who became a high official directly under Hatshepsut. The practice of using men like him continued under Thutmose. By c. 1450 BC Thutmose was bringing back the sons of the chiefs to Egypt where they could be educated in Egyptian ways. Ultimately, they would be returned to their homes to rule them as Egyptian client-states. Over a century later one of these men was remembered in a letter from Addumari, a king of Nuḫašše (in north-west Syria), to Amenhotep III or Akhenaten which reads:

> When Manaḫpiya (= Menkheperre, Thutmose III), the king of Egypt, your ancestor, made Taku, my ancestor a king in Nuḫašše, he put oil on his head and spoke as follows: 'when the king of Egypt has made a king [and on whose head] he has put [oil] . . . (rest of this sentence lost) . . .'[21]

Addumari still regarded himself bound in fealty to the king of Egypt as part of the tradition stretching back to Thutmose III's reign. In return he begged the Egyptian king's attention either in person or via one of his 'advisers'. The same applied to the inhabitants of the city of Tunip (a state in western Syria) who continued to 'fall at the feet' of the Egyptian king as they had done since Thutmose III's time.[22]

The Annals routinely itemized with casual indifference the thousands of human lives reduced to bald statistics with all the other booty, like the '1,796 male and female slaves with their children' taken at one point in the first campaign.[23] Those slaves would be followed by many more. Nameless and almost invariably undetected in the archaeological record, they disappeared into Egypt on countless unsung tasks from labouring in the fields, serving in the army and working as artisans, to hacking out stone in the quarries or being rented out. They were essential to Egypt's march to power and wealth, reflecting widely accepted practices of the era.[24]

Egypt's ambitions were also helped by the willingness of some captives to pursue their personal and family destinies in service to Egypt. Some of them were children who could be more easily brought up to know nothing else except loyalty to the pharaoh. Others were the sons and daughters of rulers of states who handed them over as a form of living tribute, but there was room for men of talent to rise. They are often given away by their Asiatic names like Pas-Ba'al, named after the Syrian solar cult of Ba'al, who appears to have been captured during one of Thutmose III's wars. His talents led him to become chief architect at Karnak, with his descendants succeeding him in the post for at least six generations. Such people left no trace of their origins in the archaeological record. Their culture was left behind as a condition of becoming Egyptian, their names remaining the only evidence of where they had come from.[25]

Occasionally there was a happy ending of a sort, even if it was far from the place the slaves had once called home. Sabastet was a barber whose tiny statue offering records that he formally handed over his occupation to a Nubian slave called Amen-iywy whom he had captured and been given in one of Thutmose III's wars. Sabastet allowed the man the right to marry his blind niece, the girl perhaps being impossible to provide for any other way.[26] This was how the everyday experience of foreigners gradually eroded everyday prejudice against non-Egyptians among the wider population. It also helped undermine the relentless state depiction of foreigners as degenerate and evil and opened the way for more foreign influences.[27]

The Nubian Maiherpri was another acquisition. His tomb in the Valley of the Kings (KV36) is undated, but his mummy was wrapped in cloth that carried Hatshepsut's throne name, Maatkare. This means Maiherpri died during her reign as king or under Thutmose III. The latter is far more likely. The evidence from Tutankhamun's tomb is that items from previous reigns, including cloth, were routinely available from palace stocks to be used as needed.

Maheirpri's well-preserved mummy and paintings of him in his exceptionally fine copy of the Book of the Dead make it clear he was a Nubian. He possessed high-quality items such as an Asiatic-style quiver and vessels. His tomb was thus a metaphor for Egypt's role as a cosmopolitan imperial state acting as a pivot around which other contemporary nations orbited. Culture and ethnicity were slowly becoming blurred in Egypt.

Maiherpri died in his twenties. He had grown up to become a royal flag-bearer on the king's right, but before that had been a 'child of the [royal] nursery'. Maiherpri was probably the son of a Nubian chieftain or prince brought to the court to be 'Egyptianized'. He was evidently so valued that he was accorded the exceptional privilege of burial in the royal necropolis. The entrance faced south directly towards the wadi that led up to Thutmose III's tomb, a further clue that he died during the warrior king's sole reign or not long after.

An oddity of Maheirpri's burial was the presence of a third, unused, coffin. Funeral planning could be remarkably disorganized, even for Egyptian high society and despite the colossal investment of time and resources. Maheirpri's body was brought to the tomb in his third (innermost) coffin, where the plan was to insert it into the two outer coffins prepared and waiting for him. Only then did it emerge that no one had bothered to check if all three coffins fitted inside one another. The third coffin was too large. Maheirpri's body was transferred to the second coffin which did fit inside the outermost or first coffin. The third coffin was discarded and incongruously left in the middle of the tomb floor.


## TECHNOLOGY

Another for Thutmose's success, apart from luck and audacity, was the evolving revolution in military technology. Chariots had been around long enough for the Egyptians to become skilled in their manufacture and use. The other was the composite bow, a sophisticated and powerful weapon which Thutmose himself was (naturally) a self-proclaimed expert at using. He famously demonstrated his prowess at Karnak in his 22nd regnal year, recorded on the stela found at Armant:[28]

> *When he shoots at a copper target, all wood is splintered like a papyrus reed. His Majesty offered such an example in the temple of Amun, with a target of hammered copper of three digits in thickness. When he had shot his arrow there, he caused a protrusion of three palms-width behind it, so as to cause the followers to pray for the proficiency of his arms in valour and strength. I am telling you what he did, without deception and without lie, in front of his entire army, and there is no word of exaggeration therein.*

Despite the stela's claims, the stunt is bound to have been stage-managed in some way. Firing arrows at a target while riding solo in a fast-moving chariot, however it was achieved, became a stock image for an Egyptian king and recurred several times under later kings in the 18th and 19th Dynasties. The stela goes on to explain how Thutmose, even in a rare moment of leisure out hunting, could kill seven lions 'in a moment'. The word used was the dynamic term *3t* which means not only an instant in time but also the precise moment of an attack. Thutmose had allegedly on another occasion, the stela continued, killed twelve wild bulls at breakfast time, followed by 120 elephants. There was a rhetorical element to the claims.

The 120 elephants were the ones he had hunted in Niya, but as we saw (above) Thutmose came close to losing his life before an officer stepped in to save him. The stela's claim that 'he killed 120 elephants' neatly blurred over the near-disaster and that even if all the animals had been killed, they must have died at the hands of several soldiers, not just Thutmose's. In Egyptian royal rhetoric all such acts were attributed to the king. However, while on a short punitive mission into Nubia Thutmose III found time to kill a rhinoceros (for which the Egyptian word *šꜣkb* meant literally 'hostile horn').[29]

One of the other consequences was the rising importance of horses. Horses and chariots had also become an integral component of royal imagery and status. They often formed part of the tribute levied by Thutmose III. The care of royal horses had become the subject of new and prestigious posts, such as Superintendent of the Royal Stables, held by Nebiri.[30]

Chariots became just as important, perhaps more so, during the 18th Dynasty as a badge of status for the wider elite. They widened the gulf between the king, his family and the upper classes, and everyone else. Nebamun was a minor bureaucrat and scribe around 1400–1350 BC whose duties included counting grain and supervising field boundaries. His tomb (TT17) was filled with vivid paintings of daily life. One shows the inspection by a team of scribes of a field boundary stone to make sure it had not been moved. They had arrived in chauffeur-driven chariots. Obviously, the chariots provided transport for the scribes, but they also helped add an intimidating tone of officialdom capable of turning up at speed to investigate any infractions.[31]

# OBLITERATING HATSHEPSUT

Thutmose III was the first ruler of the 18th Dynasty under whom sustained energy was expended on a malicious assault on a predecessor. The focus was on Hatshepsut's monuments as king, not those from her earlier days as regent and before that as Thutmose II's queen. The real mystery is why Thutmose III waited so long to start the job. While some of the work was concerned with erasing representations of Hatshepsut and her names, in some instances these were replaced with those of Thutmose II and less often by those of Thutmose I or III. Damage focused on the name of Amun may belong to the Amarna period (see Chapter 12).

The simplest solution for Thutmose III would have been to usurp likenesses of Hatshepsut with his own name, except for the annoying fact that for all their male attributes they quite clearly represented a woman. The 19th Dynasty king Ramesses II usurped so many monuments and statues of his New Kingdom male predecessors that to this day a large proportion bears his name in some form. Thutmose III had no such luxury. Hatshepsut's likenesses would have to be destroyed.

More than a hundred sphinxes bearing Hatshepsut's portrait lined the ramps that led up and into her temple. The destruction began first by neatly severing the uraeus from the brow of each sphinx. This symbolically removed Hatshepsut's royal status and was only followed later by a much more aggressive and systematic destruction of the sphinxes, Osiride figures, and other statuary. These were dragged out of the temple and carried to a hollow created earlier when spoil was removed for landscaping purposes and other nearby depressions or holes in the rock. These now became burial grounds for the shattered statues which had been pulverized with hammers by workers. Little attention was paid to Hatshepsut's names. This phase took place somewhere between Thutmose III's 30th and 42nd regnal years. A more concerted effort to destroy Hatshepsut's names only began around the 42nd regnal year when the king was in his mid-forties and had ceased his annual campaigning.[32]

Thutmose's motives were never explained but it must have been obvious that Hatshepsut's efforts at Karnak and Deir el-Bahari might overshadow any building projects he began. This would explain why different solutions were used to obscure or destroy

Hatshepsut's works. At Deir el-Bahari the sheer number and visibility of Hatshepsut sculptures meant they had to be destroyed, but the work was labour intensive. At Karnak it was simpler to dismantle the Red Chapel and reuse its blocks, with the unintended consequence that it has been possible to reconstruct this shrine in modern times.

Hatshepsut's 15th regnal year obelisks, the largest then standing at Karnak, were walled up as far as possible to hide them, avoiding the technical complications of taking them down. Some of the royal titles were altered to Thutmose's, but Hatshepsut's name remains prominently visible today. No doubt Thutmose's male sensibilities were offended by Hatshepsut's encroachment on kingly ithyphallic territory. The result of hiding the obelisks was that, ironically, the inscriptions on the one that still stands are mostly well preserved. Hatshepsut's earlier missing obelisks (except a surviving part of one) might be because Thutmose's engineers removed them. Another possibility is that they were lowered by the Romans and were either damaged beyond repair in the process, lost at sea on the voyage to Rome, or made it there to join many other trophy obelisks but have not yet been found.[33] Most of those known in Rome were only discovered in Renaissance times, usually buried in the ruins of stadiums where they had stood on the central *spinae*.

Another way Thutmose III tried to distance himself from Hatshepsut was to remove the body of his grandfather Thutmose I from the tomb (KV20) she shared with him. It also separated Hatshepsut from the dynastic line of descent. For this purpose, a new tomb (KV38) for Thutmose I was prepared along with new burial equipment that included a sarcophagus and canopic chest. The one Hatshepsut had provided for her father, converted from one of her own, was left behind in KV20. Although modest and uncomplicated, KV38 shares certain features with Thutmose III's own tomb, for example the cartouche-shaped burial chamber. Thutmose I's body was not to remain there, and its fate is unknown (see Chapter 5).

Thutmose might have been concerned that his mother Iset's lesser status could be used to call his line of descent into question. However, no challenge was ever made and there is nobody that we know of who could have made one.[34] Thutmose's military success and the wealth he brought to Egypt were synonymous with legitimacy, at least as long as he and his descendants could continue the tradition. It is equally possible that he developed an irrational loathing for Hatshepsut and decided to do what he could to erase as much as possible of her conspicuous presence.

Thutmose was probably responsible in the last decade of his reign for ordering the more prominent measures like the destruction of Hatshepsut's statues in her mortuary temple, covering up the obelisks and the hacking out of reliefs. Other desecration such as that in the tombs of Senenmut and Djehuty might have been second-wave or incidental destruction rather than necessarily having been ordered by the king. There was no concerted or centralized programme to expunge any relics of Senenmut's life and career.

By the latter part of the reign, statues of Thutmose III were produced more in the style of his father and grandfather but apart from his more masculine physical appearance little was done to emphasize his appearance from Hatshepsut's, to whom he probably bore some natural resemblance. He was also inclined to usurp Hatshepsut's name on monuments and substitute their names rather than his.[35] A good example is on a wall on the north side of the doorway in the upper court at Hatshepsut's temple where what appears to be the story of Thutmose I's coronation incongruously follows a depiction of his death and worship by Hatshepsut. It is likely originally to have shown Hatshepsut's coronation, subsequently altered on Thutmose III's orders to substitute his grandfather.[36] Thutmose III was restoring the narrative in which the crown was transmitted from Thutmose I to Thutmose II and then to him, with the future Amenhotep II also being included. The process also did away with Hatshepsut's experiment with royal identity and prevented it becoming an enduring and visible precedent.

The proscription of Hatshepsut ended by the early part of Amenhotep II's reign, though it was resumed later, for example in the 19th Dynasty king lists at Abydos from which she was conspicuously omitted, and at her temple under Ramesses II. That she survived into Manetho's account shows that she was never entirely forgotten. Thutmose cannot seriously have believed he could obliterate Hatshepsut's memory any more than England's Charles II's counting of his regnal years from the date of his father Charles I's execution in 1649 could have deleted the Commonwealth and Oliver Cromwell from English history. Thutmose's purpose must have been primarily symbolic.

## THUTMOSE THE BUILDER

At Deir el-Bahari Thutmose added his own significant terraced temple to Amun (Djeser-Akhet, 'Sacred Horizon') late in the reign. It was built between and behind Hatshepsut's temple, which despite the desecration of her memory remained in use, and that of Mentuhotep II, but was later destroyed by rockfalls because it lay even closer to the cliff.

Karnak provided the king with the best opportunity to continue the 18th Dynasty's custom of greatly enriching the power of the cult of Amun. Likewise, he claimed to have been directed by Amun and it was Amun whom he credited with having made him victorious. The priests at Karnak were reaching the stage where their authority over other temples exceeded that of any other priests, but there is no evidence that they were attempting to operate as a state within a state. The cult of Amun and the king were far too closely intertwined.

Thutmose's Annals were carved on the inside of the innermost sanctuary walls in the heart of Karnak, just east of the Sixth Pylon.[37] At the time these enclosed Hatshepsut's Red Chapel barque shrine, but Thutmose replaced it with his own at around the same time as his more concerted effort was being made to desecrate her memory.[38] Other reliefs were also used to depict the huge quantities of precious metal, furniture and other valuable commodities donated by

Thutmose to the cult, as well as the dedication of one pair of his obelisks. The Seventh Pylon, on the south entrance at Karnak, was built to celebrate Thutmose's achievements. Today it still bears a prominent relief showing a giant Thutmose wearing the red crown of Lower Egypt smiting his foes. The text lists 359 cities he had allegedly captured, including 119 from his earliest campaigns.

Thutmose III added his so-called Festival Hall (named 'the Glorious Monument') which was built at the eastern end of Karnak and is still partially extant today.[39] This innovative stone basilican structure, laid out at right angles to the east-west spine of Karnak, was designed to emulate the king's campaign tent, perhaps as a form of nostalgia for his glory days. He certainly claimed to have been involved in its planning. It included a room decorated with reliefs showing the plants Thutmose had brought back with him in an echo of Hatshepsut's Punt expedition. The hall's purpose was to associate Thutmose's royal power with the creative force of Amun, in the interests of order and harmony (Maat). Like the Seventh Pylon, the building also marked Thutmose's thirtieth anniversary jubilee. In a side room on the south-west side reliefs commemorated Thutmose's royal predecessors dating back to the Old Kingdom pharaoh Djoser.

The petulant Thutmose did his best to outdo Hatshepsut with obelisks of his own. Two pairs were installed at Karnak to begin with, recorded in several ways including references to offerings being made for the four. A relief still visible at Karnak in the central cult area shows one of the pairs. The other pair, distinguished by having different inscriptions, was depicted on a relief in a private tomb.[40] One of the pairs was set up in front of his Seventh Pylon, the other apparently in front of the Fourth Pylon.[41] Only part of one of these four survives today in Istanbul where it was taken by Constantine I (AD 307–37) for the hippodrome in his new capital of Constantinople. For good measure Thutmose also took over the uninscribed northern obelisk of the pair set up by his grandfather Thutmose I, though he may have done this much earlier and perhaps when he ruled alongside Hatshepsut.[42] Another pair was erected at Heliopolis. The two were taken in the nineteenth century respectively to London and New York where they stand today.

Thutmose's obelisk plans went further but were thwarted. At Aswan the half-gestated remains of an unfinished obelisk lie in the granite quarry, probably intended for Karnak. Had it been finished and raised it would have stood 138 ft (42m) tall and been the largest obelisk ever made. Possibly commissioned during the time that Hatshepsut and Thutmose were ruling together, it was abandoned when cracks appeared and remains to this day one of the great sights of Egypt and a monument to pharaonic hubris. This vast folly was almost certainly the companion of another obelisk which was successfully extracted from Aswan and brought to Karnak. This one remained unfinished and in the care of the temple's workmen until the reign of Thutmose IV when it was finally completed and raised as a singleton in his grandfather's name (see Chapter 10). It is now in Rome (outside San Giovanni in Laterano). Today none of Thutmose III's obelisks stands or is even visible in Egypt, something that might have gratified the shade of Hatshepsut. Why the obelisk was abandoned for decades is unknown, but the reason was probably that at the time no one, including Thutmose III, had any idea what to do with an odd obelisk.

## THUTMOSE III'S WIVES

If Hatshepsut's daughter, the God's Wife Neferure, was ever one of Thutmose III's wives, then the marriage lasted only a short time. Or it may not have happened at all. The only evidence is two instances of the names of two royal women having clearly replaced someone else's. One is a cartouche of Thutmose's wife Sitiah, called God's Wife here, visible traces of the sign for Re having been erased, and another on which the name of Thutmose III's mother Iset has been cut in over a previous name.[43] Whether Neferure was the name deleted in either case cannot be determined but is possible. Pursuing the issue is futile because even if such a marriage might have made sense from Hatshepsut's perspective, Thutmose III is unlikely to have felt the same once he was ruling alone. Either way, Neferure's swift disappearance from the stage meant she played no further part in the history of the 18th Dynasty.

The most important of Thutmose III's wives was Merytre-Hatshepsut. In Thutmose's tomb an unparalleled scene on one of the columns in the burial chamber depicts Thutmose followed first by Merytre, then Sitiah and a third wife called Nebtu. The latter's name is not written in a cartouche suggesting that she was of subordinate status, but all three are labelled 'wife of the king'. Merytre's origins are virtually unknown apart from the fact that she was probably the daughter of an adoratrice-priestess called Huy. If she was not a blood relation, then her arrival can only have increased Thutmose's chance of fathering a healthy heir. That is exactly what happened. She was the mother of the successful Amenhotep II as well as several siblings.

Thutmose had a tomb cut for Merytre in the Valley of the Kings (KV42) only a few metres from his own. In plan it resembled his, and the foundation deposits make it certain it was designated as hers. In the event though she was never buried there, Amenhotep II preferring the idea of having his mother (elevated to being his great royal wife) buried in his own tomb (see Chapter 9).[44]

Thutmose's other wives included the anonymous princess of Retjenu and several other foreign women. Three were buried in a tomb cut into the Wadi Gabbanat in Western Thebes. They were called Menhet, Menwi, and Merti. Each of their names included a hieroglyph that supplied the first vowel sound but was also used as a determinative in words that mean 'give' or 'booty' and related terms. Each name starts with the owl hieroglyph for the phonetic sound *m* which forms the main consonant in the word for 'give' (*imi*).[45] This suggests that their personal birth names had been adapted in Egyptian to contain explicit allusions to their status as literal trophy wives, 'given as booty'.

Their mummies were destroyed in antiquity by floodwater

entering the tomb, which was then ransacked by local robbers after it was found in 1916. Fortunately, at least some of the contents were recovered from the stolen antiquities market. These included their elaborate headdresses which were not types worn by the Great Royal Wife or a dowager queen, thereby indicating their elite but not frontline royal status. One of these was the double-gazelle headdress which featured a pair of gazelle necks and heads in the centre of the band above the eyes instead of the vulture. Thanks to the bracelets bearing his name, the three women can be identified as members of Thutmose III's harem. Hatshepsut's name appeared on some items. Despite the desecration of her memory the court inventory of valuable goods clearly still included items from her time, both when she was Thutmose II's wife and her time as king.[46] This might have made them suitable items to dispose of in burials.

Without their bodies, the causes of the three women's deaths and their ages are obviously unknown. The only evidence for their existence is the tomb. If they bore the king children nothing is known about them. The chance that they died close enough together to be buried in the same tomb is a clue that they may have succumbed to the same illness, and that Thutmose's harem was probably considerably bigger than we can account for now.

# THE DEATH AND BURIAL OF THUTMOSE III

Thutmose died in his 54th regnal year (c. 1425 BC; see Chapter 9). He was therefore in his mid- to late fifties. His reign was long but not his life, though he reached a very respectable age for the era. The lack of any signs of violence (apart from the damage caused by tomb robbers) suggests that he died from natural causes. His eldest son Amenemhet was made Overseer of Cattle in Thutmose's 24th regnal year but disappeared thereafter. Instead, Thutmose was succeeded by a younger and very energetic son known to history as Amenhotep II, possibly already lined up as a co-regent. The vizier Rekhmire was still in post and sailed as fast as possible downriver to Hout-sekhem, about 65 miles (110 km) north of Thebes, with the new king to present him with the symbols of kingship. In return Amenhotep II confirmed him in his posts, Rekhmire hastening back to Thebes to announce the good news and be greeted by the priests.[47]

Unlike many of his major building projects, Thutmose III's mortuary temple Henkhet-Ankh ('Offering-Life') was probably begun while Hatshepsut was still regent. Located not far from her mortuary temple, it was a substantial structure that covered a larger area but in a much more conventional form. Although the plan is known the building was substantially robbed out by later kings and little remains. It may also have been overshadowed by the temple of Amun Thutmose built beside Hatshepsut's temple and was possibly never finished.

The tomb of Thutmose III (KV34) lies at the southern end of the Valley of the Kings, one of the closest to the triangular hill (El Qurn) that overlooks the Valley, and which is thought to have reminded the New Kingdom Egyptian kings of pyramids. Unlike Hatshepsut's dangerously deep and meandering tomb, Thutmose's was clearly conceived as an integrated design from the outset. It pioneered the more sophisticated architectural features and layout used in subsequent royal tombs of the necropolis.

Thutmose's tomb was reached only by clambering up a steep side of the valley wall over a gap and down into the rock behind. Anyone familiar with the Valley would have known that the occasional torrential rainstorms in the area would cause flash floods to pour off the higher ground, carrying rubble that would in time completely bury the entrance. If that was the plan it comprehensively failed. The tomb was later robbed out and lay open for long periods in antiquity.

Access was via a corridor heading south that led to a small chamber, followed by another corridor, and then the well shaft. The latter was both a security measure and a trap for water entering the tomb. The well shaft, which now requires a bridge to be crossed, is virtually the only rectangular component of the tomb. It was only dug out once Thutmose had been buried and the further chambers sealed off. From here a doorway leads into a trapezoidal room with two columns that abruptly changed the direction of the tomb by 90 degrees to the left. A flight of stairs in the chamber's north-eastern corner led down into the cartouche-shaped burial chamber. This also had two columns, and a pair of small storerooms on either side to the north and south.

Physical access to the tomb today is still quite a struggle. It bears witness to the Herculean efforts of the tomb builders that they were able to clamber up and down into the tomb to hack out the rock with their copper tools in blistering and suffocating heat while also seeing to the removal of the spoil which was discarded nearby.

The eccentric geometry of the tomb is a strange contrast to the way it looks as if it was designed to be symmetrical and based on a right-angle roughly halfway in after the well shaft. The men who cut it out seem to have had no access either to any form of measuring instrument or means of determining the direction other than by guesswork. Successive tombs followed the basic layout but were far more geometrically refined.

Only debris and the empty sarcophagus remained when the tomb was found in 1898. The ancient robbers had scarred the walls by throwing grave goods to break them. Careful planning of the remaining fragments of burial equipment showed that Thutmose had clearly been buried there. These included, for example, wooden statues of the type that flanked the blocked entrance to the burial chamber in the tomb of Tutankhamun, and a carcass of a bull.

Thutmose III ruled on his own for over thirty years, ample time to have a tomb dug and decorated though he was the first ruler buried in the Valley of the Kings to have had decoration added to the walls (except in the corridors). The shape of the burial chamber with its curved corners suggests it was designed as a canvas on which decoration in the manner of an unrolled papyrus could be laid out. The sketched outline figures and the use of hieratic were designed to emulate exactly the funerary papyri of the period. Two texts had been used: the Amduat (a sort of What's What in the Underworld or Afterlife) on the walls, and the Litany of Re on the columns. The Amduat was a twelve-hour journey through the night as the king sailed on his barque to where his mummy could be received by the gods. The Amduat was only painted after the side chambers had been filled and sealed behind wooden doors. Clearly, the process of completing a tomb could carry on for some time after a king's death.

The panel on one of the burial chamber columns depicting Thutmose leading three of his senior wives and his deceased daughter Nefertari following on behind also showed the king riding on a boat with his mother Iset. She had already been awarded the title 'King's Mother'. In this scene she was conflated with her namesake goddess Isis, being additionally shown on the far right as a tree suckling her son. The scene has no parallel. Thereafter, members of the royal family were not normally shown in the decoration of royal tombs.

Thutmose III's mummy survived in the 1881 cache of royal mummies, revealing that his body and wrappings had been equipped with amulets and other items torn out, with a bracelet being overlooked. This had either happened when the tomb was robbed, or when what was left was cleared out and taken by the Theban priest-king Pinudjem I during the 21st Dynasty (see Epilogue). The tomb lay open thereafter until at least the 26th Dynasty. An official of that time called Hapimen commissioned a sarcophagus for himself with decoration copied from Thutmose's. He was probably responsible for removing the king's canopic chest.[48] The tomb must still have been open, or had been reopened, in Graeco-Roman times because at least two burials from that period were placed in the burial chamber's side rooms. Thereafter the tomb's location became lost until its rediscovery in 1898.

# 9

# THE ARCHER KING
## c. 1425–1400 BC

### Amenhotep II (Akheperure, 'Great are the Manifestations of Re')

*Amenhotep II followed his father as a warrior king. He boasted about his achievements but went to war far less often than his father. Investment in building projects at Karnak and elsewhere were matched by his tomb, the most sophisticated to date. Some of the evidence for his life marks him out as a memorable individual. He left Egypt ever more powerful.*

Amenhotep II was in every sense his father's son. He had a reputation, promoted mainly by himself, for being physically powerful and a highly accomplished athlete. The teeth and appearance of his mummy were those of a man who had lived into early middle age. Since he died in about 1400 BC, he was probably born around 1450–1440 BC. Amenhotep II was thus no less than around eighteen years old when he succeeded his father but might already have been made co-regent. His mummy was found in its original sarcophagus in his tomb (KV35) in the Valley of the Kings, the only other one being Tutankhamun's. He stood about 5 ft 6 in (1.67 m) tall, placing him more on a par with ordinary Egyptians than his predecessors.

Amenhotep's early career as a prince in the Memphis area was recorded on a stela set up at Giza, in the temple to Horemakhet (the falcon form 'Horus in the Horizon') he built a few metres to the north-east of the Sphinx, not long after his succession when making a visit to pay homage to his remote 'ancestors' Khufu and Khafra of the 4th Dynasty.

There was, of course, no traceable family connection but that was not the point. The Sphinx's mystical antiquity had made it a powerful symbol of kingship in the form of a lion with Khafra's face. It had evolved into the focus of a royal solar cult. The Sphinx was conceived as a physical manifestation of Horemakhet and had become an important spiritual centre that attracted pilgrims including princes with an eye on the succession. Amenhotep's new temple was a significant stage in the development of the setting's importance which continued throughout antiquity and, of course, in its own way still does today.

Amenhotep's gesture was either an act of authentic piety or a more calculated attempt to follow his father's efforts to assert the bloodline's legitimacy. The personal tone of his stela's text suggests there was at least some sincerity involved. On the lintel inscription which began with his regnal name 'Great are the Manifestations of Re', he was variously described as 'son of Re', 'Dual King', 'given eternal life' and 'beloved of Horemakhet'.[1] The divine name Horemakhet was not new, but it anticipated how another manifestation of the sun, the Aten disk, would rise to prominence as a divinity in its own right under his great-grandson, Akhenaten.

Over the inscription was a representation of a winged sun disk. Amenhotep II also took the title 'ruler of Heliopolis', centre of the worship of Re.[2]

Amenhotep used the opportunity to promote himself as a superman. The stela installed at Giza boasted that he had rowed his boat for several miles upstream with an oar whereas the other oarsmen had been shattered by the effort. Perhaps they had been mostly exhausted by doing everything in their power to make Amenhotep look as impressive as possible. He was said to be able to outrun everyone else, used a bow that nobody else could pull, and was 'a connoisseur of horses' who took enormous pleasure in training them. The truth of course, whatever it was, was neither here nor there. The claims were part of the posturing of kingship. When Thutmose III heard about his son's pastimes, he was said to have instructed that the best horses in his stables were given over to the prince to take care of. Naturally, this led to the inevitable claim that Amenhotep did the job so well that his horses were unmatched for endurance and speed. His archery abilities were subsequently depicted in reliefs, including one at Karnak (see below), but the real purpose was to spell out Amenhotep's destiny. Thutmose III was quoted as saying, 'It is he who will be Lord of the Entire Land, there being no assailant for him, because he devotes his heart to valour, and rejoices in victory'.[3]

Later, one of Egypt's dignitaries boasted that he had a hand in the boy's education. Among other titles, Min was the mayor of Thinis and tutor of Amenhotep II, recording in his tomb (TT109) how he had taught the future king to use a bow. One of the wall images showed Min standing behind the youth as he pulled back on a bow to fire at a rectangular target. Min was another of those 18th Dynasty officials with an implausible array of jobs and extravagant titles.[4]

Thutmose III died on the 30th day of the 3rd month of the 2nd season (7th month of the civil calendar) in his 54th regnal year. For once we know this for a fact.[5] Amenhotep II is recorded as having succeeded on the 1st day of the 4th month of the first season (4th month of the civil calendar), almost exactly four months earlier in the calendar year, but whether this was the same year in which Thutmose died is unknown. The record of the accession in fact dates from an anniversary recorded in the king's 23rd year (the stela of Usersatet, discussed in more detail later in this chapter).[6] This problem arises frequently in Egyptian history thanks to the lack of any system of continuous year numbering other than by individual reign and often just supplying dates with only the day, month and season. This could mean that Amenhotep had a co-regency with his father for four months, sixteen months, twenty-eight months or even longer, which would certainly explain the joint monuments. This has implications for deciding how far into his sole reign a dated event like a campaign occurred. The campaign, or what passed for one, that took place in the 3rd regnal year (see below) might, for example, have occurred very soon after Thutmose III's death.

On the other hand, Thutmose III's death came on the last day of a month, while Amenhotep succeeded on the first day of a month. If the second date was a mistake and the engraver of the stela really meant the 1st day of the 4th month of the second season (the 8th month of the year), then Amenhotep succeeded the day after his father.[7] This is one of those unsatisfactory arguments that depend on assuming a mistake when there is no proof any error was made. The stela is damaged at the crucial point where the date was written anyway. Like most of these problems in Egyptian chronology the position is unresolvable. It made little or no difference since Thutmose's death is a certainty and from that moment on Amenhotep ruled alone. However, the transition was eased by keeping the vizier Rekhmire in post for the sake of continuity.

## AMENHOTEP II AT WAR

Amenhotep never troubled himself to commission anything like his father's Annals at Karnak. Instead, all we have are the texts on several stelae and other scattered references.[8] Piecing together what happened in these wars has proved to be rather difficult. Different narratives turn up in modern books about the period, thanks in no small part to the incomplete and fragmented evidence.[9] The following is an attempt to follow a plausible narrative.

Amenhotep had a vested interest in promoting his image. Fates of entire populations depended solely on a king's personal abilities.

Inaction, illness and death could all destabilize individual states and international relations in an instant. Amenhotep II had up to three campaigns into Syria. Two of these took place in his 7th and 9th regnal years and were the most important. The first apparently occurred in his 3rd regnal year and was limited in scope. Anyone choosing to delve deeper into this topic will soon find confusion. Some Egyptologists reject the idea of the 3rd regnal year campaign and attribute its events to the 7th regnal year, usually without any further explanation. In this book they will be treated as separate, for reasons that ought to become clear. However, it is impossible to be definitive.

Some of the cities that Thutmose III had captured and reduced to vassal status might have tried their luck when he died and once the news reached them but there is no evidence of a widespread immediate effort to throw off the Egyptian yoke. There were other powers in the region and the Egyptian protection racket might have seemed the least bad option.

The 3rd regnal year campaign, such as it was, turns up on stelae found at Amada and Elephantine (Aswan). The texts are vague and typically bombastic, reiterating some of the earlier claims of Amenhotep's staggering abilities. He was 'great in strength, who has no equal and for whom one cannot find a second; he is a king (with a very mighty arm), there is none who can draw his bow, neither among his soldiers nor among the rulers of the hill countries and the princes of Retjenu'. Amenhotep raged 'like a panther' (not the first to be described thus) and completely dominated the battlefield, leading from the front throughout – naturally. Colourful superlatives aside, the stelae texts record no battles, sieges, or capture of any booty, preferring to focus on the building of temples.[10]

Something important had happened because the story then moves on to announce that 'when his majesty returned . . . he slew with his own weapon the seven princes who had been in the district of Tikhsi' (somewhere in west Syria). Doubtless the hapless victims had been tied up so this could take place without mishap. This occasion was also mentioned by the old soldier Amenemheb in a passage that implies the executions came soon after Amenhotep's accession.[11] Given that the whole region did not erupt, another possibility is that Amenhotep wanted an excuse to start a war. All he needed was news of a spot of local discontent as a pretext. This way he could demonstrate to everyone who mattered what sort of king he was going to be, including to Egyptian officers and soldiers keen to enrich themselves. If he was to maintain authority at home and abroad Amenhotep needed to demonstrate as soon as possible that he was the right man for the job.

The expedition of the 3rd regnal year seems only to have involved tackling the 'seven princes' of Tikhsi as part of a punitive policing operation, probably after news of them stirring up discontent. Their bodies were brought back to Thebes hanging off the king's ship, as was the revolting custom. Six were displayed on the walls of the city while the seventh was taken upriver to the city of Napata in Kush, Egypt's most southerly permanent city close to the Fourth Cataract and home also to the Kushite cult of Amun. The purpose was explicitly to serve as a warning to everyone including the Nubians that Amenhotep II would make his borders where he pleased, but the killings probably also formed part of a more complex sacrificial ritual with magical powers of neutralizing Egypt's enemies.

Amenhotep II was less preoccupied with campaigning than his father. Part of the reason may well have been a change in policy towards peace, preferring to see Asiatic states where possible as the compliant suppliers of tribute rather than as enemies who needed military action to keep them in check. Naturally, this depended on maintaining the nuclear deterrent in the form of the prospect of a warrior king bursting out of the Nile Valley on his chariot at the head of a large and ruthless army. Policing actions were therefore unavoidable.

In his 7th regnal year Amenhotep II went to war again, heading north once more. The stelae from Karnak and Memphis that record this nominally second campaign describe it as the first, completely sidelining the exploits of the 3rd year 'campaign' probably because it had amounted to so little either in military or booty terms.[12] The source of the trouble was significantly more serious than the Tikhsi affair. One possibility is that Mitanni was no longer being kept under control by the Hittites to the north-west and was able to start throwing its weight about in the region more aggressively.

Amenhotep II began taking his men over the Orontes river in Syria on the 26th day of the 1st month of the third season in his 7th regnal year, or about 266 days into the Egyptian year, which at that point in the cycle was around the middle of April.[13] Amenhotep's forces ran straight into an attack by an army sent from Qatna, a city in central western Syria. The attack only came about because Amenhotep had already crossed the Orontes with the vanguard of his army, leaving the rest behind and dangerously exposed. Amenhotep had to turn back, making sure this was later described as an example of his brilliant tactical skill in attacking the enemy from the rear. The uncomfortable truth was that he had come close to defeat and humiliation. His age and Thutmose III's cessation of campaigning twelve years before his death means that Amenhotep cannot have had any serious combat experience and certainly not under his father's guidance. It is easy to imagine that, like his father at Megiddo, the officers must have included some who knew he was making a potentially serious mistake. Like his father, luck was on his side and the Qatna experience probably only served to convince him of his own abilities.

Over the next two weeks the Egyptians headed further north before mysteriously turning round to head south to Niya about 60 miles (100 km) north of Qatna. One school of thought would have it that Amenhotep met the Mitanni forces in battle, was defeated and had to retreat. Another suggests that, faced with the prospect of an Egyptian army led by a determined king, and the son of Thutmose III at that, the Mitanni army turned back and avoided a battle altogether, preferring to wait until the Egyptians had returned home.

The campaign was far from over. Niya capitulated as soon as the

Tetradrachm of the Roman emperor Antoninus Pius struck at Alexandria in AD 142, commemorating the four-year period (AD 139–42) when Egypt's civil calendar was synchronized with the solar calendar for the first time since 1321–1318 BC.

Stela of Kamose. Found at Karnak. c. 1550 BC.

Ahmose I. Limestone shabti from Thebes. c. 1550–1525 BC.

Ahmose I offers wine to the falcon-headed war god Montu on a lintel from the temple to the god at Armant. c. 1550–1525 BC.

Ahmes-Ibana. He was a soldier whose career biography in his tomb is a vital source for early 18th Dynasty history.

Stela of the tomb worker Qen, his wife Nefertari and their two sons worshipping Amenhotep I and his mother, the queen Ahmose-Nefertari.

Thutmose I. One of a pair of obelisks erected by the king at Karnak in front of the Fourth Pylon. Approximately 80 ft (24 m) high. c. 1504–1492 BC.

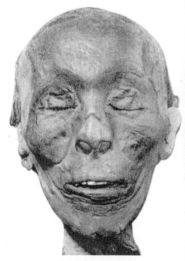

Thutmose II (1492–1479 BC), half-brother of Hatshepsut. His body was found in the cache of royal mummies found at Thebes in 1881.

Hatshepsut's birth name on her obelisk that still stands at Karnak. The upper three signs form the name of Amun, with whom she was so keen to associate herself. c. 1464 BC.

Thutmose I on the north wall of his chapel at Hatshepsut's memorial-mortuary temple at Deir el-Bahari. Painting by Howard Carter.

Hatshepsut as king kneels before Amun. A relief carving at the top of an obelisk (the pair to the one above) at Karnak, now fallen. c. 1464 BC.

Hatshepsut's memorial and mortuary temple at Deir el-Bahari. c. 1473–1458 BC.

Hatshepsut's temple at Deir el-Bahari (left), showing its terraces facing east towards Karnak.
To the right is the temple of Mentuhotep II of the 11th Dynasty. In between and set slightly back
is the temple of Hatshepsut's nephew and joint ruler Thutmose III.

Senenmut, principal steward of Hatshepsut, with Neferure, daughter of Thutmose II and Hatshepsut. From Karnak.

Myrrh trees from Punt, brought back by Hatshepsut's expedition. From her mortuary temple at Deir el-Bahari. c. 1471–1458 BC.

A barque 'way-station' shrine built originally by Hatshepsut for the Opet Festival, later usurped by Ramesses II and placed in his court at the Temple of Luxor.

Cartouches of Thutmose III (centre) and his grandson Thutmose IV (left and upper right) on the Lateran obelisk, now in Rome. c. 1400–1390 BC (completed).

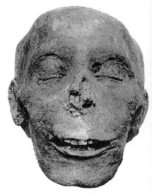

Thutmose III. His body was in the cache of royal mummies discovered in 1881.

Thutmose III and Horus. Painted relief in the temple at Deir el-Bahari. c. 1450–1425 BC.

Thutmose III, wearing the Red Crown of Lower Egypt, smites his enemies.
Karnak, Seventh Pylon. c. 1435–1425 BC.

Thutmose leads three of his senior wives (Merytre, Sitiah and Nebtu) and his deceased daughter Nefertari following on behind. Above the king rides on a boat with his mother Iset (Isis). Tomb of Thutmose III.

Chariots were a symbol of officialdom in the 18th Dynasty. A team from the temple of Karnak arrived in chariots to show their importance while surveying fields. Tomb of Nebamun. c. 1400–1350 BC.

Amenhotep II (1427–1400 BC). The superman Egyptian king showcasing his archery skills by firing arrows through a copper ingot from a chariot. From the Third Pylon at Karnak where it had been reused.

Karnak, the Eighth Pylon. Originally built by Hatshepsut, Amenhotep II modified the pylon to showcase the 18th Dynasty with colossi of his ancestors.

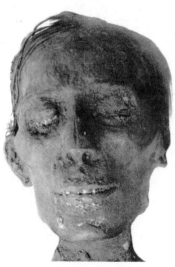

The mummy of Thutmose IV, found in the cache of royal mummies in the tomb of Amenhotep II in 1898.

Thebes, tomb of Rekhmire (TT100). Cretans bringing tribute to the vizier Rekhmire. c. 1425 BC.

Egyptians arrived, but Amenhotep had to make his way southwards from there. He plundered, received the surrender, or fought engagements against five settlements of uncertain identity and location until he reached Qadesh, at the time friendly to Egypt. Qadesh provided Amenhotep with the opportunity to demonstrate his power in several different ways. Oaths of allegiance were sworn to him.[14]

Amenhotep used the occasion to put on a public performance of his physical abilities as a hunter and as a chariot-mounted archer. Archery was Amenhotep's most significant military attribute and the one of which he was most proud. His archery skills were illustrated on several of his monuments and in his tomb. At Karnak he was shown on one relief riding a chariot having fired five arrows through a copper ox hide-shaped ingot and about to fire off a sixth as he rode past. The carving shows the king standing alone in the chariot, the bow in his left hand, his right pulling back the sixth arrow, having already fired five and surrounded by columns of hieroglyphs describing the occasion. The two horses leap forward, their back legs hovering above the ground. The composition was only partially successful and exposed the weakness of the Egyptians' reliance on stylized figures and postures. The king could not possibly have stood in an advancing chariot while firing his bow without holding on or being strapped in. The reins are shown as rigidly horizontal. The four-spoked wheel of the chariot is static. The arrow Amenhotep is about to let loose is aimed at a point in mid-air above the ingot.

The ox hide-shaped copper ingot, weighing approximately 82 lb (37 kg), was a standard unit in the region during the Bronze Age and is often found in contemporary shipwrecks. A typical size was 28 × 16 in (70.5 × 41.5 cm) and a little over 2 in (5 cm) in thickness. This matches the description of the Karnak display where the copper was the thickness of three fingers and the arrows protruded by the width of three (hand) palms. The ingot shown at Karnak appears to be larger than known examples at almost twice the size though that was surely artistic licence. Size and proportion were invariably adjusted for such reliefs to show the king to maximum advantage. This way they served as visual allegories of the way the accompanying texts also only described his achievements.

Chariot technology was advancing. Amenhotep was shown riding in an old-style chariot with four-spoked wheels. Amenhotep presented his Chief Steward Qenamun with what seems to have been a superior six-spoked chariot, depicted in the latter's tomb (TT93).[15] Amenhotep's chariot scene showed him as a superman worthy of the divine sponsorship which underpinned his rule. As an allegorical composition it proved durable, used even when a later elderly king was manifestly incapable of acting out the achievements for real (see Chapter 16). In Amenhotep II's case the imagery was closer to reality. His hunting expedition was immediately followed by the capitulation of another city, evidently so close to the forest that both events may have occurred on the same day. From here Amenhotep headed home via Megiddo, then Aruna and the Plain of Sharon. There seems to have been a Mitanni plan afoot to stir up anti-Egyptian feeling. A Mitanni messenger was captured at Aruna carrying a clay tablet round his neck. He was punished, which suggests the text on the tablet was an incitement to rebellion, and Amenhotep continued his three-week journey back to Memphis.[16] This may have led to the 9th regnal year campaign followed finally by a diplomatic breakthrough when soon after the chief of Mitanni was, with others, at Amenhotep's court soliciting the important gesture of gift exchange.

Two years passed before Amenhotep ventured out again. After he had ruled for nine years, he had carried out fewer campaigns than his father had over the same length of time, with the first not even really meriting the description. The campaign of the 9th regnal year lasted a little over four months and was conducted almost entirely in Canaan between the Jordan and the coast.[17]

Amenhotep first confronted a city called Aphek, which offered no resistance, at the southern end of the Plain of Sharon. From here, in full battle order he worked his way through one city after another and semi-nomadic settlements. The climax was the capture of two cities, one of which was called Migdal. Amenhotep claimed to have had a dream at Migdal in which Amun-Re visited him to provide him with strength and protection. This sort of oneiric intervention is not unusual in ancient accounts of battles, invariably (and obviously) composed after the event concerned and always depicted as a favourable omen that foretold victory with divine backing.

The drama unfolded. The populations of the two cities were taken prisoner, described in the text literally as 'living captives'.[18] They were corralled within a pair of ditches filled with inflammable material which was set alight and 'behold! They were filled with fire.' It would appear the prisoners were thrown into the ditches and burned alive while Amenhotep, allegedly on his own with his battle axe, kept a lone vigil at the scene all night. The atrocity was Amenhotep's grisly sacrifice in honour of, and in gratitude to, Amun. The final stages of the war included the deposition of the king at a city called Geba-Šemen and the installation of a more compliant replacement. Amenhotep collected 1,643 pounds of gold and 120,883 pounds of copper alone, together with prisoners (550 nobles and 240 wives), 210 horses and 300 chariots.[19]

The geographical extent of the 9th regnal year campaign was symptomatic of Egypt's reliance hitherto on active force to maintain control on vassal territories, ideally led in person by the king. Amenhotep's ruthlessness seems to have achieved its purpose, because now Egypt started to receive diplomatic missions from several of the regional powers, including even Mitanni, preferring peaceful relations to fighting.[20] These were arranged to perform gift-giving and exchange. Thereafter Amenhotep avoided labelling or depicting Mitanni as enemies who had now become integrated with Egypt's other allies.

Amenhotep II, so far as we know, never went on campaign again. Egyptian power and influence were now so great that war was becoming largely unnecessary, at least for the time being. The time and cost of past imperialist wars were paying off in the form of sustained tribute and obsequious overtures from neighbouring nations desperate to be on the right side of Egypt. This had no impact on the image of the warrior king – the threat of violent retribution underpinned Egyptian prestige and the ideology of the 18th Dynasty. Kings continued to be depicted regardless in the manner of a chariot-borne blitzkrieg bearing down on Egypt's foes.

# REKHMIRE

The tomb (or, better, memorial chapel) of Rekhmire (TT100) is one of the most important records of Egyptian state administration and contact with foreigners of the period (see Chapter 1).[21] Rekhmire held the position of vizier under Thutmose III and Amenhotep II, as well as serving as mayor of Thebes. He seems to have fallen out of favour under Amenhotep II and disappeared. He was an interesting example of someone else who survived the proscriptions of Hatshepsut's associates since his uncle User had served under her as vizier. The tomb paintings give a good idea of the kinds of tribute that were brought to Rekhmire whose staff would accept, assess and administer them under his supervision. For example, Syrians ('Retjenu') arrive bearing vessels containing food and drink, horses and exotic animals including an elephant, a chariot, weapons and objects that appear to be copper ox hide-shaped ingots of the type the king had so gleefully fired arrows through. Other foreigners include Nubians, those from Punt, and Cretans (called here 'Keftiu').

The paintings also depict manufacturing, the production of building materials and construction, tax collection, distribution of food to temples, vineyards and a hunting expedition with the prizes brought in. Regardless of what happened to Rekhmire, his monument preserves in exceptional detail the idealized and highly organized world Thutmose III and Amenhotep II presided over. The desecration of Rekhmire's images suggest his career did not end well, probably because the wealth and power he gained in post made him that most unreliable of all such officials, the overmighty subject with enemies. However, his body has not yet been found. The 'tomb' served only to showcase his career as a memorial chapel and included nowhere for a burial. This must have occurred elsewhere in the vicinity, assuming it had happened as he planned.

The gift of the chariot to Qenamun was a significant example of the relationship between a king and his most favoured officials. Qenamun and Amenhotep had grown up together, the king's wet-nurse having been Qenamun's mother. Qenamun's tomb itemized his exceptional portfolio of offices and honours in over eighty epithets, most of them purely symbolic, but one had a more sinister tone mentioned in the tomb inscriptions. The hieroglyphs are gratifyingly literal with two signs for the human eye, and two for the human ear, arranged around the signs for the Dual King. The 'noble' Qenamun was thus the king's 'eyes' and 'ears', and clearly therefore the man he relied on for intelligence about any disloyalty, plots, or other questionable behaviour at court.[22] The work brought him no friends. Like Rekhmire's, the tomb chapel was vandalized after his death.

Another favoured official called Sennefer, the mayor of the Southern City and cousin of the vizier of Upper Egypt, was presented with a double-heart pendant, one heart made of gold and the other silver, both bearing Amenhotep II's name. He was shown wearing the decoration in his fine and extensive tomb.[23]

Sennefer's surviving letter to a tenant farmer is surely typical of how martinets in high places like him took every opportunity to exercise their prerogatives. The farmer was told Sennefer would be coming in three days, that he should pick flowers and plants for presents and his herdsmen should prepare milk in jars. He was warned: 'Do not let me find fault with you concerning your post. Do not have it lacking in good, good order . . . Now mind, you shall not slack, for I know that you are sluggish and fond of eating lying down.'[24]

Baki, the tenant farmer, was to be left in no doubt at all about his lowly status compared to that of the high official Sennefer who did not trouble himself to add any kind of closing formula.

# BUILDING

Amenhotep's temple by the Sphinx was only one of over thirty locations where he is known to have built including (especially) at Karnak. Most of his work is represented only by scattered remains today. Even at Karnak much of his contribution was later removed or adapted as the result of the remorseless way successive pharaohs did as they pleased with their predecessors' projects. The relief from Karnak depicting his archery skills, for example, was later reused in the Third Pylon. A relief from Bubastis shows Amenhotep loyally making offerings of water or wine to Amun-Re in two panels, one being the mirror opposite of the other.[25]

One of the more prominent relics of Amenhotep's building activity today is the Eighth Pylon at Karnak, but it had been built originally by Hatshepsut. Taking it over conveniently continued his father's work erasing her memory. The main purpose was to create a suitable setting for his premature jubilee. Egyptian rulers, especially in the 18th Dynasty, regarded the jubilee as a necessary context for building projects, ignoring the theoretical need to have reigned thirty years first if it suited them.

A walled pavilion was added in front of the Eighth Pylon which was at the time the southernmost entranceway to the temple. The faces of the pylon walls were decorated with standard enemy-smiting scenes and on either side of the passageway between the two pylons were his names and his father's. Seated colossi reinforced the dynastic links, representing Amenhotep I and II (these being originally positioned nearby and not in front of the pylon where they now are), and two of Thutmose II. On the opposite side of Karnak, beyond the north precinct wall, he built his own temple to Amun. This was subsequently demolished, and the stone reused by Amenhotep III.

# FAMILY

Amenhotep II ran a simpler household than his father, having only one wife, Tia (or Tiaa), that we know of.[26] Tia was a shadowy figure and is known only for certain from records of her name and role made after his death. She emerged during the reign of her son Thutmose IV who bestowed on her the normal suite of titles appropriate for a queen (see below). Tia belonged to a time in the 18th Dynasty when the wives of living kings were deliberately marginalized. The most likely explanation is the long-term fallout of Hatshepsut's rule, making sure that, should a king die, his widowed wife would not be able to assume the throne in her own right so easily again.

Amenhotep II's mother, Merytre, was more prominent during her son's rule than she ever was when Thutmose III was alive, and even held the position of Great Royal Wife. This lay behind the apparent decision to arrange for her to be buried in her son's tomb, rather than the one prepared for her by her husband Thutmose III (KV42). This facility was never used, with the possibility that Merytre lived on into the reign of Thutmose IV only to be supplanted by her daughter-in-law, his mother Tia.

Tia, like Merytre, had no known blood connection to the ruling house and therefore her position was exclusively dependent on her son. She was never named as 'King's Daughter'. The possession of a fertile wife who remained out of sight during her sons' minorities obviously sidestepped the Hatshepsut problem, while her mother-in-law fulfilled all the official duties and prominence expected of a queen. This deliberate marginalization of the current king's wife makes the prominence of two later queens in the dynasty, Tiye and Nefertiti, even more remarkable. After Amenhotep II's death, Merytre was pushed to one side to make way for the new dowager queen Tia. Thutmose IV had Tia's name cut over Merytre's, for example on Amenhotep II's Karnak pavilion, where the term 'King's Mother' was retained, which it would not have been had Amenhotep II been responsible.[27] The 'disgrace' of Merytre is as likely to be a figment of some Egyptologists' imagination as anything else, the usurpations merely the result of adjusting the royal line-up in the new reign.

## AMENHOTEP II AT LEISURE

Amenhotep II wrote to the viceroy of Kush, a former comrade-in-arms called Usersatet, at the start of his 23rd regnal year. The message was part of commemorating his accession and is our source of evidence for the anniversary of the date his reign began (see earlier in this chapter). Usersatet preserved Amenhotep's letter by having its text carved on a stela found at a fort in the Semna region near the Second Cataract. The text is damaged and parts have had to be restored but it is a rare instance of what seems to be the actual words of an Egyptian king, expressing himself freely and candidly, apparently while settling down to relax. For once the abstract world of the superhero king cutting a swathe through hapless enemies depicted on pylon reliefs gives way to a man in his forties preparing to start drinking while addressing Usersatet as a friend and someone who understood the problems of dealing with foreign peoples on Egypt's borders:

Copy of the order which His Majesty wrote himself, with his own hand [for the viceroy Usersatet. At the time of His Majesty's glorious appearance upon the great dais] of Pharaoh when he was beginning to drink and make holiday (literally 'happy day'). Look, this order of the king is brought to you ... who are in far-away Nubia, a hero who brought booty from all foreign countries, a charioteer ... you (are) master of a wife from Babylon and a maidservant from Byblos, a young girl from Alalakh and an old woman from Arapkha. Now, these people from Tikhsi are worthless — what good are they at all? Another message for the viceroy: do not be lenient at all to the Nubians, be on your guard against their people and their magicians. Keep an eye on this servant of a commoner, for example, whom you made an official although he is not an official whom you should have suggested to His Majesty; or did you want to allude to the proverb: 'If you lack a gold battle-axe inlaid with bronze, a heavy club of acacia wood will do'? So, do not listen to their words in searching out their messages![28]

Some of the words and emphasis in the English are unavoidably absent from the original, and damaged, text and there has been a tendency to read too much into the message. The term used for Nubians is the normal one and is purely descriptive. The reference to magicians probably refers to being wary of powerful Nubian ritual execution or sacrificial practices involving captives, just as Amenhotep himself had early in his reign dealt with the Tikhsi leaders.[29] Nonetheless, there is more than just a hint of Amenhotep's personality in how he addressed his old friend.

Apart from the evidence that Amenhotep II had several pets (see below), he also had a fondness for glass, benefiting from a remarkable short-lived era of high-quality glass production in Egypt. His tomb contained the smashed fragments of seventy-six glass vessels, around 10 per cent of which bear the enamelled names of the king, the largest group known to have been in one Egyptian's possession. Other fragments of glass statues marked with his name have turned up, including a bust of the goddess Taweret. Amenhotep also used glass as a high-value gift item. He presented his son Thutmose's tutor Heqareshu with a solid glass shabti, a miniature mummiform figure intended to serve the deceased in the afterlife. Two monkey figurines marked with the king's name found their way to the Greek citadels of Mycenae and nearby Tiryns respectively, perhaps sent as part of the elaborate diplomatic gift-giving process. Amenhotep's name also appeared on a faience plaque found in the so-called 'Cult Centre' in the citadel at Mycenae.[30]

## AMENHOTEP II'S MORTUARY TEMPLE AND TOMB

Amenhotep II built a mortuary temple, but it was one of many such buildings which were robbed out by later kings. It stood close to where Ramesses II's celebrated mortuary temple, the Ramesseum, was built in the 19th Dynasty. Almost nothing is now visible on the site. Amenhotep's tomb (KV35) is one of the most interesting in the Valley of the Kings, not least because he was still in his sarcophagus when it was discovered in 1898. The tomb lies at the foot of the cliffs on the western side of the Valley. The design closely followed that of his father's but with one conspicuous modification: Amenhotep's tomb is by comparison a model of geometric order apart from minor irregularities. It was as if the plan of Thutmose III's had been stretched and pulled into shape by an architect offended by its eccentricities.[31]

A surviving architect's plan of the tomb (KV2) of Ramesses IV of the 20th Dynasty shows that tomb builders were operating by then according to a blueprint prepared in advance.[32] The difference between the tombs of Thutmose III and Amenhotep II might be because the latter was the first royal tomb cut out by workers using a similar plan. However, differences between the plan and the tomb of Ramesses IV as executed show it only served as a guide. Amenhotep II's tomb's regularity suggests that it is close to whatever was originally conceived. Amenhotep also made provision for his mother Merytre, replacing another tomb (KV42) constructed for her.[33]

Amenhotep II died no earlier than his 26th regnal year but with no specific evidence for his death and the usual opportunities to speculate, the result has been another inconclusive debate. All that can be said with safety is that he is unlikely to have lived much longer. He went to eternity with more help than his predecessors. Amenhotep II is the first pharaoh known to have been buried with a large number of shabtis (over eighty). He was also buried with his favourite bow, placed in the sarcophagus alongside him. Sadly, it was stolen after the tomb's discovery in 1898 and remains lost.

Amenhotep apparently arranged for the burial nearby of a menagerie of pets including monkeys, a dog and other animals in three small tombs (KV50–52). Their location so close to his own tomb makes him the animals' most likely owner. The burials create a colourfully eccentric image of the pharaonic court with the god king of Egypt enjoying the company of his hound, a trio of ducks and several jewel-bedecked monkeys, while he dealt with the day's business. Along with his great bow and the description of his tipsy evening's relaxation, this image makes him one of the most human but strangely overlooked of all Egypt's kings. Yet, one can never forget that he had also presided over the immolation of his Tikhsi prisoners.

The simplicity of Amenhotep II's marital arrangements did nothing to clarify the position when it came to his children. His son Thutmose IV felt a need to go to considerable trouble to assert his right to the throne (see Chapter 10). Amenhotep II may have had at least six sons and possibly as many as seven, but the evidence for them is ephemeral as it so often is for princes. It is not even certain that all of them were his offspring. A stela from Amenhotep II's temple by the Sphinx at Giza depicts a prince with erased royal titles.[34] Their removal does not suggest he died a natural death and raises the possibility that there was a disputed succession. The 18th Dynasty had a century left to run when he died. As we know all too well from our own era, a great deal can happen in ten decades and so it did in Egypt.

# 10

# THE SPHINX'S CHOSEN ONE, c. 1400–1390 BC

## Thutmose IV (Menkheperure, 'Eternal are the Manifestations of Re')[1]

*Thutmose IV manufactured an unusual destiny myth for himself, but his reign was short and uneventful. Egypt had reached the stage where the ruling house was in total control of the nation's resources. Everything was enshrined in the person of the absolutist king, even his wife having been completely marginalized. Wealth and tribute continued to pour into Egypt, most dramatically displayed in the private tombs of the elite at Thebes.*

Amenhotep II had reigned successfully over Egypt for more than a quarter of a century. The Hatshepsut episode had faded into the past. Amenhotep was also the last serious warrior king of the 18th Dynasty. Suddenly the pace slackened. The reign of his son Thutmose IV marked a period of levelling off, a scarcely noticed interlude before the reign of his own son Amenhotep III and that of his notorious grandson Akhenaten.

Undeterred by the apparent absence of any explicit instructions that he succeed his father, Thutmose moved fast to promote his claim to be king, recorded on the so-called Dream Stela found at Giza. Thutmose had several brothers to contend with, a relatively unusual situation for the Egyptian royal family in the 18th Dynasty (at least that we know of). An undisputed succession would have required all the other brothers to give way. The potential scenarios are almost unlimited. One possibility is that because Amenhotep II did not have a principal wife during his reign, he had been able to father several sons. He thereby ensured a succession, while simultaneously creating the potential for rivalry and confusion when he died.

If Thutmose IV did impose himself on the throne of Egypt, there is no evidence for any sort of spat at all, apart from the cryptic erasure of a prince's name from a stela of Amenhotep II in his temple by the Sphinx. Another possibility is that the death of an elder brother propelled Thutmose to the forefront unexpectedly. The only time Thutmose was ever named 'king's eldest son' was supposedly on a retrospective reference in a tomb painting executed during his reign where he is shown as a child on the knee of his nurse-tutor Heqareshu (TT64). However, the word for 'eldest' has been restored in published drawings of a section of the painting destroyed in antiquity and may therefore be disregarded as unreliable, though the context and format suggest that Thutmose was being shown as the senior heir.[2] Like so many similar issues in the chronology and details of the Egyptian royal families it is impossible to take this further.

Whatever machinations, if any, were involved there is certainly no evidence that Thutmose's succession was ever disputed. Much has been made of the granite Dream Stela, discovered between the front legs of the Sphinx, and erected there on Thutmose's orders.[3] In the text, which is dated to Thutmose IV's 1st regnal year, he regaled anyone who could read the text with how one day he was hunting in the desert, firing copper projectiles at lions and other animals, with only two attendants for company. No one else knew he was there, he explained, thereby supplying an essential component in a story which conveniently limited the number of authoritative witnesses to himself.

At midday Thutmose took a rest beside the 'statue of the very great Khafra', taking advantage of the shadow the huge stone figure cast across the sand. Like his father he was also associating himself with a remote ancestral king. While he slept, the god of the Sphinx, Horemakhet, came to speak with Thutmose in the manner of a father addressing his son. Inevitably he promised Thutmose the white and red crowns of Upper and Lower Egypt, and tribute from all nations. The Sphinx went on to explain that he had grown weary because of the build-up of sand. The message was clear: the gift of Egypt was in return for being relieved of the sand. Most of the rest of the text is lost but it is certain that it went on to recount how Thutmose did as the Sphinx asked, and thereby confirmed his eligibility to become king, sidelining any pretext to dispute his accession.

This type of retrospective prophecy was already a well-established 18th Dynasty tradition, especially where there was any possible room for doubt about succession to the throne. It is possible that Thutmose's Dream Stela was no more than a ritual gesture, a self-indulgent fictional validation which no one took seriously. In the context of the era, though, it is no less likely that he had such a dream and believed it, circulating the story as part of his own personal ideology of predestination.

The other most notable aspect of the Dream Stela was the omission of Amun.[4] The focus was on Horemakhet instead. That this was accidental is unlikely. Amun was the creator god who sponsored the monarch. One need only look at Hatshepsut's reign to consider the self-conscious urgency and emphasis she applied to depicting herself as Amun's chosen ruler, just as her frustrated nephew Thutmose III put about his own identity as Amun's nominee. Setting Amun to one side was then a significant gesture, though significant of what it is hard to know. Likewise, whether this was a portent for the future and the rise of solar worship in the form of the Aten, it is impossible now to say because at Karnak Thutmose seemed suitably reverential in his attitude to Amun (see below).

Even if Thutmose IV was born early in his father's reign, he is unlikely to have been past his mid-twenties when he succeeded his father and on the evidence of his mummy (see below) quite possibly up to ten years younger. That would explain further why his mother Tia played such a conspicuous role during his rule.

## THUTMOSE IV'S WARS

Thutmose IV's reign was too short for him to match the reputation of his father and grandfather, though a lack of surviving evidence might be partly responsible. He led an expedition into Mitanni territory in Syria, witnessed by one of his bodyguard who described on his tomb stela being right behind the king on the battlefield.[5] This was not so much a campaign as an opportunity for Thutmose to show himself to vassal cities and states at the head of an army. Their handing over of tribute to Egypt became an increasingly popular theme in the tombs of the king's senior officials.[6]

In his 8th regnal year Thutmose ordered an army south into Nubia when nomadic tribes entered the province of Wawat, between the First and Second Cataracts, possibly with the intention of attacking Egypt's gold-mining routes.[7] The Nubians had organized a conspiracy of 'rebels and barbarians from other countries', according to a stela that describes how Thutmose led the expedition upriver in person after 'consulting' Amun. The campaign was supposedly successful, though it would never have been described as anything else.[8] He was able to order the erection of a temple on Argo Island, south (upriver) from the Third Cataract, building work that carried on into his son's reign.[9]

Thutmose IV had little interest in proving himself in the way his predecessors had. Nor did he need to. Perhaps he had the wit to realize that so long as the tribute kept arriving there was no need to go to war. The costs were bound to outweigh the gains. Mitanni was no longer a serious threat, and the Egyptians undoubtedly had the upper hand. In his 6th regnal year, a diplomatic mission of Mitanni nobles had arrived at Thutmose IV's court.[10] They brought various gifts which included horses, bowls with artefacts of gold, and weaponry, as well as a motley collection of prisoners of war. The purpose of the embassy was probably to hand over to Thutmose his share of the booty and slaves from a Mitanni war against a third party, a far more efficient way of profiteering from violence.[11] The 6th regnal year embassy may also have been connected to negotiations for a Mitanni wife for Thutmose IV and we know he was to obtain one during the reign (see below).

A panel from Thutmose IV's chariot showing him as a
conventional 18th Dynasty warrior king singlehandedly
annihilating an Asiatic foe.

None of this prevented Thutmose IV from being depicted as a heroic warrior pharaoh, whether he ever really went to war or not. A wooden panel from a throne survived in his tomb (KV43) among the shattered debris discovered when it was found in 1903. The king was depicted as a sphinx and, naturally, trampling his enemies. The wood was once covered with gold foil, the chair perhaps having been made for Thutmose's coronation.[12] The body of one of his chariots was also recovered from the tomb. It had silver relief panels depicting him riding into battle on a chariot and scattering Asiatic enemies as he fired a fusillade of arrows at them, and another scene with him as a sphinx trampling more of the same.

The eight-spoked wheels shown on the chariot were a short-lived attempt to upgrade the six-spoked version introduced under his father but were quickly abandoned. Thereafter the six-spoked wheel remained standard. An archer's ivory cuff guard found in a house at Amarna, Akhenaten's city (see Chapter 12), shows Thutmose armed with a khopesh scimitar about to decapitate a hapless Asiatic on bended knee.[13] To the side the falcon war god Montu is shown on hand ready to pass the fearsome king another sword. That the guard was as much as half a century old when left behind at Amarna shows that the image of a king could endure for a considerable time after his death, even in a private context.

## WIVES AND CHILDREN

One of the best-known relics of Thutmose IV's reign is a granite seated dyad statue of the king with his mother Tia found at Karnak.[14] This conventional format depicting a husband and wife had its origins centuries earlier in the Old Kingdom. Both are depicted wearing heavy wigs and the uraeus. This example is a useful reminder of the fluid notion of roles in Egypt. The inscription states Tia to be 'mother of the king' and 'wife of the king'. The more literal translation, as we have seen, would be 'woman of the ruler' and from that perspective it becomes easier to understand how the king's mother could fill the role, predicated on her status as the dowager queen. She thus fulfilled the female part of the male-female composite identity of the monarch.

The idea of a principal female who was not a true wife, but who otherwise acts in the public capacity of a wife, is found at other times but normally involved a highly dominant woman who sought to rule through her son. In Egypt there was another consideration. Tia filled a necessary role that needed to be occupied by a female, ideally one who posed no dynastic threat or had any ambition other than her son's secure occupancy of the throne. That entailed serving in the nominal capacity of wife and queen and is unlikely to have occasioned any surprise at the time. Given her anonymity prior to Thutmose's reign, her elevation was entirely his doing and formed part of a programme to legitimate his succession.

Thutmose IV is known to have had several wives. One was called Nefertari, a woman of unknown origins. We do not know if she only arrived on the scene after Tia's death, but it made no difference since before long she was dead too, having left no children.[15] Another was Thutmose's sister Iaret who could have preceded or replaced Nefertari. Her name was represented by a cobra, which in this case meant the cobra uraeus worn on the brow to denote royalty (though it also served as the determinative of a serpent goddess). The addition of a determinative in her cartouche that indicated a queen made it clear she was a queen known as Iaret.[16] Epithets added that she was both the daughter and sister of a king.

Thutmose had a foreign wife acquired as part of a diplomatic arrangement with Artatama, king of Mitanni, but nothing is known about her, even her name. If this was the reason for the Mitanni embassy in the 6th regnal year, then that gives us an indication of when the marriage took place. The union is retrospectively referred to about half a century later in a diplomatic letter to Akhenaten from Mitanni.[17] Marriages to foreign princesses were now part of the standard protocol when formalizing peace treaties with other nations.

Thutmose IV's most significant wife was Mutemwiya, the mother of his son and heir Amenhotep III. She is also known only from references during her son's time as king. Mutemwiya thus held no formal status during Thutmose IV's rule and must have been a minor wife (her name was a common one). Suggestions that she was the unknown Mitanni princess-wife have always been rejected on the grounds that there is no evidence to substantiate any connection. Another possibility, which has more circumstantial basis (but no proof), is that her brother was the man called Yuya who became not only the most important courtier in the reign of Amenhotep III, but was also the father of his queen, Tiye. Mutemwiya was to rise to prominence in the early part of Amenhotep III's reign (see next chapter).[18]

Thutmose had an eldest son called Amenemhet who predeceased his father and was buried in his father's tomb along with two other children.[19] Thutmose undoubtedly had other offspring who included one daughter and son, also buried in his tomb. There were at least five more sons mentioned in Heqareshu's tomb, and at least two daughters.[20] There are other possibilities based on further evidence such as mummy labels. Like his father Thutmose had ensured a succession, but his early death had the potential to destabilize the country since none were old enough to assume the crown as adults.

## THE ADMINISTRATION OF EGYPT

As befitted Egypt's unique geography, everyday administration of the state was handled by a vizier in the north and a counterpart in the south. This had certainly been the case under Amenhotep II. During Thutmose's reign the practice continued. It was more efficient and involved less long-distance travelling. It also split the power inherent in the job and reduced the possibility of one vizier becoming over-mighty and challenging the king.

The evidence for two viziers comes from a legal papyrus dating to Thutmose IV's reign. This covered the proceedings of a court held at Thebes and involved a dispute about the revenues of a temple of Hathor at Gebelein. The officials mentioned include the treasurer Sobekhotep, who on this occasion had turned up to represent the temple (and in whose favour the court found), and the two viziers: Ptahhotep who governed the north and Hepu the south. The case shows how justice was carried out in 18th Dynasty Egypt. A soldier had alleged some sort of discrepancy in the temple accounts. Sobekhotep insisted that the revenue was unchanged from Ahmose's reign. The soldier was judged to be wrong and was punished with 100 blows to his feet. Bringing a case deemed to have wasted court time was a punishable offence and was commensurate with the sort of violence endemic in the Egyptian system.[21]

There is some evidence that moves were being made to reduce the power of the Amun cult during Thutmose IV's reign by placing them under the control of a senior military figure. Horemheb (not to be confused with the later general and pharaoh of the same name) was a very senior military officer under Thutmose IV and Amenhotep III. Like so many senior Egyptian officials he basked in an eccentric range of apparently unrelated titles, all proudly displayed in his tomb (TT78).[22] They included being responsible for the recruiting and training of troops, serving as Overseer of Birds and Fish, and Chief of the Priests of Upper and Lower Egypt. The latter was a title more commonly held in the past by the high priest of Amun. Appropriately enough, in the tomb the accomplished Horemheb was depicted presenting a floral bouquet of Amun contained in a frame to Thutmose IV. The range of Horemheb's responsibilities was illustrated on other scenes, for example one showing him taking charge of tribute donations 'from the vile land of Kush' and Asiatics. The Kushite Nubians included two princes, as well as women and children and Nubian dancers. There is no obvious explanation for Horemheb's supervisory post over priests unless it was a deliberate decision by Thutmose IV to diminish the Amun high priesthood's dominance.[23]

Nubia was too far away to be administered from Thebes and therefore was governed by the king's delegate or viceroy. The incumbent towards the end of Thutmose's reign was a man called Amenhotep who was the first to be given the title King's Son of Kush (viceroy of

Kush). He also had the additional title King's Right Hand Fanbearer. The term 'King's Son' was only notional in this context and was used to stress the importance of the position.[24]

## BUILDING WORKS

Thutmose IV expended much of his energy on commissioning building projects throughout Egypt and into Nubia, but not in ways that were especially memorable. This is undoubtedly due in part to the brevity of his reign and the willingness of his successors to remove some of his works. This certainly happened at the Temple of Luxor. A palace of his at Abydos is only known from a reference on a private stela.[25]

Karnak was Thutmose's focus but some of his efforts were soon swept away. A peristyle court built by him in front of the Fourth Pylon counted for nothing during his son Amenhotep III's reign. For a nation so often described as being built on the concept of eternity and unchanging regularity, the enthusiastic willingness to undo even the work of an immediate predecessor must have created the opposite impression. Amenhotep III had the western part of the court demolished and the stones used in the foundations of his Third Pylon to which the stone from a demolished barque shrine of Thutmose IV was added.

Thutmose ordered that Thutmose III's unfinished obelisk still lying at Karnak be completed and raised, claiming, of course, that he was acting on Amun's instructions. By then it had lingered on the south side of Karnak for thirty-five years 'in the hands of craftsmen', recorded by Thutmose IV's own explanatory inscription. Why this had happened and, more to the point, why Amenhotep II had done nothing to complete the job went unexplained. Once erected, this towering obelisk stood directly on Karnak's east-west axis and at the eastern end of the complex, instead of being one of a pair flanking the axis. The new setting, and the fact that only one obelisk was involved, could be seen as a significant statement of interest in solar symbolism and part of an evolving interest in prioritizing sun worship over other considerations at the heart of royal religious observance.[26] Alternatively, it was no less a pragmatic solution to there being only one obelisk, its likely companion having been abandoned in the quarry at Aswan where it remains.

The obelisk was known as 'the obelisk, the sole one' and was apparently the last of the 18th Dynasty.[27] Thutmose III's obelisk and one of a smaller pair erected by him at Karnak were removed on the orders of the Roman emperor Constantine I (AD 307–37) in 330 with the intention that they would stand in the hippodrome in his new capital at Constantinople. The latter reached Constantinople (Istanbul) and can be seen there today, albeit in a very truncated form. The larger solo obelisk had been left in place hitherto, so claimed the Roman historian Ammianus Marcellinus, because of its sheer size and because it had been dedicated to the sun and erected in the most sacred part of Karnak. Once at the docks in Alexandria the obelisk had to wait for preparations to be made for shipping it to Rome, but they were abandoned after Constantine's death. At some point during his son Constantius II's reign it was brought to Rome. In 357, when Constantius made his first visit to the city, he was egged on by his court lackeys to emulate Augustus and have it raised in the Circus Maximus where it formed a pair with Seti I's obelisk brought over three centuries earlier by Augustus.[28] Both eventually fell down, breaking into several pieces, and were buried there. Thutmose III's obelisk was found in 1587, repaired, and re-erected in 1588, this time outside San Giovanni in Laterano where it remains.[29] Originally 105 ft (32 m) in height, now shortened by 13 ft (4 m) by repair work after it was discovered, the obelisk was the largest at Karnak and remains the largest standing example today. By the time the obelisk was lowered at Karnak by Constantine it had stood there for seventeen centuries, a stretch it has now almost matched in Rome.

Under Thutmose IV Karnak was a good deal less sprawling than it was going to become, especially by the 19th Dynasty. It was, however, already a great deal bigger than it had been thanks to the various additions made by Thutmose's immediate predecessors. The east-west main axis's central feature remained the shrine of Amun that dated back to the Middle Kingdom. Anyone approaching from the Nile to the west arrived first at Thutmose I's Fourth and Fifth Pylons, over which Thutmose I's and Hatshepsut's pairs of obelisks towered, though the latter had been largely concealed since Thutmose III's reign. Thutmose III's Festival Hall had extended the complex to the east. A new north-south axis was being developed with the Seventh and Eighth Pylons to create a ceremonial entrance on the avenue to the precinct of Mut to the south.

It is almost impossible now to appreciate how Karnak must have appeared in those days. The pylons and reliefs on other walls featured brightly coloured depictions of kings and gods replete with panels of hieroglyphs. Gold and electrum were used to plate some features like the obelisk tips. Flagpoles with banners stood before the pylons. The courts, corridors, chambers and open spaces were packed with an ever-accumulating array of stelae and statues of kings, gods and affluent private individuals. These created an enduring headache for the priests who periodically had to clear the congestion by burying the sculptures and stelae in huge pits within the precinct. Today some survive on site, and many more probably still wait to be recovered from as-yet undiscovered underground caches. The majority of those found have been dispersed to museums in Egypt and around the world.

Thutmose IV's mortuary temple in Western Thebes was heavily robbed out in antiquity. It was made mainly of mudbrick which virtually guaranteed it would eventually disintegrate. The disciplined and symmetrical plan has been recovered. There were two pairs of pylons forming an entranceway through two courts to the main block: the peristyle court with three concentric rows of columns around an inner courtyard and the sanctuary beyond. The building was surrounded by a precinct wall which was slightly eccentric, forming a parallelogram around what was otherwise a rectangular footprint.

Thutmose IV's temple drew heavily on earlier versions, but the result was overall better proportioned. It was exactly this characteristic that is found in his tomb (KV43), making it likely that both were designed or at least constructed by the same man. He was probably Kha, who called himself in his tomb both Overseer of Works in the Great Place and Chief of the Great Place, the Great Place being the royal necropolis in the Valley of the Kings, an interesting example of the imprecise way the Egyptians used supervisory titles. His career began under Amenhotep II.[30] Thutmose IV's tomb is so similar to his father's that Kha is likely to have used the original plans but with modifications. It was a second attempt. Another tomb for Thutmose had already been begun in the adjacent Western Valley of the Kings (WV22), identified by foundation deposits in his name discovered outside its entrance. That tomb was later completed and used by his son Amenhotep III, but why it was temporarily abandoned is unknown. Thutmose IV's new tomb closely resembles the tombs of his father and grandfather with its entrance corridor, well shaft, right-angled turn to the left, first chambered hall and following corridor. The implication is that although the three had some significant differences they were all designed, and their construction overseen, by Kha.

Thutmose IV's tomb was the most accomplished royal tomb executed to date in the Valley of the Kings. The chambers and corridors were cut to a higher standard than before, completed apart from decoration during a short reign. Accuracy and proportion were hardly new in Egyptian architecture. Old Kingdom architects had established the necessary expertise and mathematical skills.[31] If anything, it is a surprise that it was well into the 18th Dynasty before tombs became more architecturally refined. The decoration abandoned the papyrus style of the previous two royal tombs. An antechamber to the burial chamber featured a more formal and complete decorative style, in this room depicting receiving the *ankh* sign of life from Osiris, Anubis and Hathor, the latter being the deity attributed with protective powers over the necropolis.

# TOMB WORKERS

Thutmose IV's tomb showcased the developing skills of the workers. By the beginning of the fifteenth century BC, Egypt's royal necropolis depended on a well-established force of professional tomb builders who lived with their families just under a mile (1.3 km) south in the village today known as Deir el-Medina and at the time as Set-Maat ('place of truth'). A sprawl of mostly contiguous stone houses, linked by a network of narrow tracks or roads, fills a slight rectangular depression between two slopes in the foothills. Overlooking the village are the tombs of the workers who used their skills to create some of the most decorative and imaginative private tombs in the area.

Today the settlement is barren and skeletal with little more than the lower footings of the individual houses surviving. The site has been largely cleared and any remaining artefacts removed, with the private tombs the most impressive sights now. The physical remains of the structures obviously represent an accretion of building over centuries rather than any kind of Pompeii-like snapshot and even include the remains of a Ptolemaic period temple dating to well over a thousand years after Thutmose IV's reign. Nonetheless, the Deir el-Medina workers' village is a striking symbol of the semi-industrial scale of the necropolis that grew up under the kings of the 18th Dynasty and especially the 19th Dynasty.

Large numbers of written records found, mainly in the form of notes scribbled on potsherds or fragments of stone, demonstrate that there was an unusually large literate component of the village's population, perhaps as much as 5 per cent – much higher than the general population.[32] These documents record a well-developed local private economy which involved the workers and their families managing livestock, actively selling their services, food, the use of equipment (including pack animals), or manufactured items to others in return for whatever the villagers needed. These 'others' undoubtedly included a type of trader known as a *šwty* (*shuty*) who served as middlemen, even to the extent of fencing precious contraband stolen from royal or other richly appointed tombs.[33] The village was in its own way a model of private enterprise operating under the umbrella of a state concern.

Whole generations of families depended on the living they made working on the royal and elite tombs in the area. The paths the workers wore out across the hills going back and forth to the cemeteries are visible today. The settlement's early life was comparatively ad hoc and it was only under Horemheb and afterwards that it became more formally administered. By the 19th Dynasty the usual Egyptian tradition of handing down jobs within families was fully established, including administrative posts that recorded the work performed by individuals. The bureaucracy made it easier for the state authorities to restrict the activities of gangs using their local knowledge to sneak out and rob the royal necropolis or dispose of their loot, an essential precaution because the sudden appearance of stolen goods from tombs could disrupt the economy.[34] The controls did not last. By the late 20th Dynasty robbing tombs, especially the royal ones, had developed into an organized industry sanctioned by officialdom (see Epilogue).

Clamping down on the inhabitants' freelance activities increased their reliance on the state. Deir el-Medina was not *prima facie* a commercial operation, not least because Egypt did not have a money economy, even though a scale of values and pricing existed. It was primarily a state facility and was fed and supplied by the state with resources gained from war, tribute and taxation. Having created that dependence on the state it was essential for the system to be maintained properly if there was not to be a breakdown in the social order. In the 20th Dynasty a series of strikes erupted in Western Thebes when routine payments to tomb workers at Deir el-Medina were not made. The underlying cause was a state overstretched by funding defence against foreign invaders while also trying to stage Ramesses III's thirtieth anniversary jubilee.[35]

The strike, although much later than the period covered by this book, showed how dependent the Egyptian state had become on an uninterrupted flow of tribute and other income. So long as it worked, the system formed part of the mechanism by which the Egyptian state redistributed some of the wealth which it controlled. This bears some comparison with the very much larger Roman state and how its activities were funded by the fruits of conquest, including the grain dole in Rome. Deir el-Medina was not the only concentration of labour involved with preparations for the afterlife. Huge quantities of resources were poured into the creation of tombs and their contents, and mummification. So integral did Deir el-Medina become to the practicalities and logistics of tomb construction and decoration that a similar settlement was developed during the Amarna period under Akhenaten at his new city (see Chapter 12).

The inhabitants of Deir el-Medina were effectively state employees. Appropriately enough, they came to regard themselves as being in the protection of the deified Amenhotep I and his mother Ahmose-Nefertari, worshipping them long into the 19th Dynasty and beyond.[36] The remains of the workers' own sometimes lavish tombs illustrate just how comfortably off some of the more enterprising and talented among them could become, especially those who reached high office. Kha, as Overseer of Works in the Great Place, oversaw the royal necropolis projects. As such, he was in his time the headman of the Deir el-Medina community. He was responsible for tomb construction and other projects, such as a shrine at the Temple of Thoth at Hermopolis. Kha's tomb (TT8) was discovered intact in 1906. Among the over 500 objects found were an inscribed gold-plated wooden cubit measuring rod presented to him by Amenhotep II, several items of furniture including a bed, stools, a lampstand in the form of a papyrus column and various boxes and an extensive array of foods and containers such as large ceramic jars. These were all packed in around the coffins of Kha and his wife, found still covered by dust sheets. Near the rock-cut tomb was his small pyramid which contained his funerary chapel.[37]

Senior men such as Kha also contributed to the modest redistribution of royal wealth further into Egyptian society. Their prominence also obscures a much larger number of labourers who are virtually invisible from the record but were surely responsible for most of the heavy work. This was no idyll. The evidence from a workers' cemetery at Amarna under Akhenaten is that these people suffered dangerous, brutal and short lives (see Chapter 12).

Kha's ability, and that of his peers, to be able effectively to write off high-value possessions and food by burying them in their relatively extravagant personal tombs (though, of course, they saw this as an investment) is another indicator of the growth in elite affluence during the 18th Dynasty. Kha was nonetheless well aware of where he lived and what went on. He took special precautions to prevent his tomb being robbed. His burial chamber was sealed behind a wooden door with a mechanical lock for which no key was provided. When the tomb was discovered, the lock had to be sawn open.

Other private tombs of this area show how the tomb workers' skills created exceptional records of everyday life. The tomb of the scribe Nakht and his wife Tawy (TT52), a chantress of Amun, can be stylistically linked to Thutmose IV's reign from other, better-dated, tombs. It contains painted decoration depicting the good life in the golden days of the 18th Dynasty.[38] These were homes for eternity and appropriately enough they replicated the structure of homes for the living, even to the extent of painting in ceiling rafters found in the flat-topped houses of a type still found in Egypt today.

The scenes in Nakht and Tawy's tomb include a sensual depiction of a banquet featuring elegantly and expensively dressed women, their physical attributes very much in evidence, and naked dancing girls. The scene is unusually vivid and dynamic. A dancing girl reaches out both her hands to one of the ladies watching, while another female guest has turned round to pass a piece of fruit(?) to another. More scenes in the tomb depict agricultural prosperity, offerings to the gods, famously beneath the couple in one scene a striped cat (surely their pet) consuming a fish, and female musicians as well as a blind male harpist. One of the other best-known scenes shows Nakht and his family hunting birds and fishing in the Nile marshes to obtain the necessary offerings. Although the overloaded vessels make it clear this is an allegorical and idealized scene, the intimate detail had clearly been gained from personal observation of and participation in similar activities.

The tomb of the soldier Horemheb (TT78) described earlier included elaborate painted panels depicting the traditional journey of the deceased from Thebes to Abydos, the mythical burial place of Osiris and thus his resurrection, and back again. Although the transport of Horemheb's body on this journey was shown in detail, it is more likely that the paintings were an allegorical representation of an expedition rather than undertaking it for real. The same applies to the pictures of an array of grave goods which included food, weaponry, furniture, chests and figurines. Horemheb's tomb was too small to contain all of these. The images must also have been symbolic rather than acting as a literal record of the tomb's inventory. Since men like Horemheb were obviously aware of the risks of tomb robbing, it stands to reason that there were other significant benefits to relying on painted equivalents instead.

## THE DEATH OF THUTMOSE IV

Thutmose IV's mummy, or at least the one labelled as his, is today one of the less ghastly looking physical remains of an Egyptian ruler. Thutmose's face still bears a strangely serene expression, his mouth slightly open as if caught between breaths in sleep, and his eyes tightly shut beneath a good head of hair. He has been described as effeminate in appearance and with aquiline features. He was about 5 ft 5 in (1.65 m) tall. Manetho allocated Thutmose IV (calling him Thmôsis) a reign of nine years and eight months. While this cannot be regarded as reliable, the duration is at least compatible with the indirect evidence for a short reign.

Thutmose IV was emaciated when he died. He was relatively young, no older than his mid-thirties at most. His teeth were so unworn that he might only have been in his mid- to late twenties, supported by other skeletal evidence, but this is questioned as has even been the identity of the mummy (of course).[39] His 8th regnal year is the highest attested. That does not prove he died then, but it is unlikely that he reigned for much more than ten to fifteen years. Thutmose IV's tomb must have been largely complete some time before his death because several of his children were buried with him (as proven by the survival of their canopic jars and at least one mummy of a child). In stark contrast to his father's and grand-father's tombs, the burial chamber and the other pillared chamber were left undecorated, probably because of his premature death. Although many other fragmentary items were found, including the chariot body mentioned earlier, the tomb had been thoroughly robbed out by the end of the New Kingdom. Thutmose's body was removed during the royal tomb clearances conducted in the 20th and 21st Dynasties and reinterred in his father's tomb, where it was found in 1898.

# 11

# THE FIRST FAMILY
## c.1390–1352 BC

### AMENHOTEP III (NEBMAATRE, 'THE LORD OF TRUTH IS RE') AND TIYE

*Under Amenhotep III the 18th Dynasty reached its pinnacle of wealth and indulgence. The king presided over state religion that became ever more focused on the sun. This was the most stage-managed reign of the dynasty to date, as well as one of the longest. The most remarkable development was the prominence of his queen Tiye and her family. The extravagance was unprecedented, but the unfinished projects suggested the 18th Dynasty's ambitions were exceeding the nation's capacity or will to meet them.*

Thutmose IV's death in c. 1390 BC may or may not have been expected but we have no idea of the cause. It was certainly untimely. With his elder brother having predeceased him, Amenhotep III was another of those kings whose accession only came about thanks to a twist of fate and whose reigns have dramatic consequences for their nations.

Amenhotep III's reign was the ultimate manifestation of a culture and state that glorified the king above all others. He stood at the apex of a society whose elite were as self-serving as the royal family. Amenhotep and Tiye enjoyed a reign of unparalleled and unregulated indulgence which also benefited her parents and other members of her family circle. They were to be followed by the extraordinary reign of their son Akhenaten whose self-absorption exceeded even theirs. The 18th Dynasty in both father and son reached its denouement.

# ACCESSION

Amenhotep III was at most about twelve when he became king, probably in late May 1390 BC (based on the date of his first jubilee thirty years later). The brevity of his father's reign makes it unlikely he was any older. The succession does not appear to have been contested, but he was too young to have managed it himself, including displacing any other brothers. One factor was to become rapidly apparent: the subsequent conspicuous presence and dominant role of his wife Tiye and her family, especially her father Yuya. Yuya and his wife Thuya did so well out of the rule of Amenhotep III that it is difficult to believe they had not played a hand in it happening. There can be no doubt that they had already gained influential and important positions at court under Thutmose IV and were conveniently on hand when he died.

Amenhotep III's mother is not known to have been his regent. Instead, the widowed Mutemwiya only temporarily fulfilled the position of Great Royal Wife, as her mother-in-law had done. Her name meant 'Mut in the sacred barque'.[1] Appropriately, she was depicted in such a barque in a rebus sculpture set up at Karnak by Amenhotep III, linking her to Mut, Amun's divine consort. Seated in the barque, Mutemwiya was wrapped in the wings of a vulture, the symbol of Mut and the hieroglyphic sign for the goddess's name.[2] The purpose was to imply that Amenhotep was the progeny of Amun and Mut, or even Mut on her own as the mother with the powers of parthenogenesis. A relief at the Temple of Luxor in the birth room built later by her son showed her being greeted by Amun-Re as Thutmose IV as he arrived to impregnate her. She was the last queen of the 18th Dynasty to be shown this way. Mutemwiya's status at this time makes it likely that Amenhotep III was not married to anyone when he became king. Her origins are a mystery but there is a very plausible explanation for her good fortune involving Yuya and his daughter Tiye, Amenhotep III's queen (see Family Matters below).

Amenhotep III was king for around thirty-eight years, the second longest reign of the 18th Dynasty after Thutmose III. Just how much he genuinely ruled the country is difficult to know. Thutmose III's much shorter time as sole king was largely characterized by the annual campaigns and associated braggadocio that played so large a part in Egypt's rise to dominance in the region and unprecedented affluence. Although two more kings had preceded Amenhotep III after his great-grandfather, it was his good fortune to pass much of his rule enjoying the wealth that had come, and continued to come, to Egypt. This was a period of exceptional building and extravagance with little inclination for, or need to turn to, war. Indeed, war was expressly avoided (see below).

The reign was the most profligate to date. To what end is not perhaps as obvious as it might seem. For all the building achievements and showcase events of Amenhotep III's time as king, the personality of the man is comparatively elusive, even by Egyptian standards. This reflected the increasing emphasis on the king as the living progeny of Amun-Re. His life was a journey towards an apotheosis on Earth before his people's very eyes, or at least that was how he was portrayed. As such, his entitlement to absolutist rule was impregnable.

Amenhotep III lived a carefree and indolent life. Several of his predecessors left some traces of the assertive individuals they undoubtedly were. The most recent ones had kept their wives in the background. That is not the case with Amenhotep III who instead was surrounded and succeeded by some far more conspicuous individuals than he ever was. Much of what happened seems to have been intended primarily to benefit them, especially his principal queen Tiye and her family.

There is a very occasional glimpse of the man himself, especially in the retained copy of a letter sent by Amenhotep to Kadašman-Enlil, king of a place called Karaduniyaš (in Babylonia). The subject was the negotiation of a daughter of Kadašman's to be a wife of Amenhotep. Kadašman was irritated by the request because his sister had already been sent as a wife and no one had heard anything about her since, or so he claimed. Amenhotep's tart response, assuming it was genuinely his composition rather than by one of his officials, was to point out that Kadašman's previous envoys had been 'nobodies' including an 'ass-herder', whom he alleged did not even know who Kadašman's sister was. Other sneering retorts to Kadašman's complaints about the various ways in which he had been disrespected followed with a final pay-off: 'are we to laugh?' The translation here is uncertain and an alternative is 'we are distressed'.[3] Amenhotep's text is sarcastic and condescending, but elements are of dubious meaning, and it is not demonstrably the text of the actual letter sent. With so little to compare it to, we cannot be sure how much personal input he had with its composition, nor when or even if it was dispatched to its disgruntled addressee. Another letter, also to Kadašman, is a routine itemization of the usual niceties and various gifts from Amenhotep III.[4] Most of the king's other extant texts were formulaic and routine.

The question of intelligence or strength of personality is rarely discussed in Egyptology unless the evidence is there to suggest that both qualities were present in a ruler. The converse is harder to confront. Amenhotep III might have been a king who succeeded to the throne because of his birth but was not necessarily a dominant, decisive, or effective personality, at least not as much as his wife was. Indeed, Tiye's remarkable visibility might have been a function of inadequacy on his part. This is an interesting phenomenon attested at other times. It does not have to result in poor or unstable government so long as those operating royal power on the monarch's behalf do so conscientiously and with sense and restraint, but the balance is a precarious one.

There is certainly no reason why a hereditary monarchy would produce one assertive, intelligent and accomplished king after another. England's Henry III (1216–72) and Henry VI (1422–61, and 1470–1) both reigned for long periods. The two men were weak individuals who were manipulated and exploited by those around them. Henry VI followed a militarily brilliant father. Both succeeded to the throne as children, an important ingredient in necessarily involving others to rule on their behalf. They reigned as kings for fifty-six years and thirty-eight years respectively (although Henry VI was deposed at that point, then subsequently briefly reinstated before being murdered). Their birthrights to rule were indisputable. Both reigns were characterized by the conspicuous presence of dominant individuals at court who managed affairs (in some cases competently). In Henry VI's case these included first his uncles and then his queen, Margaret of Anjou, who went out of her way to compensate for her husband's various problems, which included his mental health, as well as to fulfil her own sense of entitlement. Henry VI was exceptionally devout, even by the standards of the day, peaceable and well-intentioned but almost completely ineffectual. He was incapable of exercising sound judgement about those who sought to influence him. His reaction to the greatest crisis of his reign was to suffer a bout of catatonic depression that left him unable to rule for around eighteen months.[5] The two kings were useful to those who exerted influence over them and whose interests were best served by keeping them on the throne.

We do not know that Amenhotep III was a similarly weak ruler. However, the circumstantial evidence of his age at accession, the exceptional role of Tiye and her family which is at complete variance with the three previous reigns, together with signs of serious physical neglect in Amenhotep's later life, suggests it is a real possibility.

# FAMILY MATTERS

By the end of his 2nd regnal year, dated by the so-called Marriage Scarab, Amenhotep III was married to Tiye, who was probably about the same age as him, or a little younger. The scarab bore an important dynastic statement and forms one of a series of large commemorative scarabs produced during his reign.[6] This example bears Amenhotep's and Tiye's names in cartouches, together with the names of her parents Yuya and Thuya but without saying anything else about them. Including them was unprecedented. As a result, unlike so many other royal wives in the 18th Dynasty, Tiye's parentage is not in doubt. Yuya and Thuya were flagged up at every possible opportunity in ways that were remarkable and had no parallel in Egypt.[7] This was particularly incongruous under a king like Amenhotep III where his kingship and mythologized powers were promoted more avidly than ever before.

Yuya and Thuya became two of the most significant non-royals in the 18th Dynasty and perhaps all ancient Egyptian history, an impression reinforced by the discovery of their tomb. Even Hatshepsut's Senenmut had never become so embedded within the royal closed shop. Yuya and Thuya's daughter emerged rapidly into one of the most visible of all royal consorts in dramatic contrast to her predecessors and anticipating the remarkable role her daughter-in-law Nefertiti would play in the next reign. Most recent 18th Dynasty kings had done everything possible to marginalize the women necessarily brought in to bear heirs, until as dowager queens under their sons each could be safely publicized as the great royal wife.

Despite speculation that Yuya was of foreign origin (based largely on his facial features, height and unusual name), or that he was Mutemwiya's brother, there is no unequivocal evidence explaining his family's exceptional proximity to Amenhotep III.[8] Therein lies one of the great mysteries of the later part of the 18th Dynasty. That the son of a minor wife had become king was already a matter of note. If Yuya was Mutemwiya's brother and had used his proximity first to obtain her marriage to Thutmose IV, then engineer Amenhotep III's accession by whatever method necessary and his sister's promotion to Great Royal Wife, followed up after a respectable period by overseeing the boy's marriage to his daughter Tiye, much of what was to follow is explained and would match other historical instances. There is, unfortunately, no evidence that proves Mutemwiya and Yuya were related.[9]

Yuya came from a city called Akhmim downriver from Thebes about 20 miles (30 km) north of Abydos. Tiye also had property at Akhmim. Yuya's numerous titles included honorific statements of his intimacy with the king as well as asserting his social rank.[10] Many of them appear on the papyrus version of the Book of the Dead found in the Valley of the Kings tomb which he shared with his wife (KV46). The tomb, found largely intact in 1905 and yielding their spectacularly well-preserved mummies, was their final great privilege. One of Yuya's coffins was supplied 'by special favour of the king'. The contents show that Yuya and Thuya set great store by the honours they had been awarded.[11] They also show that the couple escaped the fate of some of their overmighty predecessors. They did not fall from grace before they could be buried, another sign of the extent of their importance and influence that lasted throughout their lives.

Yuya's titles are hard to define in terms that are easy to understand today. He was declared to be of 'noble status' and of foremost status at court.[12] Edouard Naville, who analysed the text more than a century ago, metaphorically wracked his brain for ideas. He cited 'prince' as a common translation but concluded vaguely that it 'certainly indicates a rank at court'.

Another of Yuya's titles used the bee sign for kingship and a seal determinative. Naville suggested 'seal-bearer' or 'chancellor'. The translations are obviously no better than best guesses. The most likely is that it was Yuya's privilege to rubber-stamp the king's decision in some regard, perhaps being made a keeper of a royal seal to do so. While this may have involved practical duties it is equally likely, and perhaps more so, that it was purely honorific.

Some of Yuya's other titles were truly nebulous, but as we have seen he was not the first to be so honoured. Amenhotep II's favoured steward and boyhood companion Qenamun had been particularly proud of his litany of honours, itemized with extravagantly colourful language in his tomb. Yuya was certainly a sound competitor. Confronted with Yuya's use of the quadrupled sign *wr* for 'great' (i.e. 'great great great great'), Naville suggested 'the great of the great ones', conceding that he did 'not know the real sense'.[13] Yuya basked in a variety of additional complimentary titles that amounted to various descriptions of his status as 'favourite' in a variety of contexts such as 'of his lord' or even Amun, as well as being the 'first friend' among the circle of those who loved the king.[14] Nothing could match the unsurpassable 'favourite of favourites'. This had religious connotations, in which Amenhotep III was the favourite of Re.[15] One might coin the title 'First Intimate' to sum up Yuya's unique position. Of more significance was Yuya's title 'Father of the God', sometimes qualified to make it clear that by 'God' the king was meant, making the title implicitly 'father-in-law of the king'. Yuya was also 'Divine Father of the Lord of the Two Lands'.

Yuya held at some point in his life a variety of other roles. He was a priest of the fertility god Min and was also Overseer of Min's Oxen at Akhmim. In addition, Yuya was Master of Horse and His Majesty's Deputy of Chariotry according to a single line on his second coffin, positions that he seems to have held under Thutmose IV and possibly even Amenhotep II.[16] Master of Horse is straightforward enough to read (though the determinative is one applicable to animals generally), but the other is typically oblique for Egyptian. The operative phrase, together with a determinative to indicate a span of animals is involved, means in this instance 'the (troop) concerned with spans of animals (horses?)'. Given that there is so little evidence for the Egyptian use of cavalry, and certainly not during the 18th Dynasty, by default the reasoning is this must mean the chariot wing of the armed forces.[17] The term seems to date back to Kamose's time when the Egyptians had to find a way of referring to chariots which at the time they had no word for. By Thutmose I's reign a word for chariot (*werret*) had come into use, which means that Yuya's title was probably an archaism.[18]

A section of the inscription on Yuya's coffin referring to his Master of Horse and His Majesty's Deputy of Chariotry titles. The second line refers to his post of Master of the Oxen of Min. The symbol that resembles a flag is the determinative indicating animals, read here as 'horses', specified at the start of the line with the word for horses (*ssmt*). The curved sign that appears at the start of each line is the ox-tongue determinative used for the word translated today in many different ways, such as 'master', 'superintendent', or 'overseer'.

There is also the interesting case of an unprovenanced and undated 18th Dynasty shabti of a similarly named man called Yey who was the God's Father and Master of Horse. His name was effectively the same as one of the many forms of Yuya's and may have been a predecessor.[19] In the absence of any corroborating evidence that Yuya ever served actively in any military capacity, the best one can say is that his horse and chariotry posts appear to be two other honours which were perhaps inherited. They were rarely used by Yuya, but they were also employed by Ay, another possible member of the family (see below).

Almost three millennia after Yuya's life, the French essayist Michel de Montaigne observed how most systems of government devise 'certain vain, and in themselves, valueless decorations, in order to honour and reward virtue'.[20] The recipients are granted all sorts of privileges such as riding in coaches, 'a special seat at public meetings', special names and titles, and symbols on their dress. He could easily have been writing about Egyptian court life, but of course the point is that it belonged to a very long tradition still evident in our own time.

There is no indication of when Yuya's various titles, which reached a comically implausible extent, were conferred though the Min ones must have belonged to his earlier career. They were probably cumulative, inherited, bestowed, or even appropriated on one occasion after another. While Yuya enjoyed exceptional privileges, his honours were mainly decorative, a cascade of 'gongs' that flattered his vanity and embellished his standing without involving him doing very much in his various capacities.

The closeness of men such as Yuya, or Rekhmire long before him, to the king meant not just having his ear and being able to influence him. It also meant possessing the power of being an intermediary between the king and others, and thus the ability to exclude those whom they considered undesirable or their personal enemies, while advancing their cronies. Such priorities were of huge significance in a court context.

For Yuya's daughter Tiye to be available to marry Amenhotep III and for her to live on well into her son's reign she must have been at least ten years of age but not much older. Yuya's body is that of an elderly man who died aged at least sixty and stood about 5 ft 5 in (1.65 m) in height. He clearly survived some way into Amenhotep III's reign but predeceased his wife Thuya because the two were mummified in different ways. One of the most striking inclusions in their tomb was Yuya's chariot. Since by the time he died he cannot have had any active military use for it (if indeed he ever had), the chariot is probably the one in which he rode around as the most exalted official in Amenhotep III's court.[21]

Thuya had also reached her fifties or sixties. The body identified by some as hers was just under 4 ft 11 in (about 1.495 m) tall, not quite as short as the body sometimes identified as her daughter's. Thuya was honoured in a manner appropriate for the mother of the queen, but her titles belong mainly to the court and temple. She was the King's Dresser and Chantress of Amun as well as Lady of Min's Harem, but most importantly Mother of the Great Royal Wife of the King.[22] The latter was repeated in multiple locations in the tomb. The purpose was to act as an apotropaic device to ward off thieves – though that would have relied on the thieves being both literate and troubled enough to desist, a reflection perhaps of Thuya's personal conceit. One possibility has always been that Thuya was in service at court and that this resulted in Tiye being given access as her child. This way Tiye became a person of interest to the new king or was pushed forward by ambitious parents. Tiye ostensibly posed no dynastic threat, and in that sense resembled Mutemwiya, Tia, and Merytre before her. There is no evidence that Yuya or his wife ever played any role in the governance of the state but that proves nothing about the extent to which they exerted influence behind the scenes, about which we would expect to know nothing.

Amenhotep III may have felt a need to hand out titles to Yuya and Thuya for a variety of reasons. The obvious questions are why and whether he was placed under pressure by others to do so. Yuya's privileges may have been at the behest of Tiye or even Yuya himself, adding to any he had inherited. His litany of honours must have provoked jealousy at court from others who saw coveted and lucrative positions being showered on a very few people. The only way this could have continued is if Yuya and his family had an iron grip on the king via Tiye or had some other unassailable link. Another possible explanation is that Yuya and his clan had either bought their way into privilege and status or perhaps, like Amenhotep II's steward and friend Qenamun, Yuya had a parent in a role close to the court during an earlier reign, probably Amenhotep II's. There is no specific evidence to support either contention, which is hardly surprising, apart from the family's exceptional status.[23] However, the evidence from other periods makes both possible.

Yuya and Thuya may have already been connected by blood to the royal family in some way. The potential Mutemwiya link is the most plausible, but not the only one. Cyril Aldred suggested that Yuya might have been related to Thutmose IV and his father Amenhotep II but did not explain why other than the circumstances of Yuya's command of the horse and chariotry under them, mentioned above.[24] The name 'Tiye' is allegedly a diminutive of Nefertari, and Tiye made much of the cult of Ahmose-Nefertari. 'Thuya', it has also been claimed, is a contraction of Ahhotep and thus suggested that there was some line of descent from the earlier members of the 18th Dynasty royal house.[25] It is a stretch to use names as the basis of arguing for a long-distance dynastic connection. However, as we shall see, it is possible that there were other family links between the royal line and Yuya and Thuya.

No commoner parents of any previous Egyptian queen had become such star personalities, so there was no tradition of the king being obliged to promote his in-laws this way. The flaunting of their privileges was so unusual that the idea they were the innocuous beneficiaries of good fortune is unconvincing. They were more likely to have played a proactive, even determined, part in soliciting their advancement by a young king unable or unwilling to obstruct them. In 1464 Edward IV of England married Elizabeth Woodville, a commoner of high provincial social status (her father was Baron Rivers at the time), but not high enough for her ambitious family who had an important royal connection. Her mother Jacquetta had previously been married to John, Duke of Bedford (d. 1435), brother of Henry V, and remained known as the Duchess of Bedford, which meant they were closely associated with the crown. Over the next few years, although in Edward's case he was a highly intelligent and capable adult king, the Woodvilles became the recipients of honours and profitable marriages deemed appropriate to the relatives of England's new queen and mother of the heir to the throne. Senior members of the aristocracy were enraged and frustrated. They saw in Elizabeth's offspring the direction of the royal line and patronage thereafter, and the cost to their own prospects.[26]

It is not hard to see how an opportunistic Yuya might have fulfilled a paternal role for Amenhotep III, recently vacated by the deceased Thutmose IV. His relative age, compared to most of the population and particularly the king and queen, would have afforded him considerable status as an elder. For how long he had been inveigling himself into the royal family will remain a mystery, as will any other dynastic connection there might have been. Nevertheless, it is possible, perhaps even likely, that Yuya was also in his own way an honourable and decent man whose presence helped the stability of Amenhotep's reign.

Yuya and Thuya's only two certain children were Tiye and her brother Anen. Both were attested as such in their parents' tomb and Tiye on other pieces such as commemorative scarabs. By the 20th regnal year Anen had reached the dizzying heights of Second Prophet of Amun, and a high priesthood of Re. There were other candidates. Ay rose to high office under Akhenaten, holding similar positions to Yuya, and served under Tutankhamun before becoming pharaoh himself. He also established a shrine to Min at Akhmim and was styled with titles used by Yuya. It has often been proposed that Nefertiti was his daughter but without any evidence to substantiate the theory. We could tentatively add a later steward of Tiye's called Huya who subsequently accompanied his mistress to Akhenaten's new city when she was dowager queen. No evidence has ever been found to confirm Ay or Huya's links to Yuya and Thuya but their names, titles and proximity to the royal circle make a good case for suggesting they were at least close kinsmen.

## THE PROMINENCE OF TIYE

There is nothing new about the idea that Tiye was a dominant figure. A century ago, Tiye was often depicted as the driving force behind the Aten revolution under her son Akhenaten, at a time when he was sometimes portrayed as a narcissistic halfwit.[27] That has changed in the light of new evidence, especially about Nefertiti (see next chapter), but for Amenhotep III's reign it is still much easier to build a case for Tiye's prominence at her husband's expense. Tiye never sought elevation to the kingship to rule alongside her husband. The reason was obvious. The posthumous denigration of Hatshepsut, and the marginalization of queens since then, told its own story. Tiye did not openly step outside her sphere as queen, even if her visibility was significantly amplified. In this regard she fulfilled the role expected of her as the female manifestation of kingship, supplemented in due course by her daughter Sitamun. That need not in any way have inhibited her ability to assert her power and influence over the state even if that was publicly conducted through the person of her husband.

Correspondence during Akhenaten's reign shows that foreign kings had come to regard Tiye as a major player by then, if not before. At least, they referred to her as if she was. She was called by them, for example, 'the Mistress of Egypt' and given precedence after Akhenaten in the obsequious list of addressees that each letter began with, as well as being the recipient of costly gifts. In one notable reference, Tushratta of Mitanni wrote to complain that gold statues promised by Amenhotep III had finally arrived but were plated wooden versions. Insulted by the attempt to fob him off with such trinkets, he said to Akhenaten, 'Tiye, your mother, knows all the words that I spoke with your father. No one else knows them. You must ask Tiye, your mother, about them so she can tell you.' Tiye was thus clearly marked out as Amenhotep III's main confidante, and thus is not surprisingly described in one letter as 'the principal and favourite wife' of Amenhotep III.[28]

Letters addressed to Amenhotep III before his death involve all the usual greetings but there is little hint beyond those of the nature of the man, in contrast to the way in which a belief in Tiye's grip on affairs was explicitly alluded to. These correspondents had not met Tiye. Their impression was based on her reputation and the eyewitness accounts brought back by their diplomats and couriers. These must have exaggerated her image to some extent but are likely to have had some basis in truth to have had currency.

The so-called 'Elder Lady' found in Amenhotep II's tomb has been identified as Tiye's. The evidence is persuasive but not conclusive. If the mummy is hers then Tiye stood no more than 4 ft 9 in (1.45 m) tall.[29] As a great royal wife she was displayed alongside her husband on temple reliefs and in sculptures to an unprecedented extent and during his lifetime, a marked divergence from the practice of the three preceding reigns. A curiosity is that Tiye was never apparently made 'God's Wife of Amun' and as a result is conspicuous by her almost total absence from the temples at Karnak and Luxor. For someone so able to assert herself, this must mean that such a role was not a priority for her or was even avoided. This raises the interesting possibility that she was involved with the growing prominence of the cult of the Aten sun disk which helped concentrate power exclusively in the hands of the monarchy at the expense of Amun.

Sitamun (literally 'Daughter of Amun'), Amenhotep and Tiye's eldest daughter, was also given unusual prominence.[30] The only female who came close to Tiye's status during Amenhotep's rule, she was also granted the title Great Royal Wife as part of the jubilee celebrations held in the 30th regnal year. She had her own suite in the palace at Malqata (see below). Yuya and Thuya's tomb contained three chairs, two of which bear Sitamun's name. She is named and illustrated on the largest chair in a panel on the back that shows her twice in receipt of offerings. Sitamun is described as the king's eldest daughter, but Amenhotep's name does not appear. The second chair was for a child. On a panel on the chair's back Tiye is shown seated in a papyrus boat, accompanied by a cat and attended by two princesses. One of them is offering lotus flowers to Tiye, referred to as the great royal wife. She is named as Sitamun (her name is also in a cartouche) together with the inscription 'daughter of the king ... favoured of the Lord of the Two Lands'.[31] It has to be assumed both chairs were personal gifts from Sitamun to her maternal grandparents (unless she had predeceased them). Her lineage via Tiye from Yuya and Thuya was given greater emphasis than descent from her father.

Sitamun's marriage to Amenhotep III was no more than a formal union in a family where a princess was allowed to marry only a king or not at all. As such, it resembled the arrangements where the king's widowed mother had formerly served as a great royal wife, but this time in a supplementary capacity to Tiye. Sitamun is not known ever to have borne children.[32] Despite her status, she was also to join the ranks of the disappeared. She is not heard of again and no trace of her burial has ever been knowingly found. A room attached to Amenhotep III's burial chamber was probably intended for her but there is no evidence it was ever used.

Panel from a chair of Sitamun showing the princess with
her mother Tiye. From the tomb of Yuya and Thuya.

Tiye's other daughters were awarded lesser titles such as King's Wife.[33] There is no more likelihood of these having been incestuous arrangements either. One of them, Iset, also became Great Royal Wife towards the end of the reign, four years after Sitamun, and another, Henutaneb, became Consort of Horus. Promoting daughters in this manner was new for the 18th Dynasty and was another way to draw more attention to the female members of the family with Tiye at their head. It turned the royal family further in on itself, by emphasizing the daughters as being beyond anyone else's reach.

As well as their daughters, Amenhotep III and Tiye had at least two sons: Thutmose, who predeceased his father, and Amenhotep IV (Akhenaten). Thutmose was described as a 'son of the king', a title taken to mean heir apparent, in our terms therefore 'crown prince'. He served in several prominent priesthoods, one of which was in the Apis bull cult at Saqqara where he was depicted with his father making an offering. Amenhotep III had created the first tomb and chapel at Saqqara for the Apis bull, believed to be a manifestation of the god Ptah, initiating a custom that lasted down to Graeco-Roman times. What happened to Prince Thutmose is not clear but the emergence of the second son as a new heir after the 30th regnal year makes it probable that he had predeceased his father.[34] If so, Thutmose's death was to have remarkable consequences.

Several foreign princesses from Babylon and the Mitanni were added to the king's harem. They helped display his formal dominance and power over other states in the region. The arrangements involved a certain amount of posturing just as under Thutmose IV, the foreign kings doing their utmost to offer a show of resistance and thereby claw back something of their autonomy. Gilukhepa, a Mitanni princess, reached Egypt in the 10th regnal year, but only after a fitful round of diplomatic negotiations that had involved six requests from Egypt. When the princess arrived to take her role as a secondary wife, she came with a showcase retinue of over 300 of her women. She is not known to have had any children by Amenhotep III, though if she was fertile and the marriage involved sexual relations this could hardly have been prevented. It is improbable that Tiye would have countenanced any prospect of a rival line of descent by a lesser wife. From that we can assume that if such children existed, they were completely ignored at any official level and disappeared from history. Gilukhepa was thus merely a trophy wife, a decorative embellishment of the court.[35]

## MAN OF PEACE

During the earlier part of Amenhotep III's reign a scarab publicity campaign portrayed the young man as a ruler cut in the mould of his more bellicose predecessors. Along with the Marriage Scarab there are other scarabs that commemorate the young king's activities. Scarabs were well-known commemorative items, but there was a more concerted attempt to advertise key events of the reign that way under Amenhotep III. They could have been issued on the king's express command, but it is no less possible, especially considering their unprecedented numbers, that they were designed to compensate for something lacking. Throughout Amenhotep III's reign there was a persistent contrast between the way the regime did everything possible to promote the king's public image and how he was overshadowed by other family members.

These scarabs include a record of Amenhotep's triumphant killing of more than a hundred lions during that time, and ninety-six bulls in the 2nd regnal year alone. The symbolism was obvious. The bull was an integral component of Egyptian religious imagery in its use as the physical manifestation of various deities such as Osiris and Re, and a wild animal represented the forces of disorder which needed controlling. The word for a bull, *ka*, was phonetically identical to the word for the 'spirit' or 'soul'. Killing bulls also provided opportunities for a brutal form of entertainment that could demonstrate the king's prowess.

The bull hunt recorded on the scarab took place after a herd was spotted in the desert in an area now known as Wadi Natrun, a depression below sea level west of the Delta in northern Egypt. The description makes it clear that the occasion was a choreographed turkey shoot and publicity stunt. This raises more questions about the extent to which the king really took part or even if the hunt ever happened at all. The location was conveniently remote and far away from unwanted eyewitnesses. Amenhotep and his entourage allegedly sailed downriver in a ship called *Appearing in Truth* before crossing overland to the depression in his chariot at the head of his army. The 170 bulls involved were corralled by digging a ditch around them before the king supposedly proceeded to kill fifty-six of the enraged animals by circling around in his chariot. He is likely to have been assisted in the task to a considerable extent. Four days followed to rest the horses before Amenhotep returned to massacre another forty bulls.[36]

There is little evidence from the rest of the reign beyond the 11th regnal year that provides any basis for a chronology of events. A major reason for this was the lack of warfare, and thus tomb records by senior officers like Ahmes-Ibana. Amenhotep III went out of his way to avoid fighting. A later diplomatic letter to Akhenaten referred retrospectively to how Amenhotep III had written constantly about peace, 'there was nothing else whatsoever that he wrote about over and over'.[37]

By the 5th regnal year Amenhotep had made an expedition into Nubia but it was the only war he ever participated in, or at least accompanied. The expedition was recorded on a stela set up between Aswan and Philae. It records how 'the wretched foe of Kush' led by someone called Ikheny had rebelled. Amenhotep had taken his army to crush the rising, successfully it seems and allowing his 'first victorious campaign' to be declared.[38] Identifying the rebel leader by name was an unusual development. Ikheny was evidently some-one to contend with and defeating him clearly worth publicizing. Allegedly, 30,000 of the enemy were captured. This figure is likely to have been as routinely rhetorical as the bombastic tone of the stela but is large enough to suggest the war was a significant one and had required the use of a sizeable Egyptian army.

The only other Nubian campaign that might have taken place is only recorded on an undated stela found at East Semna, south of the Second Cataract. Merymose, the viceroy ('King's Son') of Kush, commemorated how a rebellion had emerged in the Nubian region of Ibhet.[39] Merymose raised an army and set out to crush the insurrection. The king was not present. It does not appear to have been the same as the war of the 5th regnal year and involved only a minor engagement against one community, resulting in a small number of the enemy captured. It is possible it was a single operation during that 5th year war but could also have taken place at a different time.

The victory, which Merymose claimed took only an hour, was conducted in Amenhotep's name as 'the mighty bull' and 'fierce-eyed lion'. Allegedly, 740 people were captured alive, made up of soldiers, women, children and servants. For good measure, the stela adds the score of 312 'hands' cut from the bodies of the dead, thereby accounting for 1,052 of the enemy. This rebellion is unlikely to have involved more than a single settlement and its immediate area, if indeed it was a rebellion at all. A more convincing explanation is that it was a unilateral act of piracy by Merymose on a spurious pretext to capture slaves as well as make sure that the supply of Nubian gold to Egypt was maintained.[40] Another viceroy of Kush under Akhenaten appears to have followed suit (see Chapter 12). Given our dependence on the chance survival of evidence for exploits like this, we should probably suspect there were many other such instances of gratuitous and profiteering attacks on easy civilian targets by greedy officials. It was, after all, becoming the only way they could make good the lack of profitable participation in wars of conquest.

Thanks to the demolition of Amenhotep's mortuary temple (see below) in the 19th Dynasty and the reuse of the stone, another undated stela once displayed there has survived.[41] This was designed as a conventional depiction of the king as a warrior and crusher of his enemies. The stela refers generally to the king's defeat of the Nubians, whom he is shown driving his chariot over, but also includes a reference to defeating Naharin (Mitanni). A vague reference to such a war is mentioned by a man called Amenhotep, son of Hapu (see below). He referred to leading an Egyptian force sent against the 'Nubians and the Asiatics' and was guided by 'the plans of my lord'. This sounds metaphorical, implying that Amenhotep III was not personally involved, though there is a reference to counting all the captives.[42] Since Egypt and Mitanni were at peace, proved by the extant diplomatic correspondence, the stela is difficult to explain unless it was symbolic. As such it would have been designed as a way of depicting Amenhotep III with the appropriate credentials including a claim to have crushed Egypt's enemies to the north and south. That would also explain the usurped statue installed at the mortuary temple (see below).

# EGYPT UNDER AMENHOTEP III

Aside from the exceptional privileges afforded Yuya (who in any case died during the reign), many other trusted individuals were delegated to management roles in the promotion of the king's interests and public works. These jobs were allocated often on a regional basis, such as Amenhotep-Huy who as mayor supervised building and religious festivals at Memphis. These men were frequently drawn from the same families. Huy's brother was the same Ramose who was vizier of the south under Thutmose IV, and their father was Heby, sometime mayor of Thebes. Huy's son served as a high steward during Akhenaten's reign. This family's experience of collective success at the heart of Egyptian administrative affairs is what also makes it so likely that, despite the lack of evidence, more of the family of Yuya and Thuya was involved in state affairs than we can at present confirm.

One of Amenhotep III's most important assistants was his namesake Amenhotep, son of Hapu, who established his reputation in his hometown Athribis (Tel Atrib in Lower Egypt at the southern end of the Delta), not far from Memphis. Promoted on merit, he served in several capacities before rising to prominence under Amenhotep III as supreme Overseer of all the King's Works.[43] This also resulted in the king endowing Athribis with a temple, the most northerly constructed during the reign, though nothing of the building now remains.[44]

Amenhotep, son of Hapu, was possessed of considerable skills and vision, as well as knowledge of religious symbolism and ritual. This led to him becoming what might be called project manager of the king's first jubilee. He was responsible for supervising the construction of some of the king's more ambitious buildings. He was given the exceptional privilege of being able to erect his own mortuary temple next to the king's. So great were his achievements that he was subsequently deified in his own right and attributed with all sorts of powers including healing. Scribal statues of him at Karnak were later positioned on a processional route, emphasizing his special role as a link to the gods.[45] In Graeco-Roman times he was worshipped in his own shrine on the upper terrace of Hatshepsut's temple at Deir el-Bahari, by then ruinous and largely choked with sand but with other cult activities being maintained on the upper level. His healing cult was a remarkable long-term legacy of the 18th Dynasty.[46]

Amenhotep, son of Hapu, was not the first such architect to be so honoured in his own time and after.[47] He presided over a range of officials in charge of areas and particular monuments. Within this maze of responsibilities and overlapping interests it is impossible to work out what any one of the people really did in practice. For the most part we only have accounts by or on behalf of these individuals themselves. Naturally enough they always paint themselves in the best possible light. Earlier in the Dynasty, for example, the architect Ineni positioned himself at the epicentre of history as the king's right-hand man and left out references to anyone else. At that date he was comparatively unusual. By Amenhotep III's time the numbers of self-penned eulogies by Egyptian officials had increased greatly.

Hor and Suty were almost certainly brothers and very possibly twins, commemorated on a joint granodiorite stela with their text of a hymn to the sun.[48] The text identifies them respectively as overseers in charge of building projects on the west and east sides of the Nile at Thebes, including Amenhotep III's memorial-mortuary temple at Kom el-Hettân and Karnak. The wording suggests that they worked together. However, there was also a Meryptah who claimed to have been the overseer in charge of the Kom el-Hettân temple's construction, recorded on his tomb stela found at Saqqara.[49] They were not alone. Perhaps, given the length of the reign, some fell from favour, grew sick or died, and were replaced by someone else. Hor and Sety's stela was later damaged, their figures and names having been defaced. It is impossible to know why, but easy to envisage how professional rivalry might have been a motive.

Corruption and cronyism must have played an important part in the allocation of these roles that so often overlapped. Horemheb's programme of reform (see Chapter 17) included references to specific instances of abuse of privilege, particularly in the years leading up to his reign. Issues like these and the resulting inefficiency would certainly help explain why so many of Amenhotep III's building projects were unfinished at his death.

The programme of works bears the hallmarks of a ruling family bent on establishing the image of the king at a whole new level. It bordered on megalomania, especially the colossal statues which became a special priority under Amenhotep III. They absorbed the sort of energy and resources some of his 18th Dynasty predecessors had once devoted to obelisks (these were not resumed until the 19th Dynasty).[50]

Amenhotep III's building works clearly benefited from the development of infrastructure, administration, and a workforce by his predecessors, as well as the wealth that underwrote the projects. These also relied on the establishment of technically proficient architects and engineers, sculptors, artists and other craftsmen, and were the result of Egypt's wealth and the years of peace. That glib observation glides over the astronomical quantity of human labour, free Egyptian and captured servile, involved. It is impossible to apply figures to these projects since the workers concerned are all but invisible in the record, other than incidentally.

Building was conducted in numerous places in Egypt in Amenhotep III's name, though most of the structures now are either destroyed or survive only in fragments. Production of statues and buildings was on such a scale under Amenhotep III that there must have been a significant increase in the workforce. Each labourer had to be fed and accommodated out of resources derived from taxation and tribute, all controlled by the state. In such a context, Merymose's expedition in Nubia to capture labour makes more sense.

The tomb chapel of the vizier Rekhmire (TT100) belongs to earlier in the 18th Dynasty, but the building work and technology depicted in the detailed paintings would not have changed by Amenhotep III's time, other than in scale. They include, for example, three men polishing and finishing a twice life-size stone sphinx, and another scene showing huge mudbrick ramps being used to drag up individual blocks and column drums. The workforce involved those labouring on the production of mudbricks and stone blocks intended for statues and include depictions of Asiatics and Nubians.[51] Some would live long enough to see their work become obsolete. Amenhotep III's Third Pylon at Karnak even replaced some of his own work from earlier in the reign, a mark of the wasteful extravagance so characteristic of the era.

## AMENHOTEP III'S WESTERN THEBES

One of the principal results of the blood, sweat and tears expended under Amenhotep III and Tiye was a sprawling complex in Western Thebes that largely outclassed anything else already in existence. There the king and his queen were showcased at the height of their power. The site served as the diplomatic and cultural capital of Egypt.

Amenhotep III's neighbours constantly sought his friendship and benevolence. They took infantile pleasure in evidence of his approval and good intent in the form of his letters and gifts. They grew petulant and worried if these seemed in any way to devalue their conceits about their standing in his eyes. This would take on greater significance under Akhenaten when he showed markedly less concern about his neighbours. The relationships were in practice conducted largely by proxies in the form of ambassadors and Egyptian officials. They acted out their masters' demands or wheedling solicitations, buoyed up by their own sense of importance and relative standing.

The most southerly part was a sprawling palace city complex, now known as Malqata and in its time first as 'Palace of the Dazzling Aten' and then as Per Hai, 'House of Rejoicing'.[52] Built mainly from mudbrick, it covered between 55 and 74 acres (22–30 ha) and had its own harbour linking it to the Nile.[53] The footings of the chambers, halls, storerooms, gardens, a temple (apparently primarily used for Amenhotep's second jubilee, see below) dedicated to Amun and other gods, and further structures are still visible today. Traces of extensive painted decoration on plastered walls have been found. Separate suites existed for the king, queen, Sitamun, other members of the royal family and senior staff. Beyond and stretching south towards Medinet Habu there was an associated urban settlement.[54]

A little over a mile to the north (2 km) at Kom el-Hettân was the king's memorial-mortuary temple on the Nile's flood plain. This complex was also designed as a monumental lifetime venue for the regime in his 30th regnal year jubilee. The king's formal and formulaic dedication speech, surviving on a stela installed in the temple, announces that it was made in honour of Amun-Re and was 'filled with monuments'.[55] Another large stela triumphantly itemized the king's catalogue of building achievements there and at other locations. The text explains how the temple was filled with slaves and accommodated 'the children of the princes of all the countries of the captivity of His Majesty'. It was also surrounded by 'settlements of Syrians, colonized by the children of princes', together with vast numbers of cattle.[56] The temple precinct and its surroundings were a strange combination of a town and internment camp used to display his human possessions.

The annual inundation of the Nile was intended from the inception of the temple to form part of the annual cycle of renewal by flooding the precinct. For that reason, the temple was not designed as a cohesive single building of pylons, courts and halls. Covering over 740 acres (almost 300 ha) and thereby exceeding Karnak, the temple consisted of a vast open-walled precinct with an entrance facing east. Three pairs of freestanding pylons led the visitor through to a peristyle court beyond.

The most striking feature of the temple was the vast pair of seated statues of Amenhotep III at the easterly entrance. Much smaller figures of Tiye and his mother Mutemwiya were carved by his legs.[57] Battered and damaged, they remain perhaps the most evocative single relics of the 18th Dynasty. They stand more than 60 ft (18 m) in height and weigh over 700 tons each. Known since Graeco-Roman times as the Colossi of Memnon, they once formed part of a series of colossi on the site, most of which fell down in an earthquake around 1200 BC. Some of these have recently been excavated and re-erected. Others, including smaller statues, were removed during the 19th Dynasty and later right into modern times. The mudbrick pylons have long since been robbed out and washed away, for the most part in the aftermath of Amenhotep's reign and accelerated by the earthquake. The latter did so much damage that it saved the trouble of further demolition and created overnight a convenient quarry.

The arrangements and labour involved in sourcing the stone, carving the statues and transporting them to Thebes, let alone the other colossi erected at the temple, epitomize Egypt's staggering engineering capabilities by that time. The stone came from a major quarry at el-Gabal el-Ahmar in an area where eastern Cairo (Nasr City) is now. This entailed moving the blocks around 420 miles (675 km) to Thebes. The best clue to how this was done comes from the tomb of Djehutihotep who administered one of Egypt's regional districts (nomes) during the Middle Kingdom some five hundred years earlier.[58] The colossus shown in his tomb painting was about one-third of the height of the Colossi of Memnon and has been estimated to have weighed around 60 tons. It had been placed on a sledge, secured by ropes and pulled by 172 men in four columns while additional workers delivered a continual supply of water to be poured in front of the statue to alleviate the friction on the sand. A roughly life-size sandstone statue of Amenhotep III was found in the so-called 'cachette' of statues later buried in the Temple of Luxor. Unusually, it shows a figure of the king in walking pose on a sledge with a back pillar on a pedestal. It seems to represent not the king in person but is instead a statue of a colossus being transported.[59]

Since the Colossi of Memnon were a great deal larger and heavier than the one recorded by Djehutihotep, it is possible that as many as 2,000 men were required to pull each one. Unless they had already been completed before moving them south, both statues would have weighed considerably more than they did when finished. Water transport was involved at some point as at the very least they had to be moved across the Nile from east to west. Impressive though they still are the statues give little idea of their dramatic original appearance in front of the temple in complete and painted form, and with the flooded Nile lapping round the pylons and their plinths.

To speed up the work the officials in charge looked around for any handy reusable statues and found a colossus, about 26 ft (8 m) tall and of uncertain date – estimates range from the reign of Thutmose IV to as far back as the 12th Dynasty. The names and titles of the original king were removed and replaced with those of Amenhotep III. Only the lower legs and base survive today. Its purpose was to provide an opportunity to showcase the names of African nations to the south under Egyptian control along with depictions of prisoners. These were displayed on the sides of the base. The challenging task of moving it to Kom el-Hettân resulted in an accident, slicing off part of the front side of the base which had to be repaired with a clamp. Under normal circumstances a colossus would be completed on site, but the nature of the damage shows that Amenhotep III's names had already been carved on when this happened.[60]

Theatrical considerations were paramount. In the 11th regnal year, one of the last dated points that can be fixed in the reign, Amenhotep ordered the excavation of an artificial lake for Tiye at 'her town', a place called Djarukha, believed to have been near Akhmim where her father Yuya came from. The pointlessly ostentatious lake was to be 3,700 by 700 cubits, or about 173 acres (70 ha), more than eight times the size of the lake in Central Park, New York. The details were recorded on commemorative scarabs, now the only evidence for its existence. The work began in the 11th regnal year, the scarab's text implausibly suggesting the project was completed in fifteen days. This must mean that an existing depression was flooded. The scarab also names both Amenhotep III and Tiye and adds the names of her parents Yuya and Thuya.[61] Tiye was thus probably really the instigator. The lake was inaugurated from the royal ship *Dazzling Aten*, a title also applied to Amenhotep III as an epithet as part of the Aten sun disk's growing importance.[62] Another ceremonial lake was added at Birket Habu for the Malqata palace, at the expense of some of the palace structures which were replaced with new buildings nearby. This lake, which was never finished, was linked to the Nile with canals and its own harbour, with another harbour on the east bank.

The mortuary temple, the Malqata palace and the nearby lake were used as a vast stage on which Amenhotep's several jubilee celebrations were held. The first jubilee sed festival came in his 30th and 31st regnal years, an event that included the king riding on the lake in a solar boat and fulfilling the role of Re himself. The event, exceptional for its immoderation even for a pharaonic jubilee, was the product of years of peace which meant resources were not diverted into war and the time was available for planning. It also helped make up for the lack of military victories that could have been celebrated. Amenhotep proceeded to hold two more jubilees in his 34th and 37th regnal years.[63]

The tomb complex of Tiye's steward and royal scribe Kheruef

(TT192) included a description of some of the events at the first jubilee which took place roughly in late May on a day that is likely to have been the anniversary of the day on which Amenhotep had become king. It reads like a modern totalitarian state media's press release about the party elite on parade, overseen by the leader rewarding them for their faithfulness.

> Year 30, second month of the 3rd season, day 27, under the Majesty of Horus, mighty bull, appearing in truth, given life, the King of Upper and Lower Egypt, Lord of the Two Lands, Nebmaatre, the Son of Re, beloved of him, Amenhotep Ruler-of-Thebes, given life, at the time of celebrating the first jubilee of His Majesty: the glorious appearance of the king at the Great Double Doors in his palace of rejoicing and introducing the officials, the king's friends, the chamberlain, the men of the gateway, the king's acquaintances, the crew of the barque, the governors of the palace, and the king's dignitaries.
>
> Rewards were distributed as 'Gold of Praise', and ducks and fish of *nbwi* ('both of gold'), and they received ribbons of green linen, each person being made to stand according to his rank. (They) were fed with food of the king's breakfast: bread, beer, oxen and fowl. They were directed to the lake of His Majesty to row in the barque of the king. They grasped the tow ropes of the evening barque and the prow rope of the morning barque, and they towed the barques at the Great Place. They stopped at the steps of the throne.
>
> It was his Majesty who did this in accordance with writings of old. Past generations of people since the time of ancestors had never celebrated such rites of the jubilee. It was for the one appearing in truth, the Son of Amun, who enjoys the legacy of his father, given life like Re forever, that which was decreed.[64]

Some of Egypt's neighbours missed the point entirely. Kadašman-Enlil, king of Karaduniyaš, was aggrieved not to receive an invitation, grumbling that one had not been sent for him to 'come and eat and drink', and no suitable 'greeting gift' had been dispatched either.[65]

Amenhotep's jubilee was used to mark a form of rebirth in which visual realizations of the deified king turned back time. Demonstrating this claim as dramatically as possible was designed to create the illusion that the meeting of the divine and mortal worlds could be witnessed by ordinary people. Amenhotep was depicted as the youth he was when he became king. His person became explicitly linked with the Aten solar disk, elevating him further above and beyond the temporal world. The real purpose was to magnify the entitlement of the king to rule through the exclusivity of this relationship and the duty of his subjects to accept this without question. In the meantime the cults of other gods were celebrated but under Akhenaten they were to be pushed aside in the quest to push the idea of the king as the sole agent and inter-mediary of the sun to its ultimate form.

Among the vast number of statues at the memorial-mortuary temple were eventually around 730 of the lion-headed goddess Sekhmet carved from black Aswan granite. There was one for each day and night of the year, adding to the clutter. The black granodi-orite may have been chosen because, as the Nile subsided after the inundation, the statues would have been seen emerging from the black silt deposited by the floodwaters. Sekhmet was an interesting choice. The name meant 'the powerful one'.[66] This lion-headed goddess was therefore a divine manifestation of power, but that power could be used both for protection and destruction. The point of the cult was to ensure her protection could be directed towards Egypt and her destructive capabilities against Egypt's enemies.

Sekhmet had links to other deities including Mut, and thus Amenhotep III's mother Mutemwiyah. There is also the possibility, albeit unproven, that the large number of Sekhmet statues had come about as an effort to appease the goddess because of some affliction that had hit the nation. Correspondence between Babylon and Akhenaten some years later made a retrospective reference to a Babylonian princess-wife of Amenhotep III who had died in a plague, but without any more specific information it is impossible to know if a contagion had struck Egypt.[67] There is no parallel for Sekhmet ever being commemorated on this scale at any other time. Many of the extant statues were later moved to the precinct of the temple of Mut just south of Karnak and usurped, for example, by Sheshonq I of the 22nd Dynasty around 945 BC during the Third Intermediate Period.[68]

A limestone seated dyad of Tiye and Amenhotep III, which included the much smaller figures of three of their daughters, stood in the temple. At 23 ft (7 m) high it remains the largest such composition known though it only survives in fragments which have been heavily restored. The couple are equally sized, but thanks to her headdress Tiye's figure is taller, a feature so incongruous that it must have been deliberate. The statue therefore served as a conspicuous declaration of the queen's importance to the image of the regime.

Part of another dyad of the couple was found in the mortuary temple of Merenptah of the 19th Dynasty to which it had been moved following the destruction of Amenhotep III's temple by an earthquake. A great royal wife could now blaze her way across the firmament alongside her husband instead of being kept in the background. Tiye was not always shown on this scale. In the tomb of her steward Kheruef she is shown at the 30th regnal year jubilee *sed* festival behind the king and almost a head shorter, more in accordance with what her actual height is believed to have been.[69] On the Colossi of Memnon she was shown as a conventionally tiny figure compared to the vast figures of her husband.

Colossal portraits of Amenhotep III had evolved into highly stylized depictions of the king with the mouth forever caught in the faintest hint of a smile beneath two almond eyes. The form was human in structure but transported to the divine sphere of timeless serenity. Statues of Amenhotep, or Amenhotep and Tiye, and their setting look more like the symbols of a state personality cult than anything else, refining the depiction of the king or the royal couple as omnipotent, all-seeing quasi-divine beings presiding over the nation. At least one of the chief sculptors responsible was a man called Men from Heliopolis. He is shown on a stela at Aswan, created by his chief sculptor son Bek who worked for Akhenaten (see Chapter 12), worshipping a colossus of Amenhotep III, which must be one he had worked on himself. A head from a 30 ft (9 m) tall colossus of the king now in the British Museum, carved from sandstone quarried near Heliopolis, is likely to have been one of his creations.[70] Tiye's imposing and impassive features survive well in a granite statue usurped in the 19th Dynasty by Ramesses II for his mother Tuy, taken to Rome in antiquity where it resides now in the Vatican.[71]

The devotion of so much of Egypt's productive capacity to indulging the whims of the monarch and his wife, or perhaps primarily his wife's, has echoes in the Romanian regime of Nicolae and Elena Ceauşescu, for example with their Palace of the Parliament in Bucharest. That building remains one of the largest government buildings in the world operated by civilians though it was not completed until after the Ceauşescus' downfall. Amenhotep and Tiye escaped such a fate and there is no suggestion that their activities risked any such outcome – Egypt was obviously a very different place – but there was a similar level of extortion of a nation's human and economic resources to reinforce a regime's control with an abstract illusion of power and security.

At Karnak, the Third Pylon was added to the west towards the Nile, in part using stone taken from existing monuments and features including some erected by his father. In keeping with the glorification of the king that was a hallmark of the reign, the dedication inscription likened Amenhotep to the sun, 'making brightness for all men'. He was 'exalted above millions to lead on the people forever'. His face was a source of 'terror' to any would-be rebels. The pylon was celebrated with an account of its statistics, including cost, and the use of electrum and lapis lazuli to adorn it.[72]

The Tenth Pylon, begun by Amenhotep III but not completed

until the end of the Dynasty by Horemheb, extended the ceremonial entranceway on the road that connected Karnak to the temple of Mut. In front of the Tenth Pylon a quartzite sandstone colossus of the king was installed. It was one of the largest ever erected in Egypt and was the work of Amenhotep, son of Hapu.[73] Only its feet remain but thanks to the use of standard proportions by the Egyptians it can be shown it was probably about 69 ft (21 m) tall. It stood on two plinths elevating the gigantic figure further. It was not alone. Another colossus of Amenhotep III ended up in the temple of Khonsupakhered within the precinct of Mut, though it may originally have stood either in the mortuary temple across the river or in Karnak and was later modified probably to represent Ramesses II. Its head alone including crown is 9 ft 6 in (2.9 m) high.[74]

The main block of the Temple of Luxor today is largely Amenhotep III's work with the shrine complex to the south approached by a hypostyle hall that led into a huge solar court surrounded on three sides by a double colonnade. To the south the 'birth room' part of the temple displayed the moment of his conception when his mother Mutemwiya was visited by Amun-Re, her ensuing pregnancy, and birth of the future king. To make way, earlier work by Hatshepsut and Thutmose III was cleared away and the stone reused.

Some of Amenhotep III's building projects were unfinished when he died. Evidently, his regime's ambitions exceeded both the time and resources available. It is possible the labourers resisted the onerous demands made of them by deliberately finding ways to slow the projects down, or that squabbling officials delayed the work. Captive labour was used but freeborn Egyptians probably had no more choice in what they were put to work at. It may be too much to try and depict such activities as a form of proletarian resistance, but it is important to remember that our image of Egypt is dictated by elite sources. Conversely, there is likely to have been a certain amount of pride involved in being part of such grandiose projects. This is certainly reflected in the tombs of the elite though they, of course, did not have their noses, literally or metaphorically, to the grindstone in the same way as the workers. They also had to play their part by being seen to celebrate the conceits of the royal couple.

Sheer scale mattered ever more. In the dedication speech of the Colossi of Memnon attributed to Amenhotep, he made a specific reference to the 'great rejoicing because of their size'.[75] The buildings and their statues were designed to dwarf their predecessors. It is also easy to overlook now that these statues and buildings were brightly painted, the statues being given the colours of a living being. There was an obvious contrast with the physical presence of the real king and queen, especially if the diminutive bodies thought to be theirs have been correctly identified. Amenhotep III and Tiye and their assistants, particularly Amenhotep, son of Hapu, took competitive gigantism to new heights, both literally and figuratively. They reached or even exceeded the limits of what was possible in terms of the engineering technology of the era.

The 18th Dynasty kings had been in love with projecting themselves on a grand scale for generations but Amenhotep III and Tiye's hubris was unprecedented. The organization of resources and the workforce necessary to do these things meant professionalizing the state's abilities to an unmatched extent. Akhenaten inherited these systems, without which the realization of his building projects and founding of a whole new city would have been impossible and unthinkable (see Chapter 12). More and more of Egypt's wealth and the productive force of its people was being squandered on prodigious follies. It was just as well some were left uncompleted since it is hard to know what could have come next.

The extent of the building projects as well as the size of some royal statues raises interesting questions about the extent to which the king, and indeed the queen, were now regarded as living deities or were descending into megalomania. At Soleb in Nubia, just north of the Third Cataract, a temple was dedicated to Amun-Re, and Amenhotep III as the deified Lord of Nubia, with reliefs portraying some of the thirtieth anniversary sed festival celebrations. The work here was also incomplete when Amenhotep died and was finished by Tutankhamun. At Sedeinga nearby Tiye was worshipped as a manifestation of Hathor, the mother of Re, conflated with the moisture deity Tefnut. These cults reflected a phenomenon found more widely in Egypt during the reign in which the identity of the king was increasingly associated with that of a variety of deities, and whose solar connections were prioritized.

The Nubian examples, which were not matched in Egypt, were experiments in blurring the identity of the king first with existing deities. It was already well established in royal lore that the king was the chosen one of Amun and thus a short, but potent, leap to the idea of the king as a divinity in his own right. With the years of major wars of conquest long into the past this identity as a living deity helped replace the depiction of the king as a supremely successful warrior. There is also the question of regional tastes. The Nubian examples may represent only something deemed suitable for local consumption rather than being indicative of a more general policy. The driving force may even have been Tiye whose prominence is explained if she had an unmatched dominance of events and state policy, aided by her relatives.

## AMENHOTEP III'S TOMB

Amenhotep III was well into middle age when he discovered he was not a god after all. The only remaining question is whether he maintained sole rule until his death or whether his son Amenhotep IV (Akhenaten) was a co-regent for the last few years. The evidence for any co-regency in Egyptian history is usually limited and often ambiguous. This putative co-regency has always attracted even more attention because of the addictive nature of trying to unravel the chronology and events of Akhenaten's reign. Nothing has emerged that would resolve the problem one way or the other.

Work was restarted at Thutmose IV's abandoned tomb in the

Western Valley of the Kings (WV22). Like his palace and mortuary temple, Amenhotep III's tomb was larger than those of his predecessors though the length of his reign gave him more time. The design was a slightly modified version of Thutmose IV's second tomb and included modifications to the side chambers of the burial chamber to create additional accommodation.

The most likely intended additional beneficiaries were Tiye and Sitamun. Tiye's importance was acknowledged even in the production for the tomb of unprecedented double shabtis bearing her name and Amenhotep's in parallel strips.[76] Tiye, who outlived her husband for at least twelve years, seems to have ended up here temporarily but only after first being buried at Akhenaten's new city of Amarna and then in another tomb in the Valley of the Kings (see Chapter 13 for the movements of her body).

Amenhotep III's mummy, or at least the one identified as his from labels on the coffin lid and the body's shroud, is poorly preserved.[77] It was one of the bodies of the royal cache found in his grandfather Amenhotep II's tomb (KV35) which is interesting because another occupant of the tomb has been identified as that of Tiye (the 'Elder Lady'). How they got there by separate and circuitous routes is discussed later in the book. The mummy is that of a man around 5 ft 1 in (1.56 m) tall.[78] His baldness, lost teeth, tooth decay and abscesses suggest a neglected and prematurely aged individual in his fifties. Other evidence such as reliefs make clear, however tactfully, that he had also become obese in later life. However, some doubt will always remain that the body is his.[79]

The state of the body supposed to be Amenhotep III's is in dramatic contrast to the regime propaganda of a rejuvenated sun king, making it interesting to speculate how state occasions were managed, and his physical and possibly mental state disguised as he deteriorated. The remains add a further dimension to the evidence provided by the bodies of some of his forebears for a royal line of kings and queens who were unprepossessing in height and appearance, and a long way from the popular impression of the glamorous rulers presiding over

Egypt at the height of its power. Amenhotep III was interred in his tomb after his death in 1352 BC during or shortly after his 38th regnal year. If Sitamun ever joined him, her burial has left no trace.

A curious relic of Amenhotep III was found at Amarna, his son's new city (see next chapter). This small private stela, only just over 30 cm high, probably originated from a small household shrine. It depicts Tiye seated alongside her husband. The figure of the king is that of an overweight old man though he cannot have been much more than in his early fifties when he expired. He looks partly slumped in his throne, his right arm languidly resting on his leg and staring indifferently at a pile of offerings. One historian's verdict was that he had become 'flabby, diseased, and prematurely senile', speculating that the statue of the goddess Šauška (Ishtar) sent to Amenhotep III by Tushratta of Mitanni was to help the ailing king though this is too much to read into a single relief.[80] When the relief was carved is not known. Whether it was produced during his life or just after, it was a product of a new form of realism in Egyptian art that flowered under Akhenaten.

By the time of his death Amenhotep III and Tiye had exposed the limits of their ambition despite the almost four decades they had presided over Egypt and without the distraction of a major war or so far as we know a natural catastrophe. Their vast building projects were mostly unfinished, some more so than others. Their son and successor would under normal circumstances have seamlessly followed his father by continuing his works or transforming them in his own image. Instead, Egypt was about to change direction in an unexpected way, but which was an entirely logical development of the elevation of the king ever more to divine status.

# 12

# THE GREAT LIVING ATEN
# c. 1352–1341 BC:
# AKHENATEN AND NEFERTITI'S
# HIGH SUMMER

## AKHENATEN (NEFERKHEPERURE, 'BEAUTIFUL ARE THE MANIFESTATIONS OF RE')

*The reign of Akhenaten was only possible because the 18th Dynasty had created a fabulously wealthy absolute monarchy that ruled without restraint, and whose most recent king was presented as a god to his people. Akhenaten's religious revolution and physical relocation of the regime has always defied complete understanding and analysis. This remains the most controversial era in Egyptian history.*

'There is no statement in Amarnan studies which cannot be contradicted.'[1]

This simple but piercingly accurate observation cuts right to the heart of the problem with the strange reign of Akhenaten and his cult of the Aten solar disk, often referred to as the Amarna Period after the modern name of the site of his new capital city, Akhet-aten, known now as Tell el-Amarna. Generations of Egyptologists have continually re-examined and rearranged the limited and confusing evidence to uncover what really happened, but often going round in circles.[2] Much remains unknown.

## ACCESSION

Had Amenhotep III been succeeded by a more conventional son, Egypt might have embarked on a new era of bombast and war. Instead, he was followed by his surviving son Amenhotep IV, later known as Akhenaten and who will be referred to here by this name hereon. His upbringing, as was normal for royal princes, is a virtual blank. All we know is that Akhenaten had had an elder brother called Thutmose whose premature death left the way open for him. Akhenaten may have been appointed a co-regent before his father's death though how long (or even if) this co-regency lasted is impossible to say.[3] Given the length of his father's reign the balance of probability is that he was no younger than his middle teenage years and perhaps into his twenties when he became king.

Akhenaten had no interest in setting off immediately to assert himself in a chariot war. It was just as well because under Amenhotep III there would have been little chance to gain any military experience before his accession. Akhenaten had other things on his mind. He had seen the light. Literally. However, the reign began quite normally, with no hint of the revolution just around the corner.

Akhenaten's partner in every way was his queen Nefertiti, whom he married within four years of becoming king. Akhenaten and Nefertiti were let loose on an unsuspecting Egyptian population caught up in a whirlwind that reinvented the nature of Egyptian despotism. The caprice and passion of their rule was relatively brief, but the consequences were dramatic. Everyday life for the ordinary Egyptians did not change in substance. They still lived and laboured at the king's pleasure. The waste of Egypt's wealth and power reached an unprecedented extent, poured away on the pursuit of the whims of one young man and his wife.

## Nefertiti's Origins

Nefertiti was even more conspicuous a queen than Tiye had been. Nefertiti was so integral to the revolutionary aspects of the reign that she and Akhenaten formed the climactic expression of the Egyptian male-female king composite, effectively operating as joint monarchs which was eventually made formal. This was a concept they experimented with in sculptural representations of themselves, reflecting the endless Egyptian interest in finding imagery to represent abstract ideas.[4]

Unlike Tiye, who was exceptional for an Egyptian queen in this regard, Nefertiti's origins were never stated but this was normal. One idea, for which there is no evidence, has always been that she was a foreign princess. Her name ('the Beautiful One is come') has no special significance.[5] Given her dominant role under Amenhotep III, Tiye could never have accepted a daughter-in-law playing so important a part unless Nefertiti was already part of the royal circle, perhaps as a member of Tiye's extended family. Tiye also remained conspicuously involved in the events of her son's reign. Nefertiti was never described as 'King's Daughter', which makes it unlikely she was one of Akhenaten's sisters who had changed her name (see Chapter 15).[6] Over the years various Egyptologists have been inclined to assert their divergent views about Nefertiti's origins as fact. In 1925 Ernest Wallis Budge said that Akhenaten's 'wife Nefertiti was his half-sister, being the daughter of his father by a Mesopotamian woman' as if this was attested in the surviving records.[7] Needless to say, there is no evidence for this claim and the same goes for many others made since.

An important clue comes from several noble tombs at Amarna, including that of Tiye's steward Huya (TA1), where in some scenes Nefertiti's titles begin with the term *rpˁt*. The title has been translated, in this case as 'heiress' or 'hereditary princess', but is more nuanced than usual because it is followed by a feminized determinative for a person of particularly high rank.[8] This alluded to descent from an exalted line, being also the feminized determinative that formed part of the name of Isis. There was clearly a semi-divine tone to the title in this context, too, which might suggest that Nefertiti was descended from the royal line, however far back. This being Egypt, of course the true significance is typically opaque. It could alternatively only refer here to Nefertiti being related by blood to Tiye.[9]

Nefertiti is only known to have had a sister called Mutbenret, a similar (but not identical) name to that of the second wife and queen, Mutnodjmet, of Horemheb (see under Royal Entourage below).[10] One suggestion, often cited, is that Ay, one of Akhenaten's most senior officials who would later be king himself, was Tiye's brother and Nefertiti's father. Neither relationship has ever been proven though given Yuya and Thuya's roles and other circumstantial evidence both are plausible, with Tiye's certain brother Anen just as likely a candidate for Nefertiti's father (see previous chapter).

Akhenaten and Nefertiti presided over a dramatic change in the emphasis of Egyptian religion, and therefore the focus, but not the nature, of Egyptian culture, which began within a year of his accession. They might have found this exhilarating, but their every action upset order (Maat) throughout Egypt. This was despite the way Akhenaten explicitly sought to be 'living in Maat' in the manner of a god, by redefining order and truth in his own terms, which involved – or so he believed – an upheaval in almost every aspect of the spiritual and ritual foundations of life. Under Akhenaten Maat was spelled out phonetically, evading the convention of using the hieroglyphic sign for the goddess. The royal couple had six daughters who were prominently displayed as powerful symbols of their fecundity. They may also have had sons, including Tutankhuaten (later Tutankhamun) but he was virtually never mentioned.

The exclusive focus on the sun disk deity of the Aten was a logical development of the steady solarization of cult, including that of the king as a divinity in his own right, under Amenhotep III. The Aten had formerly been visualized in traditional form with a sun disk on a falcon-headed human figure. Under Akhenaten the Aten evolved into a solar disk only, its rays each featuring a hand holding the ankh sign of life and caressing the king and queen. Simultaneously Akhenaten transformed Egyptian religion by building it around a much simpler core relationship between one man and his god. Akhenaten and Nefertiti's exclusive status as the intermediaries between the Aten and humanity further amplified the divine power and entitlement of the 18th Dynasty Egyptian king. To some ordinary Egyptians the disruption must have had frightening implications for their own beliefs in what happened after death though such concerns are silent in the surviving record.

To find an analogy for their role as solar intermediaries, Akhenaten and Nefertiti plundered the back catalogue of Egyptian deities for their avatars. They found an answer in the Ennead of nine deities worshipped at Heliopolis, specifically Atum's children Shu (the air, and the void) and Tefnut (moisture). They had made it possible for Atum to bring about the creation. Even that was nothing new. Shu had formed part of an earlier form of the Aten's name in use at least since early in Amenhotep III's reign. Tiye had been conflated with Tefnut, among other deities, as we have already seen.[11] The effect was to help couch Akhenaten and Nefertiti's new order partly within the parameters of tradition and thereby blur the transition.

Akhenaten's fixation with achieving his version of order in a culture with an aversion to change would have consequences for how he and Nefertiti would be treated by Egyptian posterity (see Epilogue). A key ingredient was the suppression of Amun and his powerful priesthood, but whether that was a primary motivation is another matter altogether. The cult of Amun had been so integrated and politicized a component of the 18th Dynasty that it was now virtually a state within a state. There is certainly a case to be made that Akhenaten had in mind enhancing the power of the monarchy at the expense of Amun. He was, after all, only living out the endlessly asserted divinity of the king, but as never before.

## The name of the Aten

'Aten' was an abbreviation of a more complicated formulaic name, translatable in several ways. The version used in Amenhotep III's reign was elaborated by Akhenaten, taking on a more ponderous form that meant something like 'The living Re-Horakhty rejoices in the horizon in the name Shu-Re who is in Aten'. In this form Akhenaten's names and that of the Aten formed a constantly repeated decorative motif, even on functional architectural features like stair rails in the Karnak temple of the Aten.[12] The references to Horus and Shu were deleted by the 9th regnal year, the name being changed to 'The living Re, ruler of the two horizons, rejoices in the horizon in his name as Re the Father who comes in the Aten', matching the shift to portraying the god only as a radiant solar disk. In both versions the name was spread across two cartouches, in the manner of a king and with kingly epithets, unparalleled for a god. These are always shown larger than the cartouches containing Akhenaten and Nefertiti's names which usually appear alongside, clearly presenting the Aten as the supreme divine monarch who ruled with his co-regent representatives on Earth.[13]

# THE REVOLUTION BEGINS

At Karnak building work and the annual cycle of traditional religious festivals ceased. The latter had probably the greatest impact on the lives of most ordinary Egyptians. To the east of Karnak, a large new temple complex was laid out covering about 6.4 acres (2.6 ha). Named the 'Discovery of the Aten' (Gem-pa-aten, see Appendix 7), it was devoted exclusively to the cult and the promotion of Akhenaten (still known as Amenhotep at this early stage of the reign) and Nefertiti as the pivotal and rapturous agents who acted as guarantors of the Aten's power. The so-called 'Mansion of the Benben', the primordial mound of creation, formed part of the new temple complex and featured Nefertiti as the exclusive celebrant (see Appendix 7).

The 18th Dynasty state was well equipped to rake in the funds to support the new cult and the thousands of people working in it. Existing temples and towns across Egypt were faced with a new tax on metals, incense and cloth.[14] This may also have inspired corrupt officials to use the additional imposts and Akhenaten's distraction as an opportunity to worsen existing corruption by enriching themselves further.

The temple project began when Akhenaten issued orders for sandstone to be quarried by 'forced labour' under military supervision for the new temple of the Aten at Karnak. Like every other great pharaonic enterprise, the load was borne by a workforce marched to their duties at the king's pleasure.[15] The work was expedited by the innovatory mass-production technique of using a small, prefabricated rectangular block known now as a *talatat*. Each measured approximately 54 × 27 cm and 27 cm deep (1 Egyptian cubit and ½ cubit respectively). Once in place these blocks were carved with sunken reliefs in the style of the regime, the joins between them plastered over and painted. Their standard size had two unintended consequences. One was that when the temple was demolished, they could be conveniently reused as filling in post-Akhenaten projects at Karnak, thereby preserving them. The other was that by compiling electronic databases of recovered blocks in modern times it has been possible to restore some of the reliefs.[16] This has revealed that Nefertiti featured at Karnak more often than Akhenaten, raising the interesting possibility that she was in some ways the dominant partner.[17]

Colossal statues of Akhenaten, and apparently Nefertiti, embossed the piers in a colonnade around a courtyard. These famously androgynous figures deliberately blurred the royal couple's genders. The statues were originally conventional in design but were subsequently modified into the exaggerated style so characteristic of the more extreme early works of the regime's art. Some of the colossi of the king had headdresses of the feathers worn by Shu, with the possibility therefore that some were intended to represent Nefertiti as Tefnut. In their new city of Akhet-aten they were shown presenting boxes to the Aten which were decorated with the symbols of Shu and Tefnut. The royal couple also appeared on rings as the two deities.[18] The new temple complex served as the venue for Akhenaten's incongruously early sed festival, which took place in the 2nd or 3rd regnal year. This was perhaps the time when his father's 40th regnal year sed festival would have taken place had he lived. If so, the occasion was explicitly rebranded as being in honour of the Aten in which the deceased sun god king had become absorbed.

Akhenaten found work for the priests of Amun who might have been wondering what was going to happen to them. One called May was sent out to a quarry on the road between Coptos and the Red Sea. His task was to secure stone to be used for a statue of the king. Whether this means he was still also fulfilling priestly duties is not clear, but he felt no compunction about mentioning his status, despite the radical changes going on.[19]

The Theban works included a tomb at the far end of the Western Valley of the Kings (WV25), which is of a style and scale appropriate for a royal tomb but was left unfinished. It is likely this was originally intended for Akhenaten. If so, it seems there was no initial plan to relocate, but the tomb was abandoned when the decision was made to leave Thebes. Nobles at Thebes honoured the new king in their tombs, carrying on tradition. These include that of the vizier Ramose (TT55) in which Akhenaten and Nefertiti are shown giving Ramose gold and gifts beneath the beneficent rays of the Aten disk. This motif was to become a standard image in the noble tombs at Amarna. Ramose had served under Amenhotep III, carrying on in post during the first part of Akhenaten's reign.[20]

Akhenaten, still known as Amenhotep, and Nefertiti bestow the vizier Ramose with gifts early in the reign. The scene was unfinished. After Akhenaten's death the royal figures were hacked out, along with the names of the Aten, Akhenaten's throne name and Nefertiti's name. Akhenaten's birth name Amenhotep was left intact. Note the symbolic severance of the Aten's rays, carried out after Akhenaten's death to neutralize the Aten's power. From Ramose's tomb (TT55).

# THE 5TH REGNAL YEAR

By his 5th regnal year at the latest, Akhenaten and Nefertiti's first child, Meryetaten ('Beloved of Aten', sometimes called Meritaten today), had been born.[21] The other five daughters followed in rapid succession thereafter. The two others most significant for the story of the reign were the second and third, Meketaten ('Protected by Aten') and Ankhesenpaaten ('Living for the Aten'), along with their probable brother or half-brother Tutankhuaten.

That same year the royal couple made irreversible decisions. The king took the name Akhenaten, explicitly identifying himself with Aten and detaching himself from Amun. This meant 'effective/useful for the Aten' or 'Creative Manifestation of the Aten'.[22] He did not change his traditional format throne name, Neferkheperure ('Beautiful are the Manifestations of Re', often with the epithet Waenre, 'the Unique One of Re'), probably because the solar Re element remained appropriate. Akhenaten was known by his throne name in official documents, following convention.

Nefertiti was restyled Neferneferuaten-Nefertiti, augmenting her name rather than changing it. The 'nefer' component is usually translated as 'beautiful' but can also mean 'good', 'kindly', or 'happy'. In the first part of her new name, the sign was written four times, indicating something like 'the beautiful beauty of Aten' or 'the beneficent/perfect goodness of Aten'. Both Nefertiti and her husband's new names evoked abstract notions of their roles as the exclusive expressions of the Aten's purpose. They shared the responsibilities involved in promoting the new order. Nefertiti, for example, laid claim to preserving Maat and even appeared in her barge cabin as a ruler smiting Egypt's foes, recorded on a relief which showed Akhenaten in the same pose, a warrior-king convention otherwise generally absent from Amarna art (see later in this chapter).[23] Nefertiti thus participated in roles that were in more normal times fulfilled only by the king. She is most often shown wearing her blue cap-crown, of a design unknown before this time. Other cap-type crowns are only known worn by kings. It must therefore symbolize something special about her status, placing her above other queens.

Indifferent to the resources already expended on their Karnak temple, the decision was also made to move the principal centre of Aten worship to a 'tract of sacred land' downriver from Thebes and north of Abydos today, known then as Akhet-aten ('Horizon of the Aten') and now as Tell el-Amarna.[24] The Akhet- component of the new setting's name, although distinguished by a sign that depicted a horizon with the rising sun, was phonetically identical to several other words such as that for the eye of a god. It resembled the word for sunshine and the Akh- part of Akhenaten's name that meant beneficial or useful. The word 'Amarna' is now used to reference the whole reign.

## AKHET-ATEN (TELL EL-AMARNA)

Akhenaten was neither the first nor last Egyptian king to create a new city, but his was unique in being established and built during one reign and abandoned afterwards.[25] Akhenaten made it clear it was his decision to make the move to a new location, his 'place of the primeval event', and a virgin site where there were no existing monuments. Amarna's unadulterated status was its prime appeal – it did not belong to any god or goddess', proclaimed Akhenaten on his new boundary stelae. These were used to set out in some detail the king's vision for his new home. He announced that it was the Aten, my father, who advised me'. This was a predictable rhetorical claim substituting the Aten for Amun, but it is also possible that he was unwittingly alluding to hallucinations. He was determined to emphasize that it was to him alone that the Aten had revealed where the new settlement should be. He would ignore anyone else's suggestions, and even if Nefertiti had said 'look, there is a nice place for Akhet-Aten in another place', he would not listen to her.[26]

The first Amarna boundary stelae were created in the 5th regnal year, marking the initiation of the project. They were followed by more in the 6th regnal year, making a minimum total of sixteen now known, all carved into the living rock. The new stelae commemorated the progress to date and made for a more precise demarcation of the sacred zone. Both series carried extended proclamations of the king's explanation of his choice of new home, together with his intentions and oaths that were renewed in the 8th regnal year.

Boundary stelae were nothing new but carving them into the living rock was, and so was using them to provide a written rationale of the new foundation. Akhenaten's stelae were unique in both respects and were clearly intended to mark out Akhet-aten permanently, a purpose they were to serve for less than two decades. They were dotted around the huge bay on the east bank where the city developed on a curved north-south axis across the wide Amarna plain, with several more defining a much larger rectangular zone on the west bank.[27] The encircling cliffs were as much a natural fortification as a boundary. Akhenaten had embarked on a potentially dangerous path, and he could not take it for granted that his new home was safe from domestic or even external threats. He was effectively isolating himself and his immediate circle in a remote and defensible corral.

The stelae vary in size, with the largest 25 ft (almost 8 m) high, but some are less than half that. The design was consistent, with the usual curved top and a panel showing Akhenaten, Nefertiti and their two eldest daughters (each waving a sistrum) adoring the Aten. Below that was the text, dominating the stela panel. To the side of the later stelae were statues of the royal couple holding cartouches of the Aten and their own names with their two eldest daughters. All four were shown naked or mostly so. These were created by cutting the stela so far back to leave rock in front for sculptors to fashion the figures which thus protruded from the cliff. Today the stelae are so battered and weathered, with some badly damaged and two destroyed, that they give little sense of what they must once have looked like. In their original form, glittering and painted, they were powerful and highly visible symbols that demarcated the special zone in which Akhet-aten lay.

Akhenaten alluded cryptically to mounting opposition. He had heard something 'more evil than' he had already heard in the previous years of his reign, and anything experienced by his predecessors. He had also been 'caused pain' by things said from a range of sources.[28] The clear implication is that the original plan had been to recreate Thebes and Karnak as the centre of religious worship but that this had been abandoned in favour of a place untouched by tradition or past use, and free of opponents. The relocation to Akhet-aten had the advantage of physically separating the inhabitants of the new settlement from old cult centres. Many will have had no choice about being moved, especially those carrying out the heavy labour. Akhenaten said nothing explicitly about building a new city, but it was obvious one would be necessary. Akhet-aten effectively supplanted the administrative and religious roles of, respectively, Memphis and Thebes, and sidestepped direct confrontation with the vested interests at Karnak, perhaps the source of the 'offensive' threats.

## The site of Akhet-aten

The place chosen for Akhet-aten was a large bay on the eastern bank of the Nile midway between Memphis and Thebes. Archaeology has supported Akhenaten's claims that it was a virgin site, though it lay opposite Hermopolis, home to the cult of Thoth. Most of the known palaces, temples, houses and other buildings occupied a 5 mile (8 km) long zone close to the river and were linked by roads running from north to south. Noble tombs and the Boundary Stelae were located in the eastern cliffs up to 3 miles (5 km) away, with the Royal Tomb another 3 miles further in a remote wadi.

The upper part of Boundary Stela S. On both sides Akhenaten and
Nefertiti, with Meryetaten and Meketaten, adore the Aten. The
main text explaining Akhenaten's intentions continued below.

While Akhenaten and Nefertiti enlarged their family and indulged
their dream, a collection of nobles, architects, engineers, artists,
artisans and workers oversaw and built the new temples as well as
a new city which included palaces, houses, industrial facilities, and
workers' villages. Along with its north suburb, Akhet-aten stretched
out over 4.2 miles (7 km) and was about 0.6 miles (1 km) wide. The
talatat blocks were also used to accelerate the building work though
most of the structures were mainly mudbrick. Over the time that the
city was in use, it is unlikely any of the major structures were fully
executed. Reduced now to their footings and robbed out, there is no
means of working out how far the work had progressed though their
remains demonstrate the extent to which the city had been laid out

by the time the reign ended. Quarrying for some major buildings was still underway in the 16th regnal year.[29]

The huge administrative, industrial and residential settlement from the reign of Amenhotep III at Western Thebes suggests that Akhet-aten was a new version. The city has been described appropriately as a 'vast factory in the service of the king' though this did not affect how the country was already being run.[30] Like all Egyptian cities before the Graeco-Roman era it lacked any facilities for public entertainment or even a large open public meeting space. Although the main centre with its temples, palace and administrative buildings had clearly been planned, the rest of the settlement was characterized by straggling suburbs and other structures across the Amarna plain. This was not an instance of enlightened and coordinated urban planning.

The main features were the temples, their precincts and the avenues that connected them. The new temples were open-plan with none of the dark and exclusive shrines at Karnak or Luxor. The most important temple's name was the Per Aten ('House of the Aten').[31] The main entrance block's principal feature was a sequence of rectangular courts separated by pylons. This lay within a much larger walled precinct, filled with several hundred altars in rows on which sacrificial offerings could be laid out, and with the sanctuary at the far eastern end.[32] There were no obelisks, but the most obvious difference from earlier temples was the absence of cult statues. These had become redundant when the only focus was on Aten, visible throughout the day as the physical sun which the temple's design embraced. Gone were the deeper inner sanctums of the traditional Egyptian temple, congested with effigies of gods.

The design reflects the freedom to plan and build without constraint or having to absorb or clear away existing structures. This was a huge contrast with the temples at Karnak and Luxor, both of which were jumbled accumulations of different phases. Various other temples and chapels at key symbolic locations turned the city into an Aten religious theme park. There was certainly no other entertainment to be had apart from watching the king and his family in processions or participating in religious ceremonies.

In a nod to tradition and as part of the mechanism of absorbing the Heliopolitan solar cult, Akhenaten made provision at Amarna for the burial of the divine Mnevis bull, who represented the conflated force of Re and Atum. A single living bull represented the cult and on its death was traditionally buried at Heliopolis. The new burial place at Amarna has not been discovered.

There were four palaces at Amarna, the principal one being the Great Palace. It lay in the centre and was clearly the royal nerve centre with its bridge over the city's main road that connected the main complex to the so-called King's House. Its full extent has not been explored. Currently, the most instructive one is the North Palace, thought to have been used by Akhenaten's secondary wife Kiya and then his eldest daughter Meryetaten. Measuring about 377 × 476 ft (115 × 145 m), its rectangular plan was based around a longitudinal axis leading from its south-western main entrance which crossed an open court to the 'window of appearances', and beyond to a sunken garden and then the northern range of courts and rooms with a throne room on the axis. This was a classic Bronze Age palace format which obliged a visitor to advance through several zones and rooms before reaching the inner sanctum, echoed in the megarons of the roughly contemporary Mycenaean palaces in Greece, and on a small scale in the main private houses at Amarna. On either side of the building ranges of rooms provided service quarters, a dedicated courtyard for ornamental animals and an altar court.[34] The palace represented the apex of Egyptian society, and this remained true in Amarna.

One of the obvious consequences of Atenism was the suppression of worship of the vast array of other gods in the Egyptian pantheon and especially the female ones, for example Isis and Hathor. Instead of cult statues of gods in household shrines, private individuals substituted reliefs and stelae that depicted the royal couple, often with their children, engaged in activity beneath the beneficent Aten sun. The stelae embodied the king and queen's roles as the exclusive intermediaries between the temporal world and the divine, thereby supplanting the old gods.[35]

This substitution extended to the temples. At Akhet-aten there were in addition to all the other religious facilities at least seven so-called 'sunshade' temples, several of which at least were on the south-east side of the city.[36] The idea of the 'sunshade' temple was not new, but the number was. They were dedicated to sun worship, but each was in the name of one of the royal women of Amarna including Tiye, Nefertiti, some or all of their daughters and temporarily Akhenaten's lesser wife Kiya (discussed in more detail below) before her temple was usurped in favour of Meryetaten.[37] They seem also to have served as the Amarna version of memorial-mortuary chapels.[38]

Private observations of the old cults did not cease. Ordinary people at Amarna continued to believe in at least some of the traditional gods and venerated them openly. The protector dwarf god Bes remained a favourite, even turning up on a gold ring in the Royal Tomb at Amarna, while Amun and Isis retained a presence in the funerary chapels of some workers, among other gods.[39] What is not clear is the extent to which this happened, whether such practices were tolerated, or whether they represented subtle and conservatism which the state was powerless to prevent. The most likely explanation is a combination of both.[40]

# THE ROYAL ENTOURAGE AND FAMILY LIFE

Akhenaten made it clear in his boundary stelae that Akhet-aten would be where he and Nefertiti lived in their respective residences. Amarna was also where he and Nefertiti, and Meryetaten, were to be buried.[41] Meryetaten alone of their children was cited by the 5th regnal year but given the rapid appearance of siblings she was already probably at least two years old. Her sister Meketaten was added retrospectively to the stelae a year or so later. In the next few years, these two would be joined by several other sisters:

Ankhesenpaaten, Neferneferuaten-Tasherit ('the Younger', see Appendix 7), Neferneferure, and Setenpre. The Re- suffix names of the youngest two make it probable they were born and named after the name of the Aten had acquired its later form in around the 9th regnal year.

Tutankhuaten might have been born around the middle of the reign but presumably before the Aten's name change and the birth of the two younger daughters. A letter from the Mitanni king Tushratta to Akhenaten includes in its greetings a reference to 'your sons'. This implies Akhenaten had male offspring, though it could be a standard formula.[42] Tutankhuaten was undoubtedly a member of the court circle and close to Tiye (see Chapter 15 where his parentage is discussed). His virtual absence from the record at this date is frustrating, but normal for princes in the 18th Dynasty.

The most prominent surviving member of Amenhotep III's court was the dowager queen Tiye, together with her daughter Baketaten. Baketaten ('maidservant of Aten') was only ever called King's Daughter of his Body and is known principally from depictions showing her with Tiye at Amarna. Little is known about her, including her age. She is never called the King's Sister which might have been expected if she was Akhenaten's sibling.[43] Her name belonged strictly to the Atenist era, so it is feasible she was one of the known daughters of Amenhotep III, none of whom is attested during Akhenaten's reign, and had changed it.[44] This sort of ambiguity is typical of the problems that beset Egyptian royal family relationships, compounded by Baketaten later joining the ranks of the Amarna royal 'disappeared'.

Tiye appears in the Amarna tomb of her steward Huya, who had accompanied her, doubtless along with other members of her personal household, from Thebes to the new city. Huya's tomb is one of the two with reliefs depicting the 12th regnal year 'durbar' (see below), giving us an idea of at least how long she survived. Huya's titles were listed in his Amarna tomb and are certainly compatible, like his name, with the idea that he was another scion of the family of Yuya and Thuya. Huya enjoyed a range of exalted positions on her personal staff by that stage, described in his tomb at Amarna (see next chapter). Huya's name obviously had phonetic links to the names of Yuya's family – indeed, his name was a variant of Yuya's and Thuya's.[45] His proximity and loyalty to the queen in her later life makes the idea that he was another, but younger, kinsman very likely.

All Huya's titles were overseer-class supervisory posts, regardless of the different ways this word is translated today, showing that he was in charge of the royal harem, treasury, and 'House of the Great Royal Wife' (Tiye).[46] Tutankhuaten may have been brought up in the royal harem at Gurob in the Faiyum where the famous bust of Tiye was found (see below), suggesting that during her time as queen and then as dowager she presided over the establishment, which dated back to Thutmose III's reign.

For all his idealism, Akhenaten and Nefertiti toured their new home with military escorts. They, their daughters and their attendants rode around Akhet-aten in a cavalcade of chariots, followed by the similarly mobilized and gleeful elite, maintaining the well-established 18th Dynasty style of displaying status. Their chariot wheels spinning as they cruised along the Amarna Strip, the vehicles and their passengers made for a new form of religious pageantry that substituted the living god and his family for the old processions of cult statues. Meanwhile, the populace prostrated themselves as the luminaries passed, or at least were portrayed as doing so. It was the only public leisure activity they were treated to.

Nefertiti and Akhenaten were depicted in palace settings engaged in unparalleled intimate poses and settings, often with their daughters. The intensity of some of the scenes of Akhenaten and Nefertiti suggests they were sexually infatuated with one another, emphasized by flaunting their progeny. That was not the only way they advertised their interest in one another. On a pair of talatat blocks from Karnak the two were shown arm in arm sidling towards their marital bed, an image more reminiscent today of a pair of narcissistic celebrities smugly posing in their bedroom for a gossip magazine.[47]

In a scene in the tomb of the dedicated loyalist Mahu (TA9), Chief of Police at Amarna, Akhenaten and Nefertiti were shown riding in a chariot with Meryetaten.[48] The child uses a stick to egg the horses on while her naked father at the reins turns back to face Nefertiti, similarly unrobed, seemingly about to kiss her.[49] While hardly the same as a lucky paparazzi photograph, the scene must have been based on commonplace displays by the family. The royal couple and their children presented themselves unclothed at the 'window of appearances' in the palace to bestow gifts on favoured officials. Such uninhibited displays would be compatible with the ideology of the regime in which fertility was so important. Even in reliefs where they are shown dressed, the garments were as revealing as possible. These scenes were exceptional in royal art and were not followed afterwards other than briefly under Tutankhamun with his queen.

## Nefertiti's sister Mutbenret

Nefertiti had brought with her a sister called Mutbenret (sometimes read as Mutnodjmet and leading to the suggestion she eventually became Horemheb's queen – see Chapter 17 and Appendix 5; both names meant the same: 'Mut is sweet'). Mutbenret made occasional appearances in reliefs depicting the royal family, usually with her nieces. She cut a raffish figure at court carrying an ostrich feather fan as a mark of her nobility, often accompanied by her familiars, a pair of male and female dwarfs who followed on behind with her personal fanbearers. Mutbenret's dwarfs had extravagant names, the female being called Queen Reneheh ('To Eternity') and the male one Mut's Father Para ('The Sun'). Both names were preceded by the word for a vizier, evidently awarded to make them figures of fun – the English terms 'His Excellency' and 'Her Excellency' are probably a close equivalent in this context.[50] They may have belonged to a pygmy tribe such as the Libyan Nasamonians described as 'dwarfs' by Herodotus.[51] Mutbenret seems not to have married during the Amarna period, which is unsurprising since a husband might have proved intrusive or a threat. She was never depicted participating in Atenist rites even though she was clearly present during ceremonies. Against the weighty symbolism of Akhenaten's world Mutbenret's idiosyncratic style must have added some colour as perhaps the faintly unsuitable and eccentric younger sister of the queen.

The nuclear family was not quite as nuclear as the idyllic reliefs made it look. The Amarna Letters include references to foreign princesses being sent to Akhenaten's court. One was Tushratta of Mitanni's daughter Tadukhepa, mentioned in a letter from him that also referred to 'the rest of your wives'.[52] Tadukhepa was the niece of Amenhotep III's lesser wife Gilukhepa.

By the 9th regnal year Akhenaten had acquired a wife called Kiya, attested on various artefacts and reliefs from Amarna.[53] Kiya was prominent enough for her name to appear on monuments dedicated in her name, including a sunshade temple. Kiya had at least one daughter who appears on reliefs with her and Akhenaten, her name deleted and usurped, and wearing a plaited sidelock. Kiya was known, exceptionally, as 'Great Beloved Wife of the King of Upper and Lower Egypt' and as 'the noblewoman', but despite these titles she did not last long.[54] Nor did she ever find a role as an intermediary with the Aten; that remained the exclusive preserve of Akhenaten and Nefertiti.

Kiya's origins are unknown. Various theories have been mooted, including that she was a Mitanni princess, perhaps even Tadukhepa, but there is no real substance to any of these. Her name resembles one of the Egyptian words for a monkey (*ky*) and was perhaps a pet name.[55] If so, Kiya may have had a more formal original name that was not normally used and which we do not know. Kiya has been proposed as the mother of Tutankhamun but there is nothing in the record to support this idea (see Chapter 15 for the controversial DNA evidence).

Two more girls of the Amarna royal circle, the ephemeral Meryetaten-Tasherit and Ankhesenpaaten-Tasherit (both 'The Younger'), are attested on inscribed blocks from Hermopolis, and a few other instances.[56] Nothing of any substance is known about them except that one was apparently born to a mother who was a daughter of a Great Royal Wife.[57] That has led to speculation Akhenaten fathered them by his elder daughters of the same names. Given the royal couple's enthusiastic flaunting of their fertility within the context of a cult, and the lack of any Egyptian taboos about incest, one must accept this as a possible explanation among several others. However, it is doubtful the elder Meryetaten and Ankhesenpaaten were old enough to bear children unless the pregnancies occurred very late in the known length of the reign. By then Meryetaten was married to the mysterious Smenkhkare anyway. The alternative is that the names were invented as a means of replacing Kiya and her daughter after their disappearance, minimizing the modifications needed to the reliefs. The Tasherit girls are only known in contexts where they were substituted for Kiya and her anonymous daughter, and all at around the same time.[58] Without any other evidence for these children's lives their story has nowhere to go.

## LIFE AT AKHET-ATEN

Building Akhet-aten was the most profligate exercise engaged in by any 18th Dynasty king to date. It was only possible because the king was wholly unaccountable. Temple revenue was diverted there away from Amun to Aten (in practice Akhenaten), to whom it now belonged, along with the income from new taxes and from his patrimony.

Establishing Akhet-aten rendered obsolete most of what had been built before at Thebes. Akhenaten and Nefertiti proceeded

on their ecstatic course, oblivious to or unconcerned by the consequences either for individuals or Egypt. For some, of course,
mainly certain members of the elite who had spotted the chance
to gain office and honours if they supported the regime or even the
artisans allowed to experiment with new styles of expression, there
were opportunities.

Decamping to Amarna had relied from the outset on the involvement of several high officials like Huya, some of whom would play
important roles after Akhenaten's reign. Their responsibilities,
recorded in their new Amarna tombs (see below), showed that the
system of patronage and reward carried on as normal, including
officials to manage Akhenaten's patrimony. Ramose was a military
commander and scribe who also supervised the administration of
Amenhotep III's estate. Any, another scribe, was the Steward of the
Estate of Amenhotep II. Other officials who were resident at Amarna
held titles familiar from earlier times like Mahu, Chief of Police,
and May, whose various posts included being Overseer of Cattle on
the Estate of Re at Heliopolis (see below).[59] Mahu's duties included
supervising guards on Amarna's perimeter, marked out by the stelae,
dealing with any trouble in the workers' villages as well as in the city
proper and providing security for royal processions. The Amarna
dream was not immune to potentially dangerous levels of dissent
and opposition.

## The high official Ay

One of the new leading lights at Amarna was Ay, at the time a
senior military officer whose titles were listed in his tomb (TA25).[60]
These included several titles such as the King's beloved scribe, the
King's Right-Hand Standard-Bearer, and Master of all the King's
Horse, which were carried on into the reign of Tutankhamun.[61]
These resemble very closely the panoply of colourful titles enjoyed

by Yuya, Tiye's father, especially the additional honorific ones of the king's 'friend' and 'principal companion', and especially the crucial God's Father, a cryptic term that seems to have included father-in-law of the king among its implicit meanings.[62] Such titles strengthen the case for claiming Ay was Akhenaten's maternal uncle, and even that he might have been Nefertiti's father, just as Yuya had been Tiye's.

Ay's vowel-based and unusual name certainly resembled Yuya's. Modern transliterations tend to obscure the fact that Ay and Yuya were phonetically similar, and so were Tiye and Thuya.[63] Their written forms in hieroglyphs varied more than usual for names, suggesting that those who wrote them down were uncertain how to express them. The names are obviously not identical, but they are more like each other than they are other Egyptian names. Ay's profile in reliefs and paintings supposedly bears some comparison with Yuya's, though this is a very unreliable basis for arguing a connection.[64] With Tiye as queen her family was already so dominant that they would have been unlikely to want the spoils to be shared with anyone else. This factor alone, by default, makes Ay's membership of the family a possibility. He was also married to a woman known now for convenience as Tey, but which was in Egyptian the same as Tiye, perhaps another relative.[65]

Unfortunately, unlike Tiye, Nefertiti never made any reference to her parents, making it impossible to confirm whether Ay had a blood connection to her. Ay made a great deal of the fact that his wife (and future queen) Tey only served as 'wet-nurse of the Good God's [i.e. king's] Great Wife Neferneferuaten-Nefertiti'. This apparently rules Tey out as a candidate for Nefertiti's mother but suggests by virtue of her post that she was another key to Ay's success.[66] Given the precedent of Ahmose-Nefertari's nurse Rai, who seems to have been a relative of that queen (based on their both possessing the congenital overbite), it is possible Tey was also connected to the royal line by descent through some route.[67] One thing is certain though: whatever his origins, Ay would rise to succeed Tutankhamun as king, and with Tey by his side, and this fact alone suggests that he had some special qualification or entitlement. If Tutankhamun's unusually small tomb (KV62) was formerly Ay's, the case for him being a close relative of Yuya and Thuya's is even stronger (see Chapter 16).

Akhenaten also created his own 'new men', a familiar tactic for a new regime wishing to ensure a fresh batch of loyalists. The only concession to tradition was the appointment of one known high priest of the Aten, Meryre i (there were two important officials of this name at Amarna), whose origins are unknown. Meryre's tomb reliefs made it clear that he was subordinate in the cult to Akhenaten, in whose reported speech the king said, 'Behold, I am giving you to myself, to be the Greatest of Seers of the Aten of the House of Aten'. This was done out of 'love' for Meryre and because he was a 'servant, who listens to the instruction'. His wife Tenro was attributed with saying that Akhenaten, 'master of lifetime', was the source of time itself.[68]

May, the King's Right-Hand Fanbearer (and several other titles, including General of the Lord of the Two Lands), gave thanks to Akhenaten for plucking him from the obscurity of poverty and rewarding him with office and status. Joining in with Akhenaten's dream must have been an easy decision for May to make. No wonder he praised the new city as 'great, the big, the beloved . . . the mistress of favour, rich in possessions'.[69] Some of these people, however loyal they might have seemed at the time, were equally quick to switch horses when the wind changed a few years later. Others went down with the ship.

'All the world, they do their work,' said Akhenaten in his Hymn to the Aten, proceeding to paint a picture of a rustic idyll with no mention of the forced labour necessary to realize his vision.[70] The Amarna workforce had to be housed and fed, and then there were the logistics needed to service a new city with a transplanted population that ran into tens of thousands. The prodigious capacity of the Egyptians to pull off vast engineering projects has always staggered later ages; but there were limits, as had become evident under Amenhotep III. The work must have been rushed, compromised and was ultimately incomplete.

There was nothing egalitarian about Akhenaten's revolution. Workers' villages have been identified, linked to the city by a network of roads. One, for the labour force creating the new tombs, lacked access to water and cultivatable land. Effectively a forced labour camp, it was equipped with features to make sure the residents could not leave and were under constant surveillance by the army.[71] Archaeology in recent years has begun to uncover evidence of the price paid by some of the workers involved whose remains were deposited in dedicated pit-grave cemeteries. It is impossible to know how many of them were indigenous Egyptians and how many were slaves, or the descendants of slaves, seized in Egypt's wars.

Many of the bodies showed signs of a lack of nutrition resulting in characteristic underdevelopment of teeth enamel, evidence of childhood starvation. Scurvy was also present. The general stress under which the Amarna population lived resulted in an adult population unusually short in stature for dynastic times when compared to studies from other sites and periods. Men averaged 5 ft 4 in (1.63 m) and women 5 ft 0 in (1.52 m).[72] Signs of bone and muscle conditions including injury and degenerative joint disease were also common, the latter visible in over 77 per cent of adult bodies, and with over 67 per cent having fractured bones. These were all consequences of accidents and carrying heavy loads. Many of the individuals had died young, one study finding that over half (57 per cent) of the bodies examined were aged seven to fourteen years (more than a quarter of whom had suffered fractures of some sort). Few of the adults were older than their mid-twenties at death.[73] Mummification in these poor graves had not taken place – it was always the preserve of the better-off – and grave goods were mainly limited to pottery vessels.[74] The nature of the burials was thus dramatically different from those of the upper classes.

Circumstances at Amarna were not necessarily any better at other times in the New Kingdom, but the height difference suggests that conditions there were worse than usual. However, physical injuries such as fractures and skeletal wear from heavy lifting, and a variety of ailments caused by heavy labour, are known from human remains belonging to the general Egyptian population, in marked contrast to the bodies of the elite, especially upper-class women.

Zealots like Akhenaten never pay the social rent, but then nor for the most part had any of his predecessors. He had been brought up in a phenomenally wealthy and privileged court that included a mother whose ego was in inverse proportion to her size and a father whose smiling colossi portrayed him as semi-divine. The exploitation of the workforce to pursue pharaonic ambitions was nothing new. If we were only able to associate other cemeteries with projects such as Hatshepsut's memorial-mortuary temple the same phenomenon would surely be found.

## HOUSING

The houses of the elite at Amarna are the only such examples surviving from the New Kingdom. They illustrate another way in which all Akhenaten had done was relocate the opportunities for the elite, rather than change Egyptian society. Built of mudbrick with timber fittings, they suffered from having been partially dismantled and cleared out when the city was abandoned. Their plans show an unsurprising emphasis on formal and public reception areas. These villas sat within walled compounds containing support structures like granaries and accommodation for livestock, resembling the haciendas of Latin America, and were surrounded by the far more unprepossessing residences of the ordinary people who were thus constantly reminded of their relative status.[75]

The house of the vizier Nakht (or Nakhtpaaten) is one of the largest and better known. Located in the south of the city, its central feature was a four-columned hall that aped in miniature form palace architecture. Such designs made use of public architectural features to draw attention to the owner's formal status.[76] Accordingly, the structure was built on a raised platform. The house had an eight-pillared loggia, administrative rooms and private residential areas, which included bedrooms and even a bath. The decoration featured loyalist art in stone showing the king worshipping the Aten and an inscription itemizing Nakht's achievements and qualities much in the way that the tomb chapel of Rekhmire had listed his years before. Accommodation was not included for servants or slaves who must therefore either have lived in a separate structure or made do with floors or any other available space.[77] Other elite houses mirrored the design and loyalist decorations, with the key factor in scale being the owner's ranking. The richest examples had upper floors.[78]

Amarna was a sprawling settlement that included packed slums as well as palatial private houses and glittering temples. Much of the city was given over to industry, the production and distribution of food, the keeping of animals and other everyday activities.[79] While Akhenaten and Nefertiti promenaded along the city's main highway in their chariots the side streets were choked with refuse. The rich might have enjoyed the benefits of primitive plumbing and had the labour to keep their homes moderately clean, but the rest of the population could do little more than throw their rubbish out of their doors. There were neither sewers nor the rainwater to flush them through. The city depended on large numbers of private and public wells.[80]

For all his religious idealism and utopian vision, Akhenaten and Nefertiti had little to offer most of their people. Nor is there any suggestion that was their intention. They relied on the existing social structure to fulfil their requirements and the traditional acceptance of their position in the hierarchy by those lower down the ladder.

Akhenaten and Nefertiti make offerings of boxes embellished
with the attributes of Shu and Tefnut, accompanied by their three
eldest daughters. The early name of the Aten is shown at top left
and top centre and on the offerings, placing this probably between
the 8th and 9th regnal years. From the tomb of Ipy (TA10).

## TOMBS AT AMARNA

To the east in a remote wadi the Royal Tomb (TA26) was begun in
accordance with Akhenaten's wishes expressed in his 5th regnal year
that he and his family be buried at Akhet-aten.[81] The eastern setting
for the royal and noble tombs, in contrast to the west bank at Thebes,
is often explained as being linked to the Atenist interest in the rising
sun. There were other reasons. The eastern cliffs and wadis were
more suitable than the west bank. The tombs were easier to cut out
and decorate using labourers based in secured settlements around

Amarna. They could also be protected more easily from robbers and any other potential threats to the regime.

The Royal Tomb was similar in concept to those in the Valley of the Kings but was laid out differently with some innovative features. The entrance was via a stairway that led to a sloping corridor off which two side ranges of rooms exited. At the bottom of the corridor was an unprecedented second stairway that led down to the well shaft room and immediately into the burial chamber. The lateral ranges leading off the main corridor were for family members.[82] The elaborate tombs of nobles including men such as Ay, Tiye's steward Huya, and the multi-office holder May, were also prepared in at least two other areas to the north and south.[83] The northern ones were connected by road to three so-called 'Desert Altars', perhaps serving as the public focus of mortuary cults for the elite deceased.[84]

The nobles' tomb reliefs are the most important source of visual evidence for life at Amarna but were dominated by various records of royal religious events. These included showing the nobles riding to these occasions in chariots and participating in the receipt of tribute from Syria and Kush and other places. Instead of them adoring the Aten, in almost every instance the reliefs show Akhenaten doing so, reflecting his exclusive status as the sole intermediary with the Aten. Another favourite subject was the distribution of largesse by the king and queen to loyalists through the 'window of appearances' at the palaces. These scenes were embellished with details of the active involvement of the noble concerned and his wife, intimate scenes of the royal couple together and with or without their children, and sometimes also with Tiye and Baketaten.[85] Ay, for example, proudly basked in Akhenaten's beneficence, portrayed in his tomb (TA25) festooned with collars thrown down at him by the naked king and his family from the 'window of appearances'.[86]

The tombs of Akhenaten's loyalist elite have no reference to the past or to wider family contexts. Their reliefs and inscriptions served only to depict the noble concerned and his wife enveloped exclusively in Akhenaten and Nefertiti's world, as grateful lesser satellites orbiting them at the centre of their solar universe.

# DESECRATING AMUN

While one army of labourers was struggling to build the new city of Akhet-aten, other work gangs were setting about the exhausting work of obliterating the efforts of their predecessors though this did not start until some way into Akhenaten's rule. Their focus was the desecration of the names of Amun, Mut and Khons (the 'Theban Triad') and thus to displace Amun from his role of presiding over other gods. Visible retribution was as important as the totemic neutralization of Amun's power, even if that included Amenhotep III's name. No evidence survives of Akhenaten issuing a general order to do this, though, of course, he might have done. A great deal of damage was done to the great medieval cathedrals and churches during the English Civil War of the 1640s. Contemporary accounts describe sporadic and opportunistic raids by soldiers conducted in the name of the parliamentary state. They were motivated as much or more by the prospect of theft, indulging in destruction for the sake of it, and emboldened by the knowledge that the government either condoned it or turned a blind eye.[87] It is unlikely many of the Atenist vandals were any different.

At Deir el-Bahari the memorial-mortuary temples, including Hatshepsut's, were attacked by gangs who smashed up carved reliefs. At the Temple of Luxor enterprising Atenists used ladders or scaffolding to reach the lintels in Amenhotep III's Sun Court to hack out references to Amun. Their efforts paled into insignificance compared to the daredevils who obliterated images and the name of Amun on the top of Hatshepsut's obelisks at Karnak. Thutmose III's giant solo obelisk was also assaulted, the damage still visible in modern Rome where it stands today. A surviving granite lintel from Bubastis depicts identical but opposed panels of Amenhotep II presenting gifts of water or wine to Amun-Re. The figures of Amun-Re and his name were hacked out, and not replaced until the reign of the 19th Dynasty pharaoh Seti I.[88] Given the conservative sensibilities most people nurse for cherished institutions and beliefs, this was a dangerous game. The damage might temporarily have helped suppress the worship of Amun publicly but risked bitterness. However, no other god was treated this way, reflecting the evidence for other traditional cults surviving in some private settings.

The damage done to Amun's name provides interesting instances of the minimal level of literacy that prevailed. The roving iconoclasts knew exactly what they were looking for, or at least thought they did. While they recognized the name of Amun they also sometimes became confused when the same hieroglyphs appeared in other words, hacking them out, too. This occurred typically with words containing the paired hieroglyphs for *mn*, suggesting the gangs had been given instructions they did not fully understand. They played safe by hacking out other nouns and verbs that to them resembled Amun, which were in fact irrelevant.[89]

Almost all the royal tombs in the Valley of the Kings that existed by this time were subsequently robbed out. This nefarious work, which had probably already been underway for some time, might have increased during the Amarna period, taking advantage of the reduced state and security presence in the Theban area. The thieves may even have convinced themselves that robbing tombs filled with effigies and representations of traditional gods was legitimate under Akhenaten. However, it is not now possible to detect when any of these thefts took place.

## THE DURBAR

The so-called 'durbar' took place at Akhet-aten in the 12th regnal year. The term is derived from the ceremonial events held in British India at which dignitaries gathered to demonstrate their loyalty. Akhenaten's 'durbar' was depicted in at least two noble tombs, including one owned by Tiye's steward Huya. An inscription provides the date and the description of Syrian and Nubian tribute arriving as 'all foreign countries gathered as one', including 'the islands in the middle of the sea' (presumably Cyprus, Rhodes, and Crete). Akhenaten and Nefertiti were shown being carried to the celebrations on an extravagant litter in the company of large numbers of half-bowed officials, and then seated in an open-air kiosk to receive the tribute. The king and queen were illustrated as identical and barely overlapping figures holding hands and shown with six daughters, who must all have still been alive at this stage. This is taken by some to be sound evidence that Nefertiti was ruling alongside her husband as a joint monarch and sharing his divine status.[90] The public purpose of the occasion is unknown though numerous possibilities have been suggested, such as another sed festival.

There is no evidence of Akhenaten's army taking part in any war in Western Asia, for example against the Hittites who had defeated Mitanni, though this did not stop some Egyptian allies begging for help. It was not apparently forthcoming beyond routine enforcement of loyalty. Akhenaten's army was led by a man called Paatenemheb, Master of the Soldiers of the Lord of the Two Lands, known from his incomplete tomb at Amarna (TA24), but he is not attested fighting in any war.[91] Individual soldiers are attested in the city, some drawn from Egypt's vassal states like the Syrian Terura who lived at Akhetaten with his wife, or the chariotry officer Ranefer who was able to afford an impressively decorated two-storey house.[92]

The only attested military incident during Akhenaten's reign was an engagement in Nubia which took place in the 2nd or 12th regnal year, recorded on a shattered stela set up at Buhen and another at Amada. This was a punitive expedition led by Thutmose(?), the viceroy of Kush, supposedly against a Nubian rebellion. By Egypt's imperialist standards it was a piffling sideshow. Just 145 living captives were taken, and an unknown number killed.[93] The most likely explanation is that the settlement this thug attacked like a rogue medieval baron, an otherwise unknown place called Ikayta, was a target of opportunity chosen as a source of slave labour and other valuables on a spurious pretext. The action was conducted, of course, in Akhenaten's name, which gave it a semblance of legitimacy, but it is more likely the viceroy was exploiting the king's distraction with more ethereal matters to engage in some private and profitable piracy.

There were more serious potential consequences for an imperialist regime that had built its reputation on war and conquest. The long period of peace under Amenhotep III had deprived Egyptian soldiers of the chance to lay their hands on booty and receive gifts of land and slaves from the crown. Any Ahmes-Ibana types missed out on the chance to enrich themselves and their descendants. Akhenaten extended the absence of such opportunities. Thutmose, the villainous viceroy of Kush, was trying to compensate for the king's negligence of his prospects. His actions were a symptom of the state losing control.

## INTERNATIONAL RELATIONS

Akhet-aten was the findspot in 1887 of the so-called Amarna Letters. The building in which they were found was identified on brick stamps as the 'House of Pharaoh's Correspondence'. These were mostly the incoming cuneiform diplomatic letters from Asiatic powers on clay tablets to Amenhotep III and Akhenaten, and some retained copies of outgoing correspondence.[94] They show that the new city was the epicentre of royal power and international diplomacy. Similarly, the presence of Mycenaean Greek pottery is proof of trading connections across the eastern Mediterranean and Aegean seas. Unfortunately, the letters cannot normally be precisely dated unless they carry an Egyptian docket. The appearance of a version of Akhenaten's regnal name, normally 'Naphurreya/Namhurya' or similar, in a few proves they were written during his reign but could have preceded the move to Akhet-aten.

The surviving archive (clearly only a small part of the original) included correspondence from a narrow world of leaders in the Near East, numbering a few dozen at most. Some were rulers of states who regarded themselves as equivalents of the Egyptian king and addressed him as 'brother', an insult for a man who was exalted in Egypt beyond comparison with any other mortal.

Other rulers of lesser states were semi-autonomous but beholden to Egypt in various ways. Their relationships with the pharaoh were largely restricted to letter and gift exchange. They and he addressed each other in elaborately respectful ways and sent each other presents. These gestures were intended to solicit an equivalent response so they could bask in the acknowledgement of their own international significance. Great weight was attached to this process, especially if the reply and gifts fell short of expectations. The process was slow. Letters arrived months or years apart. The rulers rarely if ever met in person and largely relied on emissaries to act as intermediaries. The result was that they created their own perception of the Egyptian king based on his generic image, blurred by the anecdotes from their diplomats and the tone of letters they received.

Some of the correspondents became worried that Akhenaten's Egypt was not the powerful, generous and responsive neighbour it had been under Amenhotep III and looked back with nostalgia. The dowager Tiye remained a major figure to contend with, or at least so certain correspondents believed. Her status and influence were recognized in widowhood by foreign kings who clearly believed that she was a more reliable authority figure than her son.

Tushratta of Mitanni wrote to Tiye, reminding her of the close relationship he had enjoyed with the late Amenhotep III, even though that friendship was an artefact largely of his imagination. The letter was a complaint, Tushratta alleging that Amenhotep had promised him statues of solid gold but that Akhenaten, who must have succeeded before the statues were made, had dispatched plated wooden statues. An incredulous Tushratta, who had expected Akhenaten to treat him 'ten times better' than Amenhotep III had, pointed out that since gold was 'like the dirt in your country' he wanted to know why the statues had not been sent.[95]

One agitated letter was sent to Tiye, apparently as a last resort to ask her to intercede with Akhenaten. Burra-Buriyaš of Karaduniyaš (Babylon) wrote to say that he and his brother were determined to be as friendly to Akhenaten as they had been to Amenhotep III.[96] He complained that some of his merchants had been killed in Canaan, then under Egypt's control. He demanded that the new king see to it that the culprits were apprehended and executed but enclosed a gift of lapis lazuli as an enticement.[97]

Clearly Burra-Buriyaš had believed that Egypt under Akhenaten would continue to police its subject lesser states. He also expected to receive generous gifts, moaning later that a short-measure present of gold had arrived, with less than a quarter appearing when melted and even that 'looked like ashes'. Less picky than Tushratta, he asked for wooden models of animals, even secondhand ones that could be dispatched immediately. This letter also discusses the transport of a Karaduniyaš princess to Akhenaten supervised by his envoy Ḥaya. Burra-Buriyaš's main concern was that Ḥaya had brought an unsuitably small number of chariots and soldiers and demanded a better-sized escort for the princess. Burra-Buriyaš was placated by a vast consignment of goods including numerous gold, silver, ivory and ebony items, furniture, vessels, linen, statuettes, and valuable substances like oil.[98]

There is a hint here that Akhenaten was not bothered about keeping these rulers happy or maintaining cordial relations. Nor is it even apparent that he personally engaged in the correspondence. Akizzi, mayor of the city of Qatna in Syria, was in fear of one Aziru, ruler of Canaan, who was in league with the Hittite king Shuppiluliuma I. He begged Akhenaten to send troops or else 'the country will be in fear of Aziru'. It was not the only such plea he made, explaining that 'the king, my lord, will not come forth'.[99] Egypt's new king had other things on his mind than sending out armies to fight in Egypt's interests or to protect vassal states.

# THE IDEOLOGY OF ATENISM

Until the accession of Akhenaten, royal religious ideology of the 18th Dynasty was largely based on the notion of the king as Amun's chosen one. This maximized his chance of maintaining control over the population. He repaid that by endowing the cult of Amun with some of the wealth obtained through divinely sponsored warfare and the resultant tribute. Other deities in the Egyptian pantheon were integrated into this wider vision of Egypt's destiny, benefiting in varying degrees from similar gifts that amounted to a vast proportion of the nation's human resources.

Akhenaten's displacement of Amun, Osiris and other key state deities after his accession had the potential to undermine the whole legitimacy of the state and the dynasty. He also threatened the vast institution of Amun worship, its temples and most importantly its influential and powerful priesthood. One could be forgiven for suspecting that Akhenaten was at least a little mad. He was certainly both a narcissist and an obsessive. Akhenaten and Nefertiti ploughed on, buoyed up by the certainty of fanatics and bankrolled by having almost unlimited resources at their disposal.

Early on in his reign, Akhenaten had given a speech at Karnak about his beliefs. Only a fragment survives from the relief that recorded it, but it explains a core part of his reasoning. He had noted, he said, how the representations and temples of the old gods eventually came to nothing, regardless of what they were made from. Their transient nature was in complete contrast to a visible solar god that had been its own progenitor and whose mysteries were beyond anyone to know. He was refuting the whole basis of Egyptian theology, the pantheon of gods and equally importantly of the priests who claimed to be party to the claimed mysteries of these deities made of wood, stone and gold. In a few lines Akhenaten dismissed the idolatrous edifice of traditional Egyptian religion. He presented his country with a far more abstract notion of a god who was above and beyond all, and unknowable. Only he was the messenger and the intermediary.[100]

This was a new idea that was starting to have wider currency across the region, and had echoes in the Old Testament, close to the time Akhenaten made his speech, such as this line from the Book of Isaiah: 'Behold, the Lord rides upon a swift cloud, and shall come into Egypt: and the idols of Egypt shall be moved at his presence, and the heart of Egypt shall melt in the midst of it.'[101] One can only try and imagine the impact when Akhenaten delivered his speech with its similar sentiments to a throng of incredulous priests and officials. In the imagery of Atenism members of the royal family were transmuted into animated cult idols in place of all the old inert ones, their public appearances serving as choreographed *tableaux vivants* of royal divinities in new ceremonies and parades. These were matched by statues and reliefs that depicted only the royal family, for example on the boundary stelae.

Akhenaten's religious ideology was expressed within his so-called 'Hymn to the Sun'. This amounted to a religious and cultural manifesto in which the absolute power of light and its daily renewal was the central theme.[102] Written as if it was Akhenaten speaking to the Aten, he may have composed it himself, but it is just as likely his thoughts were put into its leaden verse by a court poet. The Hymn has also been long likened to the Old Testament's Psalm 104 with which it bears some comparison in its celebration of the beneficent and creative powers of a single deity. This impression is, however, at least in part the result of the way the Egyptian has been translated into modern languages. The similarities between Atenism and ideas emerging in the Old Testament do not mean they were directly connected. They may both be manifestations of a parallel development which grew out of the similar state of cultural and religious evolution in the region.

The Hymn's overall tone is more reminiscent of the late Roman imperial panegyrics composed by a palace lickspittle, amounting more to a grand rhetorical exercise than anything else. Appropriately enough, the Hymn begins with a fulsome list of the Aten, Akhenaten and Nefertiti's names and titles, and at the end reiterates the royal couple's names and titles but in extended form. These are usually left out of modern quotes from the Hymn, thus overlooking this important feature of the composition. In between, the ponderous text describes how the beautiful Aten (identified with Re) rises every day as the force behind all life, dispersing the forces of darkness that preside over the inert landscape of night. Through his rays the Aten is the source of fertility and the infinite range of living beings. The Aten presides over all nations, with all the peoples of the world in places and roles designated by him, meaning that all living entities are in essence depictions of the Aten.

In an interesting evolution of Egyptian thought, Syria and Nubia are cited alongside Egypt, each nation having its rightful place under the Aten's beneficent gaze, 'foreign peoples' being equally entitled to share in the 'inundation in heaven'. There was no expression of hostility towards other deities and therefore we do not know if Akhenaten expressly refuted them, apart from the objection to Amun's traditional role as the supreme creator god amalgamated with the solar deity Re.

Akhenaten's Hymn to the Aten lacks above all else a direction. There was no expectation of a millenarian-style upheaval in the world order or a messianic coming, either of which might have been expected from a cult founded on ecstatic revelations. Instead, the Hymn described an idealized state of affairs, reflected in the boundary stelae that literally set in stone the temporal setting of his spiritual paradise, rather than serving as a guidebook for the journey to a promised land.

Typical for a religious cult is the human agent on Earth, in this instance Akhenaten himself. He alone had been admitted to the innermost mysteries by being made uniquely aware of the Aten's intentions and power. 'There is no one that knows *You*, except your son Neferkheperure-Waenre, because you have told him of your plans and strength,' claimed Akhenaten.[103] This exclusivity is a familiar ingredient in cults, validating the entitlement of the enlightened one to impose his will on others. In Akhenaten's case it also consolidated the absolutism his father and mother had developed.

Atenism arose out of the intense dogmatic and jubilant certainty of two young people, convinced they alone had been enlightened. Nefertiti was probably as important as Akhenaten in constructing the ideology, even if it was all expressed in his words and name. She was manifestly integral to its promotion and reinforcement though her husband always claimed to be the supreme authority. While Akhenaten may have persuaded other people of the truth of his cause, he was unusual as a revolutionary cult leader in also already being a king. He was not a rival authority to the state – he *was* the state. This meant that it was in the interests of those with ambition, or positions to protect, to go along – even play along – with the king's desires, at least for as long as necessary. They were the party faithful, at least so long as it suited them to be, in every sense of the term. In this respect the Aten cult had something in common with modern political movements built around utopian dreams. Unfortunately for Akhenaten, participation in this kind of cult tends to lack resilience. Disappointment and disillusion are common consequences of enlightened visions of paradise, especially once the realization spreads that there is nowhere to go.

The Hymn to the Aten likened night to a fleeting state of death triumphantly defeated by the new dawn, the world reinvigorated beneath the solar rays. The Egyptian theology of death had always been founded on that concept. The process of death and rebirth was managed and overseen by the old gods, each with a dedicated task, and the tribunal presided over by Osiris. The construction of tombs at Amarna, the traces of grave goods like the shabtis in Akhenaten's own tomb, and his expressed determination to be buried there, showed the resilience of core Egyptian funerary practices and Akhenaten's own conservatism. Earlier in Akhenaten's reign an Overseer of the Granaries at the 'Mansion of the Aten' at Karnak, presumably a synonym for Akhenaten's Gem-pa-aten temple, called Hatiay had managed to combine traditional exhortations to the old gods alongside his Atenist credentials on his coffin. Hatiay was buried at Thebes, along with his wife who was a chantress of Amun at Karnak.[104]

The expulsion of most of the old gods was soon to leave the process of death and burial bereft of its traditional agents. Their absence is a conspicuous feature of the Amarna tombs. In Ay's tomb (TA25) the funerary texts invoke a story of a solo journey to the afterlife. 'May you stride through the gates of the underworld', one passage reads before describing the prospect 'of all gifts in the necropolis when your Ba (the unique soul of the deceased's individual personality) rests in your tomb'.[105] With the loss of Osiris and Horus the significance for the king was even more profound. Atenism provided, so far as we know, no theological guidance for the death of a king and the succession. The boundary stelae texts made it clear Akhenaten understood he and his family would die, but he never seems to have made provision for who or what might follow him or even to have envisaged the circumstances in which that would be necessary. The remaining traces of decoration in Akhenaten's burial chamber in the Royal Tomb at Amarna (TA26) conformed only to the routine depictions of the king and queen making offerings to their god.

In the tomb of Tiye's steward Huya (TA1) his lonely mummy is portrayed standing before a pile of offerings from the king while a priest officiates in the company of mourners. Female family members are seen wailing behind the mummy. Under normal circumstances Huya might have been shown adoring Osiris, and having his heart weighed before Osiris by Anubis, but there was no possibility of either for a court loyalist at Amarna.[106] Only the light of Aten mattered as a divine force and context. Death was repositioned as a temporary nocturnal state in anticipation of the new dawn instead of a journey to an afterlife, the mummy becoming an overnight repository for the deceased's soul. This obviously created difficulties with the reality of death and where the deceased was supposed to subsist during the daytime. The latter years of the reign show several signs of stress which may have begun with the deaths of Tiye and Meketaten, especially if the loss of other royal children occurred (see next chapter), and an uncertainty about how to handle the losses.

There was no evangelical or proselytizing zeal to Atenism. The boundary stelae and security patrols helped contain, even symbolically incarcerate, the revolution within the protective confines of Amarna. The old temples might have been shut, but there is little or no evidence that the wider population of Egypt either bought into Atenism or were even encouraged (or forced) to do so. Instances of possible Aten temples elsewhere in Egypt are rare.[107] Akhenaten and Nefertiti never left Amarna once they had moved there, as far as is known. The overwhelming impression is that Atenism was a private club for the royal couple and their trusted familiars, and that their concerns were primarily for the immediate.

Consequently, Akhenaten and Atenism's eventual disappearance was total. There was no admiring folk memory of him and his milieu. No Atenist tradition endured. In part this was attributable to a key flaw. Atenism relied on the king and queen being the exclusive agents through whom the Aten flowed. When they were gone, Atenism went with them. They left no one to inherit their roles and had planned no future for the cult. No 'Pseudo-Akhenaten' ever emerged from the sands of Amarna to revive their ideas.

## THE IMAGE OF THE REGIME

Based on the skeletal remains of Tutankhamun and his predecessors, Akhenaten is unlikely to have stood much more than 5 ft 4 in tall (1.63 m). If the mystery body found in tomb KV55 is Akhenaten's (see Chapter 14) its size is certainly consistent with this and is of a man only a little taller than Amenhotep III.[108] The body believed by some to be that of Nefertiti is of a woman about 5 ft 2 in (1.58 m) in height, the so-called Younger Lady (see Chapter 15). A shattered life-size seated official dyad from Amarna shows Nefertiti significantly shorter than her husband.[109] A small dyad statue of

Akhenaten and Nefertiti showing the couple walking side by side, hand in hand, suggests that she was a little smaller.[110] The obvious objection to this is that the dyad may have followed a stylistic convention of women being depicted smaller than men, and this was certainly the case with some reliefs of the couple while others show them as being equally sized. Non-Amarna Egyptian dyad statues usually represented couples with equal or similar heights (for example in the colossal dyad of Amenhotep III and Tiye from his mortuary temple, or the approximately contemporary dyad of the treasurer Maya and his wife Meryt from Saqqara).[111] Either way, the Amarna royal couple did not make for an imposing pair. Their physical presence relied to a large extent on the theatrical impact of their elaborate headpieces which significantly increased their heights, riding in chariots, and appearing from on high at the 'window of appearances'.

Akhenaten's unusual appearance in many of his reliefs and sculptures has always excited the most comment, including wild speculation especially in the nineteenth and early twentieth centuries.[112] To begin with he was depicted in a conventional way. A 25 in (64 cm) high yellow limestone (but uninscribed) statuette identified as being Akhenaten, which once formed half of a seated dyad, provides what is probably one of the most lifelike depictions of the king.[113] The unusual features are all there, especially his sagging belly and wide hips, but are restrained. This deformation, probably inherited, makes sense of Akhenaten's appearance even though it was subsequently exaggerated in many of his representations. The natural state of his body was apparently treated as evidence of his exceptional qualities and attributes. The head size and features suggest a young man plump and short in stature and unprepossessing in appearance, compatible with the idea that he became king in his late teens or early twenties.[114] His female partner's figure is lost and only one of her arms survives around his back. She might be Nefertiti but if Akhenaten was as young as he looks in this statue, then it was more likely to have been Tiye. This would be consistent with several of his predecessors who were shown with their mothers as the great royal wife early in their reigns.

Egyptian art was traditionally very stylized and although there were distinct differences from era to era it was relatively easy for one generation of artists after another to replicate the work of their predecessors. They were helped by standard grids of proportions, stock poses, and routine compositions. Akhenaten's stylized art introduced a dramatic new level of intimacy and realism in terms of context and setting, especially in the relaxed depictions of the king and queen with their family, as well as incorporating a contradictory and physiologically implausible representation of the human form. Akhenaten's exaggerated features were transposed to representations of other members of his family to reinforce their specialness. This concept is well known in more modern art, often developed for political purposes and to create a strong visual image for the regime in question. An 'Amarna' grid of proportions was devised to help adapt conventional compositions to the new styles. Conspicuous by their rarity are scenes of the king attacking his enemies, so characteristic of earlier reigns in the 18th Dynasty, even though military escorts were occasionally shown.[115] The image of the warrior king had become temporarily obsolete in an age when active conquest had receded into the past, replaced with a new vision of the king whose powers were as an intermediary with his god and whose physical features enhanced his special qualities.

A simple experiment was made with photographs of the well-known bust from Gurob in the Faiyum (and location of one of the royal harem residences) believed to be of Tiye and a sculpted head of Akhenaten from a composite statue (an innovative design created at Amarna), both now in Berlin.[116] These showed that by only modifying slightly the vertical dimension of his face to restore more normal proportions, Akhenaten's unusual features are a surprisingly good match for his mother's though, of course, she may have been depicted in his image (see second colour plate section). At the very least it makes it very unlikely the Tiye bust is of anyone other than her.

From the outset the most obvious difference from earlier official Egyptian art was the ubiquitous presence of the Aten sun disk at the top of each panel, its rays radiating out across the scene, each ending in a hand that metaphorically caressed the king and queen and other people in the scene who were engaged in the activities portrayed. Gone were the conventional gods depicted in human form standing behind or being greeted by the king.

One of the most fascinating consequences was the way prominent individuals adopted the new style and the king's features. A self-portrait of the senior sculptor Bek ('Servant') and his wife from Amarna shows him with the same distended belly exhibited by Akhenaten and Nefertiti, but this is also found on reliefs in tombs of other Amarna officials. The combination of Bek's full, round belly and pleated skirt resembles the image of the Aten solar disk with its radiating rays found at the top of depictions of Akhenaten and his family worshipping the god. This was surely deliberate; he can hardly have failed to notice. Bek's father had worked for Amenhotep III in the same capacity (see Chapter 11). On a stela from Aswan, Bek says he was the apprentice whom Akhenaten 'taught'.[117] This was a typically obsequious claim, and an inscription of the usual sort in which a man of some consequence positioned himself as the exclusive focus of the king. It is more likely Bek, who grew up in Heliopolis where sun worship was paramount, was one of those responsible for 'realizing' the distinctive early so-called 'revolutionary' style of Akhenaten's regime, including the astonishing colossi at Karnak.[118] Bek's work helped create a radical new normal for the image of the regime that would exhibit the exceptional qualities of the royal family and set them apart from others. Exaggeration helped to achieve the desired result, hence the 'stretched' form of Akhenaten's bust and other characteristics like the distended belly and wide hips so typical of the earlier Aten period.

The sculptor Thutmose was another creative force in the Amarna era. He produced artistic works in the latter part of the reign that aspired to a more natural and realistic style. The contents of

Thutmose's studio at Akhet-aten, abandoned along with the rest of the city, included portrait busts of some of the principal players in the drama, but most importantly Akhenaten and Nefertiti. It is clear from the celebrated bust of Nefertiti found in Thutmose's studio, and now in Berlin, that he was eminently capable of producing accomplished works easily comparable with Graeco-Roman classical sculpture. Recent work on the bust has identified modifications that had been made to enhance its visual perfection from what was probably a truer likeness beneath the surface. An unfinished bust of Nefertiti from the same source is a less flattering portrait, but still striking and perhaps truer to life.[119] The famous bust was probably intended as a model for the use of sculptors in the studio to copy. There is also the small limestone standing figure of an older Nefertiti, found likewise in Thutmose's house, that sensitively but authentically depicts the figure of an ageing woman who has borne children.[120] These examples make it more likely that earlier artists such as Bek were deliberately exaggerating royal features for stylistic purposes.

There were other artists at work in Akhet-aten. Iuty was pictured creating a statue of Baketaten on a relief in the tomb of Tiye's steward Huya which we know belonged to the 12th regnal year or later. His proximity to the dowager queen means he is less likely to have played a major role in radicalizing art. Nonetheless, the figure of Baketaten has some of the characteristic features of Amarnan style, including the pot belly, showing that Iuty followed the trend.[121] Alongside these were the artists who produced the astonishingly lifelike and jubilant depictions of the natural world such as birds taking to the air, or fish in the Nile.

The more extreme earlier Amarnan style was thus a matter of stylistic choice rather than an attempt to be realistic. The dynamic naturalism of a flock of birds bursting out of Nile reeds cannot be treated as 'proof' that the exaggerated style must therefore be an equally accurate depiction of its subject. If there was a 'message' it is lost to us. Although huge significance could be attached to the symbolism and intent, and therefore also the change of style during the reign, these were probably the ideas of a very few individuals. The artists of this 'school' were presented with an opportunity to indulge their creative skills by experimenting with defining an era through their work, and they seized the chance. The result perhaps then was Bek being one of those able to dominate to begin with, but either his death or a change in tastes and requirements opened the door to other artists, including Thutmose. One might here consider the enormous influence Arno Breker (1900–91) had on defining the style of sculpture so prized by senior figures of the Nazi regime.[122]

Akhenaten and Nefertiti used theatre and illusion to present themselves as dominant figures and satisfy their own narcissism. Both techniques were well established in Egyptian monumental royal art. Under Akhenaten, royal portraiture was developed into a truly idiosyncratic form based on his authentic appearance but elaborated into an extravagant caricature before reverting to something closer to reality. Akhenaten emerges as one of those historical figures whose minds were absorbed by their radical ideas and ambitions. He escaped the mediocrity of his physical appearance by adopting an image that made him seem otherworldly, above and beyond ordinary human beings. In this respect he was following a tradition that had been steadily evolving under his predecessors even if he had now taken it in a radical new direction.

The temporary projection of Atenism on Egypt was a flash in the pan when set against the wider backdrop of Egyptian culture and history, and it relied on much that had gone before. Akhenaten and Nefertiti's new order contained the seeds of its own destruction. By undermining traditional beliefs, they created uncertainty. They destabilized the Egyptian expectation that an individual king's reign would be conflated with a renewal of the mythological cycle of kingship and belief and upset the legitimization of the dynasty's hold on power. Their innovations overwhelmed what had always been seen as permanent and immutable. This was obviously unsustainable, but unexpected events were about to have a dramatic impact.

# 13

# LATTER DAYS AT AMARNA
## c. 1341–1336 BC

### AKHENATEN, SMENKHKARE
### AND NEFERNEFERUATEN

*Unravelling the events of the final years of Akhenaten's reign and their imme-diate aftermath has taxed Egyptologists for generations. The deaths of Tiye and Akhenaten's daughter Meketaten changed the tone at court dramatically and marked the first uses of the Royal Tomb. Akhenaten died not long after his 16th regnal year and was buried at Amarna with Tiye. He may already have been ruling with a co-regent called Smenkhkare, but he too appears to have died. Regardless of what else happened, including the probable brief co-regency with Nefertiti as a king and then her sole rule, the outcome was the accession of Tutankhuaten, who changed his name to Tutankhamun.*

In less than two decades the ruling dynasty that had once seemed in complete control of Egypt had reached a cliff edge. The story of the latter days of Akhenaten and their immediate aftermath is a remarkable one, and worth documenting in some detail. It is as much a tale of Egyptology as anything else but is not for the faint-hearted. At no other point in Egyptian history has the available evidence been scavenged to produce so many theories, from the plausible and inspired at best to the absurd at worst and involving some that can only be regarded as unasinous.[1] The controversies go nowhere because the evidence does not exist to resolve them. If we set aside the more eccentric cul-de-sacs that have plagued the study of this period, the essential story is relatively simple. The stakes boiled down to who was going to rule Egypt after Akhenaten and what he (or she) would do about the king's religious revolution.

# THE DEATHS OF TIYE AND MEKETATEN

Tiye is last attested alive in Akhenaten's 12th regnal year in reliefs in the tomb of her steward Huya (TA1). Her death is unrecorded though her passing was alluded to in one of the Amarna Letters.[2] She was buried in the Royal Tomb (TA26) at Amarna but did not remain there (see Chapter 14). Fragments of a sarcophagus found in the tomb have been identified as hers.[3] Given her active role in royal life at Amarna, Tiye's death must have had a considerable impact on the regime. When news reached foreign states, their concerns about the ability of Egypt under Akhenaten to fulfil their expectations probably increased. Her loss was soon to be followed by a much more poignant family tragedy.

By the 12th regnal year or soon after Meketaten, the second oldest Amarna princess, was also dead. Her passing was more than just a family tragedy. In his 6th regnal year Akhenaten's second series of boundary stelae had included his oath that such was his heart's gratification with Nefertiti and their children she and Meryetaten and Meketaten, the only ones born by that time, would be caused to live to 'old age'.[4] The hope was more significant than it would be today. His daughter's death must have been a blow to Akhenaten's beliefs and wider confidence in his regime. There is good reason to believe that two of Meketaten's youngest sisters also died around this time. These family catastrophes resulted in an unusual series of commemorative reliefs carved on the walls of the second of the two spur burial suites leading off the main shaft of the Amarna Royal Tomb. Tiye had probably predeceased Meketaten since she is absent from these scenes.

Akhenaten, Nefertiti and their surviving daughters mourn an effigy of the deceased Meketaten. Room γ of the Royal Tomb, wall B.

The furthest room in this spur (Room γ) was used for the burial of Meketaten. One scene showed an effigy of Meketaten, named as her, being mourned by her parents and Meryetaten, Ankhesenpaaten, and Neferneferuaten-Tasherit.[5] A second scene showed the deceased princess, her grieving parents and courtiers and a mysterious baby being carried away by nurses. In this second scene the text next to the dead Meketaten labelled her as 'daughter of the king, of his body, his beloved Meketaten, child of', followed by the lost name and titles of Neferneferuaten-Nefertiti. A similar text was placed next to the nurse carrying away the baby to whom she offers her breast. Although this second passage was more damaged, the name of Neferneferuaten was undoubtedly there and is visible in an old photograph, and so are two hieroglyphic

283

signs compatible with the name of Meketaten.[6] Clearly this relief could only have been conceived of and executed *after* Meketaten's death, rather than being part of the longer-term programme to decorate the tomb.

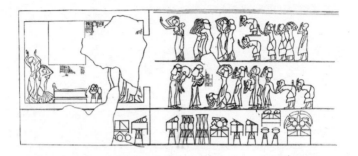

The deceased Meketaten is mourned by her parents and other courtiers. In the lower register of mourners to the right, a baby is being carried away by a wet-nurse. Room γ of the Royal Tomb, wall A.

Two similar scenes were included on the walls of the first room in this range (Room α). Both show the mourning king and queen, along with a group of similarly distressed attendants. One shows another infant being carried away, the other an unidentifiable deceased child on a bier. Despite the damage, the general similarity of the compositions makes it likely that both also showed a deceased child and a baby being carried away but with no surviving key texts, neither can be identified.

The analysis of the scenes has always focused on whether they were intended to be literal representations of real events, which they certainly look like, or were symbolic. Given the context, the likelihood is that they were both but to what degree in either way remains an intractable problem.

The two additional scenes of mourning, the upper one including a baby being carried away, but another was probably shown in the lower register originally. Only the figures of Nefertiti and Akhenaten are identifiable. The dead children involved are unnamed. Room α of the Royal Tomb, wall F.

The simplest explanation is that each of the three scenes depicted the death of one of Akhenaten and Nefertiti's daughters, each of whom was interred in the Royal Tomb, rather than multiple versions of Meketaten's death.[7] This would explain why only three daughters are portrayed honouring the statue of Meketaten. The other two, by elimination, would have to be Neferneferure and Setenpre, both attested earlier in the reign but who later disappear. Plague has been suggested but in a pre-modern society losing several children from different causes was not unusual. The likelihood is that the deaths occurred over a relatively short period of time.

The evidence of the boundary stelae is that Meketaten was born by the 6th regnal year. Unless her death did not come until the 16th regnal year at least it is unlikely she was old enough to bear a child, though it is not impossible. Nonetheless, a theory has long circulated that the baby was Tutankhuaten, though there is nothing to support this.[8] Akhenaten's fifth and sixth daughters Neferneferure and Setenpre (if the other two deceased children were them) were certainly too young to have had children by then.

The scenes were irretrievably damaged by vandals in 1934, so any further discussion relies on early drawings and photographs. One theory is that the Meketaten death scene includes her symbolic rebirth after death.[9] This is not as bizarre as it sounds and might also explain the other two scenes, each thereby including a phantasm baby of each dead princess. There is no precedent in Egyptian funerary art for this format, but Atenism had done away with the old gods presiding over death and rebirth, without substituting any alternative.

Atenism had brought in a different emphasis on realism from which some older forms of symbolism had been expelled. One of these was the nursing of an infant king, symbolizing his ka (soul or spirit), by goddesses, each of whom offer the baby a breast. Hatshepsut and her ka were shown being suckled by two Hathors at her mortuary temple. Another twelve children, each representing another ka of Hatshepsut, are shown held by nurses.[10] Amenhotep III was depicted retrospectively several times this way on a relief at the Temple of Luxor while his mother Mutemwiya looked on.[11] In this conventional form the nursed child-god rulers symbolized the regeneration of kingship, just as the sun was reborn every day.

The connection to Atenist solar beliefs is obvious. 'You rise in perfect beauty from the sky's horizon, the living Aten who begins life', Akhenaten had written in his Hymn, comparing night to death, and how sunrise brought renewal and triggered life in a mother's womb. The posthumous scenes in Meketaten's suite in the Royal Tomb might thus be revising an obsolete but reassuring concept for Atenism. If so, then the babies symbolized the nurturing of the ka of each dead princess, her divine origins and her rebirth. Here, then, might be an attempt to realize the Atenist ideology of death as a temporary nocturnal state. There may have been, indeed almost certainly was, considerable uncertainty about how to handle this in Akhenaten's new order, especially as what little we know about his theology had made no provision for such eventualities. This more easily explains the incongruities in the design which are confusing and opaque to us and perhaps also to those who executed the reliefs (this might also apply to many other peculiarities of the Amarna period that now apparently defy a logical explanation). Nothing like these compositions was ever produced again.

Whatever the unrecoverable truth, no historical significance can be attached to the babies since they cannot be linked to the drama that followed, and neither can the daughters who had died. All we can infer is that Meketaten's death had traumatized the royal family and was probably followed soon after by the deaths of her two youngest sisters. Meketaten's body has never been found, and of her burial only fragments of her sarcophagus, and pieces of a vase and a statuette both bearing her name, have been recovered.[12]

# THE DISAPPEARANCE OF KIYA

Akhenaten's 'Great Beloved Wife' Kiya is not heard of after his 11th regnal year, one of many of the Amarna players to disappear without explanation in the later part of the reign. Her likenesses and name were mostly usurped in favour of Akhenaten's two surviving eldest daughters, indicating that Kiya's disappearance came after Meketaten's death. The usurpations included inscriptions on columns from the North Palace at Amarna, where her name was replaced with Meryetaten's and likewise in her sunshade temple.[13] These usurpations perhaps also included renaming her anonymous daughter as variously the fictitious offspring of Meryetaten and Ankhesenpaaten (see Chapter 12). Some of Kiya's funerary equipment was pressed into service for another burial altogether (see Chapter 14).[14]

Kiya's fate, especially the apparent denial of a royal burial, goes unexplained but that is unsurprising. The deletions of her name imply that she had fallen from grace. Given Nefertiti's prominence in her lifetime compared to so many of her predecessor queens, one possible explanation is that Kiya had borne Akhenaten a son (Tutankhuaten?). Since previous kings had celebrated their birth mothers at the expense of their fathers' other wives, in the Amarna context Nefertiti might have become alarmed at the prospect of marginalization by the mother of the male heir. At the time she was in the process of becoming even more powerful a figure and eventually co-regent with her husband. Removing Kiya meant getting rid of a potential rival. It might also mean that if Tutankhuaten was Kiya's son he was never aware of the fact – he never mentioned her, let alone reinstated her memory. Of course, this is purely speculative. It remains no less likely that Nefertiti was Tutankhuaten's mother.[15]

The family deaths were not the only signs of stress after the 12th regnal year. Most of the Amarna noble tombs were never used.[16] The steward Any's tomb (TA23) was one of the few that was. The rest were abandoned unfinished about this time. One explanation is that confidence in the regime was crumbling, leading to some of the elite to start absenting themselves from what they guessed might be the ill face of things to come. From this point on the murk on the Amarna stage thickens into an impenetrable fog inhabited by elusive shadowy figures and the rapid vaporization of most of the remaining members of the cast.

# A BRIEF OUTLINE OF EVENTS AT THE END OF AKHENATEN'S REIGN

On 14 May 1338 BC in what might have been Akhenaten's 15th regnal year (this depends entirely on the chronology being followed) a total eclipse of the sun passed over the site of Akhet-aten. It took place in the early afternoon, five weeks prior to the summer solstice. Totality lasted about 4 minutes and 50 seconds. Since we can be as good as certain that the sky was free of clouds this extraordinary event must have been as overwhelming as it is possible for a solar eclipse to be.[17]

The path of totality missed Thebes where the eclipse was around 99 per cent, still enough to bathe Karnak in pallid and eerie sunlight.[18] Whether this eclipse happened in Akhenaten's 15th regnal year or not is unlikely ever to be known and nor is the impact it might have had on a city built round the worship of the sun. No Egyptian account of the occasion has survived. Given the emphasis placed by Akhenaten on the absolute power of Aten's light, the blotting out of the sun cannot have seemed like approval – *if* it took place during his reign. It is even possible the eclipse was a decisive moment in the unravelling of the revolution.[19] Either way, in an historical era of endless uncertainty, it is moderately gratifying to know for certain that the eclipse occurred at that moment in time and at that place, whenever it fell in the historical sequence of events.

There is at least one piece of evidence that seems to be beyond doubt. A graffito from the Deir Abu Hinnis quarry a few miles north of Amarna names Akhenaten as Neferkheperure, and Nefertiti as Neferneferuaten, Great Royal Wife. The graffito was only found in 2004 and required sophisticated digital enhancement to become legible. It was dated to the 15th day of the 3rd month of the first season (flood), placing it at sixty-five days into the civil calendar in the 16th regnal year. In or around 1337 BC the civil calendar was almost back in alignment with the solar calendar, making the time of year concerned about the end of our September.[20]

Akhenaten and Nefertiti were thus still in position as king and queen in his 16th regnal year, supplying a *terminus post quem* for his death. The discovery annihilated a litany of theories about Nefertiti based on the idea she had disappeared from the record several years earlier.[21] All we can say is that Akhenaten died later in the 16th year or afterwards, but not when. Whether Akhenaten was still in a fit state to rule or not (assuming he ever had been) is another matter altogether. The text refers to stone being sourced for the smaller of the two great Aten temples at Amarna, the 'Mansion of the Aten'. Since it was written by a royal scribe in charge of the work, his date must have been correct.

The normal claim is that Akhenaten died in his 17th regnal year, based solely on a docket on a honey jar from Amarna that refers to a '17th regnal year' but does not name a king. This was partly overlaid by a similar docket marking reuse of the jar for wine in the 1st regnal year of a subsequent unnamed king, though how long after his predecessor's 17th regnal year it is impossible to say.

The 17th regnal year docket is useless as evidence despite it being constantly trotted out as if it was a public announcement of the death of Akhenaten posted at the entrance of the Great Palace.[22] The length of the reign after the 16th year will remain open-ended until or if any more evidence such as the quarry graffito turns up. Akhenaten had to survive long enough to allow time for ensuing events. This makes it possible he lived for several years longer than is normally claimed today and would make it much easier to fit in what we know or believe to have happened (explained below and including Nefertiti's elevation to the kingship as a co-regent). Akhenaten was omitted from all subsequent king lists and cannot be reliably identified in Manetho, denying us other sources of information about the possible true length of his reign. This is a critical difference between Akhenaten and many other rulers but is usually overlooked. For example, Senusret III of the 12th Dynasty was apparently recorded in the Turin Canon as having reigned for thirty-five years, but his 19th regnal year is the highest known from other evidence.[23]

Even when Akhenaten did die the court is bound to have been thrown into disarray since so far as we know he had done nothing to provide any dogma or theological framework or ritual to replace the old beliefs about a royal death and succession. This was likely to have resulted in confusion at court and possibly even a temporary concealment of his death (well attested in numerous other historical contexts where the succession was uncertain).

Around this time Smenkhkare came into view, but only just. Smenkhkare apparently ruled alongside Akhenaten briefly as a co-regent, taking the throne name Ankhkheperure, 'Living are the Manifestations of Re'. Like many Egyptian royal names, the meaning of Smenkhkare is cryptic. Possibilities include 'Ennobled is the Soul of Re' and 'Potent is the Soul of Re'. The structure and nature of Smenkhkare is incongruously that of another throne name rather than a birth name. It may therefore have been a name taken on accession and which replaced an earlier personal name unknown to us. This cannot be easily explained unless he was a member of the royal circle who was promoted.[24] Manetho lists several rulers called 'Acencheres' at the end of the 18th Dynasty, almost certainly a surviving memory of the name Ankhkheperure but without any useful or compatible information about when or for how long these individuals reigned (see Appendix 4). But he does at least suggest that there was more than one ruler who bore this name at around the same time.

There is no other figure for whom the emergence of unequivocal information about who he was, what he was, what happened to him, and even just verification of his existence, would not cause more relief among Egyptologists. In an ideal world Smenkhkare-Ankhkheperure could be forgotten about, but although his role was little more than a walk-on one, he played an important part in the Amarna finale. Smenkhkare is unknown from any earlier reference to his presence at the Amarna court or before. Almost all the claimed instances of Smenkhkare are by the Ankhkheperure name only.

The other principal theory is that Smenkhkare was really Nefertiti's alter ego, a male identity as king that she briefly adopted while serving as Akhenaten's co-regent and short-lived successor before reverting to Neferneferuaten, or the other way round.[25] The basis for this argument is that Nefertiti was so prominently and obviously effectively ruling alongside Akhenaten the only credible scenario is her taking on the role of co-regent and then briefly as sole ruler after his death until the accession of Tutankhuaten.

Why Nefertiti might have felt the need to change her name to Smenkhkare is not explained, and neither is the evidence that both she and Smenkhkare reigned for separate periods of at least three regnal years. Neither Sobekneferu nor Hatshepsut changed their names when they became kings since their new status was conceived as a preordained modification of their existing identities.

In one of the current versions of events the new co-regent Smenkhkare married Akhenaten's eldest daughter Meryetaten who took the title Great Royal Wife. Co-regencies helped to ensure a smooth succession, though they remain notoriously hard to prove. Tutankhuaten, whoever his parents were, was too young to succeed safely had he needed to do so. This was a possible motive for appointing an adult co-regent and successor, perhaps in the belief he would act as a guarantor for maintaining Atenism. Another is that Akhenaten was ill and not expected to live long, but we know nothing of that.

Since Smenkhkare married Meryetaten, it is inconceivable that he was an outsider or even a foreigner, assuming family tradition was being followed. However, this leaves several possibilities: that he was Akhenaten's brother, half-brother, son, or even a cousin descended from a son of one of Amenhotep III's predecessors. The latter would obviate any difficulties arising from trying to reconcile an adult Smenkhkare with the traditionally accepted timespan of Akhenaten's reign.[26] Another possibility is, assuming the theory Nefertiti and Ay were members of the Yuya clan is correct, that royal family tradition was adapted by admitting a brother of Nefertiti's as an expedient co-regent and restyling him accordingly with a manufactured name. The obvious weakness of that suggestion is that there is no evidence for a brother of Nefertiti, but that was hardly unusual at a time when male relatives in the royal circle usually went unmentioned. Consequently, the idea is no better or worse than any other.[27]

Meryetaten and the spectral Smenkhkare appear with their names once barely legible in the tomb of an official at Amarna. Smenkhkare's figure resembled Akhenaten's but stylistically he was bound to be shown like the king. He and his young queen were only shown as preparatory drawings, the relief being left unfinished though the inscriptions had been carved.[28] The other obvious possibility is that since all the other scenes in the tomb show Akhenaten and Nefertiti, they were originally the intended figures. After all, rebranding reliefs and sculpture by changing the names was one of Egypt's most established royal traditions. Several eyewitnesses drew the damaged, badly carved and possibly modified cartouches in the early 1800s before their destruction in the 1880s. All struggled to read the one believed to have said Smenkhkare, though the Ankhkheperure name was much clearer.[29] Smenkhkare-Ankhkheperure was named on a relief from a temple of Aten at Memphis, but the upper parts of the names were not on the surviving fragment, which has been lost anyway.[30]

The only legible artefacts with the names Smenkhkare and Ankhkheperure side by side in cartouches that could be tracked down today are clay seals from Amarna, one also bearing the crucial royal titles Dual King and Lord of the [Two Lands]. The very few other recorded examples are far from certain, and generally lost or destroyed. A few rings vaguely described as having been 'found in the town', and specifically not the palace unlike most of the Ankhkheperure rings, at Amarna are virtually the only instances of the name Smenkhkare that are (or were) readable in full.[31] Wine was made on an estate in Smenkhkare's name at Amarna, recorded on several wine jars.[32] Smenkhkare allegedly had one known monument at Amarna, a hall of unknown function attached to Akhenaten's Great Palace It has been identified from bricks only bearing the name Ankhkheperure, which also appears on rings found at Amenhotep III's Malqata palace.[33] Ankhkheperure and Meryetaten's names appear together on gold sequins on a linen garment that ended up in Tutankhamun's tomb.[34] The famous relief, now in Berlin, of an Amarna king and queen is often described as Meryetaten and Smenkhkare but it bears no inscription and is just as likely to be Akhenaten and Nefertiti.[35]

One of the few pieces of evidence to support the idea of a

co-regency is a globular calcite vase from Tutankhamun's tomb. It bears an almost entirely erased inscription consisting of two pairs of kings' names side by side. Despite there being virtually no remaining traces of hieroglyphs, the inscription has been restored to show the names of Akhenaten and Smenkhkare side by side. The heavily restored names were produced without the benefit of either direct physical examination of the vase or the production of very high-quality photographs under varying light angles or scientific examination. If the result therefore seems tenuous, indeed it is, but in Amarna studies such examples carry enormous weight.[36] Such restorations rely on precise assumptions about the layout and execution of the original inscription, a technique that overlooks how messy and crude similar and more complete examples are.[37] The real oddity is that, like the tomb relief supposedly showing and naming Smenkhkare and Meryetaten, there is only one example of a vase allegedly with his name. Smenkhkare can only be read on either example by using elaborate reconstruction.

Smenkhkare's attributed significance today is in inverse proportion to anything supposedly known about him or his importance at the time. Not a single possession or grave good of his with Smenkhkare on it has ever been found. Smenkhkare is like a mirage, shimmering elusively in the distance and dissipating the moment anyone approaches him. Despite that, Smenkhkare has maintained a resilient presence. Someone who used that name was undoubtedly a figure in the Amarna royal circle, but only briefly. This may be frustrating for us, but in the broader context of subsidiary male members of the Egyptian royal family, especially those who died young, his obscurity is not unusual.

Smenkhkare did not last long, whoever he was. Most Egyptologists believe that Smenkhkare-Ankhkheperure died in his 1st regnal year towards the end of Akhenaten's reign.[38] One of the wine jars in Smenkhkare's name for that year is said to bear the 'true of voice' epithet, usually applied only to the deceased.[39] However, Petrie recorded twenty-five oil jars of the 2nd regnal year of (allegedly) Smenkhkare and one of his 3rd regnal year at Amarna, suggesting he survived as co-regent until at least then, but these are generally ignored today and are certainly untraceable now.[40]

Smenkhkare was replaced as king and co-regent by Nefertiti, presumably in the absence of any alternative option and with Tutankhuaten still too young to act as a reliable successor. This makes most sense if there was a prevailing belief that Akhenaten was suffering from a mental incapacity or was not going to survive until Tutankhuaten came of age. There is no specific evidence for either, but in the context of cult fanaticism and the demoralizing deaths of some of his daughters both are obviously plausible.

The elevation of Nefertiti, already by then known as Neferneferuaten, from queen to king was marked by modifying her names on some reliefs to add the throne name Ankhkheperure, the very throne name used by Smenkhkare, perhaps to maintain continuity and sometimes feminized in the form Ankhetkheperure. This must have come after the quarry graffito of the 16th regnal year. The feminized form is only known from examples 'linked with Akhenaten', reinforcing the idea that two different people calling themselves Ankhkheperure were involved.[41] Neferneferuaten adopted various significant epithets, sometimes in the female form, including 'beloved of Waenre', part of one of Akhenaten's names. One of the epithets, which can be translated as 'effective for her husband' (but also in another way), has been used to argue for further proof of Nefertiti serving her husband as a female co-regent.[42] Another version of her Neferneferuaten name included the *heqa* symbol for a ruler.[43] A stela found in the North Palace at Amarna was clumsily modified so that her double cartouches of a king now appeared, and some of her statues were adapted to show her wearing a king's crown.[44]

Correspondingly, a strip of wood found in the filling of the entranceway to Tutankhamun's tomb, broken off from an heir-loom box found in the tomb proper, names both Akhenaten and Neferneferuaten as kings, and Meryetaten as Great Royal Wife, their daughter thus transferring her role to the service of her parents in that formal capacity after the death of Smenkhkare. It was a new variant on how Sitamun had served her father Amenhotep III.[45]

An alternative theory is that Nefertiti was king and co-regent *before* Smenkhkare. In theory that was possible, but unlikely. Sobekneferu and Hatshepsut had made themselves kings only when there was no available or suitable successor. If Smenkhkare was available to succeed Nefertiti, then he must have previously been available to serve as Akhenaten's co-regent.

A curiosity is that despite her prominence Nefertiti was unmentioned by name in the extant Amarna Letters, but Meryetaten seems to turn up twice in them called Mayatu (the only daughter of Akhenaten's to be so), though at an earlier date and with no mention of a marriage. She is referred to in letters to Akhenaten, specifically as 'your daughter', and was clearly regarded as a figure of note to whom gifts were sent. In one of these two instances a reference to the 'mistress of the house' is the only possible acknowledgement of Nefertiti who is thereby explicitly distinguished from Mayatu.[46]

## THE DEATH OF AKHENATEN

In this version of events Nefertiti continued as king of Egypt briefly after her husband's death (whenever that really happened), perhaps overseeing the accession of Tutankhuaten/Tutankhamun, but before long had disappeared, too, as had Meryetaten (and all her surviving sisters except Ankhesenpaaten). That she never appears with her name modified to Meryetamun makes it unlikely she survived much beyond Tutankhamun's accession or retreated into obscurity. A small number of her personal possessions found their way into his tomb. Her own burial is unknown. It would have been logical for Nefertiti to continue to rule on her own after his death, given Nefertiti's prominence from the outset of the reign when she served effectively as a joint monarch with Akhenaten long before she became formally a co-regent.[47]

The shattered fragments of Akhenaten's grave goods in the Royal Tomb, including fragments of the smashed sarcophagus (on which Nefertiti's likeness had replaced the traditional goddess at each corner), over 200 shabtis and pieces of a canopic chest, as well as structural modifications to accommodate his shrines, make it certain that he died at Akhet-aten and was originally buried there, joining Tiye and up to three of his daughters.[48] Death from natural causes is the simplest explanation for Akhenaten's disappearance in or following his 16th regnal year. There is nothing to substantiate suicide or assassination, though both are serious possibilities in the peculiar circumstances of his reign. We cannot even assume that Akhenaten was still in control by then. The contradictory evidence for this confusing period may well be a function of the regime unravelling.

There is good evidence, including a deep cut to the neck on his body, that Ramesses III (1184–1153 BC) of the 20th Dynasty was murdered by a palace conspiracy.[49] He was by no means as controversial a figure as Akhenaten. There are numerous examples across history of monarchs, especially those who were inadequate or who imposed unwelcome change, being assassinated. One might consider the fate of the Roman emperor Elagabalus who imposed his own brand of sun worship on the Roman Empire in AD 218 and was murdered four years later in return for upsetting the established order. The weak and pious Henry VI of England was eventually murdered in 1471 with the connivance or even active involvement of his cousin and successor Edward IV.[50] In Akhenaten's case the limited or non-existent opportunities to profit from wars of conquest is also hardly likely to have endeared him to the military. Moreover, the evidence of the physical remains now believed by some to be Nefertiti's is that she died violently (see Chapter 15). If Tutankhuaten was considered by others to be old enough to be planted on the throne, that might have been all those who were keen to remove Akhenaten needed.

Akhenaten and Tiye were later disinterred and taken to Thebes. The Royal Tomb was emptied and its Atenist decoration desecrated, though the latter may have occurred much later. The clearance must have included removing Meketaten and the two younger sisters who had probably shared her dedicated suite. The well shaft was filled with rubble and bricks to facilitate the removal of burials and funerary equipment from the main burial chamber.[51] Only Tiye's reburial at Thebes can be tracked with tolerable certainty (see below). Smenkhkare's Amarna burial place has not been found, assuming he had one.

A graffito on the wall of a tomb at Western Thebes (TT139) was written in the 3rd regnal year of the reign of the king Neferneferuaten (Nefertiti) with her throne name Ankhkheperure, both names with epithets (partially lost).[52] There is no reference to Akhenaten, who may have died by then. The 3rd regnal year referred to could have been Nefertiti's in her own right or Tutankhamun's, with Nefertiti serving as his co-regent and sharing the regnal year count.[53] The latter is plausible but there is nothing to confirm this in the way there is for Hatshepsut and Thutmose III. The text, which included a prayer to Amun, was composed by a priest of Amun called Pawah and his brother. The two served in the *Hewet* of Ankhkheperure (with no epithet) at Thebes. In the context of a royal name *Hewet* means the temple of a royal mortuary cult.[54] The lack of an epithet for this name suggests the cult was that of Smenkhkare, but it does not really matter apart from implying he was dead. The important point is a reference to the memorial-mortuary temple, which has not been located, of either of the last rulers of the Amarna phase.[55] It would also appear that observances of Amun were resuming openly.

There is one more fleeting glimpse of this period, found on a box that was to end up in Tutankhamun's tomb. The lid inscription had once included the names and full titles of Nefertiti as the king Neferneferuaten, and of her daughter and great royal wife Meryetaten. These had served as palimpsests for the names of

Tutankhamun and his queen, Meryetaten's sister Ankhesenamun, which replaced them.[56] It seems indeed that Nefertiti had ruled for a time on her own after Akhenaten's and Smenkhkare's deaths, but like Meryetaten she soon disappeared from history.[57]

This short summary makes some sense of what little is known but that does not mean it is correct. Egyptologists have scoured the scrappy and ambiguous evidence for this period in the hope that somewhere enshrined within lies a clear explanation for what really took place at the end of Akhenaten's reign and its immediate aftermath. Thus far the search has been in vain and will remain so. The result has been irreconcilable and sometimes fractious differences of opinion, with none vested in anything solid.[58]

The evidence from other periods of disorder, for example the aftermath of the suicide of Nero in AD 68, or the death of Edward IV of England in 1483, is for chaotic and often spontaneous developments including the emergence of rival factions, and a temporary descent into violence before order and stability were restored.[59] Both these episodes are much better documented than the end of the Amarna period, but they remain subject to great difficulties of interpretation, not least because even those involved, as well as witnesses, were not fully aware of what was happening in different places and at different times as events unfolded rapidly and could never have been so.

If no one at the time really knew what was going on in Egypt after Akhenaten's disappearance it is no surprise at all that the evidence is irrevocably confused and contradictory. The perpetual quest for a definitive resolution and narrative is thus a lost cause. Since this episode was described by Horemheb as a 'storm' only a few years later (see Chapter 17), the best we can ever do is accept that for a while Egypt was temporarily at the mercy of competing interests whose protagonists acted ruthlessly in pursuit of power, and who probably operated as much on impulse in the light of fast-moving circumstances as with any strategic intent. The people involved included surviving members of the royal family and senior officials with the mood intensified by uncertainty, fear, suspicion and the high stakes. We will never know anything more specific, and it is a delusion to believe otherwise.

The most obvious point of all is usually overlooked: most of the key players disappeared in short order. The Aten was restored to its former role as a subsidiary member of the Egyptian pantheon. The only individuals of any importance left when the dust settled that we know of were Tutankhuaten and Ankhesenpaaten, both still children, the senior court official Ay to whom they may have been related, and the general Horemheb. Tutankhuaten became king, changed his name to Tutankhamun and married Ankhesenpaaten, who changed hers to Ankhesenamun. Tutankhamun, or rather those who controlled him, presided over the beginning of the restoration of the old order. In him and them the fortunes of the 18th Dynasty were now vested. However, before turning to his reign we need to consider the mysterious tomb called KV55.

# 14

# THE STRANGE CASE OF THE TOMB KNOWN AS KV55

*In the murky drama of Akhenaten's aftermath and the first few years of Tutankhamun's reign the small and scrappy Valley of the Kings tomb known as KV55 and its wrecked contents are never offstage. The controversies, bolstered by recent scientific evidence which has only muddied the waters further, have rumbled on ever since the tomb was found. However, the surviving evidence of the deposit suggests it was originally a reburial of Tiye and Akhenaten whose bodies were brought from Amarna by Tutankhamun for safety. Subsequent clearance work left behind only one male body of indeterminate identity, but undoubtedly a close relative of Tutankhamun's, along with cluttered and damaged remnants of funerary equipment.*

KV55 is a tomb in the Valley of the Kings that contained a cache of material and bodies brought from Amarna after Akhenaten's reign. It lies only about 120 ft (36 m) across the valley floor from Tutankhamun's tomb (KV62). No other two 18th Dynasty royal tombs are so close to one another but neither had been designed originally as a royal tomb. They were far too small, corresponding to the tombs of nobles allowed the privilege of a burial in the Valley, such as Yuya and Thuya's. Tutankhamun's was subsequently modestly enlarged to squeeze in the paraphernalia of a king but KV55 was not.

KV55 consists only of an entrance corridor, a rectangular burial chamber, and a small niche annexe. There were no dockets or decoration that might have explained whose tomb it was. It had suffered from a chaotic burial of at least two bodies, after which it was reopened. Some of the contents were removed, leaving only one body behind in a royal coffin and some funerary equipment. Deliberate damage was caused to what was left behind, made worse by later water ingress and structural collapse.

The tomb had the misfortune to be found in 1907 by a team led by Edward Ayrton, then working for a wealthy American hobbyist Egyptologist called Theodore Davis who pressured them to make a hasty removal of the contents. The tomb was not recorded properly, or a plan made. Some small pieces were stolen and rapidly appeared on the local antiquities market. The result was to compromise permanently analysis of the assemblage though sterling efforts since have made good some of the lost information.[1]

Nevertheless, the tomb yielded some important but controversial evidence.[2] The most conspicuous relics were panels from a gilded wooden shrine intended for the burial of Tiye, commissioned for her by Akhenaten. The shrine had been in the process of being removed during the clearance work that took place within two centuries of the original deposit, but the job was abandoned when it became too difficult to drag the panels up through the corridor. The shrine parts were damaged, but they still bore scenes decorated with figures of Akhenaten and Tiye in the Amarna style. Akhenaten's name had been cut out but the surviving inscriptions on the shrine described Tiye as Amenhotep III's queen. The Aten's name had not been touched.

There were four magic mudbricks. Three were in their niches in the burial chamber, and one apparently displaced in the little annexe. Akhenaten's throne name Neferkheperure was still visible on two of the bricks, most clearly on the 'northern' brick.[3] Such bricks were a common inclusion in New Kingdom tombs and carried protective spells connected to birth, and thus the rebirth of the deceased. The texts on these bricks were the conventional ones from Chapter 151 of the Book of the Dead and had no mention of the Aten. The spells resemble, for example, those found in the tomb of Thutmose IV.[4]

The tomb contained a royal coffin with a badly preserved mummy of an adult male reduced to a skeleton. The only names still visible on gold foil with the body were those of the Aten. Anything that might have identified the man had been carefully removed. There were also four canopic jars, each bearing portrait bust stoppers of a royal woman wearing the 'Nubian wig', popular towards the end of the 18th Dynasty. Each bust had been modified by adding the cobra uraeus symbol of royalty, subsequently removed. The inscriptions on the jars had been deliberately rubbed off, with only traces remaining.

There were other items, but few were inscribed. Those that were mostly carried the names of Tiye and/or Amenhotep III. The sole exceptions were a collection of clay seals carrying Tutankhamun's throne name Nebkheperure. There were no objects that carried Smenkhkare's or Nefertiti's names, or their shared throne name Ankhkheperure. Nor was there anything that could be linked to Meryetaten or other members of the Amarna royal family.

So much for what we know. What we can infer takes the story a little further. The battered shrine panels were of dimensions compatible with a restoration of Tiye's sarcophagus from fragments found in the Royal Tomb at Amarna.[5] It seems Tiye's body had been removed along with the shrine and her other burial goods and taken to Thebes for reburial in KV55. Tutankhamun's seals make it likely this was his decision; it certainly took place in his name. The shrine inscriptions had gone through two phases of desecration. The first must have occurred at Amarna during Akhenaten's reign once the proscription of Amun's name had begun, with the first part of Amenhotep III's name being erased. The second phase, probably when the shrine was taken from Amarna to Thebes for KV55, reversed the process by deleting Akhenaten's name and replacing it with Amenhotep III's throne name Nebmaatre in red ink. The name of the Aten in its two cartouches was left untouched. This can be explained if at the beginning of Tutankhamun's reign the Aten was still recognized, albeit marginalized by the restoration of Amun's primacy (see Chapter 15).[6]

The magic bricks of Akhenaten were probably made at Thebes for KV55 in the knowledge or *belief* that another body being reburied was Akhenaten's and to serve in the ritual of that reburial. Alternatively, they had been left in store from the beginning of his reign when a burial at Thebes had still been expected.[7] It is inconceivable that the bricks with their orthodox texts were made at Amarna during the Aten ascendancy. Crucially, at least one of the Akhenaten bricks referred to Akhenaten as the Osiris. This would have served a useful purpose for Tutankhamun. If his father had died and ascended as Osiris then he was validated as the Horus, fulfilling and restoring the royal religious mythological cycle. However, since Akhenaten had failed to fulfil that role in life there was no credible means of presenting this dogma in public. The furtive burial of Akhenaten in KV55 with a modicum of traditional decorum therefore makes more sense. Akhenaten had been posthumously restored to the fold in secret and was in no position to object.

This does not preclude the possibility of the burial or reburial of other individuals in KV55 as part of the process, but only the one male body remained after the subsequent clearance. There is a tenuous possibility the female body known as the 'Younger Lady' was also deposited in KV55 along with Akhenaten and Tiye by Tutankhamun before the removals and rearrangements. It was later to end up with what some believe to be Tiye's mummy in the royal cache in the tomb of Amenhotep II (see Chapter 15 for the theory that the Younger Lady was Nefertiti).

The bust stoppers of the four canopic jars did not necessarily belong to the jars originally. While the wigs resemble the one that Kiya wore, the faces' profiles resemble most closely Nefertiti's (or by extension one of her daughters).[8] The erased jar inscriptions left traces compatible with the names of the Aten, Akhenaten and a reference to Kiya's unique title Greatly Beloved Wife.[9] However, the traces really are just that. The only part of her title detectable on the jars now is the sign for wife, but barely, and is not definitive on its own. Kiya's personal name is not visible and nor is her special title. Moreover, the restoration of her name and titles is founded on the assumption they were accurately laid out originally and did not replace an earlier text. As viable evidence this restored text is another non-starter.[10] The erasure of the inscriptions was probably to prepare the jars for use in KV55 for the male burial. The best that might be said is that the jars were possibly Kiya's but might have been fitted with stoppers bearing portraits of Nefertiti or another female member of the royal family. Although very similar in appearance, the stoppers are not identical. They may even have been manufactured as *generic* portraits of Nefertiti or her daughters, intended for any one of them who needed the equipment.

The coffin inscriptions were changed or defaced in two phases. The inscriptions on the coffin's front and inside have the word Maat in the traditional form of the hieroglyph for the eponymous goddess. On the coffin's foot the word is spelled out phonetically, an Atenist characteristic of the latter part of Akhenaten's reign also found on Tiye's shrine that avoided a direct reference to a divinity of the old order. The technicalities and restorations of the coffin's modified texts are extremely complicated, but a plausible original owner was Kiya, after which the coffin was repurposed for a king in preparation for his reburial in KV55. This king's names were themselves subsequently removed. Those on the lid of the coffin were neatly cut out from the cartouches in a way that suggests the plan might have been to replace them with someone else's names, a procedure that was never completed. This work left in place key Atenist epithets used for Akhenaten, such as the 'perfect little one of the living disk', suggesting that the intended third(?) owner of the coffin was someone for whom these would be suitable.[11]

Thus, the coffin was most likely once a lesser wife's before probably being reused for Akhenaten or Smenkhkare, or both. It is not possible to say which and nor would either necessarily determine whose body was found in the coffin. There was nothing unusual about reusing coffins and canopic jars. Possible contexts are that either Kiya's burial equipment had never been used, or there was a general clearance of Amarna tombs during Tutankhamun's reign which freed them up for redeployment.

Armed with this information it is possible to imagine some of what might have happened. On Tutankhamun's instructions Tiye and Akhenaten were removed from the Royal Tomb at Amarna, together with selected portable funerary equipment drawn from their original burials.[12] Other available pieces which might have included some of Kiya's were added. These and the two bodies were taken to Thebes and reburied in KV55, possibly joined at some point by the 'Younger Lady'. If so, Tutankhamun was therefore seeing to the burial of his parents, or at least those whom he *believed* to be his parents, and his grandmother. An effort was made to create a conventional 18th Dynasty royal burial, hence the magic bricks, and thus also reassert the dynasty's entitlement to rule. The disappearance from the Amarna Royal Tomb of the remains of Meketaten and her younger sisters, and virtually all their burial equipment, makes it possible another reburial is still waiting to be found. It is also probable that some of the royal funerary goods taken from Amarna were set aside to be used in later burials, including eventually Tutankhamun's.

Later, tomb KV55 was reopened, but whether as the result of an accidental discovery or by intent is unknown. The most likely context is during the reign of Horemheb when the Valley was being systematically inspected, a time when Atenist monuments were being dismantled and memory of the period suppressed (Chapter 17). If so, the plan was probably to remove Tiye and rebury her with Amenhotep III in his tomb in the Western Valley of the Kings, thus detaching her from Akhenaten and thereby placing her in the suite originally provided for her by her husband.[13] If the 'Younger Lady' was in KV55 she was removed, too (see Chapter 15 for the shabti in

Nefertiti's name from the Royal Tomb). These mummies remained in their new locations until the major clearances of the royal tombs took place in the late 21st Dynasty when they were transferred to the royal mummy cache in Amenhotep II's tomb (KV35, see Epilogue).

As part of the task, the KV55 working party picked out anything with either of Akhenaten's names on it, which they mostly erased, but not his throne name on the magic bricks. This may or may not have included some of the name deletions and symbols of royalty on the coffin unless those had already taken place at or before the time of the original deposit. The team gave up on Tiye's shrine. They left the dismantled panels where they fell but defaced them (if they had not been already), removing both Akhenaten's names and his figure but did not touch the names of the Aten. This suggests they were following exact instructions and were working under supervision. They also abandoned the male body which they did not damage. If the body was not already in the coffin, this was when it was placed there.

These activities and the fact that gold, including decorative elements of the coffin, was left behind show that the clearance team were not primarily thieves and must have been acting in an official capacity (obviously, we have no idea of what they might have privately helped themselves to). The treatment of KV55 shows that Akhenaten was remembered, but that there was a clear intention to suppress his name.

Enough survives of the skeleton to be certain it is that of an adult male who was a member of the royal family. He was closely related to Tutankhamun, sharing what was at the time a relatively unusual blood group (A2/MN) and physical appearance which included the large pelvis, though this connection did not become apparent until after Tutankhamun's body was unwrapped in 1923.[14] No physical remains have been found in the Royal Tomb at Amarna, while the magic bricks made it possible, even likely, that Akhenaten's body or a body believed to be his had been reburied in KV55 at some point.[15]

By default, Smenkhkare is the only alternative candidate to Akhenaten that we know of, apart from Akhenaten's older brother

Thutmose who had long predeceased Akhenaten's accession to the throne.[16] The only circumstantial physical inference we can draw from what little we know about Smenkhkare is that he was younger than Akhenaten and was a close family member. Nothing found in KV55 belonged to him, and even the material in Tutankhamun's tomb that might have been his is not demonstrably so. Without the unidentified body and the deleted names on the coffin there would never have been any suggestion Smenkhkare had been buried in KV55, unlike Tiye and Akhenaten.

No named sculpture of Smenkhkare is known, so it is impossible to compare the skull with representations of him and Akhenaten.[17] The identification debate has been based around the body's estimated age at death, and most recently DNA which has been used to claim that the body, regardless of its identity, is that of Tutankhamun's father (see Chapter 15), adding to the evidence of the shared blood type. This leaves unresolved the 'highly contentious issue' of Akhenaten's family circle.[18] One of the main reasons is that the only bodies whose identity is not in doubt are those of Yuya, Thuya, and Tutankhamun. Some believe that the KV55 body is that of a young man aged in his early to mid-twenties. Others prefer the idea that the age at death was thirty-five to forty, which is more consistent with what happened during Akhenaten's reign but is not essential.[19] That two such incompatible estimates continue to subsist inspires little confidence in the evidence.

Sticking with the lower range for age at death means those in favour of the body being Akhenaten's arguing that his reign, religious revolution and large family, and all the known events, were packed into his adolescence and young adulthood.[20] This is not impossible, especially given that becoming king as a child or an adolescent was common in the 18th Dynasty (or indeed in antiquity in general). In Akhenaten's case, however, it is difficult to believe he was only in his mid-twenties by the time he had ruled for an absolute minimum of sixteen years in such an epoch-changing reign. Either way, nothing helps the case for Smenkhkare, who is the alternative solution for explaining the alleged youthfulness of the KV55 body, while sometimes also suggesting that he was Tutankhamun's father but without any corroborating evidence.[21] Had Smenkhkare been his father it would be necessary to assume also that Meryetaten was Tutankhamun's mother. Since we know Tutankhamun died in his late teens after a reign of a little under a decade, he must therefore have been born around the 8th to 10th regnal year of Akhenaten at the latest, and when Meryetaten was still only eight or nine years old at most. This stretches the credibility of the case beyond breaking point.

Much more likely is that for different reasons the various estimated ages of the KV55 body at death and the DNA evidence are unreliable. DNA does not name or identify individuals. DNA markers can be used to identify potential relationships but cannot, for example, distinguish siblings. For example, one body's DNA may be compatible with being the father of another but could also be an uncle. In a family with multiple consanguineous unions over several generations the potential for other options is even greater, involving cousin relationships that are now untraceable. In Chapter 15 this is discussed in more detail in connection with Nefertiti's descent. The techniques used to estimate age at death are notoriously prone to major error for a variety of reasons, including the lack of any controls in ancient populations. These techniques do not name or identify individuals either. They have been demonstrated to be prone to significant error with a blind study conducted on the bodies of known age (specified on coffin plates) from burials in the crypt at Christ Church, Spitalfields, in London. No investigation of the KV55 body, which includes examination of the bones (for example, the fusion of the epiphyses) and teeth, has led to agreement.[22] Since many Egyptologists are disinclined to accept any of these unpalatable truths except where to do so allows them to refute someone else's theory, the result has been a ceaseless and wholly unresolvable controversy about the KV55 body and other human remains from this period.

Anyone who starts reading the relevant literature in depth

will be confounded by the claims and counter-claims which are driven almost entirely by a personal preference for Akhenaten or Smenkhkare.[23] Consequently, none of the information (such as it is) yielded by the body can be tied conclusively to either candidate. Nor does any of the physiological or DNA evidence affect the view that whether the body is Akhenaten's or not, it would still be the case that Akhenaten is the strongest candidate for the *original* burial in KV55 along with Tiye, and that Tutankhamun was most likely Akhenaten's son and the one who reburied him in the Valley of the Kings in KV55.

Like a gun without a serial number, the anonymous body in KV55 only leads back to itself. The evidence needed to answer the question conclusively has either not survived or has not yet been found. After all, the whole intention was to deny the body its identity, a job that was done very efficiently and that tells us a great deal on its own.[24] Moreover, when the tomb was found it housed only the remnants of a cache. We have no idea what else it once contained. Clearly there is something very wrong either with our understanding of what might have happened or the nature of the body, or both. Another mistake is to assume that the family relationships and the identities of the bodies were all correctly known to those involved in the original extractions from the Royal Tomb at Amarna and the reinterments in KV55, Tutankhamun himself, and especially those responsible for the subsequent removals and rearrangements. Therefore, the endlessly recycled arguments in favour of the body being either Akhenaten or Smenkhkare have gone everywhere and got nowhere.[25]

## The case for Richard III

The case of the skeleton of England's Richard III (reigned 1483–5), found in Leicester in 2012, makes for a sobering comparison. Like the KV55 body it was unlabelled but contemporary evidence provided information about his possible scoliosis of the spine, age at death, place and cause of death, postmortem injury, and burial location which all matched the remains. Paintings also provided a comparison for Richard's physical appearance. The DNA evidence obviously did not name the skeleton but was compatible with descent from Richard's mother, trackable to modern family members descended from Richard's siblings. Crucially, there was also no alternative known candidate for the body. All these factors made its identification as Richard III's remains overwhelmingly likely. This is a conclusion that would have been drawn even if the discovery had been made before DNA analysis was available. These corroborating factors are not available for the KV55 body and cannot now be made good.

Those obsessed with KV55's human remains consistently miss the point, which would be to ignore the body and concentrate instead on what the original assemblage was supposed to be. The mistake has always been to believe that an anonymous skeleton is the key to the history of this confusing episode. It can never be so. KV55 was apparently part of the wider effort under Tutankhamun to shut down Amarna by reburying the remains of Tiye and Akhenaten, and possibly others with them, in the Valley of the Kings. This clandestinely honoured tradition and protected the bodies from being robbed and desecrated had they remained at Amarna. It was a sensible precaution and means that there were probably other reburials elsewhere, for example of the deceased daughters of Akhenaten, which have never been found and may no longer exist. The subsequent partial clearance of KV55 and erasure of the remaining body's identity have only served to divert attention from the original historical context of the deposit, apart from showing that the body was that of a prominent male member of the royal family in the Amarna period whose identity had to be obscured in perpetuity.

*

Anyone who chooses to pursue the musical-tombs story of KV55 will find that the arguments say far more about Egyptology than they do about the events and personalities enshrined in what was left of its rotted contents. The short period between Akhenaten's death and Tutankhuaten's accession injected only a minor delay in ending the Amarna period. For all the talk of graves, of shrines, and epithets, the child Tutankhuaten was so far as we know the only dynastically eligible royal male left to fill Egypt's hollow crown. His accession secured the regime's hold on power, at least for the moment, and Amun was restored. This indisputable turn of events rendered the possible fleeting tenure of the throne by any intermediaries, regardless of their order (or even attempting to rule at the same time) or who they were, during the last part of Akhenaten's reign and its immediate aftermath neither here nor there.

The crisis was, however, only just beginning. The overwhelming issue was whether as Tutankhamun and Ankhesenamun the new king and his young queen would live long enough to secure the dynasty's future and maintain the grip on power that had already lasted well over two centuries. In that endeavour they were to fail.

# 15

# THE KING WHOSE NAME THE WHOLE WORLD KNOWS c. 1336–1327 BC[1]

## Tutankhamun (Nebkheperure, 'Lord of the Manifestations of Re')

*Tutankhamun's reign lasted almost a decade and ended with the creation of a tomb that stopped the world in its tracks when it was discovered a century ago. For all his modern fame, however, Tutankhamun is barely detectable today as an historical personality, his tomb having added little to the minimal surviving evidence for his reign. Even his parentage remains uncertain. He married Akhenaten's daughter Ankhesenamun and presided over the first phase of undoing the Amarna era. His death, without an heir, occasioned a succession crisis.*

Egypt's most successful royal line to date was in a tight corner. Everything relied on the child Tutankhuaten growing up to be an effective adult king, restoring the nation's prestige and authority, and fathering an heir. In fact, the 18th Dynasty's track record had hitherto been remarkably successful in those regards. From Thutmose

II on, every new king had either been a child or at most barely into adulthood, but each had lived and reigned at least long enough to father an heir (assuming Akhenaten was Tutankhuaten's father). In the post-Amarna turmoil, though, the circumstances were far more challenging, and nor does Tutankhuaten appear to have been in good health. Only a fool would have banked on him living long enough to produce a successor. In the event his reign did no more than postpone the crisis. If Nefertiti stage-managed Tutankhuaten's accession and oversaw the first part of his reign, evidence of her role has not survived.

## BIRTH AND ORIGINS

Tutankhuaten ('Living Image of Aten') was born during the Amarna years perhaps about eight years into the reign. He became king around a decade later and married Akhenaten and Nefertiti's third daughter Ankhesenpaaten ('Living for Aten'). At the time he still bore the name Tutankhuaten.[2] As Tutankhuaten he had already been shown on a private stela at Amarna busily making an offering to Amun and Mut.[3] Within a short time, the royal couple changed their names respectively to Tutankhamun and Ankhesenamun, another public sign that the regime had turned its back on Atenism.[4] Tutankhamun also adopted the title now included in his new cartouche, Ruler of southern Heliopolis (Karnak).[5] This publicly associated him with Amun. Given his age, the assumption must be that the agenda was being driven by others in the court circle.

A piece of an inscribed relief found across the Nile from Amarna at Hermopolis bears the name Tutankhuaten labelled as 'King's Son' though this, as we have seen, is not definitive proof of his parentage.[6] It is virtually the only evidence for his existence before accession. This was not unusual for a prince in the 18th Dynasty but since Akhenaten had apparently failed to make any Atenist theological provision for the succession Tutankhamun's childhood invisibility is even less surprising.

The study of Tutankhamun's body and clothing, stashed in significant quantities in his tomb, has shown that he exhibited some of Akhenaten's unusual physical characteristics, including being pigeon-chested, and had unusually wide hips.[7] Since the Hermopolis block includes an unnamed princess, described as 'King's Daughter', the two might have been siblings. Various efforts have been made to restore her name, of which only the first hieroglyph of the -aten suffix survives, but its positioning matches Ankhesenpaaten best.[8] This evidence cannot deliver anything conclusive but has contributed to the common, but not universal, assumption that Tutankhamun was the son of Akhenaten and probably Nefertiti.

A surveying instrument of Tutankhamun's found in an unknown location probably in Western Thebes carries an inscription stating that Thutmose IV was his 'father of his fathers'.[9] Similarly, one of a pair of granite lions at Soleb belonged to a temple commissioned by Amenhotep III that needed completion or restoration. Tutankhamun saw to this and dedicated it to 'his father'. This was not a literal statement of parentage, though some have mistaken it for one. Lacking precise terms for grandfather and other similar relationships, the Egyptians freely used the word we translate as 'son' as a synonym.[10] The important point is that the boy was presented as a direct descendant of the male royal line, the simplest explanation being that he was. Tutankhamun's skull also exhibits the characteristic overbite seen in other members of the dynasty.

The only other evidence linking Tutankhamun directly to the royal family was the inclusion of a lock of Tiye's plaited hair in his tomb. It was contained within the smallest of a nest of miniature coffins, the last bearing her name. The tomb also contained a pair of ivory clappers, one inscribed for Tiye and the other for her granddaughter Meryetaten.[11] The most logical relationship for Tutankhamun to have had with Tiye was as her grandson. If so, then it follows that at least one of Tutankhamun's parents was the child of Tiye and Amenhotep III. Microprobe analysis linked this lock of hair to the 'Elder Lady' found in the KV35 royal mummy cache with the conclusion that the body is Tiye's, since then supposedly supported by the DNA evidence.[12] That does not affect inevitably inferring from the lock of hair (which unlike the Elder Lady's body was labelled as Tiye's) that Tutankhamun was surely descended from Tiye, regardless of the contradictory and inconclusive scientific evidence.

Tutankhamun's attitude to his mother, whoever she was, differed from that of his predecessors in a crucial way: she is never mentioned in any surviving monument, unlike previous queen mothers such as Tia (mother of Thutmose IV) or Mutemwiya (mother of Amenhotep III). His father goes unmentioned, too, other than Tutankhamun's routine claim that he was the son of Amun. Of course, this could be because any such references were subsequently destroyed, but there is nothing from his tomb either. At the very least this probably means his mother died before his accession or not long after.

The idea Kiya was Tutankhamun's mother is partly based on perceived facial similarity and as the most prominent lesser wife, but that was founded on identifying the canopic jar bust stoppers in KV55 as Kiya's. As discussed in Chapter 13 there is no reason to assume the stoppers necessarily belonged to the jars. They are more plausibly seen as generic portraits of Nefertiti (whom the bust stoppers resemble most closely) and her daughters. This raises all sorts of questions about who most of these pieces, including Tutankhamun's gold mask and coffins, really represented. This involves considering the extent to which being manufactured by the same group of artists, influenced by 'house style' and repetitious practices, as well as seeking to produce idealized portraits of members of the same family, resulted in producing pieces that were similar in appearance. They may not therefore be reliable indicators of individuality and were possibly never intended to be.[13] After all, the portraits on the coffins of Yuya and Thuya bear no meaningful resemblance to their exceptionally well-preserved mummies (whose identity is beyond doubt).[14] The congenital overbite, so evident in several of the other royal mummies of the 18th Dynasty, including Tutankhamun's, is invariably absent in sculpture or paintings of the same people, amply demonstrating that they are not wholly authentic personal likenesses.

DNA analysis has been used in recent years to argue that the 'Younger Lady' and the KV55 body were not only siblings but also Tutankhamun's parents.[15] This overlooked the possibility that in a royal family where multiple consanguineous unions have occurred two cousins may exhibit the same coincidence of DNA markers as siblings in more normal contexts.[16] The same study assumed the KV55 body was Akhenaten's and excluded Nefertiti as a candidate for the Younger Lady on the grounds that she is never called King's Sister, claiming instead that the Younger Lady must have been a hitherto unknown and anonymous daughter of Amenhotep III and Tiye. The Younger Lady was found next to the 'Elder Lady' (Tiye?) in the royal mummy cache in Amenhotep II's tomb (KV35). Since Tiye was originally buried in KV55 it is likely the Younger Lady was once buried there, too (see Chapter 13). With only three of the bodies involved identified with absolute certainty (Yuya, Thuya and Tutankhamun), and many other key individuals missing entirely (including most or all of Akhenaten's daughters, Kiya, Mutbenret, and Ay) the potential for error is compounded further.

Another study which examined the physical remains of the Younger Lady concluded that she was Nefertiti, based on the physical appearance of the mummy. There is also the improbability that a sister of Akhenaten had managed to grow to adulthood and bear him a future king without making any detectable appearance in the records. After all, several other sisters of Akhenaten such as Sitamun are attested, but only in their father's lifetime. However, the Younger Lady's skull has the dynasty's congenital overbite visible in several royal mummies back to and including Ahmose and Ahmose-Nefertari, suggesting that she was related to the royal line of descent in some way.[17]

None of this need be as contradictory and confusing as it looks. England's Edward III (1327–77) fathered nine children, several of whom lived to adulthood and had offspring. Within five generations (about 125–150 years) he had over 320 attested descendants and within two centuries theoretically several thousand.[18] Given the length of time that had elapsed since the beginning of the 18th Dynasty it ought to be immediately apparent that the extended Egyptian royal family could have been, and probably was, considerably larger by Akhenaten and Nefertiti's lifetimes than we will ever know. Indeed, there is a case to be made that the coincident DNA markers exhibited by the bodies believed to be those of Amenhotep III and Tiye are at the least consistent with them being cousins through Yuya's family, but without determining any route.[19] Based on all the circumstantial evidence it is therefore feasible that the Younger Lady is Nefertiti, that she was a member of the 18th Dynasty bloodline through a long-term route unknown to us but most likely also including a link to Tiye's family, especially Yuya and Thuya, and that she and Akhenaten were cousins and the parents of Tutankhamun. However, this is only one of several possible explanations (see below for the foetuses found in Tutankhamun's tomb).

There is now no means of producing a definitive answer, and it is too easy to be beguiled by the prospect of scientific evidence providing a magic solution. However, the picture that is emerging from all this evidence is of a royal family with extensive dynastic links and lines of descent through the 18th Dynasty nobility that cannot now be traced and involving potentially far more individuals than we know about.[20] Such a general picture is unlikely to be improved on, however frustrating that is. The family of Edward III and its dominance of the crown, nobility and high office, as well as feuding that led to the Wars of the Roses (also known as the Cousins' War precisely because so many of the protagonists were closely related), for generations after his death offers a useful parallel. It also illustrates amply just how much more information we would need to reconstruct the multiple possible lineages that led to Nefertiti and other members of the royal circle.

This identification of the Younger Lady as Nefertiti, helped by a facial reconstruction, has received more support of late along with the interesting possibility that damage to the body, which included being struck in the face with a weapon and a major wound to the torso, was ante mortem.[21] Indeed, this is the potentially most important part of the Younger Lady saga. If Nefertiti was assassinated, perhaps after overseeing the early part of Tutankhamun's reign as his co-regent in the manner of Hatshepsut with Thutmose III and thereby provoking concerns she might remain in control for decades, the agencies involved must have been those who saw in Tutankhamun the chance to rule Egypt through a child and reverse the changes of recent years more quickly, and to their advantage.[22] Given her track record, Nefertiti was far more likely to have been murdered than a nameless and otherwise unknown sister of Akhenaten, even if her intentions were to protect and preserve the crown until Tutankhamun came of age.

This version of events, which is plausible and would explain a great deal, rests on a series of interdependent opinions and theories rather than facts and is obviously suppositious. Regardless of her fate or whether the Younger Lady is her, Nefertiti disappeared from history. She had planned a conventional burial. An unprovenanced calcite shabti of Nefertiti as a king, and now in two pieces, probably came from the Royal Tomb at Amarna.[23] This does not prove she was buried there at all, but it is compatible with the possibility that she died and was interred there before Tutankhamun's accession or shortly after. If so, then her body as the Younger Lady was then subsequently taken from Amarna to KV55, too, with the remains of Akhenaten and Tiye. This, of course, is purely speculative. Some of Nefertiti's burial equipment possibly found its way eventually to Tutankhamun's tomb. This included a few shabtis which had been renamed but their appearance makes it likely they had been made for a woman, but none bears a trace of a previous name (see Chapter 15).

Egypt has always been subject to fanciful notions of buried treasure. In the 1800s one of the boundary stelae at Amarna was blown up by local people convinced a haul of gold and valuables lay hidden behind it.[24] The latest manifestation of this myth is the proposition that the unadulterated burial of Nefertiti, surrounded by riches, lurks concealed beyond the walls of Tutankhamun's burial chamber. To date no amount of high-tech radar scanning has found anything. Fortunately, today there is no chance of high explosives being wheeled in to tear the walls down.[25] For that at least we can be grateful.

The identity of Tutankhamun's mother was deliberately, and successfully, suppressed along with that of his father. There is one possible simple explanation. The prevailing dogma of the 18th Dynasty which went back to its earliest days and beyond was that the king's mother had been impregnated by Amun in the guise of his father. In Tutankhamun's case no such claim was ever made, and nor could it have been if Akhenaten and Nefertiti were his parents. Since Tutankhamun was made king, despite his age and with nothing else to recommend him, his winning card must have been his lineage. That trumped the ambitions of anyone else left in the court circle, but he could not express or illustrate that lineage in any of the traditional ways. Casting a veil over his parents, whoever they were, was a convenient means of symbolically closing the door on Amarna, clearly deemed essential for the path back to stability, even if he took the trouble to make provision for their burial.[26] His accession made it possible for the royal line to continue, at least for the time being.

## ACCESSION AND RULE

Soon after his accession, whether under Nefertiti's supervision or not, Tutankhamun's court was set up at the palace of Thutmose I in Memphis, recorded on his Restoration Stela set up at Karnak (see below).[27] The move to Memphis formed part of a concerted restoration of the old order. Tutankhamun was depicted retrospectively as a child on the lap of his wet-nurse Maia on a relief in her Saqqara tomb chapel while wearing the khepresh crown in a relief that postdated his name change. The composition was symbolic, recalling Maia's time with him when he was a small child but showing him as king to emphasize her important role in his upbringing.[28] Rings and scarabs found at Amarna bear Tutankhamun's name, including the new -amun form, suggesting that the city was still functioning at least into the early part of his reign.[29] He may therefore have moved between the cities before Amarna was given up.

Significant members of the new regime included the general and future king Horemheb and the treasurer Maya. Both built new tombs in the Memphite necropolis at Saqqara, a significant decision that symbolized the shift in power away from Amarna. The most important, at least in his own view, was Ay. Already in high office under Akhenaten he managed the seamless transition to the new regime and might have been promoted to vizier, though this is disputed.[30] Another Ay, probably a relative, was Second Prophet of Amun and high priest of Mut at Karnak under Tutankhamun.[31]

One of Horemheb's titles was Hereditary Prince or Noble, later repeated on his Coronation Text (see Chapter 16 and Appendix 7). This might indicate he was the nominal heir until or if Tutankhamun produced an heir.[32] If so, Horemheb was to be displaced by Ay senior but only temporarily. However, it is easy to interpret these titles too literally or narrowly. It could just as easily have been used to indicate Horemheb's elite status as a servant of the crown.[33]

Tutankhamun's immaturity did not automatically mean he was only a puppet, and nor was his age at accession unusual in the 18th Dynasty. The difference was that Ahmose, Thutmose III and Amenhotep III all lived well into adulthood. England's Edward VI succeeded to the throne in 1547 at nine years old, about the same age as Tutankhamun had been. Highly educated, Edward rapidly demonstrated that he was not only dedicated to promoting the Protestant religious cause but also to determining who would succeed him. Fully aware of his prerogative as monarch, Edward was quite capable of asserting himself in a historically significant manner, even once he knew he would die young. While this does not mean Tutankhamun was of the same calibre or even educated to a comparable level, Edward nonetheless shows that an educated child of the same age brought up within a royal family could have sought to impose his will, even if that meant a battle with courtiers.

The adult-sized golden throne from Tutankhamun's tomb had clearly belonged to a predecessor but had been modified for his use when still Tutankhuaten, this name appearing prominently on the right outer arm and on the backrest struts.[34] The throne seatback depicts the queen attending to the seated king, but their facial features are virtually identical. They are bathed in the Aten's rays. The queen wears the so-called Nubian wig, which became fashionable during the Amarna period and was itself clearly the result here of a modification (the truncating of the wig is obviously an alteration). On either side of the Aten disk are identical but mirror-reversed pairs of cartouches bearing the two names of the Aten in the form characteristic of the later part of Akhenaten's reign.[35] It was then partially updated. The figures on the throne back are labelled as Tutankhamun and Ankhesenamun, having been easily changed from the -aten versions, yet the Tutankhuaten cartouches on the right arm and the back were left untouched. Ankhesenamun's name on the back had been changed from Ankhesenpaaten but retained its original Aten-period layout in which the -aten element came last in the cartouche. This minimized the necessary changes but omitted the honorific transposition that should have placed Amun at the beginning of her name as seen on new items made during the reign.

Howard Carter believed that either Tutankhamun was not personally committed to the restoration of Amun, or that token efforts to update the throne were considered sufficient.[36] There were several other heirloom objects found in the tomb that bear undamaged names from Akhenaten's reign, showing that such material had survived into Tutankhamun's possession without being altered either during his life or for use in his burial.[37] Another explanation is that the Aten had been reintegrated with the old gods in its traditional role as a form of the sun god. As such it would have been acceptable to see the Aten's name alongside other deities, just as it appeared twice within the inscriptions on the back of a table-shaped wooden box found in the tomb.[38] A further possibility is that Tutankhamun's burial provided a handy opportunity to get rid of any portable property still bearing the Aten name rather than destroy it. There is even some evidence that Aten worship lingered on briefly at Amarna, at least until Horemheb's reign, which means there cannot have been a comprehensive prohibition of the cult.[39]

## Tutankhamun's unborn children

A pair of unlabelled miniature high status coffins found in a box in Tutankhamun's tomb treasury contained the mummies of two miscarried foetuses.[40] The foetuses were of about five and at least eight months' gestation. They have no exact parallel in an Egyptian royal tomb (though given that all the other tombs had been ransacked in antiquity that is unsurprising), but the burial in the king's tomb of royal children who predeceased their fathers is attested, for example in Amenhotep II's and Thutmose IV's tombs.

We have no idea when the miscarriages occurred but obviously one had been stored for many months longer than the other. The cartonnage mask prepared for one of the foetuses was too small. It was set to one side and later deposited along with other used embalming material in the corridor of the tomb. After necropolis officials discovered the tomb had been robbed (the first of two such occasions), the mask was removed with all the other items left there to a nearby pit (KV54, see below). The similarity in the design of their coffins, and the last-minute discovery that one of the masks did not fit, as well as one of the coffins having to have its feet cut back to fit into the box used for them, suggests that the bodies were only prepared for interment with Tutankhamun once he had died, but had been embalmed and stored to await that event. They bore no explanatory inscriptions to identify them or their parents, and instead carried only ritual funerary formulae.[41]

The elder of the two foetuses had several congenital deformities including scoliosis. The foetuses were included in the recent DNA analysis of the royal mummies. The results were consistent with them being Tutankhamun's children, which might have been assumed anyway, and the grandchildren of the KV55 body. The DNA markers also indicated that their descent further back included Yuya and Thuya, and the bodies identified as Amenhotep III and Tiye. Their maternal descent was less certain because the DNA sequencing was incomplete, and very much biased to markers attributed to Tutankhamun. This appeared to indicate that the KV55 body could not also be that of their maternal grandfather. This creates problems with the obvious assumption being that they were Ankhesenamun's children and that she and Tutankhamun at least shared a father. However, as has been suggested by Marc Gabolde, the imbalance is so great it suggests instead that some of the mother's DNA in the foetuses was identical to Tutankhamun's and was misattributed to him by mistake. If so, that would support the parents being siblings or at least half-siblings, restoring the idea that Ankhesenamun was the mother and that therefore Tutankhamun was also a child of Akhenaten's. Nevertheless, there is nothing to confirm that she was the mother, and it would have been perfectly normal for Tutankhamun to have had at least one secondary wife.[42] So many other objections have been raised about the DNA study, some of which have already been mentioned, that it is impossible to accept conclusions drawn from it at face value.[43]

Nothing can alter the commonsense observations that Tutankhamun and Ankhesenamun were likely to have been half-siblings at least, and that Tutankhamun fathered the foetuses either by Ankhesenamun or a lesser wife.

The depictions of Tutankhamun and Ankhesenamun in the tomb are routinely affectionate in the Amarna style and suggest that they enjoyed a normal marriage. These include those on the throne, and, for example, panels on the gilded model shrine of the vulture mother goddess Nekhbet (a patron deity of Egypt) with a variety of scenes including the king pouring water into the queen's hands.[44] Another showing Tutankhamun seated on a stool and firing an arrow at wildfowl while Ankhesenamun sits on the ground in front of him passing him extra ammunition probably represents a favourite pastime. The large number of bows, boomerangs, clubs and other weapons found in the tomb were appropriate equipage for a king. One of Tutankhamun's chariots and other pieces of his equipment show signs of regular use. His clothing included garments designed to brace and secure him in a chariot in the manner of a safety harness. The huge number of walking sticks and fighting sticks (more than 130) found in the tomb are difficult to account for unless the former were practical walking aids for a young man who had mobility issues as indeed his body suggests (see below). Tutankhamun even helped himself in this regard, specifically cutting a reed for use as a stick while out on an expedition which was then inscribed to record the fact.[45]

## TUTANKHAMUN AND EGYPT'S NEIGHBOURS

Tutankhamun made a fleeting appearance in the Amarna Letters, at least one of which was addressed to him by Burra-Buriyaš of Karaduniyaš (Babylon), another piece of evidence for Amarna remaining in use at least for part of the reign. It was a routine pleading that the Egyptian king send gold, offering other goods in return, and must come from early in the reign.[46] There is some evidence that Egypt soon returned to active warfare. The well-known 'painted box' from the tomb with its battle scenes of Tutankhamun in a chariot firing arrows at Asiatic enemies restored the essential stock pose for an Egyptian king.[47] In a relief at the Temple of Luxor Tutankhamun wears the khepresh blue 'war' crown making offerings.[48]

A fragment of gold leaf found in the Western Valley of the Kings shows Tutankhamun smiting a foe while Ankhesenamun looks on, but this is a standard image of a king and of no other significance.[49] More graphic are the reused blocks found in the Temple of Luxor and at Karnak, some probably originating in Tutankhamun's mortuary temple, that include war scenes of Tutankhamun leading in his chariot in an assault on an Asiatic fortress. Both these were probably symbolic representations of his involvement in a war that may have taken place for real, but not necessarily with him in person. The purpose was to recreate the public image of a warrior king, lost during Akhenaten's time. Tutankhamun's general Horemheb included reliefs in his Saqqara tomb that depicted Syrian and Hittite prisoners. Their primary purpose was to magnify Horemheb's achievements as supreme commander of the Egyptian army, albeit ostensibly in honour of Tutankhamun. The reliefs are among the finest surviving examples of the genre, but also commemorated the cruelty suffered by the captives. Paraded with their hands and arms tied up, punched in the face, or tormented by gesticulating Egyptian soldiers, they were hauled before Tutankhamun and his queen as the climax of their humiliation.[50]

The conquering hero Horemheb, bedecked with gold collars, was shown in the presence of Tutankhamun and Ankhesenamun symbolically larger than his attendants and the crowd of manacled and humiliated captives. The reference in the accompanying texts to a regnal year (the actual year date is lost) suggests the events depicted were real ones.[51] Evidently fighting led by Horemheb took place against Asiatic enemies during Tutankhamun's reign. The context would have been Egypt trying to recover dominance in the region after the Hittites defeated Mitanni during Akhenaten's reign and became the main threat to Egyptian influence and vassals in western Asia.

# RESTORING EGYPT

Meanwhile, gradual demolition of Akhenaten and Nefertiti's temple complex at Karnak began. The relief sculptures of the Akhenaten temple were not defaced, as one might have expected. Some of the talatat blocks also found their way into Tutankhamun's building work, flipped over and with new scenes on the other side.[52] The order made by Tutankhamun, or someone on his behalf, to remove Tiye and Akhenaten (at least) from the Royal Tomb at Amarna and rebury them in the Valley of the Kings in KV55 was another part of restoring order (see Chapter 14).[53]

Reliefs in the abandoned and unfinished noble tombs at Amarna were defaced, the favourite target being likenesses of Akhenaten.[54] The desecration extended to Thebes. The tomb of the vizier Ramose (TT55) was entered and the depictions of Akhenaten and Nefertiti from early in the reign were chiselled out. So, too, were names of the Aten and Nefertiti, and Akhenaten's throne name Neferkheperure, but not his birth name Amenhotep by which he was still known at the time. Care was taken to hack through the Aten's rays which were always shown caressing Akhenaten and his family. Severing these was an important symbolic gesture that neutralized the Aten's powers.

The Restoration stela of Tutankhamun at Karnak recorded the programme that had 'repaired what was ruined' and 'repelled disorder from the Two Lands'.[55] The announcement that 'when his Person appeared as king' is the only reference to his origins, his parentage again neatly sidestepped. Once more a ruler of Egypt embarked on discarding the efforts of his predecessor and the human labour involved, though there was little alternative if normality was to return. The programme of restoration began early in the reign:

> *The temples of the gods and goddesses from Elephantine to the marshes of the Delta . . . had fallen into decay. Their shrines had become desolate and had become mounds overgrown with [weeds]. Their sanctuaries were as if they had never been.*

*Their buildings were just thoroughfares. The land was in distress. The gods were ignoring this land.*[56]

Praying to the gods had become futile in those dark days, so the text said. They 'had turned their backs upon this land' and 'their hearts were hurt in their bodies'. Tutankhamun had dealt with the 'deceit' that had afflicted Egypt, setting in place laws that made any repetition of such 'falsehood' an 'abomination of the land', cryptically reducing Akhenaten to a malevolent force that had betrayed the gods. It continued:

*His Majesty sought counsel with his heart, searching for any beneficial deed, seeking out acts of service for his father Amun . . . Then His Majesty made monuments for the gods [making] their cult-statues of authentic electrum . . . building their sanctuaries anew and monuments for the ages of eternity . . . The hearts of the gods and goddesses who are in this land are in joy; the possessors of the shrines are rejoicing.*

The text boasted of an increase in the number of carrying poles used to transport the image of Amun. Tribute to the temples was 'doubled, trebled, quadrupled'. The whole tone, inevitably, was of restoration that 'surpassed' what had gone before. It was a routine claim. Portraying a scene of ruin made the achievement of rebuilding more impressive, symbolizing rebirth. It is unlikely that the traditional temples across Egypt had become quite so decrepit after less than twenty years, especially given the remarkable state of preservation of some today.

The reference to the rejoicing gods was, of course, the final divine endorsement and made a dramatic contrast with the earlier reference to the way the hurt gods had turned their backs on Egypt. The point being made was an obvious one. Amun was fully restored, and the royal house was fully recommitted to supporting the cult. Statues of Amun were erected with Tutankhamun's features, some surviving in the temple today but bearing the names and titles of his successors who usurped them. They had served to reinforce the blurring of the new king's identity with the principal god of the traditional Egyptian pantheon and thus further obliterate the Aten interlude.

At the Temple of Luxor, Tutankhamun completed Amenhotep III's colonnade and commissioned a decorative scheme depicting the Opet Festival. Elsewhere in Egypt, and even into Nubia, Amenhotep III's work was finished or restored.[57] Memphis was probably a major focus of new building or restoration, but the site is so denuded today that little evidence survives beyond fragments.[58] The work was carried out with the assistance of Tutankhamun's most senior officials. Maya, later to be one of the very few officials to be given the privilege of contributing to Tutankhamun's tomb, recorded his contribution:

> I carried out the plans of the King of my time without neglecting anything that he had commanded. I made splendid the temples fashioning the images of the gods for whom I was responsible . . . [I was] the King's mouthpiece in order to furnish the temples and to fashion the cult images of the gods.[59]

One peculiar occasion was recorded in the tomb (TT40) of the noble Amenhotep, nicknamed Huy, who served as a viceroy of Kush under Tutankhamun.[60] The tomb paintings show Huy being invested with his office and presiding over the ceremonial submission of tribute. Tutankhamun is depicted and named. The oddity is that Huy was specifically shown being in receipt of tribute not only by representatives from Nubia but also from Western Asiatic nations.[61] Given his sphere of responsibilities this was incongruous, especially as the two handovers are quite distinct. The ritualized format of these scenes makes it possible the artist used some sort of pattern reference work to copy that resulted in an at least partially symbolic representation of what might or might not have been a genuine event.

Of all the mysteries surrounding Tutankhamun, one more is worth mentioning. Two of his chariots were found in the tomb's treasury and with them a whip handle inscribed 'King's Son, troop commander, Thutmose'.[62] This man appears to have been a prince of the royal household, unless, like the viceroy of Kush, the 'King's Son' element was honorific. Whether he was alive or dead at the time of Tutankhamun's burial it is impossible to say. Likewise, if the whip handle was an heirloom item belonging to Akhenaten's deceased elder brother Thutmose there is no means of proving that since he is not otherwise attested in this post.

The enigmatic Thutmose is a further reminder that there were other players, and likely family members, in the drama of the Amarna period and its aftermath about whom we know nothing. Their presence and actions might have had a material effect on events and relationships that we cannot unravel.


# THE DEATH OF TUTANKHAMUN

Tutankhamun died in his late teens during his 9th regnal year or shortly afterwards.[63] In his case his body makes it certain his death could not have come much later, but its cause is far from straight-forward. His clothes had been tailored to fit someone who had unnaturally wide hips for a male and a narrow waist.[64] An old idea that skull damage was evidence of foul play has been rejected after it was realized this occurred during mummification, leaving displaced fragments. He had a club left foot and hypophalangism (where a pha-lanx is missing) in his right foot. These, together with the walking sticks found in the tomb, suggest he had mobility problems. He also had malaria, traces of the disease's DNA being present in his body. This might have caused his death, but the unhealed fracture of one of his legs may have severely weakened him first, compounding the existing effects of 'multiple physical disorders'.[65] There were also the possible health consequences of descent through a family in which several consanguineous marriages had occurred, and which had caused his unborn children to miscarry.

Several hundred arrows were recovered from the tomb, many of which had been fired, and a decorated tapestry quiver still full of arrows. There was also the well-used chariot, and a folding camp bed that had seen service. His clothing included pieces clearly designed for sports use. The hunting scenes were found in several contexts in the tomb, for example a gilded wooded ostrich-feather fan with a scene showing Tutankhamun in his chariot shooting at fowl with a dog ready to grab the prey.[66] Therefore it is possible Tutankhamun suffered an accident while riding in a chariot on one of these occasions, or even while accompanying a campaign. The trauma of the leg fracture, which had occurred around the time of death or very shortly before, combined with the malaria and a generally weakened constitution is one possible explanation for his early demise, but is by no means conclusive.[67]

When Tutankhamun died, Egypt was still in conflict with the Hittites. Around this time the city of Amqa (or Amka, near Qadesh), controlled by Egypt, was assaulted by a Hittite chariot force in retaliation for an Egyptian chariot attack on Hittite possessions. Perhaps Egypt was starting to struggle to hold on to its prestige in the region. The Hittite description of the event makes it sound far more like an opportunistic raid ('deportees, cattle and sheep' were taken) than any kind of major disaster, even if it humiliated Egypt. According to the Hittite source the Egyptian people were 'afraid' when they heard about it, but that was an inevitable claim which the Hittites could never have substantiated.[68]

What mattered to the Egyptians was not the cause of Tutankhamun's death but the fact that the nation had abruptly lost a young and inexperienced king without a blood heir. This catastrophe had occurred when the nation's power and stability were still being restored. There can be little doubt that Tutankhamun's accession and reign had been overseen by powerful individuals at court. With their young charge suddenly gone, the long-term prospect of ruling through him had evaporated too. Egypt now had only a childless and widowed queen. There was no dynastic successor Ankhesenamun could have acted as regent for. The 18th Dynasty bloodline had abruptly failed. The queen could only have sustained it if she remarried and had children. If Horemheb was still fighting the Hittites, then he was out of the frame for the moment. The scene was set for an extraordinary series of events.

# 16

# THE WIDOWED QUEEN AND THE GOD'S FATHER
## c. 1327–1323 BC

### ANKHESENAMUN AND THE REIGN OF AY

*Another period of confusion followed the death of Tutankhamun. The childless Ankhesenamun began an ill-advised and dangerous attempt to solicit a foreign prince to become her new king and fend off the factions at court. She failed. With Horemheb nowhere to be seen, Tutankhamun's elderly official Ay took the crown and accelerated the process of restoring the power of Amun and the interests of the elite.*

Tutankhamun was the first 18th Dynasty king to die when no appropriate male heir was available within the family circle. A lateral solution had to be found as fast as possible. The most obvious tactic would have been to withhold announcing Tutankhamun's death while backstage manoeuvring took place. Those with vested interests at court were not about to see their power and influence lost to an interloper, and certainly not to a foreign invader taking advantage of the interregnum.

Under normal circumstances, burial was expected to follow the seventy days of mummification. After that, the body was transferred onto a bier to be taken to the tomb, followed by the mourning, the mouth-opening ceremony and other incantations prior to interment.[1] That was the theory. For a private citizen there were none of the political complications surrounding the death of a king and especially one so young and with no heir. Nor were there the practical issues of readying a royal tomb during such a crisis.[2] The new king also needed to be available to officiate over the burial, including the ritual 'Opening of the Mouth'. If no successor was available or had not yet been decided on, then clearly the process could not be concluded.

The discovery of garlands of flowers on Tutankhamun's body, flowers that mostly only appear in March/April, was used by Howard Carter to argue that Tutankhamun must have been buried around that time and had therefore died late the previous year, seventy days earlier. Water lilies included in the garlands only flower between July and November. Carter decided vaguely that if the lilies were 'cultivated in garden tanks at Thebes' they would 'flower much earlier in the year', a classic instance of making the evidence fit the theory as well as being conveniently imprecise.[3]

More collars had been found in the embalming cache originally from the tomb (KV54, see below). Some of the collars and garlands from both sources also had blue glass and faience beads sewn into the rows.[4] Making them was an elaborate process that separated the time of picking the flowers from the earliest date at which they could be used. They were so well preserved, and the conditions so favourable, that most of the species could be identified.

Tutankhamun's intricate floral collars were of types also found in other high-status graves. This either means those who died at any other time of the year had to do without or, as is surely more likely, the wreaths were manufactured when the flowers were available and then set aside to be installed in burials as needed. The presence of the water lilies is much more easily explained that way. The

Egyptian climate would certainly have facilitated such a practice. The Egyptian funerary industry was organized around a continuous production process and stockpiling of material.[5]

As evidence for the date of Tutankhamun's burial, the flowers are thus of no matter. Tutankhamun's mummification was therefore not necessarily followed immediately by the funeral obsequies and sealing the tomb. The complicated circumstances meant that a delay was far more likely, but it is pointless to try and construct a specific timetable. There is good reason to believe that the succession and arrangements for his funeral were far from settled when Tutankhamun died.[6]

# THE EGYPTIAN QUEEN'S CORRESPONDENCE

One of the most important pieces of evidence from this period is a series of fragmented cuneiform tablets found at the Hittite settlement of Hattusa (Bogazköy) in Turkey.[7] They included a text named as the 'Deeds of Shuppiluliuma as told by his son Mursili II'. The Hittite attack on the Egyptian vassal city of Amqa, described in the account, was a sign of the mounting tension.

There then came an extraordinary twist. Following the sudden death of a king, a widowed Egyptian queen was floundering. In anxious expectation of a solution, she sent off dispatches to Shuppiluliuma, copies of the texts of which have – extraordinarily – survived. These are in the form of incidental references and quotes supplied by the son of Shuppiluliuma who was mainly concerned with recounting the story of his father's capture of Carchemish. They are not the original documents, which lays them open to omissions, modifications, and mistakes. Some of the requests are given as the queen's own words, but others are in the words of courtiers (who are otherwise unknown) on her behalf, repeating the same request. They apparently refer to actual events but are not necessarily wholly reliable.

The irritatingly similar throne names used by Egyptian kings of the period have made it difficult to work out exactly who was involved from the Hittite version. The only two serious possibilities are Akhenaten and Tutankhamun. Even the Hittites may not have been fully aware of whom they were dealing with. They called the queen Dakhamunzu, their phonetic rendition of the Egyptian words for queen.[8]

The correspondence found at Amarna shows that three months for a letter to travel one way to or from Western Asia to Egypt counted as express mail.[9] Therefore, the Egyptian queen might have waited six months or more for a reply. Clearly, drawing conclusions about the exact sequence of events in Egypt over weeks or months is impossible. The messages were almost certainly out of date when they reached Shuppiluliuma, let alone when his replies reached Memphis or Thebes.

There are only three realistic candidates for the widowed queen: Nefertiti, Meryetaten and Ankhesenamun. She stated she had no son, meaning there was no male heir on hand. Only in Ankhesenamun's case was this true. For Nefertiti and Meryetaten, Tutankhamun was available to succeed following Akhenaten's death (and a possible short tenure of the throne by Nefertiti), which was exactly what he had done. Therefore, on the face of it Ankhesenamun is most likely to have been the queen concerned and thus the deceased king Tutankhamun.[10] That of course is not the same as a certainty.

The widowed Egyptian queen made no bones about her predicament, begging Shuppiluliuma to provide one of his own sons to replace her husband and make good the lack of an heir. She insisted that under no circumstances would she choose a husband from among her servants, by which she meant senior men in the court and army circle. The eventual failure of the queen's subterfuge meant that precisely what she was trying to avoid occurred: the elderly court official Ay became king.

The queen was completely isolated, trusting no one around

her. The succession was clearly still unsettled and dangerously so – she said she was afraid. There was much at stake. Whoever ended up ruling Egypt would become the most powerful leader in the region. Her tactic breached one of the great taboos of the 18th Dynasty royal family. A foreign husband, and thus a king, was unthinkable.

Since the passages concerned are so unusual, they are reproduced here with some modifications. They have been edited for clarity into Mursili II's narrative and the reported speech of both the Egyptian queen and Shuppiluliuma. The dates given are estimates. No dating information exists in the originals apart from some references to the time of year. The correspondence began no later than the late summer because it refers to Shuppiluliuma being on campaign when the first request from the Egyptian queen with the news of her husband's death arrived. It continued after winter into the following spring, to which there is an explicit reference.

## LATE SUMMER/AUTUMN 1327 BC

MURSILI: But when the people of Egypt[11] heard of the attack on Amka [by Shuppiluliuma's forces], they were afraid. And since, in addition, their lord Niphururias [Tutankhamun?] has died, therefore the queen of Egypt who was Daḫamunzu, sent a messenger to my father [Shuppiluliuma] and wrote to him thus:

THE QUEEN: *My husband died. A son I have not. But to you, they say, the sons are many. If you would give me one son of yours, he would become my husband. Never shall I pick out a servant of mine and make him my husband . . . I am afraid.*

MURSILI: When my father heard this, he called forth the Great Ones for council (saying):

SHUPPILULIUMA: *Such a thing has never happened to me in my whole life.*

MURSILI: So, it happened that my father sent forth to Egypt the chamberlain Hattušaziti (with this order):

SHUPPILULIUMA: *Go and bring you (his chamberlain Hattušaziti) back to me the true word. Maybe they are deceiving me. Maybe they do in fact have a son of their lord. You bring the true word back to me.*

EARLY 1326 BC – Hattušaziti returns from Egypt with a new letter from the queen, and accompanied by an Egyptian official called Hani:

MURSILI: But when it became spring, Hattušaziti [came back] from Egypt, and the messenger of Egypt, Lord Hani, came with him. Now, since my father had, when he sent Hattušaziti to Egypt, given him orders as follows:

SHUPPILULIUMA: *Maybe they have a son of their lord? Maybe they deceive me and do not want my son for the kingship?*

MURSILI: Therefore, the queen of Egypt wrote back to my father in a letter thus:

THE QUEEN: *Why did you say 'they deceive me' in that way? Had I a son, would I have written about my own and my country's shame to a foreign land? You did not believe me and have even spoken thus to me. He who was my husband has died. A son I have not. Never shall I take a servant of mine and make him my husband. I have written to no other country, only to you have I written. They say your sons are many. To me he will be husband but in Egypt he will be king.*

MURSILI: So, since my father was kind-hearted, he complied with the word of the woman and concerned himself with the matter of a son.

In the next tablet, Shuppiluliuma addresses Egypt's Lord Hani, who repeats the queen's problem:

SHUPPILULIUMA: *You keep asking me for a son as if it was my duty. He will in some way become a hostage, but [king] you will not make him.*

MURSILI: Hani spoke thus to my father:

HANI: *Oh, my Lord. This is . . . our country's shame. If we had [a son of the king?] at all, would we have come to a foreign country, asking for a lord for ourselves? Niphururias [Tutankhamun?], who was our lord, died; a son he has not. Our lord's wife is solitary. We are seeking a son of our Lord*

> *for the kingship in Egypt, and for the woman, our lady, we seek him as*
> *her husband. Furthermore, we went to no other country, only here did we*
> *come. Now, oh our Lord, give us a son of yours.*

MURSILI: So, then my father concerned himself on their behalf with
the matter of a son.

Despite the prospect of effectively joining the Hittite nation and
Egypt into one, Shuppiluliuma smelled a rat and asked for clarification. He gambled on having been told the truth and ordered
his son Zannanza to head for Egypt and make his approaches
to the queen. To Shuppiluliuma's fury Zannanza was killed, or
died, on the journey, recorded on a later document (see below),
and convincing him that he had been the victim of Egyptian
duplicitousness.[12]

The now-damaged tablets had been prepared for copying onto
bronze tablets which are long lost. Fortunately, the sections referring
to the Egyptian queen are among the best preserved. Working out
which pieces belonged where and their order involved meticulous
work. It is possible that the passages referring to the queen's correspondence are not in the correct chronological order.

Most of the problems arise from the names, or lack of. Since
the queen is not identified by a personal name, the key word is the
name of the recently deceased Egyptian king. This read Niphururias
or Nibḫururiya.[13] The two Egyptian throne names to which this
is closest are Neferkheperure (Akhenaten) or Nebkheperure
(Tutankhamun).[14] Some Egyptologists prefer to believe the name
represented is Akhenaten's Neferkheperure, but this is largely
because they want evidence for the idea Nefertiti ruled in her own
right after his death.[15] There is good reason to believe she did, but
since Tutankhamun was available the succession crisis could not
have applied to Nefertiti.

Just as Tutankhamun as king never referred to his parentage, neither did the Hittites refer to the lineage of Nibḫururiya.
However, since the Hittites were likely to have been confused by

the similar throne names of Akhenaten and Tutankhamun, especially given that the tablet texts are not the original texts, there is nothing to be gained by trying to pin the names down definitively.[16] More importantly, only the widowed Ankhesenamun's circumstances, so far as we understand them, properly fit the events described in the tablets but in Egyptology that will never be enough to settle the matter. However, for the purposes of this book it will be assumed hereon that the letters were sent by Ankhesenamun.

# BURYING TUTANKHAMUN

Young, childless and widowed, Ankhesenamun had nothing to offer her country. Any plans to marry a foreigner were bound to be resisted. Ankhesenamun's wishes were ignored. So were Tutankhamun's since he was quite clearly not interred in a royal tomb. The one in which Tutankhamun was eventually buried (KV62) was much smaller and simpler than was usual for a king. The tomb was also very close to KV55 where at the time Tiye and Akhenaten(?) were still buried. In its original form it consisted of no more than a corridor and single chamber (known today as the antechamber), resembling Yuya and Thuya's tomb (KV46). To prepare it for Tutankhamun's use it was extended by cutting out three additional rooms, but they were not sufficient to prevent the tomb being congested with jumbled grave goods intended for a much larger facility.

Tutankhamun was thus buried in what might once have been planned as a noble's tomb, one perhaps being prepared for Ay as a special honour.[17] If KV62 was originally Ay's tomb it replaced his earlier tomb at Amarna (TA25) which had been abandoned along with all the other tombs there. If Ay was Yuya and Thuya's son, then his high status under Tutankhamun might very well have led to the privilege of a tomb in the Valley of the Kings not far from theirs. Some of the burial chamber's decoration was laid out on the Amarna grid of proportions, but the rest was completed on the restored traditional grid. Tutankhamun's intended tomb is most likely to have been the one in the Western Valley of the Kings later used by Ay (WV23). It was built in a style and on a scale suitable for a royal tomb.[18]

Tutankhamun's burial equipment, including special items and pieces from his everyday life, was carried to the Valley of the Kings in the funeral procession through what was then a narrow and winding track. One of the first items to go in was the heavy quartzite sarcophagus, as well as items designated for the treasury beyond.[19] This was a secondhand piece, but it is impossible now to tell from the adapted carving and new inscriptions who the original owner was.[20] No one had bothered to check if it was suitable for Tutankhamun's three coffins. The outer coffin's feet protruded upwards from the sarcophagus which meant that the sarcophagus lid cracked when it was lowered into place. The end of the coffin's foot was summarily hacked off with an adze before replacing the lid and using plaster to cover up the crack. Evidently there was no time available to do anything else.

Once Tutankhamun's body and coffins were secured in the sarcophagus, the shrine panels were brought in and partially (and incorrectly) assembled. Only then was a partition wall built to close off the burial chamber but with an access doorway incorporated so that final items could be installed there and in the treasury beyond. The burial chamber's wall paintings were executed, or at least completed, and only then was the doorway to the burial chamber sealed.[21]

In the haste to pack out the tomb, calcite jars containing vintage oils and unguents were cleared out from palace stores. They included examples that had been passed over for previous burials. They clearly had not been intended for tomb use and had seen long service. Some were broken and repaired, with one dating back to Thutmose III.[22] The tomb also contained some pieces designated for other burials that had either never been used or that had been removed from some of the cleared Amarna burials. This sort of ad hoc assemblage, especially if a king died sooner than expected, may well have been normal up to a point. These included some valuable and important items, their origins allegedly betrayed by trace palimpsests of the throne name Ankhkheperure used by Smenkhkare and Nefertiti, for example on the miniature coffins that held Tutankhamun's viscera.[23] His names on a pectoral of Nut had undoubtedly replaced others, one probably being Ankhkheperure and the other possibly Neferneferuaten.[24] The second gilded wooden shrine of the four used to encase the sarcophagus originally belonged to someone whose name ended -aten, a particularly tantalizing clue to its former owner, with only Smenkhkare being easily ruled out.[25] This sort of reuse may well have been normal for a royal tomb, at least up to a point, but in Tutankhamun's case all the evidence points to a rushed job.

Some other repurposed items include a gilt wooden statuette of a king wearing the crown of Upper Egypt. The figure is that of an adult woman standing on a base set on the figure of a walking leopard, yet an inscription identifies the person as Tutankhamun. Nefertiti was a likely original owner, and perhaps also of some of the shabtis.[26] The second coffin is often said to have facial features unlike those of the other two coffins or any other named likenesses of Tutankhamun, the alternate candidate usually cited (without any possible means of verification) as the elusive Smenkhkare. A simple experiment overlaying an image of the golden mask over the second coffin's portrait told a different story. The proportions of the features of the two faces are almost identical. The differences in detail are trivial and far fewer than the similarities.[27] The gold mask as originally designed had ear piercings but was installed in the tomb with gold discs used to patch over the holes. Other material had been taken over by Tutankhamun for use in his lifetime. One was a box that was clearly once inscribed for Neferneferuaten as king and Meryetaten as her great royal wife but had been relabelled for

Tutankhamun and Ankhesenamun. The box even bore a hieratic docket indicating that it had been earmarked for the funeral procession, and unwittingly a voyage through time to the twentieth century.[28]

At the very least, Tutankhamun's tomb emerges as a likely partial repository of items drawn from the Amarna period and its aftermath, conveniently disposed of on a permanent basis by including them in the inventory. There is one other striking point to note. Just like KV55, nothing in Tutankhamun's tomb demonstrably belonged to the elusive Smenkhkare.[29]

Thanks to haste and disorganization, mistakes were made in assembling the gilded shrines resulting in some of the panels being incorrectly orientated. Brute force was used to make them fit.[30] The shrine that contained the canopic jars was assembled incorrectly, with two of the four figures of the guardian goddesses misplaced. It was left by the carpenters and joiners responsible in the company of a pile of wood chips they did not trouble themselves to clean up, confident that once the tomb was sealed no one else would know (or care).[31]

The errors extended to other pieces in the tomb. The antechamber contained three animal-sided gilt wooden ritual beds. One of these bore an inscription for the cow goddess Mehetweret, but the bed concerned had lioness heads. The cow-headed bed, conversely, had an inscription referring to the lioness goddess Isis-Mehtet.[32] If this was a simple transposition mistake that happened while preparing the components it would have been an easy one to make, especially if the artisans involved were only semi-literate. The observation might seem a trivial one, but in Egypt enormous significance could be attached to a single word or phrase. The demonstrable errors made in the tomb of a king, even one whose burial had required the urgent rustling up of the necessary funerary equipment, leave open the possibility that some incongruous or cryptic inscriptions found in other contexts might also contain mistakes and thus render conclusions drawn from them quite wrong. The Egyptians may seem confusing to us, but sometimes the people they most confused were themselves.

Further complications lurk in the wall paintings of the burial chamber.[33] Based on the inscriptions, an implausibly youthful Ay is depicted on the burial chamber's wall paintings carrying out the Opening of the Mouth ceremony, raising questions about whether the figures had originally been painted to represent others. The ritual, which symbolically reanimated a mummy, dated back to the earliest days of pharaonic history. The procedure took place outside the tomb before the mummy was interred. Thus revived, the mummy could once more consume food and drink and thereby have the strength to maintain the soul (ka) of the deceased. In this royal context it also marked out Ay as Tutankhamun's heir, but the scene was unprecedented for a royal tomb even though it was known in surface buildings. The painted version served as a permanent record of what must have happened at the entrance to Tutankhamun's tomb. Ay appears to have been particularly concerned to take every opportunity to assert his right to rule, however incongruous that must have seemed. This was another instance of how Egyptian royal identity and protocols were vested in symbolism, managed as a sort of parallel alternate reality.

Apparently Ay's succession had been settled upon by the time the wall paintings were finished and may very well have been by the time the decision was made to go ahead with the burial in KV62. However, the Osiris figure of the deceased Tutankhamun has been claimed to have 'feminine' features and incongruously holds two flails instead of the conventional kingly crook and flail. This has led to the suggestion that the tomb and its paintings were originally prepared for Nefertiti with her as Osiris, and Tutankhamun opening her mouth (explaining the youthful features of the new king Ay). In that scenario, Tutankhamun's entire burial would have occasioned the clearance of Nefertiti's assemblage in his favour on Ay's orders, explaining the reused burial goods, the iconography and the inscriptions. The scene in this version therefore originally showed

Tutankhamun opening the mouth of the deceased Nefertiti.[34] However, as was pointed out earlier, facial features are not a reliable means of distinguishing individuals within the context of art being produced for a narrow royal circle, and especially where symbolic youth was more important. Egyptian artisans would have had no basis or precedent for showing Ay as a man in his sixties and nor would it have been in his interests to be so, which is why he also usurped statues of Tutankhamun.

None of this makes any difference to the facts that Nefertiti died or was killed at some point, Tutankhamun had ruled, died and been succeeded by Ay. It had been several decades since anyone had been called on to prepare a conventional royal tomb with traditional themes. Mistakes and novelties were possible, such as the twin flails which in any case made for attractive symmetry over the Osiride shoulders, as was the way artistic workshops often rely on replicating imagery, especially generic portraits in the politicized context of state art.[35]

Some of the most important related pieces to be installed in the tomb were Tutankhamun's chariots. In a world where these vehicles had become the most conspicuous accessory for a king, this was unsurprising. Appropriately for a king he was therefore buried with six while his noble forebear Yuya had been buried with only one. It was obvious from its axle grease and worn components that at least one of the two placed in the treasury (the other four being placed in the antechamber) had been used in life.

Ever since its discovery, the tomb of Tutankhamun has been regarded as the glamorous climax of Egyptian royal burial customs. This is based largely on the fact that no other royal tomb of the period has ever been found in such a relatively undisturbed state and excellent preservation. The tomb of the 21st Dynasty king Psusennes I (1039–991 BC), which was also found intact at Tanis in 1940, paled by comparison.[36]

The extravagant contents of Tutankhamun's tomb reached their height with the solid gold inner coffin, weighing 243 lb (110 kg, at the time of writing over US$6.5 million in bullion value alone), and the solid gold mask. The honorific formulae that embellished so many of the contents were explicit references to the extent of his divinity as a manifestation of Osiris that positioned him way beyond other mortals. They epitomize the emphasis placed on the importance of the person of the pharaoh that he merited such treatment, and the hold the royal family had over Egypt's wealth and the ability to write it off in tombs.

Nevertheless, the chaotic way in which key items were installed would have completely negated their magical function. This had even included ignoring the written instructions on the components and the care that had been taken to manufacture them. This begs the question of just how important any of this potent symbolism really was, and why the work was executed so badly by people whose apparent concern was only to finish the job. One could forgive the workmen concerned for ignorance of the correct protocols, but not those who must have been in charge.[37] The process of filling the tomb also surely provided opportunities for the light-fingered among the workers to filch small items. If not, they still went away armed with vital intelligence about what the tomb contained, a highly saleable commodity on its own.

The last stage was to fill the antechamber and annexe with remaining items before the final rituals. After that the tomb was closed, residual items were left in the corridor and the entrance stairway filled with rubble and covered over. The chaos discovered in parts of the tomb by Howard Carter, especially in the annexe, has always been attributed to the two break-ins by tomb robbers. They were certainly responsible for some of the damage, but not necessarily all of it. Considering the sloppy work so evident in the treasury and elsewhere, it is quite possible some of the jumble dated to the original burial.

The discovery of a pit nearby (KV54) in 1907 shed more light on the completion and closure of the tomb.[38] The contents were the remains of a funerary meal held at the real tomb, put into about a dozen jars along with materials such as bags of natron salts used in the king's mummification, and some floral collars worn by those attending the wake. These had been placed originally in the corridor to the tomb immediately after the antechamber was closed. Only the staircase was filled with rubble, the doorway to the corridor being sealed.

After the first robbery, which only affected the antechamber and annexe, all these items, together with the cartonnage mask belonging to one of the miscarried foetuses, had been removed and reburied in the pit. Meanwhile, the tomb corridor was filled with rubble to dissuade (unsuccessfully) any more robbers from gaining access. This would also have inhibited any subsequent official inspections which were operating in the Valley a few years later. The second robbery was more organized and probably involved a series of entries over consecutive days or nights. The thieves had to dig their way through the filled corridor but were eventually able to make their way throughout the tomb and had begun to open the sealed doors to the shrines surrounding the sarcophagus when it appears they were caught. Even so, it is inconceivable that they had got that far without the connivance of some of the officials in charge of the necropolis. Those responsible for subsequently clearing up the robbers' mess and resealing the tomb for the last time made no more than a perfunctory stab at the task and for all we know also helped themselves to items while on the task.

The robbers also obviously exhibited no sentimentality about Tutankhamun's welfare in the afterlife or those who had provided for it. Apart from portable valuables, the key targets included the valuable unguents which were decanted from the fifty or so calcite vases into containers, such as skins.[39] Practically untraceable, these liquids would have been relatively easy to sell on. Had the thieves involved in the second break-in not been apprehended they would have eventually opened all the shrines and then forced their way into the sarcophagus to reach the coffins in search of jewels and gold.

Meanwhile, Tutankhamun was consigned to the ages. For a while his posthumous cult was maintained but it does not seem to have lasted long. A 'pure priest' at the 'temple of Tutankhamun' called Pairy is attested in the role on a shabti from his own tomb, and a stela records Userhat who served the cult and that of Amenhotep III.[40] The mortuary temple, known as 'The Mansion of Nebkheperure', has never been found though statues from it were used by his successor Ay in his own temple and talatat blocks possibly from it have turned up at the Temple of Luxor.[41] Meanwhile, temporal events were moving fast and before too long any official memory of his reign would be wiped out, too.

# THE REIGN OF AY 1327/6–1323 BC (KHEPERKHEPERURE, 'EVERLASTING MANIFESTATIONS OF RE')

The Hittite king Shuppiluliuma might have deduced from the original letters he received from the queen that there were rival factions at the Egyptian court. If so, he did not appreciate just how vulnerable she claimed to be, preferring to believe that he was the one under threat. At some point Ay appears to have waded into the exchanges with Shuppiluliuma because correspondence between the Hittite ruler and a new king of Egypt followed.

Shuppiluliuma blamed Egypt for his son Zannanza's death, likening him to a chick killed by a falcon, the falcon symbolizing Horus as the predatory state of Egypt. He threatened revenge which the new Egyptian king responded to by promising to fight back and mocked suggestions of a peace agreement. Ay is not named in the documents. Therefore, it can only be assumed that he was the subject of the correspondence, but with good reason.[42] Shuppiluliuma died not long afterwards, apparently killed by a plague among the prisoners he brought back from Egypt's vassal states that he had attacked. He was followed to the grave a year later by his heir Arnuwanda II, the disaster having a serious impact on Hittite power for some time to come.[43]

The enemies at court whom Ankhesenamun feared must have been galvanized by the discovery of what she had been up to, especially if they had their own plans. Doubtless dismayed by the prospect of Egypt becoming a divided or vassal state, and even more by the thought of the loss of their own privileged positions, it would have been natural to take action to deal with Zannanza as he travelled towards the Egyptian border. It is easy to imagine Ay sending a hit squad out to deal with the foreign prince and stage-managing his own accession. However, the road south into Egypt from Hittite territory was long and dangerous, and the possibility remains that Zannanza was taken out by armed robbers. The consequences were the same: the correspondence achieved nothing for Ankhesenamun who was shortly to become as irrelevant as the rest of her birth family already had.

Ay's stellar career had made him, so far as we know, the most dominant and best-placed official when Tutankhamun died.[44] He might once have expected to live out his days exerting influence over and directing Tutankhamun throughout his reign. The young king's premature death put paid to that plan, making for unexpected opportunities. If Ay had a blood connection back through the family of Yuya, however tenuous, this may have clinched his claim. As we have seen, the circumstantial evidence for this is strong but not conclusive. Ay had just as likely applied himself to displacing Horemheb as a potential heir, perhaps because the latter was absent fighting the Hittites.

Ay had acquired or appropriated his 'God's Father' title by Akhenaten's reign, an honour of potentially decisive significance, and possibly also the viziership though this is not certain.[45] In a bizarre twist Ay had by succeeding Tutankhamun also become the King's Son. It was a nonsense of course, given that he was old enough to be Tutankhamun's grandfather (and possibly was his actual grandfather), but in the world of Egyptian royal relationships what mattered was the label, not the reality. A succession crisis had been at least temporarily evaded.[46]

Gold leaf depicting Ay as 'God's Father' while Tutankhamun
smites a foe and Ankhesenamun looks on.

Ay succeeded to the throne well into later life, something he
could surely not have expected. He remained married to Tey. Ay's
accession sealed Ankhesenamun's fate. She had lost control and soon
disappeared. The beleaguered queen goes unmentioned thereafter
apart from a single blue faience ring that bore her name alongside
Ay's regnal name. It was found in the Nile Delta at an unknown site
and bears no statement of relationship or occasion.[47] The ring only
makes sense if it refers to a marriage after Ay's accession. Whether it
was something that had happened or was planned is impossible to
say without any other evidence to substantiate the union.

If the ring is evidence that Ankhesenamun married Ay (perhaps
under coercion), the arrangement did not last. No child appeared.
Ay is only ever shown with Tey. The stillborn children found in
Tutankhamun's tomb would have done nothing to recommend
Ankhesenamun's fertility, assuming they were hers. Her foiled
attempts to find a foreign husband would have discredited and marginalized her. Neutralized and irrelevant, history thereafter passed

her by, and she, too, was deleted from monuments by Ay's successor Horemheb. Apart from items associated with her in Tutankhamun's burial, Ankhesenamun has like her sisters otherwise vanished.[48]

Given Tutankhamun's youth, and the disappearance of Nefertiti, it is hard not to imagine that Ay had been the one really in charge, even if Tutankhamun was developing ideas of his own. Ay was well placed to manage his own succession. He seems to have ruled unchallenged apart from a possible brief and little-known war against the aggrieved Shuppiluliuma's army. Ay cannot have led that in person, Horemheb being far more likely.[49] Ay certainly posed on his monuments as 'Suppressor of Asia', capitalizing on the publicity.[50] One of the other remnants that turned up in Pit 58 (KV58) in the Valley of the Kings suggests Ay knew how to pose as a warrior king even if he had never been one. A piece of gold foil that had clearly once been in his tomb was decorated with the ageing king shown as a warrior in a pose more suited to Amenhotep II's glory days, an irony given how long it had been since there had been any such king. Ay as king stands in a chariot firing arrows at a copper ingot, four of which had already pierced the target. Another depicts the usual foreigners prostrating themselves before him as king.[51] However, court artisans were also accustomed to turning out pieces with stock images like this on them.

Ay had a son or grandson called Nakhtmin whose mother was a woman called Iuy, Chantress of Isis and an Adoratrice of Min.[52] Iuy's name and association with Min raise the possibility that she was yet another member of Yuya's clan, and perhaps even Ay's daughter. Nakhtmin was old enough to hold several high offices and therefore well placed to succeed Ay. He was already present in the court circle in a senior military capacity by the time Tutankhamun died. Nakhtmin was on hand to commission several shabtis for Tutankhamun's tomb. Horemheb did not contribute any shabtis, perhaps because he was out of the country fighting. Nakhtmin was not yet called 'King's Son' at the time – the title only appears on the remains of a broken statue.[53] He must have been awarded the title after Tutankhamun's death and only once Ay had become king.[54] The availability of Nakhtmin as a putative successor would have helped Ay's accession and strengthened his tenure of the throne. If that was the plan, it came to nothing because Nakhtmin was another high-profile individual who disappeared.

Ay indulged briefly in bestowing patronage on his loyal supporters. One, whose name and title are lost, received a gift of land in Ay's 3rd regnal year while the king was in Memphis. Ay lasted into his 4th regnal year at least.[55] The subsequent destruction or usurpation of most of Ay's monuments guaranteed that few records of his activities would survive.

Ay's main pastimes were completing the tomb he had helped himself to in the Western Valley (WV23) and usurping his young predecessor's statues and other monuments, including almost certainly Tutankhamun's mortuary temple. It may even have been cleared away to make room for Ay's, and then taken over later by Horemheb.[56] Rebranding Tutankhamun's statues as his was a quick way for Ay to increase his profile and appear youthful. It had taken Amenhotep III thirty years and a jubilee to achieve rejuvenation.[57] Ay managed it far more easily but barely lived long enough to enjoy the experience.

Ay's appropriated tomb was unfinished when he died. Ay's bourgeois origins betrayed themselves in some of the painted scenes in the burial chamber. One, unique for the tomb of a king, included his queen Tey watching her husband hunt. Incongruous for a royal burial chamber, the husband and wife composition and its setting were more appropriate for the walls of a noble's tomb (though similar scenes had appeared on the Nekhbet shrine in Tutankhamun's tomb). Other painted scenes in the burial chamber are unknown elsewhere in the Valley of the Kings. Just as with Tutankhamun's tomb the artists were still in the throes of reviving pre-Aten funerary iconography and were both uncertain and imaginative in their approach.[58] One of these novel scenes was of the four sons of Horus. They were all shown holding only flails in the manner of a hieroglyph used as a determinative for revered persons.[59]

Ay's tomb was later comprehensively vandalized by robbers, leaving little to be recovered in modern times (it was found in 1816) and making it impossible to evaluate the burial. The few fragments of bone recovered, not necessarily even his, can say nothing about Ay's cause of death. It is also impossible now to compare these with the remains of the Elder Lady or Yuya and Thuya, which might have gone some way to confirm whether Ay was a close relative of theirs. His age was the most likely reason for Ay's death, but it also made him vulnerable. The decision to remove Ay forcibly by those keen to bring the whole Amarna era to a permanent end and place a more dynamic character on the throne is a plausible scenario.

This overmighty subject had achieved the unimaginable. Being an Egyptian king was much more about the posturing than the reality. Nothing could turn back time for Ay, even usurping Tutankhamun's statues. If Ay was a member of Yuya's family, his death marked the end of the clan's dominance of the royal circle and the last blood link to the dynasty. Now the self-professed outsider Horemheb could make his move.

The elderly Ay depicted as a warrior king in a stock pose firing arrows through a copper ingot. A piece of gold foil found in Pit 58 in the Valley of the Kings, but which had originated in his tomb in the Western Valley.

There is one final mystery surrounding Ay. A blue faience pommel from a walking stick or box knob bearing his throne name was found in the tomb of Nefertari-Meryetmut, the principal queen of Ramesses II.[60] By the time she died in the mid-thirteenth century BC Ay had been dead for around seventy-five years. There is no demonstrable connection, but the possibility remains that the queen was descended from or related to Ay and that the pommel had been retained as an heirloom. If so, Nefertari was the last link with Yuya's family. None of her children were to succeed Ramesses II.

# 17

# THE ENLIGHTENED DESPOT
## c. 1323–1295 BC

### Horemheb (Djeserkheperure Setenpre, 'Holy are the Manifestations of Re, Chosen of Re')

*The accession of Horemheb was the last turning point for the 18th Dynasty. Although Horemheb sought to delete permanently any record of his immediate predecessors and restore the crown's power and prestige, he had an enlightened sense of the contract between the king and the population. His reforms had no precedent. His choice of successor determined Egypt's future direction.*

The reign of Ay was only possible because of the unfortunate circumstances surrounding Tutankhamun's premature death and the absence of an heir. Ay's rule represented a tenuous brand of continuity, but he was tainted by association with Akhenaten and Nefertiti. The disappearance of Nakhtmin, Ay's son or grandson and intended successor, left the way open to Horemheb. A successful general under Tutankhamun and Ay, Horemheb was one of the most conspicuous officials of the time.[1]

Horemheb's rise from obscurity was a result of ability and strength of character. These were attributes less likely to arise in a hereditary monarchy other than by sheer luck. Horemheb was that rare royal commodity, a king who had the ability and intelligence to rule on his own merit. This made him unusual by 18th Dynasty standards. Horemheb had the political acumen to see that Egypt needed a line drawn in the sand. He must have seemed especially appealing after a time of instability. Experienced, dynamic, and educated, he would also have appeared much more intimidating to foreign rulers than his immediate predecessors.

With the elderly Ay on the throne it is also easy to see how much more attractive a prospect as king a man of Horemheb's calibre might have been to those with an eye on the future. If Ay was assassinated in a coup designed to place Horemheb on the throne we know nothing of it, but given the ageing Ay's dubious claim on the throne a plot to get rid of him is plausible. Either way, unlike most of the 18th Dynasty kings Horemheb came to power at a more appropriate age, with experience of statecraft and the professed determination to use it properly. Whether he had any 'right' to take the throne is entirely academic in the context of the period, even with his title Hereditary Prince. Opportunity and circumstance were the decisive factors, especially when there was no dynastic heir available, at least that we know of.

Horemheb's Hereditary Prince title (see previous chapter) only indicated that he might have been earmarked to become king if Tutankhamun died childless. If so, he had been temporarily out-manoeuvred by Ay. Horemheb now took great trouble to present himself as the rightful king and the restorer of Egypt (see below).[2] It was Egypt's good fortune that the best man for the job had been found though few at the time can have had a clear idea of what the job was. This was just as well because there is no evidence that anyone else was available.

Horemheb was later portrayed as succeeding Amenhotep III, deleting Akhenaten, Tutankhamun and Ay from the king lists. No one now seems quite sure whether to place Horemheb in the 18th or 19th Dynasty and he would have been uncertain himself. Apart from the tenuous possibility that his queen Mutnodjmet was Nefertiti's sister, Horemheb had no connection to the 18th Dynasty bloodline.[3] In Egyptology the reading of a single hieroglyphic sign, or the similarity of a name, can lead to inspiration, confusion, or both. As a result, the assumption that Nefertiti's sister had the same name led to the theory that Horemheb had positioned himself by marrying as close to the royal family as possible during the Amarna period. It now seems Nefertiti's sister was really called Mutbenret and was probably a different person (see Chapter 12 and Appendix 5).[4] Even if they were one and the same, Horemheb was the third king in a row to leave no descendants, so the bloodline failed regardless. He established the 19th Dynasty but had no family connection to those who succeeded him.

Horemheb created his own fantasy destiny myth. In his Coronation Text, Horemheb claimed to have been plucked from obscurity by his father Horus, Lord of Hut-nesu (the Egyptian name for Herakleopolis, meaning 'child of the king'). Herakleopolis was a town near the Faiyum Oasis, presumably where Horemheb came from. Horus, who may be either the god or a predecessor king in the guise of the god, brought Horemheb to Karnak to be embraced as king by his father Amun in the Opet Festival. The ambiguity was deliberate, as was making sure he was crowned king during that powerfully symbolic annual event. It obscured how he had really come to power.[5]

Horemheb had to prove his right to rule. Not to have claimed he was Amun's chosen one would have been incongruous. The theological framework was sufficiently flexible and reliant on symbolism to accommodate the passage of the crown to a successor of non-royal origins. It went with the territory. However, Horemheb avoided the traditional claim of descent from a queen impregnated by Amun. Even the most imaginatively contrived yarn could not have concealed his lack of royal blood. The contrast between the reality and the fiction was blatant though it is very unlikely this made any difference to most of the population. He reinforced his position with other symbols. A tableau found in the Temple of Luxor shows Horemheb kneeling before the creator god Atum making an offering in recognition of the gift of kingship.[6]

At Hatshepsut's Deir el-Bahari temple, which he restored, Horemheb referred to Thutmose III as 'the father of his fathers'. It was the closest he came to claiming membership of the dynasty. Horemheb is very unlikely to have belonged to Thutmose III's blood-line, however distantly, or else he would have made much of the connection. The claim of dynastic descent made here was to recreate a sense of continuity in the royal line after the Amarna episode.[7] Horemheb understood the symbolism of the succession and that the father-son progression could be a fiction. In time he used the same method to arrange his own successor.

## THE RESTORATION OF EGYPT

In his Coronation Text Horemheb emphasized how the 'king' had 'set him to be supreme chief of the land to steer the laws of the two regions [the opposite banks of the Nile] as hereditary prince of this entire land' and that he was unique in this capacity. The 'king' here is usually assumed to have been Tutankhamun. It is no less possible that the reference to Horemheb's predecessor was deliberately vague and generic. Horemheb went on to explain how he had been sum-moned before the king when the palace 'had fallen into a storm'. The word for a storm has a subtle range of meanings related to a major weather disaster. In this instance it seems to be used as a metaphor for a state of enragement or chaos – we might say 'at a time when a tornado had ripped through the palace'. The obvious context might be the aftermath of Akhenaten's reign, though no details are given, and the phrase may be rhetorical.[8]

Appropriately, Horemheb compared himself to Thoth, the god of knowledge and wisdom, an analogy which fitted well with how

Tiye, Amenhotep III's queen. Created late in Tiye's life or shortly after her death. c. 1360–1330 BC. Height 22.5 cm.

Amenhotep III and Tiye limestone dyad statue from the mortuary temple at Kom el Hettân. Height 7 m. c. 1361 BC.

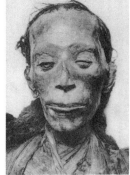

Marriage scarab of Amenhotep III and Tiye, also naming her parents Yuya and Thuya.

The astonishingly well-preserved mummies of Yuya and Thuya, Tiye's parents, after their discovery in tomb KV46. Their titles and honours made them commoners of huge and unprecedented significance.

The Colossi of Memnon at Amenhotep III's mortuary temple. Height 60 ft (18 m). c. 1361 BC.

Statue of Sekhmet, originally from Amenhotep III's mortuary temple. Now at Ramesses III's mortuary temple, Medinet Habu.

Akhenaten. Upper part of a colossal statue from his temple to the Aten at Karnak. c. 1352–1347 BC.

Cartouches of Akhenaten (left) and the Aten (right) from a lintel originally in his temple to the Aten at Karnak. Found in the Second Pylon (built by Horemheb). c. 1352–1347 BC.

Amarna. One of the boundary stelae (U) that marked out the territory of Akhenaten's new city. This one was created in the 6th regnal year.

A composite photograph of busts of Tiye and Akhenaten showing their remarkable similarity. The vertical dimension of the Akhenaten bust has been slightly adjusted to reduce its distorted proportions.

Akhenaten, Nefertiti and their three eldest daughters Meryetaten, Meketaten and Ankhesenpaaten. Found at Amarna.

Amenhotep III's throne name Nebmaatre in a cartouche. The epithet 'beloved of Amun-Re' has been damaged by Atenists, on the capital of a column in his sun court at the Temple of Luxor. Original carving c. 1390–1352 BC, damage c. 1352–1336 BC.

Pottery fragments with distinctive painted decoration from Mycenae in Greece. Found at Amarna, c. 1347–1336 BC.

Nefertiti becomes king. Akhenaten's names are to the left. Nefertiti's single cartouche has been obviously, and crudely, modified from one to two to give her the names and titles of a king. North Palace, Amarna.

Alabaster relief from Amarna showing Nefertiti as queen and one of her daughters, probably Meryetaten. From the main palace, Amarna. c. 1345 BC.

The celebrated painted limestone and plastered bust of Nefertiti. From the workshop of the sculptor Thutmose at Amarna.

Relief carving of a king and queen, perhaps either Akhenaten and Nefertiti, or Smenkhkare and Meryetaten. Amarna. c. 1345–1336 BC.

Corner fragment from Akhenaten's sarcophagus depicting Nefertiti rather than one of the traditional goddesses. c. 1347–1336 BC.

The shattered dereliction that greeted the discoverers of the tomb known as KV55. This view shows the badly damaged and defaced royal coffin which contained skeletal remains, usually identified as either those of Akhenaten or Smenkhkare.

Composite image of (l–r): Tiye, KV55 canopic jar stopper, Tutankhamun and Nefertiti. The resemblance of the latter three to one another is obvious, raising the possibility that all three were related and that the Tutankhamun gold mask was not originally made for him. The resemblance of the stopper bust to Nefertiti is particularly strong in the nose and upper face, making it feasible that Nefertiti or one of her daughters was the subject. Alternatively, the three busts may have once represented the same person or appear similar because they were made in the same workshop by artists affected by habit.

Calcite jar from Gurob in the Faiyum bearing the names of (l–r): Ankhesenamun, and Tutankhamun-Nebkheperure. The difference in the -amun part at the top of the left two cartouches is an object lesson in how precarious reconstructions of damaged texts can be since the same hieroglyphs in reality could be executed and positioned quite differently.

Tutankhamun as Amun at Karnak. The statue was later usurped but the youthful features make it very likely it was carved during his reign.

Brutalizing Egypt's traditional enemies. Asiatic captives are brought before Tutankhamun by Horemheb's soldiers, their hands secured in wooden yokes so they could be pulled along. From Horemheb's Saqqara tomb. c. 1336—1327 BC.

Portraits of Horemheb from his Saqqara tomb complex, constructed when he was still a general under Tutankhamun. c. 1336—1327 BC. In the relief (above) the uraeus serpent symbol of royalty has been added to update his status as king.

Dyad of Ay and Tey as Amun and Mut in the Temple of Luxor. Probably originally Tutankhamun and Ankhesenamun. Usurped by Horemheb. c. 1336–1323 BC.

Relief of Tutankhamun at the Temple of Luxor. Usurped by Horemheb, whose names have been substituted. c. 1336–1327 BC.

Section of one of the king lists from Abydos reading from right to left, the throne names of Thutmose IV, Amenhotep III, Horemheb and Ramesses I. The reigns of Akhenaten, Tutankhamun and Ay, between Amenhotep III and Horemheb, had been expunged from the official records. c. 1294–1279 BC.

Thutmose III strides towards Amun on a granite relief cut down in Graeco-Roman times to serve as a mill-stone wheel. Found at Dendera, but original location of the relief unknown.

Horemheb saw himself and liked to be seen. He was described as having 'reorganized this land; he adjusted to the time of Re. He restored the temples.'[9] In Egyptian the word for restoration could also mean 'to strengthen' or 'to perpetuate' and was linked to similar sounding words that meant setting right wrongs or making everything flourish.[10] Not surprisingly, in Horemheb's version of events his success led seamlessly to him being chosen as heir. This was to be a period of renewal.[11]

The new king set about recreating a sense of normality and stability, which in practice meant making certain the crown resumed control of the country, its resources, and its people. The claim was contradictory since by deleting any reference to his immediate predecessors and positioning himself as Amenhotep III's successor there ought to have been no need to restore anything. It did not matter. The symbolism was all-important.

Horemheb was also a political pragmatist. For all his reactionary gestures, he took advantage of the opportunity to strengthen his position. The Amun priesthood was re-established though, of course, this must have started under Tutankhamun. The difference now was that their numbers were drawn from the 'choicest of the army', or so he claimed in his coronation inscription. This was an aspiration and not a description of a fulfilled policy. His intention was to make sure the priests were military men he knew and could trust.[12]

This policy went hand in hand with a more general claim that Horemheb had restored temples throughout Egypt from the Delta to Nubia. He accelerated the work with the fastest method. His names were carved over those of Tutankhamun and Ay on suitable monuments or statues of theirs. Horemheb's targets included Tutankhamun's Restoration Stela. Ay's memorial-mortuary temple, which had probably replaced Tutankhamun's, was taken over by Horemheb and completed in his name. Horemheb also appeared in new statues. One now in Turin shows Horemheb with features that resemble Tutankhamun's but there are no signs of erasures or usurpation, suggesting the sculptor replicated youthful features he was familiar with, or perhaps the statue had been finished but not inscribed. The result matched usurped statues of Tutankhamun and reinforced an image of Horemheb as a vigorous young man, in this case depicted standing by a seated and larger figure of Amun, as the successor of Amenhotep III.[13]

The systematic demolition of Akhet-aten probably started under Horemheb, if it had not already begun. This even extended to cutting out Akhenaten's names from carvings in private houses. Talatat blocks from public buildings were carted off to Hermopolis for reuse, preserving many of them. The work only needed to progress so far – the sand would do, and indeed did, the rest, burying the remains of most of the houses, temples and palaces until the first systematic exploration of the site in the 1800s.

Ay's tomb was entered, and any images of the former king hacked out. His sarcophagus was bludgeoned to pieces (it has been restored in modern times). The work was so aggressive that it would make sense if Horemheb had issued the order, but it is no less possible that it took place during the 19th Dynasty at a time when the Ramesside pharaohs were doing their best to pose as the legitimate descendants of Horemheb and as protectors of Egypt's sacred traditions, or even later. This might explain how Ramesses II's queen came into possession of the pommel bearing Ay's name (see end of Chapter 16). Little was left in the tomb but just enough, including some bones, to suggest that Ay and probably Tey had still been buried there when the attack took place.

Horemheb's officials checked up on existing royal tombs, anticipating much greater regulation and control of the necropolis and the tomb workers' village in the 19th Dynasty. In Horemheb's 8th regnal year, Maya, Overseer of the Treasury who was also in charge of the 'Festival of Amun' in Karnak, made his way into Thutmose IV's tomb (KV43). In the first pillared chamber (Room F) at the bottom of the entrance corridor Maya left a record of the visit which was 'to renew the burial' of Thutmose IV.[14] This was part of a general programme of inspection to make good any damage or theft committed during the Amarna period when normal supervision had probably been lax, if it existed at all. The inspections may have been enough to dissuade any further gangs from trying their luck with Tutankhamun's tomb. Eventually, its location was lost beneath flood debris anyway.

Horemheb recommenced traditional gigantism building work, beginning by extending Karnak along both its axes. He commissioned the Second Pylon at Karnak which advanced the temple towards the Nile. To help build it, blocks from Akhenaten's demolished Aten temple in East Karnak were used. Today some of those carrying the names of Aten and Akhenaten are still visible in the fill. Behind the Second Pylon Horemheb probably planned what would become one of the most awe-inspiring architectural achievements in Egyptian history, the great hypostyle hall, but this was not executed until the reigns of Seti I and Ramesses II. He completed the Tenth Pylon and built what is now called the Ninth Pylon behind it. To speed up the work and hide more evidence of Akhenaten the remaining parts of the Aten temple to the east were dismantled, and the talatat blocks used as additional filling and reinforcement for the hollow Tenth Pylon.

## HOREMHEB'S WARS

Given his history as a professional warrior, one might have expected Horemheb to have seized the opportunity to blaze a path as a warrior king. There is little evidence to suggest he had any such ambitions. A relief from Karnak's Tenth Pylon refers to and illustrates Asiatic captives being brought before Amun, Mut, and Khons, but this may only have been generic and was perhaps just transference of his achievements as a general under Tutankhamun.[15] It was not until the 21st regnal year of Ramesses II that a peace treaty (the so-called 'Eternal' or 'Silver' treaty of Qadesh) was signed between Egypt and the Hittites, reflecting a long period of tension that included Horemheb's reign, but not one that had included major warfare until then.[16]

More convincing are Horemheb's reliefs in his rock-cut temple (the so-called 'Great Speos') at Gebel el-Silsila, about 25 miles (40 km) north of Aswan. These record a war in Kush but include generic references to victory in the Asiatic north. African captives are illustrated along with statements about Horemheb's triumph. They could hardly be described as especially informative or unequivocal.[17] Back at Karnak, Horemheb also commemorated an expedition to Punt. This was probably routine and unlikely to have been a special initiative unless it was intended to resume the supply lines thanks to disruption during the Amarna era and its aftermath.[18]

# HOREMHEB'S EDICT

Unlike his royal predecessors Horemheb had experience of practical administration. Under Tutankhamun or Ay he had commissioned a statue of himself as a military scribe, probably found in or near Memphis.[19] The symbolism was important because it showed he wanted to be seen as a member of the literate elite.

Horemheb's so-called Great Edict was carved on a stela in front of his Tenth Pylon.[20] In its text he anticipated some of the ideas of the English political philosopher Thomas Hobbes (1588–1679): the people accept the state in the person of the king so long as he insulates them against disorder, instability, and injustice. Although some kings of the 18th Dynasty had acted in this way, such as Ahmose I's response to the terrible storm during his reign, Horemheb articulated the principle and applied it more generally. Unlike some of his predecessors, Horemheb understood that being king brought with it a sense of duty and obligation.

Horemheb's reforms have the tone of a policy brought to bear on deep-rooted problems which had become exacerbated under Akhenaten rather than serving as an expression of a theory of government. Horemheb sought to rectify a series of specific grievances that had been represented to him, generally involving the heavy-handed exaction of revenue and tribute by various bodies including the crown, the army, and the temples. These abuses had become embedded as a matter of precedent and often involved officials siphoning off goods for themselves while acting in the name of the state. They were symptomatic of the exploitation and corruption that underwrote the 18th Dynasty crown and ruling elite. The problems bear some comparison with the so-called English 'bastard feudalism' of the Middle Ages when wealthy and powerful aristocrats could use their retainers to do as they pleased and ignore or even defy the crown.

Horemheb's Edict described a country afflicted by violence and oppression. Of course, it suited him to depict the past as degenerate and therefore himself as the saviour. Making claims of this sort were routine for an Egyptian king (or indeed almost any other leader at any time), just as Ahmose I had done and Tutankhamun more recently. How much truth there was at the time is much harder to evaluate, but Horemheb's claims are specific. The detail is likely only to have arisen from scrutinizing repeated representations made by the aggrieved. If royal authority had dwindled during Akhenaten's time and afterwards, some localized misbehaviour was to be expected. After all, Akhenaten had isolated himself and his court in a new home.

The Edict referred to various criminal activities, including taxes being appropriated by tax collectors for themselves and requisitioning slaves for their own use, and specified some of the punishments. The army is described as stealing cattle and hides from villagers whom they beat up for good measure. Horemheb decreed that any such soldier who was caught doing this was to be subjected to a hundred blows, five wounds, and to have the hides seized back from him. Villagers had also been subjected to the robbery of vegetables by officials who turned up and told them the seizures were in the name of the king. Soldiers involved in ripping off dues that were supposed to be paid to the royal harem or temples were liable to have their noses cut off and then be sent to the fortress of Tjaru (Sile) on the road into Canaan, a bleak frontier outpost manned by criminals. It was not the only crime punished this way.[21]

The Edict said that during the journey to and from Memphis for the Opet Festival in Thebes the staff of the queens and their harems (a euphemism for their entourages) had become accustomed from Thutmose III's time to making unreasonable demands on the local communities they passed. These people had used the pretext that they were simply enforcing the legitimate impost of the king. The abuse was a classic manifestation of how poisonous an absolute monarchy can become in its effect on the wider population. Although it is unclear to what extent the queens themselves had been complicit, the effect on the villages and farmers was the same, discrediting the crown in a way that Horemheb professed to be trying now to rectify.[22] The reforms also included the reorganization of the regional judiciary panels, the *kenbets*.[23]

The picture that Horemheb's reforms paints is of an Egypt which had become wearily accustomed to a culture in which the king, or those claiming to act with his authority, had contemptuously treated the wider population. Absolute monarchies have exhibited the same tendencies throughout history. One need only consider how the crown and elite of late Tsarist Russia behaved. What was new for Egypt, or so it seems, was a king who was conscious of the injustices and the need for him to bring in reforms. Some of his predecessors had justified their actions and rule by claiming to be acting on the will of Amun, or in Akhenaten's case the Aten. Horemheb understood that there was a better way to legitimate the office of king.

Horemheb's solutions were pragmatic and potentially long-lasting. The use of regional administrators was not new – Egypt's geography made that unavoidable – but he formalized the system with a vizier in both Memphis and Thebes. They were warned not to transgress, Horemheb asking 'how then shall those like you judge others, when one of you is committing a crime against justice?' Any such infringement was to be a capital crime. This was mirrored in the army, the command of which was also placed under two legates who represented his power.[24] By splitting the military command that way he diminished the chances that one or the other would use the armed forces to mount a coup. Horemheb knew the country well and claimed to have explored it in its entirety. Given his military career this is plausible; he is likely to have been far more familiar with Egypt's true everyday nature than many of the kings who preceded him.

Horemheb insisted he had ordered regular distribution of food to be made from royal storehouses to the officials and soldiers sent out to make inspections on the state's behalf. It was a simple solution to the corruption, intended to make it unnecessary, or at least indefensible, for any of these men to run extortion rackets.[25] The Edict was a necessary solution that made amends for what seems to have been decades of institutionalized abuse. Horemheb's Edict reads as unusually enlightened by the standards of the time, but then it was supposed to.

There was obviously a rhetorical element to the claims, and possibly a major one. Horemheb could only go so far in rewriting history. There is no evidence that Egypt had collapsed into anarchy by the end of Akhenaten's rule and during the reigns of Tutankhamun and Ay, though perhaps it seemed that way at the time. The deletion of Akhenaten and his successors from the record was a component of the restoration of fairer governance, and not just petty retribution. It is equally easy to see Horemheb using claims of reform as a way of restoring the Egyptian crown to its sense of entitlement to exert total and unquestioning control over the nation, its people, and its resources. With no dynastic claim to the throne, he had to invent ways to legitimate his rule. Perhaps he was that paradox of absolute monarchies and dictators, the enlightened despot, and thus Egypt's Frederick the Great (1740–86). If so, Horemheb's successful balance still depended on his own personality, illustrating the vulnerability of the system to the abuse that had riven the 18th Dynasty.

With no heir of his own, Horemheb could afford to choose a senior military commander called Paramessu, who also served as a vizier and held various titles resembling those Horemheb had held under Tutankhamun. Paramessu came from Avaris and a long family tradition of involvement with the cult of Seth.[26] Scribal statues of Paramessu were placed alongside those of Amenhotep, son of Hapu, by Horemheb's Tenth Pylon at Karnak, to form components of a processional route, marking him as a man with special access to the gods.[27]

The promotion of Paramessu to royal heir avoided the uncertainty that followed both Akhenaten's and Tutankhamun's deaths. Paramessu is known to history as Ramesses I, the first true king of the 19th Dynasty. Ramesses was the father of Seti I and grandfather of Ramesses II, both of whom were on hand when he was chosen by Horemheb. Ramesses I thus provided dynastic security, and in his son and grandson a future, together with the necessary age and maturity to handle the transition.

# THE TOMBS OF HOREMHEB

Horemheb's Saqqara tomb and chapel became redundant for his own needs. He saw to it that a royal uraeus symbol of kingship was added to any depictions of him on its fabulous reliefs. The idea was to leave no doubt that even as a successful general under Tutankhamun he was destined to rule. Any depictions of Tutankhamun in the tomb were also renamed for Horemheb. This meant the conquering hero ended up being congratulated and decorated with gold collars by himself. In the curious rhetorical and symbolic world of Egyptian royal imagery this existential paradox is a reminder of how elastic the Egyptian notion was of identity or achievement.

These alterations were made because in an unprecedented move the Saqqara tomb was repurposed for his queen Mutnodjmet. This established a new tradition for queens who in the 18th Dynasty had not usually had their own tombs (with a very few exceptions). She had enjoyed some prominence during her husband's reign, sustaining the new higher profile of late 18th Dynasty queens during their husbands' lifetimes, and been portrayed in colossi alongside Horemheb. A mummy that was probably Mutnodjmet's, shattered by robbers, was found in the tomb hall where her body had been dragged from the burial chamber along with the remains of a baby that had either gone almost to term or died shortly after birth. She was in her late thirties or early forties and had already experienced several pregnancies, as well as losing all her teeth due to disease, another salutary reminder of the truth behind the illusion of glamour Egypt so often evokes today.[28]

The length of Horemheb's reign is the last great puzzle of the 18th Dynasty. No reference to his death has survived. He had ordered an impressive new tomb in the Valley of the Kings (KV57). It was never finished though he had clearly been buried in it. Most of the dockets on several dozen wine jars in his tomb record Horemheb's 13th and 14th regnal years, so he had ruled at least that long, but like all such pieces of evidence they do not set a maximum length.[29] The pivotal evidence for the longer reign is a mysterious reference to Horemheb's 59th regnal year on the wall of a scribe's tomb at Saqqara. This could only make sense if it included the approximately thirty-one years of Akhenaten, Tutankhamun and Ay which if subtracted leave twenty-eight years for Horemheb's reign (to c. 1295).[30] There is no other such example, but by the 19th Dynasty the formal succession of the 18th Dynasty routinely omitted Hatshepsut and the Amarna and post-Amarna rulers, for example in a relief at Ramesses II's mortuary temple depicting his predecessors.[31] Manetho may have included Horemheb as his 'Ôrus' with a reign of thirty-six years and five months (see Appendix 4).

There was something eerily apposite about the state of Horemheb's tomb when it was found in 1908 by Theodore Davis and his companions. The 18th Dynasty's last blast of sepulchral glitter had been wrecked by tomb robbers, followed by debris that had tumbled down through the corridors and rooms over the centuries that followed. Theodore Davis's assistant Edward Ayrton had to scramble over the fill to find an inscription that confirmed it was Horemheb's tomb. The group of excited explorers struggled through the stifling heat, crammed between the stones and sand and the ceiling. Along their way they found that the well chamber had been equipped with a false painted wall to fool tomb robbers. The plan had failed. The wall had clearly been breached as soon as the robbers, almost certainly armed with advance information and the necessary equipment, reached it.

Davis's expedition made their way on down another 180 ft (55 m) to the burial chamber, fascinated by the shattered grave goods lying all around and state of the incomplete decoration ranging from finished painted elaborate reliefs (the use of relief sculpture was an innovation for the Valley of the Kings, and made decorating the tomb far more challenging) to the sketched schemes nearby on some of the burial chamber's walls. These included a unique depiction of the Book of Gates, a funerary text never normally incorporated in such schemes. Once in the furthest part of the burial chamber they were confronted with the sarcophagus and a few bones left in it, the remains of two women on the floor nearby and those of a man in one of the further chambers – all three were intrusive later burials. They were greeted in the unfinished last chamber by a unique painted figure of Osiris in a single panel.

The battered finds included a wooden statue of the king resembling those found in Tutankhamun's tomb guarding the blocked entrance to his burial chamber. Horemheb's canopic chest was of the solid variety (as was Tutankhamun's), with cylindrical recesses cut into the chest for the king's viscera, each capped by a conventional-style bust stopper in the form of the head of a king from the solid canopic chest. The two surviving stoppers are very similar, but not identical. While they may be intended to represent Horemheb they are as stylistically generic 18th Dynasty royal items as they are individualized. Both are youthful looking, making it possible they were drawn from an existing royal inventory of funerary paraphernalia.[32]

The paintings in his tomb depicted the low-born Horemheb absorbed into the canonical tradition of a king's funeral. In the room leading into the hall and burial chamber beyond he was shown being greeted by Anubis, god of the necropolis, with Isis, Horus, Hathor, and Osiris. It was a clear expression of the restoration of order, though there was some modification of detail. The quality was high but despite the residual traces of the animated realism pioneered at Amarna the purpose was clearly to revive and re-establish older traditions. The events of recent years had had some impact on the availability of the necessary skills, which took some years to mature, reaching their climax in the tomb of Seti I a quarter of a century later.[33]

Despite what Horemheb had done to restore Egypt to order and stability he was treated the same way as almost all his predecessors. His tomb was inspected in Year 4 and Year 6 of the so-called 'renaissance' period during the reign of Ramesses XI when the first major bout of official removals and reburials of kings was undertaken while despoiling the bodies and tombs. The two graffiti correspond in content with more specific records of body removal at other royal tombs.[34] If Horemheb's mummy was taken to one of the royal caches it has never been found (see Epilogue).

Without Horemheb's body it is impossible to estimate his age at death. Perhaps that is some small consolation. Instead of the grisly bandaged remains of so many of the other 18th Dynasty kings, Horemheb lives on in his magnificent Saqqara tomb reliefs made when he was in his prime, the high-quality painted decoration that had been completed in his Theban tomb, and some of the outstanding statuary from both his pre-royal career and when he was king.

Horemheb's real legacy was bringing the 18th Dynasty to an end without allowing Egypt to descend into civil war or the instability of a disputed succession resulting from the failure of the bloodline. Securing the future was no mean achievement, given the epic events of recent decades. For a brief time, the weaknesses of Egypt's hereditary absolute monarchy were tempered by a king of high ability who had no choice but to select his successor from the best men available.

# EPILOGUE

*No city under the sun has ever been so adorned by votive offerings, made of silver and gold and ivory, in such number and of such size, by such a multitude of colossal statues, and, finally, by obelisks made of single blocks of stone.*[1]

Diodorus Siculus describes Thebes
in the first century BC

By the time of Horemheb's death there can have been few people left alive with any meaningful memory of Akhenaten's revolution or its aftermath. Akhet-aten was becoming a wind-blown ghost town, its last remnants already disappearing beneath the sand though casual occupation of the site lingered on. Oddly, Akhenaten's boundary stelae escaped defacement in antiquity. Despite the huge damage wrought by weathering and later vandalism they remain the most visible remaining features of Akhenaten's dream. The earlier 18th Dynasty must have seemed even more remote. There would never be another king called Amenhotep or Thutmose.[2]

Once Horemheb was gone the elderly Ramesses I of the 19th Dynasty reigned for less than two years at the end of a long life that must have stretched back at least as far as the Amarna period. He took steps to create his own version of continuity. By adapting his name to Ramesses from his birth name Paramessu, he emphasized the primacy of Re. His throne name Menpehtyre ('Enduring in the Strength of Re') was a one-off revival of the structure of Ahmose's throne name Nebpehtyre ('Lord of the Strength of Re'), replacing the 'Manifestations of Re' suffix of most of the 18th Dynasty throne names.[3]

Ramesses I expired in or around 1294 BC, his son Seti I already having been appointed his co-regent. The male dynastic line was now actively promoted, this time in the form of a prince Ramesses who succeeded Seti as Ramesses II in 1279 BC and ruled until 1213 BC.[4] The shattered remains of Ramesses II's colossi at Thebes and Abu Simbel have become the most enduring symbols of the era. The obsessive usurpation by Ramesses II of his predecessors' monuments was an expression of both his own narcissism and the importance of cloaking change with a sense of timeless permanence, but this work is most evident in the extant monuments at Karnak and Luxor.

Ramesses II created a new capital for the 19th Dynasty at Pr-Ramesses close to the Thutmosid complex on the site of Avaris, but very little remains visible there today thanks to the Nile's movements. For this reason, Pr-Ramesses was supplanted by yet another new capital at Tanis further west in the Delta by the end of the 20th Dynasty to which Pr-Ramesses's monuments were laboriously moved. It also compensated for the loss of access to Thebes as Egypt fell into another period of political turmoil in the Third Intermediate Period. Tanis was abandoned by the Graeco-Roman period. Today its scattered and fallen relics are completely outclassed by the temples at Thebes, creating the impression to Diodorus Siculus and others ever since that it was and always had been Egypt's greatest city.[5]

At Karnak and Luxor, the 18th Dynasty elements and cluttered statues and stelae were slowly overwhelmed when both complexes were substantially enlarged during the 19th Dynasty. Luxor, for example, received a vast new northern court and pylon fronted by seated statues of Ramesses II and obelisks. It featured a shrine that reused the parts of one made by Hatshepsut. Karnak continued to grow, most obviously with the gigantic hypostyle hall built by Seti I and Ramesses II. Nonetheless, the obelisks of Thutmose I, Hatshepsut and Thutmose III remained prominent features. The clearance of Akhenaten's temple at Karnak may have been to destroy his memory but would probably have happened anyway, even if it had been devoid of any special notoriety. The vast accumulation of statues in Karnak was periodically tidied up by the priests, desperate to claw back space. Some were buried in pits that have yielded remarkable discoveries of well-preserved sculpture.[6] Other monuments, such as Tutankhamun's Restoration Stela, usurped by Horemheb, were hacked up for reuse.

Some pre-Amarna monuments were restored to something like their original appearance. Seti I was particularly conscientious, even replacing restoration work under Tutankhamun and Ay with his own. The figure of Amun, for example, was restored to the obelisks of Hatshepsut defaced by Atenists. By this time Akhenaten was remembered vaguely as 'the enemy of Akhet-aten', and as the 'schismatic' (or 'rebel'), continuing to serve as terms of reference for the past despite the official proscription of his name, but without making any specific reference to what he had done.[7]

Most of the royal mortuary temples of the 18th Dynasty were soon ransacked for stone to be used in new monuments if they had not been already. Amenhotep III's vast sprawling memorial-mortuary temple complex in Western Thebes was gradually dismantled, hastened by an earthquake and the annual inundation of the Nile which spread across the precinct and had obviously been intended to do so. The monumental stela that recorded his building works had been largely obliterated by Atenists. Seti I had the text restored, though when the remains of the temple were demolished by his grandson Merenptah it was removed and reused. Today the only 18th Dynasty mortuary temple with meaningful remains is Hatshepsut's, which has been substantially restored. The others now visible are those of

Seti I, Ramesses II, and Ramesses III. The latter, known as Medinet Habu, is particularly well preserved, easily explained by the fact that no more mortuary temples of that scale were built (and thus not requiring robbed stone to build them), and because it served as the administrative headquarters of Western Thebes thereafter.[8]

One of the most remarkable phenomena of the 18th Dynasty is the survival of many royal bodies, but with some notable exceptions. The story of how these made it down to modern times is astonishing though difficult to unravel. A curious paradox of ancient Egypt is that the kings and queens, unless they were delusional, invested heavily in constructing monuments in the knowledge that their temples might be demolished, their statues removed or usurped and the tombs broken into and robbed. Some were complicit in this practice themselves.

# TOMB ROBBERS

The general assumption about tomb robbers in Egypt is that they were corrupt locals, including some tomb workers and officials acting in concert. This impression has been gained largely from extant accounts of trials of thieves. Under Ramesses IX of the 20th Dynasty the robbery of the tomb of Sobekemsaf II of the 17th Dynasty was uncovered by Paser, the mayor of Eastern Thebes. He ordered an inspection of ten royal tombs to find out the extent of the thefts. The main target seems to have been Paweraa, the mayor of Western Thebes, suspected of being one of the criminal masterminds in the tomb-robbing mob. The investigation, manipulated by Paweraa, concluded that the only tomb of the ten looked at (including Amenhotep I's) which had been desecrated was Sobekemsaf II's. Despite a further inspection, and subsequent executions of robbers, Paweraa successfully dismissed Paser's accusations, and held on to his office.[9]

At times the desecration was approved, even ordered, from the top. The 18th Dynasty rulers and their successors must have been aware of the extent of the thefts in their own time, especially as we know that officials were inspecting royal tombs under Horemheb. In the Third Intermediate Period the robbing of tombs received royal approval. The tomb of Psusennes I of the 21st Dynasty at Tanis included some items taken from royal burials, most conspicuously the innermost sarcophagus removed from the tomb of Merenptah (KV8), over two centuries after the original burial at Thebes in 1203 BC.[10]

It is inconceivable that those handling the stolen goods, however far down the line, were unaware of their origins. The prospect of torture and execution seems to have done little to dissuade the thieves. It would hardly have been feasible for a gang to remove a solid gold royal coffin and melt it down without attracting some attention when selling on the proceeds. This becomes far easier to understand if arrangements were in place at the highest levels to process the bullion or other key items for reuse. The recycling so evident in KV55 and Tutankhamun's tomb may have been more customary than is now appreciated. This would certainly help explain the phenomenon in the past of the Valley of the Kings of Egyptologists discovering remains of items belonging to earlier kings in the tombs of their successors.

The two robberies of Tutankhamun's tomb took place probably within a few years at most of the burial. Following the burial procession and sealing of the tomb, its location must have been widely known. It is also unimaginable that its entrance could not have been uncovered and dug down into without attracting attention. Both break-ins must have been carried out with the assistance of at least some necropolis officials. Those involved may have included some experience of robbing royal tombs at Thebes during the Amarna period.

The larger burials of pharaohs like Thutmose III and Amenhotep III needed to be robbed on several occasions to empty them. This work could only have been carried out by suitably equipped and organized teams. The recent discovery in the Western Valley of the

Kings of dozens of glass inlays suitable for a late 18th Dynasty rishi (feather decoration) coffin is either evidence of an on-site manufactory of funerary equipment or a processing facility for organized tomb robbing where burial items from a tomb were dismantled into reusable components or materials. One at least was probably Amenhotep III's tomb (WV22) because a ring with his name was found among the debris. The unfinished and unused tomb of Ramesses XI (KV4), last ruler of the New Kingdom, was pressed into service for the same work, a coffin of Hatshepsut's being among the valuables taken to pieces by a team stationed there.[11]

The officially sanctioned and final serious ransacking of the royal tombs was a symptom of the state of Egypt during the late 20th Dynasty. The country was breaking apart. In the south the high priest of Amun at Thebes and Pinhasi, the viceroy of Kush, had come to blows, starting a regional war. Ramesses sent a general called Piankh to tackle the crisis. Piankh managed to push Pinhasi back and made himself high priest of Amun and viceroy of Kush, effectively creating a semi-autonomous enclave, but the expensive war against Pinhasi carried on. This period was optimistically known at the time as the 'renaissance', meaning that order of a sort had replaced a period of turbulence.[12] Piankh realized that the Valley of the Kings had the potential to yield valuables that would fund his army, and ordered it to be scoured for tombs.

A letter by the powerful and wealthy scribe Butehamun, Opener of the Necropolis Gates, to Piankh tells us how they had carried out their instructions.[13] The Valley of the Kings and surrounding areas were explored by Butehamun's scouts who left markers at promising locations to guide the recovery teams. The extracted mummies were stripped of any valuables by cutting their wrappings open. Any valuable burial equipment was similarly hacked about.[14] Afterwards Butehamun was one of those who presided over what passed for a restoration and reconsecration of the bodies.

The necropolis had turned into a state-managed bullion and jewel mine, regardless of how exalted the kings and other dignitaries buried in the Valley of the Kings had once been. It was a new twist in the ancient Egyptians' willingness to despoil each other, but an inevitable development given the availability of valuable commodities in the royal necropolis. Not all the tombs were found. Yuya and Thuya's had been robbed at some point but most of its contents remained and it must have subsequently been overlooked. Tutankhamun's, of course, escaped largely unscathed apart from the two early robberies. This was a small tomb, only saved by the subsequent concealment of the entrance beneath rock washed down by floods, but Tutankhamun was omitted from king lists and was so obscure that Butehamun's men probably had no idea it existed.

Amenhotep II and Tutankhamun alone of the 18th Dynasty kings remained in their own tombs until modern times. Amenhotep's tomb (KV35, found in 1898) had been ransacked like all the others but when the tomb was finally closed he was left along with several other royal mummies deposited there for safekeeping. These included bodies labelled as Thutmose IV and Amenhotep III, and the ones now identified as Tiye (the 'Elder Lady') and the 'Younger Lady' (Nefertiti?). These accounted for some of the kings and queens of the later 18th Dynasty, along with several other kings of the 19th and 20th Dynasties, though the identities of quite a few of the bodies are unknown. The date of the final closure of this cache cannot predate the aftermath of the reign of Ramesses VI, whose body was the latest included.

Amenhotep II's tomb contained only one of several caches of royal bodies created during the rule of the Theban priest-king Pinudjem I (c. 1070–1032 BC, concurrently with the early 21st Dynasty). Pinudjem was Piankh's son or grandson, loyally following the family tradition of ripping off royal tombs. He added some decorum by calling the work restoration, but still helped himself to two coffins made for Thutmose I. The work was a strange combination of respectability and robbery. There was another curious attraction to the funerary items of long-dead great kings. Some items like royal shabtis were adapted for the personal use of later owners, who perhaps saw in them the same type of totemic power attributed to holy relics in the Middle Ages.[15]

The KV35 royal cache was supplemented around sixty years later with the reused tomb (TT320) of Pinudjem II, another priest-king of southern Egypt who died around 969 BC. During the reign of Sheshonq I, the first king of the 22nd Dynasty, this tomb was adapted to accommodate a much larger collection of royal mummies from the 17th to 21st Dynasties, some drawn from previous caches. They had been recovered from their original tombs or intermediate deposits, rewrapped and docketed, and sometimes installed in replacement coffins taken from other royal burials.

Deprived of their long-stolen treasures (apart from a few overlooked pieces embedded in their bandages), these bodies were stacked up in their new home. There they remained until 1881. They included Seqenenre Tau II, Ahmose-Nefertari, Amenhotep I, Thutmose II and III, as well as kings from the 19th Dynasty and other unidentified individuals. Several kings' mummies remain missing, among them Ay, Horemheb, and Thutmose I. If these have not already been destroyed by tomb robbers, they may still be awaiting discovery in another cache, just as Tutankhamun's was until 1922. Inspections of Horemheb's tomb (KV57) by officials who left written notes, and disarticulated remains of several unidentifiable bodies, may be evidence of its use as a royal cache, subsequently ransacked by yet more thieves. A cache of 18th Dynasty princesses is attested on a 21st Dynasty docket found in a robbed tomb, but the bodies had long gone.[16] Tomb KV21 contained two now very badly preserved royal female mummies of the 18th Dynasty, a clue that there may be, or at least were, many other burials of the 18th Dynasty in the Valley.[17]

During the 20th Dynasty Egypt entered a protracted but by no means continuous decline. There were phases when a few later kings revived the country's dominance in the region, for example a major revival of Egyptian power and prestige during the 26th (Saite) Dynasty (672–525 BC) and under the early Ptolemies. Karnak was still being added to under the Ptolemies whose building programme across Egypt included some of the best-preserved of all Egyptian temples constructed in traditional style. This continued under the Romans. At Dendera, not far to the north of Thebes, the Temple of Hathor took on its final manifestation with a complex built by the Ptolemaic pharaohs and Roman emperors. From among the debris of earlier buildings at Dendera, perhaps brought from another site, a granite relief of Thutmose III striding towards Amun was hacked up to create a millstone. The king who had once ground down his enemies a thousand years before was now pressed into service to grind grain.

The monuments of the 18th and 19th Dynasties continued to be scavenged. Their remains and mythologized kings were viewed with a mixture of fascination and confused respect. In the 26th Dynasty artisans scoured the remnants of Hatshepsut's memorial-mortuary temple for inspiration. They copied parts of the reliefs in tombs they had been commissioned to work on.[18]

In the first century BC the Greek historian Diodorus Siculus was intrigued to be told by the priests that forty-seven tombs of kings had once existed in the vicinity of Thebes, but only fifteen were still known.[19] Of the city itself he said:

> Of four temples erected there the oldest is a source of wonder for both its beauty and size, having a circuit of 13 stades (2.4 km), a height of 14 cubits (6.4 m), and walls 24 feet (7.3 m) thick. In keeping with this magnificence was also the embellishment of the votive offerings within the circuit wall, marvellous for the money spent upon it and exquisitely wrought as to workmanship.[20]

In the latter days at Karnak an imperial cult temple of deified Roman emperors stood outside the First Pylon. The Temple of Luxor became integrated within the plan of a late Roman fort. At Amarna, the long-abandoned tomb (TA6) of an official of Akhenaten's called Panehsy was pressed into service as a Coptic church, neatly turning the story of monotheism full circle.

The Valley of the Kings had become by Roman times a popular tourist destination, the visitors scrawling the walls of the few remaining open tombs, which they called 'syringes', with words like 'marvel!'[21] The burial practices of more than a millennium earlier were a source of fascination. In the Graeco-Roman cemeteries in the Faiyum and Bahariya oases among others, some of the more affluent invested in bizarre pastiches of New Kingdom royal burial practices, handed down by the intervening generations. Their bodies were sometimes equipped with cartonnage masks and breastplates made of linen and secondhand papyrus soaked in plaster, painted gold and decorated with traditional funerary motifs, but no hieroglyphs. The results were crude and peculiar conflations of Egyptian and classical traditions, ranging from three-dimensional masks to painted portraits. More importantly, they were made from materials not worth stealing.

The supreme irony is that the king whose successors did so much to erase him from Egypt's consciousness is the one on whom more ink has been spilled than any other pharaoh in modern times. Little or nothing was known about Akhenaten by Graeco-Roman times even though in those days various travellers visited Amarna and left their comments in the tombs of the nobles there, giving thanks for having journeyed thus far in safety, no doubt guided there by locals following what must be Egypt's oldest profession.[22] They were greatly impressed by the reliefs they found and regarded the place with awe but seem to have had no idea they were looking at something with special significance.[23]

It was only the unravelling of the Egyptian language in the 1800s that brought the inscriptions and battered remnants of Amarna back to life. Studies of the 18th Dynasty today are dominated by works about Akhenaten and his circle, but he has also long moved into wider culture in numerous historical works, novels and other treatments. Sigmund Freud argued that Moses had been a follower of Akhenaten and discovered monotheism that way. In Mika Waltari's novel *The Egyptian* (1945) and the motion picture version (1954) he was depicted as an epileptic, pacifist, madman, and proto-Christian. By 1983 Akhenaten had even become the subject of an opera by the composer Philip Glass, sung in Egyptian (or what passes for it). Akhenaten's rehabilitation as an historical figure has been miraculous, albeit one constantly adapted and redrawn. He and his milieu remain enveloped in mystery and unanswerable questions, preyed upon by those desperate to project their own agendas onto the Amarna era.[24] Yet, Akhenaten was only a small part of the astonishing 18th Dynasty's history, simultaneously exceptional and integral to the path that line of kings and queens weaved through Egypt's Bronze Age climax.

Amenhotep III's Colossi of Memnon were covered with Graeco-Roman graffiti, some left by members of the emperor Hadrian's entourage in AD 130. A fault in the northern statue had led it to emit a curious creaking noise when warmed by the morning sun, a phenomenon enthusiastically sought out by visitors into the second century AD when another earthquake toppled the upper part of the statue. The enterprising Romans arranged for the fallen part of the colossus to be repaired but it was the kiss of death. Thereafter it never made the sound again. The silent faceless statues still greet every visitor to Western Thebes. Even in their battered state they bear witness to the grand sense of theatre the 18th Dynasty kings pioneered in one of the world's first great historical eras. They also symbolize the transient nature of posturing and power, the eternal truth that history is driven by chance and circumstance and by the appearance on the stage of unique and idiosyncratic personalities whose conceits and ambitions help determine the fate of those they rule.

The 18th Dynasty had more than its fair share of such people. Their time deserves to stand alongside any of the other great ruling dynasties in world history whose lives, accomplishments, and failings have always proved to be a source of undying fascination to later ages. They brought their own people security, stability, and a sense of confident superiority but as in all imperialist states those benefits came at enormous cost both to the Egyptians and their neighbours. Their legacy was their history, temples, tombs, and works of art of the 18th Dynasty which the world has looked upon in awe ever since, all the while sobered by the wreckage and decay, and the lone and level sands stretching far away. In that, if we are honest, we can also see the relics of our own time and our hubris in some far distant future.

*My imagination runs riot wondering what the common people who see my monument in the years to come will say. Beware of saying 'I know not, I know not why this was made and a mountain fashioned entirely from gold like an everyday event'. I swear as Re loves me, as my father Amun favours me . . . I shall be eternal like the star that never sets.*

Hatshepsut, on her obelisks at Karnak[25]

# APPENDICES

## 1. PRONOUNCING TRANSLITERATED EGYPTIAN

The following table gives an indication of how to pronounce some of the transliterated Egyptian terms featured in this book. Some are familiar enough in English, others not.

| | |
|---|---|
| *ꜣ* | glottal stop as in German before a vowel |
| *i* | pronounced as consonantal y |
| *y* | y |
| *ꜥ* | guttural sound made at the back of the throat, e.g. in Arabic |
| *w* | w |
| *b* | b |
| *p* | p |

| | |
|---|---|
| *f* | f |
| *m* | m |
| *n* | n |
| *r* | r |
| *h* | h |
| *ḥ* | hard, emphatic h |
| *ḫ* | soft ch as at the end of words like *loch* |
| *ẖ* | as in the German *ich* |
| *s* | s |
| *š* | sh |
| *ḳ* | k |
| *g* | hard g as in 'get' or 'growl' |
| *t* | t |
| *ṯ* | tsh |
| *d* | d |
| *ḏ* | dj |

## 2. TIMELINE OF EVENTS

Although the dates below are given as calendar years, these are *not* absolute dates, only approximations. The chronology here is therefore only relative, giving an idea of each period and reign and major events, and even these are subject to potential variation, especially the death of Akhenaten and the aftermath. Only the 18th Dynasty is given in detail here. Egyptologists constantly adjust their estimation of the dates and considerable disagreement remains. Until the Late Period the sole exceptions are total eclipses like the one of 1338 BC and the Sothic Cycle synchronization of 2761–2758 BC and 1321–1318 BC, though the latter are open to dispute. These are absolute dates and indicated here *.

| | |
|---|---|
| 3100 BC | Accession of Narmer. Unification of Egypt |
| 2781–2778 BC | *Heliacal rising of Sirius coincides with the Egyptian New Year (19 July) |
| 2686 BC | Old Kingdom begins with the reign of Nebka |
| 2558–2532 BC | Reign of Khafra (Greek: Chephren) |
| 2181 BC | End of the Old Kingdom. Beginning of the First Intermediate Period |
| 2055 BC | End of the First Intermediate Period. Beginning of the Middle Kingdom under Accession of Mentuhotep II (2055–2004 BC) of the 11th Dynasty |
| 1855 BC | Accession of Amenemhet III (1855–1808 BC) of the 12th Dynasty |
| 1799 BC | Accession of Sobekneferu (1799 –1795 BC) ends the 12th Dynasty |
| 1650 BC | Beginning of the Second Intermediate Period |

## THE 18TH DYNASTY

| | |
|---|---|
| 1550 BC | End of the Second Intermediate Period. Beginning of the New Kingdom |
| | Expulsion of the Hyksos under Ahmose I. Beginning of the 18th Dynasty |

| | |
|---|---|
| 1525 BC | Death of Ahmose I. Accession of Amenhotep I |
| 1504 BC | Death of Amenhotep I. Accession of Thutmose I |
| 1492 BC | Death of Thutmose I. Accession of Thutmose II with his sister-queen Hatshepsut |
| 1479 BC | Death of Thutmose II. Accession of Thutmose III with Hatshepsut as regent, counted as 1st regnal year for both |
| 1478 BC | *1 June: total eclipse of the sun visible at Thebes (Luxor) |
| 1473 BC | Hatshepsut assumes the kingship in her own right (7th regnal year, hereafter RY) and rules with Thutmose III though in reality she was the dominant partner |
| 1471 BC | Expedition to Punt (9th RY) |
| 1468 BC | Nubian Campaign (12th RY) |
| 1465 BC | Hatshepsut's sed festival. Second pair of obelisks begun |
| 1464 BC | Last record of Senenmut (16th RY) |
| 1458 BC | Death of Hatshepsut. Thutmose III's sole reign continues |
| 1457 BC | Thutmose III's first campaign (Megiddo) (22nd RY) |
| 1427 BC | Possible appointment of Amenhotep II as co-regent |
| 1425 BC | Death of Thutmose III (54th RY). Accession of Amenhotep II |
| 1425/23 BC | First campaign into Nubia (3rd RY) |
| 1421/19 BC | Second campaign into Nubia (7th RY) |
| 1419/17 BC | Third campaign (9th RY) |
| 1410 BC | *25 September: total eclipse of the sun visible across central Egypt and Memphis (not Thebes) |

| 1400 BC | Death of Amenhotep II. Accession of Thutmose IV |
|---|---|
| 1399 BC | *1 March: annular eclipse visible at Thebes |
| 1390 BC | Death of Thutmose IV. Accession of Amenhotep III |
| 1389 BC | Amenhotep III's hunting expedition. Marriage to Tiye |
| 1389 BC | *9 February: annular eclipse visible across central Egypt (not Memphis or Thebes) |
| 1386 BC | Nubian campaign (5th RY) |
| 1382 BC | Arrival of Gilukhepa at Amenhotep III's court (10th RY) |
| 1380 BC | Djarukha lake dug out for Tiye (11th RY) |
| 1378 BC | *5 July: annular eclipse visible at Thebes |
| 1361 BC | Amenhotep III's first sed festival jubilee (30th RY) |
| 1357 BC | Second Jubilee (34th RY) |
| 1356 BC | *27 October: annular eclipse visible at Elephantine |
| 1354 BC | Third Jubilee (37th RY) |
| 1352 BC | Death of Amenhotep III. Accession of Amenhotep IV |
| 1348 BC | Amenhotep IV changes name to Akhenaten (5th RY) |
|  | Akhet-aten (Amarna) founded |
| 1341 BC | Death by this year (12th RY) of Tiye |
|  | Death of Meketaten, and two younger sisters(?) |
| 1338 BC | *14 May: total eclipse of the sun, visible at Amarna (partial at Thebes) |
| 1337 BC | Akhenaten and Nefertiti alive and ruling together (16th RY), their last attested reference, as king and queen |

Co-regency with Smenkhkare?

Accession of Nefertiti/Neferneferuaten as joint king?

Death of Akhenaten after this year, followed by indeterminate series of events possibly including sole reign of Nefertiti and then accession of Tutankhamun

| | |
|---|---|
| 1327 BC | Death of Tutankhamun. Accession of Ay (possibly delayed) |
| 1323 BC | Death of Ay. Accession of Horemheb |
| 1321–1318 BC | *Heliacal rising of Sirius coincides with the Egyptian New Year (19 July) |
| 1316 BC | Thutmose IV's tomb inspected on Horemheb's orders |
| 1295 BC | Death of Horemheb. End of the 18th Dynasty |
| | Accession of Ramesses I and the beginning of the 19th Dynasty |
| 1294 BC | Death of Ramesses I. Sole reign of Seti I begins |
| 1279 BC | Death of Seti I. Sole reign of Ramesses II begins (this is a key example of a date for which other estimates have been made, especially 1265 BC) |
| 1213 BC | Death of Ramesses II |
| 1184 BC | Accession of Ramesses III of the 20th Dynasty |
| 1153 BC | Assassination of Ramesses III |
| 1099 BC | Accession of Ramesses XI. During his reign Piankh organizes the systematic robbing out of Theban royal tombs |
| 1069 BC | Death of Ramesses XI. End of the 20th Dynasty and the New Kingdom |

|  | Beginning of the 21st Dynasty and Third Intermediate Period |
|---|---|
| 1054 BC | Pinudjem I, high priest of Amun at Karnak, begins rule of southern Egypt |
|  | Oversees clearance of royal tombs and safe deposit of royal mummies in a first cache (in the tomb of Amenhotep II, KV35) |
| 1039 BC | Accession of Psusennes I (1039–991 BC) of the 21st Dynasty |
| 1032 BC | End of Pinudjem I's 'reign' at Thebes |
| 945 BC | Accession of Sheshonq I (945–924 BC) of the 22nd Dynasty |
| 747 BC | Late Period begins under the Kushite 25th Dynasty |
| 672–525 BC | Under the 26th (Saite) Dynasty Egypt enjoys a revival of its prestige |

Dates below are absolute:

|  |  |
|---|---|
| 525 BC | Egypt falls under Persian rule |
| 504 BC | Persian rule ends |
| 332 BC | Conquest of Egypt by Alexander the Great |
| 305 BC | Accession of Ptolemy I Soter |
| 31 BC | Cleopatra VII and Mark Antony's fleet defeated at Actium by Octavian (later Augustus) |
| 30 BC | Roman conquest of Egypt. End of Egypt as an independent state |
| AD 139–42 | Heliacal rising of Sirius coincides with the Egyptian New Year (19 July) |
| 357 | Thutmose III's tallest obelisk erected in the Circus Maximus, Rome, by Constantius II |

| 1588 | Thutmose III's obelisk re-erected outside San Giovanni in Laterano, Rome |
| 1799 | Discovery of Amenhotep III's tomb (WV22), and the Rosetta Stone |
| 1816 | Discovery of Ay's tomb (WV23) |
| 1878 | One of Thutmose III's Heliopolis obelisks erected in London (Cleopatra's Needle) |
| 1881 | First royal mummy cache found (TT320) |
| | Another of Thutmose III's Heliopolis obelisks erected in New York |
| 1887–8 | Discovery of Akhenaten's tomb at Amarna (TA26) |
| 1898 | Discovery of Thutmose III's tomb (KV34) and Amenhotep II's (second royal mummy cache) (KV35) |
| 1899 | Discovery of Thutmose I's second tomb (KV38) |
| 1903 | Discovery of Thutmose IV's tomb (KV43) |
| | Carter begins clearance of Thutmose I and Hatshepsut's tomb (KV20) |
| 1905 | Discovery of Yuya and Thuya's tomb (KV46) |
| 1907 | Discovery of tomb KV55 |
| 1908 | Discovery of Horemheb's tomb (KV57) |
| 1922 | Discovery of Tutankhamun's tomb (KV62) |

# 3. LIST OF 18TH DYNASTY KINGS

The following list is based on official king lists compiled and displayed at Abydos in the 19th Dynasty, and a similar list displayed on a relief at Ramesses II's mortuary temple, the Ramesseum. This list provides most of the 18th Dynasty kings in the correct order but omitted those deemed inappropriate to commemorate, including Hatshepsut and Akhenaten and his immediate successors. Hatshepsut's reign, which took place during Thutmose III's official period of rule, was thus ignored, and Horemheb's was extended backwards to claim that he had succeeded Amenhotep III. This added around thirty years to Horemheb's reign. Some authorities regard Horemheb as the first king of the 19th Dynasty, a line which he certainly established but which was not descended from him.

The Abydos list supplies only the throne name, the official name by which kings were also known in diplomatic correspondence. The birth names were widely attested in association with these throne names at other locations and are those most familiar today.

| Throne name | Birth name | Dates BC (approximate only) | Principal queen |
| --- | --- | --- | --- |
| Nebpehtyre | Ahmose I | 1550–1525 | Ahmose-Nefertari |
| Djeserkare | Amenhotep I | 1525–1504 | Meritamun |
| Akheperkare | Thutmose I | 1504–1492 | Ahmose |
| Akheperenre | Thutmose II | 1492–1479 | Hatshepsut |
| Menkheperre | Thutmose III | 1479–1425 | Merytre-Hatshepsut |
| * Maatkare | Hatshepsut | 1473–1458 | N/A |
| Akheperure | Amenhotep II | 1427–1400 | Tia |

| Throne name | Birth name | Dates BC (approximate only) | Principal queen |
|---|---|---|---|
| Menkheperure | Thutmose IV | 1400–1390 | 1. Nefertari<br>2. Iaret |
| Nebmaatre | Amenhotep III | 1390–1352 | Tiye |
| *Neferkheperure | Akhenaten (Amenhotep IV) | 1352–1336 | Nefertiti |
| *Ankhkheperure | 'Smenkhkare' | 1339–1337? | Meryetaten |
| *Ankhetkheperure | Nefertiti as Neferneferuaten | 1338/7–1335? | Meryetaten |
| *Nebkheperure | Tutankhamun | 1336–1327 | Ankhesenamun |
| *Kheperkheperure | Ay | 1327–1323 | Tey |
| Djeserkheperure Setenpre | Horemheb | 1323–1295 | Mutnodjmet |

* Rulers omitted from official king lists.


# 4. MANETHO'S 18TH DYNASTY

Manetho's account of the 18th Dynasty exists only in quotations provided by later authors, in particular Josephus of the late first century AD. This table provides Manetho's names and comments on the left and the names by which these rulers are known today. Manetho's reign lengths may include periods of co-regency. As is evident, his list bears only a very approximate resemblance to what is now known of the 18th Dynasty, the names listed on the Abydos king lists (see Appendix 3). Any overlap is as likely to be coincidence as any genuine compatibility. There are many ambiguities and contradictions which cannot be resolved.* The relationships included for some are

* See MTA no. 111, p. 241, for one interpretation of Manetho's version of the late 18th Dynasty.

unreliable, but the genders possibly not. The multiple kings named as Acenchêrês are most likely connected with the Ankhkheperure name used by Smenkhkare and Nefertiti but are obviously badly confused. Since all three are attributed with reigns of twelve years they may well represent only one king, but as one is said to have been female the obvious explanation is she was Nefertiti. In the 19th Dynasty Manetho placed a king called 'Amenophis' who reigned for nineteen years and six months. This man did not exist and illustrates the consummate unreliability of Manetho.

| Manetho | Reign | Modern name |
|---|---|---|
| Tethmosis 'the king who drove [the Shepherds = Hyksos] out of Egypt' | 25 years 4 months | Ahmose |
| Chebrôn | 13 years | Not known, but see Thutmose II |
| Amenôphis | 20 years 7 months | Amenhotep I |
| | | Thutmose I |
| Chebrôn displaced? (garbled Akheperenre?) | | Thutmose II (Akheperenre) |
| Amessis | 20 years 7 months | Hatshepsut, based on attributed reign length |
| Mêphres (= Menkheperre?) | 12 years 9 months | Thutmose III? Length of reign obviously completely wrong |
| Mêphratuthmôsis | 25 years 10 months | Amenhotep II |
| Thmôsis | 9 years 8 months | Thutmose IV |
| Amenôphis | 30 years 10 months | Amenhotep III |

| Manetho | Reign | Modern name |
|---|---|---|
| Ôrus | 36 years 5 months | Most likely Horemheb as per Abydos king lists? But displaced |
| Acenchêrês (i) | 12 years 1 month | 'Daughter' of the previous. Nefertiti as Ankhkheperure displaced? |
| Rathôtis | 9 years | Tutankhamun? 'brother' of the previous |
| Acenchêrês (ii) | 12 years 5 months | 'Son' of the previous. Not possible if Rathôtis was Tutankhamun. Possibly partly confused with Acenchêrês (i), or perhaps Smenkhkare as Ankhkheperure displaced |
| Acenchêrês (iii) | 12 years 3 months | 'Son' of the previous. Unidentifiable and possibly a duplicate of the previous, given the suspiciously similar reign length |
| Harmaïs | 4 years 1 month | Ay? This is based purely on the attributed reign length. Name possibly confused with a variant form of Horemheb |

# 5. LIST OF PRINCIPAL PERSONALITIES (NOT INCLUDING KINGS, EXCEPT AY AND HOREMHEB)

Egyptian names can be exceptionally confusing. Firstly, they are generally unfamiliar forms to modern eyes. Secondly, many sound or look the same, and indeed are. There is little consistency in the modern spelling of these names, whether in books or in museums. Sometimes names which are identical in Egyptian are deliberately transliterated differently today to help distinguish them. The following list is intended to act as a quick reference while reading the book to individuals of note. The list is not comprehensive.

## ADDUMARI

A king in Nuḫašše (in north-west Syria), correspondent of Amenhotep III or Akhenaten.

## AHHOTEP

Widow of Seqenenre Tao, mother of Ahmose I for whom she served as regent after the death of Kamose (q.v.) until he came of age and expelled the Hyksos.

## AHMES (sometimes known as AHMES B)

One of Thutmose I's wives, mother of Hatshepsut. Hatshepsut claimed that Ahmes had been impregnated by Amun in the guise of Thutmose I. Held the titles Great Royal Wife and King's Sister. See also Mutnofret (q.v.).

## AHMES-IBANA (Ahmes, son of Ibana)

A senior soldier and naval commander who served under Ahmose (including the fall of Avaris), Amenhotep I and Thutmose I. His El Kab tomb texts provide his detailed biography and as a result form a crucial resource for the early history of the 18th Dynasty. Ahmes-Ibana routinely depicts himself in the centre of the action, ignores the achievements of others and is thus typical of the rhetorical nature of much Egyptian historical evidence.

## AHMOSE-NEFERTARI (also AHMOSE-NEFERTARY)
Queen and sister of Ahmose I. Mother of Amenhotep I, with whom she was the focus of a major posthumous cult.

## AHMOSE PEN-NEKHBET
A senior military officer and official who served under Ahmose, Amenhotep I, Thutmose I, Thutmose II, and into the reigns of Hatshepsut and Thutmose III. He rose to serve in several state offices, and finally as Neferure's nurse. His tomb biography is a key source for the period.

## AMENEMHEB
Soldier who served under Thutmose III and recorded his role in his tomb (TT85). Claimed to have saved Thutmose during the hunt of 120 elephants.

## AMENEMHET
Eldest son of Thutmose III. Not heard of again after Thutmose's 24th regnal year when he was made Overseer of Cattle. Possibly the son of a lesser wife called Sitiah.

## AMENHOTEP (temp. Hatshepsut)
Overseer of Works (or sometimes called Chief Steward) under Hatshepsut, specifically (among other posts) Overseer of Works on the two great obelisks, and apparently successor of Senenmut (q.v.). Main focus seems to have been the preparation for her jubilee. Known primarily from his tomb (TT73).

## AMENHOTEP, SON OF HAPU (temp. Amenhotep III)
Amenhotep III's principal official who came from Athribis and rose to be placed in charge of all the king's works. Revered not only for his technical skills but also his personal wisdom. He was commemorated with a statue at Karnak; the dedication inscription of work records his career and long life which lasted till he was

eighty. He was apparently deified and was also known to Manetho. This was recorded by Josephus thus 'in virtue of his wisdom and knowledge of the future, was reputed to be a partaker in the divine nature'. Manetho also recorded a legend involving Amenhotep, son of Hapu, who had supposedly advised a king called Amenophis (Amenhotep) that he would see the gods if he (the king) cleared Egypt of lepers and other diseased people. Overcome with fear of divine retribution for this advice, Amenhotep, son of Hapu, committed suicide.*

## ANKHESENAMUN
Third daughter of Akhenaten and Nefertiti. Named Ankhesenpaaten at birth. Survived the Amarna period to become Tutankhamun's queen, he being surely at least her half and possibly full brother. Changed her name to Ankhesenamun. She had two miscarriages during the reign, outlived Tutankhamun and may briefly have married Ay, his successor. Disappeared and no grave or body known for certain.

## ANKHESENPAATEN, see ANKHESENAMUN

## AY (1327–1323 BC)
Holder of multiple high offices under Akhenaten and Tutankhamun whom he succeeded as king, reigning for three to four years. Origins unknown but possibly related to Yuya and Thuya who may have been his parents. Buried in WV23. Body not found. Father or grandfather of Nakhtmin who did not survive him. No known descendants.

## BAKETATEN (temp. Amenhotep III and Akhenaten)
Youngest daughter(?) of Amenhotep III and Tiye, called King's Daughter. Her name meant 'Maidservant of Aten'. Featured in reliefs

---

* Manetho, see Fr. 54.223, and 235 ff (Loeb edition p. 123ff).

with her widowed mother during Akhenaten's reign. Her age and fate are unknown, no body or tomb having been found.

### BEK (temp. Amenhotep III and Akhenaten)

Senior sculptor whose career spanned two reigns. He may have been responsible for the exaggerated style so characteristic of Amarna art.

### BURRA-BURIYAŠ

King of Karaduniyaš (Babylonia), and correspondent with Akhenaten's court.

### DJEHUTY (also THUTIYE)

Overseer of the Treasury, literally the 'double houses of silver and gold', and other duties including building under Hatshepsut. Succeeded Ineni (q.v.). Known from the career inscription in his tomb (TT11) and at Deir el-Bahari.

### DJEHUTY (temp. Thutmose III)

A general who served in Thutmose III's Asiatic wars, gaining fame in Egyptian culture for his supposed trickery in gaining entry to Joppa for his soldiers and thereby seizing the city. His tomb was found intact at Saqqara in 1824, yielding items of great value which demonstrate the sort of gifts and favours showered on such men.

### HAPUSENEB (temp. Hatshepsut)

Senior official, and First Prophet of Amun under Hatshepsut with building and treasury responsibilities between the 2nd and 16th regnal years. Claimed to have been responsible for one of Hatshepsut's tombs. His grandfather Imhotep had been vizier under Thutmose I.

### HOREMHEB (temp. Thutmose IV, Amenhotep III)

Senior military officer under Thutmose IV and Amenhotep III. Like so many senior Egyptian officials he held multiple titles, all

398

proudly displayed in his tomb (TT78). Not to be confused with the senior officer of the same name under Tutankhamun (see next entry).

## HOREMHEB (1323–1295 BC)

General under Tutankhamun. Succeeded Ay as king and then backdated his reign to the death of Amenhotep III. Regarded as the last king of the 18th Dynasty or the first king of the 19th Dynasty or both. Parentage unknown. Married twice(?): possibly to Amenia, and his queen Mutnodjmet (q.v.). Left no descendants and arranged to be succeeded by Ramesses I. Buried in KV57, his earlier Saqqara tomb being repurposed for his wives.

## HUYA

Tiye's Chief Steward and possible kinsman during her time as dowager queen at Amarna with Akhenaten. Holder of various supervisory offices: the royal harem, treasury and Tiye's house. Known from his Amarna tomb (TA1).

## INENI

Engineer and architect in charge of major pharaonic building projects and tombs from Amenhotep I to the time of Hatshepsut and Thutmose III's joint reign. His career inscription from his tomb (TT81) is the principal source of information about him.

## ISET (ISIS)

Mother of Thutmose III and celebrated only during his reign. Lesser wife or harem girl of Thutmose II.

## KHERUEF (temp. Amenhotep III and Tiye)

Tiye's Steward of the Great Royal Wife in the Domain of Amun. Witness of the 30th regnal year sed festival of Amenhotep III. Also a royal scribe, bearer of the royal seal, among other titles. His tomb (TT192) was desecrated under Akhenaten.

## KIYA (temp. Akhenaten)

Woman of unknown origins. Lesser wife of Akhenaten, and uniquely known as 'Great Beloved Wife of the Dual King', often the only basis of identifying her possessions including key burial equipment found in KV55. Disappeared during his reign. Had at least one daughter, her name and fate unknown. Believed by some to have been Tutankhamun's mother, for which there is no evidence.

## MAHEIRPRI (temp. Thutmose III/Hatshepsut)

Young man of Nubian origin buried in the Valley of the Kings (KV36, found essentially intact). Served as a royal flag-bearer on the king's right, probably under Hatshepsut and/or Thutmose III.

## MEKETATEN (temp. Akhenaten)

Second daughter of Akhenaten and Nefertiti. Died at Amarna in or after the 12th regnal year and was buried in the Royal Tomb (TA26) in a dedicated lateral suite of three rooms. A series of mysterious reliefs in those rooms include one explicitly depicting her death, discussed in the main text.

## MENHET, MENWI and MERTI (temp. Thutmose III)

Minor foreign wives of Thutmose III. Their tomb was found at Wadi Gabbanat in Western Thebes.

## MERYETAMUN (temp. Ahmose I)

Daughter of Ahmose I and his sister Ahmose-Nefertari. Wife, sister and queen of Amenhotep I. Body recovered from the 1881 cache of royal mummies (TT320).

## MERYETATEN (temp. Akhenaten), also known today as Meritaten

Eldest daughter of Akhenaten and Nefertiti. Born by the 5th regnal year. Married to Smenkhkare. After his death(?) became Great Royal

Wife to her parents as joint kings, and then perhaps only to her
mother. Disappeared after the reign. Fate unknown. No body and
no tomb known.

## MERYTRE-HATSHEPSUT (temp. Thutmose III and Amenhotep II), also known as HATSHEPSUT-MERYTRE

Wife of Thutmose III. Mother of Amenhotep II from whose reign she
is principally known. She was apparently designated by Thutmose
III for burial in KV42, but the plans seem to have been changed to
bury her in Amenhotep II's tomb (KV35), though identification of
the remains is uncertain.*

## MUTBENRET

Sister of Nefertiti. Sometimes shown in the company of two male
dwarfs. She appears to have remained a spinster. Discussed in full
in Chapter 12. Her fate is unknown. Sometimes believed to have
been called Mutnodjmet and the wife of Horemheb. Her name is
quite clear as Mutbenret in the tomb of Ay at Amarna (TA25).† See
Mutnodjmet's entry below for an analysis of the names.

## MUTEMWIYA (temp. Thutmose IV)

Wife of Thutmose IV. Mother of Amenhotep III and celebrated as
such, with most evidence for her dating to his reign. Possibly the
sister of Yuya (q.v.).

## MUTNOFRET (temp. Thutmose I)

Wife of Thutmose I. Mother of Thutmose II. King's Sister and the
King's Daughter.

---

* Reeves and Wilkinson (1996), 100, 199, referring to remains found in the
chamber Ea to the side of the base of the well shaft, ibid., the plan on p. 101.
† Davis (1908), pl. XXVI.

## MUTNODJMET (temp. Tutankhamun and Horemheb)

Wife and then queen of Horemheb. Died c. 1310–1309 BC (13th regnal year). If she had any surviving children, they are not known. She may have died in childbirth since her probable body showed signs of multiple pregnancies. The possibility has been suggested that she was the same woman with a similar name who was Nefertiti's sister. In Egyptian her name read *mw.t-nḏm.t*. Nefertiti's sister's name, in the tomb of Parennefer (TA7), relies on a drawing made in the 1850s that appears to have mistaken one sign for another though both mean 'sweet' and may have been interchangeable (Gardiner's M30 *bnr* but giving M29 *nḏm*, confused also with V28).* It either represents Mutnodjmet written differently from the queen's name, or instead actually reads *bnr-t-mwt*, 'Benretmut' or 'Mutbenret', 'Sweet is Mut', which is as it appears in the tomb of Ay (TA25) (see above).

## NEFERTITI

Queen of Akhenaten, and mother of six daughters and probably Tutankhamun. Her origins are wholly unknown, but she is likely to have come from a family with close links to the crown, perhaps that of Yuya and Thuya. Her name was adapted to Neferneferuaten-Nefertiti. She may have ruled as Akhenaten's co-regent and then even briefly as king in her own right after his death, taking the throne name Ankhkheperure/Ankhetkheperure. Her fate is unknown, and her grave has never been found. It has been claimed the 'Younger Lady' in KV35 is her, but this is refuted by those who accept the controversial DNA evidence.

## NEFERURE (temp. Hatshepsut)

Daughter of Hatshepsut and Thutmose II. May have been married briefly to Thutmose III but she did not survive long after her mother. Elevated to the position of God's Wife under her mother.

---

* See Aldred (1991), 222, fig. 20, for the ambiguous drawing of her name.

## NEHSI (temp. Hatshepsut)

'The Nubian' (*nḥsy* – 'the Nubian'). Senior official ('wearer of the royal seal') under Hatshepsut in charge of dispatching the Punt expedition in the 9th regnal year.

## QENAMUN (temp. Amenhotep II)

Holder of numerous posts, son of Amenhotep II's wet-nurse and his childhood companion in the royal harem. Rose to become Amenhotep's intelligence chief.

## SENENMUT (or SENMUT) (temp. Hatshepsut)

Of modest origins but was in court service by Thutmose II's reign and serving as nurse to Thutmose and Hatshepsut's daughter Neferure. Under Hatshepsut he was the most senior state official as her Chief Steward, playing a conspicuous and important role in realizing Hatshepsut's ambitions and his own. Disappeared before the end of the reign. Fate unknown. Tomb and chapel (TT71, 353) never used, but subsequently desecrated.

## SENNEFER (temp. Amenhotep II)

Mayor of the Southern City under Amenhotep II and holder of other posts.

## SHUPPILULIUMA (temp. Akhenaten and Tutankhamun)

Hittite king whose assistance was solicited by a widowed Egyptian queen (probably Ankhesenamun), seeking a husband who would prevent her forced marriage to a servant (Ay?).

## SITAMUN (temp. Amenhotep III)

Eldest daughter of Amenhotep III and Tiye, rising to the position of Great Royal Wife. No other marriage for her is known. Prominently featured on her parents' monuments and in items in the tomb of her maternal grandparents Yuya and Thuya (q.v.) (KV46). No children known. Fate unknown, no body or tomb ever having been found.

### SITIAH (temp. Thutmose III)
Lesser wife of Thutmose III. Possibly the mother of Thutmose III's eldest son Amenemhet.

### 'SMENKHKARE' (temp. Akhenaten)
The spectral co-regent and son-in-law of Akhenaten, married to Meryetaten. Parentage unknown. Some believe the body in KV55 to be his, others that he never existed at all and was simply an alter ego of Nefertiti. Nothing in the tomb of Tutankhamun demonstrably belonged to him, despite claims that it did. Much confusion has resulted from his use of the throne name Ankhkheperure, the same used by Nefertiti when she became king either after him or before. The problems with this name and the history of how it was found and read are discussed in detail in the notes for Chapter 13.

### TADUKHEPA
Tushratta (q.v.) of Mitanni's daughter, sent to the court of Akhenaten. Believed by some possibly to be Kiya, Akhenaten's most important subsidiary wife, but with no serious basis.

### TEY
Only known wife of Ay, who served as queen alongside him when he became king after Tutankhamun. No children known. Probably buried with her husband.

### THUTIYE, see DJEHUTY

### THUTMOSE (temp. Amenhotep III)
Eldest son of Amenhotep III and Tiye. Predeceased his parents and younger brother Akhenaten. Served as a priest at Memphis.

## THUTMOSE (temp. Akhenaten)

Sculptor at Amarna whose workshop has been found. Contents included a number of important portrait pieces, including the celebrated Nefertiti bust.

## THUYA (also TJUYU and variants) (temp. Thutmose IV and Amenhotep III)

Wife of Yuya. Mother of Tiye. Holder of various honours as mother of the queen. Tomb (KV46) largely found intact.

## TIA (also TIAA) (temp. Amenhotep II and Thutmose IV)

Wife of Amenhotep II. Mother of Thutmose IV only under whom she gained any prominence as Great Royal Wife and Mother of the King. Most of the evidence for her existence comes only from Thutmose IV's reign. Her name usurped that of Merytre-Hatshepsut (q.v.), her mother-in-law, on certain monuments, for example at Karnak.

## TIYE (temp. Amenhotep III and Akhenaten)

Daughter of Yuya and Thuya (q.v.). Queen of Amenhotep III. Mother of Akhenaten, Sitamun, Baketaten and others. Played an exceptionally prominent role in her husband's reign and during her son's. Buried at Akhet-aten and later removed to Thebes (KV55), ending up (apparently) in KV35.

## TJENENY (also sometimes given as TJENNUNY or THANUNY) (temp. Thutmose III)

Military scribe whose journal formed the basis of Thutmose III's so-called Annals at Karnak, recounting his campaigns.

## TUSHRATTA (temp. Amenhotep III and Akhenaten)

Mitanni king and correspondent whose letters feature in the Amarna Letters archive.

## YUYA (temp. Thutmose IV and Amenhotep III)

Husband of Thuya (q.v.). Father of Tiye and Anen, and possibly Ay. Father-in-law of Amenhotep III. Possibly also brother of Mutemwiya (q.v.). Holder of an extravagant range of titles, almost all honorific, which denoted his intimate proximity to the throne and hugely prestigious status. Monuments or relics with Tiye's name frequently cited her parents' names, an exceptional practice. Buried with his wife Thuya in KV46, found almost intact.

# 6. GLOSSARY OF PLACES

The names of various places and locations in Egypt are referred to often with variant spellings and sometimes with different names. This varies from book to book and can be very confusing. The following list may help resolve some of those ambiguities and difficulties.

| Abydos | Major Egyptian religious centre north of Thebes. Believed to be the birthplace of Osiris. |
| --- | --- |
| Akhet-aten | Egyptian: *iḥt-itn* ('Horizon of the Aten'). Akhenaten's new capital city now known as Tell el-Amarna. |
| Argo | Island south of the Third Cataract. |
| Armant | About 12 miles (19 km) south of modern Luxor (Thebes). Findspot of the well-known Armant Stela of Thutmose III. Armant was the centre of the cult of the war god Montu, whose name is preserved in the place name. |
| Aruna | The road to Aruna was the one taken by Thutmose III in his campaign against Megiddo in his 22nd and 23rd regnal years. |

Avaris — The Greek name for the Hyksos capital in the Delta. Known to the Egyptians as Hutwaret (*ḥwt-wʿrt*). Renamed Perunefer after the Hyksos were pushed out. The 19th Dynasty Ramesside capital Pr-Ramesses was built on part of the site.

Bahariya — Oasis in the Western Desert to the south-west of the Faiyum (q.v.) and about 180 miles (300 km) south-west of Memphis.

Buhen — Egyptian fortress and settlement in Nubia, north (downriver) of the Second Cataract.

Carchemish — City in Mitanni territory.

Cusae — City and border control point in Egypt about halfway between Thebes and Memphis. Modern El Quseyya.

Deir el-Bahari — Hatshepsut's memorial and mortuary temple. Located in Western Thebes aligned on Karnak. Also known now as Deir el-Bahri.

Deir el-Medina — Workers' village in Western Thebes. Known as *Set-Maat* (*st-mȝʿt*, 'Place of Truth').

Dendera — City and temple site about 40 miles (65 km) downriver from Thebes. Best known today for the Graeco-Roman temple of Hathor from when it was known as Tentyris.

Dra Abu'l-Naga — Necropolis zone in Western Thebes on the slopes of hills that form the northern side of the approach to Deir el-Bahari (q.v.). Used by the 17th Dynasty kings.

Egypt — Called by the Egyptians *kmt* (Kemet, 'The Black Land', a reference to the Nile silt), and *tȝ-mri* (Tameri, 'The Beloved Cultivated Land'). Also *ḥwt-kȝ-ptḥ*, which sounded

something like *ḥwt-kꜥ-ptꜥḥ*, the phonetic
origin of the Graeco-Roman *Aegyptos* and
thus Egypt. This meant 'Mansion of the
Spirit of Ptah'. The Hittites called Egypt Mizri
(*Mi-iz-ri*).

| | |
|---|---|
| El Kab | Location of the tomb of Ahmes-Ibana. About 50 miles (80 km) south of Thebes on the east bank of the Nile. |
| Elephantine | Island in the Nile at Aswan on the border between Egypt and Nubia. It was called by the Egyptians *ꜣbw*, 'Elephant' or 'Ivory' (the word is the same), sometimes with a determinative that indicated foreign territory. Large rocks along the island's edge resemble elephants in the water and are probably the reason for the name. Home to the ram-headed god Khnum. |
| Faiyum | Depression and major oasis settlement west of the Nile near Memphis (q.v.). Location of Gurob, home to one of the royal nurseries and harems. |
| Gurob | See Faiyum (q.v.). |
| Hatnub | Alabaster quarries about 40 miles (65 km) east of the modern city of el-Minya. |
| Hatti | Kingdom of the Hittites. Located in what is now eastern Turkey. |
| Hermopolis | Graeco-Roman name for a city on the west bank of the Nile opposite the site of Akhet-aten. |
| Itj-tawy | 13th Dynasty capital in the Faiyum region (q.v.). Exact location unknown. |
| Kadesh | See Qadesh. |

| | |
|---|---|
| Karnak | Principal cult centre of Amun. Known to the Egyptians as *ʾIpt-swt*, 'Most Select of Places', though *swt* (Q1) could also mean 'seat'. There was also *nst-t3wy*, 'Throne of the Two Lands'. The tripling of the *nst* sign ('throne' or 'seat', W11) means that a more literal translation would be the 'Throne of Thrones of the Two Lands'. Amun was sometimes called *nb-st-t3wy*, 'Lord of the Throne of the Two Lands'. |
| Khent-hen-nefer | See Kush (q.v.). |
| Konosso | Island near Aswan and the First Cataract. |
| Kurgus | Between the Fourth and Fifth Cataracts in Nubia. Declared by Thutmose I to be Egypt's most southerly border. |
| Kush | Egyptian: *k3š*. Egyptian name for Nubia. Often referred to as *ḫtsy*, 'wretched' or 'vile', an adjective often employed for any foreign state Egypt had fought. Also known as *Ḫnt-ḥn-nfr* (Khent-hen-nefer) when referring to land south (upriver) of the Second Cataract; this name has a meaning linked to the idea of there being two sides, i.e. the place on the other side of the Cataract, perhaps 'the place beyond that which is beautiful/good [i.e. Egypt]'. |
| Luxor | Modern city on the site of ancient Thebes (q.v.). |
| Medinet Habu | Mortuary temple of Ramesses III. |
| Megiddo | City in Retjenu, conquered by Thutmose III. Called by the Egyptians *Myktw*.* |

---

\* For example, at URK IV.660, line 8 (far right).

| | |
|---|---|
| Memphis | Ancient administrative capital of Egypt. Called by the Egyptians *mn-nfr*, 'Established and Beautiful', after *mn-nfr-ppy*, 'Pepi is established and beautiful', the Old Kingdom name for the nearby necropolis at Saqqara from that pharaoh's time (2321–2287 BC). Also *ḥwt-k3-ptḥ* which meant 'Mansion of the Spirit of Ptah' and was later used to refer to all Egypt, for which it is the phonetic origin of the Graeco-Roman term *Aegyptos* (q.v.). |
| Mitanni | See Naharin. |
| Naharin | Egyptian: *nhrn*. Enemy and then ally of Egypt. Located in modern Syria. Known also now as Mitanni. |
| Nefrusy | Location of battle between Kamose and the Hyksos. Near Cusae (q.v.). |
| Nubia | See Kush, but also sometimes called *T'-pḏt* (Tapedet?), 'Land of the Bow'. |
| Punt | Egyptian: *pwnt*. Kingdom further south by the Red Sea coast or on the Horn of Africa. Destination of Hatshepsut's celebrated expedition and a well-established source of exotic flora and fauna, for example myrrh trees. |
| Qadesh | Major city in Syria. |
| Retjenu | Egyptian: *rtnw*. Egyptian name for Canaan and Syria from the Negev Desert to the River Orontes. |
| Saqqara | Pyramid royal necropolis of Memphis. |
| Serabit el-Khadim | Temple site in Sinai, dedicated to Hathor. |
| Sharuhen | Fortress in Palestine. Possibly modern Tel Abū Hureirah. |

*Appendices*

| | |
|---|---|
| Shasu | Egyptian: *š3sw*. In Sinai or Palestine. |
| Sudan | Modern country name for the land the Egyptians knew as Kush (q.v.). |
| Tell el-Amarna | Modern name for the site of Akhenaten's city Akhet-aten. |
| Thebes | Egypt's religious capital in the New Kingdom. Known to the Egyptians at this time as *W'st* ('sceptre district'), which referred to the administrative zone in which the city lay. Western Thebes is the modern name sometimes used for the west bank where the mortuary temples and tombs lie. |
| Tikhsi | Location or region in Syria from which Amenhotep II seized seven 'princes' and executed them. |
| Tombos | A collection of sites close to the Third Cataract of the Nile in Nubia (Sudan), including a fortress. Location of victory stela of Thutmose I. |
| Two Lands | Egyptian: *t3wy*, the opposite sides (West and East) of the Nile. For example, 'Lord of the Throne of the Two Lands', a term for the king. |
| Wawat | Egyptian: *w3w3t*. An Egyptian name for the territory of northern Nubia between the First and Second Cataracts. |
| Yehem | Khirbet Yemma in the Sharon. Place at which Thutmose III stopped to plan his next move in his first campaigning season. |

411

# 7. GLOSSARY OF TERMS

This list is not comprehensive but covers some of the more important terms used in the book. The phonetic transliteration of the hieroglyphs is supplied. Owing to the way different hieroglyphs could sometimes be used to represent the same sounds, for example *m*, a word could appear in multiple different forms but apparently sound the same. Gardiner's sign-list numbers are indicated thus: e.g. L2.

**Aten**

The name of the Aten had two versions under Akhenaten, the earlier giving way to the later in or around his 9th regnal year which removed the references to Horus and Shu. Both are cryptic:

Egyptian (early version), 1st cartouche: ꜥnḫ-rꜥ-ḥrw-ꜣḫt-ḫꜥi-m-ꜣḫt ('The Living Re-Horakhty [Horus of the two horizons] rejoices in the horizon …'); 2nd cartouche: *m-rn-f-šw-rꜥ-nty-m-itn* ('… in the name Shu-Re who is in Aten').

Egyptian (later version), 1st cartouche: inḫ-rꜥ-ḥkꜣ-ꜣḫt-ḫꜥi-m-ꜣḫt ('The Living Re, ruler of the two horizons, rejoices in the horizon …'); 2nd cartouche: *m-rn-f-f-m-it-rꜥ-ii-m-itn* ('… in his name as Re the Father who comes in the Aten').*

These names are sometimes abbreviated in modern works as Hor-Aten and Heka-Aten (for example in Murnane 1995).

**brother**

Egyptian: *sn*, using the phonetic sign of a two-barbed arrowhead (T22); also used in the word for two (*snw*) with which it was related.

---

* Based on Gunn (1923) but modified after studying the cartouches in the light of his comments. The second cartouche of the later version can be seen in the second colour plate section.

## cartouche
Oval-shaped rectangular frame with a line at one end used for royal birth and throne names, and also for the name of the Aten under Akhenaten.

## Chamberlain
Egyptian: *ḥr-tp-nsw*, 'the first man under the king', and *imy-ḫnt*, 'he who is front of [others?]'. Also, sometimes the translation given for *bity-sḏꜣwty* – see Chancellor (q.v.).

## Chancellor
Egyptian: *bity-sḏꜣwty*, 'Royal Treasurer' where the words (L2, S19) mean literally 'Bearer of the Precious Seal of the King'; *bity* is the symbol of kingship in the mortal sphere and *sḏꜣwty* is represented by a cylinder seal on a necklace. Placed in charge of administering royal domains. See Chamberlain (q.v.).

## chariot
Egyptian: *wrryt*. This had phonetic links to the word for 'great' (*wr*), reflecting the elite use of chariots. A less common word was *mrkbt*.

## chariotry
Egyptian: *t-nt-ḥrt*, 'the (troop) concerned with teams/spans of horses' (for example Yuya, see King's Deputy q.v.) or indeed any animal teams.

## Chief
Egyptian: *ḥry*, for example, 'Chief of the Great Place [i.e. the royal necropolis]' (*ḥry-st-ꜥꜣ*). Also used to indicate any position where the incumbent was placed above others in a supervisory or leadership capacity.

## Controller
See Leader.

## daughter
Egyptian: *sȝt*, represented by a pintail duck (G39) which shared the same phonetic value with the feminizing *t* (X1), and sometimes with a female determinative (B1), for example *nsw-sȝt*, 'King's Daughter', or the princess *sȝt-imn*, Sitamun 'Daughter of Amun'. The word thus served as both a literal statement of a blood offspring relationship, and a metaphorical one. See also son (q.v.).

## Discovery of the Aten
See Gem-pa-aten temple (q.v.).

## father
Egyptian: *it* but written as *it-f*. By repeating the *f* multiple generations could be indicated, for example *it-f.f.f.f.* ('father of my fathers'?), but it is not known if the number was a literal reference to the exact number of generations concerned.

## favourite
Egyptian: *ḥsw*, 'favourite', an adjective linked to *ḥsi*, 'praised one'.

## friend
Egyptian: *smr*, 'friend' or 'courtier', or *smr-wʿty*, 'sole friend', commonly applied to courtiers. An intimate of the king with other variants suggesting primacy. This term seems to have been directly transmitted to Ptolemaic Egypt where it appeared in Greek as πρωτος φιλος, 'first friend'.*

## Gem-pa-aten temple
Egyptian: *gm-pȝ-itn* (Gem-pa-aten) = usually given as 'Discovery of the Aten', or 'The Sun Disk is Found'. Akhenaten's Aten temple at Karnak. The verb *gem* (*gm*, 'find', Gardiner G28) is translated here normally as a passive verb or as a verbal noun. The word has

---

* Gardiner (1947), 20, and (1959) §260.

a wider range of meanings than the normal translations offered. For example, it can indicate an enabling or being able, and a use or using. Thus, among other possibilities, the full term could mean also 'The Enabling of the Aten'. For the hieroglyphs, see, for example, Sandman (1938), 150, CL and CLI, translated at MTA nos 10-B, C, p. 35.

### General (military)

Egyptian: *imy-r-šwᶜ*, 'Overseer of the Army' (= General), or even *imy-r-šwᶜ-wr*, 'Great Overseer of the Army (= supreme commander of the armed forces).

### God, the Perfect/Good

Egyptian: *nṯr-nfr*, or feminized as *nṯrt-nfr*. Applied to the king.

### God's Father

Egyptian: *it-nṯr*, 'God's Father', meaning the king's father-in-law.

### God's Wife

Egyptian: *ḥmt-ntr*. First held by Ahmose-Nefertari. Indicated a principal royal wife. Used by Hatshepsut and transferred to her daughter Neferure.

### Great Place

Egyptian: *st-ᶜ₃*. The royal necropolis. See Chief and Overseer (q.v.).

### harem

Egyptian: *ḥnt* and *ḥnrt* (and other words). Essentially this is now used to refer to the queen's enclosed household and entourage, but the Egyptian word was the same as the one for a prison, both being connected to *ḥnr*, 'restraint'. The connotations are obvious, as is that 'harem' is not an entirely successful translation. Also, *ipt nsw*, 'king's harem' (see O45). Phonetically the word *ipt* had several different meanings, one of which was the 'secret chamber' of a temple. It is probably this idea of an enclosed and protected zone that related to the 'harem'.*

**Hathoric crown**
Crown with cow horns and a solar disk, often worn by queens, a symbol of the sky and mother deity Hathor.

**Hereditary Prince**
Egyptian: *rpˁt* (or sometimes transliterated as *iry-pˁt*) where *pˁt* means 'hereditary' and *r* indicates a person of nobility or high position such as what we could call a prince or princess. Sometimes translated as 'noble'. It seems to have had variable meanings, depending on context and the subject, for example denoting an heir to the throne (Horemheb?) or serving as one of the many nebulous titles of elite status (Djehuty, under Hatshepsut). The addition of a special determinative suggested descent from an exalted line, as in Nefertiti's case where this was also feminized.

**jubilee**
See sed festival (q.v.).

**kenbet**
Egyptian: *ḳnbt* (or *ḳnbtˁꜣt*) = 'corner', used for regional judiciary panels or courts, a fascinating example of Egyptian terminology. It meant literally a 'corner', its relevance to the context now quite lost. It probably referred to how the men concerned were seated to hear cases in a room or area being used for a court. There is no direct English equivalent but perhaps the closest in spirit is the use of the term 'full bench' when judges of a court sit together to hear a case. Sometimes spelled *qenbet* in English.

---

* See Faulkner (1962), 16–17.

## khepresh crown

A ceremonial crown, originated under Ahmose I. Hatshepsut wears it on the apex of her obelisks at Karnak (see colour plate section) with Amun, suggesting it also evoked the king's divine power. Sometimes called the blue 'war crown' but it was not limited to this context by any means.

## King

Egyptian: *nsw*, 'he of the land of the sedge plant', in the divine sense of ruling

Egyptian: *bity*, 'he of the bee', in the temporal sense of ruling

Egyptian: *nfr-ntr*, 'the Good/Perfect God'

Egyptian: *ḥkꜣ*, 'ruler', 'rule'

Note that the *nsw* and *bity* titles normally appear together and indicated the combined divine and temporal manifestations of kingship. They were formally translated as 'King of Upper and Lower Egypt', but today 'Dual King' is the more accepted version. The formula appears much later on the Ptolemaic Rosetta Stone which included the Greek translation βασιλευς τε ανω και των κατω χωρων ('Ruler of the Upper and Lower Land'). This was once taken to be a literal reference to Egypt's geography by distinguishing the Nile Valley (Upper Egypt) from the Delta (Lower Egypt), but the Greek terms can also mean respectively 'up in heaven' and 'in the country', hence the modern reading.* See also Pharaoh (q.v.).

## King's Deputy

Egyptian: *ḥm-idnw*, 'His Majesty's deputy', in charge of e.g. Chariotry (q.v.) as in Yuya's case.

---

* Gardiner (1957), 73, for the old reading. Manley (2012), 87, defines the new reading but does not explain the way this is compatible with the Greek of the Rosetta Stone.

## King's Son of Kush

Egyptian: *s3-nsw-n-kšy*. See Viceroy (q.v.).

## Leader

Egyptian: *ḥrp*, 'he who is in control/charge'.

## Lord of the Two Lands

Egyptian: *nb-t3wy*, 'Lord of the Two Lands' (the opposite banks of the Nile, and/or Upper and Lower Egypt). Frequently appended to a king's names and other titles. Feminized as *nbt-t3wy* for queens.

## Mansion of the Benben

Egyptian: *ḥwt-bnbn* = 'Mansion [or 'House'] of the Benben', together with Gardiner O25 *tḫn* for an obelisk. This building was in the Aten complex at Karnak under Akhenaten. The Benben was the primordial mound on which the creator god Atum had settled. Its protuberance meant it was the first place where the sun's rays fell and became the basis for the Benben stones, also represented by the capstones of pyramids and the tops of obelisks. See also Aldred (1988), 225, and Sandman (1938) no. CL, translated at MTA no. 10-B, p. 35.

## Master of Horse

Egyptian: *imy-r-ssmt* (e.g. Yuya) using the same word as for e.g. 'Overseer' (q.v.) and several similar terms. Could be augmented with *nb-ḥm.f*, 'all of His Majesty's', i.e. 'Master of all His Majesty's Horse' (as in Ay's case).

## Mayor

Egyptian: *ḥ3ty-ᶜ*, 'the Foremost One', for example 'the Foremost One in Thebes'. Also translated as 'prince'.

## mistress

Egyptian: *nb-t*, literally 'she-Lord'. Also, *ḥnwt*.

## Mother of the King

Egyptian: *mwt-nsw*, 'Mother (of the) King', applied to some dowager queens during the reigns of their sons, for example Merytre-Hatshepsut (q.v.) and Tia (q.v.), providing them with honour and prominence that had not been awarded during their obscurity under their husbands.

## nemes headdress

Egyptian: *nms*. Headdress of a king made of a striped headcloth. Most familiar now as the one worn by Tutankhamun on his gold mask and three coffins.

## Nubian

Egyptian: *nḥsy*. The word was spelled out phonetically in Egyptian, usually either with a determinative showing a captive or a warrior, which suggests it was based on a Nubian term. It appears also as a personal name, for example Hatshepsut's high official Nehsi. Nubians were also sometimes known as *styw*, a word frequently applied to Asiatics and often in association with the idea of enemy bowmen.

## nurse

Egyptian: *mn* and *mnˁt*, the latter being a wet-nurse, literally 'she of the breast'. As *mnˁ* it could be applied to a man, also translated as a nurse, but perhaps better in English as guardian, tutor or nurturer since the task involved all three.

## obelisk

Egyptian: *ṯn*. A tapering four-sided monolith with a pyramidion-shaped top, usually raised in pairs, one on either side of the entrance through a temple pylon. Many were removed by Augustus and later Roman emperors, and others at later dates. See also Mansion of the Benben (q.v.).

**offering**

There were many Egyptian words which can be translated in ways related to this gesture. One, *ḥnk*, was written as a determinative sign showing an extended arm with a hand holding a bowl and indicated the making of a present. The same sign could be added to another word, *drp*, which meant 'offer'.* However, there were other words such as *ḥtp* which meant 'altar' and which were incorporated into a longer word meaning 'offerings to the god', probably by association with the idea of placing the offering (or a symbol of the offering) on an altar in a temple.† The making of an offering did not necessarily involve handing over anything. There was also the possibility of a symbolic transference of ownership to the god even if in reality the donator retained whatever was being offered.

**Opet Festival**

Annual festival for which Hatshepsut was largely responsible. Took place in the 2nd month of the season of flood and connected therefore to fertility and renewal. By Thutmose III's time it ran for eleven days but was lengthened by the 19th Dynasty into several weeks. It involved the transportation of Amun's image from Karnak to Luxor for a series of ceremonies and then its return. Named after the first part of Karnak's name *ʾIpt-swt*, 'most select of places'.

**Overseer**

Egyptian: *imy-r*, 'he who is in the mouth [of his underlings?]'. Essentially, a man appointed to a senior position in charge of a project, palace, or department. The same word is also found translated as steward, master and various other supervisory titles but essentially all meant the same in Egyptian. A 'specification of office' often followed, for example *imy-r-pr-wr*, 'Great High Steward'. Also, 'Overseer of Works in the Great Place' (*imy-r-kȝt-st-ʿȝ*), the royal necropolis. In

---

* See Gardiner D36.
† See Gardiner U4.

practice it could be abbreviated to *imy*, and even reduced often to being represented only by the simple determinative for an ox tongue.* This same word is also translated as 'master', as in the title 'Master of Horse'.† See also General (q.v.) and Master of Horse (q.v.).

## Pharaoh

Egyptian: *pr-ʿȝ*. Literally 'Great House', thus effectively 'palace'. By the 18th Dynasty the word had become a synonym for the king. An example of its usage is: *nb-pr-pr-ʿȝ ʿnḫ-wdȝ-snb*, 'Lord Pharaoh, may he live, be prosperous, be healthy', the latter usually abbreviated now to l.p.h.

## Police, Chief of

Egyptian: *ḥrt-mḏȝw* = 'Chief of the Medjay', where Medjay was a term for militarily able people of the Eastern Desert which had been adopted as a generic term for state security personnel.

## priest

Various Egyptian terms including *ntr-ḥm*, 'the god's servant/slave', sometimes also translated as 'prophet', and *mry-ntr*, 'beloved of the god' (the latter for example in the tomb of Amenhotep-Huy under Tutankhamun). Another, *wnwt*, had a variety of meanings associated with duty and service and could also be used to refer to a priest.

## prophet

See priest (q.v.).

---

* Gardiner F20. This sign also had a quite independent phonetic value *ns*.
† As in the case of Yuya – see specifically Gardiner (1957), 31, and Ay (as in his Amarna tomb TA25). The determinative is Gardiner F20.

# pylon

Egyptian: *bḫnt* or *sbꜣ*, the gateway into a temple made of a pair of trapezoidal towers flanking a narrow passageway. Usually fronted by a pair of obelisks (q.v.) and colossal statues of the king and sometimes his queen and his predecessors.

# Queen

Egyptian: *ḥmt-nsw*, literally 'woman/wife of the king', sometimes amplified by *wrt*, 'great', thus *ḥmt-nsw-wrt*, 'Great Wife of the King' or 'Great Royal Wife'; *ḥmt* survived into Coptic as *hime*, ϹϨⲓⲘⲉ. There was no specific word that denoted 'queen' in our terms, but *iꜥrt* (iaret), the cobra uraeus worn on the brow to denote royalty, could also indicate a queen. See also sovereign (q.v.).

# regnal year

Egyptian: *ḥꜣt-sp*, literally 'year of time', meaning year of the reign and accompanied by a number. Counted from the accession of an individual ruler. Hatshepsut backdated her accession as king to Thutmose III's accession and thus the two shared the same regnal year count. It is not clear whether other co-regents had their own individual regnal year counts or shared one.

# sed festival

Egyptian: *ḥb-sd*, 'festival feast'. A rejuvenation celebration of a king's thirtieth anniversary (jubilee), restoring him to the vitality and dynamism of youth. Preparations could take years and the events were characterized by extravagance and special building preparations. In practice kings could hold a sed festival whenever they wished. Subsequent jubilees could be laid on at far shorter intervals, as under Amenhotep III.

# shabti

Egyptian: *šwbty*. Model figure for installation in the tomb where it would perform labour on behalf of the deceased in the afterlife. Also

known today as an ushabti or shawabti. Amenhotep II's tomb was the
first royal tomb to feature these in numbers.

### sister
Egyptian: *snt*, for example *nsw-snt*, 'King's Sister', using the feminized phonetic sign of a two-barbed arrowhead used for a brother
(T22) (q.v.).

### son
Egyptian: *s3*, represented by a pintail duck (G39) which shared the
same phonetic value, and sometimes with a male determinative
(A1), for example *s3 re*, 'son of Re'. The word thus served as both
a literal statement of a blood offspring relationship and a metaphorical one, which can be confusing especially where there was
a blood connection but not necessarily a true father-son one. See
also daughter (q.v).

### sovereign
Egyptian: *ity*, the feminized version being *ityt* ('queen regnant',
obviously linked to *bity*, see King q.v.), which is normally translated
as 'sovereign' in either a male or female sense.

### Steward
See Overseer (q.v.).

### tasherit
Egyptian: *t3-šr.t*, 'the Younger' (or 'the Little'), here feminized, applied
for example to Akhenaten's fourth daughter Neferneferuaten-Tasherit,
to distinguish from her mother Neferneferuaten-Nefertiti.

### Treasurer
See Chancellor (q.v.)

**troop commander**
Egyptian: *ḥry-pḏt*. Literally he who is over or above the troops, using a hieroglyph for a bow (Gardiner T10) as a collective term for soldiers.

**true of voice**
Egyptian: *mꜣꜥ-ḫrw*. An honorific epithet usually added to the name of a deceased person. Also translated as 'justified'.

**Viceroy**
Egyptian: *sꜣ-nsw-n-Kšy*, 'King's Son of Kush', the governor of Kush (Nubia). The reference to 'son' was honorific, not literal.

**Vizier**
Egyptian: *ṯꜣyty*, 'he of the curtain'. The most senior official under a king, usually on a regional basis, who received detailed submissions from officials which he then reported to the king.

**Warrior of the Ruler**
Egyptian: *ꜥḥwti-n-ḥkꜣ*, 'Warrior of the Ruler', where the word for 'ruler' (*ḥkꜣ*) is also the word for 'rule'.

**worthy**
Egyptian: *zꜣb*, a generic word for a 'worthy' or 'dignitary', someone of esteemed status, but not a specific post. Applied as a nebulous form of compliment in the absence of any more substantive office.

# NOTES

## FOREWORD

1  *ḥwt-kꜣ-ptḥ* = Hewet-ka-Ptah, leading ultimately to *Aegyptos*. The word *hewet* can also mean temple.
2  *kmt* = Kemet, and *Tꜣ-mri* = Tameri.
3  *mḏ-r* = 'walled-in place of treasure'.

## 1. EGYPT IN THE 18TH DYNASTY

1  William Shakespeare, *Cymbeline* III.3.
2  The text of 'The Immortality of Writers', composed in the 19th Dynasty, is written on the verso of the Chester Beatty IV papyrus, BM acc. no. EA10684–5 (https://www.britishmuseum.org/collection/object/Y_EA10684-5).
3  Papyrus Prisse. Now in the British Museum acc. no. EA10435.1 (https://www.britishmuseum.org/collection/object/Y_EA10435-1).
4  *wꜣḏ wr* = 'The Great Green'. Multiple possible meanings, including the lakes and waterways of the Delta.
5  As described in the tomb chapel of Rekhmire (TT100), see BAR (ii) §675.
6  For example, Henry VIII's appointment of relatives from his mother's Yorkist descent.
7  Colton, C. (2013), 'Orthopaedic challenges in Ancient Egypt', *Bone and Joint*, 360, vol. 2, no. 2. Accessed at: https://online.boneandjoint.org.uk/doi/full/10.1302/2048-0105.22.360124?journalCode=bj360&
8  Breasted (1980) provides the full text and commentary.
9  For example, the Ebers Papyrus, compiled under Amenhotep I. See Bryan

(1974). His text of the Ebers Papyrus is available online at: https://babel.
hathitrust.org/cgi/pt?id=coo.31924073200077&view=1up&seq=1

10 Late 18th Dynasty. Ruma's stela is in Copenhagen, Ny Carlsberg Museum
(acc. no. ÆIN 0134).

11 Martin (1991), 71, ill. 40. See colour plate section 2.

12 BAR (iv) §499–556 supplies examples of various investigations into
robberies of royal tombs, including confessions and punishments.

13 The house of the vizier Nakht at Akhet-aten is the best example of
how houses were used in much the same way as the tomb to promote
the owner's status. See Kemp (1991), 241. The term 'prodigy' used here
is derived from its application to the 'prodigy houses' of Elizabethan
England, see Summerson (1993), 59–60.

14 Herodotus 2.100ff, and 2.142. Herodotus is online at: https://penelope.
uchicago.edu/Thayer/E/Roman/Texts/Herodotus/2B*.html

15 These are compiled in the Loeb Classical Library edition of Manetho.

16 The Turin Canon is ME acc. no. Cat. 1874 (viewable at: https://collezioni.
museoegizio.it/en-GB/material/Cat_1874/). For an Abydos king list
see BM acc. no. EA117 (https://www.britishmuseum.org/collection/
object/Y_EA117).

17 From the Greek στήλη (stele), a generic term for an inscribed block of
stone.

18 The text and a translation of Ahmes-Ibana's tomb autobiography is
available at https://mjn.host.cs.st-andrews.ac.uk/egyptian/texts/corpus/
pdf/urkIV-001.pdf. See also BAR (ii) §24–29, 38–39, 78–82.

19 Shattered reliefs at Abydos also recorded Ahmose's campaign but cannot
be reconstructed into a historical narrative. Ahmose II ruled in the 26th
Dynasty, a millennium later.

20 Murnane (1989).

21 Van Dijk (2002), 292, accepts a Hittite reference to an attack on the
Egyptian ally city of Amka not only at face value, but interprets it as a
'major confrontation' and 'disaster'. The Hittite source paints a much less
dramatic image of the event but even so was still probably exaggerated
by them. See Chapter 15. Likewise, Wilkinson (2010), 300, called the 18th
Dynasty 'one of the most glorious dynasties ever to rule Egypt, progenitor
of great conquerors and dazzling rulers', an assessment apparently based
on a face-value acceptance of 18th Dynasty royal propaganda.

22 The best example is the latter part of Akhenaten's reign and its
immediate aftermath (see Chapter 13).

23 T. Jacobsen (1957), 'Early Political Development in Mesopotamia',
*Zeitschrift für Assyriologie*, vol. 52, 94–5, cited by Murnane (1977), 236–7.

24 The problems with the 18th Dynasty royal mummies have been argued
over ever since their discovery and the disagreements show no signs
of abating. Tutankhamun is the sole 18th Dynasty king whose body's

identification is beyond any doubt. The identities of all the other surviving ones have all been questioned in some way, based on querying the dockets on the mummies, and physiological and DNA evidence.

25 Historical nihilism is a term coined in modern China for anyone who dares to question the state's version of events.

26 For example, the texts on a statue of Senenmut from the temple of Mut. There are three published transcriptions of the hieroglyphs but all three differ in some way, with a significant impact on attempts to translate them. Clearly, at least two must be wrong. See Chapter 7, n. 31.

27 Ward, W. A., in *Journal of Near Eastern Studies*, vol. 50, no. 3, July 1991, reviewing Manuelian, P. (1987), *Studies in the Reign of Amenophis II*, Gerstenberg Verlag (Hildesheimer Ägyptologische Beiträge 26), Hildersheim, 1987. Accessed at: https://www.journals.uchicago.edu/doi/pdf/10.1086/373503

28 NASA, *Five Millennium [sic] Catalog of Solar Eclipses* (https://eclipse.gsfc.nasa.gov/SEsearch/SEsearchmap.php?Ecl=-14770601 and https://eclipse.gsfc.nasa.gov/SEsearch/SEsearchmap.php?Ecl=-13370514). Note that the astronomical dates, which includes a year 0 are 1477 and 1337 BC. These are adjusted to 1478 and 1338 BC for true dates.

29 These eclipses can all be located on the NASA Five Millennium Solar Eclipses site (https://eclipse.gsfc.nasa.gov/SEcat5/SE-1399--1300.html), but note that this gives the astronomical dates to which BC events must have one year added for a true calendar year. For example, the astronomical date of the 1312 BC eclipse is 24 June '1311' BC. See also Huber (2001) for these instances, and especially Gautschy (2014) for just how complex and inconclusive trying to associate attested 'eclipses' with actual astronomical events is.

30 Diodorus Siculus 1.50.2.e

31 Gilmore and Ray (2006), 191–2.

32 Cassius Dio 62.16.4–5 (Loeb edition vol. VIII, p. 73); Anglo-Saxon Chronicle (trans. and ed. by G. N. Garmonsway, section E1135).

33 Diodorus Siculus 1.50.2 and Strabo 17.1.46 (C816) both note that the Egyptians calculated the solar year at 365¼ days. Neither observed that the Egyptian civil calendar only ran for 365 days.

34 Flood = *ȝḥt*, growth = *prt*, and low water = *šmw*.

35 Gardiner (1957), 204–5.

36 It took 1,461 Egyptian civil calendar years before it aligned with solar calendar, the additional year needed to make up for the annual shortfall of ¼ day.

37 Sear (2002), no. 4348. The reverse legend is **AIωN** ('Epoch' or 'Era'). The bird is the Benu bird, a form of heron used in late antique Egypt as a symbol of both the sun and of renewal, and not a phoenix as commonly stated in coin catalogues.

38  Censorinus, *de Die Natali Liber* 18.10.

39  The Ebers calendar reference is in hieratic and appears to supply the throne name of Amenhotep I, Djeserkare (*ḏsrkȝrꜥ*), albeit with a fourth additional sign. An image of this section is viewable online at: https://nilescribes.org/2017/12/20/the-ancient-egyptian-calendar/

40  This and other instances of the heliacal rising of Sirius are listed by Long (1974), 263.

41  Gautschy (2014) is an excellent case in point of a phenomenally complicated and ultimately completely inconclusive and impenetrable discussion based on an array of astronomical (mainly lunar) evidence which then blurs into making chronological deductions dependent on all sorts of assumptions.

42  Dodson (2018), 168–9, provides a useful table of approximate parallel chronologies of regimes in the later 18th Dynasty.

43  Dodson (2003, 141) and (2016, 148) dates the 18th Dynasty as respectively 1549–1298 BC and 1540–1278 BC. Not only are the dates different but the overall length of the Dynasty has been extended by eleven years and reflects ongoing revision of the ambiguous evidence. Clayton (1994) dates the 18th Dynasty to 1570–1293 BC while Fletcher (2015, 373) supplies 1550–1295 BC, which are also the dates supplied by Shaw (2002, 481).

44  Pliny the Elder, *Natural History* 36.14.65 (Loeb vol. X, p. 51).

45  Höflmayer (2016) summarizes the position with Egyptian radiocarbon dating.

46  For example, *EA* 3. See also *EA* 51 for Thutmose III and Moran (1992), 122. Pliny the Elder, *Natural History* 36.14.64ff (Loeb vol. X, pp. 51ff) supplies a number of pharaonic royal names as he understood them in the AD 70s, providing yet more variants.

47  Ahmes was written as *iꜥḥms*. A modern biography of Hatshepsut (Tyldesley, 1998) calls her 'Hatchepsut' even though there is no obvious phonetic reason for this, the key sign being Gardiner's A51 *špsi* 'shpsy'.

48  Dodson and Hilton (2010), 137.

49  The closest Egypt has to a canonical series of texts are those published by James Breasted more than a century ago (abbreviated throughout here as BAR). These are only translations and obviously lack many more recently discovered sources such as Amenhotep II's Giza stela. Murnane (1995) produced a remarkable series of translations of texts from the Amarna period. The collection is invaluable but, despite his efforts to leave out as many as possible of the endlessly repeated formulae, the really important elements remain confused by ponderous incantations, his own confusing numbering system and other ways of translating the passages.

50  Manley (2012) is a good example of an introduction to hieroglyphs.

51  Ammianus Marcellinus 17.4.8–10. The obelisk concerned appears to have been one of Seti I's from Heliopolis, installed in the Circus Maximus. It

had been usurped by Ramesses II and Hermapion's translation reflected that. The Loeb volume (vol. I, p. 327, n. 6) is in error believing that the translated texts belong to the Lateran obelisk of Thutmose III.

52  Gardiner (1957), 434.

53  BAR (ii) §674.

54  Gardiner (1938) (ii), 125. He was discussing an obscure idiomatic phrase used by Hatshepsut on the west side of the base of her extant Karnak obelisk, 'my mind travelled this way and that'.

55  The horse determinative (Gardiner E6) could be replaced by the cow hide (Gardiner F27) which referred more generically to mammals, but after *ssmt* (horse) still meant a horse or horses.

56  The transliterated form of Tutankhamun is *imn-twt-ʿnḥ*, 'Amun-image-living', hence 'living image of Amun'. However, where a name was changed, expediency could leave a god's name displaced.

57  Gardiner (1957), 482, M23.

58  The two obvious examples were Amenhotep III's daughter Sitamun, and Akhenaten's daughter Meryetamun.

59  Troy (1986), 3: '[the queen] provides the continuity of the kingship in its multi- generational composition as daughter, sister-wife and mother. And it is used to present the sovereignty of the kingship as a male-female composite and thus as a correlate to the androgynous form of the creator with the generative powers of that status'.

60  See Manetho Fr. 9 and Fr. 10 (Loeb edition p. 39) for 'Biophis, in whose reign it was decided/decreed by law that women also might hold the kingly office'.

61  Known in Greek as the ψχέντ (pschent) crown, and in Egyptian as the *sḥmty* (sekhemty) crown.

62  For example, as used by Hatshepsut at Deir el-Bahari for her grandmother Seniseneb, mother of Thutmose I. See Roehrig (ed.) (2005), 8, fig. 1. The difference between 'Mistress' and 'Lady' in this context is something of a semantic point since literal translations are almost impossible. They could be, and sometimes are, translated the other way round, for example by Troy (1986). However, Gardiner (1957), 183 supplies 'mistress' for *ḥnwt*, and routinely 'lady' for *nbt*, for example ibid., 72.

63  The text of Apiy's letter can be found in Griffith (1898), vol. I, pp. 91–2, and illustrated in vol. II, pl. xxxviii. For a more general discussion see Gardiner (1957), 75.

64  See the case of Hapuseneb, chief priest under Hatshepsut (Chapter 7).

65  Published by Gardiner (1947).

66  Van den Boorn (1988).

67  Such houses do not survive other than at Amarna (Akhenaten's new city) where the house of the vizier Nakht amply demonstrates the way they were used to advertise the owner's exalted status. See Chapter 12.

68   'Greatly loved' was written ꜥꜣ-*mrwty*, and 'one greatly respected' *šfšfyty*.

69   BAR (ii) 713. Accessible online at and visible at https://www.osirisnet.net/popupImage.php?img=/tombes/nobles/rekhmire100/photo/rekhmire_tt100_cm_6519-20.jpg&lang=en&sw=1536&sh=864

70   Corruption became so established that Horemheb issued an Edict at the end of the 18th Dynasty in an attempt to stamp it out (see Chapter 16). Rekhmire's memorial chapel texts are at BAR (ii) §666ff and the speech can be accessed at: https://www.osirisnet.net/tombes/nobles/rekhmire100/e_rekhmire100_03.htm

71   Sons named here: https://www.osirisnet.net/tombes/nobles/rekhmire100/e_rekhmire100_09.htm

72   'Vizier' was written with signs that transliterate as *ṯꜣyty*. See Appendix 7. Gardiner (1947), 19, considered the use of the word 'vizier' to be 'very apt' as a translation.

73   *sꜣ-nsw-n-Kšy* = 'King's son of Kush'. See Appendix 7.

74   A 'King's son of Kush' under Thutmose IV was called Amenhotep, leading to the implausible suggestion this was his actual son, the future Amenhotep III, even though he was only a child.

75   Manley (2012), 32, suggests 'the leader in activity'.

76   Gardiner F20. This sign also had a quite independent phonetic value *ns*.

77   As in the case of Yuya – see specifically Gardiner (1957), 31 and Ay (as in his Amarna tomb TA25).

78   Gardiner 61–2, §79.

79   Gardiner S42. Applied, for example, to the architect Ineni who said he was 'in control of all craftsmen'. See p. 435 n. 4.

80   Sky sign is Gardiner N1. See also Faulkner (1962), 175, for the phonetic version. See Nebiri, 'Superintendent of the Royal Stables' under Thutmose III, on a canopic jar (QV30), and Kha, Overseer of the Great Place' (TT8). For the latter's use of both for the same title, see Chapter 10 and Vandier and Jourdain (1939), 9–11.

81   Faulkner (1962), 18–19.

82   Gardiner (1947), 21, suggesting 'generalissimo' instead, but presumably reflecting the historical context (Franco) of when he wrote, and 27.

83   Shirley (2014), 206. He is known primarily from his tomb (TT73).

84   This is exactly what happened in the case of Yuya and his possible son Ay. See Chapter 11.

85   Setau's statue is in the Louvre, acc. no. 4196, but is unnamed there (https://collections.louvre.fr/ark:/53355/cl010006346). See Roehrig (2005), catalogue no. 72, pp. 130–1.

86   BAR (ii) §675–679, 712.

87   Cassius Dio 60.17.4–9 (Loeb vol. VII, pp. 411–13).

88   See, for example, Strabo 17.2.4, and Herodotus 2.91.

## 2. TWILIGHT OF THE HYKSOS

1 The Egyptian term was *ipt-rsyt*, 'southern place'. Only fragments of the Thutmosid Temple of Luxor exist, and little is known about its form or extent, though Hatshepsut built a shrine there.

2 Karnak's names: *ipt-swt*, 'most select of places', and *nst-t3wy*, 'Throne of the Two Lands' (the opposite sides of the Nile). Compare the latter with *nb-t3wy*, 'Lord of the Two Lands'. For an instance of the latter see the immaculate conception of Amenhotep III in a relief from the Temple of Luxor, illustrated by Kemp (1991), 199, fig. 70, where Amun is labelled as 'Lord of the Throne of the Two Lands'. Kemp translates this term as Karnak on p. 198 without explaining why.

3 The Egyptians did not have the masonry arch, concrete, knowledge of how to roof large spans with timber, or the timber anyway. The inclination was therefore always to repetitive gigantism.

4 BAR (ii) §883. The temple was damaged by an earthquake, and later demolished during by the 19th Dynasty king Merenptah who also took sculpture and other items to use in his own temple.

5 Stevens (2020), 37.

6 Taylor (2001), 174, fig. 126. The paintings included depictions of caricatured workers. Parts of the scene are viewable online at https://www.osirisnet.net/tombes/nobles/nebamon_ipouky181/e_nebamon_ipouky_04.htm

7 One of the words for a priest was *ntr-ḥm*, 'the god's servant/slave'. Another, *wnwt*, had a variety of meanings associated with duty and service and could also be used to refer to a priest.

8 Amun-Re-Kamutef ('Bull of his mother') was a primeval fertility title of the god. The temple later became part of the complex of Ramesses III's memorial-mortuary temple.

9 Ramesses XI's tomb (KV4) was not finished or used for the king's burial.

10 Manetho Fr. 42, cited by Josephus, *Against Apion* 1.14.73–92.

11 *ḥḳ3-ḫ3st* = *heqa-khast*, 'rulers of hill countries'.

12 Shaw (2002), 193.

13 It was formerly believed that there was an Apepi I and an Apepi II. They are now treated as the same man.

14 The family of Ramesses I came from Avaris and was closely involved in the cult.

15 The king responsible was the 13th Dynasty ruler Ay. The pyramidion is now in the Egyptian Museum, Cairo, acc. no. JE43267.

16 The Rhind Papyrus was transcribed during the reign of the Hyksos king Apophis from an original compiled under Amenemhet III. Now in the British Museum, BM acc. no. EA10058 (https://www.britishmuseum.org/collection/object/Y_EA10058).

17  Bietak in Roehrig (2005).

18  The so-called 'war', which it was not, or 'blue' crown. Shown here in
    a very crudely inscribed hieroglyph in the bottom register, where the
    determinative does not show the khepresh crown, but another type.
    It did not take on its familiar form until the 18th Dynasty. See Davies
    (1982).

19  The stonemason Amenpanufer, who gave his testimony in the 16th
    regnal year of the reign of Ramesses IX. The tomb was that of the tomb
    of Sobekemsaf II and his queen Nubkhaas at Dra Abu'l-Naga. Recorded
    on the Papyrus Leopold-Amherst. Published in BAR (iv) §499ff.

20  Dra Abu'l-Naga is a spur at the end of the hill which forms the northern
    side of the approach to Hatshepsut's temple at Deir el-Bahari, and
    overlooks the site of the mortuary temple of the 19th Dynasty pharaoh
    Seti I.

21  At around the same time an investigation into tomb robbery was
    mounted by the mayor of Thebes. The Abbott Papyrus includes a
    description of the locations of five 17th Dynasty royal tombs in the
    vicinity.

22  Intef VII's coffin is the BM acc. no. EA6652 (https://www.britishmuseum.
    org/collection/object/Y_EA6652).

23  Papyrus Sallier 1, BM acc. no. EA10185.2 (https://www.britishmuseum.
    org/collection/object/Y_EA10185-2).

24  Recovered from the 1881 cache of royal mummies (TT320).

25  Missing sections are made good by the Carnarvon Tablet, a wooden
    panel with stucco found at Dra Abu'l-Naga. The inscription is in hieratic.
    The Karnak stelae are in hieroglyphics. See Gardiner (1916) for the
    Carnarvon Tablet. The text of the second stela can be accessed at http://
    egypt-grammar.rutgers.edu/TextPDF/kamose1.pdf and http://egypt-
    grammar.rutgers.edu/TextPDF/kamose2.pdf. A translation is at: http://
    www.u.arizona.edu/~afutrell/w%20civ%2002/kamose.html.

26  Walking stick: Carter no. 50 uu, decorative details of ebony, ivory, and
    glass (http://www.griffith.ox.ac.uk/gri/carter/050vv.html). Sandals: Carter
    no. 397 (http://www.griffith.ox.ac.uk/gri/carter/397.html).

27  Enmarch (2013), 253–63.

28  Quoted on the first stela of Kamose, in Redford (1997) (the stela texts are
    available online at: http://www.u.arizona.edu/~afutrell/w%20civ%2002/
    kamose.html). Northern Nubia here is referred to as Khent-hen-nefer –
    see Appendix 6 under Kush for an explanation of this term.

29  The words were *tꜣ-nt-ḥtrì* for 'this belonging to spans [of animals]';
    *nḥm* = 'carried off'. Text available on Dr Gabor Toth's Middle Egyptian
    Grammar website at Rutgers University (http://egypt-grammar.rutgers.
    edu/TextPDF/kamose1.pdf). The site includes a number of other useful
    texts.

30  Chariots are just one example of how Herodotus' assertion (2.79) that the Egyptians never adopted foreign customs is false.

31  See Dodson and Hilton (2010), 126, 128. They may have had a child called Ahmose-Sitkamose who was a lesser wife of the king Ahmose I.

32  BAR (iv) §519, 'it was uninjured'.

## 3. THE DAWN OF THE NEW KINGDOM

1  There remains some confusion about Ahhotep and whether in fact there were two, the other being the wife of Kamose (the evidence being only a single coffin), but this seems unlikely. There is certainly nothing to be gained by pursuing the matter. See Dodson and Hilton (2010), 128.

2  Text and translation by Mark-Jan Nederhof available at https://mjn.host. cs.st-andrews.ac.uk/egyptian/texts/corpus/pdf/urkIV-014.pdf

3  The dagger is in the Egyptian Museum, Luxor, acc. no. JE4666 (viewable online at: https://old.egypt-museum.com/post/186838503176/ceremonial-dagger-of-ahmose-i). Wilkinson (2010), 215, goes a stage further and even suggests there may have been a dynastic marriage between the Egyptian and Minoan royal houses, but there is no evidence to support that.

4  The fly was a hieroglyphic sign (Gardiner L3) for a fly (*ꜥff*), but seems to have had no subsidiary, alternative, or phonetic significance and was just an honorific symbol.

5  On the evidence of the stela of her steward Kares, which refers to her still being alive in the 10th regnal year of Amenhotep I, and that she was Ahmose's mother. Accessed at: https://mjn.host.cs.st-andrews.ac.uk/egyptian/texts/corpus/pdf/urkIV-014.pdf

6  Smith (1912), 15–18.

7  Ahmose started with Heliopolis in the summer, and then Tjaru in the autumn.

8  El Kab, south of Thebes, was the ancient city of Nekhen.

9  BAR (ii) §303, at the Speos Artemidos temple.

10  Harvey (1998).

11  *smꜣ = Fighting Bull*. See Gardiner (1957), 458, E2, where this term is defined.

12  See https://www.osirisnet.net/tombes/el_kab/ahmes/e_ahmes_02.htm

13  In the 3rd regnal year of Akhenaten, for example, a soldier called Menkheper offered two days' labour by a female slave to a herdsman in return for a bowl and clothing. MTA no. 19-A, p. 44.

14  Sharuhen was possibly on the site of the modern Tel Abū Hureirah.

15  Gutgesell (1998), 365.

16  Wardle and Wardle (2000), 40–1, 71.

17  The fourth chariot, no. 161 in Carter's inventory.

18  During the reign of Ramesses II, see Gardiner (1905). Neshi's position was an *imy-r* class post which has multiple possible meanings, all denoting

being in charge in some way (see Chapter 1 and Gardiner, ibid, 27, line 2 in the original inscription's S9 line).

19  See the story of Sabastet in Chapter 8.

20  Harvey (2007), 343–4.

21  'Tempest Stela of Ahmose: World's Oldest Weather Report', *Science News*, April 2014, accessed at: http://www.sci-news.com/othersciences/ linguistics/science-tempest-stela-ahmose-worlds-oldest-weather- report-01826.html#:~:text=The%20Tempest%20Stela%20of%20 Ahmose.&text=Broken%20pieces%20of%20the%20stela,stood%20over%20 1.8%20m%20tall. Also Ritner and Moeller (2014) accessed at https://www. journals.uchicago.edu/doi/abs/10.1086/675069?journalCode=jnes.

22  See Bourriau (2000), 217.

23  Pearson, C., et al., 'Annual radiocarbon record indicates 16th century BCE date for the Thera eruption', *Science Advances* 15 Aug 2018: Vol. 4, no. 8. Accessed at: https://advances.sciencemag.org/content/4/8/eaar8241

24  The Red Sea Trough brings hot, dry air into Egypt. If disrupted the effect can be high winds and rain in the region. This is infrequent but attested. See: https://journals.ametsoc.org/view/journals/apme/51/5/ jamc-d-11-0223.1.xml?tab_body=fulltext-display

25  Ahmose's other sister-queen was Ahmes-Nebta.

26  The *ḥmt-ntr*, 'God's Wife' of Amun.

27  See, for example, Betsy Bryan, 'Property and the God's Wives of Amun', Johns Hopkins University. Undated but available online on this page: https://chs.harvard.edu/CHS/article/display/1304

28  At Serabit el-Khadim.

29  Elliot Smith (1912), pls VI, VII, and X.

30  Smith (1912), 15–18.

31  From the Kares Stela. See earlier in this chapter.

32  Ahmose's grandmother was Tetisheri. BAR (ii) §34–7.

## 4. MOTHER AND SON

1  For *swsḫ* = 'widen' or 'extend', see Faulkner (1962), 218, line 6. For *t3š*, 'border', see Gardiner (1957), 599, left-hand column, and Faulkner (ibid.), 294. For *w*, 'district', Gardiner (ibid.), 559, rh column, first entry.

2  *iwnt* = 'bow'. See Gardiner, 495, bottom entry with the signs O28 T9 X1. Some published translations provide much more specific descriptions of the Kushite enemy leader, such as 'troglodyte' and 'Nubian'. These are not supported by the Egyptian text and illustrate the problem with over-free translations.

3  At the citadel site of Qasr Ibrim, which lay between Aswan and the Second Cataract on the Nile's east bank. The stela is in the BM acc. no. EA1835 (https://www.britishmuseum.org/collection/object/Y_EA1835).

4   *ḥrp ḥmwt nbt* ('in control of all craftsmen'), and *jȝwt nbt ḥr st-ḥr ḏj* ('all
     offices [were] under the supervision of my command'). Ineni's biography
     sourced at https://mjn.host.cs.st-andrews.ac.uk/egyptian/texts/corpus/
     pdf/urkIV-020.pdf

5   For example, Amenhotep III and Tiye's daughter Sitamun, and
     Akhenaten and Nefertiti's daughters.

6   Bryan (1991), 93.

7   Dodson (1990), 89.

8   The Hatnub quarries are about 40 miles or 65 km east of the modern city
     of el-Minya.

9   The candidates are tomb AN B at Dra Abu'l-Naga, and KV39 in the Valley
     of the Kings. Neither has produced conclusive evidence of ownership
     in the form of paintings or reliefs with texts or the remains of their
     contents, but material bearing the names of Ahmose, Ahmose-Nefertari
     and Amenhotep I was found at the first.

10  See Fletcher (2015), 171–2, and citing Bradbury (1985), 87. A description
     of Amenhotep I's tomb more than 350 years later, when it was inspected
     and allegedly found still intact, does not match either of these exactly,
     not least because the reference has defied conclusive translation and
     because it may not even be referring to a tomb in the Valley of the
     Kings. This occurred in the 16th regnal year of Ramesses IX of the 20th
     Dynasty, see The Abbott Papyrus, BAR (iv) §513. The claim that the tomb
     was intact is likely to have been false. See Epilogue.

11  *kȝy* = 'high place'. Aston (2015), 36, citing all the evidence including the
     cryptic reference under Ramesses IX to the location of the tomb. See also
     Dodson (2016), 62.

12  Bryan (2000), 229, points out that Meryetamun is not stated anywhere to
     have been Amenhotep I's queen. Dodson and Hilton (2010), 126, 128, take
     it for granted that she was. The upper half of the statue is in the BM acc.
     no. EA93 (https://www.britishmuseum.org/collection/object/Y_EA93).
     The lower part is still in situ.

13  For example, a painted limestone seated statue of the king found at Deir
     el-Medina and now in Turin, ME acc. no. Cat. 1372 (https://collezioni.
     museoegizio.it/en-GB/material/Cat_1372/). A stela from the same place
     shows Seti I worshipping the deceased pair, ME acc. no. Cat. 1466 (https://
     collezioni.museoegizio.it/en-GB/material/Cat_1466/).

14  As depicted in the tomb of Amenmes, a priest of the cult. Illustrated in
     Kemp (1991), 23.

15  For example, a relief of Ahmose-Nefertari and Amenhotep I now at
     Brooklyn Museum acc. no. 86.226.25 (https://www.brooklynmuseum.org/
     opencollection/objects/4247).

16  *pȝ-n-imnḥtp* = Pa-n-Amenhotep.

## 5. FIRST OF THE THUTMOSIDS

1   Dodson and Hilton (2010), 126, suggest Thutmose was a son of Ahmose-Sipairi, brother of Ahmose-Nefertari and Ahmose I, and thus Amenhotep I's first cousin.

2   BAR (ii) §58, 'the oath be established in the name of my majesty, born of the king's mother (here given as *nsw-mwt*) Seniseneb ('the breath of health'?), who is in health', where 'health' (*snb*) repeats the last part of her name and indicated she was alive at the accession. See URK IV.81, line 1.

3   BAR (ii) §70.

4   *iw*ʿ*t* = Iwat. Gardiner F44 (*iw*ʿ).

5   This Ahmes is the 'Ahmes B' of Dodson and Hilton (2010), 130.

6   Hatshepsut's sister was called Neferubity/Akhbetneferu. Although depicted at Deir el-Bahari, she played no part in events and probably died young.

7   Dodson and Hilton (2010), 126, position Mutnofret as a possible sister of Amenhotep I.

8   Dodson and Hilton (2010), 126 –8, suggest Thutmose I was Sipairi's son by Seniseneb.

9   BAR (ii) §97, with the whole text at 91–98.

10   BAR (ii) §75, by the viceroy Turi. The original canal was by the 12th Dynasty king Senusret III (1874–1855 BC). For Senusret III's work, see BAR (i) 642–9.

11   Ḫnt-ḥn-nfr. BAR (ii) §80. See Appendix 6 under Kush. Full text and translation at https://mjn.host.cs.st-andrews.ac.uk/egyptian/texts/corpus/pdf/urkIV-001.pdf

12   The process is described by Herodotus at 2.29 and required a rope on each side of the boat so it could be hauled along past the cataract.

13   ḥry-ḥnyt where ḥry means something like 'high', with the suggestion of being above others, and ḥnyt means literally 'rowers'. BAR (ii) 80 (line 31).

14   BAR (ii) 80 (line 32). The word here for 'panther' is ȝby, but this is another example of uncertainty with Egyptian: it can also be translated as leopard. ḥbyt = 'carnage' or 'massacre'.

15   BAR (ii) §67ff.

16   As a matter of interest, some published translations also call the Nubians here 'troglodytes'. The hieroglyphs refer to fallen foreign enemy bowmen (iwnt-ḥr) together with determinatives (N25, T15, A1, A15) that make it clear a foreign enemy is involved and that they are fallen. See BAR (ii) §71 and https://mjn.host.cs.st-andrews.ac.uk/egyptian/texts/corpus/pdf/urkIV-032.pdf which both use troglodyte, presumably as a clumsy English synonym for 'ignorant' and 'backward' which the pejorative tone of the Egyptian might indirectly imply. Translations of this text vary

considerably in detail. The original Egyptian can be consulted at URK IV.84.81ff.

17   BAR (ii) §76.

18   Gardiner T14 and N25. The latter was also used to apply to Nubia – see previous note.

19   *nn ṯnwt m sḳrw-'nḫ*, '[there was] no census (or total) of captives living' followed by the words for 'brought [by] His Majesty from his victory'. Ahmes-Ibana's account, see BAR (ii) §81.

20   The negative is *nn*. The word for a number is *ḥḥ*, Gardiner C11, usually translated as 'many' or 'million', where the latter is a metaphor for a huge but unspecified total.

21   The text of the relief concerned is available at https://mjn.host.cs.st-andrews.ac.uk/egyptian/texts/corpus/pdf/urkIV-040.pdf. See also Pfälzner, P. (2016), section 33, accessed at https://journals.openedition.org/syria/5002

22   The name of the slave is *ḥdt-kwš* (Hedet-Kush).

23   BAR (ii) §83–5.

24   Vivian Davies (2010), 52.

25   Bietak (2005), 75–81.

26   At Abydos. BAR (ii) §98. Similar claims were made at Tombos, ibid., §73.

27   The Egyptian word used for Ineni's staff was *mrt* which also means 'underlings' or 'servants'. BAR §107 gives 'peasant-serfs'.

28   By Senusret III (1874–1855 BC).

29   *sḫm-f3w-imn*, 'Amun, powerful in magnificence'. Another good example of an Egyptian phrase which can be translated several different ways even if the basic suggestion is fairly clear. BAR (ii) §104 provided 'Amon, mighty in wealth'. Some translators make no attempt to turn the phrase into English. *šḫm* means 'powerful' or 'mighty', the hieroglyph being a sceptre (S42).

30   The obelisk was 120 cubits long and 40 cubits wide (180 × 60 ft, or 55 × 12 m).

31   BAR (ii) §86, and 105. The southerly one was also partially usurped in Ramesside times.

32   BAR (ii) §106.

33   *ḥrt* is the word for a tomb. The hill-country sign is Gardiner N25, where it is defined as 'sandy hill-country over [the] edge of green cultivation' – a perfect description of the general context of the Valley of the Kings. It was, for example, used as the determinative for Punt in the reliefs in Hatshepsut's temple at Deir el-Bahari.

34   The final king to have a tomb (KV4) in the Valley was Ramesses XI, the last king of the 20th Dynasty, who reigned over four hundred years later, though he was never buried in it.

35   Illustrated in Reeves and Wilkinson (1996), 91. The text includes the hieroglyphs for the dead, U2 Aa11.

36   During the reign of Seti I (1294–1279 BC). One of its chief priests was

a man called Userhat, who had been in service since at least the
reign of Horemheb. He was a loyal descendant of Thutmose I's vizier
Imhotep, recorded in Userhat's tomb (TT51). Userhat was also known
as Neferhabef. Accessed at https://www.osirisnet.net/tombes/nobles/
userhat51/e_userhat51_01.htm

37  The term 'house of corridors' is obscure. For example, *pr-n-št3* [sic?], in
the Papyrus Mayer A referring to the robbery of the tomb of Ramesses
II during the reign of Ramesses IX. See especially Peet (1915), 175, note 3,
but also BAR (iv) §545; and Budge (1920), 232 'Re-stau'. Faulkner (1962),
206, does not seem to include it and nor does Gardiner (1957).

38  Smith (1912), 25–8, pls VII, XXII, XXIV, XXVIII; for the body's youth and
rejection as Thutmose I, see Wente (1995), 2; also, Habicht et al. (2015), 5,
on evidence of sibling marriages in the royal family.

# 6. BROTHER AND SISTER

1   Two princes, Wadjmose and Amenmose, had apparently predeceased
their younger brother Thutmose II. They are known principally from the
El Kab tomb of their tutor Paheri.

2   Mutnofret was named on a statue of her son Thutmose II found at
Karnak's Eighth Pylon as 'King's Daughter, King's Sister', see URK
IV.154, line 12. Strictly speaking, the sign (T22) for 'sister' is lost but the
context and space make it a reliable restoration. The Eighth Pylon was
built by Hatshepsut but was subsequently adapted by Amenhotep II
as a showcase monument commemorating himself and his dynastic
forebears (excluding Hatshepsut). Her titles are therefore only known
retrospectively.

3   *ḥ3t-Špswt-ḥnmt-imn* = Hatshepsut-knenemet-Amun.

4   For example, on an inscription at Heliopolis. URK IV.144, line 3.

5   Bommas (2000). https://doi.org/10.11588/heidok.00003383

6   Thutmose II was also omitted by Manetho.

7   BAR (ii) §122. *T'-pḏt* (Tapedet?) = Land of the Bow.

8   Inscription at Aswan. BAR (ii) §120ff. URK IV.137, line 9ff.

9   BAR (ii) §83–5.

10  Shaw (2002) 236. *š3sw* = Shasu. Shasu is an ambiguous name because
the first part of it is represented by a lotus pool or meadow hieroglyph,
neither of which could reasonably apply to Palestine or Sinai but might
better fit a location in Nubia on the Nile. This raises the possibility that it
could just be another reference to the 1st regnal year Nubian campaign.
However, Shasu may simply be a phonetic transliteration of a foreign
place name into Egyptian.

11  Iset (Isis) appears on some reliefs beside Thutmose III, named and with
the titles *ḥmt nsw wrt*, 'Great Royal Wife'. These include those where her

name has replaced another's (possibly Hatshepsut's daughter Neferure's – discussed in Chapter 7), for example the stela now in Cairo, viewable at https://en.wikipedia.org/wiki/Iset_(queen)#/media/File:Isis-tutmosis3.jpg.

12  Davies (2004) argued that occasions where Hatshepsut seems to be taking precedence over Thutmose may simply be a misinterpretation of a stylistic convention being used to depict the two side by side to avoid one figure obscuring the other.

13  BAR (ii) §138ff.

14  Suetonius, *Augustus* 94.

15  Based on Shakespeare, *The Tempest* I.2, line 207.

## 7. KING OF EGYPT, DAUGHTER OF AMUN

1  For example, the impregnation of Mutemwiya, wife of Thutmose IV, by Amun to produce Amenhotep III, found at the Temple of Luxor. See Kemp (1991), 199, fig. 70.

2  BAR (ii) §341.

3  Hatshepsut's title here is *nbt wḏ-mdw*, literally 'the she-lord commands speaks', thus in English 'the she-lord who utters commands'.

4  Hapuseneb was another official inherited by Hatshepsut who held a variety of posts, including high priest of Amun, chief of the prophets (priests) of North and South and duties in the treasury. He was engaged on various works, among other places at Karnak and on Hatshepsut's tomb. Hapuseneb's grandfather Imhotep may have been Thutmose I's vizier, though this depends on a reading in Hapuseneb's son's tomb. Hapuseneb names his father as Hapu but is called in his descendant Userhat's tomb (TT51) the son of Imhotep the vizier. This may be a euphemism for 'grandson', in the absence of any Egyptian term to distinguish the two. However, Userhat also rose to high office in the early 19th Dynasty in the cult of Thutmose I.

5  Gardiner (1947), 18.

6  For Sobekneferu's sister's Neferuptah's coffin, see Grajetzki (2005). There were also Khentkaues I and II of the 4th and 5th Dynasties respectively. They had ambiguous titles which declared them either to be Dual Kings in their own right, or the mothers of a pair of dual kings.

7  BM acc. no. EA16581 (https://www.britishmuseum.org/collection/object/Y_EA16581). Probably connected to her contribution to her father Amenemhet III's pyramid funerary complex at Hawara, the entrance to the Faiyum. Gardiner §55, pp. 50–1. The seal is illustrated by Petrie (1917), pl. XIV, no. 29. Available at https://ia800903.us.archive.org/7/items/scarabscylinders00petr/scarabscylinders00petr.pdf

8  *nms* = nemes, literally a headcloth. For Sobekneferu's dress see, for

example, in two statues, one originally in Berlin (destroyed in the Second World War, acc. no. 14475; image at: https://en.m.wikipedia.org/wiki/File:Statue_of_Sobekneferu_(Berlin_Egyptian_Museum_14475).jpg), and the Louvre, acc. no. E27135 image at: https://collections.louvre.fr/en/ark:/53355/cl010002734

9  Auguste Mariette (1864), 'La table de Saqqarah', *Revue Archeologique* vol. 10, Paris, 168–86, pl. 17. She appears in the Turin Canon at Column 6, Row 2, called Sobeknefrure. Sobeknefru survived into at least one version of Manetho's list as his Skemiophris, attributing her a four-year reign. Manetho *Fr.* 34 'according to Africanus'. Loeb edition p. 69.

10  BAR (ii) §239.

11  See, for example, Roehrig (ed.) (2005), 99, no. 48, drawing of an inscription from Sinai (16th regnal year), where the old translation 'King of Upper and Lower Egypt' is given.

12  *ntr-nfr* ('the good/perfect god') when feminized became *ntrt-nfr* and *nb-t3wy* ('Lord of the Two Lands') became *nbt-t3wy*. Found at Deir el-Bahari. MM acc. no. 29.3.2. See https://www.metmuseum.org/art/collection/search/544450 which includes an image of the titles on the reverse. See also Roehrig (ed.) (2005), 170–1, fig. 95.

13  On a statue of Inebny, viceroy of Kush during the latter part of the joint reign of Hatshepsut and Thutmose III. Now in the BM acc. no. EA1131. Illustrated by Quirke and Spencer (1992), 42, fig. 48. He was also known as Amenemnekhu. See https://www.britishmuseum.org/collection/object/Y_EA1131. Hatshepsut's feminized titles were left untouched after her death, but her name was subsequently erased, making it clear whom Inebny had worked for.

14  Troy (1986), 3, 139–44, and Roehrig (2005), 8, fig. 1, and Roth (2005) in Roehrig, ibid., 9–12. See also the plates section of Naville (1895) for various examples, including pls IX and XIV. Conversely, Wilkinson (2010), 231, dismisses Hatshepsut as 'deeply schizophrenic', though it's not clear whether he means metaphorically or literally.

15  For example, a statue in which Hatshepsut offers Maat to Amun, Roehrig (2005), 168, no. 92. MM acc. no. 29.3.1 (https://www.metmuseum.org/art/collection/search/544449). For a statue with combined male and female titles, ibid., 170, no. 94.

16  Atum's female counterparts were Iusaas and Nebet-hetepet.

17  Wilkinson (2017), 150, 156–9.

18  *s3t-imn mrrt.f*, 'daughter of Amun, his beloved one', and *s3t r'ht.f*, 'daughter of Re, of his body', as in the tomb of Djehuty. See Galán in Galán et al. (2014), 248.

19  The last ruler of the 19th Dynasty was Tawosret (d. c. 1189 BC), another queen regent who moved herself into prime position after both her husband and stepson died. Under the Ptolemies the idea of a female ruler

became much more established but also represented a blurring of wider traditions.

20  BAR (ii) §196–8.
21  Based on the translation by Naville (1896), 17 (at the time Maatkare was transliterated as Ramaka).
22  BAR (ii) §225, 285.
23  Vivian Davies (2010), 52.
24  Navile (1894–1908), in particular his plates CLX and CLXV (no page numbers). This publication is at the time of writing accessible at https://digi.ub.uni-heidelberg.de/diglit/naville1908bd6.
25  Habachi (1957), 99, and Shirley in Galán et al. (2014), 224–5.
26  The only possible verification comes from a stela found at Armant (just south of Thebes) which lists some of Thutmose III's achievements. Allen (2010) (i), 261, inexplicably claims the stela records Thutmose III fighting two campaigns he had led into Mesopotamia and Palestine during the co-regency with Hatshepsut. This is far from evident from the surviving text of the stela which appears only to refer to campaigns in the early part of the sole rule. The text of the stela is available at: https://mjn.host.cs.st-andrews.ac.uk/egyptian/texts/corpus/pdf/ArmantTuthmosisIII.pdf. See also Mond and Myers (1940), 182–3, pl. CIII (a drawing of the stela available at https://ia800103.us.archive.org/14/items/EXCMEM43_2/MEEF%2043.2%20Mond%20Robert%20Ludwig%20-%20Temples%20of%20Armant%20%20a%20preliminary%20survey%20Armant%20Plates%20%281940%29%20LR.pdf). Text of Mond and Myers is available at: https://archive.org/stream/EXCMEM43_1/MEEF%2043.1%20Mond%20Robert%20Ludwig%20-%20Temples%20of%20Armant%20%20a%20preliminary%20survey%20Armant%20Text%20%281940%29%20LR_djvu.txt
27  Plumley (1964), 5. The obelisk is in the BM acc. no. EA1834 (https://www.britishmuseum.org/collection/object/Y_EA1834).
28  Gardiner E17 (jackal). There is an obvious phonetic similarity to the modern Arabic word *sahib*, used in several languages in the Middle East and the Indian subcontinent to mean 'companion' but in an honorific way and sometimes as an expression of recognition of rank, just as the Egyptian word was.
29  Gardiner (1947), 53; see also Roehrig (ed.) (2005), 115–16, catalogue no. 60.
30  The statue is Roehrig (2005), 124–5, catalogue no. 66, and is in Cairo, acc. no. CG579. For the text see BAR (ii) §352 (who omits the honorific epithet); Benson and Gourlay (1899), 299–309 (available online at: https://digi.ub.uni-heidelberg.de/diglit/benson1899/). The key words of line 13 in order are *mḥ-ib*, 'the one who is trusted', *wn-mꜣꜥ*, 'true/real', *ḥswti*, 'favourite/favoured'. See Faulkner (1976), pp. 113, 62, and 177, for this vocabulary.
31  BAR (ii) §353, but Breasted's translation makes little sense and ignored

some words. I have used here a far superior translation of this difficult sentence kindly provided by Dr Bill Manley, an expert in the Egyptian language, for this book. He also noted that the line recalls earlier wisdom works like the 12th Dynasty *Teaching of Ptahhotep* (pers. comm.). Published transcriptions of the hieroglyphs differ, e.g. Benson and Gourlay (1899), 309 (who did not translate this part), Borchardt (1925), 130, no. 579, and URK IV, 415, indicating one or more is in error. The line following this one is damaged beyond meaningful translation and may have had a significant impact on clarifying its meaning. For another example of Senenmut's trawling of old texts for his statues, for example an old saying about the seven cows of the Sun god and the four rudders of Heaven, see AZ (1899), 160, no. 2066 (available online at: https://archive. org/details/ausfuhrlichesver00koni/page/160/mode/2up).

32   Keller in Roehrig (ed.) (2005), 118.

33   Ibid., 117.

34   Senenmut's Maatkare statue is at Brooklyn Museum acc. no. 67.68 (https://www.brooklynmuseum.org/opencollection/objects/3759).

35   Sankiewicz (2008) discusses these in detail but see also Keller in Roehrig (ed.) (2005).

36   Senenmut and the Hathor sistrum is in the MM acc. no. 48.149.7 (https:// www.metmuseum.org/art/collection/search/544469).

37   *iry-pˁt* title = 'noble'. BAR (ii) §369ff.

38   Roehrig (ed.) (2005), 147, no. 77.

39   The original publication of the Punt reliefs is available online at https:// digi.ub.uni-heidelberg.de/diglit/naville1898bd3

40   The earliest known expedition to Punt took place in the 5th Dynasty during the reign of Sahure (2487–2475 BC) in the Old Kingdom, when myrrh and electrum were brought back. BAR (i) §161, in Sahure's 13th regnal year. See also Bard and Fattovich (2007) for a general work on Punt expeditions.

41   BAR (ii), 369.

42   Papyrus Harris 1 (The Great Harris Papyrus), quoted by Dodson (2019) (i), 46–7. Also at BAR (iv) §407. In the case of the Ramesses III expedition the final leg was 'downstream', making Memphis the likely destination. The papyrus is in the BM (acc. no. EA9999.43). It is unlikely the ships were dismantled to be transported across the desert since this would have had a dramatic impact on the workload and logistical difficulties.

43   Nehsi's transliterated name reads *nḥsy*, the word for a Nubian. See Gardiner T14, 513, and BAR (ii) §290.

44   Ruiu's sons were Djehutyhotep and Amenemhet. See Davies in Roehrig (ed.) (2005), 54.

45   Galán et al. (2010), 249, note 10, suggest that the evidence is for three pairs of obelisks, only the third pair being extant.

46  BAR (ii) §360, recorded on Sehel Island. Senenmut is depicted, rather than named.

47  Tyldesley, 161 mentions the bases of these obelisks 'at the eastern end' of Karnak.

48  BAR (ii) §330ff.

49  Shirley (2014), 206. It is possible this is the pair shown on the Red Chapel reliefs. Views on this vary.

50  BAR (ii) §315, 316, 318.

51  Bickel (2014), 28. See also Faulkner (1962), 171, and this book p. 382. However, the published translations are good examples of texts that have become virtually canonical but are exceedingly hard to reconcile with what are in my view very cryptic originals. The word for 'future', for example is *m-ḥt*, see Faulkner (1962), 198, line 20, but this seems largely to be guesswork and derives from the notion of those in attendance on a worthy who follow on afterwards, ibid., 19, lines 11–12. One translation, often cited, from the west base inscription of the extant Karnak obelisk includes the line 'Now my heart [i.e. mind] turns to and fro in thinking what will the people [i.e. of the future] say' (Urk IV.365, lines 6–7; Lichtheim 1976, 27). This derives from an obscure Egyptian idiomatic phrase concerned with erratic movement, *itt int*, in this case metaphorically. I believe it is better rendered as 'my imagination runs riot (or is all over the place) wondering what the common people who see my monument in the years to come will say', but it is obscure. See Gardiner (1938) (ii), 125 and Faulkner (1962), 34, line 14.

52  L. Gabolde (2014) provides a discussion and series of quotations on this topic.

53  BAR (ii) §376: the overseer Djehuty says in his tomb that the obelisks were 108 cubits high, meaning the cumulative total of the pair at 54 cubits each. The obelisks were in fact about 56 cubits high. At ibid. §376 he says the electrum came to 88.5 hekets, about 12 bushels.

54  Shirley (2014), 206.

55  Schulze and Sourouzian in Schulz and Seidel (1998), 176; and Bell (1985), particularly 275–6, note 128.

56  From from σπεος, 'grotto'. Presumably the unnamed shrine referred to by Djehuty as one of his achievements 'in the highlands'. BAR (ii) §374.

57  BAR (ii) §296ff, and especially 303.

58  Tomb MMA 504 in the 11th Dynasty necropolis on the north side of the wadi leading to Hatshepsut's temple.

59  See https://www.metmuseum.org/art/collection/search/545147 for Hatnefer's mask.

60  Hayes (1960), 42.

61  Tyldesley (2006), 106, is one of several Egyptologists to claim this, for example, 'A single stela, raised at Armant, tells us that Hatshepsut died

on the 10th day of the 6th month of the 22nd year of her reign', making a similar claim at (1996), 210. The stela, which is solely concerned with Thutmose III's activities, gives that date but does not mention Hatshepsut.

62 The text and translation of Thutmose III's Armant Stela are available at https://mjn.host.cs.st-andrews.ac.uk/egyptian/texts/corpus/pdf/ ArmantTuthmosisIII.pdf. See also Mond and Myers (1940), 182–3, pl. CIII (a drawing of the stela available at https://ia800103.us.archive.org/14/ items/EXCMEM43_2/MEEF%2043.2%20Mond%20Robert%20Ludwig%20 -%20Temples%20of%20Armant%20%20a%20preliminary%20survey%20 Armant%20Plates%20%281940%29%20LR.pdf). Text of Mond and Myers is available at: https://archive.org/stream/EXCMEM43_1/MEEF%2043.1%20 Mond%20Robert%20Ludwig%20-%20Temples%20of%20Armant%20%20 a%20preliminary%20survey%20Armant%20Text%20%281940%29%20LR_ djvu.txt

63 For the date see also Hornung et al. (2012), 201, citing URK 1244, line 14, and Redford (1992), 156, note 135.

64 The memory of Hatshepsut's rule endured long enough for her to be listed by Manetho as his 'Amessis' who reigned for '21 years and 9 months' (and in other versions 'Amensis' and 'Amersis' who ruled for 22 years) an almost exactly correct figure, despite Hatshepsut not being included in any of the official king lists, unlike Sobeknefru. There is no explanation for Manetho's version of her name unless he had confused Hatshepsut with Amenhotep I's mother Ahmose-Nefertari who had remained a figure of great importance for centuries long after the 18th Dynasty, unlike Hatshepsut. Manetho Fr. 50.

65 Due to the civil and calendars being out of synch and the point in the 1,460-year cycle involved. See Chapter 1 for a full discussion of this phenomenon.

66 BAR (ii) §389. Hapuseneb held several posts, including high priest of Amun, chief of the prophets (priests) of North and South and duties in the treasury. He was engaged on various works, among other places at Karnak and on Hatshepsut's tomb. Hapuseneb's grandfather Imhotep may have been Thutmose I's vizier,

67 Elevation plan of Hatshepsut's first tomb in Reeves and Wilkinson (1996), 94.

68 Thutmose I's adapted sarcophagus was found in KV20. It is now in Boston MFA acc. no. 04.278.1, and is the only 18th Dynasty royal sarcophagus outside Egypt (viewable online at: https://collections.mfa. org/objects/130720?image=8). See Roehrig (2004), 188, no. 108.

69 Reeves and Wilkinson (1996), 186.

70 The nurse was Setre-In. Hawass, Z. (2007), 'The Search for Hatshepsut and the Discovery of her Mummy', published on the author's website at: http:// www.guardians.net/hawass/hatshepsut/search_for_hatshepsut.htm

71  Hayes (1962), 8.
72  Illustrated by Dodson and Ikram (2008), 216. The key sign is Gardiner
    F4 *ḥȝt*, 'foremost', which is also the first part of Hatshepsut's name. For
    the collapse of TT71 see https://www.metmuseum.org/art/collection/
    search/549070
73  Shirley (2014), 223–4. Also known as Amenemnekhu.
74  Roehrig (ed.) (2005), 126 –7, catalogue no. 69. The statue is in Luxor Museum.
75  Attested on a dated stela from Serabit el-Khadim. Shirley in Galán et al.
    (2014), 224–5.
76  Roehrig (ed.) (2005), 103, and also 146, catalogue no. 77. Tyldesley (1998)
    describes Puyemre as an 'architect', but it would be more accurate to
    say that in his other positions he oversaw a certain number of minor
    construction projects. 'Architect' is misleading.
77  When the later female king Tawosret of the 19th Dynasty died in 1189 BC,
    leaving no obvious successor, Egypt was convulsed by a civil war lasting
    at least a year and led to the establishment of the 20th Dynasty.

## 8. WARRIOR KING

1  See, for example, Allen (2010) (i), 261, who makes this claim but see the
   previous chapter for a discussion of this which cannot be verified from
   the Armant Stela, the source he cites.
2  Martin (1991), 69. This was Horemheb, the future king.
3  This can be estimated from the civil calendar date provided in the
   Annals and the point in the Sothic Cycle by around this time.
4  BAR (ii) §409, 410. The months can be computed by setting the Egyptian
   civil dates recorded against the solar calendar based on the approximate
   point in the Sothic Cycle. By c. 1457 BC the cycle was approximately 90
   per cent of the year behind the solar year, meaning that Egyptian civil
   calendar dates were about five weeks out.
5  The line is at URK IV.649, line 4. The men are called *nḫt*, meaning
   'strong' or 'victorious'.
6  The word used is *ḏʿmw*, translated as 'fine gold' or 'electrum'.
7  BAR (ii) §432.
8  Sometimes translated as 'Encircler of Asiatics', the term is *iḥ stt* where *iḥ*
   was normally used for trapping animals in a net. It is clear the meaning
   was more than just surrounding the Asiatics: they had been corralled
   and trapped like animals. See URK IV.661, line 6, and Gardiner's T24 and
   S22.
9  BAR (ii) §430.
10 BAR (ii) §479. Strictly speaking, the Egyptian is a little less precise and
   means more literally 'herd of up-country mammals', though it is likely
   goats were meant. URK IV.697, line 15.

11 The Hittites were called by the Egyptians *Ḫ-t'*. BAR (ii) §470, 479.

12 BAR (ii) §447.

13 BAR (ii) §589.

14 Wilkinson (1992), 111. The bulti fish incubates its eggs orally and the young hatch from the mouth.

15 Djehuty's gold bowl is at the Louvre, diameter 17.9 cm (https://www.louvre.fr/en/oeuvre-notices/bowl-general-djehuty); bracelet at the Rijksmuseum van Oudheden, Leiden (https://commons.wikimedia.org/wiki/File:General_Djehuty%27s_18th_dynasty_bracelet_(Leiden).jpg). The lotus leaves on the bowl symbolized Lower Egypt and appear on one of the two heraldic columns erected at Karnak by Thutmose III. See Schulz and Seidel (1998), 161.

16 On the verso of the Papyrus Harris 500 (BM Papyrus acc. no. EA10060), of 19th or 20th Dynasty date.

17 In the Annals, the city's name is given as *'Inrṯ,-ʿn-rȝ-ṯw*. There are variant forms. See also BAR (ii) §470 for this occasion.

18 It was not unknown during the Roman Empire for populations to accept Roman rule in preference to existing despotic rule by kings or tribal chieftains.

19 The lowest part of the surviving text of the Stela refers to the 29th regnal year. The text and translation of Thutmose III's Armant Stela are available at https://mjn.host.cs.st-andrews.ac.uk/egyptian/texts/corpus/pdf/ArmantTuthmosisIII.pdf. See also Mond and Myers (1940), 182–3, pl. CIII (a drawing of the stela is available at https://ia800103.us.archive.org/14/items/EXCMEM43_2/MEEF%2043.2%20Mond%20Robert%20Ludwig%20-%20Temples%20of%20Armant%20a%20preliminary%20survey%20Armant%20Plates%20%281940%29%20LR.pdf). Text of Mond and Myers is available at: https://archive.org/stream/EXCMEM43_1/MEEF%2043.1%20Mond%20Robert%20Ludwig%20-%20Temples%20of%20Armant%20a%20preliminary%20survey%20Armant%20Text%20%281940%29%20LR_djvu.txt

20 *EA 26.*

21 *EA 51.*

22 *EA 59.*

23 BAR (ii) §436.

24 Lilyquist in Roehrig (ed.) (2005), 62.

25 Redford (1992), 177.

26 At the temple of Bastet. She was called Ta-Kemnet, 'the blind one', see Panagiotopoulos (2006), 404. Louvre acc. no. E11673. Height 11.3 cm. http://cartelfr.louvre.fr/cartelfr/visite?srv=car_not_frame&idNotice=23775

27 Panagiotopoulos in Cline and O'Connor (2006), 370–412, in particular here 406.

28 Text and translation available at: https://mjn.host.cs.st-andrews.ac.uk/egyptian/texts/corpus/pdf/ArmantTuthmosisIII.pdf

29 At Ta-Seti. Recorded on the Armant Stela where another is depicted on the New Kingdom pylon of the Temple of Montu. A rhinoceros in Egyptian was a *šꜣḳb*, 'shaqeb' ('hostile horn' – rhinoceros is derived from the Greek words for 'horn' and 'nose'). Thiers, C. (2013), 'Armant (Hermonthis)' in Bagnall et al. (2013), 720–22. Accessed at: https://halshs. archives-ouvertes.fr/halshs-00967325/document

30 Nebiri was Superintendent of the Royal Stables' under Thutmose III and able to commission a tomb (QV30) in the Valley of the Queens where he commemorated his career. Demas and Agnew (2012), 25.

31 Nebamun's tomb paintings are in the BM. A picture of the scene concerned can be seen at Quirke and Spencer (1992), 142–3.

32 Arnold (2005).

33 A fragment of an obelisk of Seti I's was found in the harbour at Alexandria, probably as the result of an accident when loading it onto a freighter bound for Rome or Constantinople. Dodson (2019) (ii), 30, fig. 26.

34 The idea that Thutmose III was trying to discredit a rival claimant to the throne descended from Hatshepsut's mother and who might have challenged his own son Amenhotep II can be safely discounted since no such individual is known.' See Dorman in Roehrig (2013), 269.

35 Laboury in Cline and O'Connor (2006), especially 263ff.

36 Naville (1908), 8–9, pls CLXVI and CLXVII. This publication is at the time of writing accessible at https://digi.ub.uni-heidelberg.de/diglit/ naville1908bd6

37 One section of the Annals is now in the Louvre acc. no. C51 (years 29 and 35) (https://www.louvre.fr/en/oeuvre-notices/annals-thutmosis-iii). See also BAR (ii) §391, note.

38 The existing shrine in this location was inserted by Philip Arrhidaeus, half-brother of Alexander the Great, who ruled Egypt 323–317 BC.

39 *iḫ-mnw* = 'glorious monument'.

40 These obelisks feature in the tomb reliefs of Puyemre (TT39), see BAR (ii) §382 and 624.

41 BAR (ii) §382, 624, with the offerings recorded at §563 and 572. One of these pairs was commemorated by a scarab now at the MM acc. no. 14.8 (https://www.metmuseum.org/art/collection/search/554560).

42 BAR (ii) §86.

43 Dodson and Hilton (2010), 132. See also Dorman (1988), 77–8. Cairo Museum acc. no. CG 34015. Those in favour of Neferure having been Thutmose III's wife include some who suggest she was the mother of his eldest son Amenemhet. There is nothing to substantiate this. https:// en.wikipedia.org/wiki/Iset_(queen)#/media/File:Isis-tutmosis3.jpg

44 KV42 was later used for the burial of royal officials but it is not clear whether they were only redeposited here after having been buried

somewhere else first. Although evidence was found for Merytre being buried there her body was not found.

45  Their transliterated names read *M⁽nht, M⁽nwi* and *M⁽rti*. The ⁽ sign is Gardiner's D39, showing a human arm extended holding a bowl, and G17 the owl is for *m*. D39 appeared in words for 'present' and 'offer' as a determinative. See in particular also Gardiner §336 discussing words for 'give', 'come' and 'take'. The word for give is *imi*.

46  And thereby possibly explaining the appearance of Hatshepsut's name in Maheirpri's tomb.

47  Rekhmire had had a meeting with Amenhotep II at Hout-sekhem (Diopolis Parva). https://www.osirisnet.net/tombes/nobles/rekhmire100/e_rekhmire100_12.htm

48  Hapimen's sarcophagus, its decoration copied from the sarcophagus of Thutmose III, is in the British Museum acc. no. EA23 (https://www.britishmuseum.org/collection/object/Y_EA23). The sarcophagus has had a remarkable history, eventually becoming a bath in a mosque.

# 9. THE ARCHER KING

1  Now in Cairo acc. no. JE55301. Illustrated in Schulz and Seidel (1998), 324.

2  For example, on the Karnak stela line 2. BAR (ii) §782.

3  Bryan (2000) in Shaw (ed.) 2000, 249, who does not reference the source. The text of Amenhotep II's Giza stela, found in 1936, is in Hassan (1949), see pp. 181ff for the relevant part here. Hassan is available online at: http://www.gizapyramids.org/static/pdf%20library/hassan_sphinx.pdf

4  Thinis was one of Egypt's earliest capitals. The site has not been found but is known to have been near Abydos. Min's full portfolio of posts was: Mayor of Thinis, Mayor of the Oases, Supervisor of the Prophets of Osiris and Onuris, tutor of Amenhotep II, Bearer of the King's seals of Upper and Lower Egypt, Overseer of the West Bank Army, Chief Administrator of the Lord of the Two Lands, Chief Overseer of the South, and Scribe. He cannot possibly have been active in all of these simultaneously and even allowing for career progression it is likely that Min was another example of an honoured official who probably did comparatively little in practice.

5  BAR (ii) §592 in the tomb of Amenemheb (TT85).

6  The date of Amenhotep II's accession as an anniversary appears on the stela of Usersatet, viceroy of Nubia, now in Boston MFA acc. no. 25.632 (viewable at https://collections.mfa.org/objects/146139). See Hornung (1997), 291, and Darnell (2014), 249.

7  Dodson (2016), 7.

8  The stelae concerned are (Amada, Elephantine, Memphis and Karnak). The sources also include the tomb texts of Amenemheb (TT85). Amenemheb (see above) emerged from retirement to serve under

Amenhotep II at the new king's special request because had served with distinction under Thutmose III. Amenemheb's tomb texts are published in BAR (ii) §809.

9   Part of the reason seems to be that James Breasted (BAR (ii) §780–2) was one of those who believed the Karnak stela described a campaign in the 2nd regnal year and only added to this the campaign of the 3rd regnal year recorded on the Amada and Elephantine stelae. Although some books have stuck to this line it has since been possible with the Memphis stela to see that it and the damaged Karnak example are both referring to campaigns of the 7th and 9th regnal years.

10   BAR (ii) §792.

11   BAR (ii) §797 (Elephantine) and 808 (Amenemheb). The latter does not name Tikhsi. Bryan, for example (2000) (ii) 252, ignores the idea of a 3rd regnal year campaign without explanation or comment on the Tikhsi episode's inclusion on the Elephantine stela of the 3rd regnal year, attributing instead to the 7th regnal year.

12   BAR (ii) §781ff.

13   In 1421–1418 BC the Egyptian new year began on or about 14 August, which places the crossing of the Orontes 266 days later, approximately in the middle of April. See Chapter 1 for an explanation of how the 365-day Egyptian civil calendar was out of synchronization with the solar calendar in a cycle that lasted 1,460 years. In 1421 BC the civil calendar was about 93 per cent ahead of the solar calendar meaning that a civil calendar date was about twenty-five days out. If the actual time of year was approximately mid-April, then the civil calendar for that day would be at the Egyptian equivalent of 20 March.

14   Bryan (2000) (i), 76, but see also Bryan (2000) (ii) in Shaw (2002), 252, which abbreviates the former.

15   Hoffmeier (1976), 43. Experiments with eight-spoked wheels under Thutmose IV were abandoned, the six-spoke wheel remaining the standard. Thutmose IV was shown riding a chariot with eight spokes on the chariot body found in his tomb. See Chapter 10.

16   Yeivin (1967), 125.

17   Recorded on stelae found at Memphis and Karnak. URK 1299–1309 (Memphis) and 1310–1316 (Karnak). The latter can also be found at BAR (ii) §781–90.

18   *skз-w-ꜥnḫ* = 'living captives'.

19   BAR (ii) §790, citing the Karnak stela which at the time Breasted attributed to the 2nd regnal year. See also Yeivin (1967) and Dodson (2016), 10, for a discussion of this campaign and more detailed references.

20   On the Memphis stela. Bryan (2000) in Shaw (ed.) (2000), 252.

21   The tomb is fully covered online at: https://www.osirisnet.net/tombes/ nobles/rekhmire100/e_rekhmire100_03.htm

22  URK 1395, line 15. Qenamun is also known as Ken-amun.

23  Sennefer was 'mayor of the Southern City' and was cousin of the vizier of Upper Egypt, Amenemopet. Sennefer's tomb (TT96) can be explored online, this part at https://www.osirisnet.net/tombes/nobles/sennefer/e_sennefer_04.htm

24  Caminos (1963), 31. The letter is unprovenanced and was still sealed with a royal seal. It had thus presumably not ever been sent or received, unless the farmer, Baki, discarded it without reading it.

25  BM acc. no. EA1103 (https://www.britishmuseum.org/collection/object/Y_EA1103).

26  This is the 'Tia A' of Dodson and Hilton (2010), 132, 140.

27  *mwt-nsw* = 'King's Mother'. Dodson and Hilton (2010), 139, 140; Dodson (2016), 12; Bryan (1991), 98–9.

28  The term for holiday is *hrw-nfr*, 'day-happy'. For the full text and discussion see Hornung (1997), 291, and Darnell (2014), 248ff, and especially the latter's warnings at 240 about misleading translations. In fact, the Egyptian for holiday has been largely restored. The stela is in Boston MFA acc. no. 25.632 (viewable at https://collections.mfa.org/objects/146139/stele-of-usersatet-viceroy-of-nubia). The 'happy day' phrase is on the left-hand side of the second row of hieroglyphs.

29  The word used for Nubians is the conventional *nḥsy* (*nehsi*). The word for magicians is *ḥk3w*.

30  Schlick-Nolte et al. (2011), 21ff, 26, 28, 33. For the plaque, see French (2002), pl. 17.

31  The man responsible for Amenhotep II's mortuary temple was probably Kha, 'Overseer of Works in the Great Place'. For his tomb (TT8), found intact, see Chapter 10.

32  The plan was drawn c. 1150 BC. Turin, ME acc. no. Cat. 1885 (viewable at: https://collezioni.museoegizio.it/en-GB/material/Cat_1885/).

33  Amenhotep II's tomb (KV35) also has a pair of square subsidiary chambers on either side of the burial chamber. These rooms would play a role much later in the tomb's history as repositories for other royal bodies removed for safety to form a second cache, including the probable body of Amenhotep III's queen Tiye.

34  Illustrated by Dodson (2016), 24, fig. 19. There were at least two others, One, Webensu, was to be buried in his father's tomb and evidently had predeceased him. Another, also called Amenhotep, seems to have been more prominent than his brothers but disappeared.

## 10. THE SPHINX'S CHOSEN ONE

1  Menkheperure, the regnal name of Thutmose IV, was the same as Thutmose III's but with the triplicating addition of the hieroglyphic

determinative for plurality III (Gardiner Z2) to the *ḫpr* ('manifestation')
component. A modern convention is to distinguish the name from
Thutmose III's Menkheperre by inserting a 'u' before the -re suffix but it
is unlikely that in Egyptian it was vocalized any differently.

2   *smsw* = eldest. Heqareshu's son Heqaerneheh would go on to serve in
the same capacity for Thutmose's own sons. Bryan (2000), 254, claims
(without referencing the source painting) that Heqareshu was described
as nurse of 'the king's eldest son'. See Dodson (2016), 28, fig. 23, who
reproduces a drawing of the painting in TT64 showing that the relevant
section has been lost and been restored.

3   The text of Thutmose IV's Dream Stela is at BAR (ii) §812ff.

4   Amun's consort Mut is included as well as other deities such as Sekhmet,
making the omission of Amun even more obvious.

5   Unhelpfully also named Amenhotep. BAR (ii) §818.

6   The Theban tomb of Sobekhotep (TT63) had painted decoration
including scenes of Western Asiatic tribute bearers arriving in Egypt.
Sobekhotep was a state treasurer, and his wife was nurse to Thutmose
IV's daughter Tiaa.

7   The episode is attested on the Konosso Stela, from the island of Konosso
near Aswan, and is also the evidence for the king's highest recorded
regnal year. BAR (ii) §825–9.

8   Thutmose was shown being in receipt of Nubian tribute in the tomb of
the senior officer Horemheb (TT78). Not to be confused with the general
under Tutankhamun and later king.

9   Today the temple is only known from the reused blocks in a new
temple built by Taharqa of the 25th Dynasty that name Thutmose and
Amenhotep.

10  Recorded in the tomb of Nebamun, standard-bearer and captain of
police in Western Thebes, where he calls them the 'chiefs of Nahary'
(TT90). Not to be confused with the scribe of the same name (TT17).

11  A similar division of the spoils is described under Amenhotep III in a
letter from Tushratta of the Mitanni who reported a war against the
Hittites and itemized what he was sending to Egypt. *EA* 17.

12  Davis (1904), pl. VI. Now at the MM, New York acc. no. 30.8.45a–c (https://
www.metmuseum.org/art/collection/search/544826).

13  From house P48.1. (Image viewable at: https://commons.wikimedia.
org/wiki/File:Bracer_of_Pharaoh_Thutmose_IV._From_Amarna,_
House_P_48.1,_Egypt._1397-1388_BCE._Neues_Museum.jpg). Now in
Berlin Egyptian Museum acc. no. ÄM21685.

14  Bryan (1987), 3, no. 1, who rejects the argument that the figure of the
king had been usurped from Amenhotep II.

15  Dodson and Hilton (2010), 135, call her 'Nefertiry C'.

16  *iˁrt* = 'iaret'. Gardiner I12, and B7.

17 The letter was from Tushratta, king of Mitanni, Artatama's grandson, writing to Akhenaten. He said, 'When [Thutmose IV], the father of Nimmureya (Amenhotep III), wrote to Artatama, my grandfather, he asked for the daughter of [my grandfather]'. Tushratta's letter goes on to explain that Artatama was no pushover and that Thutmose IV had to write seven times before the girl was sent to Egypt. *EA* 29, lines 16ff. There is no doubt that Thutmose IV is meant due to the reference to Amenhotep III. The damaged text would have given his throne name Menkheperure, or a version of.

18 Aldred (1991), 220. This speculation is linked to a complicated series of potential links between the family of Amenhotep III's queen Tiye and various ancestral members of the 18th Dynasty royal family, ibid., 140–1.

19 Named in the tomb of the royal nurse-tutor Heqaerneheh (TT64) which records his father Heqareshu as the nurse-tutor of the young Thutmose IV. The boy was the elder brother of Amenhotep III.

20 Tiaa, whose nurse was the wife of the treasurer Sobekhotep, and Tentamun who was buried with her father.

21 The soldier was called Mery. Papyrus Munich 809. Hepu is also known as the owner of TT66. Bryan (1991), 245–6, copied by O'Connor and Cline (2001), 60. See: https://books.google.co.uk/books?id=MzVszHxO3JoC&pg=PA60&lpg=PA60&dq=papyrus+munich+809&source=bl&ots=RRmvqNLeaa&sig=ACfU3U1h3YBkqKewoEAS6mszSa3ndz9igQ&hl=en&sa=X&ved=2ahUKEwiEnPvlhrzsAhWOiFwKHWjaDY0Q6AEwDXoECAYQAg#v=onepage&q=papyrus%20munich%20809&f=false

22 The tomb may be explored online at: https://www.osirisnet.net/tombes/nobles/horemheb78/e_horemheb78_01.htm

23 Bryan (1991), 244.

24 His name led to the implausible (and over-literal) belief by some today that this Amenhotep was the same man as Thutmose IV's son and heir. This is in spite of other evidence that when Amenhotep III became king he was still a child. For the source, see Bryan (1991), 250–1.

25 The stela of Neferhat, 'chief of works'. BAR (ii) §839. Now in the BM acc. no. EA148 (https://www.britishmuseum.org/collection/object/Y_EA148) and Bryan (1991), 165 (who does not mention the palace). An official called Sapair, who managed Thutmose IV's royal fleet navigators, is also attested at Abydos. BM acc. no. EA906 (https://www.britishmuseum.org/collection/object/Y_EA906).

26 BAR (ii) §831ff.

27 *thn-w'ti* = 'the obelisk, the sole one'.

28 Ammianus Marcellinus 17.4.12–15.

29 Seti I's obelisk was repaired and re-erected in the Piazza del Popolo where it stands today.

30   See Vandier and Jourdain (1939), 9, and 11, for the use of the two titles in
      Kha's tomb (TT8): *imy-r-k3t- st-ʿ3* and *ḥry-st-ʿ3* (Overseer of Works in
      the Great Place' and 'Chief of the Great Place').
31   In particular, Imhotep of the 3rd Dynasty who designed and built
      Djoser's Step Pyramid.
32   Zinn, K., 'Literacy, Pharaonic Egypt', in Bagnall et al. (2013), 4101, who
      quotes a number of estimates of literacy. Available online at: https://core.
      ac.uk/download/pdf/96773662.pdf
33   See Faulkner (1962), 263; also, Kemp (1991), 257.
34   This was reflected in modern times when tomb robbing resulted in high
      value antiquities abruptly becoming available, often revealing to the
      authorities that a clandestine but major discovery had been made. This
      was how the 1881 royal mummy cache (TT320) was tracked down.
35   Under Ramesses III (1186–1155 BC). See Mark, J. (2017), 'The First
      Labor Strike in History', at https://www.ancient.eu/article/1089/
      the-first-labor-strike-in-history/
36   A sculptor called Qen who worked there during the 19th Dynasty saw to
      it that a stela was installed in his own tomb showing him and his family
      worshipping them. In the MM, New York acc. no. 59.93. (https://www.
      metmuseum.org/art/collection/search/549536).
37   Tomb discovered in 1906. Its contents are now in Turin acc. no. 8647.
      Kha lived on into the reign of Amenhotep III. See Porter and Moss
      (1960), 16, no. 8. http://www.deirelmedina.com/lenka/TurinKha.html
      provides a useful series of pictures of the Turin Museum display, but
      this is out of date and the collection's display has been rearranged
      several times since.
38   Nakht and Tawy's names meant literally 'Strong' and 'Two Lands'. The
      word for chantress is *šmʿyt* or *šmʿt*, a term linked to others for musician
      and the making of music. Their tomb can be explored online at:
      https://www.osirisnet.net/tombes/nobles/nakht52/e_nakht_01.htm
39   G. Elliot-Smith, 'The Physical Characteristics of the Mummy of
      Thoutmôsis IV', in Davis (1904), xliii, estimated an age of twenty-five.
      See also Bryan (1991), 11, for a more detailed and modern discussion
      drawing attention to the problems created by the discrepant nature
      of the evidence. Also, see Wente (1995) for one study questioning the
      craniofacial sequencing of the royal mummies, including the identity of
      the mummy said to be Thutmose IV's.

## 11. THE FIRST FAMILY

1   *mwt-m-wi3* = 'Mut in the sacred barque', Mutemwiya.
2   BM acc. no. EA43 (https://www.britishmuseum.org/collection/
     object/Y_EA43).

3  *EA* 1, and in particular note 38. The letter was found at Amarna where it had been archived during Akhenaten's reign.

4  *EA* 5. It should be noted that Amenhotep III's(?) name on this letter is very incomplete and has been restored as [Nibmuar]ey[a].

5  The crisis was the loss of Bordeaux in 1453, the climax of a series of territorial losses in France.

6  See Blankenberg and Van Delden (1969). Various examples are known today, for example in the MM, New York, 10.130.1643. See: https://www.metmuseum.org/art/collection/search/548625

7  It is a comment on just how variable the treatment of Egyptian history is in modern works that Yuya and Thuya go unmentioned in Wilkinson (2010), despite a chapter being devoted to the reign and the discussion earlier of several of Amenhotep II's favourites. Tiye is mentioned only in passing, with no comment on her exceptional and unprecedented prominence.

8  Aldred (1957), 31, discusses Yuya's possible foreign origins.

9  Although Yuya's body is one of the best-preserved 18th Dynasty mummies, Mutemwiya's has not knowingly survived and thus no comparison can be made (though one of the female bodies in KV21 has been proposed). Nor has her tomb, if one ever existed, been found either. The only personal possession known of Mutemwiya is an unprovenanced wooden spoon in the form of a goose head and lotus-flower bowl, now in the Louvre (acc. no. E3671, https://collections.louvre.fr/en/ark:/53355/cl010008482, catalogued under Moutemouia). This may have originated in her burial, but probably from a robbery in antiquity rather than a modern one. Since it bears the title 'Great Royal Wife' it must date from Amenhotep III's reign, rather than his father's, under which it is erroneously catalogued.

10  The information about Yuya's titles, coffin and the titles of Thuya that follow, is largely taken here (but adapted) from Maspero in Davis (1907), xiv–xvii, and Naville (1908), 2–4, published in the same volume in the Duckworth reprint of 2000.

11  Yuya and Thuya's tomb (KV46) at the time was the most north-easterly in the Valley, lying in a small easterly branch. No other tombs were dug in the vicinity until the 20th Dynasty. The closest 18th Dynasty tombs were KV55, and KV62 (Tutankhamun), both created several decades later.

12  One of Yuya's titles transliterates as *rpʿ-ḥȝtyʿ*, words that meant respectively a 'noble' and 'foremost'.

13  Naville (1908), 2.

14  *ḥsw* = 'favourite', and *smr-tpy* = the 'first friend'.

15  MTA no. 58-B.8, p. 119, in the tomb of Ay at Amarna (TA25), 'May you exit and enter like [Re's] favourite'.

16  Aldred (1991), 219.

17    *t-nt-ḥtr* is the key phrase here for a span of animals. Faulkner (1962), 180 (bottom), itemizes the usages of this term but does not explain its literal meaning. Gardiner (1947) (i), 113, provides the rational basis for translating it as chariotry rather than cavalry. He was of course unaware of the burial of the Abydos Dynasty king Senekbay, found in 2014, whose body bears injuries commensurate either with having been on horseback or in a chariot, but this is exceptional. Yuya's version of these titles in hieroglyphic form can be found in Newberry (1907), 7, at the top of the page. In fact, there is no specific word for horses in the chariotry element, but instead a reference to animal teams or spans. It is a matter of interest that during the research for this book several sources were consulted to track down Yuya's titles. Although these two were referred to on several occasions, not one of the sources ever identified where they came from, merely repeating the translations. Eventually they were found in Newberry, *op. cit.* where he neither identifies nor translates them. A similar phrase appears on Kamose's second stela from Karnak.

18    The word for chariot was *wrryt* (werret). It could be represented phonetically, or with the determinative Gardiner T17 (a picture of a chariot). The word appears for example in the biography of Ahmes-Ibana.

19    *ii-iy* = Yey. Aldred (1957), 31, 33; ibid. (1991), 140, who suggested Yey's shabti was 'mid-Eighteenth Dynasty'. At present it is catalogued as being of late 18th Dynasty date. The piece is in the MM acc. no. 45.4.7 but is not listed under any personal name (https://www.metmuseum.org/art/collection/search/545972). The relevant part of the text is split across the second (left) and third (lines) of text.

20    Michel de Montaigne (1533–92), *Essays* II.7 (see the Penguin edition, translated by M.A. Screech, p. 428).

21    Images of Yuya's chariot are widely available online (for example: https://www.bridgemanimages.com/en/asset/660322/summary).

22    *nsw-mwt-ḥmt-nsw-wrt* = 'mother of the great royal wife of the king'.

23    Elizabeth I (1558–1603) raised money by charging patent holders for control of lucrative monopolies, though this was normal and accepted practice.

24    Aldred (1991), 219.

25    Ibid., 141.

26    Correctly, as it happens: through Elizabeth Woodville's daughter Elizabeth of York virtually every royal line in Europe is descended from her. Edward IV's premature death in 1483 meant he was to be succeeded by his son Edward V, still a child. The throne was usurped by Edward IV's brother Richard, Duke of Gloucester, who succeeded as Richard III. The Woodvilles become implicated in plots to get rid of Richard III and ensure both Edward V's accession and their continued privileged status. Edward V was murdered by persons unknown, but certainly with

Richard III's connivance, thwarting the Woodville plans. In 1485 Richard was killed in battle and succeeded by another cousin, Henry Tudor, as Henry VII, who married Elizabeth of York. One might also consider the Vandal general Stilicho, married to the niece of the Roman emperor Theodosius, who became a guardian for the underage emperor Honorius (AD 393–423), and married his daughter to him.

27  Montserrat (2003), 146. Since then, the discovery of more information about Nefertiti has displaced Tiye as a dominant force in Akhenaten's reign.

28  *EA* 26.1, 30–48 (the gold statues); 27; 28.7; 29, especially 29.6–10.

29  The principal evidence is the claim that the hair on the mummy is identical to the lock of hair found in Tutankhamun's tomb and which was explicitly labelled as hers.

30  The name Sitamun had also been given to a sister of Amenhotep I, a daughter of Ahmose-Nefertari.

31  Gardiner's W14, M17 (twice), making the word *ḥsy(t)*.

32  This has not stopped eccentric speculation. Fairman (1972) concluded that Amenhotep III and Sitamun were the parents of Smenkhkare and Tutankhamun. Had Sitamun been Tutankhamun's mother, we might have expected him to have commemorated her in some way. Her memory was not, so far as we know, proscribed as Nefertiti's was and nor would there have been any reason to.

33  Amenhotep III and Tiye's other daughters were Iset (the king's wife), Henuttaneb, Nebetiah, and Baketaten.

34  *s3 nsw* = 'son of the king' (crown prince). Dodson (1990), 88; also, Dodson (2016), 44–5, 75–6. The third body in a side chamber found in the royal cache in Amenhotep II's tomb may be this prince Thutmose's.

35  *EA* 17.26, 29.16–27. Gilukhepa was a daughter of Shuttarna II of Mitanni, and sister of Tushratta.

36  BAR §864. A more recent translation is available online at: https://mjn.host.cs.st-andrews.ac.uk/egyptian/texts/corpus/pdf/ScarabAmenophisB.pdf

37  *EA* 29, lines 6–10. From Tushratta of Mitanni.

38  BAR (ii) §845. This campaign may also have been described on a stela from Bubastis, ibid. §847–50.

39  Merymose's sarcophagus, found in TT383, is displayed in the BM acc. no. EA1001 (https://www.britishmuseum.org/collection/object/Y_EA1001_1).

40  BAR (ii) §851–5, referring to the findspot as 'Semneh'; Van Gils (undated). The stela is in the BM acc. no. 657 (https://www.britishmuseum.org/collection/object/Y_EA657).

41  BAR (ii) §856–9.

42  BAR (ii) §916. Now in Cairo's Egyptian Museum acc. no. JE 31409.

43  BAR (ii) §917.

44   BAR (ii) §919.

45   By Horemheb's Tenth Pylon. See Schulz and Seidel (1998), 164, fig. 28 where the statues are shown in situ.

46   Łajtar (2019), 177.

47   The reputation of Amenhotep, son of Hapu, recalls that of the celebrated and deified Imhotep under Djoser in the Old Kingdom.

48   Now in the BM acc. no. EA826 (https://www.britishmuseum.org/ collection/object/Y_EA826). The exact findspot is unknown.

49   Now at Leiden (no. V.14).

50   Thutmose IV was the last to raise an obelisk, and even that was only his grandfather's unfinished obelisk. Amenhotep III raised no obelisks that we know of, and nor did any of the remaining kings of the dynasty. Obelisks were not resumed until the 19th Dynasty.

51   Viewable at: https://www.osirisnet.net/tombes/nobles/rekhmire100/e_ rekhmire100_07.htm

52   *pr-ḥꜥi* = 'House of Rejoicing'; *pr-itn-t̠ḥn* = 'House of the Dazzling Aten'.

53   Koltsida (2007).

54   The so-called 'Lost Golden City', a grand new discovery heralded in 2021 which was not a new discovery at all. (https://www.bbc.co.uk/news/ world-middle-east-56686448).

55   BAR (ii) §905, 906.

56   *ḫ'rw* = 'Kharu'. Kharu was a generic term for Palestinians and Syrian nationals. See Budge (1920), 532.

57   Strabo 17 C816 (Loeb vol. VIII, p. 123) describes them.

58   The tomb is at Deir el-Barsha, near the modern city of Mallawi.

59   In Luxor Museum acc. no. J838 (https://commons.wikimedia.org/wiki/ File:%C3%84gypten_1999_(274)_Luxor-Museum-_Statue_Amenhotep_ III._(28449254662)_(2).jpg). The statue appears to have been originally fitted with gilded accessories such as armbands and a decorative collar. It was defaced during the Amarna period, but not restored.

60   Now in the Louvre acc. no. A18, Room 324. See also BAR (ii) §842.

61   BAR §869. Kozloff and Bryan (1992), no. 2. The sign that indicates the duck and fish were of gold is Gardiner S12, a collar of beads, *nbw* with the sign || (Z4) to indicate to indicate duality. See also BAR (ii) §869.

62   MTA no. 2F, p. 21.

63   The tomb of Kherouef (TT192) includes a particularly detailed depiction of the 37th regnal year jubilee. See: https://www.osirisnet.net/tombes/ nobles/kheru/e_kherouef_04.htm

64   Epigraphic Survey (1980), 43.

65   *EA* 3.13–22.

66   Hence the Egyptian word *sḫmt* for power.

67   *EA* 11.5–15.

68   Most of the Sekhmet statues at the Temple of Mut are damaged in some

way, many fragmenting. Many major Egyptology museum collections include one or more of the better examples such as BM acc. no. EA63 (https://www.britishmuseum.org/collection/object/Y_EA63). Others were removed in antiquity to different places, such as Ramesses III's memorial-mortuary temple.

69    Epigraphic Survey (1980), pls 42–3. TT192.

70    Aldred (1991), 93; the colossus is in the BM acc. no. EA7 (https://www.britishmuseum.org/collection/object/Y_EA7), and currently on display in the Lower Egyptian Gallery.

71    The statue is 2.27 metres tall. Vatican acc. no. 22678. Viewable online at: https://www.museivaticani.va/content/museivaticani/en/collezioni/musei/museo-gregoriano-egizio/sala-v--statuario/statua-della-regina-tuia.html

72    BAR (ii) §900–3.

73    As stated on the dedication of Amenhotep son of Hapu's own statue at Karnak. BAR (ii) §917.

74    Currently displayed in the BM acc. no. EA15 (https://www.britishmuseum.org/collection/object/Y_EA15).

75    BAR (ii) §906.

76    Reeves and Wilkinson (1996), 114.

77    Smith (1912), 46. It should be noted that the coffin itself has a painted inscription inside with the names of Ramesses III (ibid., pl. XXXII), but his body was identified separately in the tomb (ibid., pp. 84ff).

78    Smith (1912), 51; Aldred (1991), 106.

79    Wente (1995), discusses in detail his belief that there are serious problems with the craniofacial morphology of the mummies supposed to be Amenhotep II, Thutmose IV, Amenhotep III, Akhenaten, Smenkhkare, and Tutankhamun. For example, his observation was that the body labelled as Thutmose IV bore by far and away the closest resemblance to Tutankhamun's. Rearranging the skulls based on his understanding of a more plausible sequence suggests some of the bodies were mislabelled by those processing them for installation in the royal caches. However, his conclusions have not met with universal agreement (naturally).

80    BM acc. no. EA57399 (https://www.britishmuseum.org/collection/object/Y_EA57399). Illustrated in various books, for example Aldred (1991), pl. 26. The link between Ishtar and the relief may be quite false. The statue had also been invoked by Tushratta in the hope that his daughter would be pleasing to Amenhotep III. See, for example, *EA* 19.24.

## 12. THE GREAT LIVING ATEN

1    Ridley (2019), 11. But see also MTA, pp. 1–2.

2    See, for example, Weigall (1922 edition the most useful now, first

published in 1910), whose biography of Akhenaten confronted most of
the problems with understanding this period. Surprisingly little has
changed.

3   Murnane (1977), 231, 'none of [the evidence for a co-regency] can
be reckoned as convincing proof', arguing that most of it was
commemorative rather than literal. Also, Ridley (2019), 25–6.

4   Troy (1986), 9.

5   *nfr-t-ii* = Nefertiti, 'the Beautiful One is come'.

6   This has huge implications for those who believe Nefertiti's body is that
of the 'Younger Lady', found in KV35, and those who have used DNA
evidence to suggest the woman concerned was Akhenaten's sister and
mother of Tutankhamun, but *not* Nefertiti.

7   Wallis Budge (1925, reissued in 1989), 58.

8   Egyptian: *rpˁt*. Aldred (1988), 221–2, calls her 'The Heiress', MTA no.
66.4, p. 133, 'the hereditary princess', typical of variant translations with
significantly different meanings in English. The important determinative
is Gardiner's H8 (which was not apparently vocalized), feminized with
X1. The scene from Huya's tomb (south wall, west side) is illustrated by
Davies (1905), vol. III, pl. 6, where the title is very clear. Budge (1911), 235,
translates the term as 'hereditary tribal chief'. See Appendix 7.

9   'Hereditary prince' was also an honorific title, for example held by
Horemheb when a general under Tutankhamun who was by his own
admission of low birth (see Chapters 14 and 15). The only difference in his
case was that there was no determinative for exalted descent. The term
*rpˁt* is cited in Horemheb's Coronation Text, see Gardiner (1953), 14, for
line 6.

10  There are some differences in how the two names were written. See her
entry in Appendices, List of Principal Personalities. For a more detailed
discussion of Nefertiti's possible connections see Dodson and Hilton
(2010), 144–5, Ridley (2019), 183ff, and Dodson (2020), 18–20.

11  Dodson (2016), 52, 73. The connections between Shu and Tefnut and their
associated manifestations and divine remits are unsurprisingly both
arcane and complex.

12  An example from the Karnak temple is in Turin, ME acc. no. Cat. 1378
(https://collezioni.museoegizio.it/en-GB/material/Cat_1378/).

13  See MTA, p. 5, for the 'coregency' of Akhenaten and Nefertiti with the
Aten. I have adapted slightly the translations here from Gunn (1923),
176. A full transliteration of the names can be found in the Glossary
of Terms. Readers may find the later name of the Aten translated in
different or abbreviated ways (for example, Dodson, 2018, 10) but Gunn's
translation is the truer to the hieroglyphs. This is especially so of one
version that provides 'in his name of Re/light' instead of 'in his name as
Re the Father' (for example, Ridley, 2019, 138) – there is no word for light

in the cartouche. The names of conventional Egyptian gods were not shown normally in cartouches. These were used for the names of the king and queen only.

14    MTA no. 6, p. 30, records the fragmentary remains of a taxation decree.

15    Stela at Gebel el-Silsila, about 40 miles (65 km) north of Aswan, from where the quarried stone could easily be transported downriver by water to Karnak. MTA no. 5, pp. 29–30. However, BAR (ii) §935 provides the meaningless 'breach' where MTA supplies 'forced labour'. This appears to have resulted from mistaking the Egyptian transliteration for an abbreviated English word. The Egyptian is *bḥ*, 'forced labour', see Faulkner (1962), 83 (bottom). For the Egyptian text, see Sandman (1938), 143–4, no. CXXXVII (available online at: https://oi-idb-static.uchicago.edu/multimedia/1282/BiAe_8.pdf).

16    The Amarna Project run by Professor Barry Kemp, University of Cambridge. See https://www.digital-epigraphy.com/reading/carved-limestone-fragments-from-the-great-aten-temple.

17    Samson (1977), discusses the prominence of Nefertiti already by this early stage in the reign.

18    Depicted on the walls of the tomb of the scribe Ipy (or Apy) at Amarna (TA10), see MTA, 127, fig. 3 (viewable online at: https://www.osirisnet.net/popupImage.php?img=/tombes/amarna/tombes_amarna/photo/ipy10_xx_0692.jpg&lang=en&sw=1536&sh=864 and in Bouriant at: https://us04web.zoom.us/j/75829502237?pwd=cnptajJWbWFQOW8wdUdva3FyOUdSQT09. See Dodson (2016), 99, and also Aldred (1991), 235–6. Manniche (2010) discusses in forensic detail all the known colossi and fragments. For the rings, see Tyldesley (2006), 131.

19    MTA no. 35-A, p. 68.

20    This Ramose was probably not the man of the same name who served at Amarna and had a tomb there (Southern Tomb 11). They had different wives and titles. Website for TT55 forthcoming at https://www.osirisnet.net/tombes/nobles/ramose/e_ramose55_01.htm

21    In Egyptian her name was spelled ***Mry-t-itn*** where the first *t* makes the one who is beloved feminine. Her name was an Atenized version of the more traditional Meryetamun or Merytre ('beloved of Amun/Re').

22    *ȝḫ-n-itn* = 'effective/useful for the Aten'. See also Van Dijk (2003), 271.

23    For example, a slab from Hermopolis where it had been reused. See Dodson (2018), 37, fig. 30, and (2020), 61, fig. 68.

24    *ȝḫt-itn* = Akhet-aten. See Kemp (2012), 50.

25    Snape (2014), 155.

26    Murnane (1995), 37.4, p. 77 (para 2).

27    The 6th regnal year stelae took sufficiently long to execute that they had to be updated. To begin with, only two daughters, Meryetaten and

Meketaten, are shown with, in some cases, clear evidence that the latter had been added later during work in progress, followed by the third daughter Ankhesenpaaten. Aldred (1991), 47ff, covers the boundary stelae texts in detail; Reeves (2001), 108–11, provides extracts; Dodson (2016), 105–7, and Ridley (2019), 64–5, provide translations of the key passages. Murnane (1995), 73ff, provides full translations of both the 5th and 6th regnal year sequences of stelae. Murnane and Van Siclen (2011) is the supposed definitive publication of the stelae but in fact is poorly presented with no transliteration of the hieroglyphs and tortuous links to the translation, making the pursuit of any word or phrase immensely tedious. Davies (1903–08), vol. V provides the earliest detailed descriptions, photographs, and drawings.

28  MTA no. 4, p. 78. Murnane and Van Siclen (2011), 41–2. The verb used is *iw* which merely indicates something to be the case (see Gardiner §117). The words used were *bin* (bad or evil), more literally 'it is evil more than heard hither …', and *smr* (cause pain). Neither is explained by Murnane and Van Siclen.

29  The Deir Abu Hinnis quarry graffito (see next chapter) proves that building work on at least one major temple was still underway in Akhenaten's 16th regnal year.

30  Stevens (2020), 37.

31  *pr-itn* = Per Aten ('House of the Aten'). MTA no. 4, p. 77.

32  Snape (2014), 158, has a photograph of a model of the temple; Stevens (2020, 122, fig. 93, supplies a plan.

33  Aldred (1991), 49–50; MTA no. 4, p. 78.

34  Williams (2020), 81, fig. 57, and Whittemore (1926), pl. II.

35  Some of these small household stelae are unfinished, their texts incomplete or only featuring empty cartouches (unless the texts were originally painted on). These have driven some of the more obsessed 'Armanologists' half mad with ever more baroque theories.

36  The Egyptian word for sunshade was *šwt rᶜ*, literally 'the shadow of Re', but the word *šwt* was also closely linked to the one for 'spirit'.

37  Stevens (2020), 170–3.

38  See, for example, Murnane (1995), 133, no. 66.4 (tomb of Huya). Akhenaten is shown leading Tiye to her sunshade mortuary chapel, decorated with pairs of statues of Akhenaten and Nefertiti, and Amenhotep III and Tiye. See Davies (1905), vol. III, pl. VIII.

39  Stevens (2020), 43, and see also fig. 28. For the Bes ring, see Fletcher (2004), third colour plate section, p. 3.

40  Herodotus 2.42, states that Egyptians made personal choices about which gods they worshipped.

41  MTA no. 4, p. 77–8.

42  *EA* 29, lines 1–5.

43 *bзkt-itn* = 'maidservant of Aten'. Baketaten is best known from the reliefs of the tomb (TA1) of Huya at Amarna. Eaton-Krauss (2016), 4, discusses the theories about this princess.

44 The four known or suspected daughters of Amenhotep III and Tiye were: Sitamun, Henuttaneb, Iset and Nebetah.

45 Huya's name was written as *ḥзіі*. For Huya's name, see in particular Gardiner F18, G1, M17 and §20, 60. For the tomb, see Davies (1903–1908), vol. III (1905), 2 (for Huya's name and titles). Accessible online at: https://archive.org/details/cu31924020525360

46 Huya's titles were all listed as *imy-r* class posts (translated variously as 'Superintendent' and 'Steward') and show that he was in charge of the *nsw-ipt* (royal harem), *pr-ḥd* (treasury), and *pr-n-ḥmt-nsw-wr* ('house of the Great Royal Wife'). For the tomb, see Davies (1905), 2 (for Huya's name and titles). Accessible online at: https://archive.org/details/cu31924020525360

47 Found in the Ninth Pylon. See Laboury (2011), 7, available online at: http://digital2.library.ucla.edu/viewItem.do?ark=21198/zz0026vj6m

48 *ḥrt-mdзw* = 'Chief of the Medjay (police)', see Appendix 7.

49 Bouriant et al. (1903), pl. xlvi, available online at: https://digi.ub.uni-heidelberg.de/diglit/bouriant1903/0187

50 The title given to both dwarfs was *tзt(y)*, 'vizier'. During the European Middle Ages and later, court dwarfs were to become familiar accessories for royalty and nobility, for example Maria Bárbola, the *Enana de la Reina*, 'the Queen's Dwarf', of Mariana of Austria, queen regent of Spain (there are other examples from classical antiquity, for example Livia Augusta's freedwoman dwarf Andromeda). Mutbenret is shown in the company of Akhenaten's three eldest daughters in the tomb of Parannefer (TA7), viewable online at: https://digi.ub.uni-heidelberg.de/diglit/bouriant1903/0206 (Bouriant pl. XLV). She is at the extreme left. The dwarfs can be seen with her in the tomb of May (TA14), Davies (1908), vol. V, pl. III, where only the Mut- part of her name is visible but much better in the tomb of Ay (TA25), ibid., vol. VI, pl. XXVI (and https://digi.ub.uni-heidelberg.de/diglit/bouriant1903/0159), where Mutbenret and the names of the dwarfs are all clear; see also the discussion in Davies, vol. VI, 18. It is occasionally possible to infer Mutbenret's presence on damaged reliefs where only the dwarfs survive, see MTA no. 58-B.5, p. 116.

51 Herodotus 2.32.

52 Tadu-Ḫeba. *EA* 28.

53 *kyiз* = Kiya. This appears, for example, on a strip of wood probably from Amarna in association with Akhenaten's throne name, now at the Petrie Museum acc. no. UC24382 (the online catalogue does not reference Kiya's name, which is quite clear).

54 See Eaton-Krauss (2016), 4, who outlines the theories about this

princess, including that she was Baketaten, usually only seen in the company of Tiye. As Eaton-Krauss observes, this is a fringe theory. Kiya's titles were *t3-šps(t)* = 'the noblewoman'. In transliterated form, her other title reads: *ḥmt-mrryt-ʿ3t*, in order 'wife-beloved-greatly'. Nefertiti's title by contrast was *ḥmt-nsw-wrt*, again in order 'wife-king-greatest' where the different word for 'great', *wrt*, denoted supreme queenly status.

55 For the various theories, including that she was the 'favourite of Naharin (Mitanni)' mentioned on a funerary cone, see Davies and Macadam, *Egyptian Funerary Cones* no. 527. Aldred (1991), 286, supplies 'the favourite', but this is not borne out by other references to the word which formed part of Hatshepsut's name where it is always translated as 'noblewoman'. Faulkner (1962), 265, makes no mention of 'favourite'. Aldred (ibid.) contributed the pet name suggestion.

56 For example, on a plastered limestone block now in Brooklyn, acc. no. 60.197.6. (https://www.brooklynmuseum.org/opencollection/objects/3699), found at Hermopolis. See Dodson (2020), 51, figs 52 and 53, for Kiya's daughter and 66–7 for the -Tasherit children. Erasures and modifications of texts have completely obscured any certainty. See Dodson and Hilton (2010), 148, and Ridley (2019), 202ff. MTA provides translations at no. 45G, p. 92, and no. 51A, p. 98 (where the entire relevant phrase is restored, rendering it valueless as a source).

57 Another suggestion is that Meryetaten-Tasherit was the daughter of the Great Royal Wife Meryetaten when married to Smenkhkare (see Chapter 13 for this marriage), but since her titles are not cited this is unsustainable.

58 Dodson (2018), 40.

59 Stevens (2020), 163–6. For 'chief of police', see Appendix 7.

60 The tomb can be explored online at: https://www.osirisnet.net/tombes/amarna/ay_amarna/e_ay_amarna_01.htm

61 *imy-r-ssmt* = 'Master of Horse' plus *nb-n ḥm.f* = 'all of His Majesty's'. The title was, for example, expressed with slightly different hieroglyphs from Yuya's title, but the phonetic result was identical. The difference in Ay's case was the addition of 'all of His Majesty's'. See Newberry (1907), 7, for Yuya; Ay's tomb is covered by https://www.osirisnet.net/tombes/amarna/ay_amarna/e_ay_amarna_01.htm. Both used the ox tongue determinative as the abbreviated form of 'master' or 'overseer'. The 'all of' element is not significant.

62 Ay's Amarna tomb is in Davies (1903–8), vol. VI, in which see pl. XXIV, second row of hieroglyphs, at the bottom for *it nṯr*, 'God's Father'. For a translation of Ay's tomb texts, see MTA no. 58, pp. 108ff. Ay's tomb is in Davies (1903–8), vol. VI, in which see pl. XXIV, second row of hieroglyphs, at the bottom for *it nṯr*, 'God's Father'.

63 Ay (*iy*), Yuya (*ywiꜣ* or *iꜣꜣ* and variants), Tiye (*tyy*), and Thuya (*twiw* or *twiꜣ*).

64 Aldred (1991), 221.

65 Tiye and Tey were written as *tyy*.

66 Davies (1903–8), vol. VI, 21, right-hand column for the emphasis on Tey's post as nurse to Nefertiti. As on the wall of Ay's tomb chapel at Amarna. The text actually reads 'Tey, of the good god, wet-nurse of the chief wife Neferneferuaten-Nefertiti …' Illustrated by Dodson (2018), 97.

67 Elliot Smith (1912), pl. VI, for images of Rai's body with her overbite.

68 Tomb TA4. Murnane (1995), 151, no. 70.1; for Tenro, ibid., 157, no. 70.7, last entry. Murnane gives 'attaching' for no obvious reason. The operative sign is Gardiner D37 *imi*, 'give', here 'I am giving you to myself'. 'Attach' is a different word in Egyptian. The scene is Davies (1903), vol. I, pl. VI, with transcribed text at Sandeman (1938), pl. 1.

69 Murnane (1995), 143–5, nos 68.1–2 (from tomb TA14). May does not seem to have lasted long after his tomb was built in the 6th regnal year or later. His tomb is published by Davies (1908), vol. V, and Porter and Moss (1934), vol. IV, 225.

70 Ay's tomb is (or, rather, was) the source of the best-preserved text of Akhenaten's Hymn. See Bouriant (1930), pl. XVI (https://digi.ub.uni-heidelberg.de/diglit/bouriant1903/0157). Various translations are available; see previous note for one, or Dodson (2016), 122ff for another.

71 Woolley (1922), 46ff. Stevens (2020), 37–8.

72 Stevens (2020), 152, 154, fig. 130.

73 Kemp (2016), 7. However, one must bear in mind that estimating age at death from skeletons is notoriously unreliable.

74 For example, Kemp et al. (2013) and Kemp (2017).

75 Stevens (2020), 140–1ff.

76 The same phenomenon is found in Pompeii and Herculaneum where the atrium hall greeted visitors in a private version of public architecture.

77 Woolley (1922), 61ff. See also Aldred (1991), 55, and pl. 22.

78 Reeves (2001), 121, illustrating the plan of house T 36.11. Also, Stevens (2020), 139, and fig. 92, showing the recovery of a huge lintel with cartouches of the Aten and the royal couple from the house of the 'chief builder' Hatiay.

79 This has come about largely as a result of the Egypt Exploration Society's work since 1977 under the direction of Barry Kemp.

80 Stephens (2020), 149.

81 For the text of the relevant passage, see MTA no. 37, pp. 77–8, and Dodson (2016), 106. The Royal Tomb can be explored online at https://www.osirisnet.net/tombes/amarna/akhenaton_tombe/e_akhenaton_tombe_01.htm

82 Dodson (2016), 73–4, 82.

83 The Amarna tombs of the nobles are introduced online at https://www. osirisnet.net/tombes/amarna/tombes_amarna/e_tombes_amarna_01. htm

84 Stevens (2020), 85–6.

85 For an example of the Amarna 'window of appearances', see the relief from the tomb of Parennefer, reproduced in several books, for example Kemp (1991), 278, figure 92.

86 The scene has been heavily restored. Bouriant et elia (1903), pl. xxiii, available online at: https://digi.ub.uni-heidelberg.de/diglit/ bouriant1903/0164. Illustrated by Dodson (2016), 122–3, fig. 99. Also viewable at: https://www.osirisnet.net/popupImage.php?img=/tombes/ amarna/ay_amarna/photo/ay_ndgd_29.jpg&lang=en&sw=1536&sh=864

87 For example, the bouts of desecration conducted at Peterborough Cathedral. See Cobb (1980), 94–5, including an account of how brass fittings were broken up and sold, and tombs robbed and rifled.

88 Now in the BM acc. no. EA1103 (https://www.britishmuseum.org/ collection/object/Y_EA1103).

89 For example, in the tomb of Amenemhet (TT82) where along with the name of Amun, *imn*, the verb 'establish', *mn*, had been erased, too. See Der Manuelian, P., 'Semi-literacy in Egypt: some erasures from the Amarna Period.' In Teeter and Larson (1999), 285–98. Available online at: https://www.academia.edu/2189348/_Semi-literacy_in_Ancient_Egypt_ Some_Examples_from_the_Amarna_Period._

90 Particularly in the tomb of Meryre ii, see Samson (1977), 89–90, with huge implications for Nefertiti's role after Akhenaten's death. The durbar reliefs from TA1 and TA2 are published in several books, for example Dodson (2016), 140, fig. 112, (2020), 60, fig. 67, and Ridley (2019), 108–9. Text at Murnane (1995), 134–5, no. 66.6. The carrying of Akhenaten and Nefertiti to the durbar is viewable online at: https://www.osirisnet. net/popupImage.php?img=/tombes/amarna/tombes_amarna/photo/ houya1_xx_1137.jpg&lang=en&sw=1536&sh=864. The seated Nefertiti and Akhenaten side by side can be viewed at: https://archive.org/details/ rocktombsofelama14davi/page/n165/mode/2up

91 It was suggested, e.g. Martin (1991), 30, that Paatenemheb was Horemheb in an earlier Atenesque guise but this no longer seems to have any currency. There is certainly no means of proving a connection.

92 Stevens (2020), 23, fig. 10, 72, fig. 47. Terura is in the Egyptian Museum, Berlin acc. no. ÄM14122 (http://www.smb-digital.de/ eMuseumPlus?service=direct/1/ResultLightboxView/result.t1.collection_ lightbox.$TspTitleImageLink.link&sp= 10&sp=Scollection&sp=SfieldValue&sp=0&sp=7&sp=3&sp= Slightbox_3x4&sp=0&sp=Sdetail&sp=0&sp=F&sp=T&sp=9).

93 Dodson (2016), 134. Some see this war as more significant, for example

Van Dijk (2003), 277–8. The viceroy was probably a man called Thutmose, the only attested viceroy of Kush under Akhenaten. Ridley (2019), 153.

94 At the time of discovery in 1887 by locals, the significance of the Amarna Letters was not recognized. Many were destroyed and the rest, some damaged, widely dispersed among museums and private collectors. The 382 recorded by Moran (1992) represent only a tiny part of the archive that once have must existed.

95 *EA 26.*

96 Akhenaten here is referred to as Napḫu'rureya = Neferkheperure.

97 *EA 8.*

98 *EA 10, 11, 14.*

99 *EA 53, 55.*

100 MTA no. 7, p. 31.

101 Isaiah 19.1. See also Leviticus 19.4 and numerous other examples.

102 For example, Dodson (2016), 122ff. See Bouriant (1903), pl. XVI, for a copy of the original text made before being damaged (https://digi.ub.uni-heidelberg.de/diglit/bouriant1903/0157). The text survives today in a few versions, including the most complete version in the tomb chapel of Ay (TA25).

103 The most complete version of the text survived in the Amarna tomb of Ay (TA25). Now badly damaged, it was fortunately recorded by Bouriant (1903), pl. XVI (https://digi.ub.uni-heidelberg.de/diglit/bouriant1903/0157).

104 'Mansion of the Aten' is certain, given as *ḥwt-pꜣ-itn*. Translation at MTA no. 34-D.1, pp. 67–8. I am grateful to Joann Fletcher for directing me to Daressy (1891), 2–5, who published the coffin texts, a reference given but not linked to by MTA. Tyson Smith (1992), 229, cites *ḥwt-pꜣ-itn* as Gem-pa-aten in error. Hatiay's name meant 'The Foremost One'; his wife was Henwt-Wedjebu, meaning 'Mistress of the Riverside Lands'. She is described on her coffin as a *šmꜥt* (female 'musician', or 'chantress') and *nbt* ('Lady') of the house of Amun, the first part of her name being another word for mistress. His coffin is in Cairo, hers in St Louis.

105 MTA no. 58, p. 120.

106 Both scenes appear in the funeral papyrus of Yuya, of whom Huya may have been a kinsman. Naville (1908), pls I and XXII. Yuya is also seen in Re's boat with Isis, Thoth and Shu, pl. XXIX).

107 For example, a possible Sunshade temple at Memphis. See Pasquali (2011).

108 Elliot Smith (1912), 55.

109 Thompson (2006).

110 In the Louvre acc. no. 15593 (https://www.louvre.fr/en/oeuvre-notices/akhenaton-and-nefertiti). The piece is 22.2 cm high.

111 Under Tutankhamun. More information about Maya's tomb is available at: https://mag.rochester.edu/teachers/picturing-the-story/the-tomb-of-an-egyptian-nobleman-named-maya/

112 Reeves (2001), 149ff, has some useful discussion of the wilder fancies.

113 Acc. no. N831 (and AF109). Viewable online at https://collections.louvre.fr/en/ark:/53355/cl010007436

114 A plaster bust of the king from Amarna (House P47.2, room 19) depicts a similarly full-faced and possibly slightly overweight young Akhenaten. Now in Berlin acc. no. ÄM21299. Viewable online at: https://www.flickr.com/photos/menesje/48242523932. See also Gabolde (2009), 116, n. 60.

115 As seen earlier, Nefertiti and Akhenaten were seen on at least one relief at Amarna smiting their foes, but this seems to have been very unusual.

116 Egyptian Museum acc. nos ÄM21834 (Tiye), ÄM21351 (Akhenaten).

117 *sbꜣ* = 'taught'. The stela is illustrated by Aldred (1998), 93, fig. 13, in a drawing and with a photograph by Dodson (2016), 93, fig. 77. Bek's self-portrait statue is in Berlin acc. no. ÄM31009. There are numerous photographs of the piece available online, for example https://old.egypt-museum.com/post/180423039831/stele-of-sculptor-bek-with-his-wife-taheret

118 Aldred (1991), 94.

119 Hawass et al. (2010), 644. The famous bust is Berlin acc. no. ÄM21300, the less flattering unfinished one Berlin acc. no. ÄM21352 (http://www.smb-digital.de/eMuseumPlus?service=direct/1/ResultLightboxView/result.t1.collection_lightbox.$TspTitleImageLink.link&sp=10&sp=Scollection&sp=SfieldValue&sp=0&sp=1&sp=3&sp=Slightbox_3x4&sp=444&sp=Sdetail&sp=0&sp=F&sp=T&sp=445).

120 Height 11.8 in (40 cm). Egyptian Museum, Berlin acc. no. ÄM21263.

121 A drawing of this scene can be found in Ridley (2019), 112, fig. 65.

122 See also Montserrat (2003), 48.

## 13. LATTER DAYS AT AMARNA

1 It may be of interest to the reader new to this subject that this chapter and the next took more time to write than the rest of the book put together, simply because of the extent of the published material.

2 *EA* 11 includes a restored line 5 reading: [*After the wife of*] of your father had been mourned ...'

3 Brock (1996); Ridley (2019), 287, fig. 107.

4 MTA no. 38, p. 83. Also Murnane and Van Siclen (2011), pp. 89, and VI-A, p. 101. The word used for 'old age' is *iꜣwy*, 'old'. It appears twice, once for Nefertiti and once for the princesses but the first time is spelled out with a determinative (A19), whereas the second time it is spelled out phonetically only. Even in full form the spelling between the stelae differs (Stela A: *iꜣw* Stela U: *iwy*). This illustrates very well how Egyptian inscriptions were prone to variation even when identical texts were supposed to be being produced.

5    Photograph of this scene as it survives today in Dodson (2020), 65, fig. 72; a
     truncated drawing is in Aldred (1990), 284, fig. 28.

6    In Bouriant (1903), pl. IX (available online at https://digi.ub.uni-
     heidelberg.de/diglit/bouriant1903/0150).

7    Vandersleyen (1993).

8    Eaton-Krauss (2016), 5, outlines the theories.

9    Van Dijk (2009). It is remarkable how the idea of reincarnated dead princesses
     has become (at least temporarily) mainstream, largely in preference
     to acknowledging that the conundrum cannot be resolved due to the
     compromised evidence. See Dodson (2020), 63–4, for a fuller explanation.

10   Naville (1896), 17–18, and pl. LIII.

11   Wilkinson (1992), 32, fig. 3, supplies a drawing of this scene. Similar scenes
     became progressively more common in later Egyptian history.

12   For the sarcophagus, see MTA no. 46, p. 94 (D), and van Dijk (2009), 83,
     note 1. For the vase and statuette which only probably originated in
     the Royal Tomb, see Gabolde (2008), 38, note 9. A palette of Meketaten's
     almost certainly came from Tutankhamun's tomb, MM acc. no. 27.71295
     (https://www.metmuseum.org/art/collection/search/544694).

13   For example, Reeves (1988), figs 4 and 5 showing a column fragment
     with Meryetaten replacing Kiya. Accessible at: https://journals.sagepub.
     com/doi/abs/10.1177/030751338807400108. Also Stevens (2020), 170, for the
     Sunshade usurpation.

14   Reeves (1988) provides a list of items and inscriptions naming Kiya. MTA
     no. 45, p. 90, supplies the Kiya texts.

15   The controversial DNA evidence (see Chapters 14 and 15) does not appear
     to allow for Tutankhuaten having a mother outside the immediate royal
     family.

16   For example, the tomb of Neferkheperuhersekheper ('Neferkheperure
     [Akhenaten] makes me live') (TA13). A large section of the columned hall
     remained to be cut out.

17   Time was about 1410 hours. Note that the astronomical date is 1337 BC.
     Astronomical dates include a year 0. Therefore, BC dates have to
     have '1' added to each, hence 1338 BC for the true calendar date. Full
     details can be found on the NASA, *Five Millennium [sic] Catalog of Solar
     Eclipses* online at https://eclipse.gsfc.nasa.gov/SEsearch/SEsearchmap.
     php?Ecl=-13370514

18   It is a striking fact that the sheer intensity of sunlight means that even a
     pinprick of the solar disk being still visible is completely different from
     totality when all sunlight is gone. The author writes from personal
     experience of a total eclipse at a similar time of day in a blue sky in
     summer in Nebraska in August 2017.

19   McMurray (2004), 3.

20   Van der Perre (2014), and also Dodson (2020), 72, fig. 80, who provides

a picture of the graffito, written in hieroglyphics and hieratic. Van der Perre provides a useful summary of the evidence for Smenkhkare.

21 Van der Perre (2014), 71ff, lists out the older theories about Nefertiti's 'disappearance'.

22 The only evidence that this docket has anything to do with Akhenaten's death is the apparent partial erasure of 'Regnal Year 17 honey' and then next to and partially over this 'Regnal Year 1 wine', though in fact the first date remains quite clear (MTA no. 93-B, p. 207). It has not been crossed out as some claim. No kings' names are mentioned though clearly two reigns are being referred to, the second not necessarily immediately following the first. The possibility that the jar was an old one reused a few years later (a residual piece) is never considered, yet this is elementary archaeology. Since Tutankhamun's tomb included wine from a 31st regnal year that can only be Amenhotep III's, it is obvious that in this case without names the docket is worthless as historical evidence (see MTA no. 101-D, p. 223). Some Egyptologists treat the docket as firm proof of the year of Akhenaten's death which it manifestly is not. Wilkinson (2010), 298, does not even bother to mention the docket and simply announces that Akhenaten died in his 17th regnal year after the grape harvest, following Aldred (1991), of whom one might have expected better. Montserrat (2003), 26, despite pointing out how little reliable evidence exists for the Amarna period, calls the jar a 'certain' reference to Akhenaten, even though it obviously is not. Now in the Petrie Museum, London. Image available online at: https://petriecat. museums.ucl.ac.uk (enter acc. no. UC32931).

23 Shaw (2002), 12, points out that the Middle Kingdom rulers Senusret II and III were allocated 19 and 35 years respectively by the Turin Canon but the highest regnal years known from other evidence are the 6th and 19th. However, this relies on restoring the names of the kings concerned to the badly damaged text.

24 Ridley (2019), 249–55, itemizes all the evidence for the co-regency. The unusual name Smenkhkare had supposedly been used once before in Egyptian royal history, during the 13th Dynasty. Even that relies on restoring most of the name: [Smenkh]kare Imyremeshaw, attested on the Turin Canon (6.21) but only the -kare part survives, a suffix known from several Middle Kingdom names. Its format with the -re suffix makes it much more like a throne than a birth name and indeed the -kare component is a familiar part of several throne names from the Middle Kingdom. The structure of Smenkhkare's name as currently read was *smnḫ-kꜥ-re ḏsr-ḫprr-re*, 'Ennobled is the Soul of Re, Become Holy in Re'. The *smnḫ* component is a causative term with a range of meanings all involving making something distinguished, effective, or set in order and suggests that it was a name acquired on accession, replacing a

birth name now unknown to us. Habicht (2019) (back cover) calls him 'a constructed identity'. See also ibid., 10, for a discussion of the 'two' throne names.

25  Reeves (2001), 172–3, and Fletcher (2015), 218–25, both support the case for Nefertiti and Smenkhkare being the same person, an idea that goes back to the work of Samson in the 1970s and 1980s, see her (1977), and (1982) papers. Wilkinson (2010), 298, says it is 'more likely' that Smenkhkare was Nefertiti's 'third manifestation', offering no explanation for why she felt the need to change her identity on multiple occasions. Anyone reading more widely will rapidly discover that this version is flatly contradicted by many other Egyptologists. It is, incidentally, a passing curiosity that no one apparently has proposed Smenkhkare was an alter ego of Akhenaten's, given the apparently endless speculation Smenkhkare has provoked.

26  Given the prominence of Tiye's family there is a technical possibility Smenkhkare was related by that route and had been given his contrived sounding name when elevated to the co-regency. This, however, is hard to reconcile with the longer family tradition of a royal closed shop.

27  The only tenuous piece of supporting evidence is that Manetho (Fr. 50.96) refers to a female Acencheres (Nefertiti?) reigning around this time and followed by 'her brother Rathotis' (Smenkhkare?). The only value of this is that it preserves some sort of a tradition of sibling rulers. Manetho lists an implausibly large number of rulers for the period between Amenhotep III and Horemheb.

28  In Davies (1903–1908), Part II: *The Tombs of Panhesy and Meryra II* (1905), pl. XLI, viewable online at: https://archive.org/details/cu31924020525352/page/n179/mode/2up also published in various books on the period, for example Dodson (2020), 68, fig. 74. It is of interest that a large panel of decoration adjacent to this scene and covering a whole wall features Akhenaten and Nefertiti seated and clutching hands, with all six daughters behind them, one holding a pet animal. Evidently, the decoration of the tomb had extended over several years, this scene clearly preceding Meketaten's death. Davies (ibid.), pl. XXXVIII (https://archive.org/details/cu31924020525352/page/n169/mode/2up).

29  These cartouches in Meryre ii's tomb (TA2), already damaged, were seen by Robert Hay in 1830. They show three royal cartouches alongside the two names of Aten in its later form. The latter were clear and so was the Ankhkheperure cartouche. The other two were already damaged enough to be very difficult to discern, but the usual claim is that one read Smenkhkare and the other Meryetaten. While all those who saw the inscription in the early 1800s agreed on the Ankhkheperure name, they were very unsure about the other two cartouches. Each produced a different sketch of what they thought they could see. None was a

reliable version of either name, but it is certain one ended -kare, the
other -aten, and that they were *not* Akhenaten and Nefertiti. Newberry
(1928), 6, provides copies and other versions, e.g. by Lepsius made in 1845
from a squeeze. Lepsius's version of the Smenkhkare name transliterates
as Saakare (*sˤ3kˤre*), only deepening the mystery further (Gardiner's
O29 ˤ3 replacing U22 *mnḫ*). Moseley (2009), 142–7 provides excellent
reproductions of Hay's and Lepsius's records including the squeeze,
though these only show how unreliable any reading of the 'Smenkhkare'
cartouche is. In fact, the U22 can also be read as S38 *ḥk3* (ruler) in
Lepsius's squeeze, a name component far better attested in royal names,
and which is even found similarly deployed in the throne name of the
22nd Dynasty king Sheshonq II, Heqakheperure (also a co-regent). This
would make the name *sḥk3k3re*, Seheqakare. Newberry (ibid.), 6, fig. c,
records the drawing by Prisse d'Avennes who in 1843 read the sign as S38
*ḥk3* but Newberry said that all the known rings were 'quite conclusive'
in reading *mnḫ* (U22) and therefore that the name must be Smenkhkare,
borne out by the rings and wine jar dockets (see next note but one). This
illustrates amply the problems that arise from trying to make sense of
damaged and lost evidence.

30  For the Aten temple at Memphis see Newberry (1928), figs 3 and 4 – the
relief is lost and only part of the names had survived anyway. See also
Murnane (1977), 173, who speculated that the 'fly whisk' Smenkhkare is
shown holding means he was originally a non-royal figure at court, later
altered to reflect elevated status.

31  For the Smenkhkare rings and the seal (the upper parts of both names
are quite clear on the seal), see Samson (1973), also Petrie (1894), 29,
and pl. XV, nos 103–5. Reproduced by Dodson (2018), 31, fig. 23, but the
original publication is online at: https://digi.ub.uni-heidelberg.de/diglit/
petrie1894/0071. Newberry (1928), 6, fig.2, supplied drawings of five,
cryptically saying that he had 'notes of seven' and specified the source
and location of none of them. Samson (ibid.), 245, fig. 1, provides one of
the only published photographs of the rings in the Petrie Collection,
labelled by her G and H, with the seal her I. She notes the other double-
named seal recorded by Frankfort and Pendlebury (1933), 25, pl. L,
which is the one bearing the royal titles. Neither seal allows room for
Meryetaten's name. These Smenkhkare rings should not be confused
with those bearing the Ankhkheperure name (see note 33 below). None
of the rings show both names. Not all the rings recorded by Petrie and
Newberry seem to exist now, and there are some discrepancies in the
cataloguing. Crucially, the name Smenkhkare was not written the same
on each, showing that the lost cartouche in the tomb of Meryre ii could
easily have been written in one of at least two different ways.

32  For the wine jars see Wahlberg (2012), 103, also 20, 50, and 51; also, MTA

no. 95-B, p. 209: '1st regnal year. Wine of the House of Smenkhkare, Holy of Manifestations [of] the western river' – written in hieratic. Petrie (1894), 32, called him 'Rasmenkh-ka', and listed twenty-nine jars in his name, twenty-six of which were for oil.

33 Stevens (2020), 131, who does not mention that the bricks only bear the Ankheperure name, but does in her (2016), 13. It is not even certain the bricks were found in this so-called hall. For the Ankhkheperure ring bezels, see Hayes (1951), fig. 34, nos R19 and R20. Other bezels bore the throne name of Tutankhamun, the Aten version of Ankhesenamun's earlier name, as well as Amenhotep III, Tiye and Sitamun.

34 The gold sequins in KV62, which only include Smenkhkare's throne name, are Carter no. 046gg (http://www.griffith.ox.ac.uk/perl/ gi-ca-qmakedeta.pl?sid=86.185.171.255-1617043787&qno=1&dfnam=046gg-c046gg). In both cases Meryetaten's name was abbreviated to Meryaten (*mry-itn*), the first sign being Gardiner's N36 which served as a phonetic determinative.

35 Illustrated in second colour plate section.

36 There is little doubt that two pairs of kings' cartouches were once on the calcite jar, and the restoration is not inconsistent with the names of Akhenaten and Smenkhkare, but the few surviving hieroglyphs are extremely difficult to see and most of what was there has disappeared. Sadly, none of the signs *unique* to Smenkhkare's name are visible (e.g. U25 *mnḫ* for -menkh-). As evidence, the restoration is as it stands of little value. The vase needs modern forensic examination to determine whether any meaningful restoration is viable. The vase is Carter no. 405 (http://www.griffith.ox.ac.uk/gri/carter/405.html), in particular Burton photograph p1747 and card transcription 405–2. Carter believed the names were Amenhotep III's and Akhenaten's. Loeben (1994) provides the restored cartouches. See also Ridley (2019), 252, no. 7; Allen (2006), 2. Both supply further references. Dodson (2018), 30, fig. 22, illustrates the vase and restored cartouches.

37 Another such vase, found at Gurob, bears the names of Tutankhamun and Ankhesenamun quite clearly but the poor standard of execution in the friable crystalline stone, as well as the conspicuously different forming of the same signs, shows that it is impossible to produce a demonstrably reliable restoration in damaged or deliberately erased examples. The Tutankhamun vase is in the Petrie Museum acc. no. UC16021 (viewable online at https://petriecat.museums.ucl.ac.uk). See second colour plate section.

38 For example, Allen (2006), 5, and Van den Perre (2016), 82.

39 Fairman and Černý in Pendlebury (1951), figs 86 and 98. Unfortunately, the 'true of voice' (*mꜣꜥ ḫrw*) epithet appears to be entirely restored though the name Smenkhkare and 1st regnal year seem to be certain.

See Wahlberg (2012), 103, who also describes (ibid., 12) many of the problems with the 1951 publication involving a lack of facsimiles, and variable and contradictory translations. Dodson (2018), 32, cites the docket but suggests part of the epithet is readable. Either way the evidence seems unreliable and very tenuous.

40 Petrie (1894), 32, did not make it clear whether the dockets read Smenkhkare or Ankheperure but said 'these dates are the only evidence we have for the length of Ra-Smenkh-ka's (sic) reign'. He calls him Smenkh-ka-ra a few lines later.

41 Samson (1973), 246. Since Ankhkheperure was also associated with a later form of Nefertiti's name, Neferneferuaten, the idea emerged among some Egyptologists that Smenkhkare was Nefertiti. More recently it was noticed that Ankhkheperure also occasionally appeared in the female form Ankhetkheperure, and that in either form when associated with Neferneferuaten it always had one of several epithets, unlike in the few instances when it was used by Smenkhkare. The conversion of Nefertiti's names to a pair of kingly cartouches is most obvious on the 'co-regency stela', found in the Great Palace at Amarna. Illustrated by Dodson (2020), 79, fig. 90, but fully published by Martin (2009).

42 Although the idea that Neferneferuaten and Smenkhkare were two different people was always one of the most likely explanations, it is typical of Egyptology that 'confirmation' has been sought by an arcane route. The unusual and unparalleled epithet that appears with the name sometimes has now been translated as 'effective for her husband'. It is rarely the case in Egyptology that such phrases or epithets are straightforward, and this is no exception. The first two hieroglyphs can indeed mean 'effective', 'beneficial', or 'useful', with the second sign (*t*) feminizing the term. They can also mean 'become a spirit'. The three hieroglyphs translated as 'for her husband' are consistent with the phrase meaning 'effective for her husband'. However, without the determinative sign for a man the three can also function in that combination and order as the single word 'awake' or 'resurrect' which, of course, would fit well with the 'become a spirit' meaning of the first part. They would thus read *ȝḫt-nḥs*, Gardiner's signs G25 X1-N35 O4 O34. One only need consult Gardiner's own Vocabulary section (p. 628) to see the latter three together classified as the word 'wake'. Egyptian is simply not understood well enough to exclude either option in this case, so selective translation to pursue individual agendas has become commonplace.

43 *ḥḳȝ* = 'ruler'. This may be seen in Dodson (2020), 74, 'F', and is discussed by Allen (2009), 12, and Van den Perre (2014), 96.

44 It is not clear from the stela what the new cartouches replaced, since the Neferneferuaten name ought to have been the third cartouche originally, but is now the fourth, the third being filled with Nefertiti's

throne name as king. The new fourth cartouche may have overlaid one for Meryetaten. For the 'effective for her husband' epithet, see Dodson (2018), 36–7, and for the stela see (2020), 77–9, fig. 90. See especially Allen (1988), 118, fig. 1, and Allen (2010) (ii), 27–41, where he argues that the stela once named Akhenaten, Nefertiti, and Meryetaten. See also another unfinished stela, Reeves (2001), 169, where a fourth cartouche seems to have been added to accommodate Nefertiti's new status.

45    The inscription does not mention Smenkhkare, which is difficult to account for unless he was dead. See Ridley (2019), 252, no. 6, and Dodson (2020), 73, fig. 81. This piece of wood, which can be read quite clearly, lists in order Akhenaten, Neferneferuaten and Meryetaten, the latter described as wife of the king. Both kings have their birth and throne names, Neferneferuaten's throne name being in this instance Ankhkheperure with the epithet 'beloved of Neferkheperure [Akhenaten]'. Carter no. 001k-3. (http://www.griffith.ox.ac.uk/gri/carter/001k-c001k-3.html). This fragment also rules out Meryetaten being Neferneferuaten, which has been suggested.

46    *EA* 10.46 mentioning gifts sent to her specifically as 'daughter' of Akhenaten, 11.26 (reverse) where she is clearly distinguished from 'mistress of the house' (Nefertiti?) in the previous line. Her name was given as Ma-i-ia-a-t-i. Meryetaten is the only possible candidate. Anyone interested in a completely different version of events can pursue Marc Gabolde's theories, outlined at http://www.bbc.co.uk/history/ancient/egyptians/amarna_01.shtml, in which Smenkhkare is a Hittite prince, and Meryetaten rules on her own until the accession of Tutankhamun. This is not a perspective shared by many other Egyptologists, largely because there is nothing to substantiate it, but this is hardly unusual in Amarna studies.

47    The discovery of a scarab bearing the name Neferneferuaten-Nefertiti in a shipwreck at Ulu Burun off the Turkish coast has been treated by some as evidence of her sending out an embassy to the Hittites during this time. It was recovered with a collection of material that included two Near Eastern cylinder seals. Several other Egyptian items were recovered from the wreck which included at least two probable Second Intermediate Period scarabs, and an 18th Dynasty steatite plaque inscribed to Ptah. This is better evidence for the Nefertiti scarab forming part of the stock of a member of the ship's crew who had bought the scarab in Egypt while in port, intending to sell it on as a curio. Stevens (2020), 136, suggests that the presence of incense resin in 150 amphorae from the Ulu Burun ship might be evidence that it was in fact en route to Egypt, with the incense designated for use in the Amarna Aten temples.

48    Ridley (2019), 281, lists the finds in and just outside the Royal Tomb (TA26). Also, Stevens (2020), 112. Dodson (2020), 41, fig. 35 illustrates

the reconstructed fragments of the sarcophagus, but some pieces are in Berlin (e.g. acc. no. ÄM 14524). Reeves (2001), 129, describes the structural alterations but has since changed his mind about Akhenaten and believes now (2017, 426, n. 16) that the king's *primary* burial was in KV55. The tomb can be visited online at: https://www.osirisnet.net/tombes/amarna/ akhenaton_tombe/e_akhenaton_tombe_01.htm and https://www. youtube.com/watch?v=33G5_VPjdlE

49 Dodson (2019) (i), 148. See also BAR (iv) §416ff for the event and the court proceedings that followed the uncovering of the plot.

50 Egypt also supplies the Ptolemaic dynasty which saw the probable murder of Ptolemy III (246–222 BC) by a lover and her brother, the poisoning of his sister-wife Arsinoe, and the murder of Ptolemy V (205–180 BC).

51 At the time of writing, the tomb can be explored online at: https://www. youtube.com/watch?v=33G5_VPjdlE

52 The second part of each epithet had been lost by the time the graffito was first recorded. They both began *mri-i*[-], 'beloved of A-'. In the context of the graffito a possible restoration is 'beloved of Amun' (Dodson 2020, 74, titulary D), an epithet formerly used for example in some cartouches of Amenhotep III, but neither is now legible. There are also those who believe Neferneferuaten was Meryetaten. There is even less evidence for this suppositious claim than the others. See Gabolde (2009), 118, who believed that the *mri-i*[-], 'beloved of A-' epithets were the first part of Meryetaten, her name being subjoined to Ankhkheperure and Neferneferuaten. This hypothetical reconstruction ignores other, to my mind much clearer, evidence that clearly shows Neferneferuaten and Meryetaten as different people, such as the inscribed strip of wood from Tutankhamun's tomb, discussed earlier in this chapter.

53 See Dodson (2018), 45.

54 *ḥwt* = Hewet, a word with a variety of meanings, including temple, chapel and estate. Dodson (2020), 80–2, supplies the graffito's text and a discussion. See also Ridley (2019), 274–5, who explains the massive confusion this graffito has generated. Pawah was blind, the graffito being written for him by his brother Batjay.

55 The cult could have been an active one for the deceased Smenkhkare, or the preparation of Nefertiti's. The building is unknown now.

56 Carter no. 574 (http://www.griffith.ox.ac.uk/gri/carter/574.html). This box lid carries a hieroglyphic inscription which had been clearly altered for Tutankhamun and Ankhesenamun from Neferneferuaten-Ankhkheperure-mery-Neferkhperure ('Neferneferuaten, beloved of Neferkheperure [Akhenaten]'), and Meryetaten. There is no mention of Akhenaten in his own right. There is no room for another name. It is interesting that Tutankhamun's name here includes the statue

determinative A22, effectively repeating the *twt* component of his name given above rather than the more usual 'ruler of Thebes' epithet.

57 The unknown body CG 61076 found in the 1881 royal mummy cache has been proposed as a possible candidate for Meryetaten, Ankhesenamun, or Baketaten. Habicht (ed.) 2020, 'she might well be one of the daughters of Akhenaton (sic) and Nefertiti ...'. Without any evidence to support any one candidate there is nowhere to go with this.

58 The reader is advised to turn to Ridley (2019) and Dodson (2020) to pursue this further.

59 Nero's suicide in 68 was followed by a period of civil war that lasted well into 69 and saw the accession of four emperors. Edward III's death in 1483 was followed by the deposition of his son Edward V by his uncle Richard who usurped the throne as Richard III, executing opponents and probably murdering Edward V. In 1485 he was defeated in battle by Henry Tudor at Bosworth who succeeded as Henry VII.

## 14. THE STRANGE CASE OF THE TOMB KNOWN AS KV55

1 For example, Bell (1990), who has amassed all the evidence. Aldred (1962), 162, covers the stolen objects.

2 Listed by Daressy (1910) in the original publication of the find.

3 Fairman (1961), 37, re-examined the KV55 bricks and concluded that the name Neferkheperure was quite clear on one but not the other. See also Allen (1988), 121–2. Bell (1990) lists the bricks in her Catalogue no. 17. The 'northern' brick is now identified as the western brick.

4 Compare Thutmose IV's bricks in Carter and Newberry (1904), 9, with KV55's in Daressy (1910), 26–7, and pl. XXII. See also Roth and Roehrig (2002), 126. Akhenaten's name was only given as his throne name Neferkheperure on the bricks, further avoiding mention of the Aten. Conversely, Thutmose IV's magic bricks included both his birth and throne names.

5 Brock (1996).

6 See Daressy's catalogue of the objects from the tomb in Davis (1910) 13, no. 1 and pls XXXI and XXXII, also a haematite vase with Tiye's and both Amenhotep III's names, Amen- having been erased, 35–6, no. 41 and pl. IV.3.

7 The magic bricks, being conventional in form and texts, are unlikely to have been taken from Amarna where the burial chamber does not even apparently have the necessary niches in each of the four walls.

8 Dodson (2020), 51, figs 52 and 53, provides two illustrated examples. For a discussion about who the stoppers represent, see https://www.metmuseum.org/art/collection/search/544689 and the associated photographs.

9   Krauss (1986), in particular figs 7 and 8. See Ridley (2019), 217, for the
    details of Kiya's titles.
10  Attributing the canopic jars to Kiya relies on the rest of the restored
    inscription resembling, or at least not conflicting with, a complete
    version on an unprovenanced calcite unguent vase which does
    name Kiya. MM acc. no. 20.2.11. See: https://www.metmuseum.org/
    art/collection/search/544530. Kiya's name and titles also appear on
    a fragment of another calcite jar in the British Museum (EA65901),
    illustrated by Fairman (1961), 30, fig. 2.
11  Beyond this the argument descends into the nether regions of debating
    the relevance of epithets on the coffin considered more appropriate to
    Akhenaten. The epithet was 'beloved of Waenre' ('One in Re'), Waenre
    being part of one of the versions of Akhenaten's full throne name.
    Allen (1988), 123, illustrates and analyses the coffin inscription and
    provides a suggested restoration. Fairman (1961), 36, had previously
    restored the inscription to read 'the king's daughter Meritaten, justified'.
    Gabolde (2009), 117, rejects the idea the epithets referred to anyone else
    (i.e. Smenkhkare). Eaton-Krauss (2016), 8, explains the sequence of
    modifications made to the coffin texts.
12  The remnants abandoned at Amarna in TA26 included his shabtis and,
    most remarkably of all, broken pieces of a diorite bowl from the reign
    of Khaefre of the 4th Dynasty. Ridley (2019), 281. Montserrat (2003), 40,
    is more enthusiastic in his speculation about the significance of this
    antique being included in Akhenaten's tomb.
13  Fragments of shabtis in Tiye's name in Amenhotep III's tomb at Thebes
    (WV22) raise the possibility she was buried there first after removal from
    Amarna. WV22 included a suite that had surely been intended for her by
    her husband. However, Bell (1990), 136, suggests that on the evidence of
    glass said to have been found in KV55 which originated from vessels in
    KV35 that Tiye's body was moved to the latter directly.
14  For the physical similarities see Reeves (1990), 117–18. The body was
    described at the time of discovery as having an 'abnormal pelvis' which
    had led to an initial assumption the skeleton was female and thus Tiye's.
    This was very rapidly corrected when shown to the anatomist G. Elliot
    Smith soon afterwards. Davis (1910), 3, later recounted in more detail
    by G. Elliot Smith in the 1930 Introduction to C. P. Bryan's 1974 edition
    of *Ancient Egyptian Medicine. The Papyrus Ebers*, Ares Publishers, Chicago, p.
    xxx, 'to my intense surprise I found not the bones of an old lady but of a
    young man', supplying an age range at death of twenty-three to thirty.
    Available online at https://babel.hathitrust.org/cgi/pt?id=coo.31924073200
    077&view=1up&seq=32. For the blood group, see Aldred (1988), 202.
15  Some of the royal bodies interred in the royal caches (TT320 and KV35)
    were not identified by label, which includes those now believed by some

to be Tiye and Nefertiti, the 'Elder Lady' and 'Younger Lady' respectively or were misidentified (for example, the body thought by the priests to be that of Thutmose I).

16  This is feasible. For example, a 'Thutmose' stated to be '*the King's son, troop commander, Thutmose*' is attested in Tutankhamun's tomb but is not known from any other evidence. See Chapter 15.

17  One of the plaster busts from the Amarna workshop (building P47.2) of Thutmose sometimes identified as Smenkhkare closely resembles busts of Akhenaten, which means that even if the bust is of Smenkhkare then the two men looked so like each other no firm conclusion could ever be drawn either way. The 'Smenkhkare' bust is in Berlin acc. no. ÄM21340, but is not identified as such in the catalogue(http://www.smb-digital.de/eMuseumPlus?service=direct/1/ResultLightboxView/result.t1.collection_lightbox.$TspTitleImageLink.link&sp=10&sp=Scollection&sp=Sfield Value&sp=0&sp=7&sp=3&sp=Slightbox_3x4&sp=204&sp=Sdetail&sp=0&sp=F&sp=T&sp=206). Another plaster bust in the collection is also sometimes identified as Smenkhkare, again with no evidence, Berlin acc. no. ÄM21354 (where it is not linked to Smenkhkare), illustrated by Ridley (2019), 265, fig. 99.

18  Eaton-Krauss (2016), 1.

19  Van der Perre (2014), 86.

20  FAPAB (Forensic Anthropology, Paleopathology, Bioarchaeology Research Center) KV55 Akhenaton Press Release 8 March 2021 (accessed at https://www.academia.edu/s/af98667610). Gabolde (2013), 180–1, is one of the exponents of the idea that Akhenaten came to the throne aged little more than ten to twelve years old, described as 'untenable' by Eaton-Krauss (2016), 11.

21  Those who deny Smenkhkare existed at all, other than as Nefertiti with a new name, have an obvious advantage in one sense: the KV55 body can then only be Akhenaten's (or that of some entirely unknown person). But that leaves various other pieces of the mystery hanging in mid-air and unexplained, in particular 'Smenkhkare and Meryetaten' in the tomb of Meryre ii and their cryptic cartouches.

22  This is because we have no idea how old the real Akhenaten was when he died, whether Smenkhkare was his brother or son or related in some other way, their causes of death, or whether there are other explanations for a delayed fusion of the epiphyses. Anyone wishing to explore these further is advised to consult Ridley (2019), 290ff, and 302, who discusses the array of arguments and different positions adopted about the KV55 body. For over-ageing younger bodies see Christ Church, Spitalfields, where round 70 per cent of the bodies were incorrectly aged, sometimes by decades, and could be proved to have been so with coffin plate inscriptions. See Reeve and Adams (1993), Dodson (2016), 166, and

Ridley (2019), 306, 310. Kemp and Zink (2012), 17–18, regardless of their conclusions, provide a convenient summary of the DNA findings, given in far more detail by Hawass et al. (2010). Dodson (2016), 163ff, discusses the DNA evidence, noting most importantly that the lack of any control samples plus a range of other assumptions made during the DNA study seriously affect any conclusions that might be drawn from it. These assumptions also overlooked the effect of repeated first-cousin marriages.

23 Gabolde (2009), 119, is an excellent example of the remarkable and uncompromising certainty some Egyptologists exhibit: 'From the epigraphic evidence it now appears that the king buried in KV55 is none other than Akhenaten whose age at death was approximately 26–28 years.' It may be Akhenaten, but if so this requires Akhenaten's revolution to have begun when he was ten years old or even younger, and to have fathered Meryetaten by the time he was thirteen.

24 More to the point, the available evidence is so thin and inconclusive that it has been easily and freely presented simultaneously as the tenuous foundation for a theory and the means of demolishing it. Typical of the type of *argumentum ex silentio* persistently wheeled out is 'Close and extensive studies of the art, the inscriptions, the archaeology and the history of this period produces *nothing* to contradict the conclusion that Neferneferuaten and Smenkhkare were one and the same person', Reeves (2001), 173. The same could equally be said of the exact opposite point of view.

25 Habicht (2019) summarizes some of the possibilities for explaining Smenkhkare but only serves to show how inconclusive the quest has been.

## 15. THE KING WHOSE NAME THE WHOLE WORLD KNOWS

1 The chapter title is taken from Carter and Mace (1923), vol. I, 41.

2 A crook found in his tomb bears the name Tutankhuaten and his throne name Nebkheperure, showing he became king still using the Aten form of his name. Carter no. 269h calling it a *Hekat* sceptre. Found in the Treasury. Illustrated in British Museum Catalogue of the 1972 Exhibition held in London, no. 45 (http://www.griffith. ox.ac.uk/gri/carter/269h.html). A gold palette found in the tomb also bears the Tutankhuaten name and the throne name, Carter no. 271 (e) 2 (http://www.griffith.ox.ac.uk/perl/gi-ca-qmakesumm. pl?sid=86.175.244.15-1618261177&qno=1&curr=271e(2)).

3 The stela is in Berlin acc. no. ÄM14197. Illustrated by Dodson (2020), 86, fig. 97, and (2018), 49, fig. 37.

4 Tutankhuaten was easily converted to Tutankhamun, 'the living image

of Amun', by deleting the sign for the '*t*', substituting '*mn*', and removing the sun disk determinative. Thus, *itn* (-aten) became *imn* (-amun). The *n* in Aten was conveniently retained because in Amun the *n* is repeated after the *mn* as a stylistic convention.

5   *ḥḳȝ-rsy-iwnw* = 'ruler of southern Heliopolis (Karnak).

6   For the chequered history of the Hermopolis block see Eaton-Krauss (2016), 3.

7   Vogelsang-Eastwood (1999).

8   Eaton-Krauss (2016), 4, 5. The slab's format is compatible with a tableau that would have shown the pair facing each other across an altar in the company of their parents, all participating in venerating the Aten. See Dodson (2018), 15, fig. 12, and (2020), 49, figs 50 and 51.

9   The formula was *it.f.f.f* which tripled *it.f*, meaning perhaps 'his father's father's father Menkheperure', with the latter in the form used by Thutmose IV. See Allen (2006). It is now in the Oriental Institute Museum at the University of Chicago acc. no. E12144 (https://oi-idb. uchicago.edu/id/06bbd735-90de-4102-80cd-192b01170a61). See Reeves (1982), and Rittner (2019), and for its origins see Wilkinson (2000), 28.

10  The Prudhoe Lions: BM acc. no. EA2 (https://www.britishmuseum.org/collection/object/Y_EA2). Found at Napata near the Fourth Cataract to where they had been removed a thousand years after being made. Fairman (1972), 17, explains why 'father' cannot be taken here, or more generally, as an indication of a specific relationship other than one of more general descent or ancestry. Text available in MTA, 217, no. 100-E. This clarification has not swayed a few Egyptologists from claiming that Amenhotep III was Tutankhamun's father, requiring him to have ruled alongside Akhenaten for a decade or more to do so, and by an unknown mother.

11  For the lock of hair, see Carter no. 320e (http://www.griffith.ox.ac.uk/gri/carter/320e.html), and the clappers ibid., no. 620 (13).1 (http://www.griffith.ox.ac.uk/gri/carter/620(13)1-c620(13)1.html).

12  Harris et al. (1978). For the DNA see Hawass et al. (2010), 641. Naturally, the identification of the Elder Lady as Tiye has been questioned. See Dodson and Hilton (2010), 157, who say it 'is very unlikely', but Dodson (2020), 100, later acknowledges the conclusions of the hair and DNA evidence. Ridley (2019), 214, summarizes some of the contradictory views about the Elder Lady which only leave the reader in despair.

13  Hawass et al. (2010), 644, describe how the Nefertiti bust had been deliberately equipped with an additional veneer to produce a much more idealized and beautiful portrait. As for Kiya, rather than assuming the stopper busts were of Kiya and concluding she was a sister of Nefertiti's, it is more likely either that they represented Nefertiti or one of her daughters.

14 The lack of similarity between the coffin portraits of Yuya and Thuya and their mummies is obvious at the most elementary level by simply overlaying a picture of the former on the latter and includes features and proportions. The coffin portraits are best treated as generic examples from the period, not as likenesses.

15 Hawass et al. (2010), and Harris et al. (1979).

16 The necessary relationships would have to include Akhenaten and Nefertiti being first cousins through Tiye and Ay being siblings and Ay being Nefertiti's father, Mutemwiya and Yuya being siblings, thus making Amenhotep III and Tiye first cousins. There would also have to be another cousin relationship involving Nefertiti's unknown mother, but this has not been identified (see Dodson 2016, 167).

17 Personal communication Joann Fletcher, who, of course, studied the body in person.

18 Work by Andrew Millard of Durham University, see http://community. dur.ac.uk/a.r.millard/genealogy/EdwardIIIDescent.php

19 Gabolde (2013), 192.

20 The single instance of Richard Neville, 16th earl of Warwick (1428–71), is instructive. Descended from Edward III through his grandmother, Neville assiduously pursued his dynastic ambitions by acting as a prime protagonist in the Wars of the Roses, changing sides between supporting Edward IV and Henry VI, and seeking advantageous marriages for his daughters, both of whom married brothers of Edward IV, one ending up as Richard III's queen. A casual glance at the genealogy of Neville's family shows the complexity of the links between royalty and nobility at the time.

21 Luban (1999), Fletcher (2004), especially 372ff. See also Ridley (2019), 214–15, who discusses the refutation of Luban's and Fletcher's cases. The identification as Nefertiti has since gained wider acceptance even from former critics. See Burzacott (2018), and now Dodson (2020), 94–5, fig. 109, and 129–31. Those who interpret the DNA evidence as being far more specific continue to refute Nefertiti as a candidate.

22 Much later, two ex-slaves, Eulaeus and Lenaeus, made themselves the guardians of the then boy-king Ptolemy VI (1st reign 180–164 BC) in the interests of profiting out of the arrangement.

23 Dodson (2020), 89, fig. 102. One piece of the shabti is now in Brooklyn acc. no. 33.51 (see https://www.brooklynmuseum.org/opencollection/objects/35964). The other piece is in the Louvre acc. no, AF9904 (https://collections.louvre.fr/en/ark:/53355/cl010035903).

24 Boundary stela P. See Murnane et al. (1993), 183.

25 The claim was made by Nicholas Reeves (2015). It has continued to rumble on and is obviously incompatible with the identification of the

'Younger Lady' as Nefertiti. Brockman (2016) provides some particularly scathing commentary, 'another car crash of reputations driven by over-hyped claims and data'. At the time of writing, new theories about hidden chambers have emerged. See Burzacott (2018), in *Nile Magazine*, a publication that seems to specialize in an Amarna 'revelation' with almost every edition, and *Nature*, 'Is this Nefertiti's tomb?', 19 February 2020.

26 Bodies aside, Tiye's lock of hair and Thutmose IV's surveying instrument are enough to tell us that Tutankhamun was a member of the royal family in the direct line of descent. Those, and his name, make it likely he was either a sibling or half-sibling of Ankhesenamun, or at the very least a first cousin. Much the most probable is that they were brother and sister but did not necessarily share the same mother. None of the examination of the bodies has changed that.

27 For a possible greeting from the Hittite king Shuppiluliuma, see *EA* 41, addressing him as Ḫuriya, the Hittite version of the latter part of Tutankhamun's throne name Nebkheperure.

28 Eaton-Krauss (2016), 13, and pl. II. Dodson (2018), 50, fig. 38, illustrates the relevant part of the relief. If Nefertiti played any part in his accession and early rule, no evidence has survived.

29 Whittemore (1926), 4. And see also Petrie's finds UC 12520 and 23789 bearing Tutankhamun's throne name Nebkheperure, found at Amarna, and UC1937, a mould for making rings with the name Tutankhamun. The collection includes similar material from Memphis. For the catalogue, see https://petriecat.museums.ucl.ac.uk/

30 MTA no. 100-K, p. 221, who disputes their attribution to Ay. The vizier title appears on an anonymous piece of gold foil allegedly found in association with other fragments bearing his name and positions which had originated in his royal tomb and probably referred to him. Newberry (1932), 52, F (9). Other pieces from this assemblage are discussed below. Dodson (2018), 79, suggests that Ay's tenure as a vizier is incongruous and may have held it in an 'extraordinary manner' (whatever that means).

31 Ay the Younger's block statue is in Brooklyn acc. no. 66.174.1 (https://www.brooklynmuseum.org/opencollection/objects/3752). For this man, see Dodson and Hilton (2010), 154, their 'Ay B'.

32 *iry-pꜥt*, translated as either 'hereditary prince' or 'noble'. Gardiner (1953), 14, and pl. II, line 6, and Dodson (2018), 111, for the Coronation Text. For the Saqqara tomb, see Martin (1991), 52, and Van Dijk (1993), 13. Dodson, ibid., 101 says '*iry-pꜥt* during the New Kingdom can imply "crown prince"', which is another way of saying it does not always mean that.

33 Hatshepsut's senior official Djehuty described himself as 'hereditary prince' on fifteen occasions in his tomb and there is no indication that he was lined up to be a successor. BAR (ii) §371.

34 Eaton-Krauss (2016), 24, figs 6, 7.

35 Reading 'Re, ruler of the two horizons, who rejoices in the horizon' and 'In the name of his light, which is the Aten'.

36 Carter and Mace (1923), vol. I, 110.

37 Carter nos 620.41 and 42 (blue faience bracelets); 596a-1 (fan stock); 261-a, a piece of linen but the 'reading of cartouche very doubtful', whereas another at 281a-3 seems to be certain. See http://www.griffith.ox.ac.uk/ gri/carter/ and choose numbers from the options on the page. Reeves (1990), 169, provides a checklist of 'Heirloom' items included in the tomb. There is no need to assume these were necessarily gifts from the original owners who may, like Meryetaten, have been dead by the time they came into Tutankhamun's possession.

38 Carter no. 403 (http://www.griffith.ox.ac.uk/perl/gi-ca-qmakesumm. pl?sid=84.188.244.8-1243676544&qno=1&curr=403). The text is published by MTA no. 101-A, p. 221, giving the Cairo Exhibition no. 738, and supplies other instances of the incidental survival of the Aten name in the tomb.

39 Dodson (2018), 123.

40 See Carter no. 317a (http://www.griffith.ox.ac.uk/gri/carter/317a.html) for the group.

41 Carter nos 320 and 320a. Strictly speaking the foetuses are only *assumed* to be the children of Tutankhamun *and* Ankhesenamun since there was no inscription to that effect. The inscriptions only referred to an anonymous Osiris (Tutankhamun?) accompanied by the 'revered one' (*imȝḫw*) and 'true of voice' (*mȝꜥ-rḫw*) and other formulae normally applied to the deceased. See Carter and Mace (1933), vol. III, 88.

42 Gabolde (2013), 186–7.

43 Hawass et al. (2010), 641, fig. 1, for the allele data from the foetuses, and fig.1 note b for the idea that the KV55 body is Akhenaten's. See Dodson (2016), 163ff for objections, which include the lack of control samples and circular arguments. The problems are also usefully summarized by Matić (2018), 113, and in more detail by Eaton-Krauss (2016), 6ff.

44 In this scene on the Nekhbet shrine Ankhesenamun's titles are incorrectly depicted. She is called 'Lord of the Two Lands' whereas elsewhere the title has been appropriately feminized for her.

45 Reeves (1990), 178; Carter no. 229, with card no. 229–2 with a transcription (http://www.griffith.ox.ac.uk/gri/carter/229.html).

46 *EA* 9. Addressed to Nibḫurrereya (Nebkheperure? Tutankhamun's throne name).

47 Carter no. 21 (http://www.griffith.ox.ac.uk/gri/carter/021.html).

48 North wall of colonnade hall. Later usurped by Horemheb.

49 Daressy (1912), 128, no. 4. This originated in Ay's tomb.

50 Dodson (2018), 58–9, figs 44 (Horemheb's tomb), 45 (Tutankhamun's

monument), and pp. 67–8. Martin (1991), 67ff, provides commentary and photographs (and drawings) of the extant scenes at Horemheb's tomb, especially on pp. 71 and 74–5.

51 Martin (1991), 72–3. For a more recent overview of torture in the New Kingdom, see Matić (2019).

52 After his reign some of these blocks were reused once more as filling for later additions to the main Karnak complex, especially Horemheb's Tenth Pylon. These reused blocks were noted long before Tutankhamun's tomb was discovered. See Maspero (1912) (ii), 112, and more recently Johnson (2010). The military scenes were only one aspect of the Tutankhamun reliefs. Johnson distinguishes two separate buildings, claiming one was Tutankhamun's demolished mortuary temple that had reused talatat blocks from Akhenaten's Karnak temple. Dodson (2018), 58, fig. 45, illustrating the same relief as Johnson describes it as 'Tutankhamun's Karnak monument'.

53 That Tutankhamun was responsible is clear from the sealings found in the tomb bearing his name.

54 For example, in the tomb of Mahu (TA9), including a scene of Akhenaten and Nefertiti in a chariot. Although the scene was generally well preserved and the cartouches barely touched, Akhenaten's face has been chiselled out. Bouriant (1903), pl. XLVII. See https://digi. ub.uni-heidelberg.de/diglit/bouriant1903/0188. The damage has been compounded by bouts of vandalism down to modern times.

55 For the source, see the next note. Subsequently Tutankhamun's Restoration stela was usurped by Horemheb when he became king. This was part of his programme to delete any memories of the Amarna era, including its collateral members in the form of Tutankhamun and Ankhesenamun, and take all the personal credit. Tutankhamun's name was deleted, and Ankhesenamun's images were removed.

56 Text available in MTA no. 99, p. 212; also, at Nederhof, M-J. (2006), 'Restoration Stela of Tutankhamun', published online by St Andrews University at https://mjn.host.cs.st-andrews.ac.uk/egyptian/texts/corpus/pdf/RestorationTutankhamun.pdf

57 For example, at Soleb (the lions mentioned earlier in this chapter) and Kawa. See Dodson (2018), 71.

58 Dodson (2018), 72–3.

59 In his tomb at Saqqara. Quoted by Martin (1991), 173.

60 There is some confusion about this man's name. It appears to have been 'Amenhotep-written-Huy', i.e. 'Amenhotep called Huy'. It was originally thought that these names represented two brothers who served as joint viceroys (see BAR (ii) §1027ff for translations).

61 A picture can be viewed online of the tribute at: https://es.m.wikipedia.org/wiki/

Archivo:Nubian_Tribute_Presented_to_the_King,_Tomb_of_Huy_
MET_DT221112.jpg

62   *sꜣ-nsw ḥry-pḏt* = 'King's son, troop commander'. Carter no. 333. See
     Carter Card no. 333–01, with the hieroglyphic inscription (http://www.
     griffith.ox.ac.uk/gri/carter/333.html). Also, Carter and Mace (1933),
     vol. III, 97. This appears in Reeves (1990), 169, 'Heirlooms', but without
     comment.

63   The latest date from Tutankhamun's tomb is a wine jar, apparently of
     his 10th regnal year, though the highest to specify his name is of the 9th
     regnal year. This is commensurate with the age at death of the skeleton
     and his estimated accession at around the age of eight or nine. MTA no.
     101–D, p. 223.

64   Tutankhamun's waist measured 29 in (74 cm) but his hips were unusually
     wide for a male at 43 in (109 cm), possibly indicative of a congenital
     condition. Vogelsang-Eastwood (1999).

65   Kemp and Zink (2012), 19–22.

66   Carter no. 242 (http://www.griffith.ox.ac.uk/gri/carter/242.html).

67   Eaton-Krauss (2016), 104ff, discusses the theories about Tutankhamun's
     death.

68   Güterbock (1956), 93–5 (A ii 1, A iii 1). This is called a 'disaster' and
     'a major confrontation' by Van Dijk (2002), 292, both seemingly
     overdramatic readings of the Hittite source. Egypt was called *Mi-iz-ri*.

## 16. THE WIDOWED QUEEN AND THE GOD'S FATHER

1   The seventy days comes from an inscription found in the 18th Dynasty
    tomb of Djehuty (TT 11). Davis and Gardiner (1915), 56, and pl. 36. An
    adapted translation is in Ikram and Dodson (1998), 16. See also Herodotus
    2.86, and the Bible, Genesis 50.2–3.

2   Carter and Mace (1923–33), vol. II, 103, specifically acknowledge the
    likelihood of complications affecting the timing of a royal burial.

3   Dodson (2018), 88, notes that the flowers can only be evidence for a
    March/April burial 'if they were used fresh', which, of course, cannot be
    proven. See also Carter and Mace (1932–3), vol. II, Appendix III, 196.

4   Tomashevska (2019), 8–9, who wisely makes no attempt to estimate the
    date of picking the flowers or time of year of the burial.

5   Van Dijk (1993), 53, and Carter and Mace (1923–33), vol. II, 103.

6   Eaton-Krauss (2016), 103, points out that a 'longer interval is more likely'
    and that it was possible the funeral was delayed because of the 'unusual
    circumstances'.

7   Published by Güterbock (1956). Available online at: https://www.
    jstor.org/stable/1359041?seq=1 (part II), and https://www.jstor.org/
    stable/1359312?seq=1 (part III) – requires login.

8  From the direct transliteration *Da-ḫa-mu-un-zu-uš* = *ta ḥmt nsw* (*tɜ ḥmt nsw*). In other words, the Hittites just addressed her as 'the wife of the Egyptian king', using the female definite article *tɜ* (*tɜ*, which like the male definite article *pɜ,* was rarely used in Egyptian). Claims that the definite article can only mean Nefertiti on the grounds of her superior status to the others rests on the Hittites being aware of, and using, subtle aspects of Egyptian title protocols to distinguish Egyptian queens. It is far more likely that Dakhamunzu was a generic term that the Hittites used for any Egyptian queen without understanding the precise significance of the format. The term does not appear in the queen's reported speech. It is hard to imagine any Egyptian queen deliberately downgrading her status, especially one desperate to secure a husband and king from another nation. Reeves (2001), 176, explains these in detail though does not comment on how unusual it was to use a definite article. See Gardiner §21, 110, and 112.

9  *EA* 27, Tushratta to Akhenaten. Those who want the queen to be Nefertiti or Meryetaten can, of course, rustle up various arguments to support their cases, none of which alter the case in Ankhesenamun's favour.

10  Dodson (2020), 83ff. This is ignored by Egyptologists who prefer one of the other candidates.

11  Egypt's is given on the tablets as *Mi-iz-ra*, one of its ancient names.

12  Long-distance journeys were hazardous. Messengers were liable to be pursued by lethally dangerous locals, such as the Suteans in Canaan. At best they might be delayed, at worst killed. See *EA* 16.37–42.

13  Ní-ip-ḫu-ru-ri-ia-aš, equivalent to Nibḫururiya – these consonants are interchangeable in Hittite.

14  It was understood by the translator to be a Hittite version of Nebkheperure, for Tutankhamun, in Egyptian *nb-ḫpr-w-rˁ* = Nebkheperure Tutankhamun). See also Güterbock (1956), 94, 98 and 123. Some of the Amarna tablets include cuneiform letters from the Mitanni king Tushratta addressed to Napḫurreya. This was undoubtedly Akhenaten because he is consistently identified on the letters as the son of Amenhotep III and Tiye. The resemblance of the transliterated Nibḫururiya of the Shuppiluliuma tablets to Tutankhamun's throne name is marginally stronger, but manifestly not definitive.

15  For example, Reeves (2001), 176. He blurs the Hittite ḫ with the modern h which combined with a p sounds like 'f' in English and thereby leading the reader to associate it with the 'f' in Akhenaten's Neferkheperure. The letter ḫ is closest to kh in English, not h, and in cuneiform 'p' is not distinguished from 'b'. It is obvious therefore that exact equivalency is impossible to work out.

16  See also Bryce (1990). All this, of course, cuts no ice with some experts

such as Gautschy (2014), 151–2, who rejects Tutankhamun as a candidate for the recently deceased pharaoh, preferring Smenkhkare, and also concludes the body in KV55 was Akhenaten.

17   More recently it has been suggested KV62 was intended for Nefertiti (see below), based in part on the idea that the right turn at the end of the corridor towards the burial chamber is supposedly a characteristic of a queen's tomb whereas a king's tomb turns left. This ignores the facts that Amenhotep III's tomb turns left and then right, that there are no contemporary queens' tombs to compare it with and that thereafter most New Kingdom royal tombs were straight, including those in the Valley of the Queens, except for Ramesses II's which swung right (KV7). The idea is that of Reeves (2015), 19, which ended up circulating in the international press. Even the most casual scrutiny of royal tomb plans shows that KV62 is unlike any other and in my opinion was not designed as a royal tomb in the first instance. In my view, the claim is a classic example of wishful thinking, desperate to see a pattern where there is none, and in the belief that the pattern is a portal to hidden secrets.

18   The stylistic similarities of the wall paintings make it likely the same artists were involved. They were perhaps told to suspend work in WV23 and head to KV62 to prepare it for Tutankhamun, returning later to complete WV23 and adapt its decoration for Ay who had in the meantime succeeded Tutankhamun. This is by far and away the simplest explanation.

19   Eaton-Krauss (2016), 89–92. Possibilities include Smenkhkare, Nefertiti, or Tutankhamun when still Tutankhuaten.

20   One possible explanation is that Tutankhamun's sarcophagus was intended for Akhenaten *before* he ordered the move to Amarna and was left behind at Thebes unfinished.

21   The 19th Dynasty tomb of Ipuy (TT217) included a scene of a royal shrine (or 'catafalque') being manufactured. MM acc. no 30.4.116 (viewable online at: https://www.metmuseum.org/art/collection/search/548572). The scene features an indolent worker loafing on the shrine and being chided by a colleague.

22   Carter no. 404 (http://www.griffith.ox.ac.uk/perl/gi-ca-qmakesumm.pl?sid=86.145.83.12-1629123191&qno=1&curr=404). This jar was not only at least ninety years old when buried but had also been repaired twice in antiquity. See also Carter and Mace (1933), vol. III, 144.

23   Gabolde (2009), 118, and fig. 10, who also claims that Neferneferuaten is detectable in one instance. The coffinette concerned is the one associated with Neith, line 7 of the interior text of the back half of the coffin. Image available in Edwards (1979), 165. There is certainly a visible basis for arguing Tutankhamun's name has replaced someone else's because of traces of deleted hieroglyphs. The restoration of Neferneferuaten

there, together with the so-called 'effective for her husband' epithet is
plausible but optimistic, especially the epithet. In lines 9 and 12 the name
Tutankhamun recurs but there are no similar traces of a deleted name.
The most recent suggestion is that by the time they reached KV62 the
coffinettes were thirdhand, having been made originally for Smenkhkare
but were not used, were then adapted for Nefertiti, and finally modified
for Tutankhamun. Allen (2010) (ii), but see also Dodson (2018), 36–7, and
now (2020), 92, for the suggestion they were thirdhand. This will never be
proven one way or the other.

24  Gabolde (2009), 119, and Habicht (2019), 23. Carter no. 261p
(1) (http://www.griffith.ox.ac.uk/perl/gi-ca-qmakesumm.
pl?sid=86.131.241.119-1618312534&qno=1&curr=261p(1)).

25  See the Carter archive at the Griffith Institute in Oxford, in particular
photograph p1922
(http://www.griffith.ox.ac.uk/php/am-makepage1.
php?&db=burton&view=gall&burt=p1922&card=&desc=&strt=1&what=
Search&cpos=1&s1=imagename&s2=cardnumber&s3=&dno=25).
Also visible on the back wall of the second inner shrine, illustrated
on p. 102 of Edwards (1979). See also Reeves (1990), 104.

26  Carter no. 296b (http://www.griffith.ox.ac.uk/gri/carter/296b.html). The
pedestal has Tutankhamun's throne name Nebkheperure in yellow
paint. Dodson (2020), 90–1. Carter no. 289a (http://www.griffith.ox.ac.uk/
gri/carter/289a.html). For reused shabtis, see Dodson (ibid.), 94, fig. 108.

27  There is certainly no means of arguing one way more convincingly than
the other and it is the same problem that affects many 'portrait' items
from this short period of time made to represent a small number of
people from the same family and made by the same people in the same
royal workshops. In many cases they cannot be reliably distinguished,
and certainly not in terms of specific individuals, as noted earlier for
the coffins of Yuya and Thuya. Dodson (2018), 42, fig. 31, and (2020), 93,
believes the coffin was made for Smenkhkare and like the coffinettes then
adapted for Neferneferuaten. Habicht (2019), 21, is less convinced. Reeves
(1990), 109, was circumspect.

28  Carter no. 574 (http://www.griffith.ox.ac.uk/gri/carter/574.html), see
Chapter 13. The docket, which Carter struggled to understand fully
seems to read something like 'This same likewise carried (*rmn*) for the
king Nebkheperure, which is in the funeral procession'. The first line is
very obscure.

29  Apart from the calcite jar mentioned earlier that bears what might be his
heavily abraded cartouches alongside Akhenaten's (see Chapter 13).

30  Carter called it 'slovenliness'. Carter and Mace (1923–33), vol. II, 48.

31  Carter and Mace (1923–33), vol. II, 50–1.

32  Edwards (1979), 59, and Reeves (1990), 147.

33  KV62's wall paintings can be scrutinized at: https://www.osirisnet.net/tombes/pharaons/toutankhamon/e_toutankhamon_01.htm

34  It is impossible to confirm that hypothesis and the related theory that Nefertiti's own undisturbed burial lies hidden beyond Tutankhamun's burial chamber. This has even now extended to the extraordinary theory that Howard Carter made secret exploratory soundings in the north wall of the burial chamber in search of hidden rooms (presumably unsuccessfully), necessitating his clandestine repainting of one of the figures, given away by differing detail from the original photographs. Burzacott (2019) (ii), 59. That Howard Carter, an outstanding and meticulous artist, is unlikely to have made such mistakes is not considered and nor is the possibility of an unrecorded bout of innocuous but incompetent restoration work. The differences in the detail are nonetheless quite clear.

35  Huber (2018) who typically claims that the evidence cited proves KV62 was originally created for Nefertiti. See also Reeves (2015). The Osiris figure can be viewed online at: https://www.osirisnet.net/popupImage.php?img=/tombes/pharaons/toutankhamon/photo/tta_unidia-bs_35413.jpg&lang=en&sw=1536&sh=864

36  More correctly Pasebkhaniut. Psusennes is the Greek version, used by Manetho, and is more commonly employed today.

37  Manley (2012), 111, describes the canopic chest shrine of Tutankhamun admiringly as evidence of the 'faith and commitment' involved in burying a king. While that might have been true of the manufacturing work, it most certainly is not of the way the tomb was put together.

38  Davis (1912) was convinced that KV58, which his team found in 1909, was the tomb of Tutankhamun. KV54 was recognized to contain items from the funeral.

39  Guide to the London 1972 Tutankhamun Exhibition, item no. 3.

40  The shabti is in the BM acc. no. EA38121 (https://www.britishmuseum.org/collection/object/Y_EA38121). For Userhat's stela see MM acc. no. 05.4.2 (https://www.metmuseum.org/art/collection/search/544776).

41  Recent archaeological work to try and find Tutankhamun's temple near Medinet Habu uncovered an extensive settlement in the area dating to Amenhotep III's reign which had been given up during Akhenaten's rule, or so it was claimed. The settlement was already known to exist. For the talatat blocks allegedly from the temple, see Johnson (2010).

42  Murnane (1990), 25–8, especially 26.

43  Shuppiluliuma was succeeded briefly by his son Arnuwanda II who succumbed within a year to the disease, being succeeded in turn by Mursili II, presumably a brother of the dead Zannanza. In Mursili II's 10th regnal year, or in other words about a decade after Tutankhamun's

death (if he has been correctly identified as the husband of the widowed queen), a solar eclipse supposedly occurred when Mursili was about to attack a place called Azzi, but without any precision in the description ('the Sun-God made an omen'). Attempts have been made to associate this event with known eclipses, principally the one of 24 June 1312 BC in Hittite territory, and thus work back to calculate an absolute date for the death of Tutankhamun. These have been inconclusive because there were several possible eclipses, and the opaque reference may not even be to an eclipse. The plague is recorded in the 'Hittite Royal Prayers' or 'Plague Prayers', published by O. R. Gurney (1940), *Hittite Prayers of Mursili II*, University of Oxford, Oxford. Huber (2001) discusses the source text and context. These eclipses can all be located on the NASA Five Millennium Solar Eclipses site (https://eclipse.gsfc.nasa.gov/SEcat5/SE-1399--1300.html), but note that this gives the astronomical dates to which BC events must have one year added for a true calendar year. For example, the astronomical date of the 1312 BC eclipse is 24 June '1311' BC.

44  Newberry (1932), 52, itemizes Ay's remarkable litany of titles. His name was *Iy-it-ntr* = 'Ay, God's Father'.

45  This is how Ay was described on a small piece of gold leaf found in a pit in the Valley of the Kings (KV58) showing Ay, holding a fan as a sign of his status, admiring Tutankhamun smiting enemy. The pit contained debris removed from Ay's Theban royal tomb in the Western Valley of the Kings. Daressy (1912), 128, no. 4; and see also Dodson (2018), 67. Davis (1912) published KV58 as the Tomb of Tutankhamun. Not to be confused with KV54, the cache of embalming materials from KV62's corridor, removed after the first robbery and reburied. The same source yielded the fragment of gold leaf with title of vizier under Tutankhamun.

46  See Newberry (1932), 52, for a list of Ay's titles.

47  Newberry (1932), 50; MTA no. 103-A, p. 224. The ring might even have been manufactured speculatively by an artisan in the hope the union would come off.

48  The Hawass et al. (2010) DNA study tentatively identified a mummy found in KV21 as the mother of the miscarried foetuses in Tutankhamun's tomb, and thus Ankhesenamun but could obviously instead be any one of her sisters, or indeed an earlier relative. Nothing in the tomb suggested the bodies found there belonged to the late 18th Dynasty. Gabolde (2013), 191, proposed Mutemwiya, a rather optimistic deduction.

49  Murnane (1990), 29.

50  MTA nos 103-C and 103-D, pp. 225–6.

51  Daressy (1912), 127, no. 3, 129, no. 5.

52  Van Dijk (1996), 33.

53  From Western Thebes. Illustrated and described by Dodson (2018), 98–9.

54  On the shabtis his name appears in the reverse form Minnakht, with a reference to his army role. For example, Carter no. 330k (http://www.griffith.ox.ac.uk/gri/carter/330k.html) where he is named Min-nakht.

55  For the 3rd regnal year, see BAR (ii) §1042, from a stela found by the Great Pyramid; also published as MTA no. 103-C, p. 225. For the 4th regnal year, MTA no. 103-D, p. 226.

56  See earlier this chapter for the priest Pairy who served the cult of Tutankhamun. Blocks probably from Tutankhamun's mortuary temple ended up at Karnak and Luxor, reused by Horemheb.

57  Wilkinson (2000), 193; Dodson (2016), 76–7, 214, fig. 18. For the reused statues, see Reeves (1990), 28.

58  Tomb WV23 can be explored online at: https://www.osirisnet.net/tombes/pharaons/ay/e_ay_pharaon_02.htm

59  Gardiner A50. The four sons of Horus scene in Ay's tomb can be viewed online at: https://www.osirisnet.net/popupImage.php?img=/tombes/pharaons/ay/photo/ay_cd_41.jpg&lang=en&sw=1536&sh=864

60  This queen is Dodson and Hilton's Nefetiry D Meryetmut (2010), 172. The tomb is QV66, found by Ernesto Schiaparelli in 1904. The pommel is now in Turin's Egyptian Museum Suppl. 5162. There is no question about its reading. Image available here: https://www.researchgate.net/figure/Knob-head-or-pommel-with-the-throne-name-Kheper-Kheperu-Ra-of-King-Ay-Museo-Egizio_fig1_309770532

## 17. THE ENLIGHTENED DESPOT

1  The idea has long circulated that Horemheb was the same man as Akhenaten's general Paatenemheb (see Chapter 12). There is no means of connecting the two apart from the similarity of their names, which mean 'Aten/Horus in Festival' respectively, and their positions.

2  BAR (iii) §31.

3  A chantress of Amun called Amenia who was on the scene before Horemheb became king is named on a column at his Saqqara tomb. She is often assumed to be his first wife, who died before he became king, but may instead have been a female relative since the relationship is not specified. An unnamed female burial in the tomb may be hers. Martin (1991), 46, 84, 94. Amenia was recorded at the tomb, but not her body. She may or not be depicted in dyads with her husband installed in the tomb, too, one of which is now in the BM, unless this is Mutnodjmet. BM acc. no. EA36 (https://www.britishmuseum.org/collection/object/Y_EA36).

4  Dodson (2018), 98. The ambiguous drawing of Nefertiti's sister's name is in Aldred (1991), 222, fig. 20. Aldred assumed the two women were the same individual.

5  BAR (iii) §22–32.

6   Now in Luxor Museum acc. no. 1A3-EG-LM-2-A3 (http://isida-project.
    org/egypt_april_2018/luxor_museum_en.htm).

7   Maspero (1912) (i), 7, and Dodson (2018), 109, fig. 78, reproducing an old
    drawing. The original relief is lost.

8   *w3r.f nšni* = 'had fallen into a storm', where *nšni* = storm. Horemheb's
    Coronation Text is on the back of a statue in Turin (ME acc. no. Cat.
    1379; statue and text viewable at https://collezioni.museoegizio.it/it-IT/
    material/Cat_1379). Published by Gardiner (1953), 14, and BAR (iii) §22–32.
    This phrase (line 7) has been translated in several different ways, often
    incongruously, each creating a quite different sense and making it
    difficult to believe one is reading the same passage. Van Dijk (1996), 35,
    has 'when chaos broke out in the palace'. BAR (iii) §25 supplies 'when
    he was summoned before the king, the palace, it began to fear', while
    Gardiner uses 'rage'. None of these sources transliterate the words,
    though Gardiner does at least provide a picture of the Egyptian text,
    which made isolating the key word in what is a complicated construction
    difficult; *nšni* is Gardiner N35 N37 N35.

9   BAR (iii) §31. See Brand (1999) for coverage of Horemheb's work, especially 120.

10  *srwḏ* = 'restore' or 'strengthen'.

11  There was a potential additional reason for claiming renewal, though
    this depends on whether the chronology is correct which will never
    be established. In 1321 BC the heliacal rising of Sirius coincided once
    more with the Egyptian New Year and lasted until 1318 BC, briefly
    resynchronizing the civil and solar calendars. If that was what happened
    shortly after Horemheb's accession, the coincidence would have been
    convenient. The heavens and Egypt were once more in alignment. The
    same would not recur until AD 139. But whether the dates used here
    (or anywhere else) for Horemheb's reign are correct is unknown. Other
    modern versions of Egyptian chronology include those that place 1321 BC
    at the beginning of Tutankhamun's reign. For example, Dodson (2019) (i),
    154.

12  BAR (iii) §31. It is surprising how often Horemheb's expressed intention
    is taken as proof that this is what he achieved in practice. Apart from his
    choice of successor, we do not know.

13  ME acc. no. Cat. 768 (viewable at: https://collezioni.museoegizio.it/en-GB/
    material/Cat_768/).

14  Porter and Moss (1964), 560, no. (4). The text is also illustrated and
    translated by Reeves and Wilkinson (1996), 108.

15  BAR (iii) §34–6, who erroneously attributes this to a non-existent
    Eleventh Pylon. Much instead rests on Hittite sources, including the
    appearance of the name Ar-ma-a, believed by some to be Horemheb
    and rejected by others on the grounds that the Hittites would have
    represented the name as Ḥarmaḫa. Devecchi and Miller (2011), 148.

16 BAR (iii) §370ff. Under Ḫattušili III.

17 BAR (iii) §41–4.

18 BAR (iii) §37–8.

19 Horemheb's statue as a scribe is in the MM, New York acc. no. 23.10.1 (https://www.metmuseum.org/art/collection/search/544692).

20 BAR (iii) §45–67. The whole text is also in MTA no. 108, pp. 235ff.

21 BAR (iii) §51, 54, 57.

22 BAR (iii) §58.

23 BAR (iii) §65.

24 BAR (iii) §63 and 54 respectively.

25 BAR (iii) §66.

26 Seth was the enemy of Maat in his role as a god of violence and disorder. But his powers of strength and cunning were venerated, and this was the basis of the Ramesside interest in Seth. For Paramessu's titles, see Dodson (2015), 1.

27 See Schulz and Seidel (1998), 164, fig. 28.

28 Martin (1991), 97–8. A wine docket from the grave suggests Mutnodjmet had died in her husband's 13th regnal year or within a few years afterwards.

29 Half of the sixty dockets have complete years, and they are all Year 13 or 14. Van Dijk (2008) itemizes the jar docket evidence along with other evidence that suggests Horemheb's reign was much shorter than sometimes believed. There are several dated pieces of evidence from earlier in his reign, like the inspection of the tomb of Thutmose IV, but virtually nothing later. BAR (iii) §71 records Horemheb's 3rd regnal year, tomb of Neferhotep, §32B the 8th regnal year inspection of Thutmose IV's tomb.

30 MTA no. 109, p. 241. The tomb of the scribe Mose, from the reign of Ramesses II with a retrospective reference to a lawsuit. Egyptologists who support the longer reign accept the Mose text and point out that a statue docket from Horemheb's mortuary temple at Medinet Habu mentions a 27th regnal year, perhaps when sculpture was being removed from Ay's mortuary temple. Those who prefer a shorter reign reject the Mose text as a scribal 'error' or that it refers to Ramesses II's reign and insist that the wine jar dockets mean he cannot have lived past the 14th regnal year, overlooking that the dockets show the minimum length of his reign, not the maximum. Dodson (2018), 129, and Van Dijk (2008), 199, take completely opposed positions. Dodson supplies some other supporting evidence for a twenty-eight-year reign. See also Bryan (2015) for a wider discussion. The wine jar dockets serve as a *terminus post quem*: Horemheb reigned at least this long and died at some point afterwards but does not tell us when. This is an excellent example of how imprecise the chronology of Egyptian rulers is, particularly in this period, despite the best efforts to resolve the problems.

31 As on the Abydos king lists. The Ramesseum relief is illustrated by Dodson (2018), 133, fig. 98. See also Phillips (1977) for an ostracon that similarly omits undesirable kings.

32 Horemheb's canopic chest and stoppers are illustrated and described in Davis (1912), 97–100, pls LXXIV–LXXVI, reissued now by Duckworth.

33 Maspero (1912), (i) 63.

34 Reeves (2017), 430ff.

# EPILOGUE

1 Diodorus Siculus 1.46.1.

2 This was partly by chance. For example, one of Ramesses II's many sons was called Amenhotep, and another Thutmose. Some of the 18th Dynasty throne names recurred in later dynasties.

3 Dodson (2019) (ii), 12–13.

4 These 19th Dynasty dates are as disputed as those of the 18th Dynasty. See Dodson (2019) (iii), 181ff.

5 Snape (2014), 204–5.

6 Clearances went on for centuries. The Temple of Luxor cache, found in 1989, consisted of statues buried by the Romans (http://isida-project.org/egypt_april_2018/luxor_museum_en.htm).

7 In the tomb of the scribe Mose (temp. Ramesses II), and on a Ramesside tax record. MTA nos 109 and 110, p. 241. See Gardiner (1938) (i), 124. The word used was *sbi*, usually translated as 'rebel' (or 'rebellion', and phonetically identical to that for 'to drink'), but in this context clearly equated Akhenaten with having led split the state with an insurrection that we know was religious in tone, hence schismatic.

8 The 18th Dynasty subsidiary (and original) temple at Medinet Habu, which is extant, remained a cult centre into Graeco-Roman times.

9 Recorded on the Abbott Papyrus. The transcripts are published by BAR (iv) §511ff.

10 Dodson (2016), 87. The tomb of Psusennes I was found intact. Correctly, Pasebkhaniut I. Psusennes is the Greek version but is more commonly used.

11 Burzacott (2019) (i), and Reeves and Wilkinson (1996), 172–3.

12 *wḥm-mswt* = 'renaissance', the literal meaning of the Egyptian being 'repeating of birth', just as in the French word used in English, thus here 'born again'.

13 Butehamun's remarkable career is covered by Wood (2020).

14 Reeves (2017), 433–4, provides the text of Butehamun's letter and a graphic account of the treatment of the mummies. Also, Reeves and Wilkinson (1996), 204–5.

15 See Reeves and Wilkinson (1996), 206.

16   Reeves and Wilkinson ibid., 204.
17   One of these KV21 bodies is the proposed mummy of Ankhesenamun
     based on DNA evidence, see Chapter 15, but this is far from conclusive.
     See also Reeves and Wilkinson (1996), 115, for a description of the tomb.
18   For example, in the tomb of Psammetichus (Psamtik) I's vizier
     Nespekashuty, constructed close to the Deir el-Bahari temple (TT312).
     (The reliefs are viewable online at: https://www.metmuseum.org/art/
     collection/search/548338).
19   Diodorus Siculus 1.46.7.
20   Ibid., 1.46.1–3.
21   Rutherford (2019), 708–9.
22   Herodotus 2.124 recounted a tale of a pharaoh who had closed all the
     temples and denied his people the right to practise their religion, but
     there is nothing that would tie the story to Akhenaten specifically.
23   Montserrat (2003), 55–6, summarizes some examples of tomb graffiti at
     Amarna left in Graeco-Roman times.
24   Excellently summarized by Montserrat (2003). There have been many
     more since.
25   BAR (ii) §317–18; URK IV.365–7; Lichtheim (1976) 28. The word for star
     (*sk*), see URK IV.366 line 11, is an abbreviation of a longer term sometimes
     translated as 'indestructible star'. In fact, the adjective is absent from the
     hieroglyphic text here, though normally appears in translations because
     the star referred to is thought to be a circumpolar star, i.e. one that never
     sets, and that is how I have translated it.

# ABBREVIATIONS

AUC         AUC Press, Cairo
ÄM          Äegyptisches Museum, Berlin. Searchable database at:
            https://www.smb.museum/en/museums-institutions/
            aegyptisches-museum-und-papyrussammlung/
            collection-research/the-collection/
AZ          Ausführliches Verzeichnis der Aegyptischen
            Altertümer und Gipsabgüsse, Königliche Museen zu
            Berlin, Speman, Berlin (1899). Online at: https://archive.
            org/details/ausfuhrlichesver00koni/page/n3/mode/2up
BAR         Breasted, J. H. (1906–7), *Ancient Records of Egypt: Historical
            Records*, Chicago (volumes: i–v), in particular vol.
            ii (Eighteenth Dynasty), and vol. iii (Nineteenth
            Dynasty). Available online, see under Websites below
BM          British Museum
Carter      Catalogue of items from Tutankhamun's tomb held at
            the Griffith Institute, University of Oxford. These are
            accessible online, see under Websites below
DB          Deir el-Bahari area tomb series, usually now classified
            under TT (q.v.)
EA          Amarna Letters, see Moran (1992) in Further Reading
Gardiner    Gardiner hieroglyphic sign catalogue in Gardiner
            (1957) below

| JARCE | *Journal of the American Research Center in Egypt* |
| JEA | *Journal of Egyptian Archaeology* |
| JEH | *Journal of Egyptian History* |
| KV | Valley of the Kings tomb series |
| ME | Museo Egizio, Turin. Searchable database at: https://collezioni.museoegizio.it/en-GB/search/ |
| MM | Metropolitan Museum of Art, New York City |
| MTA | Murnane, W. J. (1995), *Texts from the Amarna Period in Egypt*, Society of Biblical Literature Writings from the Ancient World Series, vol. 5, Scholars Press, Atlanta |
| QV | Valley of the Queens tomb series |
| TA | Tell el-Amarna (Akhet-aten) tomb series |
| TT | Theban tomb series (sometimes including numbers also given as DB, q.v.) |
| URK | Urkunden der ägyptischen Altertums (G. Steindorf). These volumes catalogue and illustrate inscriptions in a continuous numbered series edited and compiled by several different individuals. These are most conveniently listed at http://www.egyptologyforum.org/EEFUrk.html with links to online versions of most of the volumes, but see also Helck (1955–58) and Sethe (1906–9) below |
| WV | Western Valley of the Kings tomb series |

# FURTHER READING

The number of publications, including both books and academic papers, concerned with just this one period of Egyptian history is enormous. Those listed here were the most important used in the preparation of this book.

## 1. WEBSITES

Ancient Egypt is very well served by websites. The following are some of the most useful. In the endnotes other links are cited, especially where an article is most easily accessed online, or an image of a key object. These were correct at the time of going to press, but of course links can and do change in time. Moreover, many of the articles in the main list below are available online merely by searching with the appropriate bibliographical entry.

### a) Museum collections

Museums are increasingly placing the bulk of their collections online in searchable catalogues. In this book links have been provided in the notes to many of the pieces referred to. The following is a list of the most useful museum catalogues that include 18th Dynasty items. It is not exhaustive:

Berlin, Egyptian Museum: https://www.smb.museum/
    en/museums-institutions/aegyptisches-museum-un
    d-papyrussammlung/collection-research/the-collection/
Boston, Museum of Fine Arts: https://collections.mfa.org/collections
London, British Museum: https://www.britishmuseum.org/collection
London, Petrie Museum: https://petriecat.museums.ucl.ac.uk/
New York, Metropolitan Museum of Art: https://www.metmuseum.org/
    art/collection/search/
Paris, Louvre: https://collections.louvre.fr/en/
Turin, Museo Egizio: https://collezioni.museoegizio.it/
There is also the Global Egyptian Museum: http://www.
    globalegyptianmuseum.org/

## b) Publications

https://www.academia.edu/ – this website is used by scholars to post
    papers and other documents. Many useful articles about Egypt can
    be found there.
https://www.jstor.org/ – this website is a vast electronic library of articles
    going back over a century, including some used for this book.
    Although it is subscription-based some articles can be read online for
    free. Membership of a society or institution (such as being an alumnus
    of a university) may give you free access to the whole archive.
http://etana.org/sites/default/files/coretexts/14897.pdf – James Breasted's
    corpus of Ancient Records of Egypt is available here.
https://digi.ub.uni-heidelberg.de/diglit/naville1898bd3 is Edouard Naville's
    publication of Hatshepsut's Punt reliefs. Other volumes are available
    at:
    https://digi.ub.uni-heidelberg.de/diglit/naville1895bd1
    https://digi.ub.uni-heidelberg.de/diglit/naville1896bd2
    https://digi.ub.uni-heidelberg.de/diglit/naville1901bd4
    https://digi.ub.uni-heidelberg.de/diglit/naville1905bd5
    https://digi.ub.uni-heidelberg.de/diglit/naville1908bd6
http://www.griffith.ox.ac.uk/discoveringtut/ is a free site offering total
    access to the tomb of Tutankhamun.
Bouriant (1903) on the tombs at Amarna: https://digi.ub.uni-heidelberg.
    de/diglit/bouriant1903/0001

Rock-cut tombs at Amarna (Huya): https://archive.org/details/
    cu31924020525360
Tutankhamun, Howard Carter's records at the Griffith Institute, Oxford
    of the tomb's contents at: http://www.griffith.ox.ac.uk/gri/carter/

Searching many of the works listed in the section below will throw
up online versions or downloadable texts.

## 2. BOOKS AND ARTICLES

Aldred, C. (1957), 'The End of the El-'Amārna Period', *JEA*, vol. 43
    (December 1957), 30–41

Aldred, C. (1962), 'The Harold Jones Collection', *JEA*, vol. 48 (December
    1962), 160–2

Aldred, C. (1991), *Akhenaten. King of Egypt*, Thames & Hudson, London
    (same as 1988 edition)

Allen, J. P. (1988), 'Two Altered Inscriptions of the Late Amarna Period',
    *JARCE*, vol. 25, 117–26

Allen, J. P. (2006), *The Amarna Succession*, Brown University, published online

Allen, J. P. (2010) (i), 'After Hatshepsut. The Military Campaigns of
    Thutmose III', in Roehrig (ed.) (2010), 261–2

Allen, J. P. (2010) (ii), 'The Original Owner of Tutankhamun's Canopic
    Coffins', in Hawass, Z., and Houser Wegner, J. (2010), *Millions of
    Jubilees: Studies in Honor of David P. Silverman*, vol. 1, 27–41, Conseil
    Suprême des Antiquités, Cairo

Arnold, D. (2005), 'The Destruction of the Statues of Hatshepsut', in
    Roehrig (ed.) (2005), 270–6

Aston, D. A. (2015), 'TT358, TT320 and KV39. Three Early Eighteenth
    Dynasty Queen's [sic] Tombs in the vicinity of Deir el-Bahari', in:
    *Polish Archaeology in the Mediterranean 24/2, Special Studies: Deir el-Bahari
    Studies* (edited Z. E. Szafrański)

Bagnall, R. S., Brodersen, K., Champion, C. B., Erskine, A., and Huebner,
    S. (2013), *The Encyclopedia of Ancient History*, 1st edition, Blackwell
    Publishing, Oxford

Bard, K. and Fattovich (eds) (2007), *Harbor of the Pharaohs to the Land of Punt.
    Archaeological Investigations at Mersa/Wadi Gawasis, Egypt 2001–2005*,
    Università degli Studi di Napoli 'l'Orientale', Naples

Bell, L. (1985), 'Luxor Temple and the Cult of the Royal Ka', *Journal of Near Eastern Studies*, vol. 44, no. 4 (Oct. 1985), 251–94

Bell, M. R. (1990), 'An Armchair Excavation of KV55', *JARCE*, vol. 27, 97–137

Benson, M., and Gourlay, J. (1899), *The Temple of Mut in Asher: an account of the excavation of the temple and of the religious representations and objects found therein, as illustrating the history of Egypt and the main religious ideas of the Egyptians*, John Murray, London

Bickel, S. (2014), 'Worldview and Royal Discourse in the Time of Hatshepsut', in Galán et al. (2014), 21–32

Bietak, M. (2005), 'Egypt and the Aegean. Cultural Convergence in a Thutmoside Palace at Avaris', in Roehrig (ed.) (2007), 75–81

Blankenberg-Van Delden, C. (1969), *The Large Commemorative Scarabs of Amenhotep III*, E. J. Brill, Leiden

Bommas, M. (2000), *Der Temple des Chnum der 18. Dyn. Auf Elephantine*, unpublished PhD thesis, Macquarie University, Sydney

Borchardt, L. (1925), *Statuen und Statuetten von Königen und Privatleuten im Museum von Kairo*, Nr 1–1294, Teil 2, Reichsdruckerei, Berlin

Bouriant, U., Legrain, G., and Jéquier, G. (1903), *Monuments pour servir à l'étude du culte d'Atonou en Egypte*, vol. 1, *Les tombes de Khouitatonou*, Memoires de l'Institut Français D'Archéologie Orientale de Caire (the complete volume is available online at the Universitätbibliothek Heidelberg)

Bourriau, J. (2000), 'The Second Intermediate Period (c. 1650–1550 BC)', in Shaw (ed.) (2000), 184–217

Bradbury, L. (1985), 'Nefer's inscription: On the death date of Queen Ahmose-Nefertary and the deed found pleasing to the King', *JARCE*, 22, 73–95

Brand, P. (1999), 'Secondary Restorations in the Post-Amarna Period', *JARCE*, vol. 36 (1999), 113–34

Breasted, J. H. (1906–7), *Ancient Records of Egypt: Historical Records*, Chicago (volumes i–v) (widely available as reprints)

Breasted, J. H. (1980), *The Edwin Smith Surgical Papyrus*, Oriental Institute, University of Chicago Press, Chicago

Brock, E. (1996), 'The Sarcophagus of Queen Tiye', *Journal of the Society for the Study of Egyptian Antiquities*, vol. 26, 8–21

Brockman, A. (2016), 'Nefertiti off the Radar in Tutankhamun Tomb

Row', *The Pipeline* (available online at http://thepipeline.info/
  blog/2016/06/14/nefertiti-off-the-radar-in-tutankhamun-tomb-row/)

Bryan, B. (1987), 'Portrait Sculpture of Thutmose IV', JARCE, vol. 24, 3–20

Bryan, B. (1991), *The Reign of Thutmose IV*, Johns Hopkins University Press,
  Baltimore

Bryan, B. (2000) (i), 'The Egyptian Perspective on Mittani [sic]', in Cohen
  and Westbrook (2000), 71–84

Bryan, B. (2000) (ii), 'The 18th Dynasty before the Amarna Period (c.
  1550–1352 BC)', in Shaw (ed.) (2000), 218–71

Bryan, C. P. (1974), *Ancient Egyptian Medicine. The Papyrus Ebers*, Ares
  Publishers, Chicago

Bryce, T. (1990), 'The Death of Niphururiya and its Aftermath', *JEA*, vol.
  76 (issue 1)

Bryson, K. M. (2015), 'Some Year Dates of Horemheb in Context', *JARCE*,
  vol. 51, 285–302

Budge, E. A. Wallis (1920), *A Hieroglyphic Vocabulary to the Theban Recension of the
  Book of the Dead*, Kegan Paul et al., London

Budge, E. A. Wallis (1925), *The Mummy. A Handbook of Egyptian Funerary
  Archaeology*, Cambridge University Press, Cambridge (reissued in 1989
  by Dover Publications, Mineola, New York)

Burzacott, J. (2018), 'Is this Nefertiti?', *Nile Magazine* no. 14, June–July 2018,
  46ff

Burzacott, J. (2019) (i), 'Tomb Robbers' Workshop at Luxor', *Nile Magazine*
  no. 22, Nov.–Dec. 2019, 6ff

Burzacott, J. (2019) (ii), 'KV62 The New Evidence', *Nile Magazine* no. 22,
  Nov.–Dec. 2019, 47ff

Caminos, R. (1963), 'Papyrus Berlin 10463', *JEA*, vol. 49 (Dec. 1963), 29–37

Carter, H., and Mace, A. C. (1923–33), *The Tomb of Tut.ankh.Amen* (three
  volumes), Cassell, London. Note that vol. 3, *The Annexe and Treasury*
  (1933), is credited only to Carter

Clayton, P. (1994), *Chronicle of the Pharaohs*, Thames & Hudson, London

Cline, E. H., and O'Connor, D. (2006), *Thutmose III. A New Biography*,
  University of Michigan Press, Ann Arbor

Cobb, G. (1980), *English Cathedrals. The Forgotten Centuries*, Thames & Hudson,
  London

Cohen, R., and Westbrook, R. (2000), *Amarna Diplomacy: The Beginnings of
  International Relations*, Johns Hopkins University Press, Baltimore

Daressy, M. G. (1891), 'Rapport sur la Trouvaille de [Hatiay]',
    *Annales du Service des Antiquités de l'Égypte*, vol. II, Cairo, 1–13
    (available online at: https://ia600205.us.archive.org/30/items/
    annalesduservice02egypuoft/annalesduservice02egypuoft.pdf)

Darnell, J. C. (2014), 'The Stela of the Viceroy Usersatet (Boston MFA
    25.632), his Shrine at Qasr Ibrim, and the Festival of Nubian
    Tribute under Amenhotep II', *Égypte Nilotique et Méditerranéene*,
    vol. 7, 239–76 (available online at: http://www.enim-egyptologie.
    fr/?page=enim-7&n=11)

Davies, N. de Garis (1903–1908), *The Rock Tombs of El Amarna*, 6 volumes,
    Egypt Exploration Fund, London (available online at:
    https://archive.org/search.php?query=creator%3A%22Davies%2C+
    Norman+de+Garis%2C+1865-1941%22)

Davies, N. de Garis, and Gardiner, A. (1915), *The Tomb of Amenemhēt (No 82)*,
    Egypt Exploration Fund, London

Davies, V. (2004), 'Hatshepsut's use of Tuthmosis III in her Program of
    Legitimation', *JARCE*, vol. 41, 55–66

Davies, W. V. (2005), 'Egypt and Nubia. Conflict with the Kingdom of
    Kush', in Roehrig (ed.) (2005), 49–57

Davis, T. M. (1904) *The tomb of Thoutmôsis IV*, London (account by Carter, H.,
    and Newberry, P. E. within)

Davis, T. M. (1907), *The Tomb of Iouiya and Touyiou* [Yuya and Thuya],
    Constable, London (reprinted by Duckworth, 2000)

Davis, T. M. (1912), *The Tombs of Harmhabi and Touatânkhamanou*, Constable,
    London (reprinted by Duckworth, 2001)

Demas, M., and Agnew, N. (2012), *Valley of the Queens Assessment Report*. Vol.
    1: *Conservation and Management Planning*, Getty Conservation Institute,
    Los Angeles

Devecchi, E., and Miller, J. (2011), 'Hittite-Egyptian Synchronisms and their
    Consequences for Ancient Near Eastern Chronology', in Mynářová,
    J. (ed.) (2011), *Egypt and the Near East – the Crossroads*, Proceedings of an
    International Conference on the Relations of Egypt and the Near East
    in the Bronze Age, Prague, 1–3 September 2010, Charles University in
    Prague Czech Institute of Egyptology, Faculty of Arts

Dodson, A. (1990), 'Crown Prince Djhutmose [Thutmose] and the Royal
    Sons of the Eighteenth Dynasty', *JEA*, vol. 76, 87–96

Dodson, A. (2014), *Amarna Sunrise*, AUC, Cairo

Dodson, A. (2015), *Poisoned Legacy. The Fall of the Nineteenth Egyptian Dynasty*, AUC, Cairo

Dodson, A. (2016), *The Royal Tombs of Ancient Egypt*, Pen and Sword, Barnsley

Dodson, A. (2018), *Amarna Sunset*, AUC, Egypt

Dodson, A. (2019) (i), *Ramesses III. King of Egypt. His Life and Aftermath*, AUC, Cairo

Dodson, A. (2019) (ii), *Sethy I. King of Egypt. His Life and Aftermath*, AUC, Cairo

Dodson, A. (2019) (iii), *Afterglow of Empire. Egypt from the Fall of the New Kingdom to the Saite Renaissance*, AUC, Cairo

Dodson, A. (2020), *Nefertiti. Queen and Pharaoh of Egypt*, AUC, Cairo

Dodson, A. (2022), *Tutankhamun, King of Egypt: his life and afterlife*, AUC, Cairo

Dodson, A., and Hilton, D. (2010), *The Complete Royal Families of Ancient Egypt*, Thames & Hudson, London

Dorman, P. F. (1988), *The Monuments of Senenmut: Problems in Historical Methodology*, Kegan Paul International, London

Dorman, P. F. (2013), 'The Proscription of Hatshepsut', in Roehrig (ed.) (2005), 267–9

Eaton-Krauss, M. (2016), *The Unknown Tutankhamun*, Bloomsbury, London

Edwards, I. E. S. (1979), *Tutankhamun: His Tomb and its Treasures*, Gollancz, London (an adaptation of the Metropolitan Museum of Art edition, *The Treasures of Tutankhamun*, 1976)

Enmarch, R. (2013), 'Some Literary Aspects of the Kamose Inscriptions', *JEA*, vol. 99, 253–63

Epigraphic Survey (1980), *The Tomb of Kheruef. Theban Tomb 192*, Oriental Institute Publications no. 102, University of Chicago

Fairman, W. H. (1961), 'Once Again the So-Called Coffin of Akhenaten', *JEA*, vol. 41 (Dec. 1961), 25–40

Fairman, W. H. (1972), 'Tutankhamun and the end of the 18th Dynasty', *Antiquity* 46, Issue 181 (March 1972), 15–18

Faulkner, R. O. (1962), *A Concise Dictionary of Middle Egyptian*, Griffith Institute, Oxford

Fletcher, J. (2000), *Chronicle of a Pharaoh: The Intimate Life of Amenhotep III*, Oxford University Press, Oxford (also as Egypt's Sun King: Amenhotep III – An Intimate Chronicle of Ancient Egypt's Most Glorious Pharaoh, Duncan Baird Publishers)

Fletcher, J. (2004), *The Search for Nefertiti*, Hodder & Stoughton, London

Fletcher, J. (2015), *The Story of Egypt*, Hodder & Stoughton, London

Frankfort, H., and Pendlebury, J. D. S. (1933), *The City of Akhenaten*. Part II:

The North Suburb and the Desert Altars. The Excavations at Tell el Amarna during the seasons 1926–1932, Egypt Exploration Society, London

French, E. (2002), Mycenae. Agamemnon's Capital, Tempus, Stroud

Gabolde, L. (2014), 'Hatshepsut at Karnak: A Woman under God's Commands', in Galán et al. (2014), 33–48

Gabolde, M. (1998), D'Akenaton à Toutâhkhamon, Université-Lumierè 2, Lyons

Gabolde, M (2008), 'La redécouverte de la nécropole royale de Tell el-Amarna', Égypte, Afrique & Orient no. 52, 31–8

Gabolde, M. (2009), 'Under a Deep Blue Starry Sky', in Causing His Name to Live: Studies in Egyptian Epigraphy and History in Memory of William J. Murnane. Culture and History of the Ancient Near East, vol. 37, ed. Brand, P. and Cooper, L. (2009), E. J. Brill, Leiden, 109–20

Gabolde, M. (2013), 'L'ADN de la famille royale amarnienne et les sources égyptiennes De la complémentarité des méthodes et des résultats', Équipe Égypte Nilotique et Méditerranéenne, vol. 6, 177–203

Galán, J. M. (2014), 'The Inscribed Burial Chamber of Djehuty', in Galán et al. (2014), 247–72

Galán, J. M., Bryan, B. M., Dorman, P. (2014), 'Creativity and Innovation in the Reign of Hatshepsut', Papers from the Theban Workshop 2010. Studies in Ancient Oriental Civilization no. 69, University of Chicago, Chicago

Gardiner, A. (1905), The Inscription of Mes: A Contribution to Egyptian Juridical Procedure, Untersuchungen IV, Pt 3, Leipzig

Gardiner, A., (1916), 'The Defeat of the Hyksos by Kamŏse: The Carnarvon Tablet, No. I', JEA, vol. 3, No. 2/3 (Apr.–Jul. 1916), 95–110

Gardiner, A. (1938) (i), 'A Later Allusion to Akhenaten', JEA, vol. 24, 124

Gardiner, A. (1938) (ii), 'The Idiom ìt ìn', JEA, vol. 24, 124–5

Gardiner, A. (1947), Ancient Egyptian Onomastica, Oxford University Press, Oxford

Gardiner, A. (1953), 'The Coronation of King Haremhab', JEA, vol. 39, 13–31

Gardiner, A. (1957), Egyptian Grammar, 3rd edition, Griffith Institute, Ashmolean Museum, Oxford

Gautschy, R. (2014), 'A Reassessment of the Absolute Chronology of the Egyptian New Kingdom and its 'Brotherly' Countries', Ägypten und Levante, 24, 141–58

Gilmore, G., and Ray, J. (2006), 'A Fixed Point in Coptic Chronology: The Solar Eclipse of 10 March, 601', Zeitschrift für Papyrologie und Epigraphik, Bd 158, 190–2

# Further Reading

Grajetzi, W. (2005), 'The Coffin of the "King's Daughter" Neferuptah and the sarcophagus of the "Great King's Wife" Hatshepsut', *Goettinger Miszellen* 205 (2005), 55–65

Griffith, F. L. (1898), *Hieratic Papyri from Kahun and Gorub*, Bernard Quaritch, London

Gunn, B. (1923), 'Notes on the Aten and His Names', *JEA*, vol. 9, no. 3/4 (Oct. 1923), 168–76

Güterbock, H. G. (1956), 'The Deeds of Shuppiluliuma as Told by His Son, Mursili II (Continued)', *Journal of Cuneiform Studies*, 1956, vol. 10, no. 3 (1956), pp. 75–98, published by University of Chicago Press on behalf of the American Schools of Oriental Studies

Gutgesell, M. (1998), 'The Military' in Schulz and Seidel (1998), 365–9

Habachi, L. (1957), 'Two Graffiti at Sehēl from the Reign of Queen Hatshepsut', *Journal of Near Eastern Studies*, 16 (April), 88–104

Habicht, M. (2019), *Smenkhkare: Phantom-Queen/King of Akhet-Aton and the quest for the hitherto unknown chambers in the tomb of Tutankhamun (KV 62)*, epubli GmbH, Berlin

Habicht, M. (ed.) (2020), 'Facial reconstruction of the mummy Cairo CG 61076 from the Royal Mummies Cachette DB320 [TT320]. A princess from the late 18th Dynasty?', *Under the Seal of the Necropolis*, vol. 6, 11–24

Habicht, M., Henneberg, M., Öhrström, L. M., and Staub, K. (2015), 'Brief Communication: Body Height of Mummified Pharaohs Supports Historical Suggestions of Sibling Marriages', *American Journal of Physical Anthropology*, April 2015

Harris, J. E., Wente, E. F., Cox, C. F., El Nawaway, I., Kowalski, C. J., Storey, A. T., Russell, W. R., Ponitz, P. V., and Walker, G. F., (1979), 'The Identification of the "Elder Lady" in the Tomb of Amenhotep II as Queen Tiye', *Delaware Medical Journal*, 51, no. 2, 89–93 (and in *Science*, 1978, vol. 200, no. 4346)

Harvey, S. (1998), *The Cults of King Ahmose at Abydos*, Dissertation, University of Pennsylvania (available online at: https://repository.upenn.edu/dissertations/AAI9829912/)

Harvey, S. (2007), 'King Heqatawy: Notes on a Forgotten 18th Dynasty Royal Name', in Hawass, Z., and Richards, J. (2007), *The Archaeology and Art of Ancient Egypt: Essays in Honor of David B. O'Connor*, Supreme Council of Antiquities Press, Cairo, 343–56

Hassan, S. (1949), *The Sphinx. Its History in the Light of Recent Excavations*, Government Press, Cairo

Hawass, Z. et al. (2010), 'Ancestry and Pathology in King Tutankhamun's Family', *Journal of the American Medical Association*, vol. 303, no. 7, February 2010 (available online: http://www.leben-in-luxor.de/docs/Hawass_Ancestry_and_Pathology_joc05008_638_647.pdf)

Hayes, W. C. (1951), 'Inscriptions from the Palace of Amenhotep III', *JNES*, Oct. 1951, vol. 10, no. 4, 231–42

Hayes, W. C. (1960), 'A Selection of Tuthmoside Ostraca from Dēr el-Baḥri', *JEA*, 46, 29–52

Hayes, W. C. (1962), *Egypt: Internal Affairs from Tuthmosis I to the Death of Amenophis III,* Cambridge Ancient History, vol. II, ch. IX, pt 1, Cambridge University Press, Cambridge

Helck, W. (1955–58), *Urkunden der 18. Dynastie*, vols 17–22, Akademie-Verlag, Berlin

Hoffmeier, J. (1976), 'Observations on the Evolving Chariot Wheel in the 18th Dynasty', *JARCE*, vol. 13, 43–5

Höflmayer, F. (2016), 'Radiocarbon Dating and Egyptian Chronology – From the "Curve of Knowns" to Bayesian Modeling', *Oxford Handbooks Online*, Oxford. Available online at: https://www.oxfordhandbooks.com/view/10.1093/oxfordhb/9780199935413.001.0001/oxfordhb-9780199935413-e-64#oxfordhb-9780199935413-e-64-bibItem-54

Hornung, E. (1997), 'The Pharaoh' in Sergio Donadoni, *The Egyptians*, University of Chicago Press, Chicago, 1997, 240–76.

Hornung, E., Krauss, R., and Warburton, D., *Ancient Egyptian Chronology: 83*, Handbook of Oriental Studies: Section 1, the Near & Middle East, E. J. Brill, Leiden

Huber, P.J. (2001), 'The Solar Omen of Muršili II', *Journal of the American Oriental Society*, Oct.–Dec. 2001, vol. 121, no. 4, 640–4

Huber, T. (2018), 'KV62 The North Wall Part 1: The New Interpretation', *Nile Magazine* no. 14, 10ff, June–July 2018

Ikram, S., and Dodson, A. (1998), *The Mummy in Ancient Egypt. Equipping the Dead for Eternity*, Thames & Hudson, London

Johnson, W. R. (2010), 'Warrior Tut', *Archaeology*, March/April 2010, vol. 63, no. 2, 26–28

Keller, C. A. (2005), 'The Statuary of Senenmut', in Roehrig (ed.) (2005), 112–17

Kemp, B. (1991), *Ancient Egypt. Anatomy of a Civilization*, Routledge, London

Kemp, B. (2012), *The city of Akhenaten and Nefertiti: Amarna and its people*, Thames & Hudson, London

Kemp, B. (2016), 'Tell el-Amarna', *JEA*, vol. 102, issue 2, 1–11

Kemp, B. (2017), 'Tell el-Amarna', *JEA*, vol. 103, issue 2, 137–51

Kemp, B., Stevens, A., Dabbs, G. R., and Zabecki, M. (2013), 'Life, death and beyond in Akhenaten's Egypt: Excavating the South Tombs Cemetery at Amarna', *Antiquity*, vol. 87, issue 335, 64–78

Kemp, B., and Zink, A. (2012), 'Life in Ancient Egypt. Akhenaten, the Amarna Period, and Tutankhamun' in *RCC Perspectives*, No. 3, *Sickness, Hunger, War, and Religion: Multidisciplinary Perspectives*, Rachel Carson Center, 9–24

Koltsida, A. (2007), 'A Dark Spot in Ancient Egyptian Architecture: the Temple of Malkata', *JARCE*, vol. 43, 43–57

Kozloff, A. P. (2011), *Amenhotep III*, Cambridge University Press, Cambridge

Kozloff, A., and Bryan, B. (1992), *Royal and Divine Statuary in Egypt's Dazzling Sun: Amenhotep III and his World*, Cleveland Museum of Art, Cleveland

Krauss, R. (1986), 'Kiya – ursprüngliche Besitzerin der Kanopen aus KV55', in *Mitteilungen des Deutschen Archäologischen Instituts, Kairo*, Philip von Zabern, Mainz

Laboury, D. (2006), 'Royal Portrait and Ideology: Evolution and Signification of the Statuary of Thutmose III', in Cline and O'Connor (eds) (2006), 260–91

Laboury, D. (2011), 'Amarna Art', in Cooney, K., and Wendrich, W. (eds), *UCLA Encyclopedia of Egyptology*, Los Angeles (http://digital2.library.ucla.edu/viewItem.do?ark=21198/zz0026vj6m)

Łajtar, A. (2019), 'The Theban Region under the Roman Empire', in Riggs, C. (ed.) (2019), *The Oxford Handbook of Roman Egypt*, Oxford University Press, Oxford, 177–88

Lichtheim, M. (1976), *Ancient Egyptian Literature*. Volume II: *The New Kingdom*, University of California Press

Lilyquist, C. (2005), 'Egypt and the Near East. Evidence of Contact in the Material Record', in Roehrig (ed.) (2005), 60–7

Loeben, C. (1994), 'No evidence of Co-regency: Two Erased Inscriptions from Tutankhamun's Tomb', in Lacovara, P. (ed.) *Amarna Letters*, San Francisco, vol. 3, 105–9

Long, R. D. (1974), 'A Re-Examination of the Sothic Chronology of Egypt', *Orientalia* (Nova Series), vol. 34, 261–74

Luban, M. (1999), 'Do we have the Mummy of Nefertiti?', published online at: http://www.oocities.org/scribelist/do_we_have_.htm

Manley, B. (2012), *Egyptian Hieroglyphs for Complete Beginners*, Thames & Hudson, London

Manniche, L. (2010), *The Akhenaten Colossi of Karnak*, AUC, Cairo

Martin, G. T. (1991), *The Hidden Tombs of Memphis*, Thames & Hudson, London

Martin, G. T. (2009) 'The Co-regency Stela University College London 410', in *Sitting beside Lepsius: Studies in Honour of Jaromir Malek at the Grinopth Institute*, ed. D. Magee, J. Bourriau, and S. Quirke, 343–359, Peters, Leuven

Maspero, G. (1907), 'Notes on Iouiya [Yuya] and Touiyou [Thuya]' in Davis (1907)

Maspero, G. (1912) (i), 'Note on the Life and Reign of Touatânkhamanou [Tutankhamun]' in Davis (1912)

Maspero, G. (1912) (ii), 'Inscriptions and Decoration of the Tomb of Harmhabi [Horemheb]', in Davis (1912)

Matić, U. (2018), 'Eaton-Krauss, Marianne: The Unknown Tutankhamun 2016', *Orientalistische Literaturzeitung*, June 2018

Matić, U. (2019), *Body and Frames of War in New Kingdom Egypt: Violent Treatment of Enemies and Prisoners*, Harrassowitz Verlag, Wiesbaden

McMurray, W. (2004), *Towards an Absolute Chronology for Ancient Egypt*, published online at: http://www.egyptologyforum.org/EMP/ACAE1.pdf

Mond, R., and Myers, O. H. (1940), *Temples of Armant: A Preliminary Survey*, 43rd Memoir of the Egypt Exploration Society, Egypt Exploration Society, London

Montserrat, D. (2002), *Akhenaten: History, Fantasy and Ancient Egypt*, Routledge, London

Moran, W. L. (1992), *The Amarna Letters*, Johns Hopkins University Press, Baltimore

Moseley, S. (2009), *Amarna. The Missing Evidence*, Peach Pixel, Calshot

Murnane, W. J. (1977), *Ancient Egyptian Co-regencies*, Studies in Ancient Oriental Civilization no. 40, Oriental Institute, Chicago

Murnane, W. J. (1989), 'Rhetorical History? The Beginning of Thutmose III's First Campaign in Western Asia', *JARCE*, vol. 26, 183–9

Murnane, W. J. (1990), *The Road to Kadesh; A Historical Interpretation of the Battle*

*Reliefs of King Sety* [sic] *I at Karnak*, 2nd edition, Studies in Ancient Oriental Civilization no. 42, Oriental Institute, Chicago

Murnane, W. J. (1995), *Texts from the Amarna Period in Egypt*, Society of Biblical Literature Writings from the Ancient World Series, vol. 5, Scholars Press, Atlanta

Murnane, W. J., and Van Siclen, C. C. (2011), *The Boundary Stelae of Akhenaten*, Routledge, Abingdon

Naville, E. (1894–1908), *The Temple of Deir el-Bahari*, Egypt Exploration Fund, London (particularly vol. vi)

Naville, E. (1908), 'The Funeral Papyrus of Iouiya [Yuya]', included in a 2000 edition by Duckworth of Davis (1907)

Newberry, P. E. (1907), 'Description of the Objects found in the Tomb', in Davis (1907)

Newberry, P. E. (1928), 'Akhenaten's Eldest Son-In-Law "Ankheperure"', *JEA*, vol. 14, 3–9

Newberry, P. E. (1932), 'King Ay, the Successor of Tutankhamun', *JEA*, vol. 18 no. 1/2 (May 1932), 50–2

O'Connor, D., and Cline, E. H. (2001), *Amenhotep III: Perspectives on his Reign*, University of Michigan Press, Ann Arbor

Panagiotopoulos, D. (2006), 'Foreigners in Egypt in the Time of Hatshepsut and Thutmose III', in Cline and O'Connor (eds) (2006), 370–412

Pasquali, S. (2011), 'A sun-shade temple of Princess Ankhesenpaaten in Memphis?', *JEA*, vol. 11, 216–22

Peet, T. E. (1915), 'The Great Tomb Robberies of the Ramesside Age. Papyri Mayer A and B. I. Papyrus Mayer A', *JEA*, June 1915, vol. 2, no. 3, 173–7

Petrie, W. M. Flinders (1894), *Tell el Amarna*, Methuen, London

Petrie, W. M. Flinders (1917), *Scarabs and Cylinders with Names*, London School of Archaeology in Egypt, University College, London

Pfälzner, P. (2016), 'The Elephants of the Orontes', in *Syria. Archéologie, Art et Histoire* IV, 159–82

Phillips, A. K. (1977), 'Horemheb, Founder of the XIXth Dynasty?' *Orientalia* Nova Series, vol. 46, no. 1 (1977), 116–21

Plumley, J. Martin (1964), 'Qasr-Ibrim 1963–1964', *JEA*, vol. 50 (Dec. 1964), 3–5

Porter, B., and Moss, R. L. B. (1960) (2nd edition), *Topical Bibliography of*

*Ancient Egyptian Hieroglyphic Texts, Reliefs and Paintings*, Vol. I, *The Theban Necropolis, Part 1. Private Tombs*, Clarendon Press, Oxford

Porter, B., and Moss, R. L. B. (1964) (2nd edition), *Topical Bibliography of Ancient Egyptian Hieroglyphic Texts, Reliefs and Paintings*, Vol. I, *The Theban Necropolis, Part 2. Royal Tombs and Smaller Cemeteries*, Clarendon Press, Oxford

Quirke, S., and Spencer, J. (1992) (eds), *The British Museum Book of Ancient Egypt*, Thames & Hudson, New York

Redford, D. (1987), *Akhenaten: The Heretic King*, Princeton University Press, Princeton

Redford, D. (1992), *Egypt, Canaan, and Israel in Ancient Times*, Princeton University Press, Princeton

Redford, D. (1997), 'Textual Sources for the Hyksos Period,' in E. D. Oren, (ed.) (1997), *The Hyksos: New Historical and Archaeological Perspectives*, Philadelphia, 1–44

Reeve, J., and Adams, M. (1993), *The Spitalfields Project*, Vol. 1: *The Archaeology across the Styx*, Council for British Archaeology, York

Reeves, N. (1982), 'Tuthmosis IV as "Great-Grandfather" of Tutankhamun', *Göttinger Miszellen*, vol. 44, 49–55

Reeves, N. (1988), 'New Light on Kiya from Texts in the British Museum', *JEA*, vol. 74.1

Reeves, N. (1990), *The Complete Tutankhamun*, Thames & Hudson, London

Reeves, N. (2001), *Akhenaten*, Thames & Hudson, London

Reeves, N. (2015), 'The Burial of Nefertiti', *Amarna Royal Tombs Project. Valley of the Kings*. Occasional Paper No. 1. University of Arizona Egypt Expedition, Tucson

Reeves, N. (2017), 'The Coffin of Ramesses II', in Amenta, A., and Guichard, H. (2017), Proceedings First Vatican Coffin Conference 19–22 June 2013, vol. 2, Edizioni Musei Vaticani, Vatican City, 425–38

Reeves, N., and Wilkinson, R. (1996), *The Complete Valley of the Kings*, Thames & Hudson, London

Ridley, Ronald R. (2019), *Akhenaten: a Historian's View*, AUC, Cairo

Ritner, R. K. (2019), 'Astronomical Instrument of Tutankhamun', in *Highlights of the Collections of the Oriental Institute Museum*, ed. Evans, J. M., Green, J., and Teeter, E., 97, Oriental Institute Handbooks and Guides 2019. Chicago: Oriental Institute of the University of Chicago

Ritner, R. K., and Moeller, N. (2014), 'The Ahmose "Tempest Stela",

Thera and Comparative Chronology', *Journal of Near Eastern Studies*, vol. 73, no. 1

Roehrig, C. H., ed. (2005), *Hatshepsut. From Queen to Pharaoh*, MM of Art Series, Yale University Press, New York (available as a free pdf from the Museum at: https://www.metmuseum.org/art/metpublications/Hatshepsut_From_Queen_to_Pharaoh)

Rose, D. (2004), 'Where's Nefertiti?', published online at: https://archive.archaeology.org/online/reviews/nefertiti/

Roth, A. M. (2005), 'Models of Authority. Hatshepsut's Predecessors in Power', in Roehrig (ed.) (2005), 9–14

Roth, A. M., and Roehrig, C. H. (2002), 'Magical Bricks and the Bricks of Earth', *JEA*, vol. 88 (2002), 121–39

Rutherford, I. C. (2019), 'Travel and Pilgrimage', in Riggs, C. (ed.) (2019), *The Oxford Handbook of Roman Egypt*, Oxford University Press, Oxford, 701–16

Samson, J. (1973), 'Royal Inscriptions from Amarna', *Chronique d'Égypte*, vol. xlviii, 96, 243–50

Samson, J. (1977), 'Nefertiti's Regality', *JEA*, vol. 63, 88–97

Samson, J. (1979), 'Akhenaten's Successor', *Göttinger Miszellen*, vol. 32, 53–58

Samson, J. (1982), 'The History of the Mystery of Akhenaten's Successor', in Leclant, J. (ed.) (1982), *L'Egypte en 1979*, vol. 2, Centre national de la recherche scientifique, Paris, 291–7

Sandman, M. (1938), *Texts from the Time of Akhenaten*, Fondation Égyptologique Reine Élisabeth, Brussels

Sankiewicz, M. (2008), 'Cryptogram Uraeus Frieze in the Hatshepsut Temple at Deir el-Bahari', Études et Travaux XXII, Centre d'Archéologie Méditerranéenne de l'Académie Polonaise des Sciences

Schlick-Holte, B., Werthmann, R., and Loeben, C. E. (2011), 'An Outstanding Glass Statuette owned by Pharaoh Amenhotep II and Other Early Egyptian Glass Inscribed with Royal Names', *Journal of Glass Studies*, vol. 53, 11–44

Schofield, L. (2007), *The Mycenaeans*, British Museum Press, London

Schulz, R., and Seidel, M. (1998), *Egypt. The World of the Pharaohs*, Könemann, Cologne

Schulz, R., and Sourouzian, H. (1998), 'The Temples – Royal Gods and Divine Kings', in Schulz, R., and Seidel (1998), 153–215

Sear, D. R. (2002), *Roman Coins and Their Values.* Volume II. *The Accession of Nerva to the overthrow of the Severan Dynasty*, Spink, London

Sethe, K. (1906–9), *Urkunden der 18. Dynastie* (URK), Hinrichs, Leipzig

Shaw, I. (ed.) (2002), *The Oxford History of Ancient Egypt*, Oxford University Press, Oxford

Shirley, J. J. (2014), 'The Power of the Elite: The Officials of Hatshepsut's Regency and Co-regency', in Galán et al. (2014), 173–246

Smith, G. Elliot (1912), *The Royal Mummies*, Catalogue Général des Antiquités Égyptiennes du Musée de Caire (reprinted by Duckworth, London, 2000)

Snape, S. (2014), *The Complete Cities of Ancient Egypt*, Thames & Hudson, London

Stevens, A. (2016), 'Tell el-Amarna', in Wendrich, W. (ed.), *UCLA Encyclopedia of Egyptology*, Los Angeles (http://digital2.library.ucla.edu/viewItem.do?ark=21198/zz002k6x4x)

Stevens, A. (ed.) (2020), *Amarna. A Guide to the Ancient City of Akhetaten*, AUC, Cairo

Summerson, J. (1993) *Architecture in Britain 1530–1830*, 9th edition, Yale University Press, New Haven

Taylor, J. H. (2001), *Death and Burial in Ancient Egypt*, British Museum Press, London

Teeter, E., and Larson, J. A. (eds), *Gold of Praise: Studies on Ancient Egypt in Honor of Edward F. Wente*, Studies in Ancient Oriental Civilization no. 58, Oriental Institute, Chicago

Thompson, K. (2006), 'A Shattered Granodiorite Dyad of Akhenaten and Nefertiti from Tell El-Amarna', *JEA*, vol. 92, 141–51

Tomashevska, M. (2019), *Sacred Floral Garlands and Collars from the New Kingdom Period and Early Third Intermediate Period in Ancient Egypt 1550 BC–943 BC*, Master Thesis, Universiteit Leiden

Troy, L. (1986), *Patterns of Queenship in Ancient Egyptian Myth and History*, Uppsala Studies in Ancient Mediterranean and Near Eastern Civilizations no. 14, Uppsala University, Uppsala

Tyldesley, J. (1998) (i), *Hatchepsut. The Female Pharaoh*, Penguin, London

Tyldesley, J. (1998) (ii), *Nefertiti. Egypt's Sun Queen*, Viking, London

Tyldesley, J. (2006), *The Complete Queens of Egypt*, Thames & Hudson, London

Tyson Smith, S. (1992), 'Intact Tombs of the Seventeenth and Eighteenth Dynasties from Thebes and the New Kingdom Burial System',

*Mitteilungen des Deutschen Archäologischen Instituts*, vol. 48, 193–231, Cairo (available at: https://www.academia.edu/556964/Intact_Theban_tombs_and_the_New_Kingdom_burial_assemblage)

Van den Boorn, G. P. F. (1988), *The Duties of the Vizier: Civil Administration in the Early New Kingdom*, Routledge, London

Van der Perre, A. (2014), 'The Year 16 graffito of Akhenaten in Dayr Abū Ḥinnis. A Contribution to the Study of the Later Years of Nefertiti', *JEH*, vol. 7 (1), 73

Van Dijk, J. (1993), *The New Kingdom Necropolis of Memphis: Historical and Iconographical Studies*, PhD Thesis, University of Groningen, Groningen, in particular pp. 10–64

Van Dijk, J. (1996), 'Horemheb and the Struggle for the Throne of Tutankhamun', *Bulletin of the Australian Centre for Egyptology*, 7, 29–42

Van Dijk, J. (2003), 'The Amarna Period and the Later New Kingdom', in Shaw, I. (ed.) (2003) 265–307

Van Dijk, J. (2008), 'New Evidence on the Length of the Reign of Horemheb', *JARC*, vol. 44, 193–200

Van Dijk, J. (2009), 'The Death of Meketaten', in Brand, P., and Steele, L. (eds) (2009), *Causing His Name to Live: Studies in Egyptian Epigraphy and History in Memory of William J. Murnane*, E. J. Brill, Leiden

Van Gils, P. (undated), 'The Victory Stela of Amenhotep III. History or Symbolism?' published online at: https://www.academia.edu/10451192/The_victory_stela_of_Amenhotep_III_history_or_symbolism

Vandersleyen, C. (1993), 'Les scènes de lamentation des chambre *alpha* et *gamma* dans la tombe d'Akhenaton', *Revue d'égyptologie*, vol. 44, 192–4

Vandier, J., and Jourdain, G. (1939), *Deux tombes de Deir el-Médineh*, L'Institut Français d'Archaéologie Orientale, Cairo

Vivian Davies, W. (2010), 'Egypt and Nubia. Conflict with the Kingdom of Kush', in Roehrig (ed.) (2010), 49–56

Vogelsang-Eastwood, G. (1999), *Tutankhamun's Wardrobe: Garments from the tomb of Tutankhamun*, Van Doorn & Co., Rotterdam

Wahlberg, E-L. (2012), *The Wine Jars Speak. A Text Study*, MA Thesis, Uppsala University

Wardle, K. A., and Wardle, D. (2000), *The Mycenaean World*, Bristol Classical Press, London

Weigall, A. (1922, new and revised edition), *The Life and Times of Akhnaton, Pharaoh of Egypt*, Thornton Butterworth, London

Wente, E. F. (1995), 'Who Was Who Among The Royal Mummies?',
    *The Oriental Institute*, no. 144 (April 1995), Oriental Institute of the
    University of Chicago
Whittemore, T. (1926), 'The Excavations at Tell El'Amarnah, Season
    1924–5', *JEA* vol. 12, no. ½, 3–12
Wilkinson, R. H. (1992), *Reading Egyptian Art. A Hieroglyphic Guide to Ancient
    Egyptian Painting and Sculpture*, Thames and Hudson, London
Wilkinson, T. (2010), *The Rise and Fall of Ancient Egypt*, Bloomsbury, London
Wood, G. (2020), *The Life and Times of Butehamun: Tomb Raider for the High
    Priest of Amun*, Institute of Archaeology and History, Uppsala
    University (available online at: http://uu.diva-portal.org/smash/get/
    diva2:1464825/FULLTEXT01.pdf)
Woodward, S. (1996), 'Genealogy of New Kingdom Pharaohs and
    Queens', *Archaeology* Sept./Oct. 1996, vol. 5, no. 5, 45–7
Woolley, C. L. (1922), 'Excavations at Tell El-Amarna', *JEA*, vol. 8, no. ½
    (April 1922), 48–82
Yeivin, S. (1967), 'Amenophis II's Asiatic Campaigns', *JARCE, vol.* vi,
    119–128

The author's Youtube Channel 'Classical and Ancient Civilization'
includes several talks and lectures directly linked to the content of this
book: https://www.youtube.com/c/ClassicalandAncientCivilization

# ACKNOWLEDGEMENTS

This book was written during the Covid era of 2020–21. I was and will forever remain grateful for the opportunity to write this book which afforded me the chance to escape those dark days into the piercing sunlight of Egypt's 18th Dynasty. I should like to thank first Richard Beswick at Little, Brown who was interested in publishing this project from the start and provided advice and guidance along the way. I need also to thank at Little, Brown the following who played such an important part in seeing the book through production: Zoe Gullen and Marie Hrynczak, and Nico Taylor who used my photographs and concept for the cover and made it into the stunning end result. The Egyptologist Professor Joann Fletcher of the Department of Archaeology at the University of York was an ever generous, helpful and friendly ear, often assisting with a range of queries and along with her partner Dr Stephen Buckley offering advice. So, too, was Ronald Ridley, Professor Emeritus at the School of Historical Studies in the University of Melbourne. Catriona Wilson, Head of the Petrie Egyptian and Sudanese Archaeology Collection at the Petrie Museum, and her assistant Dr Alice Williams very kindly looked out such photographs of the Smenkhkare rings and guided me to other references. Dr Bill Manley of Glasgow University stepped in to help with an obscure passage of Senenmut's to provide a translation. Peter Clayton, quondam archaeological editor at Thames & Hudson and managing editor for the British Museum, was kind enough to cast an eye over an early version of the text and make some useful suggestions about tweaks. The historians Tom Holland and Dominic Sandbrook generously read an early draft of the text and made some invaluable recommendations about making it more suitable for a wider audience. The archaeologist Helen Geake during several conversations about this book made some highly perceptive observations which have found their way into the text. Kym Ramadge of KRD Graphic Design, Melbourne, cast a critical eye, making invaluable comments, and the same goes for Rachel Johnstone-Burt. I would like to make a special mention of Norah Cooper, formerly of the Western Australian Museum, a very good friend and very knowledgeable Egypt enthusiast whose journeys to the Nile Valley made her an editor *sans pareille* – her careful reading, rereading and note-taking of the text as it went through various versions picked up on numerous places where the text needed correcting or clarifying. I'm grateful to Dr Jasmine Day and others of the Ancient Egyptian Society of Western Australia (Perth) who arranged for me to lecture to the society to try out some of my ideas. The members, especially Chris Dickinson, contributed some stimulating questions that helped develop the text. My wife Rosemary is owed a debt of gratitude for accompanying me to Egypt on several occasions. She was also willing to tolerate the piles of volumes needed seven days a week for months to write this book and to listen to my endless ruminations about the acts of long-dead kings and the meaning of cryptic Egyptian words. I had the privilege of being taught Egyptology as part of my degree at Durham by the late Professor John Harris. His enthusiasm stayed with me and played a large part in my sustained interest in the subject, leading to this book. I hope he would have enjoyed it. There are countless books about Egypt available, but few modern works can match those of Aidan Dodson, Honorary Professor of Egyptology at the University of Bristol, for his assiduous attention to detail and in particular his meticulous referencing, citing and illustrating of evidence as well as consideration of divergent views. He was also kind enough to answer some of my questions and provide two of the colour plates. There are also the many institutions which in recent years have placed so many rare and valuable Egyptian excavation reports and other studies from the late 1800s and early 1900s online. Numerous Egyptologists around the world have also generously uploaded important papers and books for anyone to read. Time and time again it proved possible to explore these sources easily, more essential in 2020–21 than ever before, opening up this marvellous subject in a way never before possible.

G. de la B.

# LIST OF ILLUSTRATIONS

Line Drawings

*All Public Domain*

Ahmes pregnant with Hatshepsut p. 106. Source: Naville (1894–1908) vol. II, pl. xlix.

Thutmose IV in a chariot p. 182. Source: Carter and Newberry in Davis (1904), fig. ix.

Yuya titles p. 205. Source: Davis (1907), 7

Sitamun and Tiye p. 212. Source: Davis (1907), 43

Akhenaten and Nefertiti in the tomb of Ramose p. 242. Source: Aldred (1991), 91

Akhenaten's Boundary Stela S, p. 247. Source: Davies (1903–1908)

Akhenaten, Nefertiti and three eldest daughters in the tomb of Ipy, p. 262. Source: Bouriant (1903), pl. xl

Meketaten death statue p. 283. Source: Bouriant (1903), pl. x

Meketaten's death mourned by her parents p. 284. Source: Bouriant (1903), pl. vii

Deaths of princesses p. 285. Source: Bouriant (1903), pl. vi

Ay and Tutankhamun p. 350. Source: Davis (1912), 128

Ay as a warrior king p. 353. Source: Davis (1912), 127

*Photographs are by the author unless otherwise stated*

## SECTION ONE

Billon tetradrachm of the Roman emperor Antoninus Pius (AD 138–161) struck at Alexandria in AD 142/3. The coin shows the Egyptian Benu bird, a solar avian deity who became synonymous with Re and renewal, on the reverse and a Greek legend giving the regnal year and the word for an 'era'. A similar coin was issued in 139. The two issues commemorated the four-year period when the Egyptian civil and solar calendars coincided, which had not happened since 1321 BC (fully explained in Chapter 1). This cycle makes it possible to calculate approximate Egyptian absolute dates.

Stela of Kamose. One of two stelae erected by Kamose, the last king of the 17th Dynasty. This one records his campaign against the Hyksos and includes a reference to capturing a Hyksos messenger en route to Kush. The text is typically bombastic, but it is clear Kamose had not succeeded in ridding Egypt of the Hyksos. That would be left to Ahmose I. Found at Karnak. c. 1550 BC, and now at Luxor Museum. Photo: Kurohito

Ahmose I from a limestone shabti probably from his unlocated tomb at Thebes, and the oldest shabti known. It recalls portrait styles of the Middle Kingdom. c. 1550–1525 BC.

Ahmose I offers wine to the falcon-headed war god Montu on a lintel from the temple to the god at Armant. The homage was appropriate given Ahmose's triumph in expelling the Hyksos from Egypt and reunifying the nation. He wears here the Red Crown of Lower Egypt. A mirror panel to the left shows him wearing the White Crown of Upper Egypt. c. 1550 –1525 BC.

Ahmes-Ibana in his tomb at El Kab. The four columns of text at the right represent the start of his career, told to the onlooker in the first person, a crucial source for major military events at the start of the 18th Dynasty. In the first of these four columns the opening group of signs down to the horizontal crescent give his final rank as 'commander of the troop of rowers', the basis of sometimes today calling him an admiral. The crescent and the two signs beneath represent his name, and below those 'son of Ibana'. Photo: Olaf Tausch

Stela of the tomb worker Qen. Qen, his wife Nefertari and their two sons are shown worshipping Amenhotep I and his mother, the queen Ahmose-Nefertari. Probably 19th Dynasty in date, by which time they were deified and treated as divine guardians of the necropolis and the tomb workers. From Qen's tomb in Deir el-Medina (TT4). Photo: MM, New York (Public Domain)

Thutmose I. One of a pair of obelisks erected by the king at Karnak in front of the Fourth Pylon. Approximately 80 ft (24 m) high. c.1504–1492 BC.

Thutmose II. The king's mummified head as photographed after discovery in the 1881 cache of royal mummies in tomb TT320. c.1492–1479 BC.

Thutmose I as depicted by Hatshepsut on the north wall of his chapel at her memorial-mortuary temple at Deir el-Bahari. Thutmose is 'making the presentation of divine offerings'. He was labelled 'the Perfect Goddess' and 'Lord of the Two Lands' in an example of Hatshshepsut's retrospective allocation of female and male titles to her father to validate her own composite notion of male-female kingship. This painting by Howard Carter. Public Domain.

Hatshepsut's birth name as displayed on her sole upstanding obelisk at Karnak. The upper three signs represent Amun, with whom she was so keen to associate herself. In full, the name reads Hatshepsut-knenemet-Amun, 'the foremost among noblewomen, joined with Amun'. c.1464 BC.

The relief carving at the top of one of Hatshepsut's obelisks at Karnak. This one has fallen and is displayed on its side (the image has been rotated) by the Sacred Lake. Hatshepsut as king is endorsed here by Amun, an essential part of her entitlement to rule in her own right. The figure of Amun and his name were chiselled out during Akhenaten's reign by supporters before the obelisk fell. In the 19th Dynasty both were restored. The shallow depression around the god and to the upper left his name created for the recurving are easy to spot. c. 1464 BC.

Hatshepsut's temple at Deir el-Bahari. Possibly begun by Thutmose II but completed by Hatshepsut as her mortuary and memorial temple where she showcased her expedition to Punt and her identity as a king of Egypt. Much was later desecrated or usurped by Thutmose III. The building has been very considerably restored in recent decades by Polish Egyptologists. c. 1473–1458 BC.

Hatshepsut's temple at Deir el-Bahari (left), showing its terraces facing east towards Karnak. To the right is the temple of Mentuhotep II of the 11th Dynasty. In between and set slightly back is the temple of Hatshepsut's nephew and joint ruler Thutmose III whose reign continued for over thirty years after her death.

Senenmut, principal steward of Hatshepsut, with Neferure, daughter of Thutmose II and Hatshepsut. Senenmut's proximity to Hatshepsut is symbolized in this original piece, probably designed personally by Senenmut, one of a number of known examples. Found at Karnak and now in the British Museum. Height: 72.5 cm. Photo: Captmondo

Myrrh trees in Punt. Some were brought back by Hatshepsut's expedition which took place in her 9th regnal year (1471 BC). The trip was the central event in her reign as king and used to display her wealth and success. From her mortuary temple at Deir el-Bahari. c. 1471–1458 BC. Photo: Hans Bernard

Hatshepsut's barque 'way-station' shrine built originally by her for the Opet Festival, later usurped by Ramesses II and placed in his court at the Temple of Luxor. Its identification as hers depends on the failure by Ramesses II's masons to delete the feminized terminology in the inscriptions. c.1473–1458 and 1279–1213 BC.

Cartouches of Thutmose III (centre) and Thutmose IV (left and upper right) on the Lateran obelisk, now in Rome (outside San Giovanni in Laterano). Originally from Karnak where it was the tallest ever erected and stood alone on the temple's central axis on the eastern side. Not completed during Thutmose III's reign, it lay on the site for thirty years until Thutmose IV ordered its completion and erection. It was removed to Rome by Constantius II in AD 357 after originally having been designated for Constantinople by his father. Originally 105 ft (32 m) high when completed. c.1400–1390 BC.

Thutmose III and Horus. Painted relief in the temple at Deir el-Bahari. The king is accompanied by several stock titles such as 'King of Upper and Lower Egypt', the 'Good God' and 'Lord of the Two Lands'. The state of this relief, protected within the temple, is a reminder of the intensely colourful nature of all Egyptian temple reliefs in their original state. c.1450–1425 BC.

Thutmose III's head from his mummy, found in the TT320 cache of royal mummies in 1881. c.1425 BC.

Thutmose III, wearing the Red Crown of Lower Egypt, smites his enemies. This warrior king used Karnak as the setting for his so-called Annals that detailed his numerous military and tribute-gathering campaigns. This relief on the Seventh Pylon is typical in depicting the Asiatic enemies as diminutive and generic, reduced to a collective mass. The relief itemizes, among other conquests, the 119 Palestinian cities seized in his earliest campaigns. c.1435–1425 BC.

Thutmose leads three of his senior wives (Merytre, Sitiah and Nebtu) and his deceased daughter Nefertari following on behind. Above the king rides on a boat with his mother Iset (Isis). She had already been awarded the title 'King's Mother' and in this scene she seems to have become conflated with the goddess Isis, being additionally shown on the far right as a tree suckling her son. After Thutmose III wives were no longer normally shown in tombs. Painting on a pillar in the burial chamber in Thutmose's tomb (KV35). Photo: Public Domain.

Chariots were an important symbol of status and officialdom in the 18th Dynasty. A member of a team from the temple of Karnak arrived in chariots to show their importance while undertaking a survey of fields and boundaries. From the tomb of Nebamun at Thebes. He was the accountant in charge of grain at the temple. c. 1400–1350 BC.

Amenhotep II demonstrates his archery prowess on a relief found reused in his grandson Amenhotep III's Third Pylon at Karnak. The king fires arrows into a copper ingot. The composition is dynamic but idealized, impossible and represented a stock motif of the mobile warrior king pioneered in the 18th Dynasty. It was subsequently emulated by later kings, regardless of whether they were capable of such feats. Photo: Aidan Dodson

Karnak, the Eighth Pylon. Originally built by Hatshepsut, Amenhotep II modified the pylon to showcase the 18th Dynasty. The crumbled nearest seated figure was Amenhotep I, then Amenhotep I (beside which, but not visible here, was the figure of his sister-queen Merytre), followed by two figures of Thutmose II.

The head of the mummy of Thutmose IV (c. 1400–1390 BC), found in the cache of royal mummies in the tomb of Amenhotep II in 1898. He died relatively young.

Thebes, tomb of Rekhmire (TT100). Cretans bringing tribute to the vizier Rekhmire. Although this belongs to the time of Thutmose III, the depiction is typical of a number of scenes in private tombs of senior officials who were shown in receipt of valuable gifts to Egypt which they processed on behalf of the king. In this instance the items include an ox-hide ingot of copper, a large bowl and a kylix drinking cup. c. 1425 BC. Painting by Nina M. Davies. Photo: MM, New York (Public Domain).

## SECTION TWO

Amenhotep III and Tiye limestone dyad statue from the mortuary temple at Kom el Hettân. Not only is the queen shown at the same size as her husband but also her headdress meant she exceeded him in height. They are accompanied by figures of three of their daughters. Height 7 m. c. 1361 BC. Photo: Sailko

Bust of Tiye, Amenhotep III's queen. Found at Medinet el-Gurob at the south-eastern end of the Faiyum. Created late in Tiye's life or shortly after her death. c. 1360–1330 BC, but later modified to add a wig and sun-disk, cow-horn twin-feather headdress (not shown). The style is unusually realistic and lacks the conventional idealism of Egyptian royal sculpture and was perhaps therefore made at Amarna. Wood with precious metal and faience inlay. Now in the Egyptian Museum of Berlin. Height 22.5 cm.

Marriage scarab of Amenhotep III and Tiye. Amenhotep's names are in the fourth row. Tiye's name is in the cartouche on the fifth row and to the far left her father Yuya's name. Her mother Thuya is mentioned in the next row. Height 8 cm. c. 1390 BC. Now in the Kunsthistorisches Museum, Vienna. Photo: Alensha.

The astonishingly well-preserved mummies of Yuya and Thuya, Tiye's parents, after their discovery in tomb KV46 in the Valley of the Kings. Their titles and honours made them commoners of huge and unprecedented significance. Their ambitions may have played a large part in dominating Amenhotep III and the royal family circle in the later 18th Dynasty.

The Colossi of Memnon. These two quartzite sandstone statues of the king once flanked the entrance through the first pylon of Amenhotep III's mortuary temple at Kom el-Hettân in Western Thebes. They epitomize the monumental royal sculpture of the reign. A diminutive figure of Amenhotep's queen, Tiye, stands by the king's legs. The upper part of the further figure was rebuilt in Roman times under Septimius Severus (AD 193–211) to repair damage after an earthquake. Height 60 ft (18 m). c.1361 BC.

Statue of Sekhmet. Originally one of hundreds installed at Amenhotep III's memorial-mortuary temple at Kom el-Hettân. Now at Medinet Habu, the mortuary temple of Ramesses III to where it was removed possibly by Sheshonq I of the 22nd Dynasty around 945 BC during the Third Intermediate Period. Many others were transferred to the Temple of Mut, just to the south of the main Karnak complex.

Akhenaten. Upper part of a colossal and highly stylized sandstone statue from his temple to the Aten at Karnak. A series of at least forty statues were created for the temple ranging from 8.5 to 12.75 m in height, some apparently representing a conflated figure of Akhenaten and Nefertiti. Each was installed on one of the piers flanking recesses decorated with reliefs. They were all carved in the so-called early Amarna or revolutionary style, characterized by the gross exaggeration of Akhenaten's features and belong to the early part of the reign. c.1352–1347 BC. Photo: Gérard Ducher.

Cartouches of Akhenaten and his Aten god from a lintel originally in his temple to the Aten at Karnak. The temple was later demolished, with blocks used by Horemheb as part of the fill for his Second and Tenth Pylons. The systematic post-reign destruction of the temple resulted in large numbers of fragments being buried or reused in and around the temple complex at Karnak. From the Second Pylon. c.1352–1347 BC.

Amarna. One of the boundary stelae (U) that marked out the territory of Akhenaten's new city and incorporated his statement of intent. This one was created in the 6th regnal year. Note the remains of figures of the royal couple in recesses either side. They were accompanied originally by figures of their daughters Meryetaten and Meketaten. Photo: Aidan Dodson

Akhenaten and Tiye. A composite photograph of busts of Tiye and Akhenaten. In the latter's case the simple reduction of the vertical dimension, exaggerated in the original composition, makes it possible to show how much Akhenaten resembled his mother, or that the latter had been depicted to resemble him. There are, of course, minor differences in the angle of the eyes, the proportion of the lips and the width of the face, but these are outweighed by the conspicuous similarities. Both busts are now in the Egyptian Museum of Berlin (acc. nos ÄM 21834 (Tiye) ÄM 21351 (Akhenaten)).

Akhenaten, Nefertiti and their three eldest daughters Meryetaten, Meketaten and Ankhesenpaaten. The composition is exceptional in two ways: first, for the highly stylized depiction which has been transferred to all the individuals represented and, secondly, the exceptional intimacy of the composition which is characteristic of Amarna art. c.1348–1341 BC (the year of Meketaten's death). Found at Tell el-Amarna. Now in the Egyptian Museum of Berlin (acc. no. ÄM 14145). Height 32 cm.

Amenhotep III's throne name in a cartouche on the capital of a column in his Sun Court at the Temple of Luxor. The king's regnal name Nebmaatre is untouched but the Amun component of the epithet 'beloved of Amun-Re' has been chiselled out by Atenists. No attempt was made to restore Amun's name here though that often occurred elsewhere. Note the care taken to avoid inflicting any damage to the solar disk symbols. Original carving c.1390–1352 BC, damage c.1352–1336 BC.

Pottery fragments with distinctive painted decoration from Mycenae in Greece. Found at Amarna, testifying to the existence of trade routes across the Aegean and eastern Mediterranean. Most of the examples found are the remains of stirrup jars and flasks, thought to have been used to bring in foodstuffs and liquid commodities and discarded when finished with. c.1347–1336 BC. Now in the British Museum.

Nefertiti and one of her daughters, probably Meryetaten, on an alabaster relief from the Main Palace at Amarna. The two were shown following Akhenaten. Both are depicted with the features of Akhenaten. The scene is typical of how the royal family had supplanted depictions of traditional gods. c. 1345 BC.

Nefertiti becomes king and co-regent. Part of a damaged limestone stela from the North Palace at Amarna. On the left are Akhenaten's names. To the right are two cartouches with Nefertiti's name in the form 'Neferneferuaten-Nefertiti, beloved of her husband' and throne name, 'Ankhkheperure, beloved of Waenre', indicating her kingly status. However, it is clear both her cartouches are crude modifications from what was originally there, which can no longer be discerned. Given that this is from a royal context, the atrocious standard of execution is noteworthy. c. 1336 BC.

A painted relief carving of an Amarna king and queen, either Akhenaten and Nefertiti, or Smenkhkare and Meryetaten in the less exaggerated, more realistic style characteristic of the later part of Akhenaten's reign. From Amarna. c. 1345–1336 BC. Now in the Egyptian Museum of Berlin (acc. no. ÄM 15000).

The celebrated life-size painted and plastered bust of Nefertiti with her characteristic crown. Found in the workshop of the sculptor Thutmose at Amarna. It is possible the plaster skim was used to improve her features and create an image of perfection. Latter part of the reign. Now in the Egyptian Museum of Berlin (acc. no. ÄM 21300).

Corner fragment from Akhenaten's granite sarcophagus in his Amarna tomb. The four normal tutelary goddesses were replaced with figures of Nefertiti wearing a solar headdress. The hieroglyphs immediately to her left read 'Aten'. The sarcophagus was destroyed as part of the programme under later kings to suppress memories of the regime. From the Royal Tomb at Amarna. c. 1347–1336 BC. Now in the Egyptian Museum of Berlin.

The shattered dereliction that greeted the discoverers of the tomb known as KV55. This view shows the badly damaged and defaced royal coffin, now thought once to have been intended for Akhenaten's lesser wife Kiya, but which contained the skeletal remains of young adult male believed by most to be that of the spectral and short-lived co-regent of Akhenaten, Smenkhkare, perhaps the king's younger brother. Photo: E. Harold Jones (Public Domain).

Composite image of (l–r): Tiye, KV55 canopic jar stopper, Tutankhamun and Nefertiti. The resemblance of the latter three to one another is obvious, raising the possibility that all three were related and that the gold mask of Tutankhamun had originally been intended for either of the women. The resemblance of the canopic jar stopper to Nefertiti is particularly strong in the nose and upper face, making it feasible that instead Nefertiti or one of her daughters was the subject. Alternatively, the three busts may have once represented the same person or appear similar because they were made in the same workshop by artists affected by habit.

Calcite jar from Gurob in the Faiyum bearing the names of (l–r): Ankhesenamun, and Tutankhamun-Nebkheperure. The difference in the -amun part at the top of the left two cartouches is an object lesson in how precarious reconstructions of damaged texts can be since the same hieroglyph could be executed and positioned quite differently, depending on the skill of the engraver and the friable nature of the medium. This makes assumptions based on the precise positioning of signs and excluding others on the grounds they would be 'impossible', potentially untenable. Now in the Petrie Museum, London.

Statue of Tutankhamun as Amun at Karnak, paired with another god. The statue was later usurped probably first by Ay and then Horemheb, and now bears the names of Ramesses II, but the youthful features make it very likely it was produced originally during Tutankhamun's reign.

The traditional brutalizing of Egypt's enemies. Asiatic captives are brought before Tutankhamun by Horemheb's soldiers, their hands secured in wooden yokes so they could be pulled along and humiliated. From Horemheb's Saqqara tomb. c.1336–1327 BC. Photo: Norah Cooper

Portraits of Horemheb found in his Saqqara tomb complex, constructed for him when he was still a general during the reign of Tutankhamun. This are examples of very high-quality sculpture and relief work commissioned for the tomb that showed Horemheb's high status and wealth. After he became king, Horemheb adapted the tomb to show his new role even though the tomb was never used by him. It was instead used by his queen Mutnodjmet for whom it was converted. In the relief the uraeus serpent symbol of royalty has been added to update his status as king. Both are now in the British Museum. c.1336–1327 BC.

Dyad of Ay and Tey as Amun and Mut in the Temple of Luxor. The figures were subsequently usurped, explaining their survival, and now bear the cartouches of Ramesses II. Note the deliberately youthful features, belying Ay's age. The dyad probably started life as Tutankhamun and Ankhesenamun. c.1336–1323 BC.

Relief of Tutankhamun at the Temple of Luxor. Usurped by Horemheb, whose names have been substituted. Originally c.1336–1327 BC. Horemheb did the same to numerous monuments of Tutankhamun, renaming or dismantling most public traces of his reign.

Section of one of the king lists from Abydos reading from right to left, the throne names of Thutmose IV, Amenhotep III, Horemheb and Ramesses I. The reigns of Akhenaten, Tutankhamun and Ay had been expunged from the official records to bury any memory of the Atenist phase of the 18th Dynasty and its immediate aftermath. The list was compiled during the reign of the 19th Dynasty king Seti I (1294–1279 BC), Ramesses I's son. Now in the British Museum.

Millstone cut out of a granite relief of Thutmose III striding towards a seated Amun. The relief was probably well over a thousand years old when it was converted to everyday use. Found at the Temple of Hathor precinct at Dendera. The original source of the relief is unknown.

# INDEX

The Notes are only indexed where points of particular interest are discussed. Egyptian kings (male and female) only are in upper case

533

# PHARAOHS OF THE SUN

Memphis xii, xxii, 2, 7, 10, 32, 44, 47, 50, 52,
64, 86, 118, 123, 161, 165, 168, 217, 218,
246, 293, 320, 329, 336, 352, 362, 364, 386,
387, 404, 407, 408, 410
Men, sculptor 228
Menht, Menwi, and Merti, foreign wives of
Thutmose III 155–6
mental illness 295
MENTUHOTEP II (11th Dynasty) xiv, 43,
115, 152, 385
mercenaries 61, 65
MERENPTAH (19th Dynasty) xiv, 227,
373, 375
Meritaten, *see* Meryetaten
Mersa Gawasis 117
Meryetamun, queen of Amenhotep I 78,
400
Meryetaten, eldest daughter of Akhenaten
and Nefertiti 114, 243, 247, 249, 250, 253,
255, 282, 283, 287, 292, 293, 294, 295, 296,
298, 299, 303, 309, 315, 336, 342, 392,
400–1, 404
Meryetaten-Tasherit 255, 463
Merymose, viceroy of Kush 216, 220
Meryptah, overseer in charge of Kom
el-Hettân's construction 219
Meryre i, official at Amarna 258
Meryre ii 292, 465, 470, 471, 478
Merytre-Hatshepsut, wife of Thutmose
III, mother of Amenhotep II 155, 391,
405, 419
Messalina 39
messianic coming 117, 272
meteorites 3
Middle Ages 9, 363, 378
Middle Egyptian, language used in the
New Kingdom 27–8
Middle Kingdom 3, 13, 41, 43, 47, 54, 69, 77,
88, 117, 189, 223, 385
Migdal 169
millstone 379
Min, god 204, 205, 206, 209, 351
Min, mayor of Thinis and tutor of
Amenhotep II 162
mines and mining 2, 43, 51, 181
Minoans 3, 4, 48, 58, 63, 67, 86
miscarriages, of Tutankhamun's children
323–4, 350
Mitanni (Naharin) xiii, 3, 23, 84, 136, 140,
144, 166, 168, 169, 181, 182, 184, 185, 210,
213, 217, 251, 254, 266, 268, 326, 404, 405,
407, 410
Mnevis bull 249

monkeys 175, 176, 254
monotheism 379, 380
Montaigne, Michel de 205–6
Montu xv, 183, 406
moon 25, 138
mother, word for 33
Mother of the King 33, 183, 419
mudbrick 189, 220, 221, 222, 247, 260, 302
mummies, problem of identifying 17–18
mummies and mummification *passim* but
especially xxi, xxii, 12, 17, 48, 50, 52,
69, 75, 77, 78, 155–6, 159, 203, 259, 307,
315–16, 317, 323–4, 330, 334, 335, 347, 377,
378, 389, 400
murder, *see* assassinations
Murnane, William 16–17
Mursili II 335, 337, 489–90
music 7, 42, 194, 453
Mut, consort of Amun and her temple
(Precinct of Mut, Karnak) 33, 41, 109,
110, 111, 120, 122, 198, 226, 227, 229, 253,
264, 314, 321, 361, 402
Mutbenret, sister of Nefertiti (*see also*
Mutnodjmet) 237, 253–4, 317, 357, 401, 402
Mutemwiya, wife of Thutmose IV and
mother of Amenhotep III 184–5, 198,
199, 202, 203, 207, 208, 222, 226, 229, 286,
316, 401, 406
Mutnodjmet, queen of Horemheb (*see also*
Mutbenret, *idem*?) 237, 253, 257, 366, 367,
392, 399, 402
Mutnofret, secondary wife of Thutmose I,
mother of Thutmose II 81, 92, 395, 401
Mycenae 3, 4, 63, 175, 249, pottery from at
Amarna 267
myrrh 118, 410

Naharin, *see* Mitanni
Nakht, scribe 194
Nakht (Nakhtpaaten), vizier at Amarna
261
Nakhtmin, son or grandson of Ay 351–2,
355, 397
names, variants of 24–5
Napata 165
Napoleon xx
narcissism 11, 111, 134, 209, 252, 270, 280
NARMER (1st Dynasty) 59, 385
Nasamonians 254
Nasr City 222
National Museum of Egyptian Civilization
xxi
natural disasters 66

542

# Index

# Index